Rail Guide 2010

Colin J. Marsden

First published 2010

ISBN 978 0 7110 3457 0

Published by Ian Allan Publishing.

An imprint of Ian Allan Publishing Ltd, Hersham, Surrey KT12 4RG.
Printed in England by Ian Allan Printing Ltd, Hersham, Surrey KT12 4RG.

Visit the Ian Allan Publishing website at www.ianallanpublishing.com

Distributed in the United States of America and Canada by BookMasters Distribution Services.

Front Cover Top: *The UK's latest new motive power to enter traffic in 2009 is a fleet of General Electric Class 70 diesel-electric locos operated by Freightliner for both Intermodal and Heavy Haul duties. The first two locos delivered to the UK Nos. 70001 and 70002 are seen at Newport Docks on 8 November 2009.* **Jack Boskett**

Front Cover Bottom: *The attractive London Midland livery looks very smart on the body profile of the Class 170 'Turbostar' fleet, a considerable improvement on some of the earlier colour styles. Set No. 170506 is seen at Gloucester in the summer of 2009 with a LM service to Worcester.* **CJM**

Back Cover Top: *2010 will see the introduction of Class 380 Siemens 'Desiro' electric stock in Scotland, when a fleet of Class 380s are introduced on Ayrshire line routes. The first built driving car for set No. 380101 is seen at the Siemens production facility in Krefeld, Germany on 17 November 2009.* **CJM**

Back Cover Bottom: *Former BR Inspection Saloon No. DB999508 is now operated by Serco/Network Rail as a Track Recording Coach based at Derby. The vehicle painted in yellow livery is seen at Stratford while marshalled between a pair of Class 31s.* **CJM**

The British public's enthusiasm for railways is perhaps best typified by the longevity of the Ian Allan ABC series. Now in its seventh decade, the ABC has introduced and fostered many people's interest in Britain's railways.

Since the publication of the first book during the height of the Second World War in 1942, it has become an important tool to the railway enthusiast and has had a long association with Ian Allan. Over the generations since its inception many a school boy (and the odd girl) has used it to go out and see if they can 'spot' the variety of trains and locomotives that have operated on Britain's railways.

Many have grown up to become involved in the day to day operation of our industry or just continued to be ardent, passionate supporters - and sometimes even critical friends - of our industry.

You may ask why is the Chief Executive of the Association of Train Operating Companies writing a foreword for a book which some may perceive as being just for enthusiasts. The short answer is that anybody who takes an interest in our industry must be encouraged. We need to encourage as many supporters as possible to help ensure that our industry attracts as much talent and support as possible. Today's enthusiast could be tomorrow's manager or decision maker.

In recent years, we have seen a move away from the traditional locomotive-hauled railway, to a passenger railway which is operated by multiple units offering faster and more flexible services. We now operate a record number of trains. Since privatisation, we have seen modern rolling stock replacing life expired trains, reflecting the success of the industry in attracting new investment. We are currently looking ahead to new train fleets such as the Intercity Express Programme which will replace the HST - the workhorse of the intercity routes for over 30 years.

The introduction of new trains and locomotives will ensure that Britain's railways continue to be an interesting place for enthusiasts. Looking forward, we have the possibility of a new high speed line as well as continued investment in the classic network helping to meet the demand on a railway which is expected to double in usage over the next 30 years.

As we continue to improve and modernise, it is important that we continue to give our friends and supporters reasonable access to our railway. That is why the railway enthusiast guidelines are published on sites like www.nationalrail.co.uk as a reminder that you are welcome to pursue your hobby safely and unhindered.

Michael Roberts
Chief Executive of the
Association of Train Operating Companies

Above: *A successful 'open access' operator is Grand Central, which currently operates a regular service on the London King's Cross to Sunderland corridor using a mix of HSTs and Class 180 stock. This operator plans to expand its quality operation with additional services in 2010 and introduce further Class 180 sets. On 7 September 2009, Grand Central-liveried set No. 180112 passes Offord with a Sunderland to London King's Cross working.* **Michael J. Collins**

The new order of the day for South West Trains, where Siemens-built 'Desiro' stock in two designs now dominate the outer suburban and main line operations. On 8 September 2009 a 12-car formation of Class 450 stock (sets Nos. 450119, 450543, and 450553) approach Hook with a stock move from Siemens Northam to Wimbledon Park depot. **CJM**

Information correct to 1 January 2010.

Welcome to the new Ian Allan *ABC Rail Guide 2010*. After a break of many years the long established ABC book covering the UK railway fleets of locomotives, multiple units and coaching stock is returning.

To meet the aspirations of the modern day enthusiast and after seeking comments from many rail network followers it has been decided that the re-launch of the annual ABC numbers book should take on a radical new style; rather than just being a list of numbers from front to back, the new format is a Guide Book to the UK rail system.

Passenger, freight, infrastructure, engineering, private train operators to name but a few all have separate sections; passenger companies include a map of their network, and a brief company profile; this is then followed by the train fleet they operate.

Since privatisation of the UK rail network in the mid-1990s, huge changes have been seen in train types, passenger fleets and networks. Both passenger and freight operators have invested heavily in new train fleets, with well over 500 new main line diesel locomotives entering service, as this introduction is keyed at the end of 2009, yet more new main line diesel locos are arriving in the UK, the first examples of General Electric rail technology to work in this country.

Although often talked down, the UK rail system has a very bright and positive future: massive growth in passenger numbers is projected over the next 20 years and after the world recession is over, freight traffic is expected to increase.

A large number of new smaller operators are now to be found on our rail network. These are all detailed in *ABC Rail Guide 2010*. In the future these are likely to expand with more 'open access' operators granted operating licences.

As Editor of *ABC Rail Guide 2010*, I would like to thank the many people from within the

rail industry who have provided invaluable information for inclusion and I hope that readers enjoy the new publication.

Colin J. Marsden
Dawlish January 2010

Train Operators, The Association of Train Operating Companies, and Network Rail welcome rail enthusiasts and photographers, but in today's safety led railway and with the continued concerns about possible transport terrorism, guidelines are very important and we encourage all to follow these published guidelines as much as possible. They are available to view and download from the National Rail and ATOC websites, but are reproduced in full below to assist you with this information. ■

The Official Railway Enthusiasts Guidelines

■ Network Rail welcomes rail enthusiasts to our stations.

■ The following guidelines are designed to help you to have a safe and enjoyable experience. Please keep them with you when you are at Network Rail managed stations.

■ You may also wish to take a copy of the Railway Bye-laws which are available from the Office of Public Sector Information website.

Before you enter the platform

■ When you arrive at a station, please let the staff at the Network Rail Reception Desk know that you are on the station. This will help keep station staff informed so that they can go about their duties without concern as to your reasons for being there.

■ You may require a platform ticket to allow access to platforms.

While you are on the platform

■ You need to act safely & sensibly at all times.

- Stay clear of the platform edge and stay behind the yellow lines where they are provided.
- Be aware of your surroundings.

Please DO NOT:

- Trespass on to the tracks or any other part of the railway that is not available to passengers.
- Use flash photography because it can distract train drivers and train despatch staff and so is potentially very dangerous.
- Climb on any structure or interfere with platform equipment.
- Obstruct any signalling equipment or signs which are vital to the safe running of the railway.
- Wear anything which is similar in colour to safety clothing, such as high-visibility jackets, as this could cause confusion to drivers and other railway employees.
- Gather together in groups at busy areas of the platform (e.g. customer information points, departure screens, waiting areas, seating etc.) or where this may interfere with the duties of station staff.

■ If possible, please try to avoid peak hours which are Monday – Friday 6:00am (06.00) – 10:30am (10.30) and 3:30pm (15.30) – 7:30pm (19.30).

Extra Eyes and Ears

■ If you see anything suspicious or notice any unusual behaviour or activities, please tell a member of staff immediately.

■ For emergencies and serious incidents, either call:

The British Transport Police on 0800 40 50 40.

The Police on 999.

■ Your presence at a station can be very helpful to us as extra "eyes and ears" and can have a positive security benefit.

Photography

■ You can take photographs at stations provided you do not sell them. However, you are not allowed to take photographs of security related equipment, such as CCTV cameras.

■ Flash photography on platforms is not allowed at any time. It can distract train drivers and train despatch staff and so is potentially very dangerous.

- Tripod legs must be kept away from platform edges and behind the yellow lines. On busy stations, you may not be allowed to use a tripod because it could be a dangerous obstruction to passengers.

Railway Bye-laws

For safety & ease of travel on the railway system (which includes passengers, staff, property and equipment), the Bye-laws must be observed by everyone. A copy of the Bye-laws can be obtained at stations or downloaded from the Office of Public Sector Information website.

General

Train operators must put the safety of their passengers and staff first. You may very occasionally be asked by station staff to move to another part of the station or to leave the station altogether. Station staff should be happy to explain why this is necessary. If you are travelling by train, they may ask you to remain in the normal waiting areas with other passengers. If this occurs, please follow their instructions with goodwill as staff have many things to consider, including the safety & security of all passengers, and are authorised to use judgement in this regard.

Above: *The first privatised operator to order new trains after the split up of British Rail was Chiltern Railways, the operator of services from London Marylebone to Birmingham, Aylesbury and Stratford-upon-Avon. The company opted for the AdTranz (now Bombardier) TurboStar product, originally classified as 168. This design in a refined form later classified as Class 170 has been the backbone of new privatised DMU orders and is now seen throughout the UK. Class 168 No. 168004 is seen heading south at Banbury on 15 August 2009.* **Stacey Thew**

Contents

Arriva Trains Wales

Address: St Mary's House, 47 Penarth Road, Cardiff, CF10 5DJ
customer.relations@arrivatrainswales.co.uk
0845 6061 660
www.arrivatrainswales.co.uk

Managing Director: Tim Bell
Franchise Dates: 7 December 2003 - 6 December 2018
Principal Routes: Cardiff to Swansea and West Wales
Cardiff Valleys
Cardiff - Hereford - Shrewsbury - Crewe - Manchester Piccadilly
Cardiff - Hereford - Shrewsbury - Chester - Bangor - Holyhead
Manchester - Crewe - Bangor - Holyhead
Shrewsbury - Pwllheli / Aberystwyth
Swansea - Shrewsbury
Depots: Cardiff Canton (CF), Chester (CH), Holyhead* (HD)
Machynlleth (MH), Shrewsbury* (SX) (* Stabling point)
Parent Company: Arriva Trains

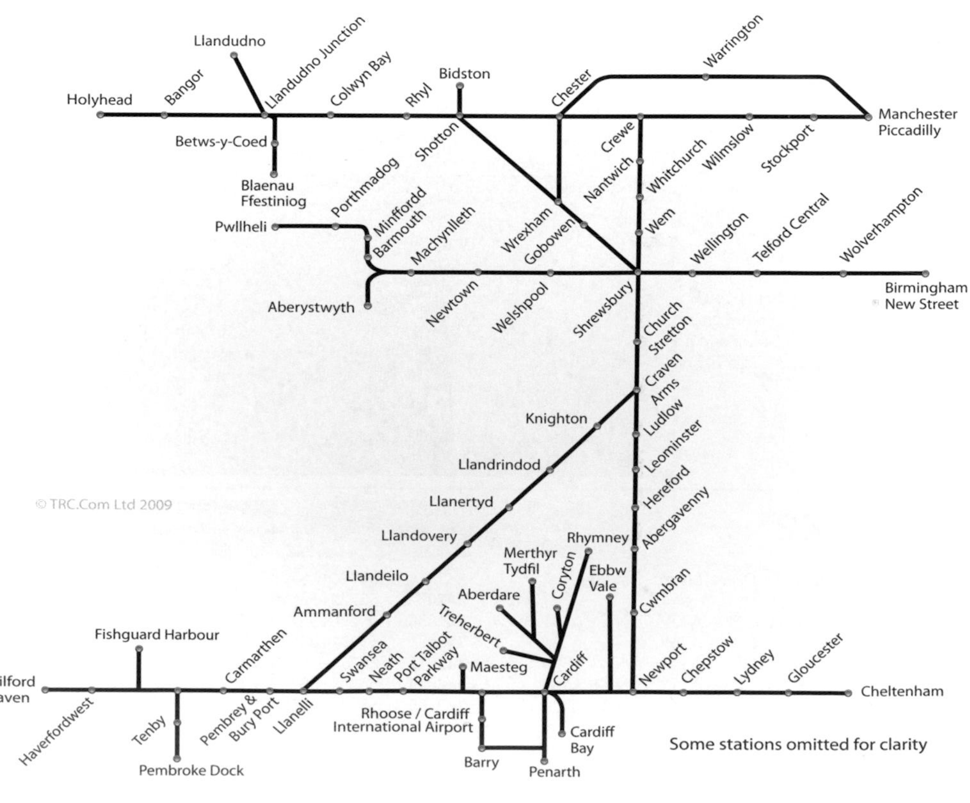

Class 57/3

Vehicle Length: 63ft 6in (19.38m)
Height: 12ft 10⅛in (3.91m)
Width: 9ft 2in (2.79m)
Engine: EMD 645-12F3B
Horsepower: 2,750hp (2,051kW)
Electrical Equipment: Brush

Number	*Depot*	*Pool*	*Livery*	*Owner*	*Operator*
57313 (47371)	***MA***	***ATTB***	***BLU***	***PTR***	***ATW/VWC***
57314 (47372)	**MA**	**ATTB**	**ATE**	**PTR**	**ATW**
57315 (47234)	**MA**	**ATTB**	**ATE**	**PTR**	**ATW**
57316 (47290)	***MA***	***ATTB***	***BLU***	***PTR***	***ATW/VWC***

Right: *Only two of the Class 57/3s available to Arriva Trains Wales for the 'executive' service linking Holyhead and Cardiff are painted in the full and branded Arriva colours - Nos. 57314/315; the other two locos are painted in all-over 'general' dark blue. No. 57315 is illustrated at Newport.* **John Wills**

■ Class 57/3 locos owned by Porterbrook and on lease to Virgin Trains, sub-leased to Arriva Trains Wales

Class 121

Length: 64ft 6in (19.66m)
Height: 12ft 8½in (3.87m)
Width: 9ft 3in (2.81m)
Engine: 2 x Leyland 150hp
Horsepower: 300hp (224kW)
Seats (total/car): 65S

Number	*Formation DMBS*	*Depot*	*Livery*	*Owner*	*Operator*	*Note*
121032	**55032**	**CF**	**ATW**	**ATW**	**ATW**	**Previously numbered 977842**

Right: *The sole example of the Arriva Trains Wales Class 121 fleet, No. 121032 is used exclusively on the shuttle service between Cardiff Queen Street and Cardiff Bay. It is illustrated from its brake van end at Cardiff Queen Street. The set receives maintenance at Cardiff Canton and if out of use is replaced by a Class 142 or Class 143.* **CJM**

Class 142

Vehicle Length: 51ft 0½in (15.55m)
Height: 12ft 8in (3.86m)
Width: 9ft 2¼in (2.80m)
Engine: 1 x Cummins LTA10-R per vehicle
Horsepower: 460hp (343kW)
Seats (total/car): 90S, 46S/44S

Number	*Formation DMS+DMSL*	*Depot*	*Livery*	*Owner*	*Operator*
142002	**55543+55593**	**CF**	**ATW**	**ANG**	**ATW**
142006	**55547+55597**	**CF**	**ATW**	**ANG**	**ATW**
142010	**55551+55601**	**CF**	**ATW**	**ANG**	**ATW**
142069(S)	**55719+55765**	**CF**	**ATW**	**ANG**	**ATW**
142072	**55722+55768**	**CF**	**ATW**	**ANG**	**ATW**
142073	**55723+55769**	**CF**	**ATW**	**ANG**	**ATW**
142074	**55724+55770**	**CF**	**ATW**	**ANG**	**ATW**
142075	**55725+55771**	**CF**	**ATW**	**ANG**	**ATW**
142076	**55726+55772**	**CF**	**ATW**	**ANG**	**ATW**
142077	**55727+55773**	**CF**	**ATW**	**ANG**	**ATW**
142080	**55730+55776**	**CF**	**ATW**	**ANG**	**ATW**
142081	**55731+55777**	**CF**	**ATW**	**ANG**	**ATW**
142082	**55732+55778**	**CF**	**ATW**	**ANG**	**ATW**
142083	**55733+55779**	**CF**	**ATW**	**ANG**	**ATW**
142085	**55735+55781**	**CF**	**ATW**	**ANG**	**ATW**

Name applied
142072 ***Myfanwy***

Arriva Trains Wales

Left: *A fleet of 15 BREL/Leyland Railbus units of Class 142 are allocated to Cardiff for Valley line duties. All are refurbished with 2+2 seating and all are painted in the latest Arriva Trains Wales bi-lingual livery. Set No. 142069 is viewed at Cardiff.* **Tony Christie**

Class 143

Vehicle Length: 51ft 0½in (15.55m)
Height: 12ft 2¼in (3.73m)
Width: 8ft 10½in (2.70m)
Engine: 1 x Cummins LTA10-R per vehicle
Horsepower: 460hp (343kW)
Seats (total/car): 92S, 48S/44S

Number	*Formation DMS+DMSL*	*Depot*	*Livery*	*Owner*	*Operator*
143601	**55642+55667**	**CF**	**ATW**	**BCC**	**ATW**
143602	**55651+55668**	**CF**	**ATW**	**PTR**	**ATW**
143604	**55645+55670**	**CF**	**ATW**	**PTR**	**ATW**
143605	**55646+55671**	**CF**	**ATW**	**PTR**	**ATW**
143606	**55647+55672**	**CF**	**ATW**	**PTR**	**ATW**
143607	**55648+55673**	**CF**	**ATW**	**PTR**	**ATW**
143608	**55649+55674**	**CF**	**ATW**	**PTR**	**ATW**
143609	**55650+55675**	**CF**	**ATW**	**CCC**	**ATW**
143610	**55643+55676**	**CF**	**ATW**	**BCC**	**ATW**
143614	**55655+55680**	**CF**	**ATW**	**BCC**	**ATW**
143615	**55657+55682**	**CF**	**ATW**	**PTR**	**ATW**
143622	**55663+55688**	**CF**	**ATW**	**PTR**	**ATW**
143623	**55664+55689**	**CF**	**ATW**	**PTR**	**ATW**
143624	**55665+55690**	**CF**	**ATW**	**PTR**	**ATW**
143625	**55666+55691**	**CF**	**ATW**	**PTR**	**ATW**

Names applied

143609 ***Sir Tom Jones***

Left: *Class 143 No. 143616 is seen arriving at Cardiff Central station on a City Line service painted in standard Arriva turquoise and cream livery.* **CJM**

Class 150/2

Vehicle Length: 64ft 9¾in (19.74m)
Height: 12ft 4½in (3.77m)
Width: 9ft 3⅛in (2.82m)
Engine: 1 x NT855R5 of 285hp per vehicle
Horsepower: 570hp (425kW)
Seats (total/car): 128S, 60S/68S

Number	*Formation DMSL+DMS*	*Depot*	*Livery*	*Owner*	*Operator*
150208	**52208+57208**	**CF**	**ATW**	**PTR**	**ATW**
150236	**52236+57236**	**CF**	**ATW**	**PTR**	**ATW**
150240	**52240+57240**	**CF**	**ATW**	**PTR**	**ATW**
150241	**52241+57241**	**CF**	**ATW**	**PTR**	**ATW**
150242	**52242+57242**	**CF**	**ATW**	**PTR**	**ATW**
150245	**52245+57245**	**CF**	**ATW**	**PTR**	**ATW**
150250	**52250+57250**	**CF**	**ATW**	**PTR**	**ATW**
150251	**52251+57251**	**CF**	**ATW**	**PTR**	**ATW**
150252	**52252+57252**	**CF**	**ATW**	**PTR**	**ATW**
150253	**52253+57253**	**CF**	**ATW**	**PTR**	**ATW**
150254	**52254+57254**	**CF**	**ATW**	**PTR**	**ATW**
150256	**52256+57256**	**CF**	**ATW**	**PTR**	**ATW**
150258	**52258+57258**	**CF**	**ATW**	**PTR**	**ATW**
150259	**52259+57259**	**CF**	**ATW**	**PTR**	**ATW**
150260	**52260+57260**	**CF**	**ATW**	**PTR**	**ATW**
150262	**52262+57262**	**CF**	**ATW**	**PTR**	**ATW**
150264	**52264+57264**	**CF**	**ATW**	**PTR**	**ATW**
150267	**52267+57267**	**CF**	**ATW**	**PTR**	**ATW**
150278	**52278+57278**	**CF**	**ATW**	**PTR**	**ATW**
150279	**52270+57279**	**CF**	**ATW**	**PTR**	**ATW**
150280	**52280+57280**	**CF**	**ATW**	**PTR**	**ATW**
150281	**52281+57281**	**CF**	**ATW**	**PTR**	**ATW**
150282	**52282+57282**	**CF**	**ATW**	**PTR**	**ATW**
150283	**52283+57283**	**CF**	**ATW**	**PTR**	**ATW**
150284	**52284+57284**	**CF**	**ATW**	**PTR**	**ATW**
150285	**52285+57285**	**CF**	**ATW**	**PTR**	**ATW**

Above: *Displaying the corporate Arriva Trains livery, set No. 150279 is viewed at Cardiff Central.* **CJM**

Class 153

Vehicle Length: 76ft 5in (23.29m)
Height: 12ft 3⅛in (3.75m)
Width: 8ft 10in (2.70m)
Engine: 1 x NT855R5 of 285hp
Horsepower: 285hp (213kW)
Seats (total/car): 72S

Number	Formation DMSL	Depot	Livery	Owner	Operator
153303	52303	CF	ATW	ANG	ATW
153312	52312	CF	ATW	ANG	ATW
153320	52320	CF	ATW	PTR	ATW
153323	52323	CF	ATW	PTR	ATW
153327	52327	CF	ATW	ANG	ATW
153353	57353	CF	ATW	ANG	ATW
153362	57362	CF	ATW	ANG	ATW
153367	57367	CF	ATW	PTR	ATW

Right: *With its small cab nearest the camera, Arriva Trains Wales Class 153 No. 153320 is seen at Bridgend on a Cardiff bound service on 2 May 2009.* **Tony Christie**

Class 158

Vehicle Length: 76ft 1¾in (23.21m)
Height: 12ft 6in (3.81m)
Width: 9ft 3¼in (2.82m)
Engine: 1 x Perkins 2006-TWH of 350hp per vehicle
Horsepower: 700hp (522kW)
Seats (total/car): 134S, 66S/68S

Number	Formation DMSL+DMSL	Depot	Livery	Owner	Operator
158818	52818+57818	MN	ATW	ANG	ATW
158819	52819+57819	MN	WAL	ANG	ATW
158820¤	52820+57820	MN	ATW	ANG	ATW
158821	52821+57821	MN	ATW	ANG	ATW
158822¤	52822+57822	MN	ATW	ANG	ATW
158823	52823+57823	MN	ATW	ANG	ATW
158824	52824+57824	MN	ATW	ANG	ATW
158825	52825+57825	MN	WAL	ANG	ATW
158826	52826+57826	MN	WAL	ANG	ATW
158827¤	52827+57827	MN	WAL	ANG	ATW
158828	52828+57828	MN	ATW	ANG	ATW
158829¤	52829+57829	MN	ATW	ANG	ATW
158830	52830+57830	MN	WAL	ANG	ATW
158831	52831+57831	MN	WAL	ANG	ATW
158832	52832+57832	MN	WAL	ANG	ATW
158833	52833+57833	MN	WAL	ANG	ATW
158834	52834+57834	MN	WAL	ANG	ATW
158835	52835+57835	MN	WAL	ANG	ATW
158836	52836+57836	MN	WAL	ANG	ATW
158837¤	52837+57837	CF	ATW	ANG	ATW
158838	52838+57838	CF	WAL	ANG	ATW
158839	52839+57839	CF	WAL	ANG	ATW
158840	52840+57840	CF	ATW	ANG	ATW
158841	52841+57841	CF	WAL	ANG	ATW

¤ fitted with operational European Rail Traffic Management System (ERTMS) equipment for operation on the Cambrian Line.

Right: *Class 158 No. 158818 painted in Arriva livery departs from Newport on a service to Gloucester.* **CJM**

Arriva Trains Wales

Class 175/0
Coradia 1000

Vehicle Length: 75ft 7in (23.06m)
Height: 12ft 4in (3.75m)
Width: 9ft 2in (2.80m)
Engine: 1 x Cummins N14 of 450hp per vehicle
Horsepower: 900hp (671kW)
Seats (total/car): 118S, 54S/64S

Number	Formation DMSL+DMSL	Depot	Livery	Owner	Operator
175001	50701+79701	CH	ATW	ANG	ATW
175002	50702+79702	CH	ATW	ANG	ATW
175003	50703+79703	CH	ATW	ANG	ATW
175004	50704+79704	CH	ATW	ANG	ATW
175005	50705+79705	CH	ATW	ANG	ATW
175006	50706+79706	CH	ATW	ANG	ATW
175007	50707+79707	CH	ATW	ANG	ATW
175008	50708+79708	CH	ATW	ANG	ATW
175009	50709+79709	CH	ATW	ANG	ATW
175010	50710+79710	CH	ATW	ANG	ATW
175011	50711+79711	CH	ATW	ANG	ATW

■ *In late 2009 set 175003 was operating as a three-car set with MS 56759 while the DM vehicles of set 175109 were repaired.*

Left: *Allocated to the Alstom-operated depot at Chester, the Class 175 fleet are the mainstay of North Wales and long distance Arriva Trains Wales workings. The design comes in both two and three car versions. Two-car set No. 175006 is seen at Newport.* **Stacey Thew**

Class 175/1
Coradia 1000

Vehicle Length: 75ft 7in (23.06m)
Height: 12ft 4in (3.75m)
Width: 9ft 2in (2.80m)
Engine: 1 x Cummins N14 of 450hp per vehicle
Horsepower: 1,350hp (1,007kW)
Seats (total/car): 186S, 54S/68S/64S

Number	Formation DMSL+MSL+DMSL	Depot	Livery	Owner	Opt'r
175101	50751+56751+79751	CH	ATW	ANG	ATW
175102	50752+56752+79752	CH	ATW	ANG	ATW
175103	50753+56753+79753	CH	ATW	ANG	ATW
175104	50754+56754+79754	CH	ATW	ANG	ATW
175105	50755+56755+79755	CH	ATW	ANG	ATW
175106	50756+56756+79756	CH	ATW	ANG	ATW
175107	50757+56757+79757	CH	ATW	ANG	ATW
175108	50758+56758+79758	CH	ATW	ANG	ATW
175109	50759+56759+79759	CH	ATW	ANG	ATW
175110	50760+56760+79760	CH	ATW	ANG	ATW
175111	50761+56761+79761	CH	ATW	ANG	ATW
175112	50762+56762+79762	CH	ATW	ANG	ATW
175113	50763+56763+79763	CH	ATW	ANG	ATW
175114	50764+56764+79764	CH	ATW	ANG	ATW
175115	50765+56765+79765	CH	ATW	ANG	ATW
175116	50766+56766+79766	CH	ATW	ANG	ATW

Below: *The three-car Class 175s offer a seating capacity for 186 standard class passengers in the 2+2 low-density style. Set No. 175104 is viewed at Flint, while operating Arriva Trains Wales 13.44 Llandudno to Manchester Piccadilly service on 6 July 2009.* **John Binch**

Class AC2E / TSO

Vehicle Length: 66ft 0in (20.11m) *Width: 9ft 3in (2.81m)*
Height: 12ft 9½in (3.89m) *Seats (total/car): 62S*

Number	*Type*	*Depot*	*Livery*	*Owner*	*Operator*
5853	TSO	CF	ATW	ATW	ATW
5869(S)	TSO	LM	ATW	ATW	-

Class AC2F / TSO

Vehicle Length: 66ft 0in (20.11m) *Width: 9ft 3in (2.81m)*
Height: 12ft 9½in (3.89m) *Seats (total/car): 60S*

Number	*Type*	*Depot*	*Livery*	*Owner*	*Operator*
5913(S)	TSO	CF	ATW	ATW	-
5965	TSO	CF	ATW	ATW	ATW
5976	TSO	CF	ATW	ATW	ATW
6013(S)	TSO	LM	ATW	ATW	-
6035(S)	TSO	LM	ATW	ATW	-
6119	TSO	CF	ATW	ATW	ATW
6137	TSO	CF	ATW	ATW	ATW
6162(S)	TSO	LM	ATW	ATW	-
6170(S)	TSO	LM	ATW	ATW	-
6183	TSO	CF	ATW	ATW	ATW

Class AE2E / BSO

Vehicle Length: 66ft 0in (20.11m) *Width: 9ft 3in (2.81m)*
Height: 12ft 9½in (3.89m) *Seats (total/car): 60S*

Number	*Type*	*Depot*	*Livery*	*Owner*	*Operator*
9503	BSO	CF	ATW	ATW	ATW
9509	BSO	CF	ATW	ATW	ATW

Class AE2F / BSO

Vehicle Length: 66ft 0in (20.11m) *Width: 9ft 3in (2.81m)*
Height: 12ft 9½in (3.89m) *Seats (total/car): 60S*

Number	*Type*	*Depot*	*Livery*	*Owner*	*Operator*
9521	BSO	CF	ATW	ATW	ATW
9524(S)	BSO	LM	ATW	ATW	-
9539	BSO	CF	ATW	ATW	ATW

For 10249 See Cargo-D leasing

Right: *Mk2f TSO No. 5976 is one of the vehicles used on the daily Holyhead to Cardiff and return service. The vehicle is owned by Arriva Trains and allocated to Cardiff Canton depot. The coach is seen at Newport.*
Nathan Williamson

Below: *Three Mk2f BSO vehicles are operated by Arriva Trains Wales. No. 9521 is illustrated from the brake end, which has been modified to accommodate bicycles.*
Nathan Williamson

Further Reading
For full technical information and class details of all traction classes covered in the Ian Allan ABC Rail Guide 2010, see our companion volume Traction Recognition.
Available from bookshops or direct from the publishers – visit www.ianallanpublishing.com for details.
TRACTION RECOGNITION
Colin J. Marsden

c2c

Address: ✉ 10th Floor, 207 Old Street, London, EC1V 9NR
c2c.customerrelations@nationalexpress.com
✆ 0845 6014873
ⓘ www.c2c-online.co.uk

Managing Director: Julian Drury
Franchise Dates: 26 May 1996 - 25 May 2011
Principal Routes: London Fenchurch Street - Shoeburyness
Barking - Pitsea via Purfleet
Ockendon branch
London Liverpool Street - Barking (limited service)
Depots: East Ham (EM), Shoeburyness*
* Stabling point
Parent Company: National Express

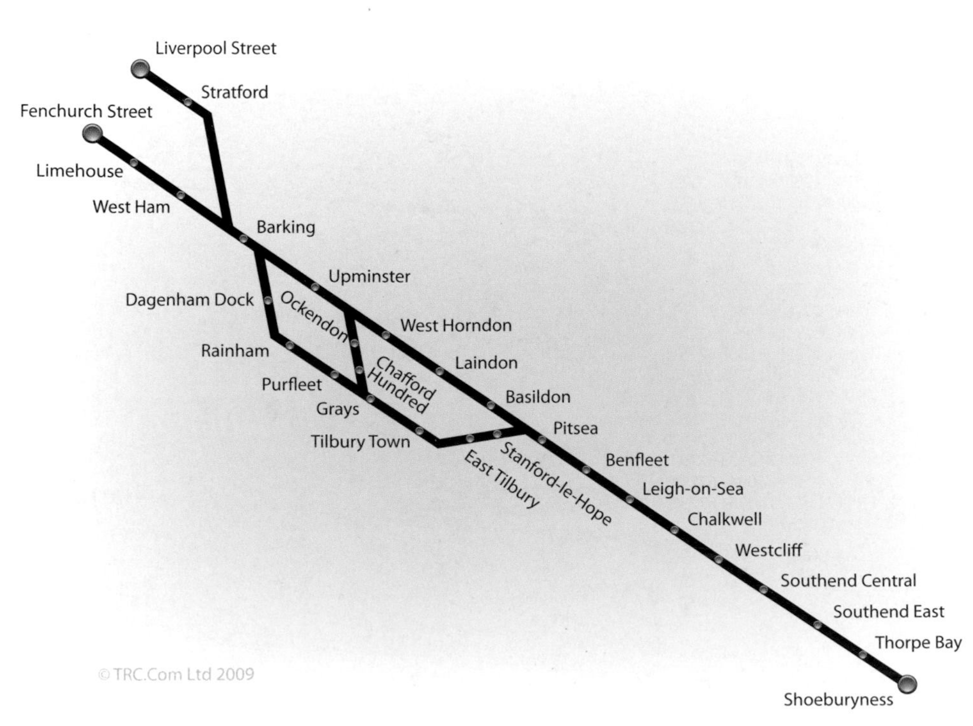

Class 357/0
Electrostar

Vehicle Length: (Driving) 68ft 1in (20.75m) (Inter) 65ft 11½in (20.10m)
Height: 12ft 4½in (3.78m)
Width: 9ft 2½in (2.80m)
Horsepower: 2,011hp (1,500kW)
Seats (total/car): 282S, 71S/78S/62S/71S

Number	*Formation* DMSO(A)+MSO+PTSO+DMSO(B)	*Depot*	*Livery*	*Owner*	*Operator*	*Name*
357001	67651+74151+74051+67751	EM	NE2	PTR	C2C	*Barry Flaxman*
357002	67652+74152+74052+67752	EM	C2C	PTR	C2C	*Arthur Lewis Stride 1841-1922*
357003	67653+74153+74053+67753	EM	C2C	PTR	C2C	*Jason Leonard*
357004	67654+74154+74054+67754	EM	C2C	PTR	C2C	*Tony Amos*
357005	67655+74155+74055+67755	EM	C2C	PTR	C2C	
357006	67656+74156+74056+67756	EM	C2C	PTR	C2C	
357007	67657+74157+74057+67757	EM	C2C	PTR	C2C	
357008	67658+74158+74058+67758	EM	C2C	PTR	C2C	
357009	67659+74159+74059+67759	EM	C2C	PTR	C2C	
357010	67660+74160+74060+67760	EM	SPL	PTR	C2C	
357011	67661+74161+74061+67761	EM	C2C	PTR	C2C	*John Lowing*
357012	67662+74162+74062+67762	EM	C2C	PTR	C2C	
357013	67663+74163+74063+67763	EM	C2C	PTR	C2C	
357014	67664+74164+74064+67764	EM	C2C	PTR	C2C	
357015	67665+74165+74065+67765	EM	C2C	PTR	C2C	
357016	67666+74166+74066+67766	EM	C2C	PTR	C2C	
357017	67667+74167+74067+67767	EM	C2C	PTR	C2C	
357018	67668+74168+74068+67768	EM	C2C	PTR	C2C	
357019	67669+74169+74069+67769	EM	C2C	PTR	C2C	
357020	67670+74170+74070+67770	EM	C2C	PTR	C2C	
357021	67621+74171+74071+67771	EM	C2C	PTR	C2C	
357022	67672+74172+74072+67772	EM	C2C	PTR	C2C	
357023	67673+74173+74073+67773	EM	C2C	PTR	C2C	
357024	67674+74174+74074+67774	EM	C2C	PTR	C2C	
357025	67675+74175+74075+67775	EM	C2C	PTR	C2C	
357026	67676+74176+74076+67776	EM	C2C	PTR	C2C	
357027	67677+74177+74077+67777	EM	C2C	PTR	C2C	
357028	67678+74178+74078+67778	EM	C2C	PTR	C2C	*London, Tilbury & Southend Railway 1854-2004*
357029	67679+74179+74079+67779	EM	C2C	PTR	C2C	*Thomas Whitelegg 1840-1922*
357030	67680+74180+74080+67780	EM	NE2	PTR	C2C	*Robert Harben Whitelegg 1871-1957*
357031	67681+74181+74081+67781	EM	C2C	PTR	C2C	
357032	67682+74182+74082+67782	EM	C2C	PTR	C2C	
357033	67683+74183+74083+67783	EM	NE2	PTR	C2C	
357034	67684+74184+74084+67784	EM	C2C	PTR	C2C	
357035	67685+74185+74085+67785	EM	NE2	PTR	C2C	
357036	67686+74186+74086+67786	EM	C2C	PTR	C2C	
357037	67687+74187+74087+67787	EM	NE2	PTR	C2C	
357038	67688+74188+74088+67788	EM	NE2	PTR	C2C	
357039	67689+74189+74089+67789	EM	NE2	PTR	C2C	
357040	67690+74190+74090+67790	EM	NE2	PTR	C2C	
357041	67691+74191+74091+67791	EM	NE2	PTR	C2C	
357042	67692+74192+74092+67792	EM	C2C	PTR	C2C	
357043	67693+74193+74093+67793	EM	C2C	PTR	C2C	
357044	67694+74194+74094+67794	EM	NE2	PTR	C2C	
357045	67695+74195+74095+67795	EM	C2C	PTR	C2C	
357046	67696+74196+74096+67796	EM	C2C	PTR	C2C	

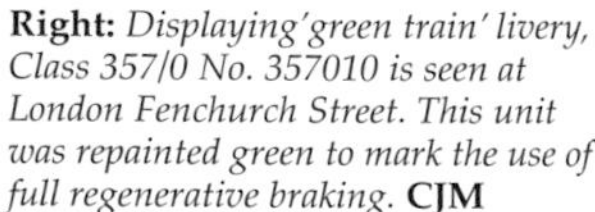

Right: *Displaying 'green train' livery, Class 357/0 No. 357010 is seen at London Fenchurch Street. This unit was repainted green to mark the use of full regenerative braking.* **CJM**

c2c

Class 357/2
Electrostar

Vehicle Length: (Driving) 68ft 1in (20.75m) (Inter) 65ft 11½in (20.10m)
Height: 12ft 4½in (3.78m)
Width: 9ft 2½in (2.80m)
Horsepower: 2,011hp (1,500kW)
Seats (total/car): 282S, 71S/78S/62S/71S

Number	Formation DMSO(A)+MSO+PTSO+DMSO(B)	Depot	Livery	Owner	Operator	Name
357201	68601+74701+74601+68701	EM	C2C	ANG	C2C	Ken Bird
357202	68602+74702+74602+68702	EM	C2C	ANG	C2C	Kenny Mitchell
357203	68603+74703+74603+68703	EM	NE2	ANG	C2C	Henry Pumfrett
357204	68604+74704+74604+68704	EM	C2C	ANG	C2C	Derek Flowers
357205	68605+74705+74605+68705	EM	C2C	ANG	C2C	John D'Silva
357206	68606+74706+74606+68706	EM	C2C	ANG	C2C	Martin Aungier
357207	68607+74707+74607+68707	EM	C2C	ANG	C2C	John Page
357208	68608+74708+74608+68708	EM	C2C	ANG	C2C	Dave Davis
357209	68609+74709+74609+68709	EM	C2C	ANG	C2C	James Snelling
357210	68610+74710+74610+68710	EM	C2C	ANG	C2C	
357211	68611+74711+74611+68711	EM	C2C	ANG	C2C	
357212	68612+74712+74612+68712	EM	C2C	ANG	C2C	
357213	68613+74713+74613+68713	EM	C2C	ANG	C2C	Upminster IECC
357214	68614+74714+74614+68714	EM	C2C	ANG	C2C	
357215	68615+74715+74615+68715	EM	C2C	ANG	C2C	
357216	68616+74716+74616+68716	EM	C2C	ANG	C2C	
357217	68617+74717+74617+68717	EM	C2C	ANG	C2C	Allan Burnell
357218	68618+74218+74618+68718	EM	C2C	ANG	C2C	
357219	68619+74719+74619+68719	EM	NE2	ANG	C2C	
357220	68620+74720+74620+68720	EM	C2C	ANG	C2C	
357221	68621+74721+74621+68721	EM	C2C	ANG	C2C	
357222	68622+74722+74622+68722	EM	C2C	ANG	C2C	
357223	68623+74723+74623+68723	EM	C2C	ANG	C2C	
357224	68624+74724+74624+68724	EM	C2C	ANG	C2C	
357225	68625+74725+74625+68725	EM	C2C	ANG	C2C	
357226	68626+74726+74626+68726	EM	C2C	ANG	C2C	
357227	68627+74727+74627+68727	EM	C2C	ANG	C2C	
357228	68628+74728+74628+68728	EM	C2C	ANG	C2C	

Below: *On 26 April 2008, c2c Class 357/2 unit No. 357225 arrives at London Fenchurch Street station with a service from Grays. The entire c2c operation is worked by East Ham-allocated 'Electrostar' Class 357 sets. These are among the most reliable EMUs operating in the UK.* **Tony Christie**

Chiltern Railways

Address: ✉ 2nd floor, Western House, Rickfords Hill, Aylesbury, Buckinghamshire HP20 2RX
Via website
✆ 08456 005165
ⓘ www.chilternrailways.co.uk

Managing Director: Adrian Shooter CBE
Franchise Dates: 21 July 1996 - 1 March 2022
Principal Routes: London Marylebone - Birmingham Snow Hill
London Marylebone - Aylesbury
Hatton - Stratford-upon-Avon
Depots: Aylesbury (AL), Wembley*
* Stabling point
Parent Company: Deutsche Bahn AG (DB Regio)

Wrexham & Shropshire services merged with Chiltern Railways from January 2010; the two trading titles will remain and the service pattern retained.

Chiltern Railways

Class 165/0 (2-car)
Networker Turbo

Vehicle Length: (driving) 75ft 2½in (22.91m), (inter) 74ft 6½in (22.72m)
Height: 12ft 5¼in (3.79m)
Width: 9ft 2½in (2.81m)
Seats (total/car): 183S, 89S/94S
Engine: 1 x Perkins 2006 TWH of 350hp per vehicle
Horsepower: 700hp (522kW)

Number	*Formation DMSL+DMS*	*Depot*	*Livery*	*Owner*	*Operator*
165001	58801+58834	AL	CRW	ANG	CRW
165002	58802+58835	AL	CRW	ANG	CRW
165003	58803+58836	AL	CRW	ANG	CRW
165004	58804+58837	AL	CRW	ANG	CRW
165005	58805+58838	AL	CRW	ANG	CRW
165006	58806+58839	AL	CRW	ANG	CRW
165007	58807+58840	AL	CRW	ANG	CRW
165008	58808+58841	AL	CRW	ANG	CRW
165009	58808+58842	AL	CRW	ANG	CRW
165010	58810+58843	AL	CRW	ANG	CRW
165011	58811+58844	AL	CRW	ANG	CRW
165012	58812+58845	AL	CRW	ANG	CRW
165013	58813+58846	AL	CRW	ANG	CRW
165014	58814+58847	AL	CRW	ANG	CRW
165015	58815+58848	AL	CRW	ANG	CRW
165016	58816+58849	AL	CRW	ANG	CRW
165017	58817+58850	AL	CRW	ANG	CRW
165018	58818+58851	AL	CRW	ANG	CRW
165019	58819+58852	AL	CRW	ANG	CRW
165020	58820+58853	AL	CRW	ANG	CRW
165021	58821+58854	AL	CRW	ANG	CRW
165022	58822+58855	AL	CRW	ANG	CRW
165023	58873+58867	AL	CRW	ANG	CRW
165024	58874+58868	AL	CRW	ANG	CRW
165025	58874+58869	AL	CRW	ANG	CRW
165026	58876+58870	AL	CRW	ANG	CRW
165027	58877+58871	AL	CRW	ANG	CRW
165028	58878+58872	AL	CRW	ANG	CRW

Class 165/0 (3-car)
Networker Turbo

Vehicle Length: (driving) 75ft 2½in (22.91m), (inter) 74ft 6½in (22.72m)
Height: 12ft 5¼in (3.79m)
Width: 9ft 2½in (2.81m)
Seats (total/car): 289S, 89S/106S/94S
Engine: 1 x Perkins 2006 TWH of 350hp per vehicle
Horsepower: 1,050hp (783kW)

Number	*Formation DMSL+MS+DMS*	*Depot*	*Livery*	*Owner*	*Operator*
165029	58823+55404+58856	AL	CRW	ANG	CRW
165030	58824+55405+58857	AL	CRW	ANG	CRW
165031	58825+55406+58858	AL	CRW	ANG	CRW
165032	58826+55407+58859	AL	CRW	ANG	CRW
165033	58827+55408+58860	AL	CRW	ANG	CRW
165034	58828+55409+58861	AL	CRW	ANG	CRW
165035	58829+55410+58862	AL	CRW	ANG	CRW
165036	58830+55411+58863	AL	CRW	ANG	CRW
165037	58831+55412+58864	AL	CRW	ANG	CRW
165038	58832+55413+58865	AL	CRW	ANG	CRW
165039	58833+55414+58866	AL	CRW	ANG	CRW

Left: *The backbone of Chiltern Railways local services is a fleet of two and three-car Class 165/0 'Networker Turbo' units, introduced in the 1980s to replace ageing DMUs. Since original introduction, all sets have been refurbished and sport standard class only accommodation. Two-car set No. 165022 departs from Banbury with a Marylebone bound service.* **Stacey Thew**

Left: *Eleven three-car Class 165/0 sets are in traffic and all sport the white and blue house colours of Chiltern Railways. Allocation of all sets is Aylesbury, but some stabling and maintenance is carried out at Wembley. Three-car set No. 165037 passes Tyseley.* **Stacey Thew**

Class 168/0
Turbostar

Vehicle Length: 77ft 6in (23.62m)
Height: 12ft 4½in (3.77m)
Width: 8ft 10in (2.69m)
Engine: 1 x MTU 6R 183TD13H 422hp per vehicle
Horsepower: 1,688hp (1,259kW)
Seats (total/car): 278S, 60S/73S/77S/68S

Number	Formation DMSL(A)+MSL+MS+DMSL(B)	Depot	Livery	Owner	Operator
168001	58151+58651+58451+58251	AL	CRW	PTR	CRW
168002	58152+58652+58452+58252	AL	CRW	PTR	CRW
168003	58153+58653+58453+58253	AL	CRW	PTR	CRW
168004	58154+58654+58454+58254	AL	CRW	PTR	CRW
168005	58155+58655+58455+58255	AL	CRW	PTR	CRW

Right: *The original five Class 168 'Turbostar' sets, the first trains ordered under privatisation, have a different front end style to the production sets and more in keeping with the Networker design. Four-car set No. 168001 is seen at Birmingham Moor Street.* **John Binch**

Class 168/1
Turbostar

Vehicle Length: 77ft 6in (23.62m)
Height: 12ft 4½in (3.77m)
Width: 8ft 10in (2.69m)
Engine: 1 x MTU 6R 183TD13H of 422hp per vehicle
Horsepower: 3/4-Car 1,266hp (944kW)/1,688hp (1,259kW)
Seats (total/car): 3-car - 208S, 59S/73S/76S, 4-car - 284S, 59S/73S/76S/76S

Number	Formation DMSL(A)+MS+MS+DMSL(B)	Depot	Livery	Owner	Operator	Notes
168106	58156+58756§+58456+58256	AL	CRW	PTR	CRW	*§ is a MSL vehicle*
168107	58157+58457+58757§+58257	AL	CRW	PTR	CRW	*§ is a MSL vehicle*
168108	58158+58458+58258	AL	CRW	PTR	CRW	
168109	58159+58459+58259	AL	CRW	PTR	CRW	
168110	58160+58460+58260	AL	CRW	PTR	CRW	
168111	58161+58461+58261	AL	CRW	HSB	CRW	*58461 was originally 58661*
168112	58162+58462+58262	AL	CRW	HSB	CRW	*58462 was originally 58662*
168113	58163+58463+58263	AL	CRW	HSB	CRW	*58463 was originally 58663*

Class 168/2
Turbostar

Vehicle Length: 77ft 6in (23.62m)
Height: 12ft 4½in (3.77m)
Width: 8ft 10in (2.69m)
Engine: 1 x MTU 6R 183TD13H of 422hp per vehicle
Horsepower: 3/4-Car 1,266hp (944kW)/1,688hp (1,259kW)
Seats (total/car): 3-car - 204S, 59S/76S/69S, 4-car - 277S, 59S/73S/76S/696S

Number	Formation DMSL(A)+MS+MS+DMSL(B)	Depot	Livery	Owner	Operator
168214	58164+58464+58264	AL	CRW	PTR	CRW
168215	58165+58465+58365+58265	AL	CRW	PTR	CRW
168216	58166+58466+58366+58266	AL	CRW	PTR	CRW
168217	58167+58467+58367+58267	AL	CRW	PTR	CRW
168218	58168+58468+58268	AL	CRW	PTR	CRW
168219	58169+58469+58269	AL	CRW	PTR	CRW

Right: *By the time the follow-on Class 168s were ordered for Chiltern, ABB/Bombardier had standardised on the Turbostar front end as used on the Class 170 design, but these sets retained the 168 classification. The two principal Class 168 front ends are shown in this study of Class 168 No. 168001 and 168111 at Birmingham Moor Street.* **John Binch**

Chiltern Railways

Class 172/1

Vehicle Length: 73ft 4in (22.37m)
Height: 12ft 4½in (3.77m)
Width: 9ft 1in (2.75m)
Engine: MTU 6H1800 of 360kW
Horsepower: 965hp (720kW)
Seats (total/car): 121S, 53S/68S

Number	Formation DMS+DMS	Depot	Livery	Owner	Operator
172101	59111+59211	AL	CRW	ANG	CRW
172102	59112+59212	AL	CRW	ANG	CRW
172103	59113+59213	AL	CRW	ANG	CRW
172104	59114+59214	AL	CRW	ANG	CRW

Sets on order scheduled for delivery spring 2010

Class 960 - Service Units

Class 121 and 122
Length: 64ft 6in (19.66m)
Height: 12ft 8½in (3.87m)
Width: 9ft 3in (2.81m)
Engine: 2 x Leyland 150hp
Horsepower: 300hp (224kW)
Seats (total/car): -

Class 117
Length: 64ft 0in (19.50m)
Height: 12ft 8½in (3.87m)
Width: 9ft 3in (2.81m)
Engine: 2 x Leyland 150hp
Horsepower: 300hp (224kW)
Seats (total/car):

Number	Formation	Depot	Livery	Owner	Operator	Notes
960010	977858	AL	MAR	NRL	CRW	Ex Class 121 55024, Sandite
960013	977866	AL	NSE	NRL	CRW	Ex Class 121 55030, Sandite
960014	977873	AL	BLG	CRW	CRW	Ex Class 121 55022, route learning/Sandite
960015	975042	AL	YEL	NRL	CRW	Ex Class 122 55019, Sandite
960021	977723	AL	RTK	NRL	CRW	Ex Class 121 55021, Sandite
960301	977987+977992+977988	AL	GRN	CRW	CRW	Ex Class 117, 51371/51375/51413 - used for water jetting

Above: *Three-car former Class 117 set No. 960301 is allocated to Aylesbury and used for autumn 'water jetting' operations to keep rails clear from leaf mulch. The set is seen stabled adjacent to Aylesbury station on 12 January 2009.* **John Binch**

Left: *Painted in full Network Rail yellow livery, former Class 122 'bubble' car No. 975042 is seen at Aylesbury from its brake van and exhaust end. This vehicle also carries the set number 960015.* **Nathan Williamson**

Class 01 (0-6-0)

Number	Depot	Pool	Livery	Owner	Operator	Name
01509 (433) RH468043	AL	MBDL	BLU	CRW	CRW	Leslie

Cross Country Trains

Address: ✉ Cannon House, 18 The Priory, Queensway, Birmingham, B4 6BS
info@crosscountrytrains.co.uk
✆ 0870 0100084
ⓘ www.crosscountrytrains.co.uk

Managing Director: Andy Cooper

Franchise Dates: 11 November 2007 - 1 May 2016

Principal Routes: Penzance/Paignton - Manchester/Edinburgh/Aberdeen
Bournemouth - Manchester/Edinburgh/Aberdeen
Birmingham - Stansted
Nottingham - Cardiff

Depots: Central Rivers (CZ), Tyseley (TS)

Parent Company: Arriva Trains

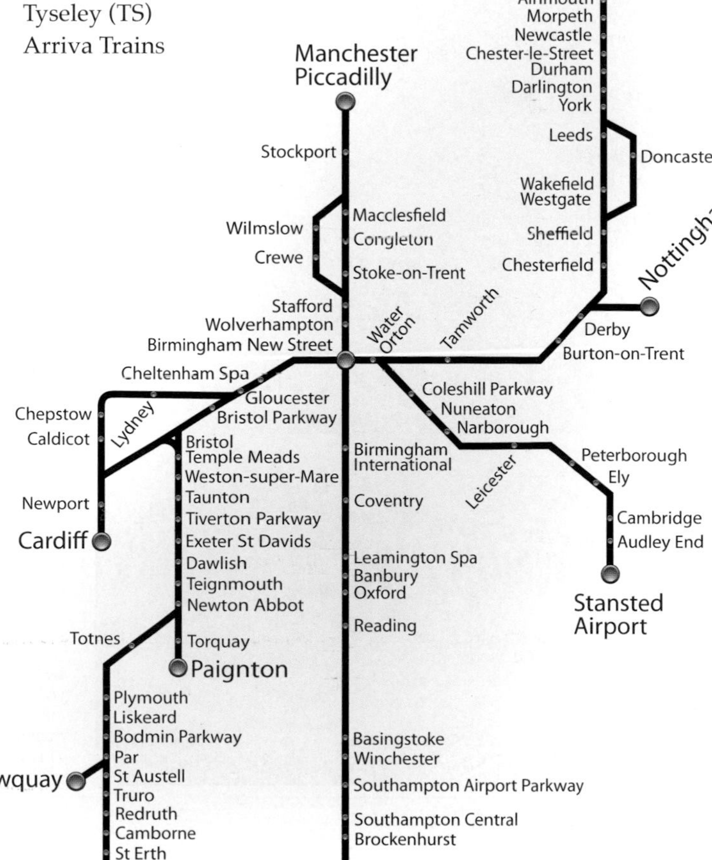

Cross Country Trains

Class 43 - HST

*Vehicle Length: 58ft 5in (18.80m)
Height: 12ft 10in (3.90m)
Width: 8ft 11in (2.73m)*

*Engine: MTU 16V4000 R41R
Horsepower: 2,250hp (1,680kW)
Electrical Equipment: Brush*

Number	Depot	Pool	Livery	Owner	Operator
43207 (43007)	EC	EHPC	AXC	ANG	AXC
43285 (43085)	EC	EHPC	AXC	PTR	AXC
43301 (43101)	EC	EHPC	AXC	PTR	AXC
43303 (43103)	EC	EHPC	AXC	PTR	AXC
43304 (43104)	EC	EHPC	AXC	ANG	AXC
43321 (43121)	EC	EHPC	AXC	PTR	AXC
43357 (43157)	EC	EHPC	AXC	PTR	AXC
43366 (43166)	EC	EHPC	AXC	ANG	AXC
43378 (43178)	EC	EHPC	AXC	ANG	AXC
43384 (43184)	EC	EHPC	AXC	ANG	AXC

Above: *The five HST sets operated on the CrossCountry network are used on the prime Scotland, North West and Yorkshire services to the West Country, easing previous overcrowding on Voyager stock. A full 2+8 set is seen at Plymouth with power car Class 43 No. 43321 nearest the camera on 13 October 2008.* **Nathan WIlliamson**

HST passenger fleet

*Vehicle Length: 75ft 0in (22.86m)
Height: 12ft 9in (3.88m)*

*Width: 8ft 11in (2.71m)
Bogie Type: BT10*

GH1G - TF *Seating 40F*

Number	Depot	Livery	Owner	
41026	EC	AXC	ANG	
41035	EC	AXC	ANG	
41193 (11060)	EC	AXC	PTR	
41194 (11016)	EC	AXC	PTR	
41195¤ (11020)	EC	AXC	PTR	¤ = TFD

GH2G - TS *Seating 82S*

Number	Depot	Livery	Owner	
42036	EC	AXC	ANG	
42037	EC	AXC	ANG	
42038	EC	AXC	ANG	
42051	EC	AXC	ANG	
42052	EC	AXC	ANG	
42053	EC	AXC	ANG	
42097	EC	AXC	ANG	
42234	EC	AXC	PTR	
42290	EC	AXC	PTR	
42342 (44082)	EC	AXC	ANG	
42366 (12007)	EC	AXC	PTR	
42367 (12025)	EC	AXC	PTR	
42368 (12028)	EC	AXC	PTR	
42369 (12050)	EC	AXC	PTR	
42370 (12086)	EC	AXC	PTR	
42371 (12052)	EC	AXC	PTR	
42372 (12055)	EC	AXC	PTR	
42373 (12071)	EC	AXC	PTR	
42374 (12075)	EC	AXC	PTR	
42375 (12113)	EC	AXC	PTR	
42376 (12085)	EC	AXC	PTR	
42377 (12102)	EC	AXC	PTR	
42378 (12123)	EC	AXC	PTR	
42379* (41036)	EC	AXC	ANG	*=TSD
42380* (41025)	EC	AXC	ANG	*=TSD

GJ2G - TGS *Seating 67S*

Number	Depot	Livery	Owner
44012	EC	AXC	ANG
44017	EC	AXC	ANG
44021	EC	AXC	ANG
44052	EC	AXC	PTR
44072	EC	AXC	PTR

GH3G - TCC *Seating 30F/10S*

Number	Depot	Livery	Owner
45001 (12004)	EC	AXC	PTR
45002 (12106)	EC	AXC	PTR
45003 (12076)	EC	AXC	PTR
45004 (12077)	EC	AXC	PTR
45005 (12080)	EC	AXC	PTR

Class 170/1
Turbostar

Vehicle Length: 77ft 6in (23.62m)
Height: 12ft 4½in (3.77m)
Width: 8ft 10in (2.69m)
Engine: 1 x MTU 6R 183TD13H 422hp per vehicle
Horsepower: 1,266hp (944kW)
Seats (total/car): 9F/191S 52S/80S/9F-59S

Number	Formation DMS+MS+DMCL	Depot	Livery	Owner	Operator
170101	50101+55101+79101	TS	AXC	PTR	AXC
170102	50102+55102+79102	TS	AXC	PTR	AXC
170103	50103+55103+79103	TS	AXC	PTR	AXC
170104	50104+55104+79104	TS	AXC	PTR	AXC
170105	50105+55105+79105	TS	AXC	PTR	AXC
170106	50106+55106+79106	TS	AXC	PTR	AXC
170107	50107+55107+79107	TS	AXC	PTR	AXC
170108*	50108+55108+79108	TS	AXC	PTR	AXC
170109*	50109+55109+79109	TS	AXC	PTR	AXC
170110	50110+55110+79110	TS	AXC	PTR	AXC

Vehicle Length: 77ft 6in (23.62m)
Height: 12ft 4½in (3.77m)
Width: 8ft 10in (2.69m)
Engine: 1 x MTU 6R 183TD13H 422hp per vehicle
Horsepower: 844hp (629kW)
Seats (total/car): 9F-111S 59S/9F-52S

Number	Formation DMS+DMCL	Depot	Livery	Owner	Operator
170111*	50111+79111	TS	AXC	PTR	AXC
170112	50112+79112	TS	AXC	PTR	AXC
170113	50113+79113	TS	AXC	PTR	AXC
170114	50114+79114	TS	AXC	PTR	AXC
170115	50115+79115	TS	AXC	PTR	AXC
170116	50116+79116	TS	AXC	PTR	AXC
170117	50117+79117	TS	AXC	PTR	AXC

* Fitted with passenger counters

Class 170/3
Turbostar

Vehicle Length: 77ft 6in (23.62m)
Height: 12ft 4½in (3.77m)
Width: 8ft 10in (2.69m)
Engine: 1 x MTU 6R 183TD13H 422hp per vehicle
Horsepower: 1,266hp (944kW)
Seats (total/car): 9F-191S 59S/80S/9F-52S

Number	Formation DMSL+MS+DMCL	Depot	Livery	Owner	Operator
170397	50397+56397+79397	TS	AXC	PTR	AXC
170398	50398+56398+79398	TS	AXC	PTR	AXC

Class 170/5
Turbostar

Vehicle Length: 77ft 6in (23.62m)
Height: 12ft 4½in (3.77m)
Width: 8ft 10in (2.69m)
Engine: 1 x MTU 6R 183TD13H 422hp per vehicle
Horsepower: 844hp (629kW)
Seats (total/car): 9F-111S 59S/9F-52S

Number	Formation DMSL+DMCL	Depot	Livery	Owner	Operator
170518	50518+79518	TS	AXC	PTR	AXC
170519	50519+79519	TS	AXC	PTR	AXC
170520	50520+79520	TS	AXC	PTR	AXC
170521	50521+79521	TS	AXC	PTR	AXC
170522	50522+79522	TS	AXC	PTR	AXC
170523	50523+79523	TS	AXC	PTR	AXC

Class 170/6
Turbostar

Vehicle Length: 77ft 6in (23.62m)
Height: 12ft 4½in (3.77m)
Width: 8ft 10in (2.69m)
Engine: 1 x MTU 6R 183TD13H 422hp per vehicle
Horsepower: 1,266hp (944kW)
Seats (total/car): 9F-191S 59S/80S/9F-52S

Number	Formation DMSL+MS+DMCL	Depot	Livery	Owner	Operator
170636	50636+56636+79636	TS	AXC	PTR	AXC
170637	50637+56637+79637	TS	AXC	PTR	AXC
170638	50638+56638+79638	TS	AXC	PTR	AXC
170639	50639+56639+79639	TS	AXC	PTR	AXC

Right: *Some form of standardisation has now emerged with the various sub-classes of Class 170 which form the CrossCountry fleet. Since the transfer of the franchise to Arriva, all sets have been refurbished and each set now has the 79xxx coach formed as a composite vehicle. Set No. 170521 is seen at Gloucester.* **CJM**

Cross Country Trains

Class 220 *Voyager*

Vehicle Length: 77ft 6in (23.62m)
Height: 12ft 4in (3.75m)
Width: 8ft 11in (2.73m)
Engine: 1 x Cummins 750hp per vehicle
Horsepower: 3,000hp (2,237kW)
Seats (total/car): 26F/174S 42S/66S/66S/26F

Number	*Formation* DMS+MS+MS+DMF	*Depot*	*Livery*	*Owner*	*Operator*
220001	60301+60701+60201+60401	CZ	AXC	HBS	AXC
220002	60302+60702+60202+60402	CZ	AXC	HBS	AXC
220003	60303+60703+60203+60403	CZ	AXC	HBS	AXC
220004	60304+60704+60204+60404	CZ	AXC	HBS	AXC
220005	60305+60705+60205+60405	CZ	AXC	HBS	AXC
220006	60306+60706+60206+60406	CZ	AXC	HBS	AXC
220007	60307+60707+60207+60407	CZ	AXC	HBS	AXC
220008	60308+60708+60208+60408	CZ	AXC	HBS	AXC
220009	60309+60709+60209+60409	CZ	AXC	HBS	AXC
220010	60310+60710+60210+60410	CZ	AXC	HBS	AXC
220011	60311+60711+60211+60411	CZ	AXC	HBS	AXC
220012	60312+60712+60212+60412	CZ	AXC	HBS	AXC
220013	60313+60713+60213+60413	CZ	AXC	HBS	AXC
220014	60314+60714+60214+60414	CZ	AXC	HBS	AXC
220015	60315+60715+60215+60415	CZ	AXC	HBS	AXC
220016	60316+60716+60216+60416	CZ	AXC	HBS	AXC
220017	60317+60717+60217+60417	CZ	AXC	HBS	AXC
220018	60318+60718+60218+60418	CZ	AXC	HBS	AXC
220019	60319+60719+60219+60419	CZ	AXC	HBS	AXC
220020	60320+60720+60220+60420	CZ	AXC	HBS	AXC
220021	60321+60721+60221+60421	CZ	AXC	HBS	AXC
220022	60322+60722+60222+60422	CZ	AXC	HBS	AXC
220023	60323+60723+60223+60423	CZ	AXC	HBS	AXC
220024	60324+60724+60224+60424	CZ	AXC	HBS	AXC
220025	60325+60725+60225+60425	CZ	AXC	HBS	AXC
220026	60326+60726+60226+60426	CZ	AXC	HBS	AXC
220027	60327+60727+60227+60427	CZ	AXC	HBS	AXC
220028	60328+60728+60228+60428	CZ	AXC	HBS	AXC
220029	60329+60729+60229+60429	CZ	AXC	HBS	AXC
220030	60330+60730+60230+60430	CZ	AXC	HBS	AXC
220031	60331+60731+60231+60431	CZ	AXC	HBS	AXC
220032	60332+60732+60232+60432	CZ	AXC	HBS	AXC
220033	60333+60733+60233+60433	CZ	AXC	HBS	AXC
220034	60334+60734+60234+60434	CZ	AXC	HBS	AXC

Below: *Since the transfer of the CrossCountry franchise from Virgin Trains to Arriva CrossCountry, the Class 220 'Voyager' sets have been extensively modified with the former shop/buffet bar removed, with catering now provided from a trolley. Set No. 220002 is seen at Reading.* **CJM**

Class 221
Super Voyager

Vehicle Length: 77ft 6in (23.62m)
Height: 12ft 4in (3.75m)
Width: 8ft 11in (2.73m)
Engine: 1 x Cummins 750hp per vehicle
Horsepower: 3,750hp (2,796kW)
Seats (total/car): 26F/236S 42S/66S/66S/62S/26F

Originally fitted with tilt system to allow higher speeds over curves. Equipment now isolated

Number	*Formation* DMS+MS+MS+MS+DMF	*Depot*	*Livery*	*Owner*	*Operator*	
221114	60364+60764+60964+60864+60464	CZ	AXC	HBS	AXC	
221115	60365+60765+60965+60865+60465	CZ	AXC	HBS	AXC	
221116	60366+60766+60966+60866+60466	CZ	AXC	HBS	AXC	
221117	60367+60767+60967+60867+60467	CZ	AXC	HBS	AXC	
221118	60368+60768+60968+60868+60468	CZ	AXC	HBS	AXC	
221119	60369+60769+60969+60869+60469	CZ	AXC	HBS	AXC	
221120	60370+60770+60970+60870+60470	CZ	AXC	HBS	AXC	
221121	60371+60771+60971+60871+60471	CZ	AXC	HBS	AXC	
221122	60372+60772+60972+60872+60472	CZ	AXC	HBS	AXC	
221123	60373+60773+60973+60873+60473	CZ	AXC	HBS	AXC	
221124	60374+60774+60974+60874+60474	CZ	AXC	HBS	AXC	
221125	60375+60775+60975+60875+60475	CZ	AXC	HBS	AXC	
221126	60376+60776+60976+60876+60476	CZ	AXC	HBS	AXC	
221127	60377+60777+60977+60877+60477	CZ	AXC	HBS	AXC	
221128	60378+60778+60978+60878+60478	CZ	AXC	HBS	AXC	
221129	60379+60779+60979+60879+60479	CZ	AXC	HBS	AXC	
221130	60380+60780+60980+60880+60480	CZ	AXC	HBS	AXC	
221131	60381+60781+60981+60881+60481	CZ	AXC	HBS	AXC	
221132	60382+60782+60982+60882+60482	CZ	AXC	HBS	AXC	
221133	60383+60783+60983+60883+60483	CZ	AXC	HBS	AXC	
221134	60384+60784+60984+60884+60484	CZ	AXC	HBS	AXC	
221135	60385+60785+60985+60885+60485	CZ	AXC	HBS	AXC	
221136	60386+60786+60986+60886+60486	CZ	AXC	HBS	AXC	
221137	60387+60787+60987+60887+60487	CZ	AXC	HBS	AXC	
221138	60388+60788+60988+60888+60488	CZ	AXC	HBS	AXC	
221139	60389+60789+60989+60889+60489	CZ	AXC	HBS	AXC	
221140	60390+60790+60990+60890+60490	CZ	AXC	HBS	AXC	
221141	60391+60791+60991+60491	CZ	AXC	HBS	AXC	*(Four-car set)*

Below: *All but one of the Class 221 'Super Voyager' sets operated by Arriva CrossCountry are five car sets, the exception being the last member of the fleet No. 221141 which was one of the original Virgin short tilting sets used on London to North Wales services. All sets are allocated to the Bombardier-operated Central Rivers depot near Burton-on-Trent and all sport CrossCountry trains silver and maroon red livery off-set by pink passenger doors. Set No. 221125 is seen passing Dawlish Warren with its first class DMF vehicle leading.* **CJM**

East Midlands Trains

Address: ✉ Midland House, Nelson Street, Derby. DE1 2SA
getintouch@eastmidlandstrains.co.uk
✆ 08457 125678
ⓘ www.eastmidlandstrains.co.uk

Managing Director: Tim Shoveller
Franchise Dates: 11 November 2007 - 31 March 2015
Principal Routes: St Pancras-Sheffield / York / Leeds / Nottingham
Norwich / Skegness / Cleethorpes - Nottingham / Crewe / Liverpool and Matlock
Depots: Derby (DY), Nottingham (NM), Neville Hill (NL)
Parent Company: Stagecoach

Class 08

Vehicle Length: 29ft 3in (8.91m)
Height: 12ft 8⅝in (3.87m)
Width: 8ft 6in (2.59m)
Engine: English Electric 6K
Horsepower: 400hp (298kW)
Electrical Equipment: English Electric

Number	*Depot*	*Pool*	*Livery*	*Owner*	*Operator*
08525	NL	EMSL	MAI	EMT	EMT
08690	NL	EMSL	MAI	EMT	EMT
08697(S)	DY	EMSL	BLU	EMT	-
08899	DY	EMSL	MAI	EMT	EMT
08908	DY	EMSL	MML	EMT	EMT
08950	NL	EMSL	MAI	EMT	EMT

Left: *East Midlands Trains maintenance is carried out at Leeds Neville Hill and Derby Etches Park depots by Maintrain. Both sites have a requirement for shunting power to re-form HST sets as required and position vehicles within the service shed for attention. No. 08525 is viewed alongside an HST powercar at Leeds Neville Hill depot.* **Tony Christie**

Class 43 – HST

Vehicle Length: 58ft 5in (18.80m)
Height: 12ft 10in (3.90m)
Width: 8ft 11in (2.73m)
Engine: Paxman VP185
Horsepower: 2,100hp (1,565kW)
Electrical Equipment: Brush

Number	*Depot*	*Pool*	*Livery*	*Owner*	*Operator*
43043	NL	EMPC	MML	PTR	EMT
43044	NL	EMPC	MML	PTR	EMT
43045	NL	EMPC	MML	PTR	EMT
43046	NL	EMPC	SCE	PTR	EMT
43047	NL	EMPC	MML	PTR	EMT
43048	NL	EMPC	SCE	PTR	EMT
43049	NL	EMPC	SCE	PTR	EMT
43050	NL	EMPC	SCE	PTR	EMT
43052	NL	EMPC	MML	PTR	EMT
43054	NL	EMPC	MML	PTR	EMT
43055	NL	EMPC	SCE	PTR	EMT
43058	NL	EMPC	SCE	PTR	EMT
43059	NL	EMPC	MML	PTR	EMT
43060	NL	EMPC	MML	PTR	EMT
43061	NL	EMPC	SCE	PTR	EMT
43064	NL	EMPC	SCE	PTR	EMT
43066	NL	EMPC	MML	PTR	EMT
43072	NL	EMPC	SCE	PTR	EMT
43073	NL	EMPC	MML	PTR	EMT
43074	NL	EMPC	MML	PTR	EMT
43075	NL	EMPC	MML	PTR	EMT
43076	NL	EMPC	MML	PTR	EMT
43081	NL	EMPC	MML	PTR	EMT
43082	NL	EMPC	SCE	PTR	EMT
43083	NL	EMPC	SCE	PTR	EMT
43089	NL	EMPC	SCE	PTR	EMT

Names applied

43048	*T. C. B Miller MBE*
43049	*Neville Hill*
43082	*Railway Children The Voice for Street Children Worldwide*

East Midlands Trains

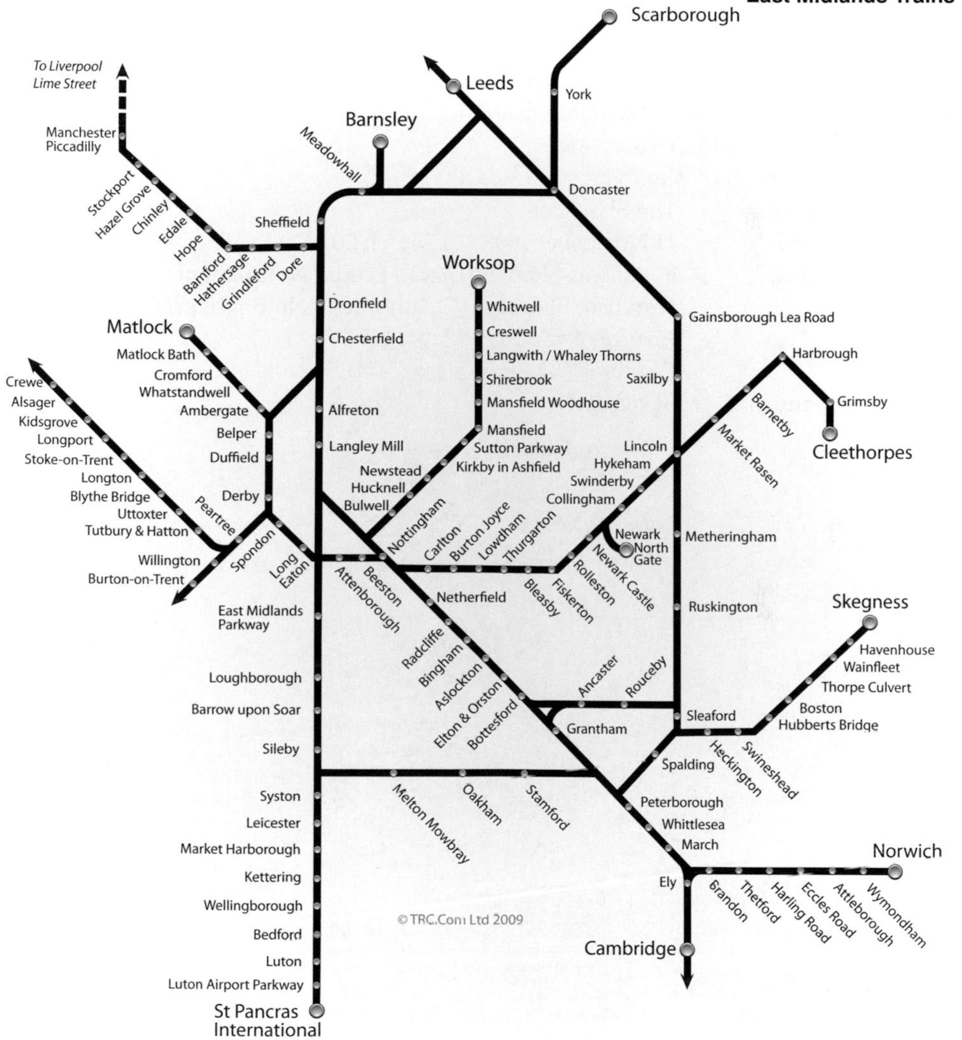

Scarborough
York
Leeds
Barnsley
Meadowhall
Doncaster
To Liverpool Lime Street
Manchester Piccadilly
Stockport
Hazel Grove
Chinley
Edale
Hope
Bamford
Hathersage
Grindleford
Dore
Sheffield
Worksop
Whitwell
Creswell
Langwith / Whaley Thorns
Shirebrook
Mansfield Woodhouse
Mansfield
Sutton Parkway
Kirkby in Ashfield
Newstead
Hucknell
Bulwell
Dronfield
Chesterfield
Alfreton
Langley Mill
Gainsborough Lea Road
Saxilby
Lincoln
Hykeham
Swinderby
Collingham
Newark North Gate
Metheringham
Ruskington
Harbrough
Grimsby
Cleethorpes
Barnetby
Market Rasen
Matlock
Matlock Bath
Cromford
Whatstandwell
Ambergate
Belper
Duffield
Derby
Crewe
Alsager
Kidsgrove
Longport
Stoke-on-Trent
Longton
Blythe Bridge
Uttoxter
Tutbury & Hatton
Willington
Burton-on-Trent
Peartree
Spondon
Long Eaton
East Midlands Parkway
Beeston
Attenborough
Nottingham
Carlton
Burton Joyce
Lowdham
Thurgarton
Fiskerton
Rolleston
Newark Castle
Bleasby
Netherfield
Radcliffe
Bingham
Aslockton
Elton & Orston
Bottesford
Ancaster
Rouceby
Grantham
Sleaford
Skegness
Havenhouse
Wainfleet
Thorpe Culvert
Boston
Hubberts Bridge
Swineshead
Heckington
Spalding
Peterborough
Whittlesea
March
Ely
Cambridge
Norwich
Brandon
Thetford
Harling Road
Eccles Road
Attleborough
Wymondham
Loughborough
Barrow upon Soar
Sileby
Syston
Leicester
Market Harborough
Kettering
Wellingborough
Bedford
Luton
Luton Airport Parkway
St Pancras International
Melton Mowbray
Oakham
Stamford

Right: *One of the most striking liveries to be applied to the iconic HST is Stagecoach East Midlands Trains red, orange, blue and white, which surprisingly suits the body profile. Viewed from the luggage van end, No. 43058 is seen at Chesterfield on 18 October 2008.* **Stacey Thew**

East Midlands Trains

Class 153

Vehicle Length: 76ft 5in (23.29m)
Height: 12ft 3⅛in (3.75m)
Width: 8ft 10in (2.70m)
Engine: 1 x NT855R5 of 285hp
Horsepower: 285hp (213kW)
Seats (total/car): 66S

Number	Formation DMSL	Depot	Livery	Owner	Operator
153302	52302	NM	EMT	ANG	EMT
153308	52308	NM	EMT	ANG	EMT
153310	52310	NM	EMT	PTR	EMT
153311	52311	NM	EMT	PTR	EMT
153313	52313	NM	EMT	PTR	EMT
153319	52319	NM	EMT	ANG	EMT
153321	52321	NM	EMT	PTR	EMT
153326	52326	NM	EMT	PTR	EMT
153355	57355	NM	EMT	ANG	EMT
153357	57357	NM	ENT	ANG	EMT
153374	57374	NM	EMT	ANG	EMT
153376	57376	NM	EMT	PTR	EMT
153379	57379	NM	EMT	PTR	EMT
153381	57381	NM	EMT	PTR	EMT
153383	57383	NM	EMT	PTR	EMT
153384	57384	NM	EMT	PTR	EMT
153385	57385	NM	EMT	PTR	EMT

Left: *Nottingham Eastcroft depot is the base for 17 Class 153 'bubble cars' deployed on lesser used local services. All are painted in East Midlands/Stagecoach outer suburban blue livery with swirl ends. Set No. 153310 is illustrated from its original 'large' cab end.* **Stacey Thew**

Class 156

Vehicle Length: 75ft 6in (23.03m)
Height: 12ft 6in (3.81m)
Width: 8ft 11in (2.73m)
Engine: 1 x Cummins NT855R5 of 285hp
Horsepower: 570hp (425kW)
Seats (total/car): 148 or 150S, 70 or 72S/78S

Number	Formation DMSL+DMS	Depot	Livery	Owner	Operator
156401	52401+57401	NM	EMT	PTR	EMT
156403	52403+57403	NM	EMT	PTR	EMT
156404	52404+57404	NM	EMT	PTR	EMT
156405	52405+57405	NM	EMT	PTR	EMT
156406	52406+57406	NM	EMT	PTR	EMT
156408	52408+57408	NM	EMT	PTR	EMT
156410	52410+57410	NM	EMT	PTR	EMT
156411	52411+57411	NM	EMT	PTR	EMT
156413	52413+57413	NM	EMT	PTR	EMT
156414	52414+57414	NM	EMT	PTR	EMT
156415	52415+57415	NM	EMT	PTR	EMT

Left: *The mainstay of longer distance outer suburban EMT services are the Class 156 or 158 fleets. 11 Class 156s are presently on the roster, all allocated to Nottingham Eastcroft and all sport the latest EMT livery. Set No. 158408 is seen at Derby.* **Tony Christie**

Class 158

Vehicle Length: 76ft 1¾in (23.21m)
Height: 12ft 6in (3.81m)
Width: 9ft 3¼in (2.82m)
Engine: 158770-813 - 1 x Cummins NT855R5 of 350hp
Horsepower: 700hp (522kW)
Engine: 158846-862 - 1 x Perkins 2006TWH of 350hp
Horsepower: 700hp (522kW)
Engine: 158863-865 - 1 x Cummins NT855R5 of 400hp
Horsepower: 800hp (597kW)
Seats (total/car): 146S - 74S, 72S

Number	Formation DMSL+DMSL	Depot	Livery	Owner	Operator
158770	52770+57770	NM	TPT	PTR	EMT
158773	52773+57773	NM	TPT	PTR	EMT
158774	52774+57774	NM	SCE	PTR	EMT
158777	52777+57777	NM	SCE	PTR	EMT

158780	52780+57780	NM	SCE	ANG	EMT
158783	52783+57783	NM	SCE	ANG	EMT
158785	52785+57785	NM	SCE	ANG	EMT
158788	52788+57788	NM	SCE	ANG	EMT
158799	52799+57799	NM	TPT	PTR	EMT
158806	52806+57806	NM	SCE	PTR	EMT
158810	52810+57810	NM	SCE	PTR	EMT
158812	52812+57812	NM	SCE	PTR	EMT
158813	52813+57813	NM	SCE	PTR	EMT
158846	52846+57846	NM	SCE	ANG	EMT
158847	52847+57847	NM	SCE	ANG	EMT
158852	52852+57852	NM	SCE	ANG	EMT
158854	52854+57854	NM	SCE	ANG	EMT
158856	52856+57856	NM	SCE	ANG	EMT
158857	52857+57857	NM	SCE	ANG	EMT
158858	52858+57858	NM	SCE	ANG	EMT
158862	52862+57862	NM	SCE	ANG	EMT
158863	52863+57863	NM	WET	ANG	EMT
158864	52864+57864	NM	WET	ANG	EMT
158865	52865+57865	NM	WET	ANG	EMT
158866	52866+57866	NM	WET	ANG	EMT

Right: *The EMT Class 158s being deemed as main line trains are painted in the Stagecoach white 'long distance' livery, similar to the South West Trains allocated sets, except the EMT allocated fleet have a 'hump' in the lower blue panel behind the cab end doors. This fleet is just completing a major refurbishment by Delta Rail, Derby. Set No. 158785 is illustrated.*
Nathan Williamson

Class 222

Vehicle Length: 77ft 6in (23.62m)
Height: 12ft 4in (3.75m)
Width: 8ft 11in (2.73m)
Engine: 1 x Cummins OSK9R of 750hp per vehicle
Horsepower: 5,250hp (3,914kW)
Seats (total/car): 106F/236S
38S/68S/68S/62S/42F/42F/22F

Number	*Formation* DMS+MS+MS+MSRMB+MF+MF+DMRFO	*Depot*	*Livery*	*Owner*	*Operator*
222001	60161+60551+60561+60621+60341+60445+60241	DY	SCE	HSB	EMT
222002	60162+60544+60562+60622+60342+60346+60242	DY	SCE	HSB	EMT
222003	60163+60553+60563+60623+60343+60446+60243	DY	SCE	HSB	EMT
222004	60164+60554+60564+60624+60344+60345+60244	DY	SCE	HSB	EMT
222005	60165+60555+60565+60625+60443+60347+60245	DY	SCE	HSB	EMT
222006	60166+60556+60566+60626+60441+60447+60246	DY	SCE	HSB	EMT

Name applied
222003 (60163) *Tornado*

Vehicle Length: 77ft 6in (23.62m)
Height: 12ft 4in (3.75m)
Width: 8ft 11in (2.73m)
Engine: 1 x Cummins OSK9R of 750hp per vehicle
Horsepower: 3,750hp (2,796kW)
Seats (total/car): 50F/190S
38S/68S/62S/28F-22S/22F

Number	*Formation* DMS+MS+MSRMB+MC+DMRFO	*Depot*	*Livery*	*Owner*	*Operator*
222007	60167+60567+60627+60442+60247	DY	SCE	HSB	EMT
222008	60168+60545+60628+60918+60248	DY	SCE	HSB	EMT
222009	60169+60557+60629+60919+60249	DY	SCE	HSB	EMT
222010	60170+60546+60630+60920+60250	DY	SCE	HSB	EMT
222011	60171+60531+60631+60921+60251	DY	SCE	HSB	EMT
222012	60172+60532+60632+60922+60252	DY	SCE	HSB	EMT
222013	60173+60536+60633+60923+60253	DY	SCE	HSB	EMT
222014	60174+60534+60634+60924+60254	DY	SCE	HSB	EMT
222015	60175+60535+60635+60925+60255	DY	SCE	HSB	EMT
222016	60176+60533+60636+60926+60256	DY	SCE	HSB	EMT
222017	60177+60537+60637+60927+60257	DY	SCE	HSB	EMT
222018	60178+60444+60638+60928+60258	DY	SCE	HSB	EMT
222019	60179+60547+60639+60929+60259	DY	SCE	HSB	EMT
222020	60180+60543+60640+60930+60260	DY	SCE	HSB	EMT
222021	60181+60552+60641+60931+60261	DY	SCE	HSB	EMT
222022	60182+60542+60642+60932+60262	DY	SCE	HSB	EMT
222023	60183+60541+60643+60933+60263	DY	SCE	HSB	EMT

East Midlands Trains

Left: *The entire fleet of Class 221/0 sets are painted in Stagecoach East Midlands white and blue livery and operate alongside the remaining HST sets on all main line services on the London St Pancras to Sheffield/ Nottingham corridor. Set No. 222017 is seen at Nottingham.* **CJM**

Class 222/1

Vehicle Length: 77ft 6in (23.62m)
Height: 12ft 4in (3.75m)
Width: 8ft 11in (2.73m)
Engine: 1 x Cummins OSK9R of 750hp per vehicle
Horsepower: 3,000hp (2,237kW)
Seats (total/car): 33F/148S 22F/11F-46S/62S/40S

Number	*Formation* DMF+MC+MSRMB+DMS	*Depot*	*Livery*	*Owner*	*Operator*
222101	**60271+60571+60681+60191**	**DY**	**SCE**	**HSB**	**EMT**
222102	**60272+60572+60682+60192**	**DY**	**SCE**	**HSB**	**EMT**
222103	**60273+60573+60683+60193**	**DY**	**SCE**	**HSB**	**EMT**
222104	**60274+60574+60684+60194**	**DY**	**SCE**	**HSB**	**EMT**

Left: *The Class 222/1 units were transferred to East Midlands Trains from Spring 2009, after Hull Trains commenced using Class 180 stock. The sets quickly lost the Hull Trains livery (and stick-on names) in favour of the Stagecoach East Midlands Trains colours. On 28 May 2009, set No. 222104 is seen at Leicester.* **John Binch**

HST Passenger Fleet

Vehicle Length: 75ft 0in (22.86m)
Height: 12ft 9in (3.88m)
Width: 8ft 11in (2.71m)
Bogie Type: BT10

GK1G - TRFB *Seating 17F*

Number	*Depot*	*Livery*	*Owner*
40700	**NL**	**MML**	**PTR**
40728	**NL**	**SCE**	**PTR**
40729(S)	**NL**	**MML**	**PTR**
40730	**NL**	**SCE**	**PTR**
40741	**NL**	**MML**	**PTR**
40746	**NL**	**SCE**	**PTR**
40749	**NL**	**SCE**	**PTR**
40751	**NL**	**MML**	**PTR**
40753	**NL**	**SCE**	**PTR**
40754	**NL**	**SCE**	**PTR**
40756	**NL**	**MML**	**PTR**

GH1G - TF *Seating 46F*

Number	*Depot*	*Livery*	*Owner*
41041	**NL**	**SCE**	**PTR**
41046	**NL**	**SCE**	**PTR**
41057	**NL**	**MML**	**PTR**
41061	**NL**	**MML**	**PTR**
41062	**NL**	**MML**	**PTR**
41063	**NL**	**MML**	**PTR**
41064	**NL**	**SCE**	**PTR**
41067	**NL**	**SCE**	**PTR**
41068	**NL**	**MML**	**PTR**
41069	**NL**	**MML**	**PTR**
41070	**NL**	**MML**	**PTR**
41071	**NL**	**MML**	**PTR**
41072	**NL**	**MML**	**PTR**
41075	**NL**	**MML**	**PTR**
41076	**NL**	**MML**	**PTR**
41077	**NL**	**SCE**	**PTR**
41078	**NL**	**MML**	**PTR**
41079	**NL**	**MML**	**PTR**
41084	**NL**	**MML**	**PTR**
41111	**NL**	**MML**	**PTR**
41112	**NL**	**SCE**	**PTR**
41113	**NL**	**MML**	**PTR**
41117	**NL**	**SCE**	**PTR**
41154	**NL**	**MML**	**PTR**

Number	Depot	Livery	Owner
41156	NL	SCE	PTR

GH2G - TS *Seating 74S*

Number	Depot	Livery	Owner
42100	NL	SCE	PTR
42111	NL	MML	PTR
42112	NL	MML	PTR
42113	NL	MML	PTR
42119	NL	MML	PTR
42120	NL	MML	PTR
42121	NL	MML	PTR
42123	NL	MML	PTR
42124	NL	SCE	PTR
42125	NL	MML	PTR
42131	NL	SCE	PTR
42132	NL	SCE	PTR
42133	NL	SCE	PTR
42135	NL	MML	PTR
42136	NL	MML	PTR
42137	NL	MML	PTR
42139	NL	MML	PTR
42140	NL	MML	PTR
42141	NL	MML	PTR
42148	NL	MML	PTR
42149	NL	MML	PTR
42151	NL	SCE	PTR
42152	NL	SCE	PTR
42153	NL	SCE	PTR
42155	NL	MML	PTR
42156	NL	MML	PTR
42157	NL	MML	PTR
42164	NL	SCE	PTR
42165	NL	SCE	PTR
42194	NL	SCE	PTR
42205	NL	MML	PTR
42210	NL	MML	PTR
42220	NL	SCE	PTR
42225	NL	SCE	PTR
42227	NL	SCE	PTR
42229	NL	SCE	PTR
42230	NL	SCE	PTR
42324	NL	MML	PTR
42327	NL	MML	PTR
42328	NL	MML	PTR
42329	NL	MML	PTR
42331	NL	SCE	PTR
42335	NL	MML	PTR
42337	NL	MML	PTR
42339	NL	MML	PTR
42341	NL	MML	PTR

GJ2G - TGS *Seating 63S*

Number	Depot	Livery	Owner
44027	NL	SCE	PTR
44041	NL	MML	PTR
44044	NL	MML	PTR
44046	NL	SCE	PTR
44047	NL	SCE	PTR
44048	NL	MML	PTR
44051	NL	SCE	PTR
44054	NL	MML	PTR
44070	NL	MML	PTR
44071	NL	MML	PTR
44073	NL	MML	PTR
44085	NL	SCE	PTR

Right: *In 2009-10 a major refurbishment of the East Midlands HST passenger fleet was underway at Leeds Neville Hill, which will see all vehicles repainted in the Stagecoach mainline white livery. One set was repainted in 2008 to match a pair of power cars. TGS No. 44047 is illustrated.* **Tim Easter**

Service Stock

HST Barrier Vehicles

Number	Depot	Livery	Owner	Former Identity
6392	NL	PTR	PTR	BG - 81588/92183
6395	NL	PTR	EMT	BG - 81506/92148
6397	NL	PTR	PTR	BG - 81600/92190
6398	NL	MAI	EMT	BG - 81471/92126
6399	NL	MAI	EMT	BG - 81367/92994

Right: *Modified from a former parcels BG van, Maintrain-owned East Midlands Trains-operated HST barrier van No. 6399 is one of five vehicles allocated to Leeds Neville Hill. The coach retains a central brake compartment. The vehicle is seen at Leeds Neville Hill.* **Tony Christie**

Class 930 Service Unit

Number	Depot	Livery	Owner	Formation
930010	DY	BLU	EMT	975600 (10988) + 975601 (10843) Former Class 405 SUB vehicles

Eurostar

Address: ✉ Eurostar, Times House, Bravingtons Walk, Regent Quarter, London N1 9AW

new.comments@eurostar.com

✆ 08701 606 600

ⓘ www.eurostar.com

Managing Director: Nicolas Petrovic / Richard Brown

Principal Routes: St Pancras International - Brussels and Paris also serving Disneyland Paris, Avignon and winter sport service to Bourg St Maurice

Owned Stations: St Pancras International, Stratford International, Ebbsfleet

Depots: Temple Mills (TI), Forest [Belgium] (FF), Le Landy [France] (LY)

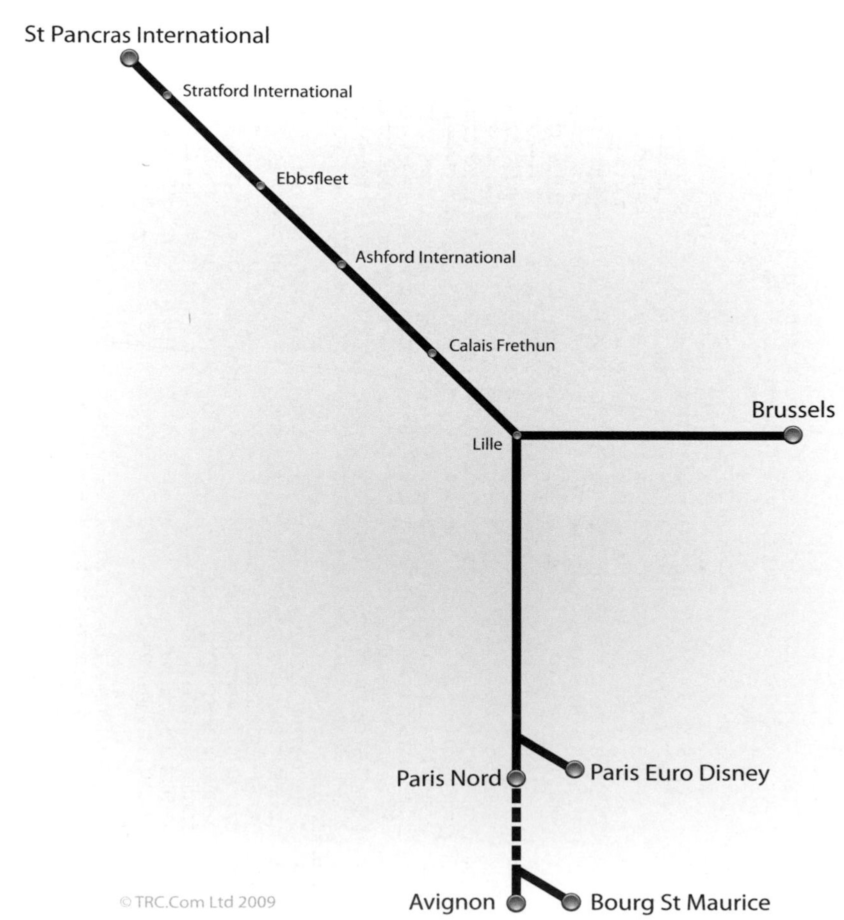

Vehicle Length: (DM) 72ft 8in (22.15m), (MS) 71ft 8in (21.84)
(TS, TBK, TF, TBF) 61ft 4in (18.70m)
Height: 12ft 4½in (3.77m)
Width: 9ft 3in (2.81m)
Horsepower: 16,400hp (12,249kW)
Seats (total/car): 103F/272S, 0/48S/56S/56S/56S/56S/0/39F/39F/24F

Number	*Formation* DM+MSO+TSO+TSO+TSO+TSO+RB+TFO+TFO+TBFO	*Depot*	*Livery*	*Owner*	*Operator*	*Name*
UK sets						
373001	3730010+3730011+3730012+3730013+3730014+3730015+3730016+3730017+3730018+3730019	TI	EUS	EUS	EUS	*Tread Lightly*
373002	3730020+3730021+3730022+3730023+3730024+3730025+3730026+3730027+3730028+3730029	TI	EUS	EUS	EUS	*Voyage Vert*
373003	3730030+3730031+3730032+3730033+3730034+3730035+3730036−3730037+3730038+3730039	TI	EUS*	EUS	EUS	
373004	3730040+3730041+3730042+3730043+3730044+3730045+3730046+3730047+3730048+3730049	TI	EUS*	EUS	EUS	
373005	3730050+3730051+3730052+3730053+3730054+3730055+3730056+3730057+3730058+3730059	TI	EUS	EUS	EUS	
373006	3730060+3730061+3730062+3730063+3730064+3730065+3730066+3730067+3730068+3730069	TI	EUS	EUS	EUS	
373007	3730070+3730071+3730072+3730073+3730074+3730075+3730076+3730077+3730078+3730079	TI	EUS	EUS	EUS	*Waterloo Sunset*
373008	3730080+3730081+3730082+3730083+3730084+3730085+3730086+3730087+3730088+3730089	TI	EUS	EUS	EUS	*Waterloo Sunset*
373009	3730090+3730091+3730092+3730093+3730094+3730095+3730096+3730097+3730098+3730099	TI	EUS	EUS	EUS	
373010	3730100+3730101+3730102+3730103+3730104+3730105+3730106+3730107+3730108+3730109	TI	EUS	EUS	EUS	
373011	3730110+3730111+3730112+3730113+3730114+3730115+3730116+3730117+3730118+3730119	TI	EUS	EUS	EUS	
373012	3730120+3730121+3730122+3730123+3730124+3730125+3730126+3730127+3730128+3730129	TI	EUS	EUS	EUS	
373013	3730130+3730131+3730132+3730133+3730134+3730135+3730136+3730137+3730138+3730139	TI	EUS	EUS	EUS	*London 2012*
373014	3730140+3730141+3730142+3730143+3730144+3730145+3730146+3730147+3730148+3730149	TI	EUS	EUS	EUS	*London 2012*
373015	3730150+3730151+3730152+3730153+3730154+3730155+3730156+3730157+3730158+3730159	TI	EUS	EUS	EUS	
373016	3730160+3730161+3730162+3730163+3730164+3730165+3730166+3730167+3730168+3730169	TI	EUS	EUS	EUS	
373017	3730170+3730171+3730172+3730173+3730174+3730175+3730176+3730177+3730178+3730179	TI	EUS	EUS	EUS	
373018	3730180+3730181+3730182+3730183+3730184+3730185+3730186+3730187+3730188+3730189	TI	EUS	EUS	EUS	
373019	3730190+3730191+3730192+3730193+3730194+3730195+3730196+3730197+3730198+3730199	TI	EUS	EUS	EUS	
373020	3730200+3730201+3730202+3730203+3730204+3730205+3730206+3730207+3730208+3730209	TI	EUS	EUS	EUS	
373021	3730210+3730211+3730212+3730213+3730214+3730215+3730216+3730217+3730218+3730219	TI	EUS	EUS	EUS	
373022	3730220+3730221+3730222+3730223+3730224+3730225+3730226+3730227+3730228+3730229	TI	EUS	EUS	EUS	
Belgian sets						
373101	3731010+3731011+3731012+3731013+3731014+3731015+3731016+3731017+3731018+3731019	FF[S]	EUS	SNB	EUS	
373102	3731020+3731021+3731022+3731023+3731024+3731025+3731026+3731027+3731028+3731029	FF[S]	EUS	SNB	EUS	
373103	3731030+3731031+3731032+3731033+3731034+3731035+3731036+3731037+3731038+3731039	FF	EUS	SNB	EUS	
373104	3731040+3731041+3731042+3731043+3731044+3731045+3731046+3731047+3731048+3731049	FF	EUS	SNB	EUS	
373105	3731050+3731051+3731052+3731053+3731054+3731055+3731056+3731057+3731058+3731059	FF	EUS	SNB	EUS	
373106	3731060+3731061+3731062+3731063+3731064+3731065+3731066+3731067+3731068+3731069	FF	EUS	SNB	EUS	
373107	3731070+3731071+3731072+3731073+3731074+3731075+3731076+3731077+3731078+3731079	FF	EUS	SNB	EUS	
373108	3731080+3731081+3731082+3731083+3731084+3731085+3731086+3731087+3731088+3731089	FF	EUS	SNB	EUS	
French sets						
373201	3732010+3732011+3732012+3732013+3732014+3732015+3732016+3732017+3732018+3732019	LY	EUS	SNF	EUS	
373202	3732020+3732021+3732022+3732023+3732024+3732025+3732026+3732027+3732028+3732029	LY	EUS	SNF	EUS	
373203¤	3732030+3732031+3732032+3732033+3732034+3732035+3732036+3732037+3732038+3732039	LY	SNT	SNF	EUS	
373204¤	3732040+3732041+3732042+3732043+3732044+3732045+3732046+3732047+3732048+3732049	LY	SNT	SNF	EUS	
373205	3732050+3732051+3732052+3732053+3732054+3732055+3732056+3732057+3732058+3732059	LY	EUS	SNF	EUS	
373206	3732060+3732061+3732062+3732063+3732064+3732065+3732066+3732067+3732068+3732069	LY	EUS	SNF	EUS	

Train Operating Companies

Eurostar

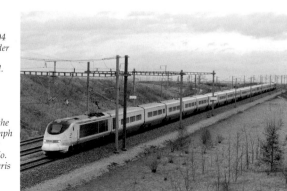

373207	3732070+3732071+3732072+3732073+3732074+3732075+3732076+3732077+3732078+3732079	LY	EUS	SNF	EUS	*Michel Hollard*
373208	3732080+3732081+3732082+3732083+3732084+3732085+3732086+3732087+3732088+3732089	LY	EUS	SNF	EUS	*Michel Hollard*
373209	3732090+3732091+3732092+3732093+3732094+3732095+3732096+3732097+3732098+3732099	LY	EUS	SNF	EUS	*The Da Vinci Code*
373210	3732100+3732101+3732102+3732103+3732104+3732105+3732106+3732107+3732108+3732109	LY	EUS	SNF	EUS	*The Da Vinci Code*
373211	3732110+3732111+3732112+3732113+3732114+3732115+3732116+3732117+3732118+3732119	LY	EUS	SNF	EUS	
373212	3732120+3732121+3732122+3732123+3732124+3732125+3732126+3732127+3732128+3732129	LY	EUS	SNF	EUS	
373213	3732130+3732131+3732132+3732133+3732134+3732135+3732136+3732137+3732138+3732139	LY	EUS	SNF	EUS	
373214	3732140+3732141+3732142+3732143+3732144+3732145+3732146+3732147+3732148+3732149	LY	EUS	SNF	EUS	
373215	3732150+3732151+3732152+3732153+3732154+3732155+3732156+3732157+3732158+3732159	LY	EUS	SNF	EUS	
373216	3732160+3732161+3732162+3732163+3732164+3732165+3732166+3732167+3732168+3732169	LY	EUS	SNF	EUS	
373217	3732170+3732171+3732172+3732173+3732174+3732175+3732176+3732177+3732178+3732179	LY	EUS	SNF	EUS	
373218	3732180+3732181+3732182+3732183+3732184+3732185+3732186+3732187+3732188+3732189	LY	EUS	SNF	EUS	
373219	3732190+3732191+3732192+3732193+3732194+3732195+3732196+3732197+3732198+3732199	LY	EUS	SNF	EUS	
373220	3732200+3732201+3732202+3732203+3732204+3732205+3732206+3732207+3732208+3732209	LY	EUS	SNF	EUS	
373221	3732210+3732211+3732212+3732213+3732214+3732215+3732216+3732217+3732218+3732219	LY	EUS	SNF	EUS	
373222	3732220+3732221+3732222+3732223+3732224+3732225+3732226+3732227+3732228+3732229	LY	EUS	SNF	EUS	
373223	3732230+3732231+3732232+3732233+3732234+3732235+3732236+3732237+3732238+3732239	LY	EUS	SNF	EUS	
373224	3732240+3732241+3732242+3732243+3732244+3732245+3732246+3732247+3732248+3732249	LY	EUS	SNF	EUS	
373225¤	3732250+3732251+3732252+3732253+3732254+3732255+3732256+3732257+3732258+3732259	LY	SNT	SNF	EUS	
373226¤	3732260+3732261+3732262+3732263+3732264+3732265+3732266+3732267+3732268+3732269	LY	SNT	SNF	EUS	
373227¤	3732270+3732271+3732272+3732273+3732274+3732275+3732276+3732277+3732278+3732279	LY	SNT	SNF	EUS	
373228¤	3732280+3732281+3732282+3732283+3732284+3732285+3732286+3732287+3732288+3732289	LY	SNT	SNF	EUS	
373229	3732290+3732291+3732292+3732293+3732294+3732295+3732296+3732297+3732298+3732299	LY	EUS	SNF	EUS	
373230	3732300+3732301+3732302+3732303+3732304+3732305+3732306+3732307+3732308+3732309	LY	EUS	SNF	EUS	
373231	3732310+3732311+3732312+3732313+3732314+3732315+3732316+3732317+3732318+3732319	LY	EUS	SNF	EUS	
373232	3732320+3732321+3732322+3732313+3732324+3732325+3732326+3732327+3732328+3732329	LY	EUS	SNF	EUS	

* **Advertising livery - London Virgins. ¤ In French domestic use.**

Left: *French and UK Eurostar sets Nos. (37)3231 and (37)3004 stand side by side under the Barlow roof at St Pancras International.* **CJM**

Right: *Travelling at the full line speed of 186mph (300km/h) a Eurostar train led by half set No. (37)3002 heads for Paris at Crosilles, south of Lille.* **CJM**

Vehicle Length: (DM) 72ft 8in (22.15m), (MS) 71ft 8in (21.84)
(TS, TBK, TF, TBF) 61ft 4in (18.70m)
Height: 12ft 4½in (3.77m)
Width: 9ft 3in (2.81m)
Horsepower: 16,400hp (12,249kW)
Seats (total/car): 103F/272S, 0/48S/56S/56S/56S/56S/0/39F/39F/24F

Number	*Formation* DM+MSO+TSO+TSO+TSO+RB+TFO+TBFO	*Depot*	*Livery*	*Owner*	*Operator*
Regional sets					
373301	**3733010+3733011+3733012+3733013+3733015+3733016+3733017+3733019**	**LY**	**EUS**	**EUS**	**SNF**
373302	**3733020+3733021+3733022+3733023+3733025+3733026+3733027+3733029**	**LY**	**EUS**	**EUS**	**SNF**
373303	**3733030+3733031+3733032+3733033+3733035+3733036+3733037+3733039**	**LY**	**EUS**	**EUS**	**SNF**
373304	**3733040+3733041+3733042+3733043+3733045+3733046+3733047+3733049**	**LY**	**EUS**	**EUS**	**SNF**
373305	**3733050+3733051+3733052+3733053+3733055+3733056+3733057+3733059**	**LY**	**EUS**	**EUS**	**SNF**
373306	**3733060+3733061+3733062+3733063+3733065+3733066+3733067+3733069**	**LY**	**EUS**	**EUS**	**SNF**
373307	**3733070+3733071+3733072+3733073+3733075+3733076+3733077+3733079**	**LY**	**EUS**	**EUS**	**SNF**
373308	**3733080+3733081+3733082+3733083+3733085+3733086+3733087+3733089**	**LY**	**EUS**	**EUS**	**SNF**
373309	**3733090+3733091+3733092+3733093+3733095+3733096+3733097+3733099**	**LY**	**EUS**	**EUS**	**SNF**
373310	**3733100+3733101+3733102+3733103+3733105+3733106+3733107+3733109**	**LY**	**EUS**	**EUS**	**SNF**
373311	**3733110+3733111+3733112+3733113+3733115+3733116+3733117+3733119**	**LY**	**EUS**	**EUS**	**SNF**
373312	**3733120+3733121+3733122+3733123+3733125+3733126+3733127+3733129**	**LY**	**EUS**	**EUS**	**SNF**
373313	**3733130+3733131+3733132+3733133+3733135+3733136+3733137+3733139**	**LY**	**EUS**	**EUS**	**SNF**
373314	**3733140+3733141+3733142+3733143+3733145+3733146+3733147+3733149**	**LY**	**EUS**	**EUS**	**SNF**

■ *These 14 short half-sets are loaned to SNCF for domestic duties until 2013.*

Right: *Built for operation on the abandoned North of London services the 14 NOL half sets saw limited use in the UK, some sets were put on short term hire to Great North Eastern Railway for use between London and Leeds/York, while other sets took part in testing of the two sections of HS1 between London and the Channel Tunnel. By 2009 the sets had been transferred to Mainland Europe and are working in France. The sets are likely to return to UK operation with projected passenger growth on UK to Mainland Europe train services. Half set No. (37)3312 is seen at Cologne Deutz.* **CJM**

Class 08

Vehicle Length: 29ft 3in (8.91m)
Height: 12ft 8⅝in (3.87m)
Width: 8ft 6in (2.59m)
Engine: English Electric 6K
Horsepower: 400hp (298kW)
Electrical Equipment: English Electric

Number	*Depot*	*Pool*	*Livery*	*Owner*	*Operator*
08948	**TI**	**GPSS**	**TTG**	**EUS**	**EUS**

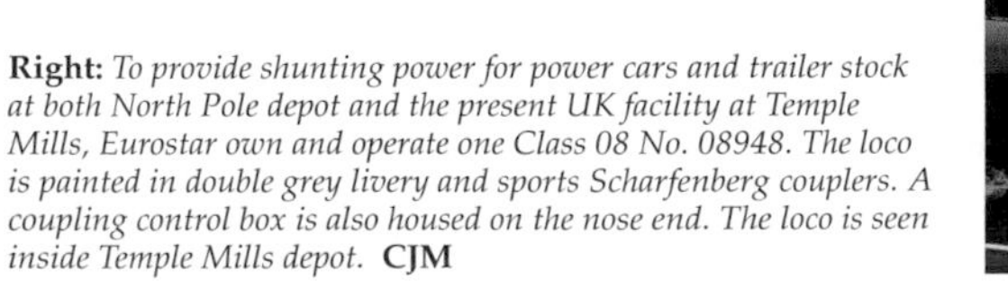

Right: *To provide shunting power for power cars and trailer stock at both North Pole depot and the present UK facility at Temple Mills, Eurostar own and operate one Class 08 No. 08948. The loco is painted in double grey livery and sports Scharfenberg couplers. A coupling control box is also housed on the nose end. The loco is seen inside Temple Mills depot.* **CJM**

First Capital Connect

Address: ✉ Hertford House, 1 Cranwood Street, London, EC1V 9QS
customer.relations.fcc@firstgroup.com
✆ 0845 026 4700
ⓘ www.firstcapitalconnect.co.uk

Managing Director: Jim Morgan

Franchise Dates: 1 April 2006 - 31 March 2015

Principal Routes: London King's Cross-King's Lynn, Peterborough/Cambridge
Moorgate- Hertford Loop and Letchworth
Bedford-Brighton (Thameslink)
Luton-Wimbledon/
Sutton (Thameslink)

Depots: Bedford Cauldwell Walk (BF),
Hornsey (HE),
Brighton (BI)*
* Stabling point

Parent Company: First Group PLC

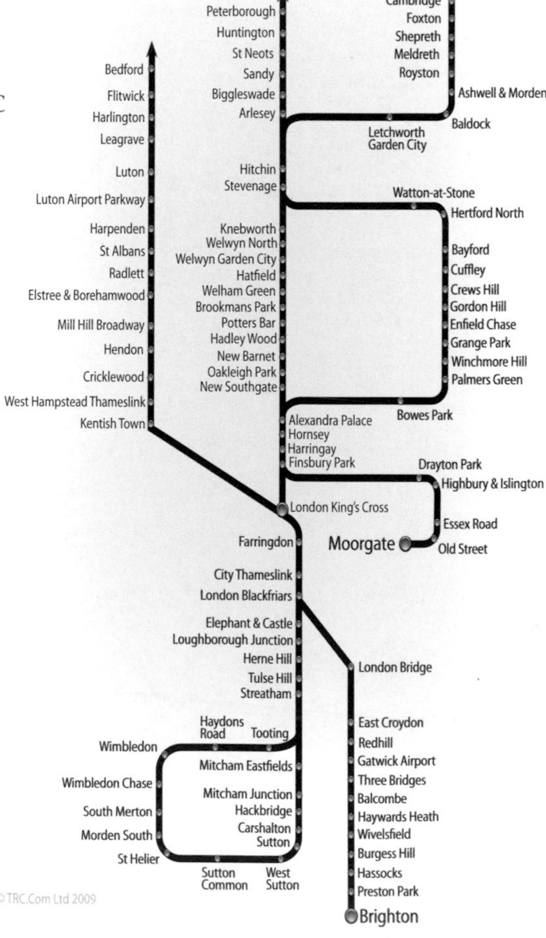

Below: *The principal maintenance facility for First Capital Connect is Hornsey in North London which is responsible for the 313, 317, 321 and 365 allocation. The site has heavy repair and day to day maintenance bays as well as stabling and carriage cleaning lines. Class 365 No. 365514 is seen inside the heavy repair shed. Note the platforms on both sides to ease vehicle access.* **CJM**

Class 313/0

Vehicle Length: (Driving) 64ft 11½in (20.75m) (Inter) 65ft 4¼in (19.92m)
Height: 11ft 9in (3.58m)
Width: 9ft 3in (2.82m)
Horsepower: 880hp (656kW)
Seats (total/car): 231S, 74S/83S/74S

Number	Formation DMSO+PTSO+BDMSO	Depot	Livery	Owner	Operator
313018	62546+71230+62160	HE	FCC	HSB	FCC
313024	62552+71236+62616	HE	FCC	HSB	FCC
313025	62553+71237+62617	HE	FCC	HSB	FCC
313026	62554+71238+62618	HE	FCC	HSB	FCC
313027	62555+71239+62619	HE	FCC	HSB	FCC
313028	62556+71240+62620	HE	FCC	HSB	FCC
313029	62557+71241+62621	HE	FCC	HSB	FCC
313030	62558+71242+62622	HE	FCC	HSB	FCC
313031	62559+71243+62623	HE	FCC	HSB	FCC
313032	62560+71244+62643	HE	FCC	HSB	FCC
313033	62561+71245+62625	HE	FCC	HSB	FCC
313035	62563+71247+62627	HE	FCC	HSB	FCC
313036	62564+71248+62628	HE	FCC	HSB	FCC
313037	62565+71249+62629	HE	FCC	HSB	FCC
313038	62566+71250+62630	HE	FCC	HSB	FCC
313039	62567+71251+62631	HE	FCC	HSB	FCC
313040	62568+71252+62632	HE	FCC	HSB	FCC
313041	62569+71253+62633	HE	FCC	HSB	FCC
313042	62570+71254+62634	HE	FCC	HSB	FCC
313043	62571+71255+62635	HE	FCC	HSB	FCC
313044	62572+71256+62636	HE	FCC	HSB	FCC
313045	62573+71257+62637	HE	FCC	HSB	FCC
313046	62574+71258+62638	HE	FCC	HSB	FCC
313047	62575+71259+62639	HE	FCC	HSB	FCC
313048	62576+71260+62640	HE	FCC	HSB	FCC
313049	62577+71261+62641	HE	FCC	HSB	FCC
313050	62578+71262+62649	HE	FCC	HSB	FCC
313051	62579+71263+62624	HE	FCC	HSB	FCC
313052	62580+71264+62644	HE	FCC	HSB	FCC
313053	62581+71265+62645	HE	FCC	HSB	FCC
313054	62582+71266+62646	HE	FCC	HSB	FCC
313055	62583+71267+62647	HE	FCC	HSB	FCC
313056	62584+71268+62648	HE	FCC	HSB	FCC
313057	62585+71269+62642	HE	FCC	HSB	FCC
313058	62586+71270+62650	HE	FCC	HSB	FCC
313059	62587+71271+62651	HE	FCC	HSB	FCC
313060	62588+71272+62652	HE	FCC	HSB	FCC
313061	62589+71273+62653	HE	FCC	HSB	FCC
313062	62590+71274+62654	HE	FCC	HSB	FCC
313063	62591+71275+62655	HE	FCC	HSB	FCC
313064	62592+71276+62656	HE	FCC	HSB	FCC

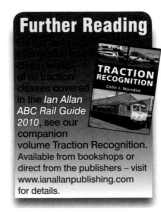

Below: *The Class 313 fleet were the first production batch of EMUs to emerge from the 1972 design high-density PEP prototype train sets. These units were designed for use on the Moorgate line and are thus dual ac/dc sets, using their ac power collection for main line operation and dc power between Drayton Park and Moorgate. Set No. 313062 is seen at Hornsey depot.* **CJM**

Passenger Train Operating Companies - First Capital Connect

First Capital Connect

Class 317/3

Vehicle Length: (Driving) 65ft 0¾in (19.83m) Width: 9ft 3in (2.82m)
(Inter) 65ft 4¼in (19.92m) Horsepower: 1,000hp (746kW)
Height: 12ft 1½in (3.58m) Seats (total/car): 22F/269S, 74S/79S/22F-46S/70S

Number	Formation DTSO+MSO+TCO+DTSO	Depot	Livery	Owner	Operator	Name
317337	77036+62671+71613+77084	HE	WAG	ANG	FCC	
317338	77037+62698+71614+77085	HE	WAG	ANG	FCC	
317339	77038+62699+71615+77086	HE	FCC	ANG	FCC	
317340	77039+62700+71616+77087	HE	WAG	ANG	FCC	
317341	77040+62701+71617+77088	HE	FCC	ANG	FCC	
317342	77041+62702+71618+77089	HE	FCC	ANG	FCC	
317343	77042+62703+71619+77090	HE	WAG	ANG	FCC	
317344	77029+62690+71620+77091	HE	WAG	ANG	FCC	
317345	77044+62705+71621+77092	HE	FCC	ANG	FCC	*Driver John Webb*
317346	77045+62706+71622+77093	HE	WAG	ANG	FCC	
317347	77046+62707+71623+77094	HE	WAG	ANG	FCC	
317348	77047+62708+71624+77095	HE	FCC	ANG	FCC	*Richard A. Jenner*

Left: *The Class 317/3 units are currently used by First Capital Connect on suburban services from London King's Cross, mainly on the Peterborough route. On 18 May 2009, No. 317347 still displaying the obsolete WAGN mauve livery but with FCC branding, is photographed at Peterborough forming the 13.18 service to London King's Cross.* **John Binch**

Class 319/0

Vehicle Length: (Driving) 65ft 0¾in (19.83m) Width: 9ft 3in (2.82m)
(Inter) 65ft 4¼in (19.92m) Horsepower: 1,326hp (990kW)
Height: 11ft 9in (3.58m) Seats (total/car): 319S, 82S/82S/77S/78S

Number	Formation DTSO(A)+MSO+TSO+DTSO(B)	Depot	Livery	Owner	Operator	Name
319001	77291+62891+71772+77290	SU	FCC	PTR	FCC	
319002	77293+62892+71773+77292	SU	FCC	PTR	FCC	
319003	77295+62893+71774+77294	SU	FCC	PTR	FCC	
319004	77297+62894+71775+77296	SU	FCC	PTR	FCC	
319005	77299+62895+71776+77298	SU	FCC	PTR	FCC	
319006	77301+62896+71777+77300	SU	FCC	PTR	FCC	
319007	77303+62897+71778+77302	SU	FCC	PTR	FCC	
319008	77305+62898+71779+77304	SU	SOU	PTR	FCC	
319009	77307+62899+71780+77306	SU	SOU	PTR	FCC	
319010	77309+62900+71781+77308	SU	FCC	PTR	FCC	
319011	77311+62901+71782+77310	SU	SOU	PTR	FCC	*John Ruskin College*
319012	77313+62902+71783+77312	SU	SOU	PTR	FCC	
319013	77315+62903+71784+77314	SU	SOU	PTR	FCC	*The Surrey Hills*

Class 319/2

Vehicle Length: (Driving) 65ft 0¾in (19.83m) Width: 9ft 3in (2.82m)
(Inter) 65ft 4¼in (19.92m) Horsepower: 1,326hp (990kW)
Height: 11ft 9in (3.58m) Seats (total/car): 18F/212S, 64S/60S/52S/18F/36S

Number	Formation DTSO+MSO+TSO+DTCO	Depot	Livery	Owner	Operator	Name
319214	77317+62904+71785+77316	SU	SOU	PTR	FCC	
319215	77319+62905+71786+77318	SU	SOU	PTR	FCC	*London*
319216	77321+62906+71787+77320	SU	SOU	PTR	FCC	
319217	77323+62907+71788+77322	BF	SOU	PTR	FCC	*Brighton*
319218	77325+62908+71789+77324	BF	SOU	PTR	FCC	*Croydon*
319219	77327+62909+71790+77326	BF	SOU	PTR	FCC	
319220	77329+62910+71791+77328	BF	SOU	PTR	FCC	

Class 319/3

Vehicle Length: (Driving) 65ft 0¾in (19.83m) Width: 9ft 3in (2.82m)
(Inter) 65ft 4¼in (19.92m) Horsepower: 1,326hp (990kW)
Height: 11ft 9in (3.58m) Seats (total/car): 300S, 70S/78S/74S/78S

Number	Formation DTSO(A)+MSO+TSO+DTSO(B)	Depot	Livery	Owner	Operator	Name
319361	77459+63043+71929+77458	BF	THM	PTR	FCC	
319362	77461+63044+71930+77460	BF	THM	PTR	FCC	
319363	77463+63045+71931+77462	BF	FCC	PTR	FCC	
319364	77465+63046+71932+77464	BF	TLP	PTR	FCC	*Transforming Blackfriars*
319365	77467+63047+71933+77466	BF	TLP	PTR	FCC	*Transforming Farringdon*
319366	77469+63048+71934+77468	BF	THM	PTR	FCC	
319367	77471+63049+71935+77470	BF	FCC	PTR	FCC	
319368	77473+63050+71936+77472	BF	FCC	PTR	FCC	
319369	77475+63051+71937+77474	BF	THM	PTR	FCC	
317370	77477+63052+71938+77476	BF	FCC	PTR	FCC	
319371	77479+63053+71939+77478	BF	THM	PTR	FCC	
319372	77481+63054+71940+77480	BF	FCC	PTR	FCC	
319373	77483+63055+71941+77482	BF	FCC	PTR	FCC	
319374	77485+63056+71942+77484	BF	FCC	PTR	FCC	*Bedford Cauldwell Walk TMD*
319375	77487+63057+71943+77486	BF	FCC	PTR	FCC	
319376	77489+63058+71944+77488	BF	THM	PTR	FCC	
319377	77491+63059+71945+77490	BF	FCC	PTR	FCC	
319378	77493+63060+71946+77492	BF	THM	PTR	FCC	
319379	77495+63061+71947+77494	BF	FCC	PTR	FCC	
319380	77497+63082+71948+77496	BF	FCC	PTR	FCC	
319381	77973+63093+71978+77974	BF	THM	PTR	FCC	
319382	77975+63094+71980+77976	BF	FCC	PTR	FCC	
319383	77977+63096+71981+77978	BF	THM	PTR	FCC	
319384	77979+63096+71982+77980	BF	THM	PTR	FCC	
319385	77981+63097+71983+77982	BF	FCC	PTR	FCC	
319386	77983+63098+71984+77984	BF	THM	PTR	FCC	

Class 319/4

Vehicle Length: (Driving) 65ft 0¾in (19.83m) Width: 9ft 3in (2.82m)
(Inter) 65ft 4¼in (19.92m) Horsepower: 1,326hp (990kW)
Height: 11ft 9in (3.58m) Seats (total/car): 12F/277S, 12F-54S/77S/72S/74S

Number	Formation DTCO+MSO+TSO+DTSO	Depot	Livery	Owner	Operator	Name
319421	77331+62911+71792+77330	BF	FCC	PTR	FCC	
319422	77333+62912+71793+77332	BF	FCC	PTR	FCC	
319423	77335+62913+71794+77334	BF	FCC	PTR	FCC	
319424	77337+62914+71795+77336	BF	FCC	PTR	FCC	
319425	77339+62915+71796+77338	BF	FCC	PTR	FCC	*Transforming Travel*
319426	77341+62916+71797+77340	BF	FCC	PTR	FCC	
319427	77343+62917+71798+77342	BF	FCC	PTR	FCC	
319428	77345+62918+71799+77344	BF	FCC	PTR	FCC	
319429	77347+62919+71800+77346	BF	FCC	PTR	FCC	
319430	77349+62920+71801+77348	BF	THM	PTR	FCC	
319431	77351+62921+71802+77350	BF	FCC	PTR	FCC	
319432	77353+62922+71803+77352	BF	FCC	PTR	FCC	
319433	77355+62923+71804+77354	BF	FCC	PTR	FCC	
319434	77357+62924+71805+77356	BF	FCC	PTR	FCC	
319435	77359+62925+71806+77358	BF	FCC	PTR	FCC	*Adrian Jackson-Robbins Chairman 1987-2007 Association of Public Transport Users*
319436	77361+62926+71807+77360	BF	FCC	PTR	FCC	
319437	77363+62927+71808+77362	BF	FCC	PTR	FCC	
319438	77365+62928+71809+77364	BF	FCC	PTR	FCC	
319439	77367+62929+71810+77366	BF	FCC	PTR	FCC	
319440	77369+62930+71811+77368	BF	FCC	PTR	FCC	
319441	77371+62931+71812+77370	BF	FCC	PTR	FCC	
319442	77373+62932+71813+77372	BF	FCC	PTR	FCC	
319443	77375+62933+71814+77374	BF	FCC	PTR	FCC	
319444	77377+62934+71815+77376	BF	FCC	PTR	FCC	
319445	77379+62935+71816+77378	BF	FCC	PTR	FCC	

First Capital Connect

319446	77381+62936+71817+77380	BF	FCC	PTR	FCC	*St Pancras International*
319447	77431+62961+71866+77430	BF	FCC	PTR	FCC	
319448	77433+62962+71867+77432	BF	THM	PTR	FCC	
319449	77435+62963+71868+77434	BF	FCC	PTR	FCC	*King's Cross Thameslink*
319450	77437+62964+71869+77436	BF	FCC	PTR	FCC	
319451	77439+62965+71870+77438	BF	THM	PTR	FCC	
319452	77441+62966+71871+77440	BF	THM	PTR	FCC	
319453	77443+62967+71872+77442	BF	THM	PTR	FCC	
319454	77445+62968+71873+77444	BF	THM	PTR	FCC	
319455	77447+62969+71874+77446	BF	FCC	PTR	FCC	
319456	77449+62970+71875+77448	BF	THM	PTR	FCC	
319457	77451+62971+71876+77450	BF	FCC	PTR	FCC	
319458	77453+62972+71877+77452	BF	FCC	PTR	FCC	
319459	77455+62973+71878+77454	BF	FCC	PTR	FCC	
319460	77457+62974+71879+77456	BF	FCC	PTR	FCC	

Left: *The Thameslink route services, operated by First Capital Connect are formed of Class 319 stock, based mainly at Bedford. The sets are presently in a period of livery transition with some sets in old Thameslink colours with First Group 'Urban Lights' corporate colours being rapidly applied. Set No. 319429 is illustrated.* **Tony Christie**

Class 321/4

Vehicle Length: (Driving) 65ft 0¾in (19.83m)
(Inter) 65ft 4¼in (19.92m)
Height: 12ft 4¾in (3.78m)
Width: 9ft 3in (2.82m)
Horsepower: 1,328hp (996kW)
Seats (total/car): 28F/271S, 28F-40S/79S/74S/78S

Number	*Formation* DMCO+MSO+TSO+DMSO	*Depot*	*Livery*	*Owner*	*Operator*
321401	**78095+63063+71949+77943**	**HE**	**FCC**	**HSB**	**FCC**
321402	**78096+63064+71950+77944**	**HE**	**FCC**	**HSB**	**FCC**
321403	**78097+63065+71951+77945**	**HE**	**FCC**	**HSB**	**FCC**
321404	**78098+63066+71952+77946**	**HE**	**FCC**	**HSB**	**FCC**
321405	**78099+63067+71953+77947**	**HE**	**FCC**	**HSB**	**FCC**
321406	**78100+63068+71954+77948**	**HE**	**FCC**	**HSB**	**FCC**

Name applied **321403** ***Stewart Fleming Signalman King's Cross***

Below: *The six Class 321/4 units inherited from London Midland began operating FCC services on 18 May 2009 to assist with growth. Having worked a service from London King's Cross, Nos. 321403 and 321401 arrive at Huntingdon prior to forming the 18.04 to London King's Cross.* **John Binch**

Class 365
Networker Express

Vehicle Length: (Driving) 68ft 6½in (20.89m) (Inter) 65ft 9¼in (20.89m)
Height: 12ft 4½in (3.77m)
Width: 9ft 2½in (2.81m)
Horsepower: 1,684hp (1,256kW)
Seats (total/car): 24F/239S, 12F-56S/59S/68S/12F-56S

Number	*Formation* DMCO(A)+TSO+PTSO+DMCO(B)	*Depot*	*Livery*	*Owner*	*Operator*	*Name*
365501	**65894+72241+72240+65935**	**HE**	**FCC**	**HSB**	**FCC**	
365502	**65895+72243+72242+65936**	**HE**	**FCC**	**HSB**	**FCC**	
365503	**65896+72245+72244+65937**	**HE**	**FCC**	**HSB**	**FCC**	
365504	**65897+72247+72246+65938**	**HE**	**FCC**	**HSB**	**FCC**	
365505	**65898+72249+72248+65939**	**HE**	**FCC**	**HSB**	**FCC**	
365506	**65899+72251+72250+65940**	**HE**	**FCC**	**HSB**	**FCC**	
365507	**65900+72253+72252+65941**	**HE**	**FCC**	**HSB**	**FCC**	
365508	**65901+72255+72254+65942**	**HE**	**FCC**	**HSB**	**FCC**	
365509	**65902+72257+72256+65943**	**HE**	**FCC**	**HSB**	**FCC**	
365510	**65903+72259+72258+65944**	**HE**	**FCC**	**HSB**	**FCC**	
365511	**65904+72261+72260+65945**	**HE**	**FCC**	**HSB**	**FCC**	
365512	**65905+72263+72262+65946**	**HE**	**FCC**	**HSB**	**FCC**	
365513	**65906+72265+72264+65947**	**HE**	**FCC**	**HSB**	**FCC**	*Hornsey Depot*
365514	**65907+72267+72266+65948**	**HE**	**FCC**	**HSB**	**FCC**	*Captain George Vancouver*
365515	**65908+72269+72268+65949**	**HE**	**FCC**	**HSB**	**FCC**	
365516	**65909+72271+72270+65950**	**HE**	**FCC**	**HSB**	**FCC**	
365517	**65910+72273+72272+65951**	**HE**	**FCC**	**HSB**	**FCC**	
365518	**65911+72275+72274+65952**	**HE**	**FCC**	**HSB**	**FCC**	*The Fenman*
365519	**65912+72277+72276+65953**	**HE**	**FCC**	**HSB**	**FCC**	
365520	**65913+72279+72278+65954**	**HE**	**FCC**	**HSB**	**FCC**	
365521	**65914+72281+72280+65955**	**HE**	**FCC**	**HSB**	**FCC**	
365522	**65915+72283+72282+65956**	**HE**	**FCC**	**HSB**	**FCC**	
365523	**65916+72285+72284+65957**	**HE**	**FCC**	**HSB**	**FCC**	
365524	**65917+72287+72286+65958**	**HE**	**FCC**	**HSB**	**FCC**	
365525	**65918+72289+72288+65959**	**HE**	**FCC**	**HSB**	**FCC**	
365526(S)	**65919+72291+72290+65960**	**HE**	**NSE**	**HSB**	¤	
365527	**65920+72293+72292+65961**	**HE**	**FCC**	**HSB**	**FCC**	*Robert Stripe Passenger's Champion*
365528	**65921+72296+72294+65962**	**HE**	**FCC**	**HSB**	**FCC**	
365529	**65922+72297+72296+65963**	**HE**	**FCC**	**HSB**	**FCC**	
365530	**65923+72299+72298+65964**	**HE**	**FCC**	**HSB**	**FCC**	*The Interlink Partnership Promoting Integrated Transport Since 1999*
365531	**65924+72301+72300+65965**	**HE**	**FCC**	**HSB**	**FCC**	
365532	**65925+72303+72302+65966**	**HE**	**FCC**	**HSB**	**FCC**	
365533	**65926+72305+72304+65967**	**HE**	**FCC**	**HSB**	**FCC**	
365534	**65927+72307+72306+65968**	**HE**	**FCC**	**HSB**	**FCC**	
365535	**65928+72309+72308+65969**	**HE**	**FCC**	**HSB**	**FCC**	
365536	**65929+72311+72310+65970**	**HE**	**FCC**	**HSB**	**FCC**	
365537	**65930+72313+72312+65971**	**HE**	**FCC**	**HSB**	**FCC**	
365538	**65931+72315+72314+65972**	**HE**	**FCC**	**HSB**	**FCC**	
365539	**65932+72317+72316+65973**	**HE**	**FCC**	**HSB**	**FCC**	
365540	**65933+72319+72318+65974**	**HE**	**FCC**	**HSB**	**FCC**	
365541	**65934+72321+72320+65975**	**HE**	**FCC**	**HSB**	**FCC**	

¤ Set No. 365526 is stored at Bombardier Crewe with extensive collision damage sustained in the Potters Bar derailment.

Right: *Hornsey depot in North London is the principal repair and stabling facility for FCC Great Northern services, with purpose built heavy repair, wheel lathe, cleaning and stabling sidings. Networker Express No. 365529 is seen inside the lifting shop on 1 July 2007.* **CJM**

Left: *Standard class interior of Class 365 'Networker Express' set, showing the 2+2 low density layout.* **CJM**

Class 377/5
Electrostar

Vehicle Length: (Driving) 66ft 9in (20.40m)
(Inter) 65ft 6in (19.99m)
Height: 12ft 4in (3.77m)
Width: 9ft 2in (2.80m)
Horsepower: 2,012hp (1,500kW) (ac), dual voltage sets
Seats (total/car): 20F-221S, 10F-48/69S/56S/10F-48S

Number	*Formation* DMCO(A)+MSO+PTSO+DMCO(B)	*Depot*	*Livery*	*Owner*	*Operator*
377501	73501+75901+74901+73601	BF	FCC	PTR	FCC *(Sub-lease from Southern)*
377502	73502+75902+74902+73602	BF	FCC	PTR	FCC *(Sub-lease from Southern)*
377503	73503+75903+74903+73603	BF	FCC	PTR	FCC *(Sub-lease from Southern)*
377504	73504+75904+74904+73604	BF	FCC	PTR	FCC *(Sub-lease from Southern)*
377505	73505+75905+74905+73605	BF	FCC	PTR	FCC *(Sub-lease from Southern)*
377506	73506+75906+74906+73606	BF	FCC	PTR	FCC *(Sub-lease from Southern)*
377507	73507+75907+74907+73607	BF	FCC	PTR	FCC *(Sub-lease from Southern)*
377508	73508+75908+74908+73608	BF	FCC	PTR	FCC *(Sub-lease from Southern)*
377509	73509+75909+74909+73609	BF	FCC	PTR	FCC *(Sub-lease from Southern)*
377510	73510+75910+74910+73610	BF	FCC	PTR	FCC *(Sub-lease from Southern)*
377511	73511+75911+74911+73611	BF	FCC	PTR	FCC *(Sub-lease from Southern)*
377512	73512+75912+74912+73612	BF	FCC	PTR	FCC *(Sub-lease from Southern)*
377513	73513+75913+74913+73613	BF	FCC	SOU	FCC *(Sub-lease from Southern)*
377514	73514+75914+74914+73614	BF	FCC	SOU	FCC *(Sub-lease from Southern)*
377515	73515+75915+74915+73615	BF	FCC	SOU	FCC *(Sub-lease from Southern)*
377516	73516+75916+74916+73616	BF	FCC	SOU	FCC *(Sub-lease from Southern)*
377517	73517+75917+74917+73617	BF	FCC	SOU	FCC *(Sub-lease from Southern)*
377518	73518+75918+74918+73618	BF	FCC	SOU	FCC *(Sub-lease from Southern)*
377519	73519+75919+74919+73619	BF	FCC	SOU	FCC *(Sub-lease from Southern)*
377520	73520+75920+74920+73620	BF	FCC	SOU	FCC *(Sub-lease from Southern)*
377521	73521+75921+74921+73621	BF	FCC	SOU	FCC *(Sub-lease from Southern)*
377522	73522+75922+74922+73622	BF	FCC	SOU	FCC *(Sub-lease from Southern)*
377523	73523+75923+74923+73623	BF	FCC	SOU	FCC *(Sub-lease from Southern)*

Left: *Twentythree of the Class 377 'Electrostar' sets originally destined for Southern were transferred to First Capital Connect to provide additional trains due to route growth. The sets are usually operated in pairs. Set No. 377504 is seen on the Midland Main Line at Millbrook forming a service bound for London.* **Mark Sheen**

First Great Western

Address: Milford House, 1 Milford Street, Swindon, SN1 1HL
fgwfeedback@firstgroup.com
08457 000125
www.firstgreatwestern.co.uk

Managing Director: Mark Hopwood

Franchise Dates: 1 April 2006 - 31 March 2016

Principal Routes: Paddington - Penzance / Paignton, Bristol, Swansea
Thames Valley local lines
Local lines in Bristol, Exeter, Plymouth and Cornwall
Bristol-Weymouth, Portsmouth / Brighton

Depots: Exeter (EX), Old Oak Common (OO), Laira (LA), Landore (LE), St Philip's Marsh (PM), Penzance (PZ), Reading (RG)

Parent Company: First Group

Class 08

Vehicle Length: 29ft 3in (8.91m)
Height: 12ft 8⅝in (3.87m)
Width: 8ft 6in (2.59m)
Engine: English Electric 6K
Horsepower: 400hp (298kW)
Electrical Equipment: English Electric

Number	*Depot*	*Pool*	*Livery*	*Owner*	*Operator*
08410	PZ	EFSH	GWG	FGP	FGW
08483	OO	EFSH	GWG	FGP	FGW
08641	LA	EFSH	FGB	FGP	FGW
08644	LA	EFSH	GWG	FGP	FGW
08645	LA	EFSH	GWG	FGP	FGW
08663	PM	EFSH	GWG	FGP	FGW
08795	LE	EFSH	GWG	FGP	FGW
08822	LE	EFSH	GWG	FGP	FGW
08836	PM	EFSH	GWG	FGP	FGW

Names applied

08484	*Dusty - Driver David Miller*
08645	*Mike Baggott*

Above: *Nine standard Class 08 shunting locomotives are operated by First Great Western: these are used for depot shunting work, mainly involving re-forming of HST and loco-hauled stock. All are fitted with drop-head HST compatible couplers. No. 08645 is seen at Laira depot, Plymouth painted in all-over FGW blue, with a First Group logo on the engine bay side door. A cast nameplate is attached to the battery box. Note that yellow/black wasp ends are applied to the front of the fuel tank and compressor cabinet.* **Stacey Thew**

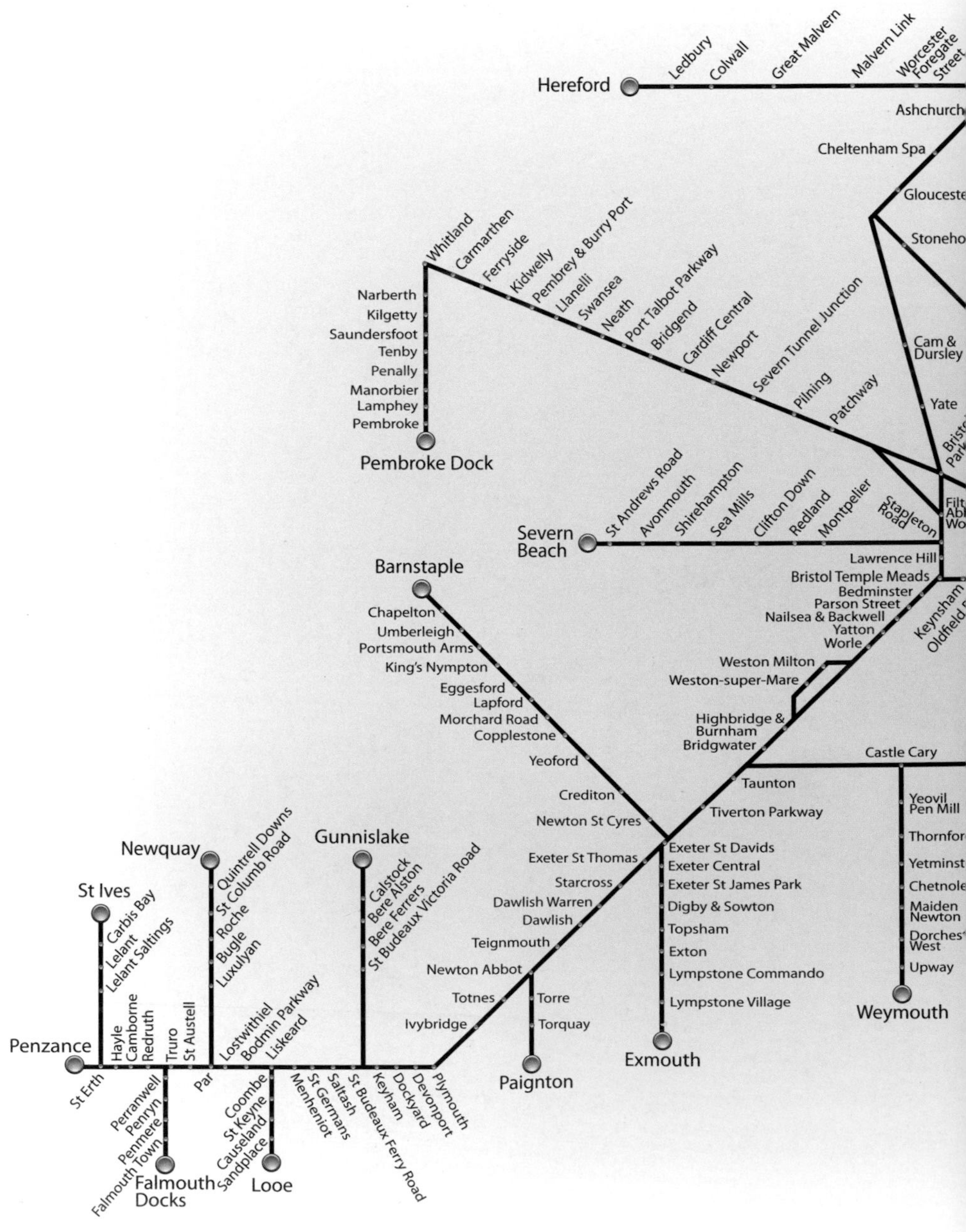
Hereford
Ledbury
Colwall
Great Malvern
Malvern Link
Worcester Foregate Street
Ashchurch
Cheltenham Spa
Gloucester
Stoneho
Cam & Dursley
Yate
Whitland
Carmarthen
Ferryside
Kidwelly
Pembrey & Burry Port
Llanelli
Swansea
Neath
Port Talbot Parkway
Bridgend
Cardiff Central
Newport
Severn Tunnel Junction
Pilning
Patchway
Narberth
Kilgetty
Saundersfoot
Tenby
Penally
Manorbier
Lamphey
Pembroke
Pembroke Dock
Severn Beach
St Andrews Road
Avonmouth
Shirehampton
Sea Mills
Clifton Down
Redland
Montpelier
Stapleton Road
Lawrence Hill
Bristol Temple Meads
Bedminster
Parson Street
Nailsea & Backwell
Yatton
Worle
Keynsham
Oldfield
Weston Milton
Weston-super-Mare
Highbridge & Burnham
Bridgwater
Castle Cary
Taunton
Tiverton Parkway
Yeovil Pen Mill
Thornfor
Yetminst
Chetnole
Maiden Newton
Dorches West
Upway
Weymouth
Barnstaple
Chapelton
Umberleigh
Portsmouth Arms
King's Nympton
Eggesford
Lapford
Morchard Road
Copplestone
Yeoford
Crediton
Newton St Cyres
Exeter St Davids
Exeter Central
Exeter St James Park
Digby & Sowton
Topsham
Exton
Lympstone Commando
Lympstone Village
Exmouth
Exeter St Thomas
Starcross
Dawlish Warren
Dawlish
Teignmouth
Newton Abbot
Torre
Torquay
Paignton
Totnes
Ivybridge
Newquay
Quintrell Downs
St Columb Road
Roche
Bugle
Luxulyan
Gunnislake
Calstock
Bere Alston
Bere Ferrers
St Budeaux Victoria Road
St Ives
Carbis Bay
Lelant
Lelant Saltings
Penzance
St Erth
Hayle
Camborne
Redruth
Truro
St Austell
Par
Lostwithiel
Bodmin Parkway
Liskeard
Menheniot
St Germans
Saltash
St Budeaux Ferry Road
Keyham
Dockyard
Devonport
Plymouth
Perranwell
Penryn
Penmere
Falmouth Town
Falmouth Docks
Coombe
St Keyne
Causeland
Sandplace
Looe

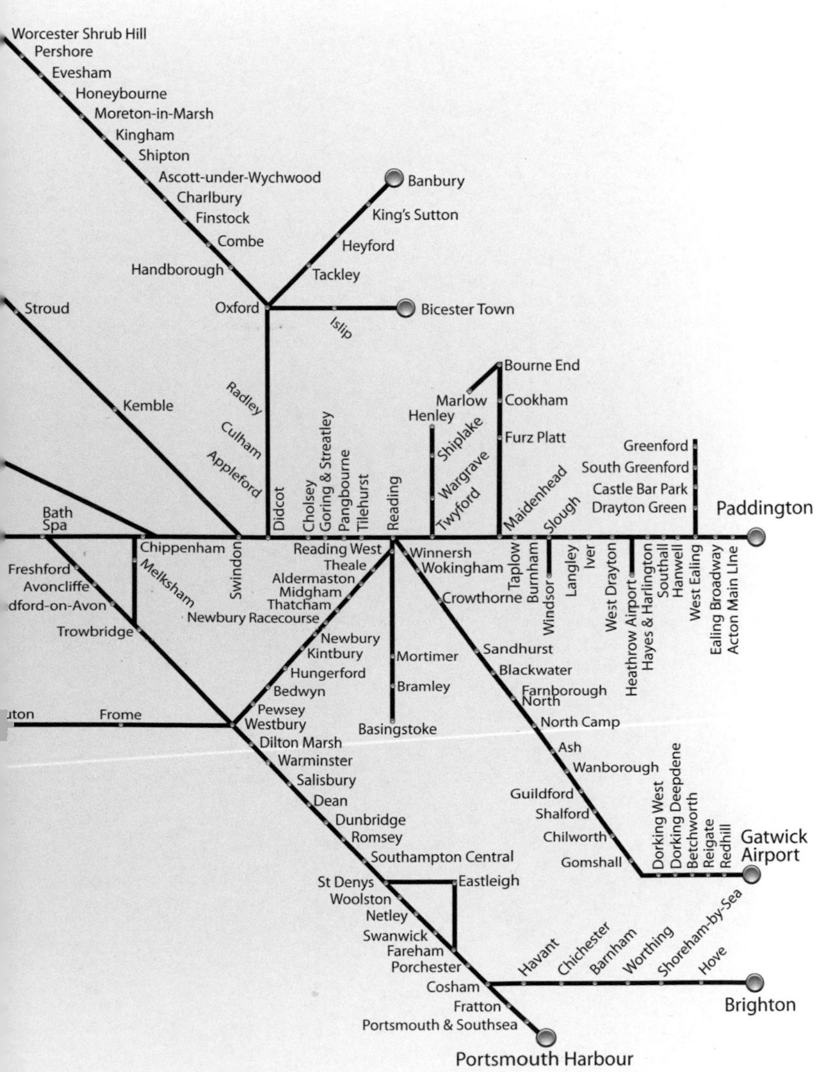
Worcester Shrub Hill
Pershore
Evesham
Honeybourne
Moreton-in-Marsh
Kingham
Shipton
Ascott-under-Wychwood
Charlbury
Finstock
Combe
Handborough
Banbury
King's Sutton
Heyford
Tackley
Oxford
Islip
Bicester Town
Stroud
Kemble
Radley
Culham
Appleford
Didcot
Cholsey
Goring & Streatley
Pangbourne
Tilehurst
Reading
Bourne End
Marlow
Cookham
Henley
Shiplake
Wargrave
Twyford
Furz Platt
Maidenhead
Slough
Greenford
South Greenford
Castle Bar Park
Drayton Green
Paddington
Bath Spa
Chippenham
Melksham
Swindon
Freshford
Avoncliffe
dford-on-Avon
Trowbridge
Reading West
Theale
Aldermaston
Midgham
Thatcham
Newbury Racecourse
Newbury
Kintbury
Hungerford
Bedwyn
Pewsey
Westbury
Winnersh
Wokingham
Crowthorne
Taplow
Burnham
Windsor
Langley
Iver
West Drayton
Heathrow Airport
Hayes & Harlington
Southall
Hanwell
West Ealing
Ealing Broadway
Acton Main Line
Mortimer
Bramley
Basingstoke
Sandhurst
Blackwater
Farnborough North
North Camp
Ash
Wanborough
uton
Frome
Dilton Marsh
Warminster
Salisbury
Dean
Dunbridge
Romsey
Southampton Central
Guildford
Shalford
Chilworth
Gomshall
Dorking West
Dorking Deepdene
Betchworth
Reigate
Redhill
Gatwick Airport
St Denys
Eastleigh
Woolston
Netley
Swanwick
Fareham
Porchester
Cosham
Fratton
Portsmouth & Southsea
Portsmouth Harbour
Havant
Chichester
Barnham
Worthing
Shoreham-by-Sea
Hove
Brighton

First Great Western

Class 43 – HST

Vehicle Length: 58ft 5in (18.80m)
Height: 12ft 10in (3.90m)
Width: 8ft 11in (2.73m)
Engine: MTU 16V4000 R41R
Horsepower: 2,250hp (1,680kW)
Electrical Equipment: Brush

Number	Depot	Pool	Livery	Owner	Operator
43002	LA	EFPC	FGW	ANG	FGW
43003	LA	EFPC	FGW	ANG	FGW
43004	LA	EFPC	FGW	ANG	FGW
43005	LA	EFPC	FGW	ANG	FGW
43009	LA	EFPC	FGW	ANG	FGW
43010	LA	EFPC	FGW	ANG	FGW
43012	LA	EFPC	FGW	ANG	FGW
43015	LA	EFPC	FGW	ANG	FGW
43016	LA	EFPC	FGW	ANG	FGW
43017	LA	EFPC	FGW	ANG	FGW
43018	LA	EFPC	FGW	ANG	FGW
43020	LA	EFPC	FGW	ANG	FGW
43021	LA	EFPC	FGW	ANG	FGW
43022	LA	EFPC	FGW	ANG	FGW
43023	LA	EFPC	FGW	ANG	FGW
43024	LA	EFPC	FGW	ANG	FGW
43025	LA	EFPC	FGW	ANG	FGW
43026	LA	EFPC	FGW	ANG	FGW
43027	LA	EFPC	FGW	ANG	FGW
43028	LA	EFPC	FGW	ANG	FGW
43029	LA	EFPC	FGW	ANG	FGW
43030	LA	EFPC	FGW	ANG	FGW
43031	LA	EFPC	FGW	ANG	FGW
43032	LA	EFPC	FGW	ANG	FGW
43033	LA	EFPC	FGW	ANG	FGW
43034	LA	EFPC	FGW	ANG	FGW
43035	LA	EFPC	FGW	ANG	FGW
43036	LA	EFPC	FGW	ANG	FGW
43037	LA	EFPC	FGW	ANG	FGW
43040	LA	EFPC	FGW	ANG	FGW
43041	OO	EFPC	FGW	ANG	FGW
43042	OO	EFPC	FGW	ANG	FGW
43053	LE	EFPC	FGW	PTR	FGW
43056	LE	EFPC	FGW	PTR	FGW
43063	OO	EFPC	FGW	PTR	FGW
43069	OO	EFPC	FGW	PTR	FGW
43070	OO	EFPC	FGW	PTR	FGW
43071	OO	EFPC	FGW	PTR	FGW
43078	OO	EFPC	FGW	PTR	FGW
43079	OO	EFPC	FGW	PTR	FGW
43086	OO	EFPC	FGW	PTR	FGW
43087	OO	EFPC	FGW	PTR	FGW
43088	OO	EFPC	FGW	PTR	FGW
43091	OO	EFPC	FGW	PTR	FGW
43092	OO	EFPC	FGW	PTR	FGW
43093	OO	EFPC	FGW	PTR	FGW
43094	OO	EFPC	FGW	PTR	FGW
43097	OO	EFPC	FGW	PTR	FGW
43098	OO	EFPC	FGW	PTR	FGW
43122	OO	EFPC	FGW	FGP	FGW
43124	LE	EFPC	FGW	ANG	FGW
43125	LE	EFPC	FGW	ANG	FGW
43126	LE	EFPC	FGW	ANG	FGW
43127	LE	EFPC	FGW	ANG	FGW
43128	LE	EFPC	FGW	ANG	FGW
43129	LE	EFPC	FGW	ANG	FGW
43130	LE	EFPC	FGW	ANG	FGW
43131	LE	EFPC	FGW	ANG	FGW
43132	LE	EFPC	FGW	ANG	FGW
43133	LE	EFPC	FGW	ANG	FGW
43134	LE	EFPC	FGW	ANG	FGW
43135	LE	EFPC	FGW	ANG	FGW
43136	LE	EFPC	FGW	ANG	FGW
43137	LE	EFPC	FGW	ANG	FGW
43138	LE	EFPC	FGW	ANG	FGW
43139	LE	EFPC	FGW	ANG	FGW
43140	LE	EFPC	FGW	ANG	FGW
43141	LE	EFPC	FGW	ANG	FGW
43142	LE	EFPC	FGW	ANG	FGW
43143	LE	EFPC	FGW	ANG	FGW
43144	LE	EFPC	FGW	ANG	FGW
43145	LE	EFPC	FGW	ANG	FGW
43146	LE	EFPC	FGW	ANG	FGW
43147	LE	EFPC	FGW	ANG	FGW
43148	LE	EFPC	FGW	ANG	FGW
43149	LE	EFPC	FGW	ANG	FGW
43150	LE	EFPC	FGW	ANG	FGW
43151	LE	EFPC	FGW	ANG	FGW
43152	LE	EFPC	FGW	ANG	FGW
43153	OO	EFPC	FGW	FGP	FGW
43154	OO	EFPC	FGW	FGP	FGW
43155	OO	EFPC	FGW	FGP	FGW
43156	OO	EFPC	FGW	PTR	FGW
43158	OO	EFPC	FGW	FGP	FGW
43159	OO	EFPC	FGW	PTR	FGW
43160	OO	EFPC	FGW	PTR	FGW
43161	OO	EFPC	FGW	PTR	FGW
43162	OO	EFPC	FGW	ANG	FGW
43163	OO	EFPC	FGW	ANG	FGW
43164	OO	EFPC	FGW	ANG	FGW
43165	OO	EFPC	FGW	ANG	FGW
43168	OO	EFPC	FGW	ANG	FGW
43169	OO	EFPC	FGW	ANG	FGW
43170	OO	EFPC	FGW	ANG	FGW
43171	OO	EFPC	FGW	ANG	FGW
43172	OO	EFPC	FGW	ANG	FGW
43174	OO	EFPC	FGW	ANG	FGW
43175	OO	EFPC	FGW	ANG	FGW
43176	OO	EFPC	FGW	ANG	FGW
43177	OO	EFPC	FGW	ANG	FGW
43179	OO	EFPC	FGW	ANG	FGW
43180	OO	EFPC	FGW	PTR	FGW
43181	OO	EFPC	FGW	ANG	FGW
43182	OO	EFPC	FGW	ANG	FGW
43183	OO	EFPC	FGW	ANG	FGW
43185	OO	EFPC	FGW	ANG	FGW
43186	OO	EFPC	FGW	ANG	FGW
43187	OO	EFPC	FGW	ANG	FGW
43188	OO	EFPC	FGW	ANG	FGW
43189	OO	EFPC	FGW	ANG	FGW
43190	OO	EFPC	FGW	ANG	FGW
43191	OO	EFPC	FGW	ANG	FGW
43192	OO	EFPC	FGW	ANG	FGW
43193	OO	EFPC	FGW	PTR	FGW
43194	OO	EFPC	FGW	FGP	FGW
43195	OO	EFPC	FGW	PTR	FGW
43196	OO	EFPC	FGW	PTR	FGW
43197	OO	EFPC	FGW	PTR	FGW
43198	OO	EFPC	FGW	FGP	FGW

Names applied

43003	*Isambard Kingdom Brunel*
43004	*First for the Future / First ar gyfer y dyfodoi*
43009	*First Transforming Travel*
43021	*David Austin - Cartoonist*
43027	*Glorious Devon*
43030	*Christian Lewis Trust*
43033	*Driver Brian Cooper 15 June 1947 - 5 October 1989*
43040	*Bristol St Philip's Marsh*
43070	*The Corps of Royal Electrical and Mechanical Engineers*
43097	*Environment Agency*
43127	*Sir Peter Parker 1924-2002 - Cotswold Line 150*
43132	*We Save the Children - Will You?*
43139	*Driver Stan Martin 25 June 1960 - 6 November 2004*
43143	*Stroud 700*
43156	*Dartington International Summer School*
43163	*Exeter Panel Signal Box 21st Anniversary 2009*
43165	*Prince Michael of Kent*
43169	*The National Trust*
43179	*Pride of Laira*
43185	*Great Western*
43198	*Oxfordshire 2007*

Above: *The entire fleet of First Great Western operated power cars or Class 43s are now refurbished and painted in corporate FGW livery. The locos are owned by a mix of Angel Trains, Porterbrook and First Group. No. 43162, one of the Angel Trains vehicles, is seen at Newton Abbot.* **CJM**

Class 57/6

Vehicle Length: 63ft 6in (19.38m)
Height: 12ft 10⅛in (3.91m)
Width: 9ft 2in (2.79m)
Engine: EMD 645-12E3
Horsepower: 2,500hp (1,860kW)
Electrical Equipment: Brush

Number	*Depot*	*Pool*	*Livery*	*Owner*	*Operator*	*Name*
57602 (47337)	**OO**	**EFOO**	**FGB**	**PTR**	**FGW**	*Restormel Castle*
57603 (47349)	**OO**	**EFOO**	**GWG**	**PTR**	**FGW**	*Tintagel Castle*
57604 (47209)	**OO**	**EFOO**	**GWG**	**PTR**	**FGW**	*Pendennis Castle*
57605 (47206)	**OO**	**EFOO**	**FGB**	**PTR**	**FGW**	*Totnes Castle*

Right: *FGW operate four Porterbrook-owned Class 57/6s to power the overnight sleeper service between London and Penzance. The locos are also used to perform other 'haulage' needs of the operator. No. 57605 is seen at Plymouth, viewed from its No. 1 end. The fleet all carry GW style cast names and numbers.* **CJM**

HST Passenger Fleet

Vehicle Length: 75ft 0in (22.86m) Width: 8ft 11in (2.71m)
Height: 12ft 9in (3.88m) Bogie Type: BT10

GN2G - TSRMB *Seating 70S*

Number	Depot	Livery	Owner
40101 (42170)	LA	FGW	PTR
40102 (42223)	LA	FGW	PTR
40103 (42316)	LA	FGW	PTR
40104 (42254)	LA	FGW	PTR
40105 (42084)	LA	FGW	PTR
40106 (42162)	LA	FGW	PTR
40107 (42334)	LA	FGW	PTR
40108 (42314)	LA	FGW	PTR
40109 (42262)	LA	FGW	PTR
40110 (42187)	LA	FGW	PTR
40111 (42248)	LA	FGW	PTR
40112 (42336)	LA	FGW	PTR
40113 (42309)	LA	FGW	PTR
40114 (42086)	LA	FGW	PTR
40115 (42320)	LA	FGW	PTR
40116 (42147)	LA	FGW	PTR
40117 (42249)	LA	FGW	PTR
40118 (42338)	LA	FGW	PTR
40119 (42090)	LA	FGW	PTR

Currently under conversion

GN1G - TRFB *Seating 23F*

Number	Depot	Livery	Owner
40204	LA	FGW	ANG
40205	LA	FGW	ANG
40207	LA	FGW	ANG
40210	LA	FGW	ANG
40221	LA	FGW	ANG
40231	LA	FGW	ANG

GK1G - TRFB *Seating 17F*

Number	Depot	Livery	Owner
40703	LA	FGW	ANG
40707	LA	FGW	ANG
40709¤	OO	FGW	ANG
40710	LA	FGW	ANG
40712¤	LA	FGW	ANG
40713	LA	FGW	ANG
40714¤	OO	FGW	ANG
40715	LA	FGW	ANG
40716	LA	FGW	ANG
40718	OO	FGW	ANG
40721	LA	FGW	ANG
40722	LA	FGW	ANG
40724¤	OO	FGW	ANG
40725¤	OO	FGW	ANG
40726¤	OO	FGW	ANG
40727	LA	FGW	ANG
40733	LA	FGW	ANG
40734	LA	FGW	ANG
40736¤	OO	FGW	ANG
40738¤	OO	FGW	ANG
40739	LA	FGW	ANG
40743	LA	FGW	ANG
40744¤	OO	FGW	ANG
40745¤	OO	FGW	ANG
40752	LA	FGW	ANG
40755	LA	FGW	ANG
40757	LA	FGW	ANG

GL1G - TRFB *Seating 17F*

Number	Depot	Livery	Owner
40801	OO	FGW	PTR
40802	OO	FGW	PTR
40803	OO	FGW	PTR
40806	OO	FGW	PTR
40807	LA	FGW	PTR
40808	OO	FGW	PTR
40809	LA	FGW	PTR
40810	LA	FGW	PTR

GN1G - TRB *Seating 23F*

Number	Depot	Livery	Owner
40900	LA	FGW	FGP
40901	LA	FGW	FGP
40902	LA	FGW	FGP
40903	LA	FGW	FGP
40904	LA	FGW	FGP

GH1G - TF *Seating 48F*

Number	Depot	Livery	Owner
41003	LA	FGW	ANG
41004	OO	FGW	ANG
41005	OO	FGW	ANG
41006	OO	FGW	ANG
41007	OO	FGW	ANG
41008	OO	FGW	ANG
41009	LA	FGW	ANG
41010	LA	FGW	ANG
41011	LA	FGW	ANG
41012	LA	FGW	ANG
41015	LA	FGW	ANG
41016	LA	FGW	ANG
41017	OO	FGW	ANG
41018	OO	FGW	ANG
41019	LA	FGW	ANG
41020	LA	FGW	ANG
41021	LA	FGW	ANG
41022	LA	FGW	ANG
41023	LA	FGW	ANG
41024	LA	FGW	ANG
41027	OO	FGW	ANG
41028	OO	FGW	ANG
41029	OO	FGW	ANG
41030	OO	FGW	ANG
41031	LA	FGW	ANG
41032	LA	FGW	ANG
41033	OO	FGW	ANG
41034	OO	FGW	ANG
41037	LA	FGW	ANG
41038	LA	FGW	ANG
41045	LA	FGW	FGP
41051	LA	FGW	ANG
41052	LA	FGW	ANG
41055	OO	FGW	ANG
41056	OO	FGW	ANG
41059	LA	FGW	FGP
41065	OO	FGW	ANG
41081	OO	FGW	PTR
41085	LA	FGW	FGP
41086	LA	FGW	FGP
41089	OO	FGW	ANG
41093	LA	FGW	ANG
41094	LA	FGW	ANG
41096	LA	FGW	PTR
41101	OO	FGW	ANG
41102	OO	FGW	ANG
41103	LA	FGW	ANG
41104	LA	FGW	ANG
41105	OO	FGW	ANG
41106	OO	FGW	ANG
41108	OO	FGW	PTR
41109	OO	FGW	PTR
41110	OO	FGW	ANG
41114	LA	FGW	FGP
41116	LA	FGW	ANG
41119	OO	FGW	PTR
41121	LA	FGW	ANG
41122	LA	FGW	ANG
41123	LA	FGW	ANG
41124	LA	FGW	ANG
41125	OO	FGW	ANG
41126	OO	FGW	ANG
41127	OO	FGW	ANG
41128	OO	FGW	ANG
41129	LA	FGW	ANG
41130	LA	FGW	ANG
41131	OO	FGW	ANG
41132	OO	FGW	ANG
41133	LA	FGW	ANG
41134	LA	FGW	ANG
41135	LA	FGW	ANG
41136	LA	FGW	ANG
41137	OO	FGW	ANG
41138	OO	FGW	ANG
41139	OO	FGW	ANG
41140	OO	FGW	ANG
41141	LA	FGW	ANG
41142	LA	FGW	ANG
41143	LA	FGW	ANG
41144	LA	FGW	ANG
41145	LA	FGW	ANG
41146	LA	FGW	ANG
41147	OO	FGW	PTR
41148	OO	FGW	PTR
41149	OO	FGW	PTR
41153	OO	FGW	PTR
41155	OO	FGW	PTR
41157	LA	FGW	ANG
41158	LA	FGW	ANG
41160	LA	FGW	FGP
41161	OO	FGW	PTR
41162	LA	FGW	FGP
41163	LA	FGW	FGP
41166	LA	FGW	FGP
41167	LA	FGW	FGP
41168	OO	FGW	PTR
41169	OO	FGW	PTR
41176	OO	FGW	PTR
41179	OO	FGW	ANG
41180	OO	FGW	ANG
41181	OO	FGW	PTR
41182	OO	FGW	PTR
41183	OO	FGW	PTR
41184	OO	FGW	PTR
41186	OO	FGW	PTR
41187	OO	FGW	PTR
41189	OO	FGW	PTR
41191	OO	FGW	PTR
41192	OO	FGW	PTR

GH2G - TS *Seating 68-84S*

Number	Depot	Livery	Owner
42003	OO	FGW	ANG
42004	LA	FGW	ANG
42005	LA	FGW	ANG
42006	LA	FGW	ANG
42007	LA	FGW	ANG
42008	OO	FGW	ANG
42009	LA	FGW	ANG
42010	LA	FGW	ANG

42012	LA	FGW	ANG
42013	LA	FGW	ANG
42014	LA	FGW	ANG
42015	LA	FGW	ANG
42016	LA	FGW	ANG
42019	LA	FGW	ANG
42021	LA	FGW	ANG
42023	LA	FGW	ANG
42024	OO	FGW	ANG
42025	OO	FGW	ANG
42026	OO	FGW	ANG
42027	OO	FGW	ANG
42028	LA	FGW	ANG
42029	LA	FGW	ANG
42030	LA	FGW	ANG
42031	LA	FGW	ANG
42032	LA	FGW	ANG
42033	LA	FGW	ANG
42034	LA	FGW	ANG
42035	LA	FGW	ANG
42039	OO	FGW	ANG
42040	OO	FGW	ANG
42041	OO	FGW	ANG
42042	OO	FGW	ANG
42043	OO	FGW	ANG
42044	OO	FGW	ANG
42045	LA	FGW	ANG
42046	LA	FGW	ANG
42047	LA	FGW	ANG
42048	OO	FGW	ANG
42049	OO	FGW	ANG
42050	OO	FGW	ANG
42054	LA	FGW	ANG
42055	LA	FGW	ANG
42056	LA	FGW	ANG
42060	OO	FGW	ANG
42061	OO	FGW	ANG
42062	OO	FGW	ANG
42066	OO	FGW	ANG
42067	OO	FGW	ANG
42068	OO	FGW	ANG
42069	OO	FGW	ANG
42070	OO	FGW	ANG
42071	OO	FGW	ANG
42072	LA	FGW	ANG
42073	OO	FGW	ANG
42074	OO	FGW	ANG
42075	LA	FGW	ANG
42076	LA	FGW	ANG
42077	LA	FGW	ANG
42078	LA	FGW	ANG
42079	OO	FGW	ANG
42080	OO	FGW	ANG
42081	OO	FGW	ANG
42083	OO	FGW	ANG
42085	OO	FGW	ANG
42087	OO	FGW	ANG
42089	OO	FGW	ANG
42092	LA	FGW	FGP
42093	LA	FGW	FGP
42094	LA	FGW	FGP
42095	LA	FGW	FGP
42096	LA	FGW	ANG
42098	OO	FGW	ANG
42099	OO	FGW	ANG
42101	OO	FGW	PTR
42102	OO	FGW	PTR
42103	LA	FGW	FGP
42105	LA	FGW	FGP
42107	LA	FGW	ANG
42108	LA	FGW	FGP
42115	OO	FGW	PTR
42118	OO	FGW	ANG
42126	OO	FGW	ANG
42129	LA	FGW	ANG
42138	OO	FGW	ANG
42143	LA	FGW	ANG
42144	LA	FGW	ANG
42145	LA	FGW	ANG
42166	OO	FGW	PTR
42167	LA	FGW	FGP
42168	LA	FGW	FGP
42169	LA	FGW	FGP
42173	OO	FGW	PTR
42174	OO	FGW	PTR
42175	LA	FGW	FGP
42176	LA	FGW	FGP
42177	LA	FGW	FGP
42178	OO	FGW	PTR
42183	LA	FGW	ANG
42184	LA	FGW	ANG
42185	LA	FGW	ANG
42195	OO	FGW	PTR
42196	OO	FGW	ANG
42197	OO	FGW	ANG
42200	LA	FGW	ANG
42201	OO	FGW	ANG
42202	OO	FGW	ANG
42203	OO	FGW	ANG
42204	OO	FGW	ANG
42206	LA	FGW	ANG
42207	LA	FGW	ANG
42208	LA	FGW	ANG
42209	LA	FGW	ANG
42211	OO	FGW	ANG
42212	OO	FGW	ANG
42213	OO	FGW	ANG
42214	OO	FGW	ANG
42216	OO	FGW	ANG
42217	OO	FGW	PTR
42218	OO	FGW	PTR
42221	OO	FGW	ANG
42222	OO	FGW	PTR
42224	OO	FGW	PTR
42231	LA	FGW	FGP
42232 ●	LA	FGW	FGP
42233	LA	FGW	FGP
42236	OO	FGW	ANG
42245	LA	FGW	ANG
42247	OO	FGW	PTR
42250	LA	FGW	ANG
42251	OO	FGW	ANG
42252	LA	FGW	ANG
42253	LA	FGW	ANG
42255	LA	FGW	ANG
42256	LA	FGW	ANG
42257	LA	FGW	ANG
42258	OO	FGW	PTR
42259	LA	FGW	ANG
42260	OO	FGW	ANG
42261	OO	FGW	ANG
42263	LA	FGW	ANG
42264	OO	FGW	ANG
42265	LA	FGW	ANG
42266	OO	FGW	PTR
42267	LA	FGW	ANG
42268	LA	FGW	ANG
42269	LA	FGW	ANG
42271	OO	FGW	ANG
42272	OO	FGW	ANG
42273	OO	FGW	ANG
42275	LA	FGW	ANG
42276	LA	FGW	ANG
42277	LA	FGW	ANG
42279	LA	FGW	ANG
42280	LA	FGW	ANG
42281	LA	FGW	ANG
42283	OO	FGW	ANG
42284	OO	FGW	ANG
42285	OO	FGW	ANG
42287	OO	FGW	ANG
42288	OO	FGW	ANG
42289	OO	FGW	ANG
42291	LA	FGW	ANG
42292	LA	FGW	ANG
42293	LA	FGW	ANG
42294	OO	FGW	PTR
42295	LA	FGW	ANG
42296	LA	FGW	ANG
42297	LA	FGW	ANG
42299	LA	FGW	ANG
42300	LA	FGW	ANG
42301	LA	FGW	ANG
42302	LA	FGW	FGP
42303	LA	FGW	FGP
42304	LA	FGW	FGP
42305	LA	FGW	FGP
42308	OO	FGW	PTR
42310	OO	FGW	PTR
42315	OO	FGW	PTR
42317	OO	FGW	PTR
42319	OO	FGW	PTR
42321	OO	FGW	PTR
42325	LA	FGW	ANG
42332	LA	FGW	ANG
42333	LA	FGW	ANG
42343	LA	FGW	ANG
42344	OO	FGW	ANG
42345	LA	FGW	ANG
42346	OO	FGW	ANG
42347	OO	FGW	ANG
42348	OO	FGW	ANG
42349	OO	FGW	ANG
42350	LA	FGW	ANG
42351	LA	FGW	ANG
42353	LA	FGW	FGP
42356	OO	FGW	ANG
42360	LA	FGW	ANG
42361	LA	FGW	ANG
42362	OO	FGW	ANG
42364	OO	FGW	PTR
42365	OO	FGW	PTR
42381 (41058)	OO	FGW	PTR
42382 (12128)	OO	FGW	PTR
42383 (12172)	OO	FGW	PTR

● Volo Television fitted

GJ2G - TGS *Seating 67-71S*

Number	*Depot*	*Livery*	*Owner*
44000	OO	FGW	PTR
44001	LA	FGW	ANG
44002	OO	FGW	ANG
44003	OO	FGW	ANG
44004	LA	FGW	ANG
44005	LA	FGW	ANG
44007	LA	FGW	ANG
44008	OO	FGW	ANG
44009	LA	FGW	ANG
44010	LA	FGW	ANG
44011	LA	FGW	ANG

First Great Western

44013	OO	FGW	ANG
44014	OO	FGW	ANG
44015	LA	FGW	ANG
44016	OO	FGW	ANG
44018	LA	FGW	ANG
44020	OO	FGW	ANG
44022	OO	FGW	ANG
44023	OO	FGW	ANG
44024	OO	FGW	ANG
44025	LA	FGW	ANG
44026	OO	FGW	ANG
44028	LA	FGW	ANG
44029	LA	FGW	ANG
44030	OO	FGW	ANG
44032	LA	FGW	ANG
44033	OO	FGW	ANG
44034	LA	FGW	ANG
44035	LA	FGW	ANG
44036	OO	FGW	ANG
44037	OO	FGW	ANG
44038	LA	FGW	ANG
44039	LA	FGW	ANG
44040	LA	FGW	ANG
44042	OO	FGW	PTR
44043	OO	FGW	ANG
44049	LA	FGW	ANG
44055	LA	FGW	FGP
44059	LA	FGW	ANG
44060	OO	FGW	PTR
44064	OO	FGW	ANG
44066	LA	FGW	ANG
44067	OO	FGW	ANG
44068	LA	FGW	FGP
44069	OO	FGW	PTR
44074	LA	FGW	FGP
44076	LA	FGW	FGP
44078	OO	FGW	PTR
44079	OO	FGW	PTR
44081	LA	FGW	FGP
44083	OO	FGW	PTR
44086	LA	FGW	ANG
44090	OO	FGW	PTR
44091	OO	FGW	PTR
44093	OO	FGW	ANG
44097	OO	FGW	PTR
44100	LA	FGW	FGP
44101	OO	FGW	PTR

¤ Due off lease

Below: *The entire FGW HST fleet has been refurbished under the present First Group franchise. Work was undertaken by Bombardier at either Derby or Ilford. All stock carries standard FGW Dynamic Lines livery. TS 42144 is illustrated.* **CJM**

Class 142

Vehicle Length: 51ft 0½in (15.55m)
Height: 12ft 8in (3.86m)
Width: 9ft 2¼in (2.80m)
Engine: 1 x Cummins LTA10-R per vehicle
Horsepower: 460hp (343kW)
Seats (total/car): 97S, 53S/44S

Number	*Formation DMS+DMSL*	*Depot*	*Livery*	*Owner*	*Operator*
142001	55542+55592	EX	FGN	ANG	FGW
142009	55550+55600	EX	FGN	ANG	FGW
142029	55570+55620	EX	FGN	ANG	FGW
142030	55571+55621	EX	FGN	ANG	FGW
142063	55713+55759	EX	FGN	ANG	FGW
142064	55714+55760	EX	FGN	ANG	FGW
142068	55718+55764	EX	FGN	ANG	FGW

Left: *Seven Class 142 'Pacer' sets are allocated to Exeter depot for South West branch line work, including the Exeter to Exmouth, Barnstaple, and Paignton lines. All sets still carry the Northern Rail blue and gold star colours. The units are scheduled to return to Northern in 2010-12. Set No. 142064 departs from Dawlish Warren with a service to Paignton on 18 March 2009.* **CJM**

Class 143

Vehicle Length: 51ft 0½in (15.55m)	Engine: 1 x Cummins LTA10-R per vehicle
Height: 12ft 2¼in (3.73m)	Horsepower: 460hp (343kW)
Width: 8ft 10½in (2.70m)	Seats (total/car): 92S, 48S/44S

Number	Formation DMS+DMSL	Depot	Livery	Owner	Operator
143603	55658+55689	EX	FGL	PTR	FGW
143611	55652+55677	EX	FGL	PTR	FGW
143612	55653+55678	EX	FGL	PTR	FGW
143617	55644+55683	EX	FGL	PTR	FGW
143618	55659+55684	EX	FGL	PTR	FGW
143619	55660+55685	EX	FGL	PTR	FGW
143620	55661+55686	EX	FGL	PTR	FGW
143621	55662+55687	EX	FGL	PTR	FGW

Right: *Eight Class 143s are allocated to First Great Western and share duties in the Exeter area with Class 142s. The sets migrated west from the Bristol suburban area in 2008, but are still frequently seen in the Bristol area. All sets have now been refurbished at Eastleigh and sport the FGW Local Lines livery. Set No. 143618 arrives at Worle Parkway forming the 17.25 Bristol Temple Meads to Weston-super-Mare on 14 June 2009.* **Chris Perkins**

Class 150/1

Vehicle Length: 64ft 9¾in (19.74m)	Engine: 1 x NT855R5 of 285hp per vehicle
Height: 12ft 4½in (3.77m)	Horsepower: 570hp (425kW)
Width: 9ft 3⅛in (2.82m)	Seats (total/car): 141S, 71S/70S

Number	Formation DMSL+DMS	Depot	Livery	Owner	Operator
150121	52121+57121	PM	SLF	PTR	FGW
150127	52127+57127	PM	SLF	PTR	FGW

Right: *A shortage of DMU rolling stock in 2006 saw a pair of off-lease ex-Silverlink Class 150/1 sets transferred to First Great Western, where the distinctive mauve, green and white livery was retained, adorned with FGW transfers. The two sets allocated to Bristol St Philip's Marsh are un-refurbished, but operate throughout the FGW network. Set No. 150121 is seen at Exeter St Davids.* **CJM**

Class 150/2

Vehicle Length: 64ft 9¾in (19.74m)	Engine: 1 x NT855R5 of 285hp per vehicle
Height: 12ft 4½in (3.77m)	Horsepower: 570hp (425kW)
Width: 9ft 3⅛in (2.82m)	Seats (total/car): 116S, 60S/56S

Number	Formation DMSL+DMS	Depot	Livery	Owner	Operator
150219	52219+57219	EX	FGL	PTR	FGW
150221	52221+57221	EX	FGL	PTR	FGW
150232	52232+57232	EX	FGL	PTR	FGW
150233	52233+57233	EX	FGL	PTR	FGW
150234	52234+57234	EX	FGL	PTR	FGW
150238	52238+57238	EX	FGL	PTR	FGW
150239	52239+57239	EX	FGL	PTR	FGW
150243	52243+57243	EX	FGL	PTR	FGW
150244	52244+57244	EX	FGL	PTR	FGW
150246	52246+57246	EX	FGL	PTR	FGW
150247	52247+57247	EX	FGL	PTR	FGW
150248	52248+57248	EX	FGL	PTR	FGW
150249	52249+57249	EX	FGL	PTR	FGW
150261	52261+57261	EX	FGL	PTR	FGW
150263	52263+57263	EX	FGL	PTR	FGW
150265	52265+57265	EX	FGL	PTR	FGW
150266	52266+57266	EX	FGL	PTR	FGW

First Great Western

Left: *FGW's fleet of 17 Class 150/2 sets are allocated to Exeter depot, but can be found operating anywhere on the non-HST routes. The sets have all received refurbishment by Pullman Rail of Cardiff and now sport FGW Local Lines livery. The sets are fully compatible with all other FGW allocated 14x and 15x class units. Set No. 150247 is seen in multiple with a Class 142 at Dawlish Warren.* **CJM**

Class 153

Vehicle Length: 76ft 5in (23.29m)
Height: 12ft 3⅛in (3.75m)
Width: 8ft 10in (2.70m)
Engine: 1 x NT855R5 of 285hp
Horsepower: 285hp (213kW)
Seats (total/car): 72S

Number	*Formation DMSL*	*Depot*	*Livery*	*Owner*	*Operator*
153305	52305	EX	FGL	ANG	FGW
153318	52318	EX	FGL	ANG	FGW
153329	52329	EX	FGL	ANG	FGW
153361	57361	EX	FGL	ANG	FGW
153368	57368	EX	FGL	ANG	FGW
153369	57369	EX	FGL	ANG	FGW
153370	57370	EX	FGL	ANG	FGW
153372	57372	EX	FGL	ANG	FGW
153373	57373	EX	FGL	ANG	FGW
153377	57377	EX	FGL	ANG	FGW
153380	57380	EX	FGL	ANG	FGW
153382	57382	EX	FGL	ANG	FGW

Left: *The First Great Western allocation of 12 single or 'bubble' cars are also allocated to Exeter depot and are principally used for branch line use or strengthening two-car formations to three at peak times. All sets have been refurbished at Eastleigh and sport FGW Local Lines colours. Set No. 153373 is seen 'on shed' at Exeter alongside a Class 142.* **CJM**

Class 158/0 (2-car)

Vehicle Length: 76ft 1¾in (23.21m)
Height: 12ft 6in (3.81m)
Width: 9ft 3¼in (2.82m)
Engine: 1 x Cummins NTA855R of 350hp per vehicle
Horsepower: 700hp (522kW)
Seats (total/car): 134S, 66S/68S

Number	*Formation DMSL+DMSL*	*Depot*	*Livery*	*Owner*	*Operator*
158745	52745+57745	PM	FGL	PTR	FGW
158763	52763+57763	PM	FGL	PTR	FGW
158766	52766+57766	PM	FGL	PTR	FGW
158767	52767+57767	PM	FGL	PTR	FGW
158769	52769+57769	PM	FGL	PTR	FGW

Left: *Bristol St Philip's Marsh depot is home to the FGW Class 158 fleet which is mainly used on the longer distance duties radiating from Bristol to Portsmouth, Weymouth and northwards to Gloucester and Cheltenham. All sets are refurbished and carry FGW Local Lines livery. Set No. 158748 is seen at Gloucester, this set has subsequently been re-formed giving one car to each of sets 158952/953.* **CJM**

Class 158/0 (3-car)

158798
Vehicle Length: 76ft 1¾in (23.21m) *Engine: 1 x Cummins NTA855R of 350hp per vehicle*
Height: 12ft 6in (3.81m) *Horsepower: 1,050hp (783kW)*
Width: 9ft 3¼in (2.82m) *Seats (total/car): 200S, 66S/66S/68S*

158950 - 158959
Vehicle Length: 76ft 1¾in (23.21m) *Engine: 1 x Cummins NTA855R of 350hp per vehicle*
Height: 12ft 6in (3.81m) *Horsepower: 1,050hp (783kW)*
Width: 9ft 3¼in (2.82m) *Seats (total/car): 204S, 66S/70S/68S*

Number	*Formation* *DMSL+MSL+DMSL*	*Depot*	*Livery*	*Owner*	*Operator*
158798	**52798+58715+57798**	**PM**	**FGL**	**PTR**	**FGW**

Number	*Formation*	*DMSL+DMSL+DMSL*	*Depot*	*Livery*	*Owner*	*Operator*
158950	**(158751/761)**	**57751+52761+57761**	**PM**	**FGL**	**PTR**	**FGW**
158951	**(158751/764)**	**52751+52764+57764**	**PM**	**FGL**	**PTR**	**FGW**
158952	**(158748/762)**	**57748+52762+57762**	**PM**	**FGL**	**PTR**	**FGW**
158953	**(158748/750)**	**52748+52750+57750**	**PM**	**FGL**	**PTR**	**FGW**
158954	**(158747/760)**	**57747+52760+57760**	**PM**	**FGL**	**PTR**	**FGW**
158955	**(158747/765)**	**52747+52765+57765**	**PM**	**FGL**	**PTR**	**FGW**
158956	**(158749/768)**	**57749+52768+57768**	**PM**	**FGL**	**PTR**	**FGW**
158957	**(158749/771)**	**52749+52771+57771**	**PM**	**FGL**	**PTR**	**FGW**
158958	**(158746/776)**	**57746+52776+57776**	**PM**	**FGL**	**PTR**	**FGW**
158959	**(158746/778)**	**52746+52778+57778**	**PM**	**FGL**	**PTR**	**FGW**

Right: *First Great Western currently operates a fleet of 11 three-car Class 158s. One set No. 158798 (illustrated) is formed with a middle MSL vehicles and the remainder are formed with three driving cars. All sets are refurbished and carry the FGW Local Lines livery, with place and group names making up the dynamic bands on vehicle sides. Set No. 158798 is seen at Westbury.* **Stacey Thew**

Class 165/1 (3-car)
Networker Turbo

Vehicle Length: (driving) 75ft 2½in (22.91m), (inter) 74ft 6½in (22.72m)
Height: 12ft 5¼in (3.79m) *Engine: 1 x Perkins 2006TWH of 350hp*
Width: 9ft 5½in (2.81m) *Horsepower: 1,050hp (783kW)*
Seats (total/car): 16F/270S, 16F-66S/106S/98S

Number	*Formation* *DMCL+MS+DMS*	*Depot*	*Livery*	*Owner*	*Operator*
165101	**58953+55415+58916**	**RG**	**FGT**	**ANG**	**FGW**
165102	**58954+55416+58917**	**RG**	**FGT**	**ANG**	**FGW**
165103	**58955+55417+58918**	**RG**	**FGT**	**ANG**	**FGW**
165104	**58956+55418+58919**	**RG**	**FGT**	**ANG**	**FGW**
165105	**58957+55419+58920**	**RG**	**FGT**	**ANG**	**FGW**
165106	**58958+55420+58921**	**RG**	**FGT**	**ANG**	**FGW**
165107	**58959+55421+58922**	**RG**	**FGT**	**ANG**	**FGW**
165108	**58960+55422+58923**	**RG**	**FGT**	**ANG**	**FGW**
165109	**58961+55423+58924**	**RG**	**FGT**	**ANG**	**FGW**
165110	**58962+55424+58925**	**RG**	**FGT**	**ANG**	**FGW**
165111	**58963+55425+58926**	**RG**	**FGT**	**ANG**	**FGW**
165112	**58964+55426+58927**	**RG**	**FGT**	**ANG**	**FGW**
165113	**58965+55427+58928**	**RG**	**FGT**	**ANG**	**FGW**
165114	**58966+55428+58929**	**RG**	**FGT**	**ANG**	**FGW**
165116	**58968+55430+58931**	**RG**	**FGT**	**ANG**	**FGW**
165117	**58969+55431+58932**	**RG**	**FGT**	**ANG**	**FGW**

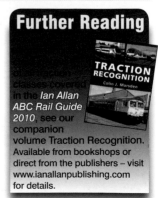

Class 165/1 (2-car)
Networker Turbo

Vehicle Length: 75ft 2½in (22.91m)
Height: 12ft 5¼in (3.79m)
Width: 9ft 5½in (2.81m)
Engine: 1 x Perkins 2006TWH of 350hp per car
Horsepower: 700hp (522kW)
Seats (total/car): 16F/170S, 16F-72S/98S

Number	Formation DMCL+DMS	Depot	Livery	Owner	Operator
165118	58879+58933	RG	FGT	ANG	FGW
165119	58880+58934	RG	FGT	ANG	FGW
165120	58881+58935	RG	FGT	ANG	FGW
165121	58882+58936	RG	FGT	ANG	FGW
165122	58883+58937	RG	FGT	ANG	FGW
165123	58884+58938	RG	FGT	ANG	FGW
165124	58885+58939	RG	FGT	ANG	FGW
165125	58886+58940	RG	FGT	ANG	FGW
165126	58887+58941	RG	FGT	ANG	FGW
165127	58888+58942	RG	FGT	ANG	FGW
165128	58889+58943	RG	FGT	ANG	FGW
165129	58890+58944	RG	FGT	ANG	FGW
165130	58891+58945	RG	FGT	ANG	FGW
165131	58892+58946	RG	FGT	ANG	FGW
165132	58893+58947	RG	FGT	ANG	FGW
165133	58894+58948	RG	FGT	ANG	FGW
165134	58895+58949	RG	FGT	ANG	FGW
165135	58896+58950	RG	FGT	ANG	FGW
165136	58897+58951	RG	FGT	ANG	FGW
165137	58898+58952	RG	FGT	ANG	FGW

Left: *The Class 165/1 sets operated by First Great Western and allocated to Reading depot are the mainstay of London-area suburban operations. The class comes in both two and three car formations. All sets now sport FGW Dynamic Lines livery with pink passenger doors. Accommodation is provided for standard and first class passengers. Set No. 165133 with its DMCL coach nearest the camera, departs from Banbury on 15 August 2008.* **Stacey Thew**

Class 166
Networker Turbo Express

Vehicle Length: (driving) 75ft 2½in (22.91m), (inter) 74ft 6½in (22.72m)
Height: 12ft 5¼in (3.79m)
Width: 9ft 5½in (2.81m)
Engine: 1 x Perkins 2006TWH of 350hp per car
Horsepower: 1,050hp (783kW)
Seats (total/car): 32F/243S, 16F-75S/96S/16F-72S

Number	Formation DMCL(A)+MS+DMCL(B)	Depot	Livery	Owner	Operator
166201	58101+58601+58122	RG	FGT	ANG	FGW
166202	58102+58602+58123	RG	FGT	ANG	FGW
166203	58103+58603+58124	RG	FGT	ANG	FGW
166204	58104+58604+58125	RG	FGT	ANG	FGW
166205	58105+58605+58126	RG	FGT	ANG	FGW
166206	58106+58606+58127	RG	FGT	ANG	FGW
166207	58107+58607+58128	RG	FGT	ANG	FGW
166208	58108+58608+58129	RG	FGT	ANG	FGW
166209	58109+58609+58130	RG	FGT	ANG	FGW
166210	58110+58610+58131	RG	FGT	ANG	FGW
166211	58111+58611+58132	RG	FGT	ANG	FGW
166212	58112+58612+58133	RG	FGT	ANG	FGW
166213	58113+58613+58134	RG	FGT	ANG	FGW
166214	58114+58614+58135	RG	FGT	ANG	FGW
166215	58115+58615+58136	RG	FGT	ANG	FGW
166216	58116+58616+58137	RG	FGT	ANG	FGW
166217	58117+58617+58138	RG	FGT	ANG	FGW
166218	58118+58618+58139	RG	FGT	ANG	FGW
166219	58119+58619+58140	RG	FGT	ANG	FGW
166220	58120+58620+58141	RG	FGT	ANG	FGW
166221	58121+58621+58142	RG	FGT	ANG	FGW

Above: *On 1 May 2009, a six-car Class 166 formation made up of units Nos. 166201 and 166211 stands at Oxford with the 16.07 FGW service to Didcot Parkway. The Class 166s are the air conditioned express variant of the 'Networker Turbo' family built by ABB for the London Paddington to Oxford / Newbury NSE routes.* **John Binch**

Mk3 Hauled Stock

Vehicle Length: 75ft 0in (22.86m)
Height: 12ft 9in (3.88m)
Width: 8ft 11in (2.71m)
Bogie Type: BT10

AJ1G - RFB *Seating 18F*

Number	*Depot*	*Livery*	*Owner*
10219	**PZ**	**FGW**	**PTR**
10225	**PZ**	**FGW**	**PTR**
10232	**PZ**	**FGW**	**PTR**

AU4G - SLEP *Comps 12*

Number	*Depot*	*Livery*	*Owner*
10532	**PZ**	**FGW**	**PTR**
10534	**PZ**	**FGW**	**PTR**
10563	**PZ**	**FGW**	**PTR**
10584	**PZ**	**FGW**	**PTR**
10589	**PZ**	**FGW**	**PTR**
10590	**PZ**	**FGW**	**PTR**
10594	**PZ**	**FGW**	**PTR**
10601	**PZ**	**FGW**	**PTR**
10612	**PZ**	**FGW**	**PTR**
10616	**PZ**	**FGW**	**PTR**

AC2G - TSO *Seating 70S*

Number	*Depot*	*Livery*	*Owner*
12100	**PZ**	**FGW**	**PTR**
12161	**PZ**	**FGW**	**PTR**

AE1H - BFO *Seating 36F*

Number	*Depot*	*Livery*	*Owner*
17173	**PZ**	**FGW**	**PTR**
17174	**PZ**	**FGW**	**PTR**
17175	**PZ**	**FGW**	**PTR**

Right: *The First Great Western Mk3 hauled stock, operated exclusively on the overnight sleeper services between London Paddington and Penzance, has all been refurbished and now carries the FGW Dynamic Lines livery with side branding reading 'Night Riviera Sleeper'. SLEP No. 10594 is illustrated at Plymouth.* **CJM**

Service Stock

HST Barrier Vehicles

Number	*Depot*	*Livery*	*Owner*	*Former Identity*
6330	**LA**	**FGB**	**ANG**	**BFK - 14084**
6336	**LA**	**FGB**	**ANG**	**BG - 81591/92185**
6338	**LA**	**FGB**	**ANG**	**BG - 81581/92180**
6348	**LA**	**FGB**	**ANG**	**BG - 81233/92963**

Right: *To allow the coupling of conventional rolling stock to the HST fleet a number of barrier coaches are allocated to all HST operators. FGW coach No. 6330, a modified BFK, is illustrated painted in un-branded FGW blue.* **CJM**

First Scotrail

Address: ✉ Atrium Court, 50 Waterloo Street, Glasgow, G2 6HQ
scotrail.enquiries@firstgroup.com
✆ 08700 005151
ⓘ www.firstscotrail.com

Managing Director: Steve Montgomery
Franchise Dates: 17 October 2004 - 31 November 2014
Principal Routes: All Scottish services, plus Scotrail sleeper services
Depots: Corkerhill (CK), Glasgow Shields Road (GW), Haymarket (HA), Inverness (IS)
Parent Company: First Group

Class 156

Vehicle Length: 75ft 6in (23.03m)
Height: 12ft 6in (3.81m)
Width: 8ft 11in (2.73m)
Engine: 1 x Cummins NT855R5 of 285hp
Horsepower: 570hp (425kW)
Seats (total/car): 142S, 70 or 72S

Number	*Formation DMSL+DMS*	*Depot*	*Livery*	*Owner*	*Operator*
156430	52430+57430	CK	FSR	ANG	FSR
156431	52431+57431	CK	FSS	ANG	FSR
156432	52432+57432	CK	FSS	ANG	FSR
156433	52433+57433	CK	FSS	ANG	FSR
156434	52434+57434	CK	FSR	ANG	FSR
156435	52435+57435	CK	FSS	ANG	FSR
156436	52436+57436	CK	FSR	ANG	FSR
156437	52437+57437	CK	FSS	ANG	FSR
156439	52439+57439	CK	FSS	ANG	FSR
156442	52442+57442	CK	FSR	ANG	FSR
156445	52445+57445	CK	FSR	ANG	FSR
156446	52446+57446	CK	FSR	ANG	FSR
156447	52447+57447	CK	FSR	ANG	FSR
156449	52449+57449	CK	FSR	ANG	FSR
156450	52450+57450	CK	FSR	ANG	FSR
156453	52453+57453	CK	FSR	ANG	FSR
156456	52456+57456	CK	FSR	ANG	FSR
156457	52457+57457	CK	FSR	ANG	FSR
156458	52458+57458	CK	FSR	ANG	FSR
156462	52462+57462	CK	FSR	ANG	FSR
156465	52465+57465	CK	FSR	ANG	FSR
156467	52467+57467	CK	FSR	ANG	FSR
156474	52474+57474	CK	FSR	ANG	FSR
156476	52476+57476	CK	FSR	ANG	FSR
156477	52477+57477	CK	FSR	ANG	FSR
156478	52478+57478	CK	FSR	ANG	FSR
156485	52485+57485	CK	FSR	ANG	FSR
156492	52492+57492	CK	FSR	ANG	FSR
156493	52493+57493	CK	FSR	ANG	FSR
156494	52494+57494	CK	FSS	ANG	FSR
156495	52495+57495	CK	CAR	ANG	FSR
156496	52496+57496	CK	FSS	ANG	FSR
156499	52499+57499	CK	FSR	ANG	FSR
156500	52500+57500	CK	CAR	ANG	FSR
156501	52501+57501	CK	CAR	ANG	FSR
156502	52502+57502	CK	FSS	ANG	FSR
156503	52503+57503	CK	FSS	ANG	FSR
156504	52504+57504	CK	CAR	ANG	FSR
156505	52505+57505	CK	FSS	ANG	FSR
156506	52506+57506	CK	CAR	ANG	FSR
156507	52507+57507	CK	FSS	ANG	FSR
156508	52508+57508	CK	CAR	ANG	FSR
156509	52509+57509	CK	FSS	ANG	FSR
156510	52510+57510	CK	FSS	ANG	FSR
156511	52511+57511	CK	CAR	ANG	FSR
156512	52512+57512	CK	FSS	ANG	FSR
156513	52513+57513	CK	CAR	ANG	FSR
156514	52514+57514	CK	CAR	ANG	FSR

Left: *A revised Scotrail identity emerged in late 2008, that of an allover blue body, offset by a stylised Scottish Saltire flag and white/blue coach side branding. The Class 156 were the first to carry these new colours, seen on set No. 156432 at Carlisle on 17 June 2009.* **Nathan Williamson**

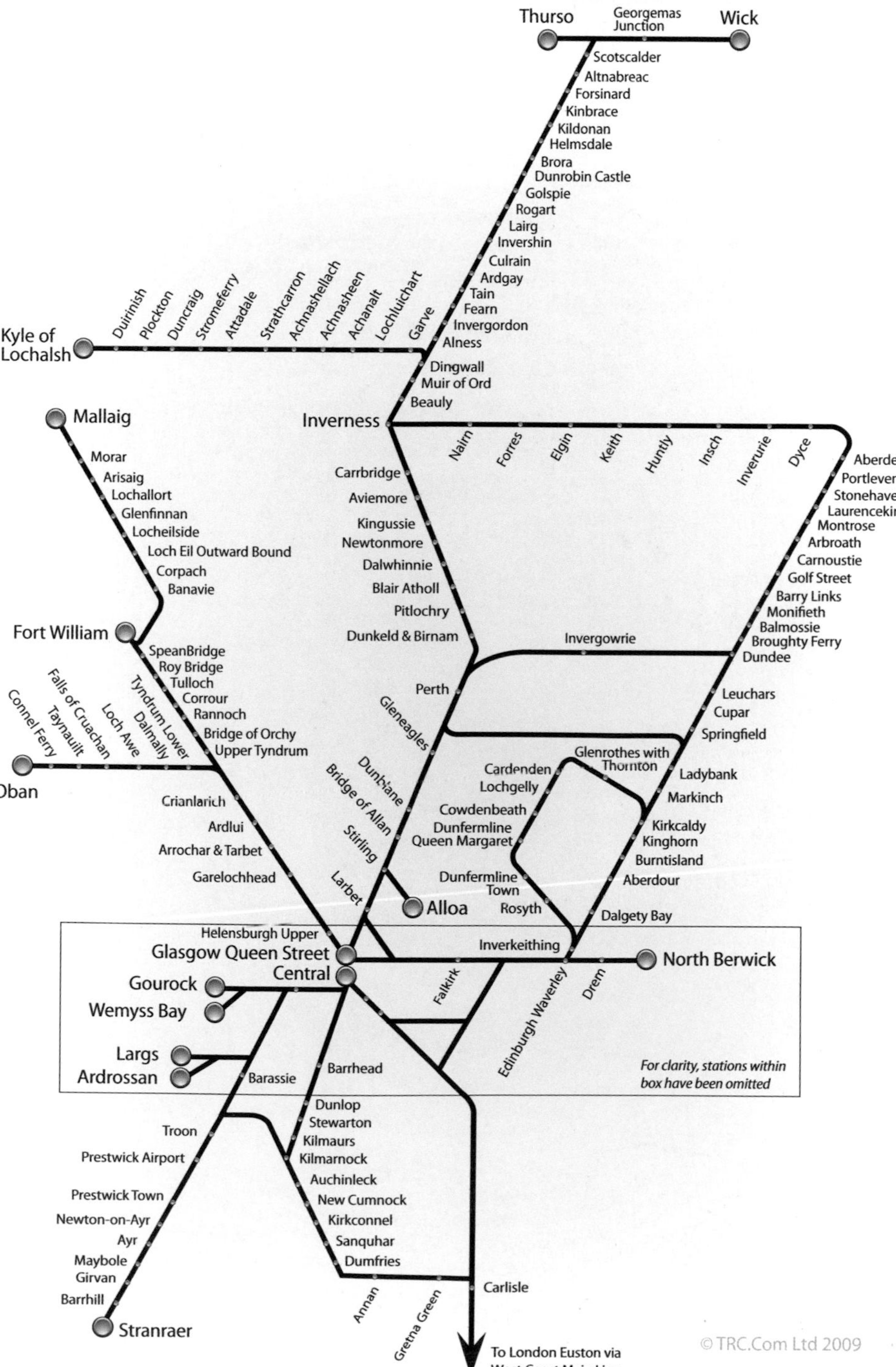
Thurso
Georgemas Junction
Wick
Scotscalder
Altnabreac
Forsinard
Kinbrace
Kildonan
Helmsdale
Brora
Dunrobin Castle
Golspie
Rogart
Lairg
Invershin
Culrain
Ardgay
Tain
Fearn
Invergordon
Alness
Dingwall
Muir of Ord
Beauly
Kyle of Lochalsh
Duirinish
Plockton
Duncraig
Stromeferry
Attadale
Strathcarron
Achnashellach
Achnasheen
Achanalt
Lochluichart
Garve
Inverness
Nairn
Forres
Elgin
Keith
Huntly
Insch
Inverurie
Dyce
Mallaig
Morar
Arisaig
Lochallort
Glenfinnan
Locheilside
Loch Eil Outward Bound
Corpach
Banavie
Fort William
Carrbridge
Aviemore
Kingussie
Newtonmore
Dalwhinnie
Blair Atholl
Pitlochry
Dunkeld & Birnam
Invergowrie
Aberdeen
Portleven
Stonehaven
Laurencekirk
Montrose
Arbroath
Carnoustie
Golf Street
Barry Links
Monifieth
Balmossie
Broughty Ferry
Dundee
SpeanBridge
Roy Bridge
Tulloch
Corrour
Rannoch
Bridge of Orchy
Upper Tyndrum
Tyndrum Lower
Dalmally
Loch Awe
Falls of Cruachan
Taynauilt
Connel Ferry
Oban
Perth
Gleneagles
Leuchars
Cupar
Springfield
Glenrothes with Thornton
Ladybank
Markinch
Cardenden
Lochgelly
Cowdenbeath
Dunfermline Queen Margaret
Kirkcaldy
Kinghorn
Burntisland
Aberdour
Dunfermline Town
Rosyth
Dalgety Bay
Dunblane
Bridge of Allan
Stirling
Larbet
Alloa
Crianlarich
Ardlui
Arrochar & Tarbet
Garelochhead
Helensburgh Upper
Glasgow Queen Street
Central
Inverkeithing
North Berwick
Gourock
Wemyss Bay
Falkirk
Edinburgh Waverley
Drem
Largs
Ardrossan
Barassie
Barrhead
For clarity, stations within box have been omitted
Troon
Prestwick Airport
Prestwick Town
Newton-on-Ayr
Ayr
Maybole
Girvan
Barrhill
Stranraer
Dunlop
Stewarton
Kilmaurs
Kilmarnock
Auchinleck
New Cumnock
Kirkconnel
Sanquhar
Dumfries
Carlisle
Annan
Gretna Green
To London Euston via West Coast Main Line
©TRC.Com Ltd 2009

Class 158

Vehicle Length: 76ft 1¾in (23.21m)
Height: 12ft 6in (3.81m)
Width: 9ft 3¼in (2.82m)
Engine: 1 x Cummins NTA855R of 350hp per vehicle
Horsepower: 700hp (522kW)
Seats (total/car): 14F/116S, 14F-46S/70S
** 138S, 68S/70S*

Number	Formation DMCL/DMSL*+DMS	Depot	Livery	Owner	Operator
158701	52701+57701	IS	FSR	PTR	FSR
158702	52702+57702	IS	FSR	PTR	FSR
158703	52703+57703	IS	FSR	PTR	FSR
158704	52704+57704	IS	FSR	PTR	FSR
158705	52705+57705	IS	FSR	PTR	FSR
158706	52706+57706	IS	FSR	PTR	FSR
158707	52707+57707	IS	FSR	PTR	FSR
158708	52708+57708	IS	FSR	PTR	FSR
158709	52709+57709	IS	FSR	PTR	FSR
158710	52710+57710	IS	FSR	PTR	FSR
158711	52711+57711	IS	FSR	PTR	FSR
158712	52712+57712	IS	FSR	PTR	FSR
158713	52713+57713	IS	FSR	PTR	FSR
158714	52714+57714	IS	FSR	PTR	FSR
158715	52715+57715	IS	FSR	PTR	FSR
158716	52716+57716	IS	FSR	PTR	FSR
158717	52717+57717	IS	FSR	PTR	FSR
158718	52718+57718	IS	FSR	PTR	FSR
158719	52719+57719	IS	FSR	PTR	FSR
158720	52720+57720	IS	FSR	PTR	FSR
158721	52721+57721	IS	FSR	PTR	FSR
158722	52722+57722	IS	FSR	PTR	FSR
158723	52723+57723	IS	FSR	PTR	FSR
158724	52724+57724	IS	FSR	PTR	FSR
158725	52725+57725	IS	FSR	PTR	FSR
158726	52726+57726	HA	FSR	PTR	FSR
158727	52727+57727	IS	FSR	PTR	FSR
158728	52728+57728	IS	FSR	PTR	FSR
158729	52729+57729	HA	FSR	PTR	FSR
158730	52730+57730	HA	FSR	PTR	FSR
158731	52731+57731	HA	FSR	PTR	FSR
158732	52732+57732	HA	FSR	PTR	FSR
158733	52733+57733	HA	FSR	PTR	FSR
158734	52734+57734	HA	FSR	PTR	FSR
158735	52735+57735	HA	FSR	PTR	FSR
158736	52736+57736	HA	FSR	PTR	FSR
158737	52737+57737	HA	FSR	PTR	FSR
158738	52738+57738	HA	FSR	PTR	FSR
158739	52739+57739	HA	FSR	PTR	FSR
158740	52740+57740	HA	FSR	PTR	FSR
158741	52741+57741	HA	FSR	PTR	FSR
158782	52782*+57782	HA	NUB	ANG	FSR
158786	52786*+57786	HA	FSS	ANG	FSR
158789	52789*+57789	HA	FSS	ANG	FSR
158867	52867*+57867	HA	WET	ANG	FSR
158868	52868*+57868	HA	WET	ANG	FSR
158869	52869*+57869	HA	WET	ANG	FSR
158870	52870*+57870	HA	WET	ANG	FSR

Left: *The First Scotrail allocation of Class 158 units is allocated between Edinburgh Haymarket and Inverness depots, with Inverness having the larger number of sets. All units are painted in First Scotrail livery, but the new Scottish Railways blue with a white Saltire will soon be applied. Set No. 158704 is shown.* **Alastair Blackwood**

Class 170/3
Turbostar

Vehicle Length: 77ft 6in (23.62m)
Height: 12ft 4½in (3.77m)
Width: 8ft 10in (2.69m)
Engine: 1 x MTU 6R 183TD13H 422hp per vehicle
Horsepower: 1,266hp (944kW)
Seats (total/car): 24F/140S, 12F-45S/43S/12F-52S

Number	Formation DMCL+MS+DMSL	Depot	Livery	Owner	Operator
170393	50393+55393+79393	HA	FSR	PTR	FSR
170394	50394+55394+79394	HA	FSR	PTR	FSR
170395	50395+55395+79395	HA	FSR	PTR	FSR

Class 170/4
Turbostar

Vehicle Length: 77ft 6in (23.62m)
Height: 12ft 4½in (3.77m)
Width: 8ft 10in (2.69m)
Engine: 1 x MTU 6R 183TD13H 422hp per vehicle
Horsepower: 1,266hp (944kW)
(170431/432 have 3 x 483hp engines giving 1,449hp)
Seats (total/car): 18F/168S 9F-43S/76S/9F-49S

Number	Formation DMCL+MS+DMCL	Depot	Livery	Owner	Operator	Name
170401	50401+55401+79401	HA	FSR	PTR	FSR	
170402	50402+55402+79402	HA	FSR	PTR	FSR	
170403	50403+55403+79403	HA	FSR	PTR	FSR	
170404	50404+55404+79404	HA	FSR	PTR	FSR	

170405	50405+55405+79405	HA	FSR	PTR	FSR
170406	50406+55406+79406	HA	FSR	PTR	FSR
170407	50407+55407+79407	HA	FSR	PTR	FSR
170408	50408+55408+79408	HA	FSR	PTR	FSR
170409	50409+55409+79409	HA	FSR	PTR	FSR
170410	50410+55410+79410	HA	FSR	PTR	FSR
170411	50411+55411+79411	HA	FSR	PTR	FSR
170412	50412+55412+79412	HA	FSR	PTR	FSR
170413	50413+55413+79413	HA	FSR	PTR	FSR
170414	50414+55414+79414	HA	FSR	PTR	FSR
170415	50415+55415+79415	HA	FSR	PTR	FSR
170416	50416+55416+79416	HA	FSR	HSB	FSR
170417	50417+55417+79417	HA	FSR	HSB	FSR
170418	50418+55418+79418	HA	FSR	HSB	FSR
170419	50419+55419+79419	HA	FSR	HSB	FSR
170420	50420+55420+79420	HA	FSR	HSB	FSR
170421	50421+55421+79421	HA	FSR	HSB	FSR
170422	50422+55422+79422	HA	FSR	HSB	FSR
170423	50423+55423+79423	HA	FSR	HSB	FSR
170424	50424+55424+79424	HA	FSR	HSB	FSR
170425	50425+55425+79425	HA	FSR	PTR	FSR
170426	50426+55426+79426	HA	FSR	PTR	FSR
170427	50427+55427+79427	HA	FSR	PTR	FSR
170428	50428+55428+79428	HA	FSR	PTR	FSR
170429	50429+55429+79429	HA	FSR	PTR	FSR
170430	50430+55430+79430	HA	FSR	PTR	FSR
170431	50431+55431+79431	HA	FSR	PTR	FSR
170432	50432+55432+79432	HA	FSR	PTR	FSR
170433	50433+55433+79433	HA	FSR	PTR	FSR
170434	50434+55434+79434	HA	FSS	PTR	FSR

Investor in People

Class 170/4
Turbostar

Vehicle Length: 77ft 6in (23.62m)
Height: 12ft 4½in (3.77m)
Width: 8ft 10in (2.69m)

Engine: 1 x MTU 6R 183TD13H 422hp per vehicle
Horsepower: 1,266hp (944kW)
Seats: 170450-170471 (total/car) 198S, 55S/76S/67S
170472-170478 (total/car) 200S, 57S/76S/67S

	DMSL+MS+DMSL				
170450	50450+55450+79450	HA	FSR	PTR	FSR
170451	50451+55451+79451	HA	FSR	PTR	FSR
170452	50452+55452+79452	HA	FSR	PTR	FSR
170453	50453+55453+79453	HA	FSR	PTR	FSR
170454	50454+55454+79454	HA	FSR	PTR	FSR
170455	50455+55455+79455	HA	FSR	PTR	FSR
170456	50456+55456+79456	HA	FSR	PTR	FSR
170457	50457+55457+79457	HA	FSR	PTR	FSR
170458	50458+55458+79458	HA	FSR	PTR	FSR
170459	50459+55459+79459	HA	FSR	PTR	FSR
170460	50460+55460+79460	HA	FSR	PTR	FSR
170461	50461+55461+79461	HA	FSR	PTR	FSR
170470	50470+55470+79470	HA	FSP	PTR	FSR
170471	50471+55471+79471	HA	FSP	PTR	FSR
170472	50472+55472+79472	HA	FSP	PTR	FSR
170473	50473+55473+79473	HA	FSP	PTR	FSR
170474	50474+55474+79474	HA	FSP	PTR	FSR
170475	50475+55475+79475	HA	FSP	PTR	FSR
170476	50476+55476+79476	HA	FSP	PTR	FSR
170477	50477+55477+79477	HA	FSP	PTR	FSR
170478	50478+55478+79478	HA	FSP	PTR	FSR

Right: *First Scotrail-operated Class 170/4 No. 170478, numerically the last member of the Scottish fleet, shows the Strathclyde carmine and cream livery, off-set by a turquoise body band.* **Alastair Blackwood**

First Scotrail

Class 314

Vehicle Length: (Driving) 64ft 11½in (19.80m) (Inter) 65ft 4¼in (19.92m)
Height: 11ft 6½in (3.58m)
Width: 9ft 3in (2.82m)
Horsepower: 880hp (656kW)
Seats (total/car): 212S, 68S/76S/68S

Number	Formation DMSO(A)+PTSO+DMSO(B)	Depot	Livery	Owner	Operator	Name
314201	64583+71450+64584	GW	FSP	ANG	FSR	
314202	64585+71451+64586	GW	FSP	ANG	FSR	
314203	64587+71452+64588*	GW	FSP	ANG	FSR	European Union
314204	64589+71453+64590	GW	FSP	ANG	FSR	
314205	64591+71454+64592	GW	FSP	ANG	FSR	
314206	64593+71455+64594	GW	FSP	ANG	FSR	
314207	64595+71456+64596	GW	FSP	ANG	FSR	
314208	64597+71457+64598	GW	FSP	ANG	FSR	
314209	64599+71458+64600	GW	FSP	ANG	FSR	
314210	64601+71459+64602	GW	FSP	ANG	FSR	
314211	64603+71460+64604	GW	FSP	ANG	FSR	
314212	64604+71461+64606	GW	FSP	ANG	FSR	
314213	64607+71462+64608	GW	FSP	ANG	FSR	
314214	64609+71463+64610	GW	FSP	ANG	FSR	
314215	64611+71464+64612	GW	FSP	ANG	FSR	
314216	64613+71465+64614	GW	FSP	ANG	FSR	

* 65488 rebuilt from 64426 and seats 74S

Left: *The 16 Class 314 units introduced for Glasgow area suburban operations were a direct derivative of the 1972 high-density stock prototypes. Now more than 30 years old these sets will be replaced by cascades of other electric stock following the 2010-11 introduction of Desiro units. Set No. 314206 is seen at Glasgow Central.* **Alastair Blackwood**

Class 318

Vehicle Length: (Driving) 65ft 0¾in (19.83m) (Inter) 65ft 4¼in (19.92m)
Height: 12ft 1½in (3.70m)
Width: 9ft 3in (2.82m)
Horsepower: 1,328hp (996kW)
Seats (total/car): 216S, 66S/79S/71S

Number	Formation DTSO(A)+MSO+DTSO(B)	Depot	Livery	Owner	Operator	Name
318250	77240+62866+77260	GW	FSP	HSB	FSR	
318251	77241+62867+77261	GW	FSP	HSB	FSR	
318252	77242+62868+77262	GW	FSP	HSB	FSR	
318253	77243+62869+77263	GW	FSP	HSB	FSR	
318254	77244+62870+77264	GW	FSP	HSB	FSR	
318255	77245+62871+77265	GW	FSP	HSB	FSR	
318256	77246+62872+77266	GW	FSP	HSB	FSR	
318257	77247+62873+77267	GW	FSP	HSB	FSR	
318258	77248+62874+77268	GW	FSP	HSB	FSR	
318259	77249+62875+77269	GW	FSP	HSB	FSR	Citizens' Network
318260	77250+62876+77270	GW	FSP	HSB	FSR	
318261	77251+62877+77271	GW	FSP	HSB	FSR	
318262	77252+62878+77272	GW	FSP	HSB	FSR	
318263	77253+62879+77273	GW	FSP	HSB	FSR	
318264	77254+62880+77274	GW	FSP	HSB	FSR	
318265	77255+62881+77275	GW	FSP	HSB	FSR	
318266	77256+62882+77276	GW	FSP	HSB	FSR	Strathclyder
318267	77257+62883+77277	GW	FSP	HSB	FSR	
318268	77258+62884+77278	GW	FSP	HSB	FSR	
318269	77259+62885+77279	GW	FSP	HSB	FSR	
318270	77288+62890+77289	GW	FSP	HSB	FSR	

Right: *Post privatisation of the 21 Glasgow area Class 318 units saw the original front gangways removed, rendering a rather unusual frontal design. All sets now have dot-matrix route displays and all are painted in carmine and cream livery. Set No. 318257 arrives at Glasgow Central.* **Nathan Williamson**

Class 320

Vehicle Length: (Driving) 65ft 0¾in (19.83m) (Inter) 65ft 4¼in (19.92m)
Height: 12ft 4¾in (3.78m)
Width: 9ft 3in (2.82m)
Horsepower: 1,328hp (996kW)
Seats (total/car): 227S, 76S/76S/75S

Number	Formation DTSO(A)+MSO+DTSO(B)	Depot	Livery	Owner	Operator	Name
320301	77899+63021+77921	GW	FSP	HSB	FSR	
320302	77900+63022+77922	GW	FSP	HSB	FSR	
320303	77901+63023+77923	GW	FSP	HSB	FSR	
320304	77902+63024+77924	GW	FSP	HSB	FSR	
320305	77903+63025+77925	GW	FSP	HSB	FSR	Glasgow School of Art 1845 – 150 – 1995
320306	77904+63026+77926	GW	FSP	HSB	FSR	Model Rail Scotland
320307	77905+63027+77927	GW	FSP	HSB	FSR	
320308	77906+63028+77928	GW	FSP	HSB	FSR	High Road 20th Anniversary 2000
320309	77907+63029+77929	GW	FSP	HSB	FSR	Radio Clyde 25th Anniversary
320310	77908+63030+77930	GW	FSP	HSB	FSR	
320311	77909+63031+77931	GW	FSP	HSB	FSR	Royal College of Physicians and Surgeons of Glasgow
320312	77910+63032+77932	GW	FSP	HSB	FSR	Sir William A Smith Founder of the Boys' Brigade
320313	77911+63033+77933	GW	FSP	HSB	FSR	
320314	77912+63034+77934	GW	FSP	HSB	FSR	
320315	77913+63035+77935	GW	FSP	HSB	FSR	
320316	77914+63036+77936	GW	FSP	HSB	FSR	
320317	77915+63037+77937	GW	FSP	HSB	FSR	
320318	77916+63038+77938	GW	FSP	HSB	FSR	
320319	77917+63039+77939	GW	FSP	HSB	FSR	
320320	77918+63040+77940	GW	FSP	HSB	FSR	
320321	77919+63041+77941	GW	FSP	HSB	FSR	The Rt. Hon. John Smith, QC, MP
320322	77920+63042+77942	GW	FSP	HSB	FSR	Festival Glasgow Orchid

Right: *The 22 strong Class 320 fleet are allocated to Glasgow Shields Road depot and operate on the Glasgow area outer suburban electrified network. All sets have been refurbished and now carry the Glasgow area carmine and cream livery. Unit No. 320305 is shown.* **Alastair Blackwood**

First Scotrail

Class 322

Vehicle Length: (Driving) 65ft 0¾in (19.83m)
(Inter) 65ft 4¼in (19.92m)
Height: 12ft 4¾in (3.78m)
Width: 9ft 3in (2.82m)
Horsepower: 1,328hp (996kW)
Seats (total/car): 291S, 74S/83S/76S/58S

Number	Formation DTSO(A)+MSO+TSO+DTSO(B)	Depot	Livery	Owner	Operator	Name
322481	78163+62137+72023+77985	GW	FSR	HSB	FSR	North Berwick Flyer 1850-2000
322482	78164+62138+72024+77986	GW	FSR	HSB	FSR	
322483	78165+62139+72025+77987	GW	FSR	HSB	FSR	
322484	78166+63140+72026+77988	GW	FSR	HSB	FSR	
322485	78167+63141+72027+77898	GW	FSR	HSB	FSR	

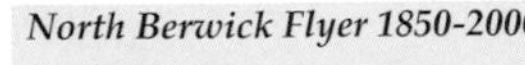

■ *Scheduled to come off-lease following delivery of Class 380 'Desiro' stock.*

Left: *Glasgow Shields Road depot is the base for five four-car Class 322 high-density sets used on the North Berwick route. The class are structurally the same as the Class 321s and were originally built in Network SouthEast days for Stansted Airport duties.* **Stacey Thew**

Class 334
Juniper

Vehicle Length: (Driving) 69ft 0¾in (21.04m)
(Inter) 65ft 4½in (19.93m)
Height: 12ft 3in (3.77m)
Width: 9ft 2¾in (2.80m)
Horsepower: 1,448hp (1,080kW)
Seats (total/car): 183S, 64S/55S/64S

Number	Formation DMSO(A)+PTSO+DMSO(B)	Depot	Livery	Owner	Operator	Name
334001	64101+74301+65101	GW	FSP	HSB	FSR	Donald Dewar
334002	64102+74302+65102	GW	FSP	HSB	FSR	
334003	64103+74303+65103	GW	FSP	HSB	FSR	
334004	64104+74304+65104	GW	FSP	HSB	FSR	
334005	64105+74305+65105	GW	FSP	HSB	FSR	
334006	64106+74306+65106	GW	FSP	HSB	FSR	
334007	64107+74307+65107	GW	FSP	HSB	FSR	
334008	64108+74308+65108	GW	FSP	HSB	FSR	
334009	64109+74309+65109	GW	FSP	HSB	FSR	
334010	64110+74310+65110	GW	FSP	HSB	FSR	
334011	64111+74311+65111	GW	FSP	HSB	FSR	
334012	64112+74312+65112	GW	FSP	HSB	FSR	
334013	64113+74313+65113	GW	FSP	HSB	FSR	
334014	64114+74314+65114	GW	FSP	HSB	FSR	
334015	64115+74315+65115	GW	FSP	HSB	FSR	
334016	64116+74316+65116	GW	FSP	HSB	FSR	
334017	64117+74317+65117	GW	FSP	HSB	FSR	
334018	64118+74318+65118	GW	FSP	HSB	FSR	
334019	64119+74319+65119	GW	FSP	HSB	FSR	
334020	64120+74320+65120	GW	FSP	HSB	FSR	
334021	64121+74321+65121	GW	FSP	HSB	FSR	Larkhill
334022	64122+74322+65122	GW	FSP	HSB	FSR	
334023	64123+74323+65123	GW	FSP	HSB	FSR	
334024	64124+74324+65124	GW	FSP	HSB	FSR	
334025	64125+74325+65125	GW	FSP	HSB	FSR	
334026	64126+74326+65126	GW	FSP	HSB	FSR	
334027	64127+74327+65127	GW	FSP	HSB	FSR	
334028	64128+74328+65128	GW	FSP	HSB	FSR	
334029	64129+74329+65129	GW	FSP	HSB	FSR	
334030	64130+74330+65130	GW	FSP	HSB	FSR	
334031	64131+74331+65131	GW	FSP	HSB	FSR	
334032	64132+74332+65132	GW	FSP	HSB	FSR	
334033	64133+74333+65133	GW	FSP	HSB	FSR	

334034	64134+74334+65134	GW	FSP	HSB	FSR
334035	64135+74335+65135	GW	FSP	HSB	FSR
334036	64136+74336+65136	GW	FSP	HSB	FSR
334037	64137+74337+65137	GW	FSP	HSB	FSR
334038	64138+74338+65138	GW	FSP	HSB	FSR
334039	64139+74339+65139	GW	FSP	HSB	FSR
334040	64140+74340+65140	GW	FSP	HSB	FSR

Right: *The Alstom-built Class 334 'Juniper' units allocated to Glasgow Shields Road depot operate on the Ayrshire Coast route, but following introduction of Class 380 'Desiro' sets from 2010 will be displaced to local routes around Glasgow. The '334s' are painted in the Strathclyde carmine and cream livery offset by a green waist height band. Set No. 334007 is seen at Preswick International Airport station.* **Stacey Thew**

Class 380
Desiro

Vehicle Length: 77ft 3in (23.57m)
Height: 12ft 1½in (3.7m)
Width: 9ft 2in (2.7m)
Horsepower: 2,682hp (2,000kW)
Seats: 3-car 208S. 4-car 282S

Number	*Formation DMSO(A)+PTSO+DMSO(B)*	*Depot*	*Livery*	*Owner*	*Operator*
380001	38501+38601+38701	GW	FSS	HSB	FSR
380002	38502+38602+38702	GW	FSS	HSB	FSR
380003	38503+38603+38703	GW	FSS	HSB	FSR
380004	38504+38604+38704	GW	FSS	HSB	FSR
380005	38505+38605+38705	GW	FSS	HSB	FSR
380006	38506+38606+38706	GW	FSS	HSB	FSR
380007	38507+38607+38707	GW	FSS	HSB	FSR
380008	38508+38608+38708	GW	FSS	HSB	FSR
380009	38509+38609+38709	GW	FSS	HSB	FSR
380010	38510+38610+38710	GW	FSS	HSB	FSR
380011	38511+38611+38711	GW	FSS	HSB	FSR
380012	38512+38612+38712	GW	FSS	HSB	FSR
380013	38513+38613+38713	GW	FSS	HSB	FSR
380014	38514+38614+38714	GW	FSS	HSB	FSR
380015	38515+38615+38715	GW	FSS	HSB	FSR
380016	38516+38616+38716	GW	FSS	HSB	FSR
380017	38517+38617+38717	GW	FSS	HSB	FSR
380018	38518+38618+38718	GW	FSS	HSB	FSR
380019	38519+38619+38719	GW	FSS	HSB	FSR
380020	38520+38620+38720	GW	FSS	HSB	FSR
380021	38521+38621+38721	GW	FSS	HSB	FSR
380022	38522+38622+38722	GW	FSS	HSB	FSR

Number	*Formation DMSO(A)+PTSO+DMSO(B)*	*Depot*	*Livery*	*Owner*	*Operator*
380101	38551+38651+38851+38751	GW	FSS	HSB	FSR
380102	38552+38652+38852+38752	GW	FSS	HSB	FSR
380103	38553+38653+38853+38753	GW	FSS	HSB	FSR
380104	38554+38654+38854+38754	GW	FSS	HSB	FSR
380105	38555+38655+38855+38755	GW	FSS	HSB	FSR
380106	38556+38656+38856+38756	GW	FSS	HSB	FSR
380107	38557+38657+38857+38757	GW	FSS	HSB	FSR
380108	38558+38658+38858+38758	GW	FSS	HSB	FSR
380109	38559+38659+38859+38759	GW	FSS	HSB	FSR
380110	38560+38660+38860+38760	GW	FSS	HSB	FSR
380111	38561+38661+38861+38761	GW	FSS	HSB	FSR
380112	38562+38662+38862+38762	GW	FSS	HSB	FSR
380113	38563+38663+38863+38763	GW	FSS	HSB	FSR
380114	38564+38664+38864+38764	GW	FSS	HSB	FSR

First Scotrail

380115	38565+38665+38865+38765	GW	FSS	HSB	FSR
380116	38566+38666+38866+38766	GW	FSS	HSB	FSR

Left: *The first set of the new Scotrail 'Desiro' train order was completed at the Siemens factory in Germany in November 2009. A driving motor vehicle for set No. 380101 - a four-car set - is seen at the Krefeld construction and static testing site.* **CJM**

Mk2 & Mk3 Hauled Stock

Mk2
Vehicle Length: 66ft 0in (20.11m) *Width: 9ft 3in (2.81m)*
Height: 12ft 9½in (3.89m) *Seats (total/car): 60S*

Mk3
Vehicle Length: 75ft 0in (22.86m) *Width: 8ft 11in (2.71m)*
Height: 12ft 9in (3.88m) *Bogie Type: BT10*

AN1F (Mk2) - BUO *Seating 31U*

Number	*Depot*	*Livery*	*Owner*
9800 (5751)	IS	FSR	HSB
9801 (5760)	IS	FSR	HSB
9802 (5772)	IS	FSR	HSB
9803 (5799)	IS	FSR	HSB
9804 (5826)	IS	FSR	HSB
9805 (5833)	IS	FSR	HSB
9806 (5840)	IS	FSR	HSB
9807 (5851)	IS	FSS	HSB
9808 (5871)	IS	FSS	HSB
9809 (5890)	IS	FSR	HSB
9810 (5892)	IS	FSR	HSB

AN1F (Mk2) - RLO *Seating 28-30F*

Number	*Depot*	*Livery*	*Owner*
6700 (3347)	IS	FSR	HSB
6701 (3346)	IS	FSR	HSB
6702 (3421)	IS	FSR	HSB
6703 (3308)	IS	FSR	HSB
6704 (3341)	IS	FSR	HSB
6705 (3310)	IS	FSR	HSB
6706 (3283)	IS	FSR	HSB
6707 (3276)	IS	FSR	HSB
6708 (3370)	IS	FSR	HSB

AU4G (Mk3) - SLEP *Comps 12*

Number	*Depot*	*Livery*	*Owner*
10501	IS	FSR	PTR
10502	IS	FSR	PTR
10504	IS	FSR	PTR
10506	IS	FSR	PTR
10507	IS	FSR	PTR
10508	IS	FSR	PTR
10513	IS	FSR	PTR
10516	IS	FSS	PTR
10519	IS	FSR	PTR
10520	IS	FSR	PTR
10522	IS	FSR	PTR
10523	IS	FSR	PTR
10526	IS	FSR	PTR
10527	IS	FSR	PTR
10529	IS	FSR	PTR
10531	IS	FSR	PTR
10542	IS	FSR	PTR
10543	IS	FSR	PTR
10544	IS	FSR	PTR
10548	IS	FSR	PTR
10551	IS	FSR	PTR
10553	IS	FSR	PTR
10561	IS	FSR	PTR
10562	IS	FSS	PTR
10565	IS	FSR	PTR
10580	IS	FSR	PTR
10597	IS	FSR	PTR
10598	IS	FSR	PTR
10600	IS	FSR	PTR
10605	IS	FSR	PTR
10607	IS	FSR	PTR
10610	IS	FSR	PTR
10613	IS	FSR	PTR
10614	IS	FSR	PTR
10617	IS	FSR	PTR

AS4G (Mk3) - SLE *Comps 13*

Number	*Depot*	*Livery*	*Owner*
10675	IS	FSR	PTR
10683	IS	FSR	PTR
10688	IS	FSR	PTR
10690	IS	FSR	PTR
10693	IS	FSR	PTR
10703	IS	FSR	PTR

AQ4G (Mk3) - SLED *Comps 11*

Number	*Depot*	*Livery*	*Owner*
10648	IS	FSR	PTR
10650	IS	FSR	PTR
10666	IS	FSR	PTR
10680	IS	FSR	PTR
10689	IS	FSR	PTR
10699	IS	FSR	PTR
10706	IS	FSR	PTR
10714	IS	FSR	PTR
10718	IS	FSR	PTR
10719	IS	FSR	PTR
10722	IS	FSR	PTR
10723	IS	FSR	PTR

Left: *A batch of 11 Brake Unclassified Open (BUO) vehicles were converted by Railcare Wolverton for Scotrail for use on the overnight sleeper services, providing the train's brake compartment and 31 unclassified seats. No. 9803, modified from TSO No. 5799, is seen at Wembley.*
Tony Christie

First TransPennine Express

Address: ✉ Floor 7, Bridgewater House, 60 Whitworth Street, Manchester M1 6LT

tpecustomer.relations@firstgroup.com

✆ 0845 600 1671

ⓘ www.tpexpress.co.uk

Managing Director: Vernon Baker

Franchise Dates: 1 February 2004 - 31 January 2017

Principal Routes: Newcastle, Middlesbrough, Scarborough, Hull, Cleethorpes to Manchester, Liverpool, Barrow, Carlisle, Edinburgh and Edinburgh

Depots: Ardwick (AK) - Siemens operated, York (YK), Crofton (XW)

Parent Company: First Group, Keolis

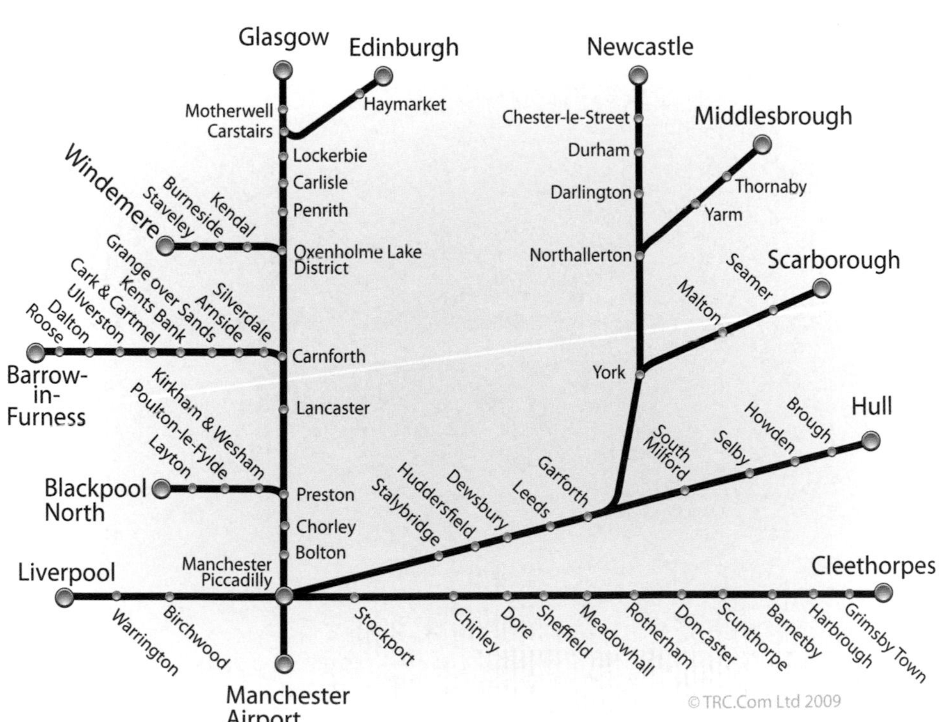

First TransPennine Express

Class 170/3
Turbostar

Vehicle Length: 77ft 6in (23.62m)
Height: 12ft 4½in (3.77m)
Width: 8ft 10in (2.69m)
Engine: 1 x MTU 6R 183TD13H 422hp per vehicle
Horsepower; 844hp (629kW)
Seats (total/car): 8F/108S 8F-43S/65S

Number	Formation DMCL+DMS	Depot	Livery	Owner	Operator
170301	**50301+79301**	**XW**	**FTP**	**PTR**	**FTP**
170302	**50302+79302**	**XW**	**FTP**	**PTR**	**FTP**
170303	**50303+79303**	**XW**	**FTP**	**PTR**	**FTP**
170304	**50304+79304**	**XW**	**FTP**	**PTR**	**FTP**
170305	**50305+79305**	**XW**	**FTP**	**PTR**	**FTP**
170306	**50306+79306**	**XW**	**FTP**	**PTR**	**FTP**
170307	**50307+79307**	**XW**	**FTP**	**PTR**	**FTP**
170308	**50308+79308**	**XW**	**FTP**	**PTR**	**FTP**
170309	**50309+79309**	**XW**	**FTP**	**PTR**	**FTP**

Below: *Originally used by South West Trains on the Waterloo to Salisbury route, these Class 170/3s were transferred north following introduction of an extended Class 159 fleet. In TransPennine livery, set No. 170305 is seen at Manchester Piccadilly on 18 June 2009.* **Nathan Williamson**

Class 185
Desiro

Vehicle Length: (driving) 77ft 11in (23.76m), (inter) 77ft 10in (23.75m)
Height: 12ft 4in (3.75m)
Width: 9ft 3in (2.81m)
Engine: 1 x Cummins OSK19 of 750hp per car
Horsepower: 2,250hp (1,680kW)
Seats (total/car): 15F/154S, 15F-18S/72S/64S

Number	Formation DMCL+MSL+DMS	Depot	Livery	Owner	Operator
185101	**51101+53101+54101**	**AK**	**FTP**	**HSB**	**FTP**
185102	**51102+53102+54102**	**AK**	**FTP**	**HSB**	**FTP**
185103	**51103+53103+54103**	**AK**	**FTP**	**HSB**	**FTP**
185104	**51104+53104+54104**	**AK**	**FTP**	**HSB**	**FTP**
185105	**51105+53105+54105**	**AK**	**FTP**	**HSB**	**FTP**
185106	**51106+53106+54106**	**AK**	**FTP**	**HSB**	**FTP**
185107	**51107+53107+54107**	**AK**	**FTP**	**HSB**	**FTP**
185108	**51108+53108+54108**	**AK**	**FTP**	**HSB**	**FTP**
185109	**51109+53109+54109**	**AK**	**FTP**	**HSB**	**FTP**
185110	**51110+53110+54110**	**AK**	**FTP**	**HSB**	**FTP**
185111	**51111+53111+54111**	**AK**	**FTP**	**HSB**	**FTP**
185112	**51112+53112+54112**	**AK**	**FTP**	**HSB**	**FTP**
185113	**51113+53113+54113**	**AK**	**FTP**	**HSB**	**FTP**
185114	**51114+53114+54114**	**AK**	**FTP**	**HSB**	**FTP**
185115	**51115+53115+54115**	**AK**	**FTP**	**HSB**	**FTP**
185116	**51116+53116+54116**	**AK**	**FTP**	**HSB**	**FTP**
185117	**51117+53117+54117**	**AK**	**FTP**	**HSB**	**FTP**

185118	51118+53118+54118	AK	FTP	HSB	FTP
185119	51119+53119+54119	AK	FTP	HSB	FTP
185120	51120+53120+54120	AK	FTP	HSB	FTP
185121	51121+53121+54121	AK	FTP	HSB	FTP
185122	51122+53122+54122	AK	FTP	HSB	FTP
185123	51123+53123+54123	AK	FTP	HSB	FTP
185124	51124+53124+54124	AK	FTP	HSB	FTP
185125	51125+53125+54125	AK	FTP	HSB	FTP
185126	51126+53126+54126	AK	FTP	HSB	FTP
185127	51127+53127+54127	AK	FTP	HSB	FTP
185128	51128+53128+54128	AK	FTP	HSB	FTP
185129	51129+53129+54129	AK	FTP	HSB	FTP
185130	51130+53130+54130	AK	FTP	HSB	FTP
185131	51131+53131+54131	AK	FTP	HSB	FTP
185132	51132+53132+54132	AK	FTP	HSB	FTP
185133	51133+53133+54133	AK	FTP	HSB	FTP
185134	51134+53134+54134	AK	FTP	HSB	FTP
185135	51135+53135+54135	AK	FTP	HSB	FTP
185136	51136+53136+54136	AK	FTP	HSB	FTP
185137	51137+53137+54137	AK	FTP	HSB	FTP
185138	51138+53138+54138	AK	FTP	HSB	FTP
185139	51139+53139+54139	AK	FTP	HSB	FTP
185140	51140+53140+54140	AK	FTP	HSB	FTP
185141	51141+53141+54141	AK	FTP	HSB	FTP
185142	51142+53142+54142	AK	FTP	HSB	FTP
185143	51143+53143+54143	AK	FTP	HSB	FTP
185144	51144+53144+54144	AK	FTP	HSB	FTP
185145	51145+53145+54145	AK	FTP	HSB	FTP
185146	51146+53146+54146	AK	FTP	HSB	FTP
185147	51147+53147+54147	AK	FTP	HSB	FTP
185148	51148+53148+54148	AK	FTP	HSB	FTP
185149	51149+53149+54149	AK	FTP	HSB	FTP
185150	51150+53150+54150	AK	FTP	HSB	FTP
185151	51151+53151+54151	AK	FTP	HSB	FTP

Above: *The first Siemens Desiro DMU sets to operate in the UK are the 51 members of Class 185, owned by HSBC Rail and operated on the First TransPennine routes. Set No. 185130 is seen departing from Preston on 30 October 2008.* **CJM**

Gatwick Express - See Southern section

Grand Central

Address: ✉ River House, 17 Museum Street, York, YO1 7DJ
info@grandcentral.com
✆ 0845 603 4852
ⓘ www.grandcentral.co.uk

Managing Director: Tom Clift
Franchise Dates: Private Open Access Operator
Principal Routes: Sunderland - London King's Cross
Depots: Heaton (HT)
Parent Company: Equisshare Partners

Sunderland
Hartlepool
Eaglescliffe
Northallerton
Thirsk
York
London King's Cross

© TRC.Com Ltd 2009

Class 43 HST

Vehicle Length: 58ft 5in (18.80m)
Height: 12ft 10in (3.90m)
Width: 8ft 11in (2.73m)
Engine: Paxman 12RP200L
Horsepower: 2,250hp (1,680kW)
Electrical Equipment: Brush

Number	*Depot*	*Pool*	*Livery*	*Owner*	*Operator*
43065	HT	GCHP	GTL	GTL	GTL
43067	HT	GCHP	GTL	GTL	GTL
43068	HT	GCHP	GTL	GTL	GTL
43080	HT	GCHP	GTL	GTL	GTL
43084	HT	GCHP	GTL	GTL	GTL
43123	HT	GCHP	GTL	GTL	GTL

Left: *Six of the original buffer fitted HST power cars are now operated by Grand Central. No. 43080 is seen at King's Cross on 11 March 2009.* **Nathan Williamson**

Class 180
Zephyrs

Vehicle Length: (driving) 75ft 7in (23.71m), (inter) 75ft 5in (23.03m)
Height: 12ft 4in (3.75m)
Width: 9ft 2in (2.80m)
Engine: 1 x Cummins OSK19 of 750hp per car
Horsepower: 3,750hp (2,796kW)
Seats (total/car): 42F/226S, 46S/42F/68S/56S/56S

Number	*Formation* DMSL(A)+MFL+MSL+MSLRB+DMSL(B)	*Depot*	*Livery*	*Owner*	*Operator*	*Name*
180101¤	50901+54901+55901+56901+59901	HT	GTL	ANG	GTL	
180105	50905+54905+55905+56905+59905	HT	GTL	ANG	GTL	
180107¤	50907+54907+55907+56907+59907	HT	GTL	ANG	GTL	
180112	50912+54912+55912+56912+59912	HT	GTL	ANG	GTL	*James Herriot*
180114	50914+54914+55914+56914+59914	HT	GTL	ANG	GTL	

¤ Grand Central to hire from Spring 2010

Above: *The first Class 180 'Zephyr' set entered traffic for Grand Central in late summer 2009, and by mid-2010 all four sets should be in traffic. Sadly devoid of its original flush front end coupling cover, set No. 180112 passes through Doncaster on the 'up' middle road on 13 October 2009.* **Derek Porter**

Mk3 HST stock

Vehicle Length: 75ft 0in (22.86m) Width: 8ft 11in (2.71m)
Height: 12ft 9in (3.88m) Bogie Type: BT10

GK2G - TRSB *Seating 33S*

Number		*Depot*	*Livery*	*Owner*
40424	**(40024)**	**HT**	**GTL**	**GTL**
40426	**(40026)**	**HT**	**GTL**	**GTL**
40433	**(40033)**	**HT**	**GTL**	**GTL**

GH1G - TF *Seating 48F*

Number		*Depot*	*Livery*	*Owner*
41201	**(11045)**	**HT**	**GTL**	**GTL**
41202	**(11017)**	**HT**	**GTL**	**GTL**
41203	**(11038)**	**HT**	**GTL**	**GTL**
41204	**(11023)**	**HT**	**GTL**	**GTL**
41205	**(11036)**	**HT**	**GTL**	**GTL**
41206	**(11055)**	**HT**	**GTL**	**GTL**

GH2G - TS *Seating 64S *TSD Seating 60S*

Number		*Depot*	*Livery*	*Owner*
42401	**(12149)**	**HT**	**GTL**	**GTL**
42402	**(12155)**	**HT**	**GTL**	**GTL**
42403*	**(12033)**	**HT**	**GTL**	**GTL**
42404	**(12152)**	**HT**	**GTL**	**GTL**
42405	**(12136)**	**HT**	**GTL**	**GTL**
42406*	**(12112)**	**HT**	**GTL**	**GTL**
42407	**(12044)**	**HT**	**GTL**	**GTL**
42408	**(12121)**	**HT**	**GTL**	**GTL**
42409*	**(12088)**	**HT**	**GTL**	**GTL**

GJ2G - TGS *Seating 67S*

Number	*Depot*	*Livery*	*Owner*
44065	**HT**	**GTL**	**GTL**
44088	**HT**	**GTL**	**GTL (Stored)**
44089	**HT**	**GTL**	**GTL**

Right: *The TS and TF vehicles operated by Grand Central are converts from former Mk3 loco hauled stock, the rebuilding being undertaken by Axiom Rail at Stoke. Some telltale signs of the former design are visible on vehicle ends, such as the blanking plate for the original TDM cable and a plate over the original buffer fixing. TF No. 41206 is illustrated; this was rebuilt from Mk3 loco-hauled coach No. 11055.* **Nathan Williamson**

Heathrow Express / Heathrow Connect

Address: ✉ 6th Floor, 50 Eastbourne Terrace, Paddington, London, W2 6LX
queries@heathrowexpress.com or queries@heathrowconnect.com
✆ 020 8750 6600
ⓘ www.heathrowexpress.com or www.heathrowconnect.com

Managing Director: Richard Robinson
Franchise Dates: Private Open Access Operator
Principal Routes: London Paddington - Heathrow Airport
Owned Stations: Heathrow Central, Heathrow Terminal 4, Heathrow Terminal 5
Depots: Old Oak Common HEX (OH)
Parent Company: Heathrow Express - British Airports Authority
Heathrow Connect - British Airports Authority / First Group

Heathrow Express

Heathrow Airport Terminal 5
Heathrow Airport Terminals 1, 2, 3
London Paddington

Heathrow Connect

Heathrow Airport Terminal 4
Heathrow Airport Terminals 1, 2, 3
Hayes
Southall
Hanwell
West Ealing
Ealing Broadway
London Paddington

Left: *The Class 332 Heathrow Express sets operate every 15 minutes throughout the day linking London Paddington with Heathrow Airport, providing a rapid, while very expensive link to the UK's main airport. Two nine car formations of Class 332 stock pass on the approaches to London Paddington; on the right an arriving set is led by unit No. 332008, while on the left a departing train heads for Heathrow, a journey of just 15 minutes.* **CJM**

Class 332

Vehicle Length: (Driving) 77ft 10¾in (23.74m)
(Inter) 75ft 11in (23.143m)
Height: 12ft 1½in (3.70m)
Width: 9ft 1in (2.75m)
Horsepower: 1,876hp (1,400kW)
Seats 4-car (total/car): 26F-148S, 26F/56S/44S/48S
5-Car (total/car): 26F-204S, 26F/56S/44S/56S/48S

Number	*Formation* DMFO+TSO+PTSO+(TSO)+DMSO	*Depot*	*Livery*	*Owner*	*Operator*
332001	**78400+72412+63400+ - +78401**	**OH**	**HEX**	**BAA**	**HEX**
332002	**78402+72409+63401+ - +78403**	**OH**	**HEX**	**BAA**	**HEX**
332003	**78404+72407+63402+ - +78405**	**OH**	**HEX**	**BAA**	**HEX**
332004	**78406+72406+63403+ - +78407**	**OH**	**HEX**	**BAA**	**HEX**
332005	**78408+72411+63404+72417+78409**	**OH**	**HEX**	**BAA**	**HEX**
332006	**78410+72410+63405+72415+78411**	**OH**	**HEX**	**BAA**	**HEX**
332007	**78412+72401+63406+72414+78413**	**OH**	**HEX**	**BAA**	**HEX**

Vehicle Length: (Driving) 77ft 10¾in (23.74m)
(Inter) 75ft 11in (23.143m)
Height: 12ft 1½in (3.70m)
Width: 9ft 1in (2.75m)
Horsepower: 1,876hp (1,400kW)
Seats 4-car (total/car): 14F-148S, 48S/56S/44S/14F
5-Car (total/car): 14F-204S, 48S/56S/44S/56S/14F

Number	*Formation* DMSO+TSO+PTSO+(TSO)+DMFLO	*Depot*	*Livery*	*Owner*	*Operator*
332008	**78414+72413+63407+72418+78415**	**OH**	**HEX**	**BAA**	**HEX**
332009	**78416+72400+63408+72416+78417**	**OH**	**HEX**	**BAA**	**HEX**
332010	**78418+72402+63409+ - +78419**	**OH**	**HEX**	**BAA**	**HEX**
332011	**78420+72403+63410+ - +78421**	**OH**	**HEX**	**BAA**	**HEX**
332012	**78422+72404+63411+ - +78423**	**OH**	**HEX**	**BAA**	**HEX**
332013	**78424+72408+63412+ - +78425**	**OH**	**HEX**	**BAA**	**HEX**
332014	**78426+72406+63413+ - +78427**	**OH**	**HEX**	**BAA**	**HEX**

Right: *The 14 Class 332 units which operate the Heathrow Express are all allocated to Old Oak Common Hex depot. Five sets are formed as five-car units and the balance as four-car sets. Unit No. 332012, a four-car set, is seen under the great Brunel roof at London Paddington.* **CJM**

Class 360/2
Desiro

Vehicle Length: 66ft 9in (20.4m)
Height: 12ft 1½in (3.7m)
Width: 9ft 2in (2.79m)
Horsepower: 1,341hp (1,000kW)
Seats (total/car): 264S, 63S/66S/74S/74S/63S

Number	*Formation* DMSO(A)+PTSO+TSO+TSO+DMSO(B)	*Depot*	*Livery*	*Owner*	*Operator*
360201	**78431+63421+72431+72421+78441**	**OH**	**HEC**	**BAA**	**HEC**
360202	**78432+63422+72432+72422+78442**	**OH**	**HEC**	**BAA**	**HEC**
360203	**78433+63423+72433+72423+78443**	**OH**	**HEC**	**BAA**	**HEC**
360204	**78434+63424+72434+72424+78444**	**OH**	**HEC**	**BAA**	**HEC**
360205	**78435+63425+72435+72425+78445**	**OH**	**HEC**	**BAA**	**HEC**

Right: *To operate the all-stations Heathrow Connect service a fleet of five, five-car Siemens Desiro units were purchased. These are based alongside the Class 332s at Old Oak Common and operate on an all-stations basis between Paddington and Heathrow Airport, providing a service aimed at Airport staff who have reduced rate travel on the trains. Set No. 360205 is illustrated.* **CJM**

Hull Trains

Address: ✉ Europa House, 184 Ferensway, Kingston-upon-Hull, HU1 3UT
customer.services@hulltrains.co.uk
✆ 0845 676 9905
ⓘ www.hulltrains.co.uk

General Manager: James Adeshiyan
Franchise Dates: Private Open Access Operator, Seven year agreement
Principal Route: London King's Cross - Hull
Depots: Crofton (XW) [Operated by Bombardier]
Parent Company: First Group

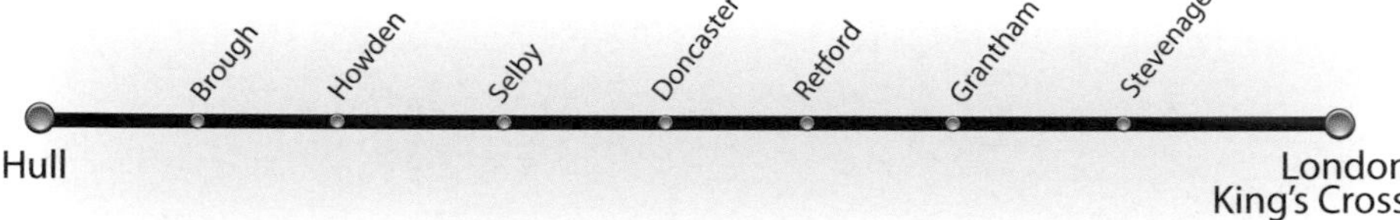

Class 180
Adelante

Vehicle Length: (driving) 75ft 7in (23.71m), (inter) 75ft 5in (23.03m)
Height: 12ft 4in (3.75m)
Width: 9ft 2in (2.80m)
Engine: 1 x Cummins OSK19 of 750hp per car
Horsepower: 3,750hp (2,796kW)
Seats (total/car): 42F/226S, 46S/42F/68S/56S/56S

Number	*Formation* DMSL(A)+MFL+MSF+MSLRB+DMSL(B)	*Depot*	*Livery*	*Owner*	*Operator*
180109	50909+54909+55909+56909+59909	XW	FHT	ANG	FHT
180110	50910+54910+55910+56910+59910	XW	FHT	ANG	FHT
180111	50911+54911+55911+56911+59911	XW	FHT	ANG	FHT
180113	50913+54913+55913+56913+59913	XW	FHT	ANG	FHT

Below: *From 2009, First Hull Trains operated its open access Hull to London service using Class 180 stock, displaced from First Great Western. The sets started to pass through Wolverton Works for refurbishment the same year and now sport First 'dynamic lines' livery. Set No. 180113 is seen at King's Cross.* **Tony Christie**

Island Line

Address: ✉ Ryde St Johns Road Station, Ryde, Isle of Wight, PO33 2BA
info@island-line.co.uk
✆ 01983 812591
ⓘ www.island-line.co.uk

Managing Director: Andy Pitt (South West Trains), **General Manager:** Andy Naylor
Franchise Dates: Part of SWT franchise 2 February 2007 - 28 February 2017
Principal Route: Ryde Pier Head - Shanklin
Owned Stations: All
Depots: Ryde St Johns (RY)
Parent Company: Stagecoach

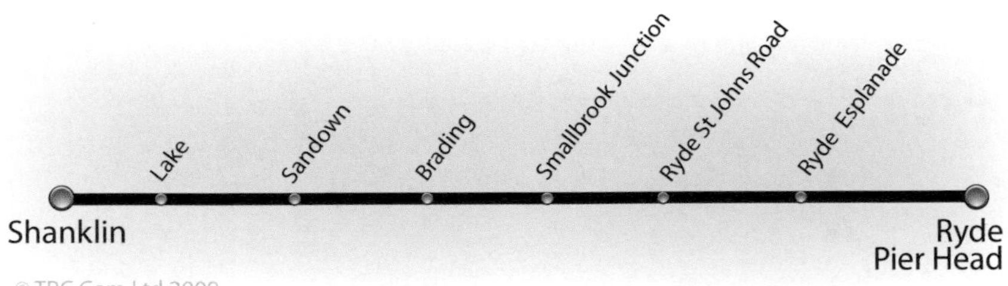

Class 483

Vehicle Length: 52ft 4in (15.95m)
Height: 9ft 5½in (2.88m)
Width: 8ft 8½in (2.65m)
Horsepower: 670hp (500kW)
Seats (total/car): 82S, 40S/42S

Number	Formation DMSO+DMSO	Depot	Livery	Owner	Operator
483002	122+224	RY	LUL	SWT	SIL
483004	124+224	RY	LUL	SWT	SIL
483006	126+226	RY	LUL	SWT	SIL
483007	127+227	RY	LUL	SWT	SIL
483008	128+228	RY	LUL	SWT	SIL
483009	129+229	RY	LUL	SWT	SIL

Below: *The wonderful little isolated network on the Isle of Wight, part of the South West Trains franchise and operated as a community railway project, uses a fleet of six two-car former London Underground tube trains. Set No. 004 is seen outside Ryde Works following repaint into mock LT red livery.* **CJM**

London Midland

Address: ✉ 102 New Street, Birmingham, B2 4JB
comments@londonmidland.com
✆ 0844 811 0133
ⓘ www.londonmidland.com

Managing Director: Mike Hodson

Franchise Dates: 11 November 2007 - 19 September 2015

Principal Routes: London Euston - Liverpool Lime Street, West Midlands routes to Stratford, Worcester, Hereford, Shrewsbury, plus Bedford and St Albans Abbey branches

Depots: Northampton (NN)*, Soho (SI), Tyseley (TS), Stourbridge Junction (SJ) * Operated by Siemens

Parent Company: Govia

Class 08

Vehicle Length: 29ft 3in (8.91m)
Height: 12ft 8⅝in (3.87m)
Width: 8ft 6in (2.59m)
Engine: English Electric 6K
Horsepower: 400hp (298kW)
Electrical Equipment: English Electric

Number	*Depot*	*Pool*	*Livery*	*Owner*	*Operator*
08616 (3785)	**TS**	**EJLO**	**LMI**	**LMI**	**LMI**
08805	**SI**	**EJLO**	**BLU**	**LMI**	**LMI**

Names applied

08616 ***Tyseley 100***	**08805** ***Concorde***

Left: *London Midland own and operate two Class 08 shunting locomotives, one is allocated to Tyseley and the other to Soho. Both are used for depot pilotage work. No. 08616* Tyseley 100 *is painted in a version of the latest London Midland livery.* **Lee Scott**

Class 139

Vehicle Length: 28ft 6in (8.7m)
Width: 7ft 8in (2.4m)
Engine: 1 x MVH420 2.0ltr LPG, flywheel hybrid
Seats (total/car): 18S

Number	*Formation DMS*	*Depot*	*Livery*	*Owner*	*Operator*
139001	**39001**	**SJ**	**LMI**	**LMI**	**LMI**
139002	**39002**	**SJ**	**LMI**	**LMI**	**LMI**

Left: *In the summer of 2009 two Type PPM60 Parry People Movers entered service on the Stourbridge Junction - Stourbridge Town 'shuttle' service. The hybrid-powered single vehicles are allocated to a single track shed at Stourbridge Junction. The vehicles while classified as Class 139 are not authorised to operate on any other section of railway and have to be transported to and from Stourbridge by road. Car No. 139002 is illustrated.* **John Binch**

London Midland

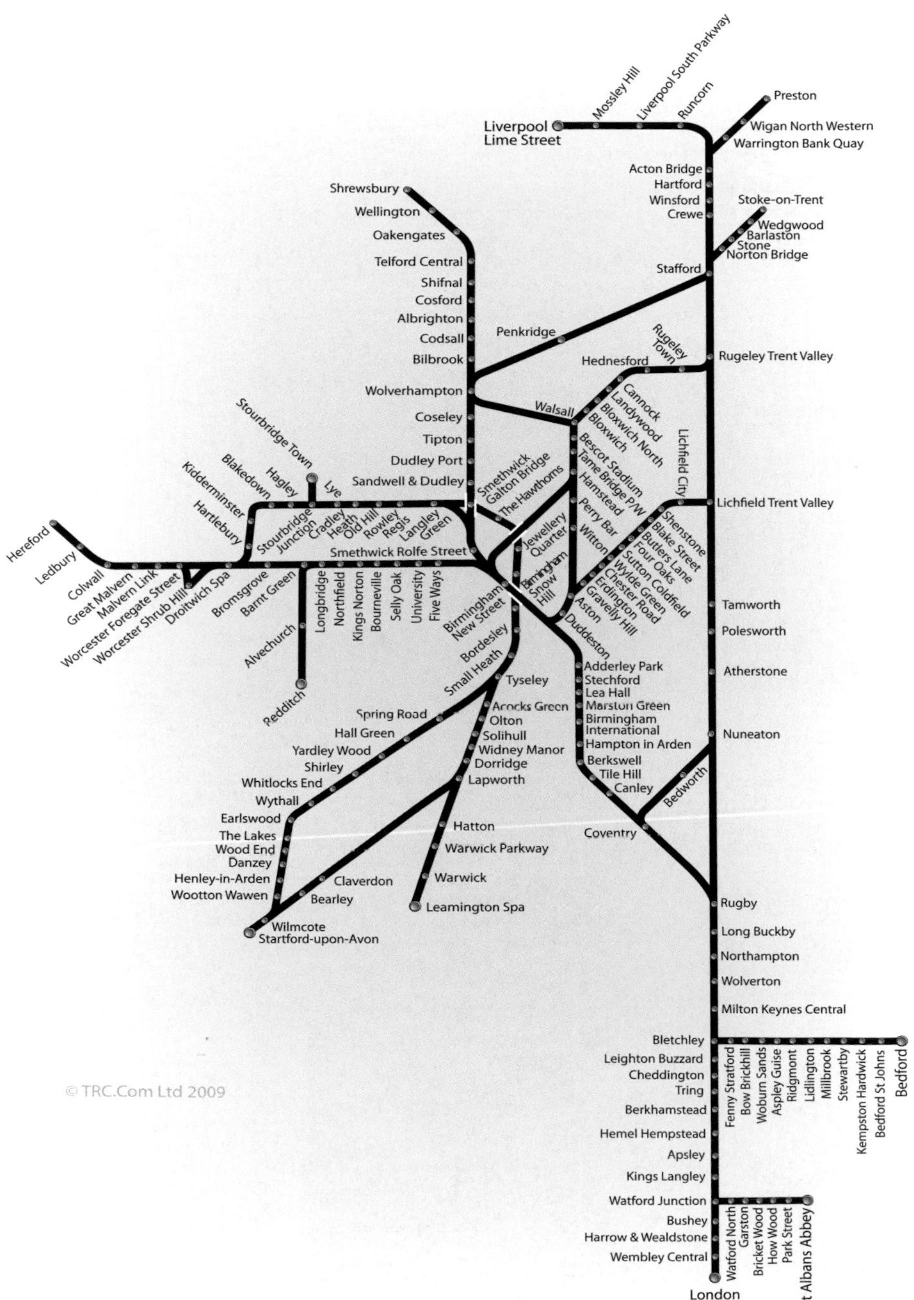

London Midland

Class 150/0

Vehicle Length: (driving) 65ft 9¾in (20.05m), (inter) 66ft 2½in (20.18m)
Height: 12ft 4½in (3.77m)
Width: 9ft 3⅛in (2.82m)
Engine: 1 x Cummins NT855R4 of 285hp per car
Horsepower: 855hp (638kW)
Seats (total/car): 240S, 72S/92S/76S

Number	Formation DMSL+MS+DMS	Depot	Livery	Owner	Operator
150001	55200+55400+55300	TS	CTL	ANG	LMI
150002	55201+55401+55301	TS	CTL	ANG	LMI

Class 150/0

Vehicle Length: 64ft 9¾in (19.74m)
Height: 12ft 4½in (3.77m)
Width: 9ft 3⅛in (2.82m)
Engine: 1 x NT855R5 of 285hp per vehicle
Horsepower: 855hp (638kW)
Seats (total/car): 224S, 76S/76S/72S
**220S, 72S/72S/76S*

Number	Formation DMSL+DMSL+DMS or DMSL+DMS+DMS*	Depot	Livery	Owner	Operator
150003	52103+52210+57106	TS	WMD	ANG	LMI
150005	52105+52210+57105	TS	CTL	ANG	LMI
150007	52107+52202+57107	TS	CTL	ANG	LMI
150009	52109+57202+57109*	TS	CTL	ANG	LMI
150010	52110+57226+57210*	TS	WMD	ANG	LMI
150011	52111+52204+57111	TS	CTL	ANG	LMI
150012	52112+57206+58112*	TS	CTL	ANG	LMI
150013	52113+52226+57113	TS	CTL	ANG	LMI
150014	52114+57204+57114*	TS	CTL	ANG	LMI
150015	52115+52206+57115	TS	CTL	ANG	LMI
150016	52116+57212+57116*	TS	CTL	ANG	LMI
150017	52117+57209+57117*	TS	CTL	ANG	LMI
150018	52118+52220+57118	TS	WMD	ANG	LMI
150019	52119+57220+57119*	TS	CTL	ANG	LMI

Class 150/1

Vehicle Length: 64ft 9¾in (19.74m)
Height: 12ft 4½in (3.77m)
Width: 9ft 3⅛in (2.82m)
Engine: 1 x NT855R5 of 285hp per vehicle
Horsepower: 570hp (425kW)
Seats (total/car): 141S, 71S/70S

Number	Formation DMSL+DMS	Depot	Livery	Owner	Operator
150101	52101+57101	TS	CTL	ANG	LMI
150102	52102+57102	TS	CTL	ANG	LMI
150104	52104+57104	TS	CTL	ANG	LMI
150106	52106+57106	TS	CTL	ANG	LMI
150108	52108+57108	TS	CTL	ANG	LMI
150122	52122+57122	TS	CTL	ANG	LMI
150124	52124+57124	TS	CTL	ANG	LMI
150125	52125+57125	TS	CTL	ANG	LMI
150126	52126+57126	TS	WMD	ANG	LMI
150132	52132+57132	TS	WMD	ANG	LMI

Class 150/2

Vehicle Length: 64ft 9¾in (19.74m)
Height: 12ft 4½in (3.77m)
Width: 9ft 3⅛in (2.82m)
Engine: 1 x NT855R5 of 285hp per vehicle
Horsepower: 570hp (425kW)
Seats (total/car): 141S, 71S/70S

Number	Formation DMSL+DMS	Depot	Livery	Owner	Operator
150214	52214+57214	TS	CTL	ANG	LMI
150216	52216+57216	TS	CTL	ANG	LMI

Left: *Three-car Class 150/0 set No. 150005 is illustrated. This was built as a two-car unit and subsequently strengthened to three-car status by adding a Class 150/2 vehicle in the middle. The train is carrying an interim livery of West Midlands Metro based on the former Central Trains colours. This unit has received modified light clusters, with a combined marker/tail light unit, rendering a blanking plate over the original marker light.* **Stacey Thew**

Class 153

Vehicle Length: 76ft 5in (23.29m)
Height: 12ft 3⅛in (3.75m)
Width: 8ft 10in (2.70m)
Engine: 1 x NT855R5 of 285hp
Horsepower: 285hp (213kW)
Seats (total/car): 72S

Number	Formation DMSL	Depot	Livery	Owner	Operator
153325	52325	TS	LMI	PTR	LMI
153333	52333	TS	LMI	PTR	LMI
153334	52334	TS	LMI	PTR	LMI
153354	57354	TS	LMI	PTR	LMI
153356	57356	TS	LMI	PTR	LMI
153364	57364	TS	LMI	PTR	LMI
153365	57365	TS	LMI	PTR	LMI
153366	57366	TS	LMI	PTR	LMI
153371	57371	TS	LMI	PTR	LMI
153375	57375	TS	LMI	PTR	LMI

Right: *London Midland operate a fleet of 10 Class 153 'bubble' cars based at Tyseley for secondary branch line use. All are now internally refurbished and painted in the latest London Midland livery. Set No. 153364 is seen at Worcester Foregate Street.* **John Wills**

Class 170/5
Turbostar

Vehicle Length: 77ft 6in (23.62m)
Height: 12ft 4½in (3.77m)
Width: 8ft 10in (2.69m)
Engine: 1 x MTU 6R 183TD13H 422hp per vehicle
Horsepower: 844hp (629kW)
Seats (total/car): 122S 55S/67S

Number	Formation DMSL+DMSL	Depot	Livery	Owner	Operator
170501	50501+79501	TS	LMI	PTR	LMI
170502	50502+79502	TS	LMI	PTR	LMI
170503	50503+79503	TS	LMI	PTR	LMI
170504	50504+79504	TS	LMI	PTR	LMI
170505	50505+79505	TS	LMI	PTR	LMI
170506	50506+79506	TS	LMI	PTR	LMI
170507	50507+79507	TS	LMI	PTR	LMI
170508	50508+79508	TS	LMI	PTR	LMI
170509	50509+79509	TS	LMI	PTR	LMI
170510	50510+79510	TS	LMI	PTR	LMI
170511	50511+79511	TS	LMI	PTR	LMI
170512	50512+79512	TS	LMI	PTR	LMI
170513	50513+79513	TS	LMI	PTR	LMI
170514	50514+79514	TS	LMI	PTR	LMI
170515	50515+79515	TS	LMI	PTR	LMI
170516	50516+79516	TS	LMI	PTR	LMI
170517	50517+79517	TS	LMI	PTR	LMI

Class 170/6
Turbostar

Vehicle Length: 77ft 6in (23.62m)
Height: 12ft 4½in (3.77m)
Width: 8ft 10in (2.69m)
Engine: 1 x MTU 6R 183TD13H 422hp per vehicle
Horsepower: 1,266hp (944kW)
Seats (total/car): 196S 55S/74S/67S

Number	Formation DMSL+MS+DMSL	Depot	Livery	Owner	Operator
170630	50630+56630+79630	TS	LMI	PTR	LMI
170631	50631+56631+79631	TS	LMI	PTR	LMI
170632	50632+56632+79632	TS	LMI	PTR	LMI
170633	50633+56633+79633	TS	LMI	PTR	LMI
170634	50634+56634+79634	TS	LMI	PTR	LMI
170635	50635+56635+79635	TS	LMI	PTR	LMI

Right: *For longer distance and outer-suburban services London Midland operate a fleet of Class 170 units, either formed as two or three car sets. Since the start of the franchise in 2007, all sets have been refreshed and now sport the latest London Midland livery, as shown on set No. 170506 at Gloucester operating a Gloucester to Worcester shuttle service.* **CJM**

London Midland

Class 172/2
Turbostar

Vehicle Length: 73ft 4in (22.37m)
Height: 12ft 4½in (3.77m)
Width: 9ft 1in (2.75m)
Engine: MTU 6H1800 of 360kW
Horsepower: 965hp (720kW)
Seats (total/car): 121S, 53S/68S

Number	Formation DMS+DMS	Depot	Livery	Owner	Operator
172211	50211+79211	TS	LMI	PTR	LMI
172212	50212+79212	TS	LMI	PTR	LMI
172213	50213+79213	TS	LMI	PTR	LMI
172214	50214+79214	TS	LMI	PTR	LMI
172215	50215+79215	TS	LMI	PTR	LMI
172216	50216+79216	TS	LMI	PTR	LMI
172217	50217+79217	TS	LMI	PTR	LMI
172218	50218+79218	TS	LMI	PTR	LMI
172219	50219+59219	TS	LMI	PTR	LMI
172220	50220+79220	TS	LMI	PTR	LMI
170221	50221+79221	TS	LMI	PTR	LMI
170222	50222+79222	TS	LMI	PTR	LMI

Sets on order awaiting delivery in spring 2010

Class 172/3
Turbostar

Vehicle Length: (Driving) 73ft 4in (22.37m)
(Inter): (76ft 7in 23.36m)
Height: 12ft 4½in (3.77m)
Width: 9ft 1in (2.75m)
Engine: MTU 6H1800 of 360kW
Horsepower: 1449hp (1080kW)
Seats (total/car): 193S, 53S/72S/68S

Number	Formation DMSO+MS+DMSO	Depot	Livery	Owner	Operator
172331	50331+56331+79331	TS	LMI	PTR	LMI
172332	50332+56332+79332	TS	LMI	PTR	LMI
172333	50333+56333+79333	TS	LMI	PTR	LMI
172334	50334+56334+79334	TS	LMI	PTR	LMI
172335	50335+56335+79335	TS	LMI	PTR	LMI
172336	50336+56336+79336	TS	LMI	PTR	LMI
172337	50337+56337+79337	TS	LMI	PTR	LMI
172338	50338+56338+79338	TS	LMI	PTR	LMI
172339	50339+56339+79339	TS	LMI	PTR	LMI
172340	50340+56340+79340	TS	LMI	PTR	LMI
172341	50341+56341+79341	TS	LMI	PTR	LMI
172342	50342+56342+79342	TS	LMI	PTR	LMI
172343	50343+56343+79343	TS	LMI	PTR	LMI
172344	50344+56344+79344	TS	LMI	PTR	LMI
172345	50345+56345+79345	TS	LMI	PTR	LMI

Sets on order awaiting delivery in spring 2010

Class 321/4

Vehicle Length: (Driving) 65ft 0¾in (19.83m)
(Inter) 65ft 4¼in (19.92m)
Height: 12ft 4¾in (3.78m)
Width: 9ft 3in (2.82m)
Horsepower: 1,328hp (996kW)
Seats (total/car): 28F/271S, 28F-40S/79S/74S/78S

Number	Formation DMCO+MSO+TSO+DMSO	Depot	Livery	Owner	Operator
321411	78105+63073+71959+77953	NN	LMI	HSB	LMI
321412	78106+63074+71960+77954	NN	LMI	HSB	LMI
321413	78107+63075+71961+77955	NN	LMI	HSB	LMI
321414	78108+63076+71962+77956	NN	LMI	HSB	LMI
321415	78109+63077+71963+77957	NN	LMI	HSB	LMI
321416	78110+63078+71964+77958	NN	LMI	HSB	LMI
321417	78111+63079+71965+77959	NN	LMI	HSB	LMI

■ *Sets Nos. 321428/430/431/433 remain on lease to London Midland until March 2010 and then transfer to National Express East Anglia.*

Left: *Class 312/4 No. 321411 became the first member of its class to receive the London Midland franchise livery. The unit received the new vinyls while being refurbished at Wabtec Doncaster in May 2009. On its first day of service 18 June 2009 the unit departs from Birmingham New Street station with the 09.53 service to London Euston (via Northampton).* **John Binch**

Class 323

Vehicle Length: (Driving) 76ft 8¼in (23.37m)
(Inter) 76ft 10¾in (23.44m)
Height: 12ft 4¾in (3.78m)
Width: 9ft 2¼in (2.80m)
Horsepower: 1,565hp (1,168kW)
Seats (total/car): 284S, 98S/88S/98S

Number	*Formation* DMSO(A)+PTSO+DMSO(B)	*Depot*	*Livery*	*Owner*	*Operator*
323201	64001+72201+65001	SI	LMI	PTR	LMI
323202	64002+72202+65002	SI	LMI	PTR	LMI
323203	64003+72203+65003	SI	LMI	PTR	LMI
323204	64004+72204+65004	SI	LMI	PTR	LMI
323205	64005+72205+65005	SI	LMI	PTR	LMI
323206	64006+72206+65006	SI	LMI	PTR	LMI
323207	64007+72207+65007	SI	LMI	PTR	LMI
323208	64008+72208+65008	SI	LMI	PTR	LMI
323209	64009+72209+65009	SI	LMI	PTR	LMI
323210	64010+72210+65010	SI	LMI	PTR	LMI
323211	64011+72211+65011	SI	LMI	PTR	LMI
323212	64012+72212+65012	SI	LMI	PTR	LMI
323213	64013+72213+65013	SI	LMI	PTR	LMI
323214	64014+72214+65014	SI	LMI	PTR	LMI
323215	64015+72215+65015	SI	LMI	PTR	LMI
323216	64016+72216+65016	SI	LMI	PTR	LMI
323217	64017+72217+65017	SI	LMI	PTR	LMI
323218	64018+72218+65018	SI	LMI	PTR	LMI
323219	64019+72219+65019	SI	LMI	PTR	LMI
323220	64020+72220+65020	SI	LMI	PTR	LMI
323221	64021+72221+65021	SI	LMI	PTR	LMI
323222	64022+72222+65022	SI	LMI	PTR	LMI
323240	64040+72340+65040	SI	LMI	PTR	LMI
323241	64041+72341+65041	SI	LMI	PTR	LMI
323242	64042+72342+65042	SI	LMI	PTR	LMI
323243	64043+72343+65043	SI	LMI	PTR	LMI

Above: *The Hunslet Transportation Project's Class 323 units are the mainstay of the Lichfield - Birmingham - Redditch 'Cross-City' line in the Midlands. On the sunny and warm 24 May 2009, No. 323213 in the latest London Midland City livery departs from Longbridge forming the 12.27 Redditch to Lichfield Trent Valley service.* **John Binch**

Class 350/1
Desiro

Vehicle Length: 66ft 9in (20.4m)
Height: 12ft 1½in (3.78m)
Width: 9ft 2in (2.7m)
Horsepower: 1,341hp (1,000kW)
Seats (total/car): 24F-209S, 60S/24F-32S/57S/60S

Number	*Formation* DMSO(A)+TCO+PTSO+DMSO(B)	*Depot*	*Livery*	*Owner*	*Operator*
350101	63761+66811+66861+63711	NN	LMI	ANG	LMI
350102	63762+66812+66862+63712	NN	LMI	ANG	LMI
350103	63765+66813+66863+63713	NN	LMI	ANG	LMI

London Midland

350104	63764+66814+66864+63714	NN	LMI	ANG	LMI
350105	63763+66815+66868+63715	NN	LMI	ANG	LMI
350106	63766+66816+66866+63716	NN	LMI	ANG	LMI
350107	63767+66817+66867+63717	NN	LMI	ANG	LMI
350108	63768+66818+66865+63718	NN	LMI	ANG	LMI
350109	63769+66819+66869+63719	NN	LMI	ANG	LMI
350110	63770+66820+66870+63720	NN	LMI	ANG	LMI
350111	63771+66821+66871+63721	NN	LMI	ANG	LMI
350112	63772+66822+66872+63722	NN	LMI	ANG	LMI
350113	63773+66823+66873+63723	NN	LMI	ANG	LMI
350114	63774+66824+66874+63724	NN	LMI	ANG	LMI
350115	63775+66825+66875+63725	NN	LMI	ANG	LMI
350116	63776+66826+66876+63726	NN	LMI	ANG	LMI
350117	63777+66827+66877+63727	NN	LMI	ANG	LMI
350118	63778+66828+66878+63728	NN	LMI	ANG	LMI
350119	63779+66829+66879+63729	NN	LMI	ANG	LMI
350120	63780+66830+66880+63730	NN	LMI	ANG	LMI
350121	63781+66831+66881+63731	NN	LMI	ANG	LMI
350122	63782+66832+66882+63732	NN	LMI	ANG	LMI
350123	63783+66833+66883+63733	NN	LMI	ANG	LMI
350124	63784+66834+66884+63734	NN	LMI	ANG	LMI
350125	63785+66835+66885+63735	NN	LMI	ANG	LMI
350126	63786+66836+66886+63736	NN	LMI	ANG	LMI
350127	63787+66837+66887+63737	NN	LMI	ANG	LMI
350128	63788+66838+66888+63738	NN	LMI	ANG	LMI
350129	63789+66839+66889+63739	NN	LMI	ANG	LMI
350130	63790+66840+77890+63740	NN	LMI	ANG	LMI

Class 350/2
Desiro

Vehicle Length: 66ft 9in (20.4m)
Height: 12ft 1½in (3.78m)
Width: 9ft 2in (2.7m)
Horsepower: 1,341hp (1,000kW)
Seats (total/car): 24F-243S, 70S/24F-42S/61S/70S

Number	*Formation* DMSO(A)+TCO+PTSO+DMSO(B)	*Depot*	*Livery*	*Owner*	*Operator*
350231	61431+65231+67531+61531	NN	LMI	PTR	LMI
350232	61432+65232+67532+61532	NN	LMI	PTR	LMI
350233	61433+65233+67533+61533	NN	LMI	PTR	LMI
350234	61434+65234+67534+61534	NN	LMI	PTR	LMI
350235	61435+65235+67535+61535	NN	LMI	PTR	LMI
350236	61436+65236+67536+61536	NN	LMI	PTR	LMI
350237	61437+65237+67537+61537	NN	LMI	PTR	LMI
350238	61438+65238+67538+61538	NN	LMI	PTR	LMI
350239	61439+65239+67539+61539	NN	LMI	PTR	LMI
350240	61440+65240+67540+61540	NN	LMI	PTR	LMI
350241	61441+65241+67541+61541	NN	LMI	PTR	LMI
350242	61442+65242+67542+61542	NN	LMI	PTR	LMI
350243	61443+65243+67543+61543	NN	LMI	PTR	LMI
350244	61444+65244+67544+61544	NN	LMI	PTR	LMI
350245	61445+65245+67545+61545	NN	LMI	PTR	LMI
350246	61446+65246+67546+61546	NN	LMI	PTR	LMI
350247	61447+65247+67547+61547	NN	LMI	PTR	LMI
350248	61448+65248+67548+61548	NN	LMI	PTR	LMI
350249	61449+65249+67549+61549	NN	LMI	PTR	LMI
350250	61450+65250+67550+61550	NN	LMI	PTR	LMI
350251	61451+65251+67551+61551	NN	LMI	PTR	LMI
350252	61452+65252+67552+61552	NN	LMI	PTR	LMI
350253	61453+65253+67553+61553	NN	LMI	PTR	LMI
350254	61454+65254+67554+61554	NN	LMI	PTR	LMI
350255	61455+65255+67555+61555	NN	LMI	PTR	LMI
350256	61456+65256+67556+61556	NN	LMI	PTR	LMI
350257	61457+65257+67557+61557	NN	LMI	PTR	LMI
350258	61458+65258+67558+61558	NN	LMI	PTR	LMI
350259	61459+65259+67559+61559	NN	LMI	PTR	LMI
350260	61460+65260+67560+61560	NN	LMI	PTR	LMI

350261	61461+65261+67561+61561	NN	LMI	PTR	LMI
350262	61462+65262+67562+61562	NN	LMI	PTR	LMI
350263	61463+65263+67563+61563	NN	LMI	PTR	LMI
350264	61464+65264+67564+61564	NN	LMI	PTR	LMI
350265	61465+65265+67565+61565	NN	LMI	PTR	LMI
350266	61466+65266+67566+61566	NN	LMI	PTR	LMI
350267	61467+65267+67567+61567	NN	LMI	PTR	LMI

Above: *The original batch of Class 350/1 sets were originally delivered painted in an SRA livery of grey with mid-blue doors being operated jointly by Central Trains and Silverlink. Following the changes to the Midland area franchises at the end of 2007, sets soon emerged in the new London Midland livery. All new Class 350/2 sets have been delivered in the new house colours. Set No. 350102 heads north at Kenton on 22 August 2008.* **Robin Ralston**

Below: *The Siemens 'Desiro' stock used by London Midland has a high quality passenger interior, providing both first and standard class seating. 24 first class seats are provided on both sub-classes, set out in the low-density 2+2 style, located in an intermediate TCO vehicle. Power sockets are provided by each seat for telephone and lap-top charging.* **CJM**

London Overground

Address: ✉ 125 Finchley Road, London NW3 6HY
overgroundinfo@tfl.gov.uk
✆ 0845 601 4867
ⓘ www.tfl.gov.uk/overground

Managing Director: Steve Murphy

Principal Routes: Clapham Junction - Willesden, Richmond - Stratford
Gospel Oak - Barking, Euston - Watford
East London Line – Dalston - West Croydon

Depots: Willesden (WN) New Cross Gate (NX)

Parent Company: Transport for London

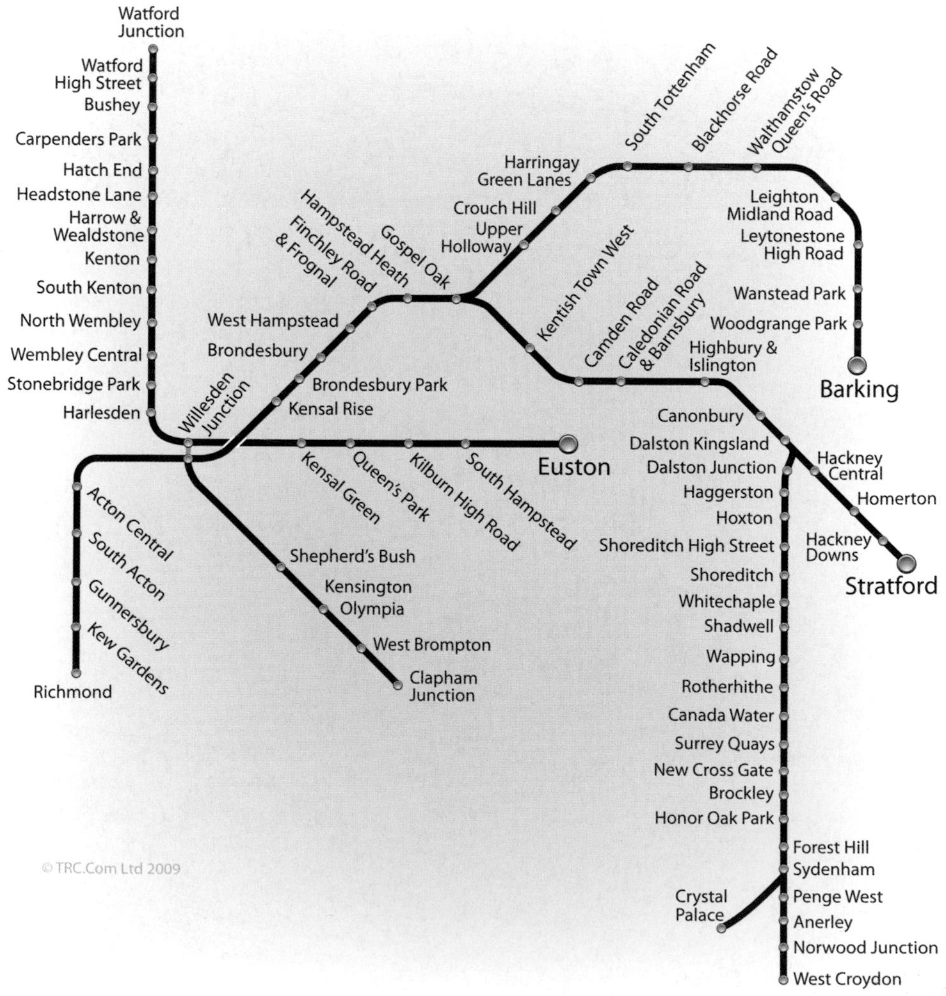

Class 150/1

Vehicle Length: 64ft 9¾in (19.74m)
Height: 12ft 4½in (3.77m)
Width: 9ft 3⅛in (2.82m)
Engine: 1 x NT855R5 of 285hp per vehicle
Horsepower: 570hp (425kW)
Seats (total/car): 144S, 71S/73S

Number	Formation DMSL+DMS	Depot	Livery	Owner	Operator	Name
150120	52120+57120	WN	SLK	ANG	LOG	*Gospel Oak-Barking 2000*
150123	52123+57123	WN	SLK	ANG	LOG	*Richard Crane*
150128	52128+57128	WN	SLK	ANG	LOG	*Bedford Bamberg 30*
150129	52129+57129	WN	SLK	ANG	LOG	*Marston Vale*
150130	52130+57130	WN	SLK	ANG	LOG	*Bedford-Bletchley 150*
150131	52131+57131	WN	SLK	ANG	LOG	*Leslie Crabbe*

Right: *The Class 150 sets currently operated by London Overground, all still painted in Silverlink colours from the previous franchise operator, will go off lease when the new Class 172 stock is delivered in early 2010. Set No. 150128 is seen at Bletchley.* **CJM**

Class 172/0
Turbostar

Vehicle Length: 73ft 4in (22.37m)
Height: 12ft 4½in (3.77m)
Width: 9ft 1in (2.75m)
Engine: MTU 6H1800 of 360kW
Horsepower: 965hp (720kW)
Seats (total/car): 121S, 53S/68S

Number	Formation DMS+DMS	Depot	Livery	Owner	Operator
172001	59311+59411	WN	LOG	ANG	LOG
172002	59312+59412	WN	LOG	ANG	LOG
172003	59313+59413	WN	LOG	ANG	LOG
172004	59314+59414	WN	LOG	ANG	LOG
172005	59315+59415	WN	LOG	ANG	LOG
172006	59316+59416	WN	LOG	ANG	LOG
172007	59317+59417	WN	LOG	ANG	LOG
172008	59318+59418	WN	LOG	ANG	LOG

Sets on order awaiting delivery in 2010

Class 313/1

Vehicle Length: (Driving) 64ft 11½in (20.75m)
(Inter) 65ft 4¼in (19.92m)
Height: 11ft 9in (3.58m)
Width: 9ft 3in (2.82m)
Horsepower: 880hp (656kW)
Seats (total/car): 202S, 66S/70S/66S

Number	Formation DMSO+PTSO+BDMSO	Depot	Livery	Owner	Operator	Name
313101	62529+71213+62593	WN	SKL	HSB	LOG	
313103	62531+71215+62595	WN	SKL	HSB	LOG	
313106	62534+71218+62598	WN	SKL	HSB	LOG	
313107	62535+71219+62599	WN	SKL	HSB	LOG	
313109	62537+71221+62601	WN	SKL	HSB	LOG	*Arnold Leah*
313110	62538+71222+62602	WN	SKL	HSB	LOG	
313111	62539+71223+62603	WN	SKL	HSB	LOG	*London TravelWatch*
313112	62540+71224+62604	WN	SKL	HSB	LOG	
313113	62541+71225+62605	WN	SKL	HSB	LOG	
313114	62542+71226+62606	WN	SKL	HSB	LOG	
313115	62543+71227+62507	WN	SKL	HSB	LOG	
313116	62544+71228+62608	WN	SKL	HSB	LOG	
313117	62545+71229+62609	WN	SKL	HSB	LOG	
313119	62547+71231+62611	WN	SKL	HSB	LOG	
313120	62548+71232+62613	WN	SKL	HSB	LOG	*Parliament Hill*
313121	62549+71233+62613	WN	SKL	HSB	LOG	
313122	62550+71234+62614	WN	SKL	HSB	LOG	
313123	62551+71235+62615	WN	SKL	HSB	LOG	
313134	62562+71246+61626	WN	SKL	HSB	LOG	*The Hackney Empire*

Above: *Until full introduction of 'Capitalstar' stock on all London Overground electrified services, the Class 313/1 sets will remain operational. After displacement some sets will transfer to the Southern franchise. Set No. 313114 is seen at Stratford, painted in Silverlink livery, with LOG branding.* **Tony Christie**

Class 378/0 (2)
Capitalstar

Vehicle Length: (Driving) (20.46m), (Inter) (20.14m) Width: 9ft 2in (3.80m)
Height: 11ft 9in (3.58m) Horsepower: 3-car (1,000kW)
Dual voltage - 750V dc third rail and 25kV ac overhead 4-car (1,500kW)
Seats 3-car (total/car): 106S, 36S/34S/36S Seats 4-car (total/car): 146S, 36S/(40S)/34S/36S

Number	*Formation* DMSO+MSO*+PTSO+DMSO	*Depot*	*Livery*	*Owner*	*Operator*
		** To be added 2010-11 sets then renumbered in 3782xx series as shown*			
378001 (378201)	38001+38201+38301+38101	WN	LOG	QWR	LOG
378002 (378202)	38002+38202+38302+38102	WN	LOG	QWR	LOG
378003 (378203)	38003+38203+38303+38103	WN	LOG	QWR	LOG
378004 (378204)	38004+38204+38304+38104	WN	LOG	QWR	LOG
378005 (378205)	38005+38205+38305+38105	WN	LOG	QWR	LOG
378006 (378206)	38006+38206+38306+38106	WN	LOG	QWR	LOG
378007 (378207)	38007+38207+38307+38107	WN	LOG	QWR	LOG
378008 (378208)	38008+38208+38308+38108	WN	LOG	QWR	LOG
378009 (378209)	38009+38209+38309+38109	WN	LOG	QWR	LOG
378010 (378210)	38010+38210+38310+38110	WN	LOG	QWR	LOG
378011 (378211)	38011+38211+38311+38111	WN	LOG	QWR	LOG
378012 (378212)	38012+38212+38312+38112	WN	LOG	QWR	LOG
378013 (378213)	38013+38213+38313+38113	WN	LOG	QWR	LOG
378014 (378214)	38014+38214+38314+38114	WN	LOG	QWR	LOG
378015 (378215)	38015+38215+38315+38115	WN	LOG	QWR	LOG
378016 (378216)	38016+38216+38316+38116	WN	LOG	QWR	LOG
378017 (378217)	38017+38217+38317+38117	WN	LOG	QWR	LOG
378018 (378218)	38018+38218+38318+38118	WN	LOG	QWR	LOG
378019 (378219)	38019+38219+38319+38119	WN	LOG	QWR	LOG
378020 (378220)	38020+38220+38320+38120	WN	LOG	QWR	LOG
378021 (378221)	38021+38221+38321+38121	WN	LOG	QWR	LOG
378022 (378222)	38022+38222+38322+38122	WN	LOG	QWR	LOG
378023 (378223)	38023+38223+38323+38123	WN	LOG	QWR	LOG
378024 (378224)	38024+38224+38324+38124	WN	LOG	QWR	LOG

Class 378/1
Capitalstar

Vehicle Length: (Driving) (20.46m), (Inter) (20.14m) Width: 9ft 2in (3.80m)
Height: 11ft 9in (3.58m) Horsepower: 4-car (1,500kW)
750V dc sets Seats (total/car): 146S, 36S/40S/34S/36S

Number	*Formation* DMSO+MSO+TSO+DMSO	*Depot*	*Livery*	*Owner*	*Operator*
378135	38035+38235+38335+38135	NX	LOG	QWR	LOG
378136	38036+38236+38336+38136	NX	LOG	QWR	LOG
378137	38037+38237+38337+38137	NX	LOG	QWR	LOG

378138	38038+38238+38338+38138	NX	LOG	QWR	LOG
378139	38039+38239+38339+38139	NX	LOG	QWR	LOG
378140	38040+38240+38340+38140	NX	LOG	QWR	LOG
378141	38041+38241+38341+38141	NX	LOG	QWR	LOG
378142	38042+38242+38342+38142	NX	LOG	QWR	LOG
378143	38043+38243+38343+38143	NX	LOG	QWR	LOG
378144	38044+38244+38344+38144	NX	LOG	QWR	LOG
378145	38045+38245+38345+38145	NX	LOG	QWR	LOG
378146	38046+38246+38346+38146	NX	LOG	QWR	LOG
378147	38047+38247+38347+38147	NX	LOG	QWR	LOG
378148	38048+38248+38348+38148	NX	LOG	QWR	LOG
378149	38049+38249+38349+38149	NX	LOG	QWR	LOG
378150	38050+38250+38350+38150	NX	LOG	QWR	LOG
378151	38051+38251+38351+38151	NX	LOG	QWR	LOG
378152	38052+38252+38352+38152	NX	LOG	QWR	LOG
378153	38053+38253+38353+38153	NX	LOG	QWR	LOG
378154	38054+38254+38354+38154	NX	LOG	QWR	LOG

Class 378/2
Capitalstar

Vehicle Length: (Driving) (20.46m), (Inter) (20.14m)
Height: 11ft 9in (3.58m)
Dual voltage - 750V dc third rail and 25kV ac overhead
Width: 9ft 2in (3.80m)
Horsepower: 4-car (1,500kW)
Seats (total/car): 146S, 36S/40S/34S/36S

Number	*Formation DMSO+MSO+TSO+DMSO*	*Depot*	*Livery*	*Owner*	*Operator*
378225	38025+38225+38325+38125	NX	LOG	QWR	LOG
378226	38026+38226+38326+38126	NX	LOG	QWR	LOG
378227	38027+38227+38327+38127	NX	LOG	QWR	LOG
378228	38028+38228+38328+38128	NX	LOG	QWR	LOG
378229	38029+38229+38329+38129	NX	LOG	QWR	LOG
378230	38030+38230+38330+38130	NX	LOG	QWR	LOG
378231	38031+38231+38331+38131	NX	LOG	QWR	LOG
378232	38032+38232+38332+38132	NX	LOG	QWR	LOG
378233	38033+38233+38333+38133	NX	LOG	QWR	LOG
378234	38034+38234+38334+38134	NX	LOG	QWR	LOG

Below: *The three and four vehicle formed 'Capitalstar' sets now operated by London Overground are more or less a main line version of an underground train, having only limited all longitudinal seats. The sets are presently allocated to the LOG depot at Willesden, but in the future will transfer to new purpose built accommodation at New Cross Gate and operate on all electrified LOG routes. Set No. 378016 is seen at Kensington Olympia forming a service to Clapham Junction from Willesden Junction on 14 December 2009.* **CJM**

Merseyrail

Address: ✉ Rail House, Lord Nelson Street, Liverpool L1 1JF
comment@merseyrail.org
✆ 0151 702 2534
ⓘ www.merseyrail.org

Managing Director: Bart Schmeink
Franchise Dates: 20 July 2003 - 31 July 2028
Principal Routes: All non main line services in Liverpool area
Depots: Birkenhead North (BD)
Parent Company: Serco/NedRailways

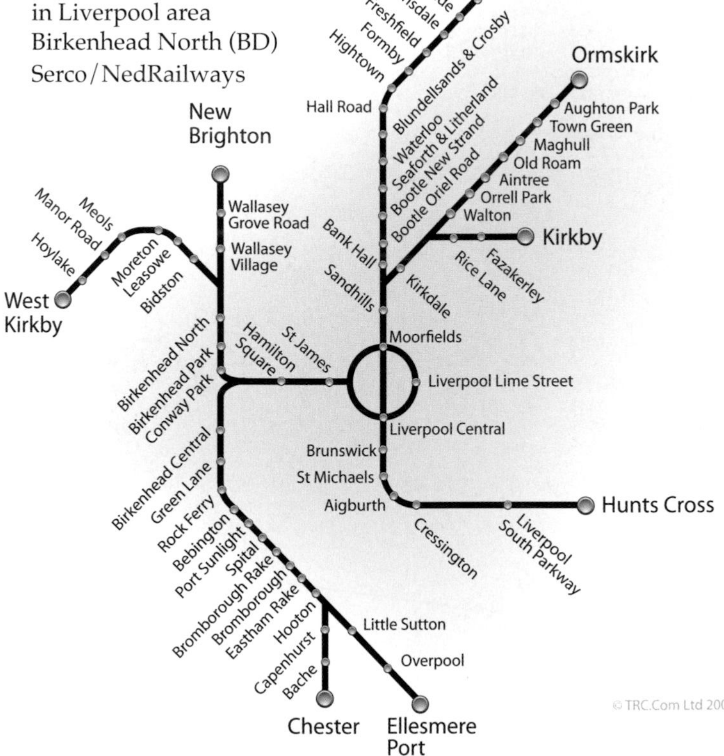

Class 507

Vehicle Length: (Driving) 64ft 11½in (19.80m)
(Inter) 65ft 4¼in (19.92m)
Height: 11ft 6½in (3.58m)
Width: 9ft 3in (2.82m)
Horsepower: 880hp (656kW)
Seats (total/car): 186S, 56S/74S/56S

Number	*Formation* DMSO+TSO+DMSO	*Depot*	*Livery*	*Owner*	*Operator*	*Name*
507001	64367+71342+64405	BD	MER	ANG	MER	
507002	64368+71343+64406	BD	MER	ANG	MER	
507003	64369+71344+64407	BD	MER	ANG	MER	
507004	64388+71345+64408	BD	MER	ANG	MER	*Bob Paisley*
507005	64371+71346+64409	BD	MER	ANG	MER	
507006	64372+71347+64410	BD	MER	ANG	MER	
507007	64373+71348+64411	BD	MER	ANG	MER	
507008	64374+71349+64412	BD	MER	ANG	MER	
507009	64375+71350+64413	BD	MER	ANG	MER	*Dixie Dean*
507010	64376+71351+64414	BD	MER	ANG	MER	
507011	64377+71352+64415	BD	MER	ANG	MER	
507012	64378+71353+64416	BD	MER	ANG	MER	

507013	64379+71354+64417	BD	MER	ANG	MER	
507014	64380+71355+64418	BD	MER	ANG	MER	
507015	64381+71356+64419	BD	MER	ANG	MER	
507016	64382+71357+64420	BD	MER	ANG	MER	
507017	64383+71358+64421	BD	MER	ANG	MER	
507018	64384+71359+64422	BD	MER	ANG	MER	
507019	64385+71360+64423	BD	MER	ANG	MER	
507020	64386+71361+64424	BD	MER	ANG	MER	*John Peel*
507021	64387+71362+64425	BD	MER	ANG	MER	*Red Rum*
507023	64389+71364+64427	BD	MER	ANG	MER	
507024	64390+71365+64428	BD	MER	ANG	MER	
507025	64391+71366+64429	BD	MER	ANG	MER	
507026	64392+71367+64430	BD	MER	ANG	MER	
507027	64393+71368+64431	BD	MER	ANG	MER	
507028	64394+71369+64432	BD	MER	ANG	MER	
507029	64395+71370+64433	BD	MER	ANG	MER	
507030	64396+71371+64434	BD	MER	ANG	MER	
507031	64397+71372+64435	BD	MER	ANG	MER	
507032	64398+71373+64436	BD	MER	ANG	MER	
507033	64399+71374+64437	BD	MER	ANG	MER	*Cllr George Howard*

Class 508

Vehicle Length: (Driving) 64ft 11½in (19.80m)
(Inter) 65ft 4¼in (19.92m)
Height: 11ft 6½in (3.58m)
Width: 9ft 3in (2.82m)
Horsepower: 880hp (656kW)
Seats (total/car): 186S, 56S/74S/56S

Number	*Formation* DMSO+TSO+DBMSO	*Depot*	*Livery*	*Owner*	*Operator*	*Name*
508103	64651+71485+64694	BD	MER	ANG	MER	
508104	64652+71486+64964	BD	MER	ANG	MER	
508108	64656+71490+64699	BD	MER	ANG	MER	
508110	64658+71492+64701	BD	MER	ANG	MER	
508111	64659+71493+64702	BD	MER	ANG	MER	
508112	64660+71494+64703	BD	MER	ANG	MER	
508114	64662+71496+64705	BD	MER	ANG	MER	
508115	64663+71497+64708	BD	MER	ANG	MER	
508117	64665+71499+64908	BD	MER	ANG	MER	
508120	64668+71502+64711	BD	MER	ANG	MER	
508122	64670+71504+64713	BD	MER	ANG	MER	
508123	64671+71505+64714	BD	MER	ANG	MER	
508124	64672+71506+64715	BD	MER	ANG	MER	
508125	64673+71507+64716	BD	MER	ANG	MER	
508126	64674+71508+64717	BD	MER	ANG	MER	
508127	64675+71509+64718	BD	MER	ANG	MER	
508128	64676+71510+64719	BD	MER	ANG	MER	
508130	64678+71512+64721	BD	MER	ANG	MER	
508131	64679+71513+64722	BD	MER	ANG	MER	
508134	64682+71516+64725	BD	MER	ANG	MER	
508136	64684+71518+64727	BD	MER	ANG	MER	*Capital of Culture*
508137	64685+71519+64728	BD	MER	ANG	MER	
508138	64686+71520+64729	BD	MER	ANG	MER	
508139	64687+71521+64730	BD	MER	ANG	MER	
508140	64688+71522+64731	BD	MER	ANG	MER	
508141	64689+71523+64732	BD	MER	ANG	MER	
508143	64691+71525+64734	BD	MER	ANG	MER	

Right: *One of the Class 508/1 fleet arried advertising livery until late)09, No. 508134, illustrated here Southport. The livery was for the erpool European Capital of Culture, had a mauve centre section, in ort of creativity.*
an Williamson

National Express East Anglia

Address: ✉ Floor One, Oliver's Yard, 55 City Road, London, EC1[illegible]
nxea.customerreleations@nationalexpress.com
✆ 0845 600 7245
ⓘ www.nationalexpresseastanglia.com

Managing Director: Andrew Chivers

Franchise Dates: 1 April 2004 - 31 March 2011

Principal Routes: London Liverpool Street to Norwich, Cambridge, Enfield Town, Hertford East, Upminster, Southend Victoria, Southminster, Braintree, Sudbury, Clacton, Walton, Harwich Town, Felixstowe, Lowestoft, Great Yarmouth, Sherringham, Stansted Airport and Peterborough

Depots: Ilford (IL), Norwich (NC)

Parent Company: National Express

Class 90/0

Vehicle Length: 61ft 6in (18.74m)
Height: 13ft 0¼in (3.96m)
Width: 9ft 0in (2.74m)
Power Collection: 25kV ac overhead
Horsepower: 7,860hp (5,860kW)
Electrical Equipment: GEC

Number	*Depot*	*Pool*	*Livery*	*Owner*	*Operator*	*Name*
90001	NC	IANA	ORN	PTR	NXA	
90002	NC	IANA	ORN	PTR	NXA	
90003	NC	IANA	NXA	PTR	NXA	*Raedwald of East Anglia*
90004	NC	IANA	ORN	PTR	NXA	
90005	NC	IANA	ORN	PTR	NXA	*Vice-Admiral Lord Nelson*
90006	NC	IANA	ORN	PTR	NXA	*Roger Ford / Modern Railways*
90007	NC	IANA	ORN	PTR	NXA	*Sir John Betjeman*
90008	NC	IANA	NXA	PTR	NXA	
90009	NC	IANA	ORN	PTR	NXA	
90010	NC	IANA	ORN	PTR	NXA	
90011	NC	IANA	ORN	PTR	NXA	*Let's Go - East of England*
90012	NC	IANA	ORN	PTR	NXA	*Royal Anglian Regiment*
90013	NC	IANA	ORN	PTR	NXA	
90014	NC	IANA	ORN	PTR	NXA	*Norfolk and Norwich Festival*
90015	NC	IANA	NXA	PTR	NXA	*Colchester Castle*

Left: *National Express corporate branding is now being applied to the East Anglia business unit. Class 90s are painted in all over grey/silver w a white angled band onto which th National Express name is applied.* 90015 Colchester Castle *is seen Ipswich.* **Nathan Williamson**

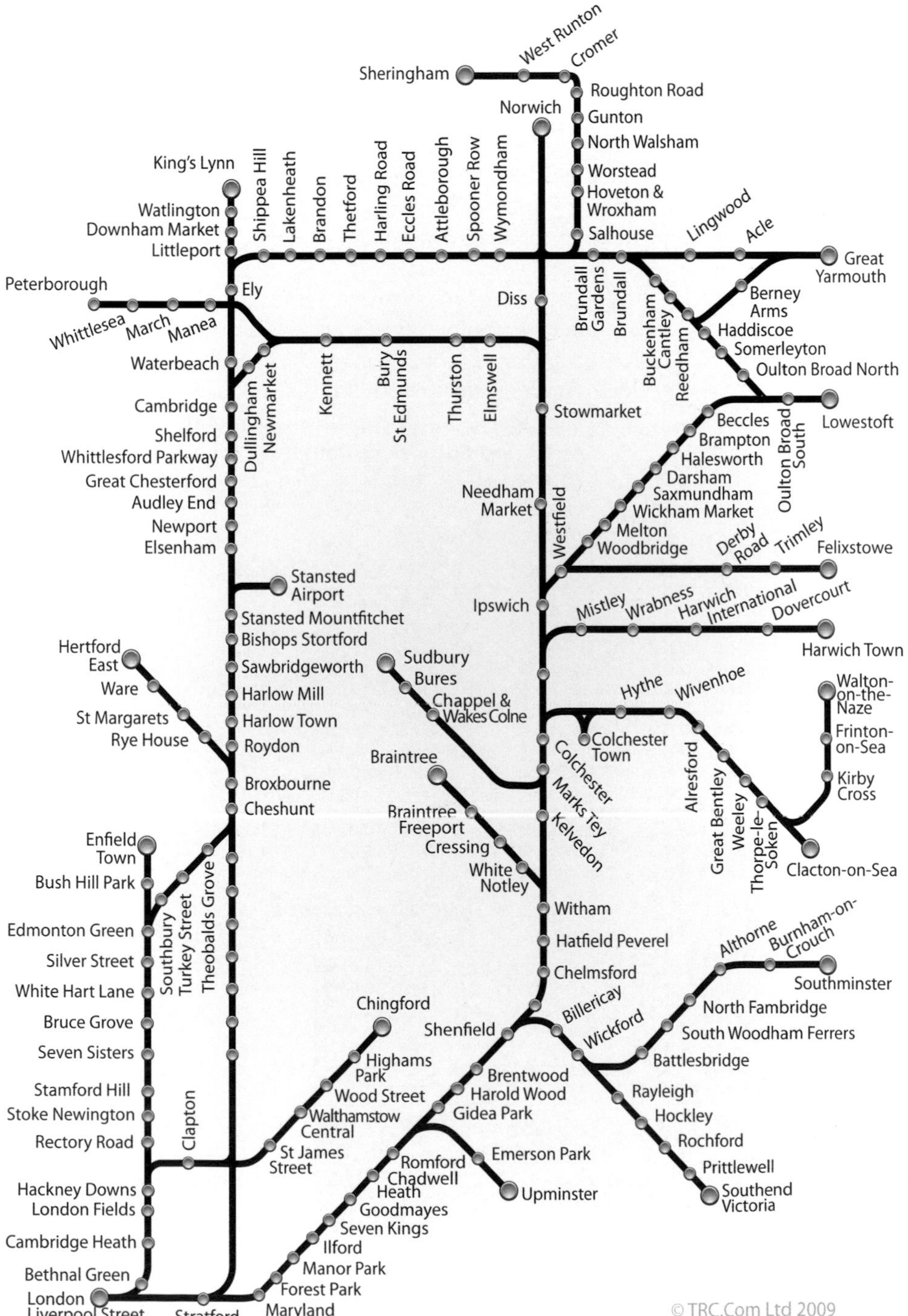

Sheringham
West Runton
Cromer
Roughton Road
Gunton
North Walsham
Worstead
Hoveton & Wroxham
Salhouse
Norwich
King's Lynn
Watlington
Downham Market
Littleport
Shippea Hill
Lakenheath
Brandon
Thetford
Harling Road
Eccles Road
Attleborough
Spooner Row
Wymondham
Lingwood
Acle
Great Yarmouth
Brundall Gardens
Brundall
Buckenham
Cantley
Reedham
Berney Arms
Haddiscoe
Somerleyton
Oulton Broad North
Lowestoft
Oulton Broad South
Peterborough
Whittlesea
March
Manea
Ely
Diss
Waterbeach
Dullingham
Newmarket
Kennett
Bury St Edmunds
Thurston
Elmswell
Stowmarket
Cambridge
Shelford
Whittlesford Parkway
Great Chesterford
Audley End
Newport
Elsenham
Beccles
Brampton
Halesworth
Darsham
Saxmundham
Wickham Market
Melton
Woodbridge
Needham Market
Westfield
Derby Road
Trimley
Felixstowe
Stansted Airport
Stansted Mountfitchet
Bishops Stortford
Sawbridgeworth
Harlow Mill
Harlow Town
Roydon
Broxbourne
Cheshunt
Ipswich
Mistley
Wrabness
Harwich International
Dovercourt
Harwich Town
Hertford East
Ware
St Margarets
Rye House
Sudbury
Bures
Chappel & Wakes Colne
Hythe
Wivenhoe
Colchester Town
Walton-on-the-Naze
Frinton-on-Sea
Kirby Cross
Braintree
Braintree Freeport
Cressing
White Notley
Colchester
Marks Tey
Kelvedon
Alresford
Great Bentley
Weeley
Thorpe-le-Soken
Clacton-on-Sea
Enfield Town
Bush Hill Park
Edmonton Green
Silver Street
White Hart Lane
Bruce Grove
Seven Sisters
Stamford Hill
Stoke Newington
Rectory Road
Hackney Downs
London Fields
Cambridge Heath
Bethnal Green
London Liverpool Street
Southbury
Turkey Street
Theobalds Grove
Clapton
Stratford
Witham
Hatfield Peverel
Chelmsford
Althorne
Burnham-on-Crouch
Southminster
Chingford
Highams Park
Wood Street
Walthamstow Central
St James Street
Shenfield
Billericay
Wickford
North Fambridge
South Woodham Ferrers
Battlesbridge
Brentwood
Harold Wood
Gidea Park
Emerson Park
Upminster
Romford
Chadwell Heath
Goodmayes
Seven Kings
Ilford
Manor Park
Forest Park
Maryland
Rayleigh
Hockley
Rochford
Prittlewell
Southend Victoria
© TRC.Com Ltd 2009

Mk 3 Hauled Stock

Vehicle Length: 75ft 0in (22.86m) Height: 12ft 9in (3.88m) Width: 8ft 11in (2.71m) Bogie Type: BT10

AJ1G - RFM *Seating 24F*

Number	*Depot*	*Livery*	*Owner*
10200 (40519)	NC	ORN	PTR
10203 (40506)	NC	NXA	PTR
10206 (40507)	NC	ORN	PTR
10214 (11034)	NC	ORN	PTR
10216 (11041)	NC	ORN	PTR
10223 (11043)	NC	ORN	PTR
10228 (11035)	NC	NXA	PTR
10229 (11059)	NC	ORN	PTR
10241 (10009)	NC	NXA	PTR
10247 (10011)	NC	ORN	PTR

AN2G - TSOB *Seating 52S*

Number	Depot	Livery	Owner
10401 (12168)	NC	NXA	PTR
10402 (12010)	NC	ORN	PTR
10403 (12135)	NC	ORN	PTR
10404 (12068)	NC	ORN	PTR
10405 (12137)	NC	ORN	PTR
10406 (12020)	NC	ORN	PTR

AD1G - FO, *FOD *Seating 48F/34F**

Number	Depot	Livery	Owner
11021 (S)	NC	VTS	PTR
11066	NC	ORN	PTR
11067	NC	ORN	PTR
11068	NC	NXA	PTR
11069	NC	ORN	PTR
11070	NC	ORN	PTR
11072*	NC	ORN	PTR
11073*	NC	NXA	PTR
11074 (S)	NC	VTS	PTR
11075	NC	ORN	PTR
11076	NC	ORN	PTR
11077	NC	ORN	PTR
11078*	NC	ORN	PTR
11080	NC	ORN	PTR
11081	NC	ORN	PTR
11082	NC	NXA	PTR
11085*	NC	ORN	PTR
11087*	NC	NXA	PTR
11088*	NC	NXA	PTR
11090*	NC	ORN	PTR
11091*	NC	NXA	PTR
11092	NC	ORN	PTR
11093*	NC	ORN	PTR
11094*	NC	ORN	PTR
11095*	NC	ORN	PTR
11096*	NC	ORN	PTR
11098*	NC	ORN	PTR
11099*	NC	ORN	PTR
11100*	NC	NXA	PTR
11101*	NC	ORN	PTR

AC2G - TSO *Seating 80S*

Number	Depot	Livery	Owner
12005	NC	ORN	PTR
12009	NC	ORN	PTR
12012	NC	ORN	PTR
12013	NC	ORN	PTR
12015	NC	ORN	PTR
12016	NC	ORN	PTR
12019	NC	ORN	PTR
12021	NC	NXA	PTR
12024	NC	ORN	PTR
12026	NC	ORN	PTR
12027	NC	NXA	PTR
12030	NC	ORN	PTR
12031	NC	ORN	PTR
12032	NC	ORN	PTR
12034	NC	ORN	PTR
12035	NC	NXA	PTR
12037	NC	ORN	PTR
12040	NC	ORN	PTR
12041	NC	ORN	PTR
12042	NC	ORN	PTR
12046	NC	ORN	PTR
12049	NC	ORN	PTR
12051	NC	NXA	PTR
12056	NC	ORN	PTR
12057	NC	ORN	PTR
12060	NC	ORN	PTR
12061	NC	ORN	PTR
12062	NC	ORN	PTR
12063 (S)	NC	VIR	PTR
12064	NC	ORN	PTR
12065 (S)	NC	VIR	PTR
12066	NC	ORN	PTR
12067	NC	ORN	PTR
12073	NC	ORN	PTR
12079	NC	ORN	PTR
12081	NC	ORN	PTR
12082	NC	ORN	PTR
12084	NC	NXA	PTR
12089	NC	ORN	PTR
12090	NC	ORN	PTR
12091	NC	ORN	PTR
12092 (S)	NC	VIR	PTR
12093	NC	ORN	PTR
12097	NC	NXA	PTR
12098	NC	ORN	PTR
12099	NC	ORN	PTR
12103	NC	ORN	PTR
12105	NC	ORN	PTR
12107	NC	ORN	PTR
12108	NC	NXA	PTR
12109	NC	ORN	PTR
12110	NC	ORN	PTR
12111	NC	NXA	PTR
12114	NC	NXA	PTR
12115	NC	ORN	PTR
12116	NC	ORN	PTR
12118	NC	NXA	PTR
12120	NC	ORN	PTR
12125	NC	ORN	PTR
12126	NC	ORN	PTR
12129	NC	NXA	PTR
12130	NC	ORN	PTR
12132	NC	NXA	PTR
12137	NC	ORN	PTR
12139 (S)	NC	VIR	PTR
12141	NC	ORN	PTR
12143	NC	ORN	PTR
12146	NC	NXA	PTR
12147	NC	ORN	PTR
12148	NC	ORN	PTR
12150	NC	ORN	PTR
12151	NC	ORN	PTR
12153	NC	NXA	PTR
12154	NC	ORN	PTR
12159	NC	ORN	PTR
12164	NC	ORN	PTR
12166	NC	ORN	PTR
12167	NC	ORN	PTR
12170	NC	ORN	PTR
12171	NC	ORN	PTR

NZAH - DVT

Number	Depot	Livery	Owner
82102	NC	ORN	PTR
82103	NC	ORN	PTR
82104	NC	ORN	PTR
82105	NC	ORN	PTR
82107	NC	NXA	PTR
82112	NC	ORN	PTR
82114	NC	ORN	PTR
82118	NC	NXA	PTR
82121	NC	ORN	PTR
82127	NC	ORN	PTR
82132	NC	ORN	PTR
82133	NC	ORN	PTR
82136	NC	ORN	PTR
82139	NC	ORN	PTR
82143	NC	NXA	PTR
82152	NC	ORN	PTR

Left: *Displaying the interim National Express East Anglia livery of one Railway blue and grey with National Express legend on a white stripe, Mk3 DVT No. 82121 departs south from Ipswich bound for London Liverpool Street on 18 November 2008.*
Nathan Williamson

Class 153

Vehicle Length: 76ft 5in (23.29m)
Height: 12ft 3⅛in (3.75m)
Width: 8ft 10in (2.70m)
Engine: 1 x NT855R5 of 285hp
Horsepower: 285hp (213kW)
Seats (total/car): 72S

Number	*Formation DMSL*	*Depot*	*Livery*	*Owner*	*Operator*	*Name*
153306	**52306**	**NC**	**ORN**	**PTR**	**NXA**	
153309	**52309**	**NC**	**ORN**	**PTR**	**NXA**	***Gerard Fiennes***
153314	**52314**	**NC**	**ORN**	**PTR**	**NXA**	
153322	**52322**	**NC**	**ORN**	**PTR**	**NXA**	***Benjamin Britten***
153335	**52335**	**NC**	**ANN**	**PTR**	**NXA**	***Michael Palin***

Right: *National Express East Anglia operate five Class 153 'Bubble' cars on rural branch line services in Norfolk. Painted in early Anglia Railways turquoise and white but now with National Express East Anglia branding, car No. 153335 leads another of the fleet, showing the later One Anglia colours. Note the brushed aluminium* Michael Palin *nameplate behind the leading door.*
Jamie Squibbs

Class 156

Vehicle Length: 75ft 6in (23.03m)
Height: 12ft 6in (3.81m)
Width: 8ft 11in (2.73m)
Engine: 1 x Cummins NT855R5 of 285hp
Horsepower: 570hp (425kW)
Seats (total/car): 146S, 70/76S

Number	*Formation DMSL+DMS*	*Depot*	*Livery*	*Owner*	*Operator*
156402	**52402+57402**	**NC**	**ORN**	**PTR**	**NXA**
156407	**52407+57407**	**NC**	**ORN**	**PTR**	**NXA**
156409	**52409+57409**	**NC**	**ORN**	**PTR**	**NXA**
156412	**52412+57412**	**NC**	**ORN**	**PTR**	**NXA**
156416	**52416+57416**	**NC**	**ORN**	**PTR**	**NXA**
156417	**52417+57417**	**NC**	**ORN**	**PTR**	**NXA**
156418	**52418+57418**	**NC**	**ORN**	**PTR**	**NXA**
156419	**52419+57419**	**NC**	**NXA**	**PTR**	**NXA**
156422	**52422+57422**	**NC**	**ORN**	**PTR**	**NXA**

Above: *A start was made in 2008 to repaint the Class 156 fleet allocated to Norwich into the latest National Express white and grey colours. Set No. 156419 is illustrated at Norwich.* **Tony Christie**

National Express East Anglia

Class 170/2
Turbostar

Vehicle Length: 77ft 6in (23.62m)
Height: 12ft 4½in (3.77m)
Width: 8ft 10in (2.69m)
Engine: 1 x MTU 6R 183TD13H 422hp per vehicle
Horsepower: 1,266hp (944kW)
Seats (total/car): 7F-173S 7F-39S/68S/66S

Number	Formation DMCL+MSL+DMSL	Depot	Livery	Owner	Operator
170201	50201+56201+79201	NC	ORN	PTR	NXA
170202	50202+56202+79202	NC	ORN	PTR	NXA
170203	50203+56203+79203	NC	ORN	PTR	NXA
170204	50204+56204+79204	NC	ORN	PTR	NXA
170205	50205+56205+79205	NC	ORN	PTR	NXA
170206	50206+56206+79206	NC	ORN	PTR	NXA
170207	50207+56207+79207	NC	ORN	PTR	NXA
170208	50208+56208+79208	NC	ORN	PTR	NXA

Vehicle Length: 77ft 6in (23.62m)
Height: 12ft 4½in (3.77m)
Width: 8ft 10in (2.69m)
Engine: 1 x MTU 6R 183TD13H 422hp per vehicle
Horsepower: 844hp (629kW)
Seats (total/car): 9F-110S 57S/9F-53S

Number	Formation DMSL+DMCL	Depot	Livery	Owner	Operator
170270	50270+79270	NC	ORN	PTR	NXA
170271	50271+79271	NC	ORN	PTR	NXA
170272	50272+79272	NC	ORN	PTR	NXA
170273	50273+79273	NC	ORN	PTR	NXA

Left: *Both two and three-car versions of the Class 170 'Turbostar' product line operate on National Express East Anglia. The three car sets are frequently seen on longer distance services working to/from London Liverpool Street, while the two-car sets principally operate in the Norwich area. National Express-branded blue livery is seen applied to set No. 170204 passing Stratford in East London.* **Tony Christie**

Class 315

Vehicle Length: (Driving) 64ft 11½in (19.80m)
(Inter) 65ft 4¼in (19.92m)
Height: 11ft 6½in (3.58m)
Width: 9ft 3in (2.82m)
Horsepower: 880hp (656kW)
Seats (total/car): 318S, 74S/86S/84S/74S

Number	Formation DMSO(A)+TSO+PTSO+DMSO(B)	Depot	Livery	Owner	Operator	Name
315801	64461+71281+71389+64462	IL	ORN	HSB	NXA	
315802	64463+71282+71390+64464	IL	ORN	HSB	NXA	
315803	64465+71283+71391+64466	IL	ORN	HSB	NXA	
315804	64467+71284+71392+64468	IL	ORN	HSB	NXA	
315805	64469+71285+71393+64470	IL	ORN	HSB	NXA	
315806	64471+71286+71394+64472	IL	ORN	HSB	NXA	
315807	64473+71287+71395+64474	IL	ORN	HSB	NXA	
315808	64475+71288+71396+64476	IL	ORN	HSB	NXA	
315809	64477+71289+71397+64478	IL	ORN	HSB	NXA	
315810	64479+71290+71398+64480	IL	ORN	HSB	NXA	
315811	64481+71291+71399+64482	IL	ORN	HSB	NXA	
315812	64483+71292+71400+64484	IL	ORN	HSB	NXA	London Borough of Newham Host Borough 2012 Olympics Bid
315813	64485+71293+71401+64486	IL	ORN	HSB	NXA	
315814	64487+71294+71402+64488	IL	ORN	HSB	NXA	
315815	64489+71295+71403+64490	IL	ORN	HSB	NXA	
315816	64491+71296+71404+64492	IL	ORN	HSB	NXA	
315817	64493+71297+71405+64494	IL	ORN	HSB	NXA	Transport for London
315818	64495+71298+71406+64496	IL	ORN	HSB	NXA	

315819	64497+71299+71407+64498	IL	ORN	HSB	NXA	
315820	64499+71300+71408+64500	IL	ORN	HSB	NXA	
315821	64501+71301+71409+64502	IL	ORN	HSB	NXA	
315822	64503+71302+71410+64504	IL	ORN	HSB	NXA	
315823	64505+71303+71411+64506	IL	ORN	HSB	NXA	
315824	64507+71304+71412+64508	IL	ORN	HSB	NXA	
315825	64509+71305+71413+64510	IL	ORN	HSB	NXA	
315826	64511+71306+71414+64512	IL	ORN	HSB	NXA	
315827	64513+71307+71415+64514	IL	ORN	HSB	NXA	
315828	64515+71308+71416+64516	IL	ORN	HSB	NXA	
315829	64517+71309+71417+64518	IL	ORN	HSB	NXA	*London Borough of Havering Celebrating 40 years*
315830	64519+71310+71418+64520	IL	ORN	HSB	NXA	
315831	64521+71311+71419+64522	IL	ORN	HSB	NXA	
315832	64523+71312+71420+64524	IL	ORN	HSB	NXA	
315833	64525+71313+71421+64526	IL	ORN	HSB	NXA	
315834	64527+71314+71422+64528	IL	ORN	HSB	NXA	
315835	64529+71315+71423+64530	IL	ORN	HSB	NXA	
315836	64531+71316+71424+64532	IL	ORN	HSB	NXA	
315837	64533+71317+71425+64534	IL	ORN	HSB	NXA	
315838	64535+71318+71426+64536	IL	ORN	HSB	NXA	
315839	64537+71319+71427+64538	IL	ORN	HSB	NXA	
315840	64539+71320+71428+64540	IL	ORN	HSB	NXA	
315841	64541+71321+71429+64542	IL	ORN	HSB	NXA	
315842	64543+71322+71430+64544	IL	ORN	HSB	NXA	
315843	64545+71323+71431+64546	IL	ORN	HSB	NXA	
315844	64547+71324+71432+64548	IL	ORN	HSB	NXA	
315845	64549+71325+71433+64550	IL	ORN	HSB	NXA	*Herbie Woodward*
315846	64551+71326+71434+64552	IL	ORN	HSB	NXA	
315847	64553+71327+71435+64554	IL	ORN	HSB	NXA	
315848	64555+71328+71436+64556	IL	ORN	HSB	NXA	
315849	64557+71329+71437+64558	IL	ORN	HSB	NXA	
315850	64559+71330+71438+64560	IL	ORN	HSB	NXA	
315851	64561+71331+71439+64562	IL	ORN	HSB	NXA	
315852	64563+71332+71440+64564	IL	ORN	HSB	NXA	
315853	64565+71333+71441+64566	IL	ORN	HSB	NXA	
315854	64567+71334+71442+64568	IL	ORN	HSB	NXA	
315855	64569+71335+71443+64570	IL	ORN	HSB	NXA	
315856	64571+71336+71444+64572	IL	ORN	HSB	NXA	
315857	64573+71337+71445+64574	IL	ORN	HSB	NXA	
315858	64575+71338+71446+64576	IL	ORN	HSB	NXA	
315859	64577+71339+71447+64578	IL	ORN	HSB	NXA	
315860	64579+71340+71448+64580	IL	ORN	HSB	NXA	
315861	64581+71341+71449+64582	IL	ORN	HSB	NXA	

Below: *The suburban units operating on National Express East Anglia (Great Eastern Lines) are all based on the 1972-design of high-density BREL York built train sets. Great Eastern sets are four-car formation of Class 315 and allocated to Ilford depot in Essex. Set No. 315857 is seen at Stratford. The set's PTSO vehicle is second from the front.* **CJM**

National Express East Anglia

Class 317/5

Vehicle Length: (Driving) 65ft 0¾in (19.83m) (Inter) 65ft 4¼in (19.92m)
Height: 12ft 1½in (3.58m)
Width: 9ft 3in (2.82m)
Horsepower: 1,000hp (746kW)
Seats (total/car): 291S, 74S/79S/68S/70S

Number	Former Number	Formation DTSO(A)+MSO+TCO+DTSO(B)	Depot	Livery	Owner	Operator	Name
317501	(317301)	77024+62661+71577+77048	IL	NXA	ANG	NXA	
317502	(317302)	77001+62662+71578+77049	IL	NXA	ANG	NXA	
317503	(317303)	77002+62663+71579+77050	IL	NXA	ANG	NXA	
317504	(317304)	77003+62664+71580+77051	IL	NXA	ANG	NXA	
317505	(317305)	77004+62665+71581+77052	IL	NXA	ANG	NXA	
317506	(317306)	77005+62666+71582+77053	IL	NXA	ANG	NXA	
317507	(317307)	77006+62667+71583+77054	IL	NXA	ANG	NXA	University of Cambridge 800 years 1209-2009
317508	(317311)	77010+62697+71587+77058	IL	NXA	ANG	NXA	
317509	(317312)	77011+62672+71588+77059	IL	NXA	ANG	NXA	
317510	(317313)	77012+62673+71589+77060	IL	NXA	ANG	NXA	
317511	(317315)	77014+62675+71591+77062	IL	ORN	ANG	NXA	
317512	(317316)	77015+62676+71592+77063	IL	ORN	ANG	NXA	
317513	(317317)	77016+62677+71593+77064	IL	NXA	ANG	NXA	
317514	(317318)	77017+62678+71594+77065	IL	NXA	ANG	NXA	
317515	(317320)	77019+62680+71596+77067	IL	NXA	ANG	NXA	

Above: *Members of the various Class 317 sub-classes are currently being repainted into the corporate National Express grey and white livery, as shown on Class 317/5 No. 317508. This set was originally numbered 317311 in its BR 'Bed-Pan' days.* **Brian Morrison**

Class 317/6

Vehicle Length: (Driving) 65ft 0¾in (19.83m) (Inter) 65ft 4¼in (19.92m)
Height: 12ft 1½in (3.58m)
Width: 9ft 3in (2.82m)
Horsepower: 1,000hp (746kW)
Seats (total/car): 24F/200S, 64S/70S/62S/24F-48S

Number	Former Number	Formation DTSO+MSO+TSO+DTCO	Depot	Livery	Owner	Operator	Name
317649	(317349)	77200+62846+71734+77220	IL	ORN	ANG	NXA	
317650	(317350)	77201+62847+71735+77221	IL	ORN	ANG	NXA	
317651	(317351)	77202+62848+71736+77222	IL	ORN	ANG	NXA	
317652	(317352)	77203+62849+71739+77223	IL	ORN	ANG	NXA	
317653	(317353)	77204+62850+71738+77224	IL	ORN	ANG	NXA	
317654	(317354)	77205+62851+71737+77225	IL	ORN	ANG	NXA	Richard Wells
317655	(317355)	77206+62852+71740+77226	IL	ORN	ANG	NXA	
317656	(317356)	77207+62853+71742+77227	IL	ORN	ANG	NXA	
317657	(317357)	77208+62854+71741+77228	IL	ORN	ANG	NXA	
317658	(317358)	77209+62855+71743+77229	IL	ORN	ANG	NXA	
317659	(317359)	77210+62856+71744+77230	IL	ORN	ANG	NXA	

Number	Former Number	Formation	Depot	Livery	Owner	Operator	Name
317660	(317360)	77211+62857+71745+77231	IL	ORN	ANG	NXA	
317661	(317361)	77212+62858+71746+77232	IL	ORN	ANG	NXA	
317662	(317362)	77213+62859+71747+77233	IL	ORN	ANG	NXA	
317663	(317363)	77214+62860+71748+77234	IL	ORN	ANG	NXA	
317664	(317364)	77215+62861+71749+77235	IL	ORN	ANG	NXA	
317665	(317365)	77216+62862+71750+77236	IL	ORN	ANG	NXA	
317666	(317366)	77217+62863+71752+77237	IL	ORN	ANG	NXA	
317667	(317367)	77218+62864+71751+77238	IL	ORN	ANG	NXA	
317668	(317368)	77219+62865+71753+77239	IL	ORN	ANG	NXA	
317669	(317369)	77280+62886+71762+77284	IL	ORN	ANG	NXA	
317670	(317370)	77281+62887+71763+77285	IL	ORN	ANG	NXA	
317671	(317371)	77282+62888+71764+77286	IL	ORN	ANG	NXA	
317672	(317372)	77283+62889+71765+77287	IL	ORN	ANG	NXA	

Class 317/7

Vehicle Length: (Driving) 65ft 0¾in (19.83m) (Inter) 65ft 4¼in (19.92m)
Height: 12ft 1½in (3.58m)
Width: 9ft 3in (2.82m)
Horsepower: 1,000hp (746kW)
Seats (total/car): 22F/172S, 52S/62S/42S/22F-16S

Number	*Former Number*	*Formation* DTSO+MSO+TSO+DTCO	*Depot*	*Livery*	*Owner*	*Operator*	*Name*
317708	(317308)	77007+62668+71584+77055	IL	NXA	ANG	NXA	
317709	(317309)	77008+62669+71585+77056	IL	NXA	ANG	NXA	*Len Camp*
317710	(317310)	77009+62670+71586+77057	IL	NXA	ANG	NXA	
317714	(317314)	77013+62674+71590+77061	IL	NXA	ANG	NXA	
317719	(317319)	77018+62679+71595+77066	IL	NXA	ANG	NXA	
317722	(317322/392)	77021+62682+71598+77069	IL	NXA	ANG	NXA	
317723	(317323/393)	77022+62683+71599+77070	IL	NXA	ANG	NXA	*The Tottenham Flyer*
317729	(317329)	77028+62689+71605+77076	IL	NXA	ANG	NXA	
317732	(317332)	77031+62692+71608+77079	IL	NXA	ANG	NXA	

Right: *The nine members of Class 317/7, allocated to Ilford and modified for London Liverpool Street to Stansted Airport workings, have a slightly revised front end layout. The roof line was straightened to incorporate a roof level headlight, while new front end lamp cluster groups were fitted. Set No. 317714 is seen inside Ilford depot.* **CJM**

Class 317/8

Vehicle Length: (Driving) 65ft 0¾in (19.83m) (Inter) 65ft 4¼in (19.92m)
Height: 12ft 1½in (3.58m)
Width: 9ft 3in (2.82m)
Horsepower: 1,000hp (746kW)
Seats (total/car): 20F/265S, 74S/79S/20F-42S/70S

Number	*Former Number*	*Formation* DTSO(A)+MSO+TCO+DTSO(B)	*Depot*	*Livery*	*Owner*	*Operator*	*Name*
317881	(317321)	77020+62681+71597+77068	IL	NXA	ANG	NXA	
317882	(317324)	77023+62684+71600+77071	IL	STN	ANG	NXA	
317883	(317325)	77000+62685+71601+77072	IL	STN	ANG	NXA	
317884	(317326)	77025+62686+71602+77073	IL	STN	ANG	NXA	
317885	(317327)	77026+62687+71603+77074	IL	STN	ANG	NXA	
317886	(317328)	77027+62688+71604+77075	IL	STN	ANG	NXA	
317887	(317330)	77043+62704+71606+77077	IL	NXA	ANG	NXA	
17888	(317331)	77030+62691+71607+77078	IL	NXA	ANG	NXA	
17889	(317333)	77032+62693+71609+77080	IL	NXA	ANG	NXA	
7890	(317334)	77033+62694+71610+77081	IL	NXA	ANG	NXA	
7891	(317335)	77034+62695+71611+77082	IL	NXA	ANG	NXA	
892	(317336)	77035+62696+71612+77083	IL	NXA	ANG	NXA	*Ilford Depot*

Class 321/3

Vehicle Length: (Driving) 65ft 0¾in (19.83m)
(Inter) 65ft [illegible]in (19.92m)
Height: 12ft 4¾in ([illegible].78m)
Width: 9ft 3in (2.82m)
Horsepower: 1,328hp (996kW)
Seats (total/car): 16F/292S, 16F-57S/82S/75S/78S

Number	*Formation* DTCO+MSO+TSO+DTSO	*Depot*	*Livery*	*Owner*	*Operator*	*Name*
321301	78049+62975+71880+77853	IL	NXA	HSB	NXA	
321302	78050+62976+71881+77854	IL	NXA	HSB	NXA	
321303	78051+62977+71882+77855	IL	NXA	HSB	NXA	
321304	78052+62978+71883+77856	IL	NXA	HSB	NXA	
321305	78053+62979+71884+77857	IL	NXA	HSB	NXA	
321306	78054+62980+71885+77858	IL	NXA	HSB	NXA	
321307	78055+62981+71886+77859	IL	NXA	HSB	NXA	
321308	78056+62982+71887+77860	IL	NXA	HSB	NXA	
321309	78057+62983+71888+77861	IL	NXA	HSB	NXA	
321310	78058+62984+71889+77862	IL	NGE	HSB	NXA	
321311	78059+62985+71890+77863	IL	NXA	HSB	NXA	
321312	78060+62986+71891+77864	IL	NXA	HSB	NXA	*Southend-on-Sea*
321313	78061+62987+71892+77865	IL	NXA	HSB	NXA	*University of Essex*
321314	78062+62988+71893+77866	IL	NGE	HSB	NXA	
321315	78063+62989+71894+77867	IL	NGE	HSB	NXA	
321316	78064+62990+71895+77868	IL	NXA	HSB	NXA	
321317	78065+62991+71896+77869	IL	NXA	HSB	NXA	
321318	78066+62992+71897+77870	IL	NXA	HSB	NXA	
321319	78067+62993+71898+77871	IL	NXA	HSB	NXA	
321320	78068+62994+71899+77872	IL	NXA	HSB	NXA	
321321	78069+62995+71900+77873	IL	NXA	HSB	NXA	*NSPCC Essex Full Stop*
321322	78070+62996+71901+77874	IL	NGE	HSB	NXA	
321323	78071+62997+71902+77875	IL	NGE	HSB	NXA	
321324	78072+62998+71903+77876	IL	NGE	HSB	NXA	
321325	78073+62999+71904+77877	IL	NGE	HSB	NXA	
321326	78074+63000+71905+77878	IL	NGE	HSB	NXA	
321327	78075+63001+71906+77879	IL	NGE	HSB	NXA	
321328	78076+63002+71907+77880	IL	NGE	HSB	NXA	
321329	78077+63003+71908+77881	IL	NGE	HSB	NXA	
321330	78078+63004+71910+77883	IL	NGE	HSB	NXA	
321332	78080+63006+71911+77884	IL	NGE	HSB	NXA	
321333	78081+63007+71912+77885	IL	NGE	HSB	NXA	
321334	78082+63008+71913+77886	IL	NGE	HSB	NXA	*Amsterdam*
321335	78083+63009+71914+77887	IL	NGE	HSB	NXA	
321336	78084+63010+71915+77888	IL	NGE	HSB	NXA	*Geoffrey Freeman Allen*
321337	78085+63011+71916+77889	IL	NGE	HSB	NXA	
321338	78086+63012+71917+77890	IL	NGE	HSB	NXA	
321339	78087+63013+71918+77891	IL	NGE	HSB	NXA	
321340	78088+63014+71919+77892	IL	NGE	HSB	NXA	
321341	78089+63015+71920+77893	IL	NGE	HSB	NXA	
321342	78090+63016+71921+77894	IL	NGE	HSB	NXA	
321343	78091+63017+71922+77895	IL	NGE	HSB	NXA	*RSA Railway Study Association*
321344	78092+63018+71923+77896	IL	NGE	HSB	NXA	
321345	78093+63019+71924+77897	IL	NGE	HSB	NXA	
321346	78094+63020+71925+77898	IL	NGE	HSB	NXA	
321347	78131+63105+71991+78280	IL	NGE	HSB	NXA	
321348	78132+63106+71992+78281	IL	NGE	HSB	NXA	
321349	78133+63107+71993+78282	IL	NGE	HSB	NXA	
321350	78134+63108+71994+78283	IL	NGE	HSB	NXA	
321351	78135+63109+71995+78284	IL	NGE	HSB	NXA	*Gurkha*
321352	78136+63110+71996+78285	IL	NGE	HSB	NXA	
321353	78137+63111+71997+78286	IL	NGE	HSB	NXA	
321354	78138+63112+71998+78287	IL	NGE	HSB	NXA	
321355	78139+63113+71999+78288	IL	NGE	HSB	NXA	
321356	78140+63114+72000+78289	IL	NGE	HSB	NXA	
321357	78141+63115+72001+78290	IL	NGE	HSB	NXA	
321358	78142+63116+72002+78291	IL	NGE	HSB	NXA	
321359	78143+63117+72003+78292	IL	NGE	HSB	NXA	
321360	78144+63118+72004+78293	IL	NGE	HSB	NXA	

321361	78145+63119+72005+78294	IL	NGE	HSB	NXA	*Phoenix*
321362	78146+63120+72006+78295	IL	NGE	HSB	NXA	
321363	78147+63121+72007+78296	IL	NGE	HSB	NXA	
321364	78148+63122+72008+78297	IL	NGE	HSB	NXA	
321365	78149+63123+72009+78298	IL	NGE	HSB	NXA	
321366	78150+63124+72010+78299	IL	NGE	HSB	NXA	

Class 321/4

Vehicle Length: (Driving) 65ft 0¾in (19.83m) (Inter) 65ft 4¼in (19.92m)
Height: 12ft 4¾in (3.78m)
Width: 9ft 3in (2.82m)
Horsepower: 1,328hp (996kW)
Seats (total/car): 16F/283S, 16F-52S/79S/74S/78S

Number	*Formation* DTCO+MSO+TSO+DTSO	*Depot*	*Livery*	*Owner*	*Operator*	*Name*
321421	78115+63083+71969+77963	IL	NXA	HSB	NXA	
321422	78116+63084+71970+77964	IL	NXA	HSB	NXA	
321423	78117+63085+71971+77965	IL	NXA	HSB	NXA	
321424	78118+63086+71972+77966	IL	NXA	HSB	NXA	
321425	78119+63087+71973+77967	IL	NXA	HSB	NXA	
321426	78120+63088+71974+77968	IL	NXA	HSB	NXA	
321427	78121+63089+71975+77969	IL	NXA	HSB	NXA	
321428	78122+63090+71976+77970	IL	NXA	HSB	NXA	
321429	78123+69031+71977+77971	IL	NXA	HSB	NXA	
321430	78124+63092+71978+77972	IL	NXA	HSB	NXA	
321431	78151+63125+72011+78300	IL	NXA	HSB	NXA	
321432(S)	78152+63126+72012+78301	IL	NXA	HSB	NXA	
321433	78153+63127+72013+78302	IL	NXA	HSB	NXA	
321434	78154+63128+72014+78303	IL	NXA	HSB	NXA	
321435	78155+63129+72015+78304	IL	NXA	HSB	NXA	
321436	78156+63130+72016+78305	IL	NXA	HSB	NXA	
321437	78157+63131+72017+78306	IL	NXA	HSB	NXA	
321438	78158+63132+72018+78307	IL	NGE	HSB	NXA	
321439	78159+63133+72019+78308	IL	NGE	HSB	NXA	
321440	78160+63134+72020+78309	IL	NGE	HSB	NXA	
321441	78161+63135+72021+78310	IL	NGE	HSB	NXA	
321442	78162+63136+72022+78311	IL	NGE	HSB	NXA	
321443	78125+63099+71985+78274	IL	NGE	HSB	NXA	
321444	78126+63100+71986+78275	IL	NGE	HSB	NXA	*Essex Lifeboats*
321445	78127+63101+71987+78276	IL	NGE	HSB	NXA	
321446	78128+63102+71988+78277	IL	NGE	HSB	NXA	*George Mullings*
321447	78129+63103+71989+78278	IL	NGE	HSB	NXA	
321448	78130+63104+71990+78279	IL	NGE	HSB	NXA	

Below: *The corporate National Express grey and white livery was applied to East Anglia repaints from mid-2008 and looks very smart. Class 321 No. 321301, the first of the build, is seen passing Stratford in August 2009.* **Tony Christie**

National Express East Anglia

Class 360/0
Desiro

Vehicle Length: 66ft 9in (20.4m)
Height: 12ft 1½in (3.7m)
Width: 9ft 2in (2.79m)
Horsepower: 1,341hp (1,000kW)
Seats (total/car): 16F/265S, 8F-59S/69S/78S/8F-59S

Number	*Formation* DMCO(A)+PTSO+TSO+DMCO(B)	*Depot*	*Livery*	*Owner*	*Operator*
360101	65551+72551+74551+68551	IL	FNA	ANG	NXA
360102	65552+72552+74552+68552	IL	FNA	ANG	NXA
360103	65553+72553+74553+68553	IL	FNA	ANG	NXA
360104	65554+72554+74554+68554	IL	FNA	ANG	NXA
360105	65555+72555+74555+68555	IL	FNA	ANG	NXA
360106	65556+72556+74556+68556	IL	FNA	ANG	NXA
360107	65557+72557+74557+68557	IL	FNA	ANG	NXA
360108	65558+72558+74558+68558	IL	FNA	ANG	NXA
360109	65559+72559+74559+68559	IL	FNA	ANG	NXA
360110	65560+72560+74560+68560	IL	FNA	ANG	NXA
360111	65561+72561+74561+68561	IL	FNA	ANG	NXA
360112	65562+72562+74562+68562	IL	FNA	ANG	NXA
360113	65563+72563+74563+68563	IL	FNA	ANG	NXA
360114	65564+72564+74564+68564	IL	FNA	ANG	NXA
360115	65565+72565+74565+68565	IL	FNA	ANG	NXA
360116	65566+72566+74566+68566	IL	FNA	ANG	NXA
360117	65567+72567+74567+68567	IL	FNA	ANG	NXA
360118	65568+72568+74568+68568	IL	FNA	ANG	NXA
360119	65569+72569+74569+68569	IL	FNA	ANG	NXA
360120	65570+72570+74570+68570	IL	FNA	ANG	NXA
360121	65571+72571+74571+68571	IL	FNA	ANG	NXA

Below: *Ordered under the previous Great Eastern route franchise operator First Group, this batch of 21 Siemens 'Desiro' units are allocated to Ilford and operate outer-suburban services. Set No. 360116 passes Stratford showing an intermediate livery of unbranded First Group colours.* **CJM**

Class 379/0
Electrostar

Thirty new Class 379/0 four-car sets are currently on order for National Express East Anglia to operate on the London Liverpool Street to Stansted route. The sets will be delivered from Bombardier Derby Litchurch Lane between March-June 2011. Funding has been arranged through Lloyds TSB General Leasing.

East Coast Main Line

Address: ✉ East Coast House, 25 Skeldergate, York, YO1 6DH
customers@eastcoast.co.uk
✆ 08457 225225
ⓘ www.eastcoast.co.uk

Managing Director: Karen Boswell
Operation Started: 13 November 2009*
Principal Routes: London King's Cross - Aberdeen/ Inverness, Edinburgh, Glasgow Hull, Leeds, Bradford, Skipton and Harrogate
Depots: Bounds Green (BN), Craigentinny (EC),
Parent Company: DfT (Directly Operated Railways Ltd)

* In the summer of 2009, it was announced that National Express were to return this franchise to the Government following the inability of the operator to reach a satisfactory financial conclusion to negotiations on the terms of the franchise.

The Government took over operation from 13 November 2009 and will continue to operate the franchise as a 'stop-gap' measure using the in place operational staff. A new franchise bid process will be launched in 2010.

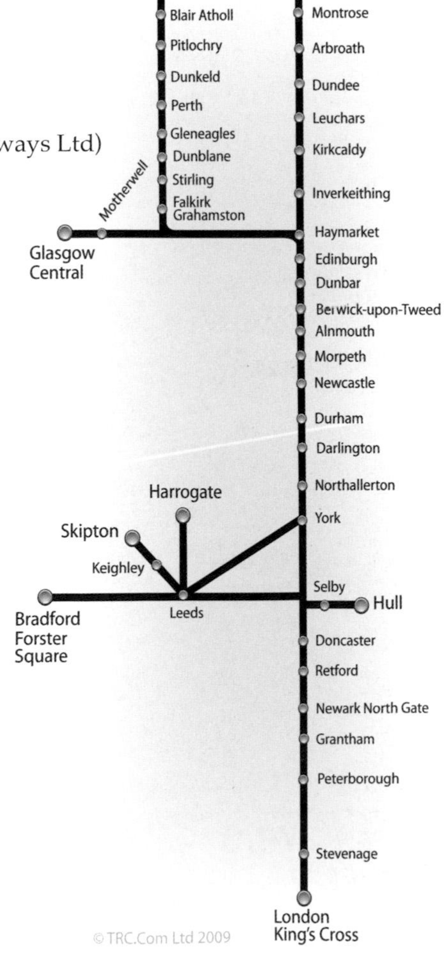

East Coast

Class 43 – HST

Vehicle Length: 58ft 5in (18.80m)
Height: 12ft 10in (3.90m)
Width: 8ft 11in (2.73m)
Engine: MTU 16V4000 R41R
Horsepower: 2,250hp (1,680kW)
Electrical Equipment: Brush

Number		Depot	Poole	Livery	Owner	Operator	Name
43206	(43006)	EC	IECP	ECT	ANG	ICE	*Kingdom of Fife*
43208	(43008)	EC	IECP	NXE	ANG	ICE	
43238	(43038)	EC	IECP	NXE	ANG	ICE	
43239	(43039)	EC	IECP	NXE	ANG	ICE	
43251	(43051)	EC	IECP	ECT	PBR	ICE	
43257	(43057)	EC	IECP	NXE	PBR	ICE	
43277	(43077)	EC	IECP	ECT	PBR	ICE	
43290	(43090)	EC	IECP	NXE	PBR	ICE	*MTU Fascination of Power*
43295	(43095)	EC	IECP	NXE	ANG	ICE	
43296	(43096)	EC	IECP	ECT	PBR	ICE	
43299	(43099)	EC	IECP	NXE	PBR	ICE	
43300	(43100)	EC	IECP	NXE	PBR	ICE	*Craigentinny*
43302	(43102)	EC	IECP	NXE	PBR	ICE	
43305	(43105)	EC	IECP	NXE	ANG	ICE	
43306	(43106)	EC	IECP	NXE	ANG	ICE	
43307	(43107)	EC	IECP	NXE	ANG	ICE	
43308	(43108)	EC	IECP	ECT	ANG	ICE	
43309	(43109)	EC	IECP	NXE	ANG	ICE	
43310	(43110)	EC	IECP	ECT	ANG	ICE	
43311	(43111)	EC	IECP	ECT	ANG	ICE	
43312	(43112)	EC	IECP	ECT	ANG	ICE	
43313	(43113)	EC	IECP	NXG	ANG	ICE	
43314	(43114)	EC	IECP	ECT	ANG	ICE	
43315	(43115)	EC	IECP	NXE	ANG	ICE	
43316	(43116)	EC	IECP	NXE	ANG	ICE	
43317	(43117)	EC	IECP	NXE	ANG	ICE	
43318	(43118)	EC	IECP	ECT	ANG	ICE	
43319	(43119)	EC	IECP	NXE	ANG	ICE	
43320	(43120)	EC	IECP	NXE	ANG	ICE	
43367	(43167)	EC	IECP	NXE	ANG	ICE	*Deltic 50 1955 - 2005 v*

Above: *As soon as the East Coast franchise was transferred from National Express ownership to East Coast, a Government owned subsidiary of Directly Operated Railways, a major operation was undertaken to remove the National Express branding from trains. Almost overnight most of the HST fleet were given the new branding, applied to the old National Express grey and white livery. Power car No. 43277 and a TGS are seen at King's Cross on the day the new company was launched - 13 November 2009.* **Brian Morrison**

Class 91

Vehicle Length: 63ft 8in (19.40m) *Power Collection: 25kV ac overhead*
Height: 12ft 4in (3.75m) *Horsepower: 6,300hp (4,700kW)*
Width: 9ft 0in (2.74m) *Electrical Equipment: GEC*

Number	*Depot*	*Poole*	*Livery*	*Owner*	*Operator*
91101 (91001)	BN	IECA	NXG	HSB	ICE
91102 (91002)	BN	IECA	NXG	HSB	ICE
91103 (91003)	BN	IECA	NXG	HSB	ICE
91104 (91004)	BN	IECA	NXG	HSB	ICE
91105 (91005)	BN	IECA	NXG	HSB	ICE
91106 (91006)	BN	IECA	NXG	HSB	ICE
91107 (91007)	BN	IECA	NXG	HSB	ICE
91108 (91008)	BN	IECA	NXG	HSB	ICE
91109 (91009)	BN	IECA	NXG	HSB	ICE
91110 (91010)	BN	IECA	NXG	HSB	ICE
91111 (91011)	BN	IECA	NXE	HSB	ICE
91112 (91012)	BN	IECA	NXG	HSB	ICE
91113 (91013)	BN	IECA	NXG	HSB	ICE
91114 (91014)	BN	IECA	NXG	HSB	ICE
91115 (91015)	BN	IECA	NXG	HSB	ICE
91116 (91016)	BN	IECA	NXG	HSB	ICE
91117 (91017)	BN	IECA	NXG	HSB	ICE
91118 (91018)	BN	IECA	NXG	HSB	ICE
91119 (91019)	BN	IECA	NXG	HSB	ICE
91120 (91020)	BN	IECA	NXG	HSB	ICE
91121 (91021)	BN	IECA	NXG	HSB	ICE
91122 (91022)	BN	IECA	NXG	HSB	ICE
91124 (91024)	BN	IECA	NXG	HSB	ICE
91125 (91025)	BN	IECA	NXG	HSB	ICE
91126 (91026)	BN	IECA	NXG	HSB	ICE
91127 (91027)	BN	IECA	NXG	HSB	ICE
91128 (91028)	BN	IECA	NXG	HSB	ICE
91129 (91029)	BN	IECA	NXG	HSB	ICE
91130 (91030)	BN	IECA	NXG	HSB	ICE
91131 (91031)	BN	IECA	NXG	HSB	ICE
91132 (91023)	BN	IECA	NXG	HSB	ICE

Right: *Before the unexpected franchise change in summer 2009, when National Express officially lost its East Coast operation, just one Class 91 No. 91111 was repainted in the National Express house colours. This was carried out at Wabtec Doncaster in mid-2008. The loco is seen at Leeds on 18 June 2009.* **Nathan Williamson**

Class 180

Vehicle Length: (driving) 75ft 7in (23.71m), (inter) 75ft 5in (23.03m)
Height: 12ft 4in (3.75m) *Engine: 1 x Cummins OSK19 of 750hp per car*
Width: 9ft 2in (2.80m) *Horsepower: 3,750hp (2,796kW)*
Seats (total/car): 42F/226S, 46S/42F/68S/56S/56S

Number	*Formation* DMSL(A)+MFL+MSL+MSLRB+DMSL(B)	*Depot*	*Livery*	*Owner*	*Operator*
180102	50902+54902+55902+56902+59902	BN	FST	ANG	ICE - Stored until mid-2010
180103	50903+54903+55903+56903+59903	NH	FST	ANG	NOR - Sub lease to Northern to 6/10
180104	50904+54904+55904+56904+59904	BN	FST	ANG	ICE - Stored until mid-2010
180106	50906+54906+55906+56906+59906	NH	FST	ANG	NOR - Sub lease to Northern to 6/10
180108	50908+54908+55908+56908+59908	NH	FST	ANG	NOR - Sub lease to Northern to 6/10

Mk3 HST Stock

Vehicle Length: 75ft 0in (22.86m) *Width: 8ft 11in (2.71m)*
Height: 12ft 9in (3.88m) *Bogie Type: BT10*

GK1G - TRFB *Seating 17F*

Number	*Depot*	*Livery*	*Owner*
40701	EC	NXE	PTR
40702	EC	NXE	PTR
40704	EC	NXE	ANG
40705	EC	NXE	ANG
40706	EC	NXE	ANG
0708	EC	ECT	PTR
711	EC	NXE	ANG
720	EC	NXE	ANG
35	EC	NXE	ANG
40737	EC	NXE	ANG
40740	EC	NXE	ANG
40742	EC	NXE	ANG
40748	EC	NXE	ANG
40750	EC	NXE	ANG
40805	EC	NXG	ANG

GH1G - TF *Seating 48F*

Number	*Depot*	*Livery*	*Owner*
41039	EC	NXE	ANG
41040	EC	NXE	ANG
41044	EC	NXE	ANG
41058	EC	NXE	PTR
41066	EC	NXE	ANG
41083	EC	NXE	PTR
41087	EC	NXE	ANG
41088	EC	NXE	ANG
41090	EC	NXE	ANG
41091	EC	NXE	ANG
41092	EC	NXE	ANG
41095	EC	NXE	ANG
41097	EC	NXE	ANG

East Coast

Number	Depot	Livery	Owner
41098	EC	NXE	ANG
41099	EC	NXE	ANG
41100	EC	NXE	ANG
41115	EC	NXE	PTR
41118	EC	NXE	ANG
41120	EC	ECT	ANG
41150	EC	ECT	ANG
41151	EC	NXE	ANG
41152	EC	NXE	ANG
41159	EC	NXE	PTR
41164	EC	NXE	ANG
41165	EC	NXE	PTR
41170(41001)	EC	NXE	ANG
41185(42313)	EC	NXE	PTR
41190(42088)	EC	NXG	PTR

GH2G - TS (*TSD) *Seating 76/62*S*

Number	*Depot*	*Livery*	*Owner*
42057	EC	NXE	ANG
42058	EC	NXE	ANG
42059	EC	NXE	ANG
42063	EC	NXE	ANG
42064	EC	NXE	ANG
42065	EC	NXE	ANG
42091*	EC	ECT	ANG
42106	EC	NXE	ANG
42109	EC	NXE	PTR
42110	EC	NXE	PTR
42116*	EC	NXE	ANG
42117	EC	NXE	PTR
42127*	EC	NXE	ANG
42128*	EC	NXE	ANG
42130	EC	NXE	PTR
42134	EC	NXE	ANG
42146	EC	ECT	ANG
42147	EC	NXE	PTR
42150	EC	ECT	ANG
42154	EC	ECT	ANG
42158	EC	NXE	ANG
42159*	EC	NXE	PTR
42160	EC	NXE	PTR
42161*	EC	NXE	PTR
42163	EC	NXE	PTR
42171	EC	NXE	ANG
42172	EC	NXE	ANG
42179	EC	NXE	ANG
42180	EC	NXE	ANG
42181	EC	NXE	ANG
42182	EC	NXE	ANG
42186	EC	ECT	ANG
42188*	EC	NXE	ANG
42189*	EC	NXE	ANG
42190	EC	NXE	ANG
42191	EC	NXE	ANG
42192	EC	NXE	ANG
42193	EC	NXE	ANG
42198	EC	NXE	ANG
42199	EC	NXE	ANG
42215	EC	ECT	ANG
42219	EC	NXE	ANG
42226	EC	NXE	ANG
42228	EC	ECT	PTR
42235	EC	NXE	ANG
42237	EC	NXE	PTR
42238*	EC	NXE	ANG
42239*	EC	NXE	ANG
42240	EC	NXE	ANG
42241	EC	NXE	ANG
42242	EC	NXE	ANG
42243	EC	NXE	ANG
42244	EC	NXE	ANG
42286	EC	ECT	PTR
42306	EC	NXE	PTR
42307	EC	NXE	PTR
42322	EC	ECT	PTR
42323	EC	NXE	ANG
42326	EC	NXE	PTR
42330	EC	NXE	PTR
42340	EC	NXE	ANG
42352(41176)	EC	NXE	PTR
42354(41175)	EC	ECT	ANG
42355(41172)	EC	NXE	ANG
42357(41174)	EC	NXE	ANG
42363(41082)	EC	NXE	ANG

GJ2G - TGS) *Seating 65S*

Number	*Depot*	*Livery*	*Owner*
44019	EC	NXE	ANG
44031	EC	NXE	ANG
44045	EC	NXE	ANG
44050	EC	ECT	PTR
44056	EC	NXE	ANG
44057	EC	NXE	PTR
44058	EC	NXE	ANG
44061	EC	NXE	ANG
44063	EC	NXE	ANG
44075	EC	NXE	PTR
44077	EC	NXE	ANG
44080	EC	NXE	ANG
44094	EC	ECT	ANG
44098	EC	NXE	ANG

Left: *By the 2009 franchise change on the East Coast route, a number of HST passenger coaches had been repainted into the white and grey National Express colours. The scheme is seen on Mk3 TS No. 42172.* **Tony Christie**

Mk4 Stock

Vehicle Length: 75ft 5in (23m) *Width: 8ft 11in (2.73m)*
Height: 12ft 5in (3.79m) *Bogie Type: BT41*

AJ2J - RSB *Seating 30S*

Number	*Depot*	*Livery*	*Owner*
10300	BN	NXG	HSB
10301	BN	NXG	HSB
10302	BN	NXG	HSB
10303	BN	NXG	HSB
10304	BN	NXG	HSB
10305	BN	NXG	HSB
10306	BN	NXG	HSB
10307	BN	NXG	HSB
10308	BN	NXG	HSB
10309	BN	NXG	HSB
10310	BN	NXG	HSB
10311	BN	NXG	HSB
10312	BN	NXG	HSB
10313	BN	NXG	HSB
10314	BN	NXG	HSB
10317	BN	NXG	HSB
10318	BN	NXG	HSB
10319	BN	NXG	HSB
10320	BN	NXG	HSB
10321	BN	NXG	HSB
10323	BN	NXG	HSB
10324	BN	NXG	HS

10325	BN	NXG	HSB
10326	BN	NXG	HSB
10328	BN	NXG	HSB
10329	BN	NXG	HSB
10330	BN	NXG	HSB
10331	BN	NXG	HSB
10332	BN	NXG	HSB
10333	BN	NXG	HSB

AD1J - FO *Seating 46F*

Number	*Depot*	*Livery*	*Owner*
11201	BN	NXG	HSB
11219	BN	NXG	HSB
11229	BN	NXG	HSB
11237	BN	NXG	HSB
11241	BN	NXG	HSB
11244	BN	NXG	HSB
11273	BN	NXG	HSB
11277(12408)	BN	NXG	HSB
11278(12479)	BN	NXG	HSB
11279(12521)	BN	NXG	HSB
11280(12523)	BN	NXG	HSB
11281(12418)	BN	NXG	HSB
11282(12524)	BN	NXG	HSB
11283(12435)	BN	NXG	HSB
11284(12487)	BN	NXG	HSB
11285(12537)	BN	NXG	HSB
11286(12482)	BN	NXG	HSB
11287(12527)	BN	NXG	HSB
11288(12517)	BN	NXG	HSB
11289(12528)	BN	NXG	HSB
11290(12530)	BN	NXG	HSB
11291(12535)	BN	NXG	HSB
11292(12451)	BN	NXG	HSB
11293(12536)	BN	NXG	HSB
11294(12529)	BN	NXG	HSB
11295(12475)	BN	NXG	HSB
11298(12416)	BN	NXG	HSB
11299(12532)	BN	NXG	HSB

AL1J - FOD *Seating 42F*

Number	*Depot*	*Livery*	*Owner*
11301(11215)	BN	NXG	HSB
11302(11203)	BN	NXG	HSB
11303(11211)	BN	NXG	HSB
11304(11257)	BN	NXG	HSB
11305(11261)	BN	NXG	HSB
11306(11276)	BN	NXG	HSB
11307(11217)	BN	NXG	HSB
11308(11263)	BN	NXG	HSB
11309(11262)	BN	NXG	HSB
11310(11272)	BN	NXG	HSB
11311(11221)	BN	NXG	HSB
11312(11225)	BN	NXG	HSB
11313(11210)	BN	NXG	HSB
11314(11207)	BN	NXG	HSB
11315(11238)	BN	NXG	HSB
11316(11227)	BN	NXG	HSB
11317(11223)	BN	NXG	HSB
11318(11251)	BN	NXG	HSB
11319(11247)	BN	NXG	HSB
11320(11255)	BN	NXG	HSB
11321(11245)	BN	NXG	HSB
11322(11228)	BN	NXG	HSB
11323(11235)	BN	NXG	HSB
11324(11253)	BN	NXG	HSB
11325(11231)	BN	NXG	HSB
11326(11206)	BN	NXG	HSB
11327(11236)	BN	NXG	HSB
11328(11274)	BN	NXG	HSB
11329(11243)	BN	NXG	HSB
11330(11249)	BN	NXG	HSB

AD1J - FO *Seating 46F*

Number	*Depot*	*Livery*	*Owner*
11401(11214)	BN	NXG	HSB
11402(11216)	BN	NXG	HSB
11403(11258)	BN	NXG	HSB
11404(11202)	BN	NXG	HSB
11405(11204)	BN	NXG	HSB
11406(11205)	BN	NXG	HSB
11407(11256)	BN	NXG	HSB
11408(11218)	BN	NXG	HSB
11409(11259)	BN	NXG	HSB
11410(11260)	BN	NXG	HSB
11411(11240)	BN	NXG	HSB
11412(11209)	BN	NXG	HSB
11413(11212)	BN	NXG	HSB
11414(11246)	BN	NXG	HSB
11415(11208)	BN	NXG	HSB
11416(11254)	BN	NXG	HSB
11417(11226)	BN	NXG	HSB
11418(11222)	BN	NXG	HSB
11419(11250)	BN	NXG	HSB
11420(11242)	BN	NXG	HSB
11421(11220)	BN	NXG	HSB
11422(11232)	BN	NXG	HSB
11423(11230)	BN	NXG	HSB
11424(11239)	BN	NXG	HSB
11425(11234)	BN	NXG	HSB
11426(11252)	BN	NXG	HSB
11427(11200)	BN	NXG	HSB
11428(11233)	BN	NXG	HSB
11429(11275)	BN	NXG	HSB
11430(11248)	BN	NXG	HSB
11998(10314)	BN	NXG	HSB
11999(10316)	BN	NXG	HSB

AI2J - TSOE *Seating 76S*

Number	*Depot*	*Livery*	*Owner*
12200	BN	NXG	HSB
12201	BN	NXG	HSB
12202	BN	NXG	HSB
12203	BN	NXG	HSB
12204	BN	NXG	HSB
12205	BN	NXG	HSB
12207	BN	NXG	HSB
12208	BN	NXG	HSB
12209	BN	NXG	HSB
12210	BN	NXG	HSB
12211	BN	NXG	HSB
12212	BN	NXG	HSB
12213	BN	NXG	HSB
12214	BN	NXG	HSB
12215	BN	NXG	HSB
12216	BN	NXG	HSB
12217	BN	NXG	HSB
12218	BN	NXG	HSB
12219	BN	NXG	HSB
12220	BN	NXG	HSB
12222	BN	NXG	HSB
12223	BN	NXG	HSB
12224	BN	NXG	HSB
12225	BN	NXG	HSB
12226	BN	NXG	HSB
12227	BN	NXG	HSB
12228	BN	NXG	HSB
12229	BN	NXG	HSB
12230	BN	NXG	HSB
12231	BN	NXG	HSB
12232	BN	NXG	HSB

AL2J - TSOD *Seating 68S*

Number	*Depot*	*Livery*	*Owner*
12300	BN	NXG	HSB
12301	BN	NXG	HSB
12302	BN	NXG	HSB
12303	BN	NXG	HSB
12304	BN	NXG	HSB
12305	BN	NXG	HSB
12307	BN	NXG	HSB
12308	BN	NXG	HSB
12309	BN	NXG	HSB
12310	BN	NXG	HSB
12311	BN	NXG	HSB
12312	BN	NXG	HSB
12313	BN	NXG	HSB
12315	BN	NXG	HSB
12316	BN	NXG	HSB
12317	BN	NXG	HSB
12318	BN	NXG	HSB
12319	BN	NXG	HSB
12320	BN	NXG	HSB
12321	BN	NXG	HSB
12322	BN	NXG	HSB
12323	BN	NXG	HSB
12324	BN	NXG	HSB
12325	BN	NXG	HSB
12326	BN	NXG	HSB
12327	BN	NXG	HSB
12328	BN	NXG	HSB
12329	BN	NXG	HSB
12330	BN	NXG	HSB
12331(12531)	BN	NXG	HSB

AC2J - TSO *Seating 76S*

Number	*Depot*	*Livery*	*Owner*
12400	BN	NXG	HSB
12401	BN	NXG	HSB
12402	BN	NXG	HSB
12403	BN	NXG	HSB
12404	BN	NXG	HSB
12405	BN	NXG	HSB
12406	BN	NXG	HSB
12407	BN	NXG	HSB
12409	BN	NXG	HSB
12410	BN	NXG	HSB
12411	BN	NXG	HSB
12414	BN	NXG	HSB
12415	BN	NXG	HSB
12417	BN	NXG	HSB
12419	BN	NXG	HSB

East Coast

12420	BN	NXG	HSB
12421	BN	NXG	HSB
12422	BN	NXG	HSB
12423	BN	NXG	HSB
12424	BN	NXG	HSB
12425	BN	NXG	HSB
12426	BN	NXG	HSB
12427	BN	NXG	HSB
12428	BN	NXG	HSB
12429	BN	NXG	HSB
12430	BN	NXG	HSB
12431	BN	NXG	HSB
12432	BN	NXG	HSB
12433	BN	NXG	HSB
12434	BN	NXG	HSB
12436	BN	NXG	HSB
12437	BN	NXG	HSB
12438	BN	NXG	HSB
12439	BN	NXG	HSB
12440	BN	NXG	HSB
12441	BN	NXG	HSB
12442	BN	NXG	HSB
12443	BN	NXG	HSB
12444	BN	NXG	HSB
12445	BN	NXG	HSB
12446	BN	NXG	HSB
12447	BN	NXG	HSB
12448	BN	NXG	HSB
12449	BN	NXG	HSB
12450	BN	NXG	HSB
12452	BN	NXG	HSB
12453	BN	NXG	HSB
12454	BN	NXG	HSB
12456	BN	NXG	HSB
12457	BN	NXG	HSB
12458	BN	NXG	HSB
12459	BN	NXG	HSB
12460	BN	NXG	HSB
12461	BN	NXG	HSB
12462	BN	NXG	HSB
12463	BN	NXG	HSB
12464	BN	NXG	HSB
12465	BN	NXG	HSB
12466	BN	NXG	HSB
12467	BN	NXG	HSB
12468	BN	NXG	HSB
12469	BN	NXG	HSB
12470	BN	NXG	HSB
12471	BN	NXG	HSB
12472	BN	NXG	HSB
12473	BN	NXG	HSB
12474	BN	NXG	HSB
12476	BN	NXG	HSB
12477	BN	NXG	HSB
12478	BN	NXG	HSB
12480	BN	NXG	HSB
12481	BN	NXG	HSB
12483	BN	NXG	HSB
12484	BN	NXG	HSB
12485	BN	NXG	HSB
12486	BN	NXG	HSB
12488	BN	NXG	HSB
12489	BN	NXG	HSB
12513	BN	NXG	HSB
12514	BN	NXG	HSB
12515	BN	NXG	HSB
12518	BN	NXG	HSB
12519	BN	NXG	HSB
12520	BN	NXG	HSB
12522	BN	NXG	HSB
12526	BN	NXG	HSB
12533	BN	NXG	HSB
12534	BN	NXG	HSB
12538	BN	NXG	HSB

NZAJ - DVT

Number	*Depot*	*Livery*	*Owner*
82200	BN	NXG	HSB
82201	BN	NXG	HSB
82202	BN	NXG	HSB
82203	BN	NXG	HSB
82204	BN	NXG	HSB
82205	BN	NXG	HSB
82206	BN	NXG	HSB
82207	BN	NXG	HSB
82208	BN	NXG	HSB
82209	BN	NXG	HSB
82210	BN	NXG	HSB
82211	BN	NXG	HSB
82212	BN	NXG	HSB
82213	BN	NXG	HSB
82214	BN	NXG	HSB
82215	BN	NXG	HSB
82216	BN	NXG	HSB
82217	BN	NXG	HSB
82218	BN	NXG	HSB
82219	BN	NXG	HSB
82220	BN	NXG	HSB
82222	BN	NXG	HSB
82223	BN	NXG	HSB
82224	BN	NXG	HSB
82225	BN	NXG	HSB
82226	BN	NXG	HSB
82227	BN	NXG	HSB
82228	BN	NXG	HSB
82229	BN	NXG	HSB
82230	BN	NXG	HSB
82231	BN	NXG	HSB

Below: *Under the original East Coast franchise holder GNER, all the Mk4 stock was fully refurbished and some new vehicle types formed. Under National Express no major overhaul work was done, so we will have to wait and see who the new franchise holder is later in the year to learn if more refurbishment is scheduled. A 46-seat FO No. 11415 is illustrated.* **Nathan Williamson**

Service Stock

HST and Mk4 Barrier Vehicles

Number	*Depot*	*Livery*	*Owner*	*Former Identity*
6340	**EC**	**NEG**	**ANG**	**BCK - 21251**
6344	**EC**	**NEG**	**ANG**	**BG - 92080**
6346	**EC**	**NEG**	**ANG**	**BSO - 9422**
6352	**BN**	**NEG**	**ANG**	**SK - 19465**
6353	**BN**	**NEG**	**ANG**	**SK - 19478**
6354	**BN**	**NEG**	**ANG**	**BSO - 9459**
6355	**BN**	**NEG**	**ANG**	**BSO - 9477**
6358	**BN**	**NEG**	**HSB**	**BSO - 9432**
6359	**BN**	**NEG**	**HSB**	**BSO - 9429**
9393	**EC**	**PTR**	**PTR**	**BG - 92196**
9394	**EC**	**PTR**	**PTR**	**BG - 92906**

Right: *To permit the coupling of conventional locomotive drawgear to HST and Mk4 passenger stock, a fleet of barrier or coupling adaptor vehicles are operated on the East Coast. Coach 6355, converted from BSO 9477 is modified for use with Mk4 stock. The coach is seen in Doncaster West Yard.* **Tony Christie**

Mk4 Set Formations

The East Coast Mk4 formations are booked to operate in fixed formations, but frequent changes are reported. This listing should be treated as a guide only.

Set No.	Loco	TSOE	TSO	TSO	TSO	TSOD	RSB	FO	FOD	FO	DVT
BN01	911xx	12207	12417	12415	12414	12307	10307	11298	11301	11401	82207
BN02	911xx	12232	12402	12450	12448	12302	10302	11299	11302	11402	82202
BN03	911xx	12201	12401	12459	12478	12301	10320	11277	11303	11403	82219
BN04	911xx	12202	12480	12421	12518	12327	10303	11278	11304	11404	82209
BN05	911xx	12209	12486	12520	12522	12300	10326	11219	11305	11405	82210
BN06	911xx	12208	12406	12420	12422	12313	10309	11279	11306	11406	82208
BN07	911xx	12231	12411	12405	12489	12329	10323	11280	11307	11407	82204
BN08	911xx	12205	12481	12485	12407	12328	10300	11229	11308	11408	82211
BN09	911xx	12230	12513	12483	12514	12308	10331	11281	11309	11409	82215
BN10	911xx	12214	12419	12488	12443	12305	10304	11282	11310	11410	82205
BN11	911xx	12203	12437	12436	12484	12315	10308	11283	11311	11411	82218
BN12	911xx	12212	12431	12404	12426	12330	10333	11284	11312	11412	82212
BN13	911xx	12228	12469	12430	12424	12311	10313	11285	11313	11413	82213
BN14	911xx	12229	12410	12526	12423	12312	10332	11201	11314	11414	82206
BN15	911xx	12226	12442	12409	12515	12309	10306	11286	11315	11415	82214
BN16	911xx	12213	12428	12445	12433	12304	10315	11287	11316	11416	82225
BN17	911xx	12223	12444	12427	12432	12303	10324	11288	11317	11417	82222
BN18	911xx	12215	12453	12468	12467	12324	10305	11289	11318	11418	82220
BN19	911xx	12211	12434	12400	12470	12310	10318	11290	11319	11419	82201
BN20	911xx	12224	12477	12439	12440	12326	10321	11241	11320	11420	82200
BN21	911xx	12222	12461	12441	12476	12323	10330	11244	11321	11421	82227
BN22	911xx	12210	12452	12460	12473	12316	10301	11291	11322	11422	82230
BN23	911xx	12225	12454	12456	12455	12318	10325	11292	11323	11423	82226
BN24	911xx	12219	12447	12425	12403	12319	10328	11293	11324	11424	82229
BN25	911xx	12217	12446	12519	12464	12322	10312	11294	11325	11425	82216
BN26	911xx	12220	12474	12465	12429	12325	10311	11295	11326	11426	82223
BN27	911xx	12216	12449	12466	12538	12317	10319	11237	11327	11427	82228
BN28	911xx	12218	12458	12463	12533	12320	10310	11273	11328	11428	82217
BN29	911xx	12204	12462	12457	12438	12321	10317	11998	11329	11429	82231
BN30	911xx	12227	12471	12534	12472	12331	10329	11999	11330	11430	82203
Spare cars		12200									82224

Northern Rail

Address: ✉ Northern House, 9 Rougier Street, York, YO1 6HZ
customer.relations@northernrail.org
✆ 0845 000125
ⓘ www.northernrail.org

Managing Director: Heidi Mottram OBE
Franchise Dates: 12 December 2004 - 31 August 2013
Principal Routes: Regional services in Merseyside, Greater Manchester, South/North Yorkshire, Lancashire, Cumbria and the North East
Depots: Newton Heath (NH), Heaton (HT), Longsight (LG),
Parent Company: Serco/NedRailways

Class 142

Vehicle Length: 51ft 0½in (15.55m)
Height: 12ft 8in (3.86m)
Width: 9ft 2¼in (2.80m)
Engine: 1 x Cummins LTA10-R per vehicle
Horsepower: 460hp (343kW)
Seats (total/car): 106S, 56S/50S

Number	Formation DMS+DMSL	Depot	Livery	Owner	Operator
142003	55544+55594	NH	NOR	ANG	NOR
142004	55545+55595	NH	NOR	ANG	NOR
142005	55546+55596	NH	NOR	ANG	NOR
142007	55548+55598	NH	NOR	ANG	NOR
142011	55552+55602	NH	NOR	ANG	NOR
142012	55553+55603	NH	NOR	ANG	NOR
142013	55554+55604	NH	NOR	ANG	NOR
142014	55555+55605	NH	NOR	ANG	NOR
142015	55556+55606	HT	NOR	ANG	NOR
142016	55557+55607	HT	NOR	ANG	NOR
142017	55558+55608	HT	NOR	ANG	NOR
142018	55559+55609	HT	NOR	ANG	NOR
142019	55560+55610	HT	NOR	ANG	NOR
142020	55561+55611	HT	NOR	ANG	NOR
142021	55562+55612	HT	NOR	ANG	NOR
142022	55563+55613	HT	NOR	ANG	NOR
142023	55564+55614	NH	NOR	ANG	NOR
142024	55565+55615	HT	NOR	ANG	NOR
142025	55566+55616	HT	NOR	ANG	NOR
142026	55567+55617	HT	NOR	ANG	NOR
142027	55568+55618	NH	NOR	ANG	NOR
142028	55569+55619	NH	NOR	ANG	NOR
142031	55572+55622	NH	NOR	ANG	NOR
142032	55573+55623	NH	NOR	ANG	NOR
142033	55574+55624	NH	NOR	ANG	NOR
142034	55575+55625	HT	NOR	ANG	NOR
142035	55576+55626	NH	NOR	ANG	NOR
142036	55577+55627	NH	NOR	ANG	NOR
142037	55578+55628	NH	NOR	ANG	NOR
142038	55579+55629	NH	NOR	ANG	NOR
142039	55580+55630	NH	NOR	ANG	NOR
142040	55581+55631	NH	NOR	ANG	NOR
142041	55582+55632	NH	NOR	ANG	NOR
142042(S)	55583+55633	NH	NOR	ANG	NOR
142043	55584+55634	NH	NOR	ANG	NOR
142044	55585+55635	NH	NOR	ANG	NOR
142045	55586+55636	NH	NOR	ANG	NOR
142046	55587+55637	NH	NOR	ANG	NOR
142047	55588+55638	NH	NOR	ANG	NOR
142048	55589+55639	NH	NOR	ANG	NOR
142049	55590+55640	NH	NOR	ANG	NOR
142050	55591+55641	HT	NOR	ANG	NOR
142051	55701+55747	NH	NOR	ANG	NOR
142052	55702+55748	NH	NOR	ANG	NOR
142053	55703+55749	NH	NOR	ANG	NOR
142054	55704+55750	NH	NOR	ANG	NOR
142055	55705+55751	NH	NOR	ANG	NOR
142056	55706+55752	NH	NOR	ANG	NOR
142057	55707+55753	NH	NOR	ANG	NOR
142058	55708+55754	NH	NOR	ANG	NOR
142060	55710+55756	NH	NOR	ANG	NOR
142061	55711+55757	NH	NOR	ANG	NOR
142062	55712+55758	NH	NOR	ANG	NOR
142065	55715+55761	HT	NOR	ANG	NOR
142066	55716+55762	HT	NOR	ANG	NOR
142067	55717+55763	NH	NOR	ANG	NOR
142070	55720+55766	HT	NOR	ANG	NOR
142071	55721+55767	HT	NOR	ANG	NOR
142078	55728+55768	HT	NOR	ANG	NOR
142079	55729+55769	HT	NOR	ANG	NOR
142084	55764+55780	HT	NOR	ANG	NOR
142086	55736+55782	HT	NOR	ANG	NOR
142087	55737+55783	HT	NOR	ANG	NOR
142088	55738+55784	HT	NOR	ANG	NOR
142089	55739+55785	HT	NOR	ANG	NOR
142090	55740+55786	HT	NOR	ANG	NOR
142091	55741+55787	HT	NOR	ANG	NOR
142092	55742+55788	HT	NOR	ANG	NOR
142093	55743+55789	HT	NOR	ANG	NOR
142094	55744+55790	HT	NOR	ANG	NOR
142095	55745+55791	HT	NOR	ANG	NOR
142096	55746+55792	HT	NOR	ANG	NOR

Left: *The largest operator of the 'Pacer' style railbus 2-car DMU stock is Northern, where sets are allocated to either Heaton or Newton Heath depots. In recent years the spartan interiors have been much improved, with the fleet still being the mainstay of local passenger services. Set No. 142027 is seen at Preston displaying Northern blue, mauve and grey livery.* **CJM**

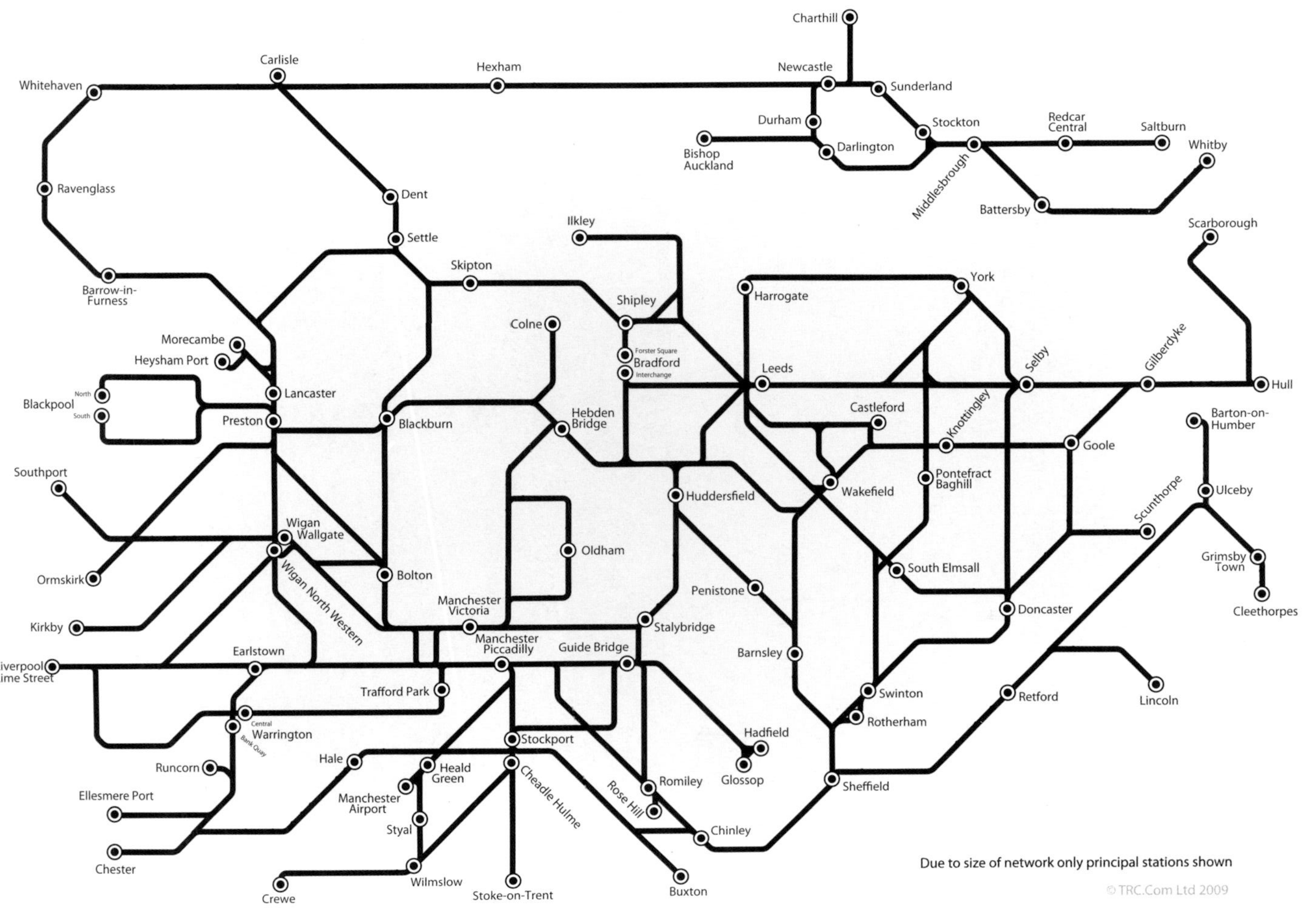
Passenger Train Operating Companies - Northern
Charthill
Whitehaven
Carlisle
Hexham
Newcastle
Sunderland
Durham
Stockton
Redcar Central
Saltburn
Whitby
Bishop Auckland
Darlington
Middlesbrough
Battersby
Ravenglass
Dent
Settle
Ilkley
Scarborough
Skipton
Barrow-in-Furness
Shipley
York
Harrogate
Colne
Morecambe
Heysham Port
Forster Square
Bradford
Interchange
Leeds
Selby
Gilberdyke
Hull
Lancaster
Blackpool North
Blackpool South
Preston
Blackburn
Hebden Bridge
Castleford
Knottingley
Barton-on-Humber
Goole
Southport
Pontefract Baghill
Huddersfield
Wakefield
Ulceby
Wigan Wallgate
Scunthorpe
Oldham
Grimsby Town
Ormskirk
Bolton
Wigan North Western
South Elmsall
Cleethorpes
Penistone
Manchester Victoria
Doncaster
Kirkby
Stalybridge
Manchester Piccadilly
Guide Bridge
Barnsley
Earlstown
Liverpool Lime Street
Trafford Park
Swinton
Retford
Lincoln
Central
Warrington
Bank Quay
Rotherham
Hadfield
Stockport
Hale
Runcorn
Heald Green
Romiley
Glossop
Cheadle Hulme
Sheffield
Manchester Airport
Ellesmere Port
Rose Hill
Styal
Chinley
Chester
Due to size of network only principal stations shown
Wilmslow
Crewe
Stoke-on-Trent
Buxton
© TRC.Com Ltd 2009

Northern Rail

Class 144

Vehicle Length: 50ft 2in (15.25m)
Height: 12ft 2½in (3.73m)
Width: 8ft 10½in (2.70m)
Engine: 1 x Cummins LTA10-R per vehicle
Horsepower: 460hp (343kW)
Seats (total/car): 87S, 45S/42S

Number	*Formation DMS+DMSL*	*Depot*	*Livery*	*Owner*	*Operator*
144001	55801+55824	NL	NOR	PTR	NOR
144002	55802+55825	NL	NOR	PTR	NOR
144003	55803+55826	NL	NOR	PTR	NOR
144004	55804+55827	NL	NOR	PTR	NOR
144005	55805+55828	NL	NOR	PTR	NOR
144006	55806+55829	NL	NOR	PTR	NOR
144007	55807+55830	NL	NOR	PTR	NOR
144008	55808+55831	NL	NOR	PTR	NOR
144009	55809+55832	NL	NOR	PTR	NOR
144010	55810+55833	NL	NOR	PTR	NOR
144011	55811+55834	NL	NOR	PTR	NOR
144012	55812+55835	NL	NOR	PTR	NOR
144013	55813+55836	NL	NOR	PTR	NOR

Name applied

144001 ***The Penistone Line Partnership***

Vehicle Length: 50ft 2in (15.25m)
Height: 12ft 2½in (3.73m)
Width: 8ft 10½in (2.70m)
Engine: 1 x Cummins LTA10-R per vehicle
Horsepower: 690hp (515kW)
Seats (total/car): 145S, 45S/58S/42S

Number	*Formation DMS+MS+DMSL*	*Depot*	*Livery*	*Owner*	*Operator*
144014	55814+55850+55837	NL	NOR	PTR	NOR
144015	55815+55851+55838	NL	NOR	PTR	NOR
144016	55816+55852+55839	NL	NOR	PTR	NOR
144017	55817+55853+55840	NL	NOR	PTR	NOR
144018	55818+55854+55841	NL	NOR	PTR	NOR
144019	55819+55855+55842	NL	NOR	PTR	NOR
144020	55820+55856+55843	NL	NOR	PTR	NOR
144021	55821+55857+55844	NL	NOR	PTR	NOR
144022	55822+55858+55845	NL	NOR	PTR	NOR
144023	55823+55859+55846	NL	NOR	PTR	NOR

Below: *In 2008-09 the entire fleet of Northern Class 144 two and three-car units were repainted into standard Northern Rail house colours, off-set by grey passenger doors. Set No. 143003 is illustrated at Doncaster.* **Nathan Williamson**

Class 150/1

Vehicle Length: 64ft 9¾in (19.74m)
Height: 12ft 4½in (3.77m)
Width: 9ft 3⅛in (2.82m)
Engine: 1 x NT855R5 of 285hp per vehicle
Horsepower: 570hp (425kW)
Seats (total/car): 124S, 59S/65S

Number	*Formation DMSL+DMS*	*Depot*	*Livery*	*Owner*	*Operator*
150133	52133+57133	NH	NOR	ANG	NOR
150134	52134+57134	NH	NOR	ANG	NOR
150135	52135+57135	NH	NOR	ANG	NOR
150136	52136+57136	NH	NOR	ANG	NOR
150137	52137+57137	NH	NOR	ANG	NOR
150138	52138+57138	NH	NOR	ANG	NOR
150139	52139+57139	NH	NOR	ANG	NOR
150140	52140+57140	NH	NOR	ANG	NOR
150141	52141+57141	NH	NOR	ANG	NOR
150142	52142+57142	NH	NOR	ANG	NOR
150143	52143+57143	NH	NOR	ANG	NOR
150144	52144+57144	NH	NOR	ANG	NOR
150145	52145+57145	NH	NOR	ANG	NOR
150146	52146+57146	NH	NOR	ANG	NOR
150147	52147+57147	NH	NOR	ANG	NOR
150148	52148+57148	NH	NOR	ANG	NOR
150149	52149+57149	NH	NOR	ANG	NOR
150150	52150+57150	NH	NOR	ANG	NOR

Right: *Northern Rail Class 150/1 unit No. 150147 stands at Platform 11 of Manchester Piccadilly station on 4 June 2009, forming the 13.17 service to Chester, via Altrincham. Note the slam type crew door on the Class 150/0 and 150/1 sets, which were replaced by single leaf sliding doors on the 150/2 build.* **John Binch**

Class 150/2

Vehicle Length: 64ft 9¾in (19.74m)
Height: 12ft 4½in (3.77m)
Width: 9ft 3⅛in (2.82m)
Engine: 1 x NT855R5 of 285hp per vehicle
Horsepower: 570hp (425kW)
Seats (total/car): 132S, 62S/70S

Number	Formation DMSL+DMS	Depot	Livery	Owner	Operator
150201	52201+57201	NH	NOR	ANG	NOR
150203	52203+57203	NH	NOR	ANG	NOR
150205	52205+57205	NH	NOR	ANG	NOR
150207	52207+57207	NH	NOR	ANG	NOR
150211	52211+57211	NH	NOR	ANG	NOR
150215	52215+57215	NH	NOR	ANG	NOR
150218	52218+57218	NH	NOR	ANG	NOR
150222	52222+57222	NH	NOR	ANG	NOR
150223	52223+57223	NH	NOR	ANG	NOR
150224	52224+57224	NH	NOR	ANG	NOR
150225	52225+57225	NH	NOR	ANG	NOR
150228	52228+57228	NH	NOR	PTR	NOR
150268	52268+57268	NH	NOR	PTR	NOR
150269	52269+57269	NH	NOR	PTR	NOR
150270	52270+57270	NH	NOR	PTR	NOR
150271	52271+57271	NH	NOR	PTR	NOR
150272	52272+57272	NH	NOR	PTR	NOR
150273	52273+57273	NH	NOR	PTR	NOR
150274	52274+57274	NH	NOR	PTR	NOR
150275	52275+57275	NH	NOR	PTR	NOR
150276	52276+57276	NH	NOR	PTR	NOR
150277	52277+57277	NH	NOR	PTR	NOR

Name applied

150268 ***Benny Rothman - The Manchester Rambler***

Right: *Painted in standard Northern Rail blue, mauve and white livery, Class 150/2 No. 150270 arrives at Warrington station on 29 May 2009 with a service for Wigan. This example has new LED type joint marker/tail lights.* **Stacey Thew**

Class 153

Vehicle Length: 76ft 5in (23.29m)
Height: 12ft 3⅛in (3.75m)
Width: 8ft 10in (2.70m)
Engine: 1 x NT855R5 of 285hp
Horsepower: 285hp (213kW)
Seats (total/car): 70S

Number	Formation DMSL	Depot	Livery	Owner	Operator
153301	52301	NL	NOR	ANG	NOR
153304	52304	NL	NOR	ANG	NOR
153307	52307	NL	NOR	ANG	NOR
153315	52315	NL	NOR	ANG	NOR
153316	52316	NL	NOR	PTR	NOR
153317	52317	NL	NOR	ANG	NOR
153324	52324	NL	NOR	PTR	NOR
153328	52328	NL	NOR	ANG	NOR
153330	52330	NL	NOR	PTR	NOR
153331	52331	NL	NOR	ANG	NOR
153332	52332	NL	NOR	ANG	NOR
153351	57351	NL	NOR	ANG	NOR

Northern Rail

153352	57352	NL	NOR	ANG	NOR
153358	57358	NL	NOR	PTR	NOR
153359	57359	NL	NOR	PTR	NOR
153360	57360	NL	NOR	PTR	NOR
153363	57363	NL	NOR	PTR	NOR
153378	57378	NL	NOR	ANG	NOR

Left: *A sizeable fleet of single car Class 153s (rebuilt from Class 155 twin-vehicle sets) are operated by Northern. All are in the latest Northern blue and mauve 'swirl' livery, illustrated on No. 153304 at Preston on 31 October 2008. This picture shows the small cab end.* **CJM**

Class 155

Vehicle Length: 76ft 5in (23.29m)
Height: 12ft 3⅛in (3.75m)
Width: 8ft 10in (2.70m)
Engine: 1 x NT855R5 of 285hp
Horsepower: 570hp (425kW)
Seats (total/car): 156S, 76S/80S

Number	Formation DMSL+DMS	Depot	Livery	Owner	Operator
155341	52341+57341	NL	NOR	WYP*	NOR
155342	52342+57342	NL	NOR	WYP*	NOR
155343	52343+57343	NL	NOR	WYP*	NOR
155344	52344+57344	NL	NOR	WYP*	NOR
155345	52345+57345	NL	NOR	WYP*	NOR
155346	52346+57346	NL	NOR	WYP*	NOR
155347	52347+57347	NL	NOR	WYP*	NOR

* *Managed by Porterbrook Leasing*

Left: *The seven West Yorkshire Class 155s are now operated in a common pool with other Neville Hill allocated units, now sporting the Northern pictogram-style livery. The sets however still retain a Metro 'M' logo on the bodyside. Set No. 155347 is seen at Leeds on 18 June 2009.*
Nathan Williamson

Class 156

Vehicle Length: 75ft 6in (23.03m)
Height: 12ft 6in (3.81m)
Width: 8ft 11in (2.73m)
Engine: 1 x Cummins NT855R5 of 285hp
Horsepower: 570hp (425kW)
Seats (total/car): 146S, 70/76S

Number	Formation DMSL+DMS	Depot	Livery	Owner	Operator
156420	52420+57420	NH	NOR	PTR	NOR
156421	52421+57421	NH	NOR	PTR	NOR
156423	52423+57423	NH	NOR	PTR	NOR
156424	52424+57424	NH	NOR	PTR	NOR
156425	52425+57425	NH	NOR	PTR	NOR
156426	52426+57426	NH	NOR	PTR	NOR
156427	52427+57427	NH	NOR	PTR	NOR
156428	52428+57428	NH	NOR	PTR	NOR
156429	52429+57429	NH	NOR	PTR	NOR
156438	52438+57438	HT	NOR	ANG	NOR
156440	52440+57440	NH	NOR	PTR	NOR
156441	52441+57441	NH	NOR	PTR	NOR
156443	52443+57443	HT	NOR	ANG	NOR
156444	52444+57444	HT	NOR	ANG	NOR
156448	52448+57448	HT	NOR	ANG	NOR
156451	52451+57451	HT	NOR	ANG	NOR
156452	52452+57452	NH	NOR	PTR	NOR
156454	52454+57454	HT	NOR	ANG	NOR
156455	52455+57455	NH	NOR	PTR	NOR
156459	52459+57459	NH	NOR	PTR	NOR
156460	52460+57460	NH	NOR	PTR	NOR
156461	52461+57461	NH	NOR	PTR	NOR
156463	52463+57463	HT	NOR	ANG	NOR
156464	52464+57464	NH	NOR	PTR	NOR
156466	52466+57466	NH	NOR	PTR	NOR
156468	52468+57468	NH	NOR	ANG	NOR
156469	52469+57469	HT	NOR	ANG	NOR
156470	52470+57470	NH	NOR	ANG	NOR
156471	52471+57471	NH	NOR	ANG	NOR
156472	52472+57472	NH	NOR	ANG	NOR

156473	52473+57473	NH	NOR	ANG	NOR
156475	52475+57475	HT	NOR	ANG	NOR
156479	52479+57479	NH	NOR	ANG	NOR
156480	52480+57480	HT	NOR	ANG	NOR
156481	52481+57481	NH	NOR	ANG	NOR
156482	52482+57482	NH	NOR	ANG	NOR
156483	52483+57483	NH	NOR	ANG	NOR
156484	52484+57484	HT	NOR	ANG	NOR
156486	52486+57486	NH	NOR	ANG	NOR
156487	52487+57487	NH	NOR	ANG	NOR
156488	52488+57488	NH	NOR	ANG	NOR
156489	52489+57489	NH	NOR	ANG	NOR
156490	52490+57490	HT	NOR	ANG	NOR
156491	52491+57491	NH	NOR	ANG	NOR
156497	52497+57497	NH	NOR	ANG	NOR
156498	52498+57498	NH	NOR	ANG	NOR

Names applied

156444 ***Councillor Bill Cameron***
156466 ***Gracie Fields***

Right: *A total of 46 Class 156s are on the books of Northern, allocated to Newton Heath (Manchester) and Heaton (Newcastle). These sets, all sporting the latest Northern blue, mauve and white livery are used on outer suburban and main line services. Set No. 156482 is illustrated at Preston.* **CJM**

Class 158

Vehicle Length: 76ft 1¾in (23.21m)
Height: 12ft 6in (3.81m)
Width: 9ft 3¼in (2.82m)
Engine: 1 x Cummins NTA855R of 350hp per vehicle
Horsepower: 1,050hp (783kW)
Seats (total/car): 208S, 68S/70S/70S

Number	*Formation DMSL+MSL+DMSL*	*Depot*	*Livery*	*Owner*	*Operator*
158752	52752+58716+57752	NL	NOR	PTR	NOR
158753	52753+58710+57753	NL	NOR	PTR	NOR
158754	52754+58708+57754	NL	NOR	PTR	NOR
158755	52755+58702+57755	NL	NOR	PTR	NOR
158756	52756+58712+57756	NL	NOR	PTR	NOR
158757	52757+58706+57757	NL	NOR	PTR	NOR
158758	52758+58714+57758	NL	NOR	PTR	NOR
158759	52759+58713+57759	NL	NOR	PTR	NOR

Vehicle Length: 76ft 1¾in (23.21m)
Height: 12ft 6in (3.81m)
Width: 9ft 3¼in (2.82m)
Engine: 1 x Cummins NTA855R of 350hp per vehicle
Horsepower: 700hp (522kW)
Seats (total/car): 138S, 68S/70S

Number	*Formation DMSL+DMSL*	*Depot*	*Livery*	*Owner*	*Operator*
158784	52784+57784	NH	NOR	ANG	NOR
158787	52787+57787	NH	NOR	ANG	NOR
158790	52790+57790	NH	NOR	ANG	NOR
158791	52791+57791	NH	NOR	ANG	NOR
159792	52792+57792	NH	NOR	ANG	NOR
158793	52793+57793	NH	NOR	ANG	NOR
158794	52794+57794	NH	NOR	ANG	NOR
158795	52795+57795	NH	NOR	ANG	NOR
158796	52796+57796	NH	NOR	ANG	NOR
158797	52797+57797	NH	NOR	ANG	NOR
158815	52815+57815	NL	NOR	ANG	NOR
158816	52816+57816	NL	NOR	ANG	NOR
158817	52817+57817	NL	NOR	ANG	NOR
158843	52843+57843	NL	NOR	ANG	NOR
158844	52844+57844	NL	NOR	ANG	NOR
158845	52845+57845	NL	NOR	ANG	NOR
158848	52848+57848	NL	NOR	ANG	NOR
158849	52849+57849	NL	NOR	ANG	NOR
158850	52850+57850	NL	NOR	ANG	NOR
158851	52851+57851	NL	NOR	ANG	NOR
158853	52853+57853	NL	NOR	ANG	NOR
158855	52855+57855	NL	NOR	ANG	NOR
158859	52859+57859	NL	NOR	ANG	NOR
158860	52860+57860	NL	NOR	ANG	NOR
158861	52861+57861	NL	NOR	ANG	NOR
158872	52872+57872	NL	NOR	ANG	NOR

Vehicle Length: 76ft 1¾in (23.21m)
Height: 12ft 6in (3.81m)
Width: 9ft 3¼in (2.82m)
Engine: 1 x Cummins NTA855R of 350hp per vehicle
Horsepower: 700hp (522kW)
Seats (total/car): 142S, 70S/72S

Number	*Formation DMSL+DMS*	*Depot*	*Livery*	*Owner*	*Operator*
158901	52901+57901	NL	NOR	HSB	NOR
158902	52902+57902	NL	NOR	HSB	NOR
158903	52903+57903	NL	NOR	HSB	NOR
158904	52904+57904	NL	NOR	HSB	NOR

158905	52905+57905	NL	NOR	HSB	NOR
158906	52906+57906	NL	NOR	HSB	NOR
158907	52907+57907	NL	NOR	HSB	NOR
158908	52908+57908	NL	NOR	HSB	NOR
158909	52909+57909	NL	NOR	HSB	NOR
158910	52910+57910	NL	NOR	HSB	NOR

Names applied

158784	***Barbara Castle***
158791	***County of Nottinghamshire***
158796	***Fred Trueman - Cricketing Legend***
158860	***Ian Dewhirst***
158910	***William Wilberforce***

Left: *Most of the original Regional Railways three-car Class 158 sets are now allocated to Northern at Neville Hill depot and still operate on the Trans-Pennine route mainly on stopping and local services. On 31 October 2008, set No. 158754 departs from Preston bound for Manchester.* **CJM**

Class 180

Vehicle Length: (driving) 75ft 7in (23.71m), (inter) 75ft 5in (23.03m)
Height: 12ft 4in (3.75m)
Width: 9ft 2in (2.80m)
Engine: 1 x Cummins OSK19 of 750hp per car
Horsepower: 3,750hp (2,796kW)
Seats (total/car): 42F/226S, 46S/42F/68S/56S/56S

Number	*Formation* DMSL(A)+MFL+MSL+MSLRB+DMSL(B)	*Depot*	*Livery*	*Owner*	*Operator*
180103	**50903+54903+55903+56903+59903**	**NH**	**FSN**	**ANG**	**NOR** - *Sub lease from ECML to 06/10*
180106	**50906+54906+55906+56906+59906**	**NH**	**FSN**	**ANG**	**NOR** - *Sub lease from ECML to 06/10*
180108	**50908+54908+55908+56908+59908**	**NH**	**FSN**	**ANG**	**NOR** - *Sub lease from ECML to 06/10*

Left: *Northern Rail introduced three Class 180 units on two daytime diagrams in late 2008. The sets are based at Newton Heath and operate on the Manchester Victoria to Blackpool North (via Wigan) corridor. On 26 January 2009, No. 180103 pulls away from Kirkham & Wesham and passes the Fox's Biscuits factory with the 13.22 Manchester Victoria to Blackpool North.* **John Binch**

Class 323

Vehicle Length: (Driving) 76ft 8¼in (23.37m)
(Inter) 76ft 10¾in (23.44m)
Height: 12ft 4¾in (3.78m)
Width: 9ft 2¼in (2.80m)
Horsepower: 1,565hp (1,168kW)
Seats (total/car) 323223-225: 244S, 82S/80S/82S
323226-239: 284S, 98S/88S/98S

Number	*Formation* DMSO(A)+PTSO+DMSO(B)	*Depot*	*Livery*	*Owner*	*Operator*
323223	**64023+72223+65023**	**LG**	**NOR**	**PTR**	**NOR**
323224	**64024+72224+65024**	**LG**	**NOR**	**PTR**	**NOR**
323225	**64025+72225+65025**	**LG**	**FSN**	**PTR**	**NOR**
323226	**64026+72226+65026**	**LG**	**FSN**	**PTR**	**NOR**
323227	**64027+72227+65027**	**LG**	**FSN**	**PTR**	**NOR**
323228	**64028+72228+65028**	**LG**	**NOR**	**PTR**	**NOR**
323229	**64029+72229+65029**	**LG**	**NOR**	**PTR**	**NOR**
323230	**64030+72230+65030**	**LG**	**FSN**	**PTR**	**NOR**
323231	**64031+72231+65031**	**LG**	**NOR**	**PTR**	**NOR**
323232	**64032+72232+65032**	**LG**	**NOR**	**PTR**	**NOR**
323233	**64033+72233+65033**	**LG**	**NOR**	**PTR**	**NOR**
323234	**64034+72234+65034**	**LG**	**NOR**	**PTR**	**NOR**

323235	64035+72235+65035	LG	NOR	PTR	NOR
323236	64036+72236+65036	LG	NOR	PTR	NOR
323237	64037+72237+65037	LG	NOR	PTR	NOR
323238	64038+72238+65038	LG	FSN	PTR	NOR
323239	64039+72239+65039	LG	FSN	PTR	NOR

Below: *Manchester Longsight is the base for the 17 Northern Class 323 sets. No. 323223 arrives at Crewe on 29 May 2008 with a train from Manchester.* **Stacey Thew**

Class 333

Vehicle Length: (Driving) 77ft 10¾in (23.74m)
(Inter) 75ft 11in (23.14m)
Height: 12ft 1½in (3.79m)
Width: 9ft 0¼in (2.75m)
Horsepower: 1,877hp (1,400kW)
Seats (total/car): 360S, 90S/73S/100S/90S

Number	*Formation* DMSO(A)+PTSO+TSO+DMSO(B)	*Depot*	*Livery*	*Owner*	*Operator*	*Name*
333001	78451+74461+74477+78452	NL	NOM	ANG	NOR	
333002	78453+74462+74478+78454	NL	NOM	ANG	NOR	
333003	78455+74463+74479+78456	NL	NOM	ANG	NOR	
333004	78457+74464+74480+78458	NL	NOM	ANG	NOR	
333005	78459+74465+74481+78460	NL	NOM	ANG	NOR	
333006	78461+74466+74482+78462	NL	NOM	ANG	NOR	
333007	78463+74467+74483+78464	NL	NOM	ANG	NOR	*Alderman J Arthur Godwin - First Lord Mayor of Bradford 1907*
333008	78465+74468+74484+78466	NL	NOM	ANG	NOR	
333009	78467+74469+74485+78468	NL	NOM	ANG	NOR	
333010	78469+74470+74486+78470	NL	NOM	ANG	NOR	
333011	78471+74471+74487+78472	NL	NOM	ANG	NOR	
333012	78473+74472+74488+78474	NL	NOM	ANG	NOR	
333013	78475+74473+74489+78476	NL	NOM	ANG	NOR	
333014	78477+74474+74490+78478	NL	NOM	ANG	NOR	
333015	78479+74475+74491+78480	NL	NOM	ANG	NOR	
333016	78481+74476+74492+78482	NL	NOM	ANG	NOR	

Right: *Siemens Class 333 No. 333008 painted in the striking Northern Rail red, white and blue livery brightens up the dull afternoon of 19 September 2009, as it passes Bingley with the 13.41 Bradford Forster Square to Skipton service. All 16 Class 333s are now in this livery and all are allocated to Leeds Neville Hill depot.* **John Binch**

South West Trains

Address: ✉ Friars Bridge Court, 41-45 Blackfriars Road, London, SE1 8NZ
customerrelations@swtrains.co.uk
✆ 08700 00 5151
ⓘ www.southwesttrains.co.uk

Managing Director: Andy Pitt
Franchise Dates: 4 December 1996 - February 2017
Principal Routes: London Waterloo-Weymouth, Exeter, Portsmouth and suburban services in Surrey, Berkshire, Hampshire
Depots: Wimbledon Park (WD), Bournemouth (BM), Clapham Junction (CJ), Salisbury (SA)
Northam (Siemens Transportation) (NT)
Parent Company: Stagecoach

Class 158

Vehicle Length: 76ft 1¾in (23.21m)
Height: 12ft 6in (3.81m)
Width: 9ft 3¼in (2.82m)
Engine: 1 x Cummins NTA855R of 350hp per vehicle
Horsepower: 700hp (522kW)
Seats (total/car): 13F-114S, 13F-44S/70S

Number	*Formation DMSL+DMSL*	*Depot*	*Livery*	*Owner*	*Operator*
158880 (158737)	**52737+57737**	**SA**	**SWM**	**PTR**	**SWT**
158881 (158742)	**52742+57742**	**SA**	**SWM**	**PTR**	**SWT**
158882 (158743)	**52743+57743**	**SA**	**SWM**	**PTR**	**SWT**
158883 (158744)	**52744+57744**	**SA**	**SWM**	**PTR**	**SWT**
158884 (158772)	**52772+57772**	**SA**	**SWM**	**PTR**	**SWT**
158885 (158775)	**52775+57775**	**SA**	**SWM**	**PTR**	**SWT**
158886 (158779)	**52779+57779**	**SA**	**SWM**	**PTR**	**SWT**
158887 (158781)	**52781+57781**	**SA**	**SWM**	**PTR**	**SWT**
158888 (158802)	**52802+57802**	**SA**	**SWM**	**PTR**	**SWT**
158889 (158808)	**52808+57808**	**SA**	**SWM**	**PTR**	**SWT**
158890 (158814)	**52814+57814**	**SA**	**SWM**	**PTR**	**SWT**

Below: *South West Trains operates a fleet of 11 two-car Class 158s, allocated to Salisbury and used alongside the Class 159 fleet. The sets are fully refurbished to SWT standards and all sport Stagecoach white main line style livery. Set No. 158886 is illustrated; this was rebuilt from the former No. 158779.* **CJM**

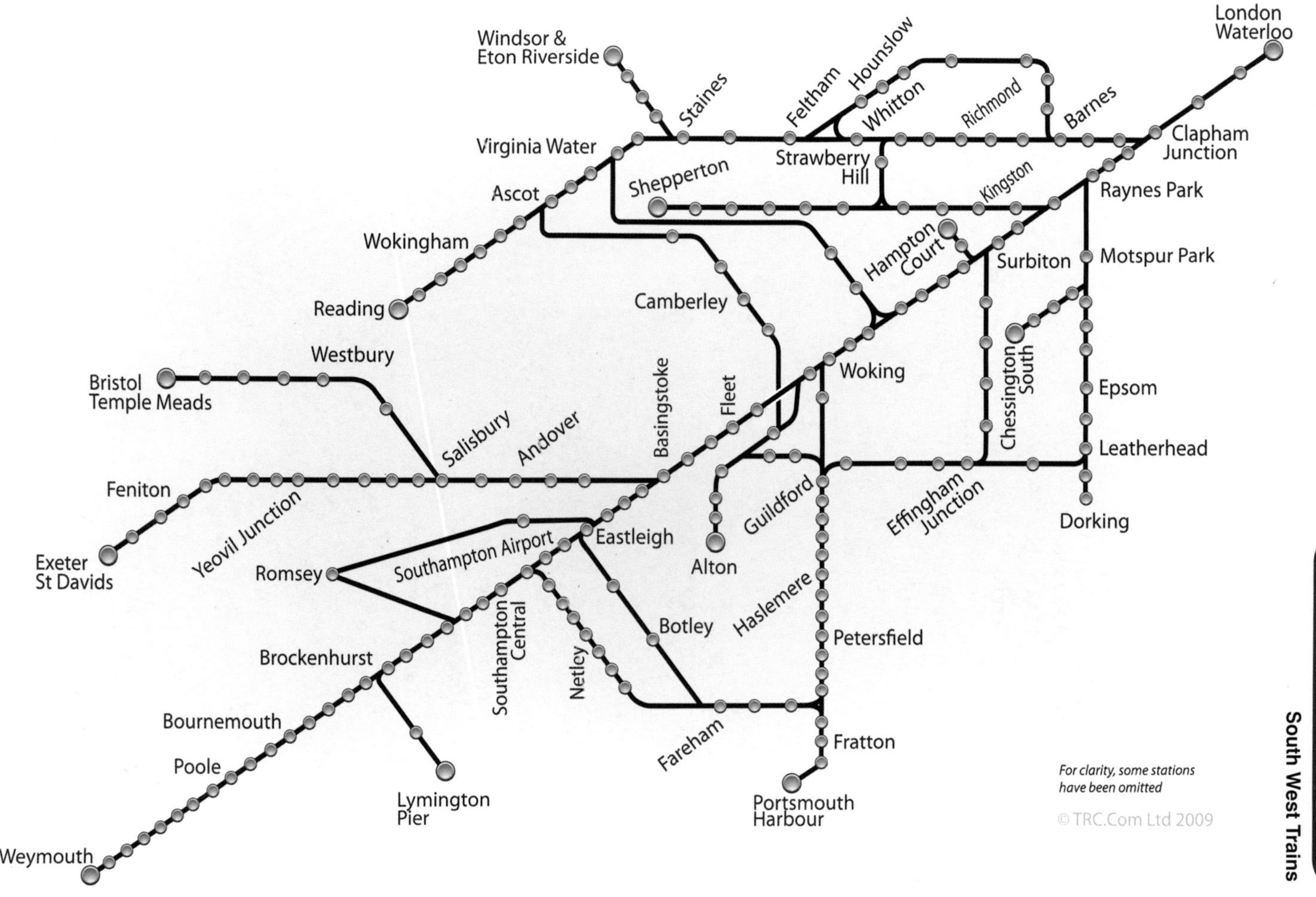
London Waterloo
Clapham Junction
Raynes Park
Motspur Park
Epsom
Leatherhead
Dorking
Barnes
Richmond
Kingston
Surbiton
Chessington South
Hampton Court
Effingham Junction
Whitton
Hounslow
Strawberry Hill
Feltham
Woking
Petersfield
Fratton
Portsmouth Harbour
Guildford
Haslemere
Staines
Shepperton
Fleet
Alton
Camberley
Basingstoke
Botley
Fareham
Windsor & Eton Riverside
Virginia Water
Ascot
Eastleigh
Netley
Andover
Southampton Airport
Southampton Central
Salisbury
Wokingham
Reading
Westbury
Romsey
Brockenhurst
Lymington Pier
Bournemouth
Poole
Yeovil Junction
Bristol Temple Meads
Feniton
Exeter St Davids
Weymouth
For clarity, some stations have been omitted
© TRC.Com Ltd 2009

South West Trains

Class 159/0

Vehicle Length: 76ft 1¾in (23.21m) Engine: 1 x Cummins NTA855R of 400hp per vehicle
Height: 12ft 6in (3.81m) Horsepower: 1,200hp (895kW)
Width: 9ft 3¼in (2.82m) Seats (total/car): 24F-172S, 24F-28S/72S/72S

Number	*Formation DMCL+MSL+DMSL*	*Depot*	*Livery*	*Owner*	*Operator*	*Name*
159001	52873+58718+57873	SA	SWM	PTR	SWT	*City of Exeter*
159002	52874+58719+57874	SA	SWM	PTR	SWT	*City of Salisbury*
159003	52875+58720+57875	SA	SWM	PTR	SWT	*Templecombe*
159004	52876+58721+57876	SA	SWM	PTR	SWT	*Basingstoke and Deane*
159005	52877+58722+57877	SA	SWM	PTR	SWT	
159006	52878+58723+57878	SA	SWM	PTR	SWT	
159007	52879+58724+57879	SA	SWM	PTR	SWT	
159008	52880+58725+57880	SA	SWM	PTR	SWT	
159009	52881+58726+57881	SA	SWM	PTR	SWT	
159010	52882+58727+57882	SA	SWM	PTR	SWT	
159011	52883+58728+57883	SA	SWM	PTR	SWT	
159012	52884+58729+57884	SA	SWM	PTR	SWT	
159013	52885+58730+57885	SA	SWM	PTR	SWT	
159014	52886+58731+57886	SA	SWM	PTR	SWT	
159015	52887+58732+57887	SA	SWM	PTR	SWT	
159016	52888+58733+57888	SA	SWM	PTR	SWT	
159017	52889+58734+57889	SA	SWM	PTR	SWT	
159018	52890+58735+57890	SA	SWM	PTR	SWT	
159019	52891+58736+57891	SA	SWM	PTR	SWT	
159020	52892+58737+57892	SA	SWM	PTR	SWT	
159021	52893+58738+57893	SA	SWM	PTR	SWT	
159022	52894+58739+57894	SA	SWM	PTR	SWT	

Left: *The original 22 Class 159/0 sets operated by South West Trains were built as the final vehicles of the Regional Railways Class 158 order and assigned to Network SouthEast to modernise the Waterloo-Exeter route. The sets are now all allocated to Salisbury and together with eight additional Class 159/1s are the backbone of the Waterloo-Exeter route, operating in either 3, 6 or 9 car formations. All sets are painted in full Stagecoach white livery and are fully refurbished internally, work carried out by Wabtec of Doncaster. Set No. 159020 passes Winchfield with a Yeovil Junction to Waterloo service.* **CJM**

Class 159/1

Vehicle Length: 76ft 1¾in (23.21m) Engine: 1 x Cummins NTA855R of 350hp per vehicle
Height: 12ft 6in (3.81m) Horsepower: 1,050hp (782kW)
Width: 9ft 3¼in (2.82m) Seats (total/car): 24F-170S, 24F-28S/70S/72S

Number	*Formation DMCL+MSL+DMSL*	*Depot*	*Livery*	*Owner*	*Operator*
159101 (158800)	52800+58717+57800	SA	SWM	PTR	SWT
159102 (158803)	52803+58703+57803	SA	SWM	PTR	SWT
159103 (158804)	52804+58704+57804	SA	SWM	PTR	SWT
159104 (158805)	52805+58705+57805	SA	SWM	PTR	SWT
159105 (158807)	52807+58707+57807	SA	SWM	PTR	SWT
159106 (158909)	52809+58709+57809	SA	SWM	PTR	SWT
159107 (158811)	52811+58711+57811	SA	SWM	PTR	SWT
159108 (158801)	52801+58701+57801	SA	SWM	PTR	SWT

Right: *As part of a major switch round of rolling stock following introduction of new DMU stock, a small batch of Class 170s operated by SWT were traded with Porterbrook in return for eight 'new' Class 159/1s, modified by Wabtec Doncaster from redundant Class 158 sets. The units are allocated alongside the original Class 159s at Salisbury and operate on the core Waterloo-Exeter route. These sets have the slightly less powerful engine, but route performance is still good. Set No. 159101 is seen at Plymouth.* **CJM**

Class 421 (3-CIG)

Vehicle Length: 64ft 9½in (19.75m)
Height: 12ft 9¼in (3.89m)
Width: 9ft 3in (2.81m)
Horsepower: 1,000hp (740kW)
Seats (total/car): 18F-146SS, 18F-36S/56S/54S

Number	*Formation* DTC(A)+MBSO+DTC(B)	*Depot*	*Livery*	*Owner*	*Operator*	*Name*
(42)1497 (1883)	**76764+62402+76835**	**BM**	**BLG**	**SWT**	**SWT**	***Freshwater***
(42)1498 (1888)	**76773+62411+76844**	**BM**	**GRN**	**SWT**	**SWT**	***Farringford***

■ *South West Trains announced in late 2009 that the two Class 421 sets would be replaced by Class 158s or 159s from May 2010.*

Right: *Just two slam-door units remain operational on South West Trains, allocated to Bournemouth and used on the Brockenhurst to Lymington Pier line. The sets, one painted in blue grey and the other in 1960s green, are likely to be withdrawn in the foreseeable future as maintenance costs are too high to justify their retention. Set No. (42)1497 is seen inside the repair shed at Bournemouth.* **CJM**

Class 444
Desiro

Vehicle Length: 77ft 3in (23.57m)
Height: 12ft 1½in (3.7m)
Width: 9ft 2in (2.7m)
Horsepower: 2,682hp (2,000kW)
Seats (total/car): 35F-299S, 35F-24S/47S/76S/76S/76S

Number	*Formation* DMCO+TSO+TSO+TSRMB+DMSO	*Depot*	*Livery*	*Owner*	*Operator*	*Name*
444001	**63801+67101+67151+67201+63851**	**NT**	**SWM**	**ANG**	**SWT**	***Naomi House***
444002	**63802+67102+67152+67202+63852**	**NT**	**SWM**	**ANG**	**SWT**	
444003	**63803+67103+67153+67203+63853**	**NT**	**SWM**	**ANG**	**SWT**	
444004	**63804+67104+67154+67204+63854**	**NT**	**SWM**	**ANG**	**SWT**	
444005	**63805+67105+67155+67205+63855**	**NT**	**SWM**	**ANG**	**SWT**	
444006	**63806+67106+67156+67206+63856**	**NT**	**SWM**	**ANG**	**SWT**	
444007	**63807+67107+67157+67207+63857**	**NT**	**SWM**	**ANG**	**SWT**	
444008	**63808+67108+67158+67208+63858**	**NT**	**SWM**	**ANG**	**SWT**	
444009	**63809+67109+67159+67209+63859**	**NT**	**SWM**	**ANG**	**SWT**	
444010	**63810+67110+67160+67210+63860**	**NT**	**SWM**	**ANG**	**SWT**	
444011	**63811+67111+67161+67211+63861**	**NT**	**SWM**	**ANG**	**SWT**	
444012	**63812+67112+67162+67212+63862**	**NT**	**SWM**	**ANG**	**SWT**	***Destination Weymouth***
444013	**63813+67113+67163+67213+63863**	**NT**	**SWM**	**ANG**	**SWT**	
444014	**63814+67114+67164+67214+63864**	**NT**	**SWM**	**ANG**	**SWT**	
444015	**63815+67115+67165+67215+63865**	**NT**	**SWM**	**ANG**	**SWT**	
444016	**63816+67116+67166+67216+63866**	**NT**	**SWM**	**ANG**	**SWT**	
444017	**63817+67117+67167+67217+63867**	**NT**	**SWM**	**ANG**	**SWT**	

South West Trains

Number	Formation	Depot	Livery	Owner	Operator	Name
444018	63818+67118+67168+67218+63868	NT	SWM	ANG	SWT	*FAB 444*
444019	63819+67119+67169+67219+63869	NT	SWM	ANG	SWT	
444020	63820+67120+67170+67220+63870	NT	SWM	ANG	SWT	
444021	63821+67121+67171+67221+63871	NT	SWM	ANG	SWT	
444022	63822+67122+67172+67222+63872	NT	SWM	ANG	SWT	
444023	63823+67123+67173+67223+63873	NT	SWM	ANG	SWT	
444024	63824+67124+67174+67224+63874	NT	SWM	ANG	SWT	
444025	63825+67125+67175+67225+63875	NT	SWM	ANG	SWT	
444026	63826+67126+67176+67226+63876	NT	SWM	ANG	SWT	
444027	63827+67127+67177+67227+63877	NT	SWM	ANG	SWT	
444028	63828+67128+67178+67228+63878	NT	SWM	ANG	SWT	
444029	63829+67129+67179+67229+63879	NT	SWM	ANG	SWT	
444030	63830+67130+67180+67230+63880	NT	SWM	ANG	SWT	
444031	63831+67131+67181+67231+63881	NT	SWM	ANG	SWT	
444032	63832+67132+67182+67232+63882	NT	SWM	ANG	SWT	
444033	63833+67133+67183+67233+63883	NT	SWM	ANG	SWT	
444034	63834+67134+67184+67234+63884	NT	SWM	ANG	SWT	
444035	63835+67135+67185+67235+63885	NT	SWM	ANG	SWT	
444036	63836+67136+67186+67236+63886	NT	SWM	ANG	SWT	
444037	63837+67137+67187+67237+63887	NT	SWM	ANG	SWT	
444038	63838+67138+67188+67238+63888	NT	SWM	ANG	SWT	
444039	63839+67139+67189+67239+63889	NT	SWM	ANG	SWT	
444040	63840+67140+67190+67240+63890	NT	SWM	ANG	SWT	
444041	63841+67141+67191+67241+63891	NT	SWM	ANG	SWT	
444042	63842+67142+67192+67242+63892	NT	SWM	ANG	SWT	
444043	63843+67143+67193+67243+63893	NT	SWM	ANG	SWT	
444044	63844+67144+67194+67244+63894	NT	SWM	ANG	SWT	
444045	63845+67145+67195+67245+63895	NT	SWM	ANG	SWT	

Left: *The main line South West Trains Class 444 fleet are finished in the Stagecoach white livery, off-set by red passenger doors and swirl ends on driving cars. The units are allocated to the Siemens-operated Northam depot near Southampton and are deployed on main line services between London, Bournemouth, Weymouth and Portsmouth. Set No. 444013 is recorded at Bournemouth.* **CJM**

Class 450/0
Desiro

Vehicle Length: 66ft 9in (20.4m)
Height: 12ft 1½in (3.7m)
Width: 9ft 2in (2.7m)
Horsepower: 2,682hp (2,000kW)
Seats (total/car): 24F-246S, 70S/24F-36S/70S/79S

Number	*Formation* DMSO+TCO+TSO+DMSO	*Depot*	*Livery*	*Owner*	*Operator*	*Name*
450001	63201+64201+68101+63601	NT	SWO	ANG	SWT	
450002	63202+64202+68102+63602	NT	SWO	ANG	SWT	
450003	63203+64203+68103+63603	NT	SWO	ANG	SWT	
450004	63204+64204+68104+63604	NT	SWO	ANG	SWT	
450005	63205+64205+68205+63605	NT	SWO	ANG	SWT	
450006	63206+64206+68206+63606	NT	SWO	ANG	SWT	
450007	63207+64207+68207+63607	NT	SWO	ANG	SWT	
450008	63208+64208+68108+63608	NT	SWO	ANG	SWT	
450009	63209+64209+68109+63609	NT	SWO	ANG	SWT	
450010	63210+64210+68110+63610	NT	SWO	ANG	SWT	
450011	63211+64211+68111+63611	NT	SWO	ANG	SWT	
450012	63212+64212+68112+63612	NT	SWO	ANG	SWT	
450013	63213+64213+68113+63613	NT	SWO	ANG	SWT	
450014	63214+64214+68114+63614	NT	SWO	ANG	SWT	

450015	63215+64215+68115+63615	NT	SWO	ANG	SWT	*Desiro*
450016	63216+64216+68116+63616	NT	SWO	ANG	SWT	
450017	63217+64217+68117+63617	NT	SWO	ANG	SWT	
450018	63218+64218+68118+63618	NT	SWO	ANG	SWT	
450019	63219+64219+68119+63619	NT	SWO	ANG	SWT	
450020	63220+64220+68120+63620	NT	SWO	ANG	SWT	
450021	63221+64221+68121+63621	NT	SWO	ANG	SWT	
450022	63222+64222+68122+63622	NT	SWO	ANG	SWT	
450023	63223+64223+68123+63623	NT	SWO	ANG	SWT	
450024	63224+64224+68124+63624	NT	SWO	ANG	SWT	
450025	63225+64225+68125+63625	NT	SWO	ANG	SWT	
450026	63226+64226+68126+63626	NT	SWO	ANG	SWT	
450027	63227+64227+68127+63627	NT	SWO	ANG	SWT	
450028	63228+64228+68128+63628	NT	SWO	ANG	SWT	
450029	63229+64229+68129+63629	NT	SWO	ANG	SWT	
450030	63230+64230+68130+63630	NT	SWO	ANG	SWT	
450031	63231+64231+68131+63631	NT	SWO	ANG	SWT	
450032	63232+64232+68132+63632	NT	SWO	ANG	SWT	
450033	63233+64233+68133+63633	NT	SWO	ANG	SWT	
450034	63234+64234+68134+63634	NT	SWO	ANG	SWT	
450035	63235+64235+68135+63635	NT	SWO	ANG	SWT	
450036	63236+64236+68136+63636	NT	SWO	ANG	SWT	
450037	63237+64237+68137+63637	NT	SWO	ANG	SWT	
450038	63238+64238+68138+63638	NT	SWO	ANG	SWT	
450039	63239+64239+68139+63639	NT	SWO	ANG	SWT	
450040	63240+64240+68140+63640	NT	SWO	ANG	SWT	
450041	63241+64241+68141+63641	NT	SWO	ANG	SWT	
450042	63242+64242+68142+63642	NT	SWO	ANG	SWT	*Treloar College*
450071	63271+64271+68171+63671	NT	SWO	ANG	SWT	
450072	63272+64272+68172+63672	NT	SWO	ANG	SWT	
450073	63273+64273+68173+63673	NT	SWO	ANG	SWT	
450074	63274+64274+68174+63674	NT	SWO	ANG	SWT	
450075	63275+64275+68175+63675	NT	SWO	ANG	SWT	
450076	63276+64276+68176+63676	NT	SWO	ANG	SWT	
450077	63277+64277+68177+63677	NT	SWO	ANG	SWT	
450078	63278+64278+68178+63678	NT	SWO	ANG	SWT	
450079	63279+64279+68179+63679	NT	SWO	ANG	SWT	
450080	63280+64280+68180+63680	NT	SWO	ANG	SWT	
450081	63281+64281+68181+63681	NT	SWO	ANG	SWT	
450082	63282+64282+68182+63682	NT	SWO	ANG	SWT	
450083	63283+64283+68183+63683	NT	SWO	ANG	SWT	
450084	63284+64284+68184+63684	NT	SWO	ANG	SWT	
450085	63285+64285+68185+63685	NT	SWO	ANG	SWT	
450086	63286+64286+68186+63686	NT	SWO	ANG	SWT	
450087	63287+64287+68187+63687	NT	SWO	ANG	SWT	
450088	63288+64288+68188+63688	NT	SWO	ANG	SWT	
450089	63289+64289+68189+63689	NT	SWO	ANG	SWT	
450090	63290+64290+68190+63690	NT	SWO	ANG	SWT	
450091	63291+64291+68191+63691	NT	SWO	ANG	SWT	
450092	63292+64292+68192+63692	NT	SWO	ANG	SWT	
450093	63293+64293+68193+63693	NT	SWO	ANG	SWT	
450094	63294+64294+68194+63694	NT	SWO	ANG	SWT	
450095	63295+64295+68195+63695	NT	SWO	ANG	SWT	
450096	63296+64296+68196+63696	NT	SWO	ANG	SWT	
450097	63297+64297+68197+63697	NT	SWO	ANG	SWT	
450098	63298+64298+68198+63698	NT	SWO	ANG	SWT	
450099	63299+64299+68199+63699	NT	SWO	ANG	SWT	
50100	63300+64300+68200+63700	NT	SWO	ANG	SWT	
0101	63701+66851+66801+63751	NT	SWO	ANG	SWT	
102	63702+66852+66802+63752	NT	SWO	ANG	SWT	
103	63703+66853+66803+63753	NT	SWO	ANG	SWT	
04	63704+66854+66804+63754	NT	SWO	ANG	SWT	
5	63705+66855+66805+63755	NT	SWO	ANG	SWT	
[illegible]	63706+66856+66806+63756	NT	SWO	ANG	SWT	
	63707+66857+66807+63757	NT	SWO	ANG	SWT	

South West Trains

Number	Formation	Depot	Livery	Owner	Operator	Name
450108	63708+66858+66808+63758	NT	SWO	ANG	SWT	
450109	63709+66859+66809+63759	NT	SWO	ANG	SWT	
450110	63710+66860+66810+63750	NT	SWO	ANG	SWT	
450111	63901+66921+66921+63921	NT	SWO	ANG	SWT	
450112	63902+66922+66922+63922	NT	SWO	ANG	SWT	
450113	63903+66923+66923+63923	NT	SWO	ANG	SWT	
450114	63904+66924+66924+63924	NT	SWO	ANG	SWT	*Fairbridge - investing in the Future*
450115	63905+66925+66905+63925	NT	SWO	ANG	SWT	
450116	63906+66926+66906+63926	NT	SWO	ANG	SWT	
450117	63907+66927+66907+63927	NT	SWO	ANG	SWT	
450118	63908+66928+66908+63928	NT	SWO	ANG	SWT	
450119	63909+66929+66909+63929	NT	SWO	ANG	SWT	
450120	63910+66930+66910+63930	NT	SWO	ANG	SWT	
450121	63911+66931+66911+63931	NT	SWO	ANG	SWT	
450122	63912+66932+66912+63932	NT	SWO	ANG	SWT	
450123	63913+66933+66913+63933	NT	SWO	ANG	SWT	
450124	63914+66934+66914+63934	NT	SWO	ANG	SWT	
450125	63915+66935+66915+63935	NT	SWO	ANG	SWT	
450126	63916+66936+66916+63936	NT	SWO	ANG	SWT	
450127	63917+66937+66917+63937	NT	SWO	ANG	SWT	

Class 450/5
Desiro

Vehicle Length: 66ft 9in (20.4m)
Height: 12ft 1½in (3.7m)
Width: 9ft 2in (2.7m)
Horsepower: 2,682hp (2,000kW)
Seats (total/car): 240S, 64S/56S/56S/64S

Number	*Formation* DMSO+TSO+TSO+DMSO	*Depot*	*Livery*	*Owner*	*Operator*
450543 (450043)	63243+64243+68143+63643	NT	SWO	ANG	SWT
450544 (450044)	63244+64244+68144+63644	NT	SWO	ANG	SWT
450545 (450045)	63245+64245+68145+63645	NT	SWO	ANG	SWT
450546 (450046)	63246+64246+68146+63646	NT	SWO	ANG	SWT
450547 (450047)	63247+64247+68147+63647	NT	SWO	ANG	SWT
450548 (450048)	63248+64248+68148+63648	NT	SWO	ANG	SWT
450549 (450049)	63249+64249+68149+63649	NT	SWO	ANG	SWT
450550 (450050)	63250+64250+68150+63650	NT	SWO	ANG	SWT
450551 (450051)	63251+64251+68151+63651	NT	SWO	ANG	SWT
450552 (450052)	63252+64252+68152+63652	NT	SWO	ANG	SWT
450553 (450053)	63253+64253+68153+63653	NT	SWO	ANG	SWT
450554 (450054)	63254+64254+68154+63654	NT	SWO	ANG	SWT
450555 (450055)	63255+64255+68155+63655	NT	SWO	ANG	SWT
450556 (450056)	63256+64256+68156+63656	NT	SWO	ANG	SWT
450557 (450057)	63257+64257+68157+63657	NT	SWO	ANG	SWT
450558 (450058)	63258+64258+68158+63658	NT	SWO	ANG	SWT
450559 (450059)	63259+64259+68159+63659	NT	SWO	ANG	SWT
450560 (450060)	63260+64260+68160+63660	NT	SWO	ANG	SWT
450561 (450061)	63261+64261+68161+63661	NT	SWO	ANG	SWT
450562 (450062)	63262+64262+68162+63662	NT	SWO	ANG	SWT
450563 (450063)	63263+64263+68163+63663	NT	SWO	ANG	SWT
450564 (450064)	63264+64264+68164+63664	NT	SWO	ANG	SWT
450565 (450065)	63265+64265+68165+63665	NT	SWO	ANG	SWT
450566 (450066)	63266+64266+68166+63666	NT	SWO	ANG	SWT
450567 (450067)	63267+64267+68167+63667	NT	SWO	ANG	SWT
450568 (450068)	63268+64268+68168+63668	NT	SWO	ANG	SWT
450569 (450069)	63269+64269+68169+63669	NT	SWO	ANG	SWT
450570 (450070)	63270+64270+68170+63670	NT	SWO	ANG	SWT

Left: *The nameplate* Desiro *as to set No. 450015.* **CJM**

Right: *Painted in Stagecoach outer-suburban blue livery, off-set by red doors and swirl ends, the Class 450 Desiro sets share allocation with the Class 444s at Northam depot and can be found throughout the SWT electrified area. Set No. 450114 is illustrated approaching Winchfield with a semi-fast Southampton to Waterloo service. Note the recess on the roof of the third vehicle from the front where a pantograph could be installed if the fleet were modified for dual-voltage operation.* **CJM**

Class 455/7

Vehicle Length: (Driving) 65ft 0½in (19.83m)
(Inter) 65ft 4½in (19.92m)
Height: 12ft 1½in (3.79m) [TSO- 11ft 6½in (3.58m)
Width: 9ft 3¼in (2.82m)
Horsepower: 1,000hp (746kW)
Seats (total/car): 244S, 54S/68S/68S/54S

Number	*Formation* DMSO(A)+MSO+TSO+DTSO(B)	*Depot*	*Livery*	*Owner*	*Operator*	
(45)5701	**77727+62783+71545+77728**	**WD**	**SWS**	**PTR**	**SWT**	
(45)5702	**77729+62784+71547+77730**	**WD**	**SWS**	**PTR**	**SWT**	
(45)5703	**77731+62785+71540+77732**	**WD**	**SWS**	**PTR**	**SWT**	
(45)5704	**77733+62786+71548+77734**	**WD**	**SWS**	**PTR**	**SWT**	
(45)5705	**77735+62787+71565+77736**	**WD**	**SWS**	**PTR**	**SWT**	
(45)5706	**77737+62788+71534+77738**	**WD**	**SWS**	**PTR**	**SWT**	
(45)5707	**77739+62789+71536+77740**	**WD**	**SWS**	**PTR**	**SWT**	
(45)5708	**77741+62790+71560+77742**	**WD**	**SWS**	**PTR**	**SWT**	
(45)5709	**77743+62791+71532+77744**	**WD**	**SWS**	**PTR**	**SWT**	
(45)5710	**77745+62792+71566+77746**	**WD**	**SWS**	**PTR**	**SWT**	
(45)5711	**77747+62793+71542+77748**	**WD**	**SWS**	**PTR**	**SWT**	
(45)5712	**77749+62794+71546+77750**	**WD**	**SWS**	**PTR**	**SWT**	
(45)5713	**77751+62795+71567+77752**	**WD**	**SWS**	**PTR**	**SWT**	
(45)5714	**77753+62796+71539+77754**	**WD**	**SWS**	**PTR**	**SWT**	
(45)5715	**77755+62796+71535+77756**	**WD**	**SWS**	**PTR**	**SWT**	
(45)5716	**77757+62798+71564+77758**	**WD**	**SWS**	**PTR**	**SWT**	
(45)5717	**77759+62799+71528+77760**	**WD**	**SWS**	**PTR**	**SWT**	
(45)5718	**77761+62800+71557+77762**	**WD**	**SWS**	**PTR**	**SWT**	
(45)5719	**77763+62801+71558+77764**	**WD**	**SWS**	**PTR**	**SWT**	
(45)5720	**77765+62802+71568+77766**	**WD**	**SWS**	**PTR**	**SWT**	
(45)5721	**77767+62803+71553+77768**	**WD**	**SWS**	**PTR**	**SWT**	
(45)5722	**77769+62804+71533+77770**	**WD**	**SWS**	**PTR**	**SWT**	
(45)5723	**77771+62805+71526+77772**	**WD**	**SWS**	**PTR**	**SWT**	
(45)5724	**77773+62806+71561+77774**	**WD**	**SWS**	**PTR**	**SWT**	
(45)5725	**77775+62807+71541+77776**	**WD**	**SWS**	**PTR**	**SWT**	
(45)5726	**77777+62608+71556+77778**	**WD**	**SWS**	**PTR**	**SWT**	
(45)5727	**77779+62809+71562+77780**	**WD**	**SWS**	**PTR**	**SWT**	
(45)5728	**77781+62810+71527+77782**	**WD**	**SWS**	**PTR**	**SWT**	
(45)5729	**77783+62811+71550+77784**	**WD**	**SWS**	**PTR**	**SWT**	
(45)5730	**77785+62812+71551+77786**	**WD**	**SWS**	**PTR**	**SWT**	
(45)5731	**77787+62813+71555+77788**	**WD**	**SWS**	**PTR**	**SWT**	
(45)5732	**77789+62814+71552+77790**	**WD**	**SWS**	**PTR**	**SWT**	
(45)5733	**77791+62815+71549+77792**	**WD**	**SWS**	**PTR**	**SWT**	
(45)5734	**77793+62816+71531+77794**	**WD**	**SWS**	**PTR**	**SWT**	
(45)5735	**77795+62817+71563+77796**	**WD**	**SWS**	**PTR**	**SWT**	
(45)5736	**77797+62818+71554+77798**	**WD**	**SWS**	**PTR**	**SWT**	
(45)5737	**77799+62819+71544+77800**	**WD**	**SWS**	**PTR**	**SWT**	
(45)5738	**77801+62820+71529+77802**	**WD**	**SWS**	**PTR**	**SWT**	
(45)5739	**77803+62821+71537+77804**	**WD**	**SWS**	**PTR**	**SWT**	
(45)5740	**77805+62822+71530+77806**	**WD**	**SWS**	**PTR**	**SWT**	
(45)5741	**77807+62823+71559+77808**	**WD**	**SWS**	**PTR**	**SWT**	
(45)5742	**77809+62824+71543+77810**	**WD**	**SWS**	**PTR**	**SWT**	
(45)5750*	**77811+62825+71538+77812**	**WD**	**SWS**	**PTR**	**SWT**	** Originally numbered (45)5743*

Left: *All Class 455/7s have now been fully refurbished and sport the South West Trains suburban red livery. During refurbishment at Ashford, the light clusters were revised to house a joint marker/tail light. Set No. (45)5740 stops at Clapham Junction with a service bound for Waterloo.* **CJM**

Class 455/8

Vehicle Length: (Driving) 65ft 0½in (19.83m)
(Inter) 65ft 4½in (19.92m)
Height: 12ft 1½in (3.79m)
Width: 9ft 3¼in (2.82m)
Horsepower: 1,000hp (746kW)
Seats (total/car): 223S, 50S/84S/84S/50S

Number	*Formation* DMSO(A)+MSO+TSO+DTSO(B)	*Depot*	*Livery*	*Owner*	*Operator*
(45)5847	77671+62755+71683+77672	WD	SWS	PTR	SWT
(45)5848	77673+62756+71684+77674	WD	SWS	PTR	SWT
(45)5849	77675+62757+71685+77676	WD	SWS	PTR	SWT
(45)5850	77677+62758+71686+77678	WD	SWS	PTR	SWT
(45)5851	77679+62759+71687+77680	WD	SWS	PTR	SWT
(45)5852	77681+62760+71688+77682	WD	SWS	PTR	SWT
(45)5853	77683+62761+71689+77684	WD	SWS	PTR	SWT
(45)5854	77685+62762+71690+77686	WD	SWS	PTR	SWT
(45)5855	77687+62763+71691+77688	WD	SWS	PTR	SWT
(45)5856	77689+62764+71692+77690	WD	SWS	PTR	SWT
(45)5857	77691+62765+71693+77692	WD	SWS	PTR	SWT
(45)5858	77693+62766+71694+77694	WD	SWS	PTR	SWT
(45)5859	77695+62767+71695+77696	WD	SWS	PTR	SWT
(45)5860	77697+62768+71696+77698	WD	SWS	PTR	SWT
(45)5861	77699+62769+71697+77700	WD	SWS	PTR	SWT
(45)5862	77701+62770+71698+77702	WD	SWS	PTR	SWT
(45)5863	77703+62771+71699+77704	WD	SWS	PTR	SWT
(45)5864	77705+62772+71700+77706	WD	SWS	PTR	SWT
(45)5865	77707+62773+71701+77708	WD	SWS	PTR	SWT
(45)5866	77709+62774+71702+77710	WD	SWS	PTR	SWT
(45)5867	77711+62775+71703+77712	WD	SWS	PTR	SWT
(45)5868	77713+62776+71704+77714	WD	SWS	PTR	SWT
(45)5869	77715+62777+71705+77716	WD	SWS	PTR	SWT
(45)5870	77717+62778+71706+77718	WD	SWS	PTR	SWT
(45)5871	77719+62779+71707+77720	WD	SWS	PTR	SWT
(45)5872	77721+62780+71708+77722	WD	SWS	PTR	SWT
(45)5873	77723+62781+71709+77724	WD	SWS	PTR	SWT
(45)5874	77725+62782+71710+77726	WD	SWS	PTR	SWT

Left: *The original build of Class 455s for BR Southern Region have the earlier type of raised centre section cab roofs, with roof mounted warnin horns. Painted in full SWT livery, N (45)5847 is seen at Vauxhall on 19 2009.* **Stacey Thew**

Class 455/9

Vehicle Length: (Driving) 65ft 0½in (19.83m)
(Inter) 65ft 4½in (19.92m)
Height: 12ft 1½in (3.79m)
Width: 9ft 3¼in (2.82m)
Horsepower: 1,000hp (746kW)
Seats (total/car): 236S, 50S/68S/68S/50S

Number	Formation DMSO(A)+MSO+TSO+DTSO(B)	Depot	Livery	Owner	Operator
(45)5901	77813+62826+71714+77814	WD	SWS	PTR	SWT
(45)5902	77815+62827+71715+77816	WD	SWS	PTR	SWT
(45)5903	77817+62828+71716+77818	WD	SWS	PTR	SWT
(45)5904	77819+62829+71717+77820	WD	SWS	PTR	SWT
(45)5905	77821+62830+71725+77822	WD	SWS	PTR	SWT
(45)5906	77823+62831+71719+77824	WD	SWS	PTR	SWT
(45)5907	77825+62832+71720+77826	WD	SWS	PTR	SWT
(45)5908	77827+62833+71721+77828	WD	SWS	PTR	SWT
(45)5909	77829+62834+71722+77830	WD	SWS	PTR	SWT
(45)5910	77831+62835+71723+77832	WD	SWS	PTR	SWT
(45)5911	77833+62836+71724+77834	WD	SWS	PTR	SWT
(45)5912	77835+62837+67400+77836	WD	SWS	PTR	SWT
(45)5913	77837+62838+71726+77838	WD	SWS	PTR	SWT
(45)5914	77839+62839+71727+77840	WD	SWS	PTR	SWT
(45)5915	77841+62840+71728+77842	WD	SWS	PTR	SWT
(45)5916	77843+62841+71729+77844	WD	SWS	PTR	SWT
(45)5917	77845+62842+71730+77846	WD	SWS	PTR	SWT
(45)5918	77847+62843+71732+77848	WD	SWS	PTR	SWT
(45)5919	77849+62844+71718+77850	WD	SWS	PTR	SWT
(45)5920	77851+62845+71733+77852	WD	SWS	PTR	SWT

Right: *By the time the final 20 Class 455s were ordered, the front end design had been cleaned up with a more streamlined roof profile, thus rendering this sub-class recognisable from the remainder of the fleet. Set No. (45)5907 stops at Berrylands on 6 October 2008 with a service to Hampton Court.* **John Binch**

Class 458
Juniper

Vehicle Length: (Driving) 69ft 6in (21.16m)
(Inter) 65ft 4in (19.91m)
Height: 12ft 3in (3.73m)
Width: 9ft 2in (2.79m)
Horsepower: 2,172hp (1,620kW)
Seats (total/car): 24F-250S, 12F-63S/49S/75S/12F-63S

Number	Formation DMCO(A)+TSO+MSO+DTCO(B)	Depot	Livery	Owner	Operator
(45)8001	67601+74001+74101+67701	WD	SWM	PTR	SWT
(45)8002	67602+74002+74102+67702	WD	SWM	PTR	SWT
(45)8003	67603+74003+74103+67703	WD	SWM	PTR	SWT
(45)8004	67604+74004+74104+67704	WD	SWM	PTR	SWT
(45)8005	67605+74005+74105+67705	WD	SWM	PTR	SWT
(45)8006	67606+74006+74106+67706	WD	SWM	PTR	SWT
(45)8007	67607+74007+74107+67707	WD	SWM	PTR	SWT
(45)8008	67608+74008+74108+67708	WD	SWM	PTR	SWT
(45)8009	67609+74009+74109+67709	WD	SWM	PTR	SWT
(45)8010	67610+74010+74110+67710	WD	SWM	PTR	SWT
(45)8011	67611+74011+74111+67711	WD	SWM	PTR	SWT
'45)8012	67612+74012+74112+67712	WD	SWM	PTR	SWT
45)8013	67613+74013+74113+67713	WD	SWM	PTR	SWT
5)8014	67614+74014+74114+67714	WD	SWM	PTR	SWT
5)8015	67615+74015+74115+67715	WD	SWM	PTR	SWT
)8016	67616+74016+74116+67716	WD	SWM	PTR	SWT

South West Trains

(45)8017	67617+74017+74117+67717	WD	SWM	PTR	SWT
(45)8018	67618+74018+74118+67718	WD	SWM	PTR	SWT
(45)8019	67619+74019+74119+67719	WD	SWM	PTR	SWT
(45)8020	67620+74020+74120+67720	WD	SWM	PTR	SWT
(45)8021	67621+74021+74121+67721	WD	SWM	PTR	SWT
(45)8022	67622+74022+74122+67722	WD	SWM	PTR	SWT
(45)8023	67623+74023+74123+67723	WD	SWM	PTR	SWT
(45)8024	67624+74024+74124+67724	WD	SWM	PTR	SWT
(45)8025	67625+74025+74125+67725	WD	SWM	PTR	SWT
(45)8026	67626+74026+74126+67726	WD	SWM	PTR	SWT
(45)8027	67627+74027+74127+67727	WD	SWM	PTR	SWT
(45)8028	67628+74028+74128+67728	WD	SWM	PTR	SWT
(45)8029	67629+74029+74129+67729	WD	SWM	PTR	SWT
(45)8030	67630+74030+74130+67730	WD	SWM	PTR	SWT

Left: *It is unlikely that the Class 458 'Juniper' units operated by South West Trains would ever win a design award. However, after several years of problems a restricted fleet is now in regular use on the Waterloo-Reading line. The sets usually operate in pairs. Two sets, led by No. (45)8028, approach Vauxhall with a Reading bound service. The front end gangway doors on these sets which were out of use for several years have now all been returned to use.* **CJM**

Class 73

Vehicle Length: 53ft 8in (16.35m)
Height: 12ft 5[5]/16in (3.79m)
Width: 8ft 8in (2.64m)
Power: 750V dc third rail or English Electric 6K
Horsepower: electric - 1,600hp (1,193kW)
Horsepower: diesel - 600hp (447kW)
Electrical Equipment: English Electric

Number	*Depot*	*Pool*	*Livery*	*Owner*	*Operator*	*Name*
73109	**WD**	**HYWD**	**SWT**	**SWT**	**SWT**	***Battle of Britain 50th Anniversary***

Left: *South West Trains still operate one Class 73 electro-diesel for depot shunting of inter-depot transfer moves, but with all Dellner coupling fitted stock now in use, the loco sees less and less work. Its long term future with the TOC is in doubt and at the end of 2009 the loco operated for a short period with Southern and for the departmental sector. No. 73109* Battle of Britain 50th Anniversary *is seen stabled at Bournemouth West depot.* **CJM**

South Eastern

Address: ✉ Friars Bridge Court, 41-45 Blackfriars Road, London, SE1 8NZ
info@southeasternrailway.co.uk
✆ 08700 000 2222
ⓘ www.southeasternrailway.co.uk

Managing Director: Charles Horton
Franchise Dates: 1 April 2006 - 31 March 2012
Principal Routes: London to Kent and parts of East Sussex, domestic services on HS1
Depots: Slade Green (SG), Ramsgate (RM), Ashford (AD*)
Parent Company: Govia
* Operated by Hitachi

Class 375/3 *Electrostar*

Vehicle Length: (Driving) 66ft 9in (20.3m) (Inter) 65ft 6in (19.96m)
Height: 12ft 4in (3.75m)
Width: 9ft 2in (2.79m)
Horsepower: 1,341hp (1,000kW)
Seats (total/car): 24F-152S, 12F-48S/56S/12F-48S

Number	Formation DMCO(A)+TSO+DMCO(B)	Depot	Livery	Owner	Operator	Name
375301	67921+74351+67931	RM	SET	HSB	SET	
375302	67922+74352+67932	RM	SET	HSB	SET	
375303	67923+74353+67933	RM	SET	HSB	SET	
375304	67924+74354+67934	RM	SET	HSB	SET	*Medway Valley Line 1856-2006*
375305	67925+74355+67935	RM	SET	HSB	SET	
375306	67926+74356+67936	RM	SET	HSB	SET	
375307	67927+74357+67937	RM	SET	HSB	SET	
375308	67928+74358+67938	RM	SET	HSB	SET	
375309	67929+74359+67939	RM	SET	HSB	SET	
375310	67930+74360+67940	RM	SET	HSB	SET	

Class 375/6 *Electrostar*

Vehicle Length: (Driving) 66ft 9in (20.3m) (Inter) 65ft 6in (19.96m)
Height: 12ft 4in (3.75m)
Width: 9ft 2in (2.79m)
Horsepower: 2,012hp (1,500kW)
Seats (total/car): 24F-218S, 12F-48S/66S/56S/12F-48S

Number	Formation DMCO(A)+MSO+TSO+DMCO(B)	Depot	Livery	Owner	Operator	Name
375601	67801+74251+74201+67851	RM	SET	HSB	SET	
375602	67802+74252+74202+67852	RM	SET	HSB	SET	
375603	67803+74253+74203+67853	RM	SET	HSB	SET	
375604	67804+74254+74204+67854	RM	SET	HSB	SET	
375605	67805+74255+74205+67855	RM	SET	HSB	SET	
375606	67806+74256+74206+67856	RM	SET	HSB	SET	
375607	67807+74257+74207+67857	RM	SET	HSB	SET	
375608	67808+74258+74208+67858	RM	SET	HSB	SET	*Bromley Travelwise*
375609	67809+74259+74209+67859	RM	SET	HSB	SET	
375610	67810+74260+74210+67860	RM	SET	HSB	SET	*Royal Tunbridge Wells*
375611	67811+74261+74211+67861	RM	SET	HSB	SET	*Dr William Harvey*
375612	67812+74262+74212+67862	RM	SET	HSB	SET	
375613	67813+74263+74213+67863	RM	SET	HSB	SET	
375614	67814+74264+74214+67864	RM	SET	HSB	SET	
375615	67815+74265+74215+67865	RM	SET	HSB	SET	
375616	67816+74266+74216+67866	RM	SET	HSB	SET	
375617	67817+74267+74217+67867	RM	SET	HSB	SET	
375618	67818+74268+74218+67868	RM	SET	HSB	SET	
375619	67819+74269+74219+67869	RM	SET	HSB	SET	*Driver John Neve*

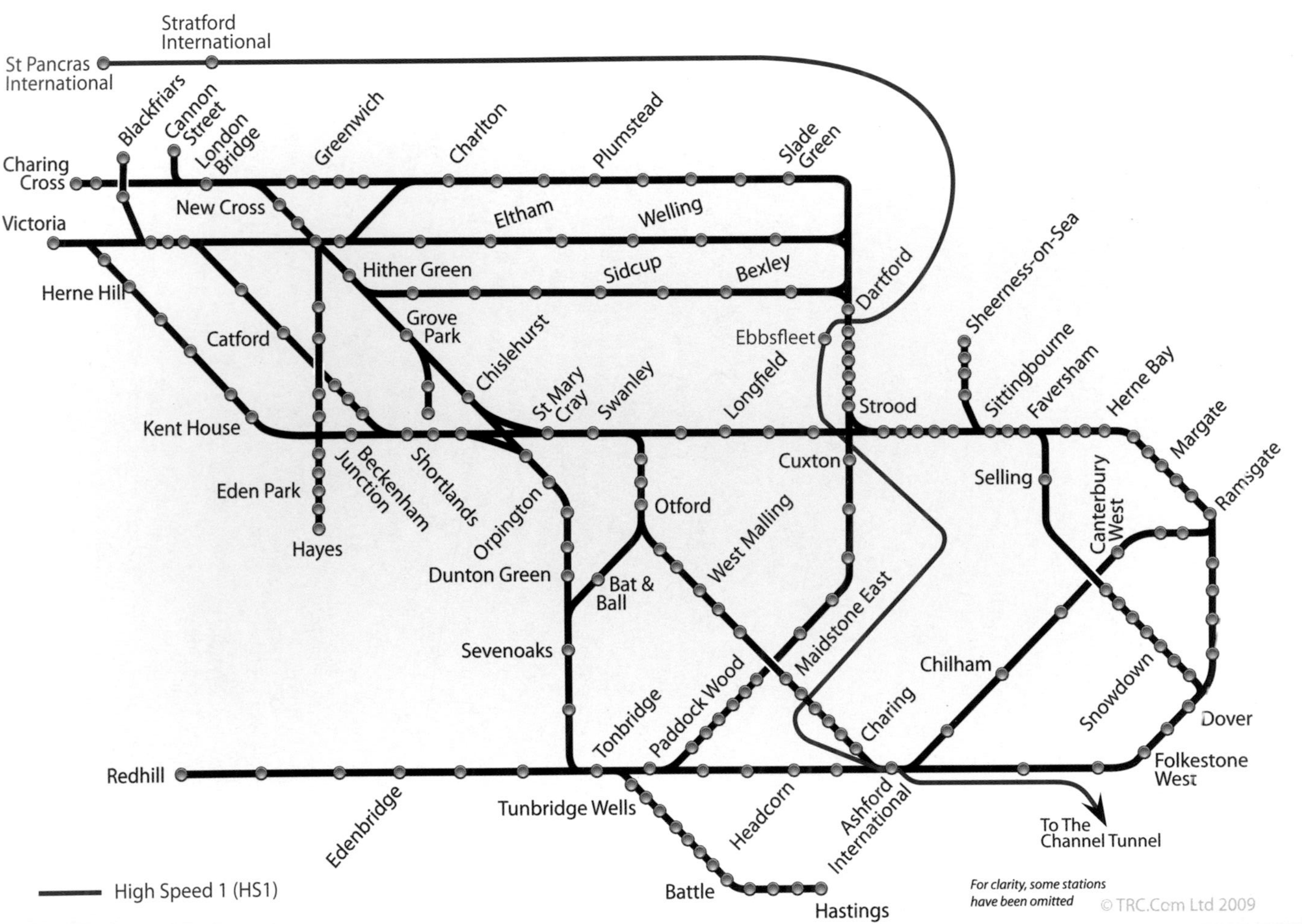
St Pancras International
Stratford International
Charing Cross
Blackfriars
Cannon Street
London Bridge
Greenwich
Charlton
Plumstead
Slade Green
New Cross
Victoria
Eltham
Welling
Hither Green
Sidcup
Bexley
Herne Hill
Dartford
Catford
Grove Park
Chislehurst
Ebbsfleet
Sheerness-on-Sea
St Mary Cray
Swanley
Longfield
Strood
Sittingbourne
Faversham
Herne Bay
Margate
Ramsgate
Kent House
Beckenham Junction
Shortlands
Cuxton
Selling
Canterbury West
Eden Park
Otford
Orpington
Hayes
Dunton Green
West Malling
Bat & Ball
Maidstone East
Sevenoaks
Chilham
Snowdown
Tonbridge
Paddock Wood
Charing
Dover
Redhill
Folkestone West
Edenbridge
Tunbridge Wells
Headcorn
Ashford International
To The Channel Tunnel
High Speed 1 (HS1)
Battle
Hastings
For clarity, some stations have been omitted
© TRC.Com Ltd 2009

375620	67820+74270+74220+67870	RM	SET	HSB	SET	
375621	67821+74271+74221+67871	RM	SET	HSB	SET	
375622	67822+74272+74222+67872	RM	SET	HSB	SET	
375623	67823+74273+74223+67873	RM	SET	HSB	SET	*Hospice in the Weald*
375624	67824+74274+74224+67874	RM	SET	HSB	SET	
375625	67825+74275+74225+67875	RM	SET	HSB	SET	
375626	67826+74276+74226+67876	RM	SET	HSB	SET	
375627	67827+74277+74227+67877	RM	SET	HSB	SET	
375628	67828+74278+74228+67878	RM	SET	HSB	SET	
375629	67829+74279+74229+67879	RM	SET	HSB	SET	
375630	67830+74280+74230+67880	RM	SET	HSB	SET	

Class 375/7
Electrostar

Vehicle Length: (Driving) 66ft 9in (20.3m)
(Inter) 65ft 6in (19.96m)
Height: 12ft 4in (3.75m)
Width: 9ft 2in (2.79m)
Horsepower: 2,012hp (1,500kW)
Seats (total/car): 24F-218S, 12F-48S/66S/56S/12F-48S

Number	*Formation* DMCO(A)+MSO+TSO+DMCO(B)	*Depot*	*Livery*	*Owner*	*Operator*	*Name*
375701	67831+74281+74231+67881	RM	SET	HSB	SET	*Kent Air Ambulance Explorer*
375702	67832+74282+74232+67882	RM	SET	HSB	SET	
375703	67833+74283+74233+67883	RM	SET	HSB	SET	*Dickens Traveller*
375704	67834+74284+74234+67884	RM	SET	HSB	SET	
375705	67835+74285+74235+67885	RM	SET	HSB	SET	
375706	67836+74286+74236+67886	RM	SET	HSB	SET	
375707	67837+74287+74237+67887	RM	SET	HSB	SET	
375708	67838+74288+74238+67888	RM	SET	HSB	SET	
375709	67839+74289+74239+67889	RM	SET	HSB	SET	
375710	67840+74290+74240+67890	RM	SET	HSB	SET	
375711	67841+74291+74241+67891	RM	SET	HSB	SET	
375712	67842+74292+74242+67892	RM	SET	HSB	SET	
375713	67843+74293+74243+67893	RM	SET	HSB	SET	
375714	67844+74294+74244+67894	RM	SET	HSB	SET	
375715	67845+74295+74245+67895	RM	SET	HSB	SET	

Class 375/8
Electrostar

Vehicle Length: (Driving) 66ft 9in (20.3m)
(Inter) 65ft 6in (19.96m)
Height: 12ft 4in (3.75m)
Width: 9ft 2in (2.79m)
Horsepower: 2,012hp (1,500kW)
Seats (total/car): 24F-218S, 12F-48S/66S/56S/12F-48S

Number	*Formation* DMCO(A)+MSO+TSO+DMCO(B)	*Depot*	*Livery*	*Owner*	*Operator*	*Name*
375801	73301+79001+78201+73701	RM	SET	HSB	SET	
375802	73302+79002+78202+73702	RM	SET	HSB	SET	
375803	73303+79003+78203+73703	RM	SET	HSB	SET	
375804	73304+79004+78204+73704	RM	SET	HSB	SET	
375805	73305+79005+78205+73705	RM	SET	HSB	SET	
375806	73306+79006+78206+73706	RM	SET	HSB	SET	
375807	73307+79007+78207+73707	RM	SET	HSB	SET	
375808	73308+79008+78208+73708	RM	SET	HSB	SET	
375809	73309+79009+78209+73709	RM	SET	HSB	SET	
375810	73310+79010+78210+73710	RM	SET	HSB	SET	
375811	73311+79011+78211+73711	RM	SET	HSB	SET	
375812	73312+79012+78212+73712	RM	SET	HSB	SET	
375813	73313+79013+78213+73713	RM	SET	HSB	SET	
375814	73314+79014+78214+73714	RM	SET	HSB	SET	
375815	73315+79015+78215+73715	RM	SET	HSB	SET	
375816	73316+79016+78216+73716	RM	SET	HSB	SET	
375817	73317+79017+78217+73717	RM	SET	HSB	SET	
375818	73318+79018+78218+73718	RM	SET	HSB	SET	
375819	73319+79019+78219+73719	RM	SET	HSB	SET	
375820	73320+79020+78220+73720	RM	SET	HSB	SET	
375821	73321+79021+78221+73721	RM	SET	HSB	SET	
375822	73322+79022+78222+73722	RM	SET	HSB	SET	
375823	73323+79023+78223+73723	RM	SET	HSB	SET	
375824	73324+79024+78224+73724	RM	SET	HSB	SET	
375825	73325+79025+78225+73725	RM	SET	HSB	SET	

375826	73326+79026+78226+73726	RM	SET	HSB	SET	
375827	73327+79027+78227+73727	RM	SET	HSB	SET	
375828	73328+79028+78228+73728	RM	SET	HSB	SET	
375829	73329+79029+78229+73729	RM	SET	HSB	SET	
375830	73330+79030+78230+73730	RM	SET	HSB	SET	*City of London*

Class 375/9
Electrostar

Vehicle Length: (Driving) 66ft 9in (20.3m)
(Inter) 65ft 6in (19.96m)
Height: 12ft 4in (3.75m)
Width: 9ft 2in (2.79m)
Horsepower: 2,012hp (1,500kW)
Seats (total/car): 24F-250S, 12F-59S/73S/59S/12F-59S

Number	*Formation* DMCO(A)+MSO+TSO+DMCO(B)	*Depot*	*Livery*	*Owner*	*Operator*
375901	73331+79031+79061+73731	RM	SET	HSB	SET
375902	73332+79032+79062+73732	RM	SET	HSB	SET
375903	73333+79033+79063+73733	RM	SET	HSB	SET
375904	73334+79034+79064+73734	RM	SET	HSB	SET
375905	73335+79035+79065+73735	RM	SET	HSB	SET
375906	73336+79036+79066+73736	RM	SET	HSB	SET
375907	73337+79037+79067+73737	RM	SET	HSB	SET
375908	73338+79038+79068+73738	RM	SET	HSB	SET
375909	73339+79039+79069+73739	RM	SET	HSB	SET
375910	73340+79040+79070+73740	RM	SET	HSB	SET
375911	73341+79041+79071+73741	RM	SET	HSB	SET
375912	73342+79042+79072+73742	RM	SET	HSB	SET
375913	73343+79043+79073+73743	RM	SET	HSB	SET
375914	73344+79044+79074+73744	RM	SET	HSB	SET
375915	73345+79045+79075+73745	RM	SET	HSB	SET
375916	73346+79046+79076+73746	RM	SET	HSB	SET
375917	73347+79047+79077+73747	RM	SET	HSB	SET
375918	73348+79048+79078+73748	RM	SET	HSB	SET
375919	73349+79049+79079+73749	RM	SET	HSB	SET
375920	73350+79050+79080+73750	RM	SET	HSB	SET
375921	73351+79051+79081+73751	RM	SET	HSB	SET
375922	73352+79052+79082+73752	RM	SET	HSB	SET
375923	73353+79053+79083+73753	RM	SET	HSB	SET
375924	73354+79054+79084+73754	RM	SET	HSB	SET
375925	73355+79055+79085+73755	RM	SET	HSB	SET
375926	73356+79056+79086+73756	RM	SET	HSB	SET
375927	73357+79057+79087+73757	RM	SET	HSB	SET

Below: *Painted in South Eastern white livery, off-set by blue passenger doors, Class 375/6 No. 375610 is seen at Canterbury West on 12 April 2008. The SET white livery has a gold/grey base band, tapered at the cab ends.* **Nathan Williamson**

Class 376
Electrostar

Vehicle Length: (Driving) 66ft 9in (20.3m)
(Inter) 65ft 6in (19.96m)
Height: 12ft 4in (3.75m)
Width: 9ft 2in (2.79m)
Horsepower: 2,682hp (2,000kW)
Seats (total/car): 216S, 36S/48S/48S/48S/36S + 116 perch

Number	*Formation* DMSO(A)+MSO+TSO+MSO+DMSO(B)	*Depot*	*Livery*	*Owner*	*Operator*
376001	61101+63301+64301+63501+61601	SG	SET	HSB	SET
376002	61102+63302+64302+63502+61602	SG	SET	HSB	SET
376003	61103+63303+64303+63503+61603	SG	SET	HSB	SET
376004	61104+63304+64304+63504+61604	SG	SET	HSB	SET
376005	61105+63305+64305+63505+61605	SG	SET	HSB	SET
376006	61106+63306+64306+63506+61606	SG	SET	HSB	SET
376007	61107+63307+64307+63507+61607	SG	SET	HSB	SET
376008	61108+63308+64308+63508+61608	SG	SET	HSB	SET
376009	61109+63309+64309+63509+61609	SG	SET	HSB	SET
376010	61110+63310+64310+63510+61610	SG	SET	HSB	SET
376011	61111+63311+64311+63511+61611	SG	SET	HSB	SET
376012	61112+63312+64312+63512+61612	SG	SET	HSB	SET
376013	61113+63313+64313+63513+61613	SG	SET	HSB	SET
376014	61114+63314+64314+63514+61614	SG	SET	HSB	SET
376015	61115+63315+64315+63515+61615	SG	SET	HSB	SET
376016	61116+63316+64316+63516+61616	SG	SET	HSB	SET
376017	61117+63317+64317+63517+61617	SG	SET	HSB	SET
376018	61118+63318+64318+63518+61618	SG	SET	HSB	SET
376019	61119+63319+64319+63519+61619	SG	SET	HSB	SET
376020	61120+63320+64320+63520+61620	SG	SET	HSB	SET
376021	61121+63321+64321+63521+61621	SG	SET	HSB	SET
376022	61122+63322+64322+63522+61622	SG	SET	HSB	SET
376023	61123+63323+64323+63523+61623	SG	SET	HSB	SET
376024	61124+63324+64324+63524+61624	SG	SET	HSB	SET
376025	61125+63325+64325+63525+61625	SG	SET	HSB	SET
376026	61126+63326+64326+63526+61626	SG	SET	HSB	SET
376027	61127+63327+64327+63527+61627	SG	SET	HSB	SET
376028	61128+63328+64328+63528+61628	SG	SET	HSB	SET
376029	61129+63329+64329+63529+61629	SG	SET	HSB	SET
376030	61130+63330+64330+63530+61630	SG	SET	HSB	SET
376031	61131+63331+64331+63531+61631	SG	SET	HSB	SET
376032	61132+63332+64332+63532+61632	SG	SET	HSB	SET
376033	61133+63333+64333+63533+61633	SG	SET	HSB	SET
376034	61134+63334+64334+63534+61634	SG	SET	HSB	SET
376035	61135+63335+64335+63535+61635	SG	SET	HSB	SET
376036	61136+63336+64336+63536+61636	SG	SET	HSB	SET

Below: *The very bland looking Class 376 'Electrostar' sets without a front gangway connection are used on the prime South-East London and Kent commuter routes where capacity issues often exist. Set No. 376005 is seen at Waterloo East forming a service to Dartford.* **CJM**

Class 395
Javelin

Vehicle Length: (Driving) 67ft 7in (20.6m)
(Inter) 67ft 6in (20.5m)
Height: 12ft 6in (3.81m)
Width: 9ft 2in (2.79m)
Horsepower: 2,252hp (1,680kW)
Seats (total/car): 340S, 28S/66S/66S/66S/66S/48S

Number	Formation DMSO(A)+MSO(A)+MSO(B)+ MSO(C)+MSO(D)+DMSO(B)	Depot	Livery	Owner	Operator	Name
395001	39011+39012+39013+39014+39015+39016	AD	HS1	HSB	SET	*Dame Kelly Holmes*
395002	39021+39022+39023+39024+39025+39026	AD	HS1	HSB	SET	
395003	39031+39032+39033+39034+39035+39036	AD	HS1	HSB	SET	
395004	39041+39042+39043+39044+39045+39046	AD	HS1	HSB	SET	
395005	39051+39052+39053+39054+39055+39056	AD	HS1	HSB	SET	
395006	39061+39062+39063+39064+39065+39066	AD	HS1	HSB	SET	
395007	39071+39072+39073+39074+39075+39076	AD	HS1	HSB	SET	
395008	39081+39082+39083+39084+39085+39086	AD	HS1	HSB	SET	
395009	39091+39092+39093+39094+39095+39096	AD	HS1	HSB	SET	
395010	39101+39102+39103+39104+39105+39106	AD	HS1	HSB	SET	
395011	39111+39112+39113+39114+39115+39116	AD	HS1	HSB	SET	
395012	39121+39122+39123+39124+39125+39126	AD	HS1	HSB	SET	
395013	39131+39132+39133+39134+39135+39136	AD	HS1	HSB	SET	
395014	39141+39142+39143+39144+39145+39146	AD	HS1	HSB	SET	
395015	39151+39152+39153+39154+39155+39156	AD	HS1	HSB	SET	
395016	39161+39162+39163+39164+39165+39166	AD	HS1	HSB	SET	*Jamie Staff*
395017	39171+39172+39173+39174+39175+39176	AD	HS1	HSB	SET	
395018	39181+39182+39183+39184+39185+39186	AD	HS1	HSB	SET	
395019	39191+39192+39193+39194+39195+39196	AD	HS1	HSB	SET	
395020	39201+39202+39203+39204+39205+39206	AD	HS1	HSB	SET	
395021	39211+39212+39213+39214+39215+39216	AD	HS1	HSB	SET	
395022	39221+39222+39223+39224+39225+39226	AD	HS1	HSB	SET	
395023	39231+39232+39233+39234+39235+39236	AD	HS1	HSB	SET	
395024	39241+39242+39243+39244+39245+39246	AD	HS1	HSB	SET	
395025	39251+39252+39253+39254+39255+39256	AD	HS1	HSB	SET	
395026	39261+39262+39263+39264+39265+39266	AD	HS1	HSB	SET	
395027	39271+39272+39273+39274+39275+39276	AD	HS1	HSB	SET	
395028	39281+39282+39283+39284+39285+39286	AD	HS1	HSB	SET	
395029	39291+39292+39293+39294+39295+39296	AD	HS1	HSB	SET	

Below: *The first Japanese trains to operate in the UK, are the 29-strong fleet of Class 395 units built by Hitachi and allocated to a new depot in Ashford, Kent for passenger use between Kent and London St Pancras International over HS1. A shadow service commenced operating in summer 2009 with a full passenger service launched in December. These sets will also be used to form 'Javelin' high speed services between St Pancras International and Stratford International for the duration of the 2012 London Olympic Games. Set No. 395001 is seen inside the purpose built Hitachi-operated depot at Ashford.* **CJM**

Class 465/0
Networker

Vehicle Length: (Driving) 68ft 6½in (20.89m) (Inter) 65ft 9¾in (20.05m)
Height: 12ft 4½in (3.77m)
Width: 9ft 3in (2.81m)
Horsepower: 2,252hp (1,680kW)
Seats (total/car): 348S, 86S/90S/86S/86S

Number	Formation DMSO(A)+TSO+TSO+DMSO(B)	Depot	Livery	Owner	Operator
465001	64759+72028+72029+64809	SG	SET	HSB	SET
465002	64760+72030+72031+64810	SG	SET	HSB	SET
465003	64761+72032+72033+64811	SG	SET	HSB	SET
465004	64762+72034+72035+64812	SG	SET	HSB	SET
465005	64763+72036+72037+64813	SG	SET	HSB	SET
465006	64764+72038+72039+64814	SG	SET	HSB	SET
465007	64765+72040+72041+64815	SG	SET	HSB	SET
465008	64766+72042+72043+64816	SG	SET	HSB	SET
465009	64767+72044+72045+64817	SG	SET	HSB	SET
465010	64768+72046+72047+64818	SG	SET	HSB	SET
465011	64769+72048+72049+64819	SG	SET	HSB	SET
465012	64770+72050+72051+64820	SG	SET	HSB	SET
465013	64771+72052+72053+64821	SG	SET	HSB	SET
465014	64772+72054+72055+64822	SG	SET	HSB	SET
465015	64773+72056+72057+64823	SG	SET	HSB	SET
465016	64774+72058+72059+64824	SG	SET	HSB	SET
465017	64775+72060+72061+64825	SG	SET	HSB	SET
465018	64776+72062+72063+64826	SG	SET	HSB	SET
465019	64777+72064+72065+64827	SG	SET	HSB	SET
465020	64778+72066+72067+64828	SG	SET	HSB	SET
465021	64779+72068+72069+64829	SG	SET	HSB	SET
465022	64780+72070+72071+64830	SG	SET	HSB	SET
465023	64781+72072+72073+64831	SG	SET	HSB	SET
465024	64782+72074+72075+64832	SG	SET	HSB	SET
465025	64783+72076+72077+64833	SG	SET	HSB	SET
465026	64784+72078+72079+64834	SG	SET	HSB	SET
465027	64785+72080+72081+64835	SG	SET	HSB	SET
465028	64786+72082+72083+64836	SG	SET	HSB	SET
465029	64787+72084+72085+64837	SG	SET	HSB	SET
465030	64788+72086+72087+64838	SG	SET	HSB	SET
465031	64789+72088+72089+64839	SG	SET	HSB	SET
465032	64790+72090+72091+64840	SG	SET	HSB	SET
465033	64791+72092+72093+64841	SG	SET	HSB	SET
465034	64792+72094+72095+64842	SG	SET	HSB	SET
465035	64793+72096+72097+64843	SG	SET	HSB	SET
465036	64794+72098+72099+64844	SG	SET	HSB	SET
465037	64795+72100+72101+64845	SG	SET	HSB	SET
465038	64796+72102+72103+64846	SG	SET	HSB	SET
465039	64797+72104+72105+64847	SG	SET	HSB	SET
465040	64798+72106+72107+64848	SG	SET	HSB	SET
465041	64799+72108+72109+64849	SG	SET	HSB	SET
465042	64800+72110+72111+64850	SG	SET	HSB	SET
465043	64801+72112+72113+64851	SG	SET	HSB	SET
465044	64802+72114+72115+64852	SG	SET	HSB	SET
465045	64803+72116+72117+64853	SG	SET	HSB	SET
465046	64804+72118+72119+64854	SG	SET	HSB	SET
465047	64805+72120+72121+64855	SG	SET	HSB	SET
465048	64806+72122+72123+64856	SG	SET	HSB	SET
465049	64807+72124+72125+64857	SG	SET	HSB	SET
465050	64808+72126+72127+64858	SG	SET	HSB	SET

Class 465/1
Networker

Vehicle Length: (Driving) 68ft 6½in (20.89m) (Inter) 65ft 9¾in (20.05m)
Height: 12ft 4½in (3.77m)
Width: 9ft 3in (2.81m)
Horsepower: 2,252hp (1,680kW)
Seats (total/car): 348S, 86S/90S/86S/86S

Number	Formation DMSO(A)+TSO+TSO+DMSO(B)	Depot	Livery	Owner	Operator
465151	65800+72900+72901+65847	SG	SET	HSB	SET
65152	65801+72902+72903+65848	SG	SET	HSB	SET

South Eastern

465153	65802+72904+72905+65849	SG	SET	HSB	SET
465154	65803+72906+72907+65850	SG	SET	HSB	SET
465155	65804+72908+72909+65851	SG	SET	HSB	SET
465156	65805+72910+72911+65852	SG	SET	HSB	SET
465157	65806+72912+72913+65853	SG	SET	HSB	SET
465158	65807+72914+72915+65854	SG	SET	HSB	SET
465159	65808+72916+72917+65855	SG	SET	HSB	SET
465160	65809+72918+72919+65856	SG	SET	HSB	SET
465161	65810+72920+72921+65857	SG	SET	HSB	SET
465162	65811+72922+72923+65858	SG	SET	HSB	SET
465163	65812+72924+72925+65859	SG	SET	HSB	SET
465164	65813+72926+72927+65860	SG	SET	HSB	SET
465165	65814+72928+72929+65861	SG	SET	HSB	SET
465166	65815+72930+72931+65862	SG	SET	HSB	SET
465167	65816+72932+72933+65863	SG	SET	HSB	SET
465168	65817+72934+72935+65864	SG	SET	HSB	SET
465169	65818+72936+72937+65865	SG	SET	HSB	SET
465170	65819+72938+72939+65866	SG	SET	HSB	SET
465171	65820+72940+72941+65867	SG	SET	HSB	SET
465172	65821+72942+72943+65868	SG	SET	HSB	SET
465173	65822+72944+72945+65869	SG	SET	HSB	SET
465174	65823+72946+72947+65870	SG	SET	HSB	SET
465175	65824+72948+72949+65871	SG	SET	HSB	SET
465176	65825+72950+72951+65872	SG	SET	HSB	SET
465177	65826+72952+72952+65873	SG	SET	HSB	SET
465178	65827+72954+72955+65874	SG	SET	HSB	SET
465179	65828+72956+72957+65875	SG	SET	HSB	SET
465180	65829+72958+72959+65876	SG	SET	HSB	SET
465181	65830+72960+72961+65877	SG	SET	HSB	SET
465182	65831+72962+72963+65878	SG	SET	HSB	SET
465183	65832+72964+72965+65879	SG	SET	HSB	SET
465184	65833+72966+72967+65880	SG	SET	HSB	SET
465185	65834+72968+72969+65881	SG	SET	HSB	SET
465186	65835+72970+72971+65882	SG	SET	HSB	SET
465187	65836+72972+72973+65883	SG	SET	HSB	SET
465188	65837+72974+72975+65884	SG	SET	HSB	SET
465189	65838+72976+72977+65885	SG	SET	HSB	SET
465190	65839+72978+72979+65886	SG	SET	HSB	SET
465191	65840+72980+72981+65887	SG	SET	HSB	SET
465192	65841+72982+72983+65888	SG	SET	HSB	SET
465193	65842+72984+72985+65889	SG	SET	HSB	SET
465194	65843+72986+72987+65890	SG	SET	HSB	SET
465195	65844+72988+72989+65891	SG	SET	HSB	SET
465196	65845+72990+72991+65892	SG	SET	HSB	SET
465197	65846+72992+72993+65893	SG	SET	HSB	SET

Class 465/2
Networker

Vehicle Length: (Driving) 68ft 6½in (20.89m)
(Inter) 65ft 9¾in (20.05m)
Height: 12ft 4½in (3.77m)
Width: 9ft 3in (2.81m)
Horsepower: 2,252hp (1,680kW)
Seats (total/car): 348S, 86S/90S/86S/86S

Number	*Formation* DMSO(A)+TSO+TSO+DMSO(B)	*Depot*	*Livery*	*Owner*	*Operator*
465235	65734+72787+72788+65784	SG	SET	ANG	SET
465236	65735+72789+72790+65785	SG	SET	ANG	SET
465237	65736+72791+72792+65786	SG	SET	ANG	SET
465238	65737+72793+72794+65787	SG	SET	ANG	SET
465239	65738+72795+72796+65788	SG	SET	ANG	SET
465240	65739+72797+72798+65789	SG	SET	ANG	SET
465241	65740+72799+72800+65790	SG	SET	ANG	SET
465242	65741+72801+72802+65791	SG	SET	ANG	SET
465243	65742+72803+72804+65792	SG	SET	ANG	SET
465244	65743+72805+72806+65793	SG	SET	ANG	SET
465245	65744+72807+72808+65794	SG	SET	ANG	SET
465246	65745+72809+72810+65795	SG	SET	ANG	SET
465247	65746+72811+72812+65796	SG	SET	ANG	SET

465248	65747+72813+72814+65797	SG	SET	ANG	SET
465249	65748+72815+72816+65798	SG	SET	ANG	SET
465250	65749+72817+72818+65799	SG	SET	ANG	SET

Class 465/9
Networker

Vehicle Length: (Driving) 68ft 6½in (20.89m) (Inter) 65ft 9¾in (20.05m)
Height: 12ft 4½in (3.77m)
Width: 9ft 3in (2.81m)
Horsepower: 2,252hp (1,680kW)
Seats (total/car): 24F-302S, 12F-68S/76S/90S/12F-68S

Number	*Formation* DMCO(A)+TSO+TSO+DMCO(B)	*Depot*	*Livery*	*Owner*	*Operator*	*Name*
465901 (465201)	65700+72719+72720+65750	SG	SET	ANG	SET	
465902 (465202)	65701+72721+72722+65751	SG	SET	ANG	SET	
465903 (465203)	65702+72723+72724+65752	SG	SET	ANG	SET	*Remembrance*
465904 (465204)	65703+72725+72726+65753	SG	SET	ANG	SET	
465905 (465205)	65704+72727+72728+65754	SG	SET	ANG	SET	
465906 (465206)	65705+72729+72730+65755	SG	SET	ANG	SET	
465907 (465207)	65706+72731+72732+65756	SG	SET	ANG	SET	
465908 (465208)	65707+72733+72734+65757	SG	SET	ANG	SET	
465909 (465209)	65708+72735+72736+65758	SG	SET	ANG	SET	
465910 (465210)	65709+72737+72738+65759	SG	SET	ANG	SET	
465911 (465211)	65710+72739+72740+65760	SG	SET	ANG	SET	
465912 (465212)	65711+72741+72742+65761	SG	SET	ANG	SET	
465913 (465213)	65712+72743+72744+65762	SG	SET	ANG	SET	
465914 (465214)	65713+72745+72746+65763	SG	SET	ANG	SET	
465915 (465215)	65714+72747+72748+65764	SG	SET	ANG	SET	
465916 (465216)	65715+72749+72750+65765	SG	SET	ANG	SET	
465917 (465217)	65716+72751+72752+65766	SG	SET	ANG	SET	
465918 (465218)	65717+72753+72754+65767	SG	SET	ANG	SET	
465919 (465219)	65718+72755+72756+65768	SG	SET	ANG	SET	
465920 (465220)	65719+72757+72758+65769	SG	SET	ANG	SET	
465921 (465221)	65720+72759+72760+65770	SG	SET	ANG	SET	
465922 (465222)	65721+72761+72762+65771	SG	SET	ANG	SET	
465923 (465223)	65722+72763+72764+65772	SG	SET	ANG	SET	
465924 (465224)	65723+72765+72766+65773	SG	SET	ANG	SET	
465925 (465225)	65724+72767+72768+65774	SG	SET	ANG	SET	
465926 (465226)	65725+72769+72770+65775	SG	SET	ANG	SET	
465927 (465227)	65726+72771+72772+65776	SG	SET	ANG	SET	
465928 (465228)	65727+72773+72774+65777	SG	SET	ANG	SET	
465929 (465229)	65728+72775+72776+65778	SG	SET	ANG	SET	
465930 (465230)	65729+72777+72778+65779	SG	SET	ANG	SET	
465931 (465231)	65730+72779+72780+65780	SG	SET	ANG	SET	
465932 (465232)	65731+72781+72782+65781	SG	SET	ANG	SET	
465933 (465233)	65732+72783+72784+65782	SG	SET	ANG	SET	
465934 (465234)	65733+72785+72786+65783	SG	SET	ANG	SET	

Right: *Under Network SouthEast, the South Eastern lines of the former Southern Region were modernised with fleets of 'Networker' EMUs introduced to replace ageing 1951 and 1957 EPB units. Built by both ABB and Alstom, the Class 465s had purpose-built depot facilities constructed at Slade Green, where the entire fleet are based. Alstom-built No. 465250 is seen approaching New Eltham.* **CJM**

Class 466 Networker

Vehicle Length: (Driving) 68ft 6½in (20.89m) Horsepower: 1,126hp (840kW)
Height: 12ft 4½in (3.77m) Seats (total/car): 168S, 86S/82S
Width: 9ft 3in (2.81m)

Number	Formation DMSO+DTSO	Depot	Livery	Owner	Operator
466001	64860+78312	SG	SET	ANG	SET
466002	64861+78313	SG	SET	ANG	SET
466003	64862+78314	SG	SET	ANG	SET
466004	64863+78315	SG	SET	ANG	SET
466005	64864+78316	SG	SET	ANG	SET
466006	64865+78317	SG	SET	ANG	SET
466007	64866+78318	SG	SET	ANG	SET
466008	64867+78319	SG	SET	ANG	SET
466009	64868+78320	SG	SET	ANG	SET
466010	64869+78321	SG	SET	ANG	SET
466011	64870+78322	SG	SET	ANG	SET
466012	64871+78323	SG	SET	ANG	SET
466013	64872+78324	SG	SET	ANG	SET
466014	64873+78325	SG	SET	ANG	SET
466015	64874+78326	SG	SET	ANG	SET
466016	64875+78327	SG	SET	ANG	SET
466017	64876+78328	SG	SET	ANG	SET
466018	64877+78329	SG	SET	ANG	SET
466019	64878+78330	SG	SET	ANG	SET
466020	64879+78331	SG	SET	ANG	SET
466021	64880+78332	SG	SET	ANG	SET
466022	64881+78333	SG	SET	ANG	SET
466023	64882+78334	SG	SET	ANG	SET
466024	64883+78335	SG	SET	ANG	SET
466025	64884+78336	SG	SET	ANG	SET
466026	64885+78337	SG	SET	ANG	SET
466027	64886+78338	SG	SET	ANG	SET
466028	64887+78339	SG	SET	ANG	SET
466029	64888+78340	SG	SET	ANG	SET
466030	64889+78341	SG	SET	ANG	SET
466031	64890+78342	SG	SET	ANG	SET
466032	64891+78343	SG	SET	ANG	SET
466033	64892+78344	SG	SET	ANG	SET
466034	64893+78345	SG	SET	ANG	SET
466035	64894+78346	SG	SET	ANG	SET
466036	64895+78347	SG	SET	ANG	SET
466037	64896+78348	SG	SET	ANG	SET
466038	64897+78349	SG	SET	ANG	SET
466039	64898+78350	SG	SET	ANG	SET
466040	64899+78351	SG	SET	ANG	SET
466041	64900+78352	SG	SET	ANG	SET
466042	64901+78353	SG	SET	ANG	SET
466043	64902+78354	SG	SET	ANG	SET

Above: *To allow the formation of two, six or ten car formations on the busy South Eastern suburban network, a batch of 43 two-car Class 466 units were built under the original NSE 'Networker' project. The sets were constructed by Alstom at Washwood Heath. Now painted in full Southeastern white and grey livery, set No. 466030 heads south at London Bridge. Since introduction these units have received anti-surfing modifications by placing a curved profile on the original front footholds.* **CJM**

Southern

Address: ✉ Go-Ahead House, 26-28 Addiscombe Road, Croydon, CR9 5GA
info@southernrailway.com
✆ 08451 272920
ⓘ www.southernrailway.com

Managing Director: Chris Burchell
Franchise Dates: 1 March 2003 - 25 July 2015
Principal Routes: London Victoria / London Bridge to Brighton, Coastway route, Uckfield / East Grinstead. Services to Surrey, Sussex and Brighton to Ashford route
Depots: Brighton (BI), Selhurst (SU)
Parent Company: Govia

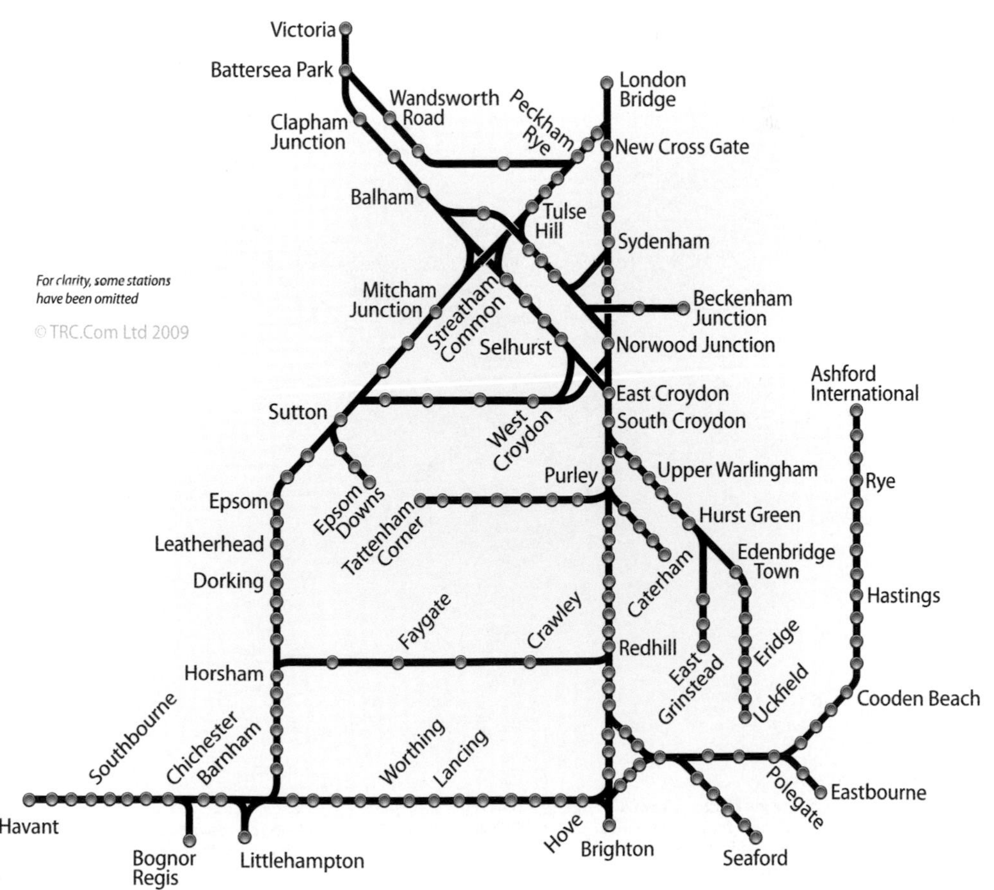

Southern

Class 171/7 Turbostar

Vehicle Length: 77ft 6in (23.62m)
Height: 12ft 4½in (3.77m)
Width: 8ft 10in (2.69m)
Engine: 1 x MTU 6R 183TD13H 422hp per vehicle
Horsepower: 844hp (629kW)
Seats (total/car): 9F-107S 9F-43S/64S

Number	Formation DMCL+DMSL	Depot	Livery	Owner	Operator
171721	50721+79721	SU	SOU	PTR	SOU
171722	50722+79722	SU	SOU	PTR	SOU
171723	50723+79723	SU	SOU	PTR	SOU
171724	50724+79724	SU	SOU	PTR	SOU
171725	50725+79725	SU	SOU	PTR	SOU
171726	50726+79726	SU	SOU	PTR	SOU
171727	50727+79727	SU	SOU	PTR	SOU
171728	50728+79728	SU	SOU	PTR	SOU
171729	50729+79729	SU	SOU	PTR	SOU
171730	50392+79392	SU	SOU	PTR	SOU

171730 Previously numbered 170392

Class 171/8 Turbostar

Vehicle Length: 77ft 6in (23.62m)
Height: 12ft 4½in (3.77m)
Width: 8ft 10in (2.69m)
Engine: 1 x MTU 6R 183TD13H 422hp per vehicle
Horsepower: 1,688hp (1,259kW)
Seats (total/car): 18F-241S 9F-43S/74S/74S/9F-50SS

Number	Formation DMCL(A)+MS+MS+DMCL(B)	Depot	Livery	Owner	Operator
171801	50801+54801+56801+79801	SU	SOU	PTR	SOU
171802	50802+54802+56802+79802	SU	SOU	PTR	SOU
171803	50803+54803+56803+79803	SU	SOU	PTR	SOU
171804	50804+54804+56804+79804	SU	SOU	PTR	SOU
171805	50805+54805+56805+79805	SU	SOU	PTR	SOU
171806	50806+54806+56806+79806	SU	SOU	PTR	SOU

Left: *The two and four-car Class 171 'Turbostar' sets operated by Southern are allocated to purpose-built facilities at Selhurst depot and operate over the non-electrified routes. The sets were built as a follow-on to the Class 170 sets and replaced a fleet of DEMU units previously used on Southern Region non-electrified routes. Set No. 171725 is shown departing from Brighton on a Coastway service to Hastings and Ashford.* **CJM**

Class 313/1

Vehicle Length: (Driving) 64ft 11½in (20.75m)
(Inter) 65ft 4¼in (19.92m)
Height: 11ft 9in (3.58m)
Width: 9ft 3in (2.82m)
Horsepower: 880hp (656kW)
Seats (total/car): 202S, 66S/70S/66S

■ Following displacement from London Overground services, after introduction of Class 378 stock, Southern are scheduled to receive a fleet of 15 Class 313s in 2010 for use on the Coastway route.

Number	Formation DMSO+PTSO+BDMSO	Depot	Livery	Owner	Operator
313101	62529+71213+62593	WN	SKL	HSB	SOU
313102	62530+71214+62594	SL	SKL	HSB	SOU
313103	62531+71215+62595	WN	SKL	HSB	SOU
313104	62532+71216+62596	SL	SKL	HSB	SOU
313105	62533+71217+62597	SL	SKL	HSB	SOU
313106	62534+71218+62598	WN	SKL	HSB	SOU
313107	62535+71219+62599	WN	SKL	HSB	SOU
313108	62536+71220+62600	SL	SKL	HSB	SOU
313109	62537+71221+62601	WN	SKL	HSB	SOU
313110	62538+71222+62602	WN	SKL	HSB	SOU
313111	62539+71223+62603	WN	SKL	HSB	SOU
313112	62540+71224+62604	WN	SKL	HSB	SOU
313113	62541+71225+62605	WN	SKL	HSB	SOU

313114	62542+71226+62606	WN	SKL	HSB	SOU
313115	62543+71227+62507	WN	SKL	HSB	SOU

Class 377/1 *Electrostar*

Vehicle Length: (Driving) 66ft 9in (20.3m) Width: 9ft 2in (2.79m)
(Inter) 65ft 6in (19.96m) Horsepower: 2,012hp (1,500kW)
Height: 12ft 4in (3.75m) Seats (total/car): 24F-218S, 12F-48(56S)/62S(70S)/52S(62S)/12F-48(56S)

Number	*Formation* DMCO(A)+MSO+TSO+DMCO(B)	*Depot*	*Livery*	*Owner*	*Operator*
377101	78501+77101+78901+78701	BI	SOU	PTR	SOU
377102	78502+77102+78902+78702	BI	SOU	PTR	SOU
377103	78503+77103+78903+78703	BI	SOU	PTR	SOU
377104	78504+77104+78904+78704	BI	SOU	PTR	SOU
377105	78505+77105+78905+78705	BI	SOU	PTR	SOU
377106	78506+77106+78906+78706	BI	SOU	PTR	SOU
377107	78507+77107+78907+78707	BI	SOU	PTR	SOU
377108	78508+77108+78908+78708	BI	SOU	PTR	SOU
377109	78509+77109+78909+78709	BI	SOU	PTR	SOU
377110	78510+77110+78910+78710	BI	SOU	PTR	SOU
377111	78511+77111+78911+78711	BI	SOU	PTR	SOU
377112	78512+77112+78912+78712	BI	SOU	PTR	SOU
377113	78513+77113+78913+78713	BI	SOU	PTR	SOU
377114	78514+77114+78914+78714	BI	SOU	PTR	SOU
377115	78515+77115+78915+78715	BI	SOU	PTR	SOU
377116	78516+77116+78916+78716	BI	SOU	PTR	SOU
377117	78517+77117+78917+78717	BI	SOU	PTR	SOU
377118	78518+77118+78918+78718	BI	SOU	PTR	SOU
377119	78519+77119+78919+78719	BI	SOU	PTR	SOU
377120	78520+77120+78920+78720	SU	SOU	PTR	SOU
377121	78521+77121+78921+78721	SU	SOU	PTR	SOU
377122	78522+77122+78922+78722	SU	SOU	PTR	SOU
377123	78523+77123+78923+78723	SU	SOU	PTR	SOU
377124	78524+77124+78924+78724	SU	SOU	PTR	SOU
377125	78525+77125+78925+78725	SU	SOU	PTR	SOU
377126	78526+77126+78926+78726	SU	SOU	PTR	SOU
377127	78527+77127+78927+78727	SU	SOU	PTR	SOU
377128	78528+77128+78928+78728	SU	SOU	PTR	SOU
377129	78529+77129+78929+78729	SU	SOU	PTR	SOU
377130	78530+77130+78930+78730	SU	SOU	PTR	SOU
377131	78531+77131+78931+78731	SU	SOU	PTR	SOU
377132	78532+77132+78932+78732	SU	SOU	PTR	SOU
377133	78533+77133+78933+78733	SU	SOU	PTR	SOU
377134	78534+77134+78934+78734	SU	SOU	PTR	SOU
377135	78535+77135+78935+78735	SU	SOU	PTR	SOU
377136	78536+77136+78936+78736	SU	SOU	PTR	SOU
377137	78537+77137+78937+78737	SU	SOU	PTR	SOU
377138	78538+77138+78938+78738	SU	SOU	PTR	SOU
377139	78539+77139+78939+78739	SU	SOU	PTR	SOU
377140	78540+77140+78940+78740	SU	SOU	PTR	SOU
377141	78541+77141+78941+78741	SU	SOU	PTR	SOU
377142	78542+77142+78942+78742	SU	SOU	PTR	SOU
377143	78543+77143+78943+78743	SU	SOU	PTR	SOU
377144	78544+77144+78944+78744	SU	SOU	PTR	SOU
377145	78545+77145+78945+78745	SU	SOU	PTR	SOU
377146	78546+77146+78946+78746	SU	SOU	PTR	SOU
377147	78547+77147+78947+78747	SU	SOU	PTR	SOU
377148	78548+77148+78948+78748	SU	SOU	PTR	SOU
377149	78549+77149+78949+78749	SU	SOU	PTR	SOU
377150	78550+77150+78950+78750	SU	SOU	PTR	SOU
377151	78551+77151+78951+78751	SU	SOU	PTR	SOU
377152	78552+77152+78952+78752	SU	SOU	PTR	SOU
377153	78553+77153+78953+78753	SU	SOU	PTR	SOU
377154	78554+77154+78954+78754	SU	SOU	PTR	SOU
377155	78555+77155+78955+78755	SU	SOU	PTR	SOU
377156	78556+77156+78956+78756	SU	SOU	PTR	SOU

Southern

377157	78557+77157+78957+78757	SU	SOU	PTR	SOU
377158	78558+77158+78958+78758	BI	SOU	PTR	SOU
377159	78559+77159+78959+78759	BI	SOU	PTR	SOU
377160	78560+77160+78960+78760	BI	SOU	PTR	SOU
377161	78561+77161+78961+78761	BI	SOU	PTR	SOU
377162	78562+77162+78962+78762	BI	SOU	PTR	SOU - *Out of use with collision damage*
377163	78563+77163+78963+78763	BI	SOU	PTR	SOU
377164	78564+77164+78964+78764	BI	SOU	PTR	SOU

Class 377/2
Electrostar

Vehicle Length: (Driving) 66ft 9in (20.3m) (Inter) 65ft 6in (19.96m)
Height: 12ft 4in (3.75m)
Width: 9ft 2in (2.79m)
Horsepower: 2,012hp (1,500kW)
Seats (total/car): 24F-222S, 12F-48/69S/57S/12F-48S

Number	*Formation* DMCO(A)+MSO+PTSO+DMCO(B)	*Depot*	*Livery*	*Owner*	*Operator*
377201	78571+77171+78971+78771	BI	SOU	PTR	SOU
377202	78572+77172+78972+78772	SU	SOU	PTR	SOU
377203	78573+77173+78973+78773	BI	SOU	PTR	SOU
377204	78574+77174+78974+78774	BI	SOU	PTR	SOU
377205	78575+77175+78975+78775	SU	SOU	PTR	SOU
377206	78576+77176+78976+78776	SU	SOU	PTR	SOU
377207	78577+77177+78977+78777	SU	SOU	PTR	SOU
377208	78578+77178+78978+78778	SU	SOU	PTR	SOU
377209	78579+77179+78979+78779	SU	SOU	PTR	SOU
377210	78580+77180+78980+78780	SU	SOU	PTR	SOU
377211	78581+77181+78981+78781	SU	SOU	PTR	SOU
377212	78582+77182+78982+78782	SU	SOU	PTR	SOU
377213	78583+77183+78983+78783	SU	SOU	PTR	SOU
377214	78584+77184+78984+78784	SU	SOU	PTR	SOU
377215	78585+77185+78985+78785	SU	SOU	PTR	SOU

Class 377/3
Electrostar

Vehicle Length: (Driving) 66ft 9in (20.3m) (Inter) 65ft 6in (19.96m)
Height: 12ft 4in (3.75m)
Width: 9ft 2in (2.79m)
Horsepower: 2,012hp (1,500kW)
Seats (total/car): 24F-152S, 12F-48/56S/12F-48S

Number	*Formation* DMCO(A)+TSO+DMCO(B)	*Depot*	*Livery*	*Owner*	*Operator*
377301 (375311)	68201+74801+68401	BI	SOU	PTR	SOU
377302 (375312)	68202+74802+68402	BI	SOU	PTR	SOU
377303 (375313)	68203+74803+68403	BI	SOU	PTR	SOU
377304 (375314)	68204+74804+68404	BI	SOU	PTR	SOU
377305 (375315)	68205+74805+68405	BI	SOU	PTR	SOU
377306 (375316)	68206+74806+68406	BI	SOU	PTR	SOU
377307 (375317)	68207+74807+68407	BI	SOU	PTR	SOU
377308 (375318)	68208+74808+68408	BI	SOU	PTR	SOU
377309 (375319)	68209+74809+68409	BI	SOU	PTR	SOU
377310 (375320)	68210+74810+68410	BI	SOU	PTR	SOU
377311 (375321)	68211+74811+68411	BI	SOU	PTR	SOU
377312 (375322)	68212+74812+68412	BI	SOU	PTR	SOU
377313 (375323)	68213+74813+68413	BI	SOU	PTR	SOU
377314 (375324)	68214+74814+68414	BI	SOU	PTR	SOU
377315 (375325)	68215+74815+68415	BI	SOU	PTR	SOU
377316 (375326)	68216+74816+68416	BI	SOU	PTR	SOU
377317 (375327)	68217+74817+68417	BI	SOU	PTR	SOU
377318 (375328)	68218+74818+68418	BI	SOU	PTR	SOU
377319 (375329)	68219+74819+68419	BI	SOU	PTR	SOU
377320 (375330)	68220+74820+68420	BI	SOU	PTR	SOU
377321 (375331)	68221+74821+68421	BI	SOU	PTR	SOU
377322 (375332)	68222+74822+68422	BI	SOU	PTR	SOU
377323 (375333)	68223+74823+68423	BI	SOU	PTR	SOU
377324 (375334)	68224+74824+68424	BI	SOU	PTR	SOU
377325 (375335)	68225+74825+68425	BI	SOU	PTR	SOU
377326 (375336)	68226+74826+68426	BI	SOU	PTR	SOU
377327 (375337)	68227+74827+68427	BI	SOU	PTR	SOU
377328 (375338)	68228+74828+68428	BI	SOU	PTR	SOU

Class 377/4
Electrostar

*Vehicle Length: (Driving) 66ft 9in (20.3m) (Inter) 65ft 6in (19.96m)
Height: 12ft 4in (3.75m)
Width: 9ft 2in (2.79m)
Horsepower: 2,012hp (1,500kW)
Seats (total/car): 20F-221S, 10F-48/69S/56S/10F-48S*

Number	*Formation* DMCO(A)+MSO+TSO+DMCO(B)	*Depot*	*Livery*	*Owner*	*Operator*
377401	73401+78801+78601+73801	BI	SOU	PTR	SOU
377402	73402+78802+78602+73802	BI	SOU	PTR	SOU
377403	73403+78803+78603+73803	BI	SOU	PTR	SOU
377404	73404+78804+78604+73804	BI	SOU	PTR	SOU
377405	73405+78805+78605+73805	BI	SOU	PTR	SOU
377406	73406+78806+78606+73806	BI	SOU	PTR	SOU
377407	73407+78807+78607+73807	BI	SOU	PTR	SOU
377408	73408+78808+78608+73808	BI	SOU	PTR	SOU
377409	73409+78809+78609+73809	BI	SOU	PTR	SOU
377410	73410+78810+78610+73810	BI	SOU	PTR	SOU
377411	73411+78811+78611+73811	BI	SOU	PTR	SOU
377412	73412+78812+78612+73812	BI	SOU	PTR	SOU
377413	73413+78813+78613+73813	BI	SOU	PTR	SOU
377414	73414+78814+78614+73814	BI	SOU	PTR	SOU
377415	73415+78815+78615+73815	BI	SOU	PTR	SOU
377416	73416+78816+78616+73816	BI	SOU	PTR	SOU
377417	73417+78817+78617+73817	BI	SOU	PTR	SOU
377418	73418+78818+78618+73818	BI	SOU	PTR	SOU
377419	73419+78819+78619+73819	BI	SOU	PTR	SOU
377420	73420+78820+78620+73820	BI	SOU	PTR	SOU
377421	73421+78821+78621+73821	BI	SOU	PTR	SOU
377422	73422+78822+78622+73822	BI	SOU	PTR	SOU
377423	73423+78823+78623+73823	BI	SOU	PTR	SOU
377424	73424+78824+78624+73824	BI	SOU	PTR	SOU
377425	73425+78825+78625+73825	BI	SOU	PTR	SOU
377426	73426+78826+78626+73826	BI	SOU	PTR	SOU
377427	73427+78827+78627+73827	BI	SOU	PTR	SOU
377428	73428+78828+78628+73828	BI	SOU	PTR	SOU
377429	73429+78829+78629+73829	BI	SOU	PTR	SOU
377430	73430+78830+78630+73830	BI	SOU	PTR	SOU
377431	73431+78831+78631+73831	BI	SOU	PTR	SOU
377432	73432+78832+78632+73832	BI	SOU	PTR	SOU
377433	73433+78833+78633+73833	BI	SOU	PTR	SOU
377434	73434+78834+78634+73834	BI	SOU	PTR	SOU
377435	73435+78835+78635+73835	BI	SOU	PTR	SOU
377436	73436+78836+78636+73836	BI	SOU	PTR	SOU
377437	73437+78837+78637+73837	BI	SOU	PTR	SOU
377438	73438+78838+78638+73838	BI	SOU	PTR	SOU
377439	73439+78839+78639+73839	BI	SOU	PTR	SOU
377440	73440+78840+78640+73840	BI	SOU	PTR	SOU
377441	73441+78841+78641+73841	BI	SOU	PTR	SOU
377442	73442+78842+78642+73842	BI	SOU	PTR	SOU
377443	73443+78843+78643+73843	BI	SOU	PTR	SOU
377444	73444+78844+78644+73844	BI	SOU	PTR	SOU
377445	73445+78845+78645+73845	BI	SOU	PTR	SOU
377446	73446+78846+78646+73846	BI	SOU	PTR	SOU
377447	73447+78847+78647+73847	BI	SOU	PTR	SOU
377448	73448+78848+78648+73848	BI	SOU	PTR	SOU
377449	73449+78849+78649+73849	BI	SOU	PTR	SOU
377450	73450+78850+78650+73850	BI	SOU	PTR	SOU
377451	73451+78851+78651+73851	BI	SOU	PTR	SOU
377452	73452+78852+78652+73852	BI	SOU	PTR	SOU
377453	73453+78853+78653+73853	BI	SOU	PTR	SOU
377454	73454+78854+78654+73854	BI	SOU	PTR	SOU
377455	73455+78855+78655+73855	BI	SOU	PTR	SOU
377456	73456+78856+78656+73856	BI	SOU	PTR	SOU
377457	73457+78857+78657+73857	BI	SOU	PTR	SOU
377458	73458+78858+78658+73858	BI	SOU	PTR	SOU
377459	73459+78859+78659+73859	BI	SOU	PTR	SOU

Southern

377460	73460+78860+78660+73860	BI	SOU	PTR	SOU
377461	73461+78861+78661+73861	BI	SOU	PTR	SOU
377462	73462+78862+78662+73862	BI	SOU	PTR	SOU
377463	73463+78863+78663+73863	BI	SOU	PTR	SOU
377464	73464+78864+78664+73864	BI	SOU	PTR	SOU
377465	73465+78865+78665+73865	BI	SOU	PTR	SOU
377466	73466+78866+78666+73866	BI	SOU	PTR	SOU
377467	73467+78867+78667+73867	BI	SOU	PTR	SOU
377468	73468+78868+78668+73868	BI	SOU	PTR	SOU
377469	73469+78869+78669+73869	BI	SOU	PTR	SOU
377470	73470+78870+78670+73870	BI	SOU	PTR	SOU
377471	73471+78871+78671+73871	BI	SOU	PTR	SOU
377472	73472+78872+78672+73872	BI	SOU	PTR	SOU
377473	73473+78873+78673+73873	BI	SOU	PTR	SOU
377474	73474+78874+78674+73874	BI	SOU	PTR	SOU
377475	73475+78875+78675+73875	BI	SOU	PTR	SOU

Class 377/5
Electrostar

Vehicle Length: (Driving) 66ft 9in (20.3m)
(Inter) 65ft 6in (19.96m)
Height: 12ft 4in (3.75m)
Width: 9ft 2in (2.79m)
Horsepower: 2,012hp (1,500kW). Dual voltage sets
Seats (total/car): 20F-221S, 10F-48/69S/56S/10F-48S

Number	*Formation* DMCO(A)+MSO+PTSO+DMCO(B)	*Depot*	*Livery*	*Owner*	*Operator*
377501	73501+75901+74901+73601	SU	FCC	PTR	FCC (Sub-lease)
377502	73502+75902+74902+73602	SU	FCC	PTR	FCC (Sub-lease)
377503	73503+75903+74903+73603	SU	FCC	PTR	FCC (Sub-lease)
377504	73504+75904+74904+73604	SU	FCC	PTR	FCC (Sub-lease)
377505	73505+75905+74905+73605	SU	FCC	PTR	FCC (Sub-lease)
377506	73506+75906+74906+73606	SU	FCC	PTR	FCC (Sub-lease)
377507	73507+75907+74907+73607	SU	FCC	PTR	FCC (Sub-lease)
377508	73508+75908+74908+73608	SU	FCC	PTR	FCC (Sub-lease)
377509	73509+75909+74909+73609	SU	FCC	PTR	FCC (Sub-lease)
377510	73510+75910+74910+73610	SU	FCC	PTR	FCC (Sub-lease)
377511	73511+75911+74911+73611	SU	FCC	PTR	FCC (Sub-lease)
377512	73512+75912+74912+73612	SU	FCC	PTR	FCC (Sub-lease)
377513	73513+75913+74913+73613	SU	FCC	SOU	FCC (Sub-lease)
377514	73514+75914+74914+73614	SU	FCC	SOU	FCC (Sub-lease)
377515	73515+75915+74915+73615	SU	FCC	SOU	FCC (Sub-lease)
377516	73516+75916+74916+73616	SU	FCC	SOU	FCC (Sub-lease)
377517	73517+75917+74917+73617	SU	FCC	SOU	FCC (Sub-lease)
377518	73518+75918+74918+73618	SU	FCC	SOU	FCC (Sub-lease)
377519	73519+75919+74919+73619	SU	FCC	SOU	FCC (Sub-lease)
377520	73520+75920+74920+73620	SU	FCC	SOU	FCC (Sub-lease)
377521	73521+75921+74921+73621	SU	FCC	SOU	FCC (Sub-lease)
377522	73522+75922+74922+73622	SU	FCC	SOU	FCC (Sub-lease)
377523	73523+75923+74923+73623	SU	FCC	SOU	FCC (Sub-lease)

Left: *Class 377/3 No. 377314 departs from sidings at Southampton on 25 February 2008. All driving cars on the Class 377 breed have first class accommodation behind the driving cab, marked by a yellow cant rail band. Some minor front end differences exist between different Class 377 builds involving the light cluster groups.* **CJM**

Class 442

Vehicle Length: (Driving) 75ft 11½in (23.15m) (Inter) 75ft 5½in (22.99m)
Height: 12ft 4in (3.81m)
Width: 8ft 11½in (2.73m)
Horsepower: 1,608hp (1,200kW)
Seats (total/car): 24F-318S, 74S/76S/24F-28S/66S/74S

Number	Formation DTSO(A)+TSO+MBC+TSO+DTSO(B)	Depot	Livery	Owner	Operator
442401	**77382+71818+62937+71841+77406**	**BI**	**SGX**	**ANG**	**SOU**
442402	**77383+71819+62938+71842+77407**	**BI**	**SGX**	**ANG**	**SOU**
442403	**77384+71820+62941+71843+77408**	**BI**	**SGX**	**ANG**	**SOU**
442404	**77385+71821+62939+71844+77409**	**BI**	**SGX**	**ANG**	**SOU**
442405	**77386+71822+62944+71845+77410**	**BI**	**SGX**	**ANG**	**SOU**
442406	**77389+71823+62942+71846+77411**	**BI**	**SGX**	**ANG**	**SOU**
442407	**77388+71824+62943+71847+77412**	**BI**	**SGX**	**ANG**	**SOU**
442408	**77387+71825+62945+71848+77413**	**BI**	**SGX**	**ANG**	**SOU**
442409	**77390+71826+62946+71849+77414**	**BI**	**SGX**	**ANG**	**SOU**
442410	**77391+71827+62948+71850+77415**	**BI**	**SGX**	**ANG**	**SOU**
442411	**77392+71828+62940+71851+77422**	**BI**	**SGX**	**ANG**	**SOU**
442412	**77393+71829+62947+71858+77417**	**BI**	**SGX**	**ANG**	**SOU**
442413	**77394+71830+62949+71853+77418**	**BI**	**SGX**	**ANG**	**SOU**
442414	**77395+71831+62950+71854+77419**	**BI**	**SGX**	**ANG**	**SOU**
442415	**77396+71832+62951+71855+77420**	**BI**	**SGX**	**ANG**	**SOU**
442416	**77397+71833+62952+71856+77421**	**BI**	**SGX**	**ANG**	**SOU**
442417	**77398+71834+62953+71857+77416**	**BI**	**SGX**	**ANG**	**SOU**
442418	**77399+71835+62954+71852+77423**	**BI**	**SGX**	**ANG**	**SOU**
442419	**77400+71836+62955+71859+77424**	**BI**	**SGX**	**ANG**	**SOU**
442420	**77401+71837+62956+71860+77425**	**BI**	**SGX**	**ANG**	**SOU**
442421	**77402+71838+62957+71861+77426**	**BI**	**SGX**	**ANG**	**SOU**
442422	**77403+71839+62958+71862+77427**	**BI**	**SGX**	**ANG**	**SOU**
442423	**77404+71840+62959+71863+77428**	**BI**	**SGX**	**ANG**	**SOU**
442424	**77405+71841+62960+71864+77429**	**BI**	**SGX**	**ANG**	**SOU**

Right: *The Southern and Gatwick Express franchises were merged in 2008 to provide an improved service on the core London Victoria to Brighton route. This included the transfer of the former Wessex Class 442s to Brighton for use on additional Gatwick Express services. Originally just a handful of sets were transferred leaving a number stored, but by late 2009 under a refranchise deal for Southern all 24 sets have now been transferred to Brighton for use. Set No. 442414 is seen at Brighton.* **CJM**

Class 455/8

Vehicle Length: (Driving) 65ft 0½in (19.83m) (Inter) 65ft 4½in (19.92m)
Height: 12ft 1½in (3.79m)
Width: 9ft 3¼in (2.82m)
Horsepower: 1,000hp (746kW)
Seats (total/car): 310S, 74S/78S/84S/74S

Number	Formation DTSO(A)+MSO+TSO+DTSO(B)	Depot	Livery	Owner	Operator
455801	**77627+62709+71657+77580**	**SU**	**SOU**	**HSB**	**SOU**
455802	**77581+62710+71664+77582**	**SU**	**SOU**	**HSB**	**SOU**
455803	**77583+62711+71639+77584**	**SU**	**SOU**	**HSB**	**SOU**
455804	**77585+62712+71640+77586**	**SU**	**SOU**	**HSB**	**SOU**
455805	**77587+62713+71641+77588**	**SU**	**SOU**	**HSB**	**SOU**
455806	**77589+62714+71642+77590**	**SU**	**SOU**	**HSB**	**SOU**
455807	**77591+62715+71643+77592**	**SU**	**SOU**	**HSB**	**SOU**
455808	**77637+62716+71644+77594**	**SU**	**SOU**	**HSB**	**SOU**
455809	**77623+62717+71648+77602**	**SU**	**SOU**	**HSB**	**SOU**
455810	**77597+62718+71646+77598**	**SU**	**SOU**	**HSB**	**SOU**
455811	**77599+62719+71647+77600**	**SU**	**SOU**	**HSB**	**SOU**
455812	**77595+62720+71645+77626**	**SU**	**SOU**	**HSB**	**SOU**

455813	77603+62721+71649+77604	SU	SOU	HSB	SOU
455814	77605+62722+71650+77606	SU	SOU	HSB	SOU
455815	77607+62723+71651+77608	SU	SOU	HSB	SOU
455816	77609+62724+71652+77633	SU	SOU	HSB	SOU
455817	77611+62725+71653+77612	SU	SOU	HSB	SOU
455818	77613+62726+71654+77632	SU	SOU	HSB	SOU
455819	77615+62727+71637+77616	SU	SOU	HSB	SOU
455820	77617+62728+71656+77618	SU	SOU	HSB	SOU
455821	77619+62729+71655+77620	SU	SOU	HSB	SOU
455822	77621+62730+71658+77622	SU	SOU	HSB	SOU
455823	77601+62731+71659+77596	SU	SOU	HSB	SOU
455824	77593+62732+71660+77624	SU	SOU	HSB	SOU
455825	77579+62733+71661+77628	SU	SOU	HSB	SOU
455826	77630+62734+71662+77629	SU	SOU	HSB	SOU
455827	77610+62735+71663+77614	SU	SOU	HSB	SOU
455828	77631+62736+71638+77634	SU	SOU	HSB	SOU
455829	77635+62737+71665+77636	SU	SOU	HSB	SOU
455830	77625+62743+71666+77638	SU	SOU	HSB	SOU
455831	77639+62739+71667+77640	SU	SOU	HSB	SOU
455832	77641+62740+71668+77642	SU	SOU	HSB	SOU
455833	77643+62741+71669+77644	SU	SOU	HSB	SOU
455834	77645+62742+71670+77646	SU	SOU	HSB	SOU
455835	77647+62738+71671+77648	SU	SOU	HSB	SOU
455836	77649+62744+71672+77650	SU	SOU	HSB	SOU
455837	77651+62745+71673+77652	SU	SOU	HSB	SOU
455838	77653+62746+71674+77654	SU	SOU	HSB	SOU
455839	77655+62747+71675+77656	SU	SOU	HSB	SOU
455840	77657+62748+71676+77658	SU	SOU	HSB	SOU
455841	77659+62749+71677+77660	SU	SOU	HSB	SOU
455842	77661+62750+71678+77662	SU	SOU	HSB	SOU
455843	776636+2751+71679+77664	SU	SOU	HSB	SOU
455844	776656+2752+71680+77666	SU	SOU	HSB	SOU
455845	776676+2753+71681+77668	SU	SOU	HSB	SOU
455846	776696+2754+71682+77670	SU	SOU	HSB	SOU

Left: *A fleet of 46 York-built Class 455/8s are operated by Southern on suburban services from London Victoria and London Bridge. All sets have been refurbished and the original unit end gangway door has been removed. The front ends now sport a single tail/marker light unit and a headlight on each side. Set No. 455809 approaches Clapham Junction.* **CJM**

Class 456

Vehicle Length: (Driving) 65ft 3¼in (19.89m)
Height: 12ft 4½in (3.77m)
Width: 9ft 3in (2.81m)
Horsepower: 500hp (370kW)
Seats (total/car): 152S, 79S/73S

Number	*Formation DMSO+DTSO*	*Depot*	*Livery*	*Owner*	*Operator*
456001	64735+78250	SU	SOU	PTR	SOU
456002	64736+78251	SU	SOU	PTR	SOU
456003	64737+78252	SU	SOU	PTR	SOU
456004	64738+78253	SU	SOU	PTR	SOU
456005	64739+78254	SU	SOU	PTR	SOU
456006	64740+78255	SU	SOU	PTR	SOU
456007	64741+78256	SU	SOU	PTR	SOU
456008	64742+78257	SU	SOU	PTR	SOU
456009	64743+78258	SU	SOU	PTR	SOU
456010	64744+78259	SU	SOU	PTR	SOU
456011	64745+78260	SU	SOU	PTR	SOU
456012	64746+78261	SU	SOU	PTR	SOU
456013	64747+78262	SU	SOU	PTR	SOU
456014	64748+78263	SU	SOU	PTR	SOU
456015	64749+78264	SU	SOU	PTR	SOU
456016	64750+78265	SU	SOU	PTR	SOU
456017	64751+78266	SU	SOU	PTR	SOU
456018	64752+78267	SU	SOU	PTR	SOU
456019	64753+78268	SU	SOU	PTR	SOU
456020	64754+78269	SU	SOU	PTR	SOU
456021	64755+78270	SU	SOU	PTR	SOU
456022	64756+78271	SU	SOU	PTR	SOU
456023	64757+78272	SU	SOU	PTR	SOU
456024	64758+78273	SU	SOU	PTR	SOU

	Name applied
465024	*Sir Cosmo Bonsor*

Right: *Built for Network SouthEast to allow the running of two, six or ten car trains, the Class 456s are operated by Southern and can be found throughout the network's suburban operation. All are painted in Southern livery and allocated to Selhurst depot. Set No. 456006 is seen departing from London Victoria.* **Tony Christie**

Class 460
Juniper

Vehicle Length: (Driving) 68ft 11½in (21.01m) (Inter) 65ft 4¾in (19.93m)
Height: 12ft 4½in (3.77m)
Width: 9ft 2¼in (2.80m)
Horsepower: 3,626hp (2,704kW)
Seats (total/car): 48F-316S, 10F/28F/9F-42S/60S/60S/38S/60S/56S

Number	Formation DMFLO+TFO+TCO+MSO+TSO+MSO+DMSO	Depot	Livery	Owner	Operator
460001	67901+74401+74411+74421+74431+74441+74451+67911	SL	GAT	PTR	SOU
460002	67902+74402+74412+74422+74432+74442+74452+67912	SL	GAT	PTR	SOU
460003	67903+74403+74413+74423+74433+74443+74453+67913	SL	GAT	PTR	SOU
460004	67904+74404+74414+74424+74434+74444+74454+67914	SL	GAT	PTR	SOU
460005	67905+74405+74415+74425+74435+74445+74455+67915	SL	GAT	PTR	SOU
460006	67906+74406+74416+74426+74436+74446+74456+67916	SL	GAT	PTR	SOU
460007	67907+74407+74417+74427+74437+74447+74457+67917	SL	GAT	PTR	SOU
460008	67908+74408+74418+74428+74438+74448+74458+67918	SL	GAT	PTR	SOU

Right: *The 2008 merger of the Gatwick Express and Southern TOCs provided an improved service on the busy London - Gatwick Airport - Brighton line. At the time Southern became the operator of the eight Class 460 sets based at Stewarts Lane. Set No. 460008 is seen passing Clapham Junction.* **Tony Christie**

■ *Sets due off-lease in 2011.*

Class 73

Vehicle Length: 53ft 8in (16.35m)
Height: 12ft 5⁵⁄₁₆in (3.79m)
Width: 8ft 8in (2.64m)
Power: 750V dc third rail or English Electric 6K
Horsepower: electric - 1,600hp (1,193kW)
Horsepower: diesel - 600hp (447kW)
Electrical Equipment: English Electric

Number	Depot	Pool	Livery	Owner	Operator	Name
73202 (73137)	SL	IVGA	GAT	PTR	SOU	*Dave Berry*

Right: *The Gatwick Express service (now Southern) operate one Class 73/2 No. 73202* Dave Berry. *This loco has received some minor modification to allow it to operate fully with Class 460 stock. The loco is used to pilot Gatwick Express stock in case of failure and is now painted in full Gatwick Express livery. The loco is seen at Kensington Olympia with a route training run from Stewarts Lane to West Ealing on 14 December 2009.* **CJM**

Virgin Trains

Address: ✉ 85 Smallbrook Queensway, Birmingham, B5 4HA
info@virgintrains.co.uk
✆ 0845 000 8000
ⓘ www.virgintrains.co.uk

Managing Director: Chris Gibb
Franchise Dates: 12 December 2006 - 31 March 2012
Principal Routes: London Euston-Birmingham, Holyhead, Manchester Liverpool, Glasgow and Edinburgh
Depots: Edge Hill* (LL), Longsight** (MA), Oxley** (OY), Wembley** (WB)
** Operated by Alstom Transportation
Parent Company: Virgin Group

Class 57/3

Vehicle Length: 63ft 6in (19.38m)
Height: 12ft $10^{1}/_{8}$in (3.91m)
Width: 9ft 2in (2.79m)
Engine: EMD 645-12F3B
Horsepower: 2,750hp (2,051kW)
Electrical Equipment: Brush

Number	*Depot*	*Pool*	*Livery*	*Owner*	*Operator*	*Name/Notes*
57301 (47845)	**MA**	**IWCA**	**VWC**	**PBR**	**VWC**	***Scott Tracy***
57302 (47827)	**MA**	**IWCA**	**VWC**	**PBR**	**VWC**	***Virgil Tracy***
57303 (47705)	**MA**	**IWCA**	**VWC**	**PBR**	**VWC**	***Alan Tracy***
57304 (47807)	**MA**	**IWCA**	**VWC**	**PBR**	**VWC**	***Gordon Tracy***
57305 (47822)	**MA**	**IWCA**	**VWC**	**PBR**	**VWC**	***John Tracy***
57306 (47814)	**MA**	**IWCA**	**VWC**	**PBR**	**VWC**	***Jeff Tracy***
57307 (47225)	**MA**	**IWCA**	**VWC**	**PBR**	**VWC**	***Lady Penelope***
57308 (47846)	**MA**	**IWCA**	**VWC**	**PBR**	**VWC**	***Tin Tin***
57309 (47806)	**MA**	**IWCA**	**VWC**	**PBR**	**VWC**	***Brains***
57310 (47831)	**MA**	**IWCA**	**VWC**	**PBR**	**VWC**	***Kyrano***
57311 (47817)	**MA**	**IWCA**	**VWC**	**PBR**	**VWC**	***Parker***
57312 (47330)	**MA**	**IWCA**	**VWC**	**PBR**	**VWC**	***The Hood***
57313 (47371)	*MA*	*IWCA*	*BLU*	*PBR*	*ATW*	*Used by Arriva Trains Wales/FGW*
57314 (47372)	*MA*	*IWCA*	*ATE*	*PBR*	*ATW*	*Used by Arriva Trains Wales*
57315 (47234)	*MA*	*IWCA*	*ATE*	*PBR*	*ATW*	*Used by Arriva Trains Wales*
57316 (47290)	*MA*	*IWCA*	*BLU*	*PBR*	*ATW*	*Used by Arriva Trains Wales/FGW*

Below: *No. 57307 is viewed from its No. 2 end. The drop-head Dellner coupling is in the raised position. The 12 locos presently operated by Virgin West Coast are all painted in 'Pendolino' style silver and red livery. This loco is unique amongst the fleet in having a pink background to its* Lady Penelope *nameplate.* **CJM**

Virgin Trains

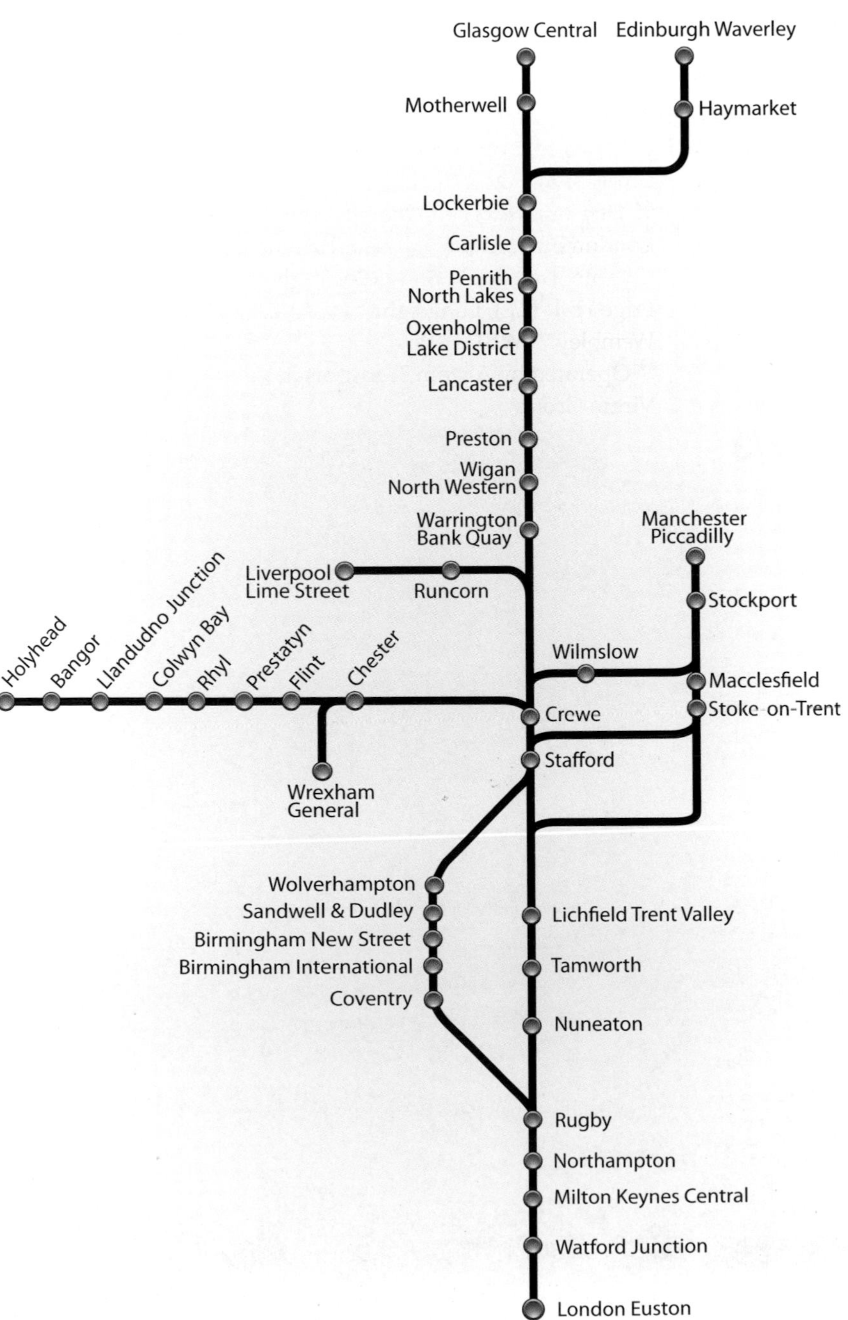
Glasgow Central
Edinburgh Waverley
Motherwell
Haymarket
Lockerbie
Carlisle
Penrith North Lakes
Oxenholme Lake District
Lancaster
Preston
Wigan North Western
Warrington Bank Quay
Manchester Piccadilly
Liverpool Lime Street
Runcorn
Stockport
Holyhead
Bangor
Llandudno Junction
Colwyn Bay
Rhyl
Prestatyn
Flint
Chester
Wilmslow
Macclesfield
Stoke-on-Trent
Crewe
Stafford
Wrexham General
Wolverhampton
Sandwell & Dudley
Birmingham New Street
Birmingham International
Coventry
Lichfield Trent Valley
Tamworth
Nuneaton
Rugby
Northampton
Milton Keynes Central
Watford Junction
London Euston

Virgin Trains

Class 221
Super Voyager

Vehicle Length: 77ft 6in (23.62m)
Height: 12ft 4in (3.75m)
Width: 8ft 11in (2.73m)
Engine: 1 x Cummins 750hp per vehicle
Horsepower: 5-car - 3,750hp (2,796kW). 4-car - 3,000hp (2,237kW)
Seats (total/car): 26F/214S 42S/60S/60S/52S/26F (*not in 4-car set)*

Number	*Formation*	*Depot*	*Livery*	*Owner*	*Operator*	*Name*
	221101 - 221118 - DMS+MS+MS+MSRMB+DMF					
	221142 - 221144 - DMS+MS+MSRMB+DMF					
221101	60351+60951+60851+60751+60451	CZ	VWC	HBS	VWC	*Louis Bleriot*
221102	60352+60952+60852+60752+60452	CZ	VWC	HBS	VWC	*John Cabot*
221103	60353+60953+60853+60753+60453	CZ	VWC	HBS	VWC	*Christopher Columbus*
221104	60354+60954+60854+60754+60454	CZ	VWC	HBS	VWC	*Sir John Franklin*
221105	60355+60955+60855+60755+60455	CZ	VWC	HBS	VWC	*William Baffin*
221106	60356+60956+60856+60756+60456	CZ	VWC	HBS	VWC	*William Barents*
221107	60357+60957+60857+60757+60457	CZ	VWC	HBS	VWC	*Sir Martin Frobisher*
221108	60358+60958+60858+60758+60458	CZ	VWC	HBS	VWC	*Sir Ernest Shackleton*
221109	60359+60959+60859+60759+60459	CZ	VWC	HBS	VWC	*Marco Polo*
221110	60360+60960+60860+60760+60460	CZ	VWC	HBS	VWC	*James Cook*
221111	60361+60961+60861+60761+60461	CZ	VWC	HBS	VWC	*Roald Amundsen*
221112	60362+60962+60862+60762+60462	CZ	VWC	HBS	VWC	*Ferdinand Magellan*
221113	60363+60963+60863+60763+60463	CZ	VWC	HBS	VWC	*Sir Walter Raleigh*
221114	60364+60964+60864+60764+60464	CZ	VWC	HBS	VWC	
221115	60365+60965+60865+60765+60465	CZ	VWC	HBS	VWC	
221116	60366+60966+60866+60766+60466	CZ	VWC	HBS	VWC	
221117	60367+60967+60867+60767+60467	CZ	VWC	HBS	VWC	
221118	60368+60968+60868+60768+60468	CZ	VWC	HBS	VWC	
221142	60392+60992+60792+60492	CZ	VWC	HBS	VWC	*Matthew Flinders*
221143	60393+60993+60793+60493	CZ	VWC	HBS	VWC	*Auguste Picard*
221144	60394+60994+60794+60494	CZ	VWC	HBS	VWC	*Bombardier Voyager*

Above: *In the franchise changes at the end of 2007, the Virgin Voyager fleet was split between Virgin West Coast and Arriva Cross Country. The Super Voyager sets remaining with Virgin were for use on North Wales line duties to cease the practice of electric Pendolino sets being loco hauled between Crewe and Holyhead. Set No. 221105 departs from Bangor on 16 February 2008 with its DMF nearest the camera.* **Stacey Thew**

Class 390
Pendolino

Vehicle Length Driving: 75ft 6in (23.01m)
Height: 11ft 6in (3.50m)
Width: 8ft 11in (2.71m)
Horsepower: 6,840hp (5,100kW)
Seats (total/car): 147F/300S, 18F/39F/44F/46F/76S/66S/48S/64S/46S
35 sets are to be strengthned to eleven vehicles and four extra Class 390 sets are to be built by Virgin Rail Projects

Number	Formation DMRFO+MFO+PTFO+MFO+TSO+MSO+PTSRMB+MSO+DMSO	Depot	Livery	Owner	Operator	Name
390001	69101+69401+69501+69601+68801+69701+69801+69901+69201	MA	VWC	ANG	VWC	*Virgin Pioneer*
390002	69102+69402+69502+69602+68802+69702+69802+69902+69202	MA	VWC	ANG	VWC	*Virgin Angel*
390003	69103+69403+69503+69603+68803+69703+69803+69903+69203	MA	VWC	ANG	VWC	*Virgin Hero*
390004	69104+69404+69504+69604+68804+69704+69804+69904+69204	MA	VWC	ANG	VWC	*Virgin Scot*
390005	69105+69405+69505+69605+68805+69705+69805+69905+69205	MA	VWC	ANG	VWC	*City of Wolverhampton*
390006	69106+69406+69506+69606+68806+69706+69806+69906+69206	MA	VWC	ANG	VWC	*Tate Liverpool*
390007	69107+69407+69507+69607+68807+69707+69807+69907+69207	MA	VWC	ANG	VWC	*Virgin Lady*
390008	69108+69408+69508+69608+68808+69708+69808+69908+69208	MA	VWC	ANG	VWC	*Virgin King*
390009	69109+69409+69509+69609+68809+69709+69809+69909+69209	MA	VWC	ANG	VWC	*Treaty of Union*
390010	69110+69410+69510+69610+68810+69710+69810+69910+69210	MA	VWC	ANG	VWC	*A Decade of Progress*
390011	69111+69411+69511+69611+68811+69711+69811+69911+69211	MA	VWC	ANG	VWC	*City of Lichfield*
390012	69112+69412+69512+69612+68812+69712+69812+69912+69212	MA	VWC	ANG	VWC	*Virgin Star*
390013	69113+69413+69513+69613+68813+69713+69813+69913+69213	MA	VWC	ANG	VWC	*Virgin Spirit*
390014	69114+69414+69514+69614+68814+69714+69814+69914+69214	MA	VWC	ANG	VWC	*City of Manchester*
390015	69115+69415+69515+69615+68815+69715+69815+69915+69215	MA	VWC	ANG	VWC	*Virgin Crusader*
390016	69116+69416+69516+69616+68816+69716+69816+69916+69216	MA	VWC	ANG	VWC	*Virgin Champion*
390017	69117+69417+69517+69617+68817+69717+69817+69917+69217	MA	VWC	ANG	VWC	*Virgin Prince*
390018	69118+69418+69518+69618+68818+69718+69818+69918+69218	MA	VWC	ANG	VWC	*Virgin Princess*
390019	69119+69419+69519+69619+68819+69719+69819+69919+69219	MA	VWC	ANG	VWC	*Virgin Warrior*
390020	69120+69420+69520+69620+68820+69720+69820+69920+69220	MA	VWC	ANG	VWC	*Virgin Cavalier*
390021	69121+69421+69521+69621+68821+69721+69821+69921+69221	MA	VWC	ANG	VWC	*Virgin Dream*
390022	69122+69422+69522+69622+68822+69722+69822+69922+69222	MA	VWC	ANG	VWC	*Penny the Pendolino*
390023	69123+69423+69523+69623+68823+69723+69823+69923+69223	MA	VWC	ANG	VWC	*Virgin Glory*
390024	69124+69424+69524+69624+68824+69724+69824+69924+69224	MA	VWC	ANG	VWC	*Virgin Venturer*
390025	69125+69425+69525+69625+68825+69725+69825+69925+69225	MA	VWC	ANG	VWC	*Virgin Stagecoach*
390026	69126+69426+69526+69626+68826+69726+69826+69926+69226	MA	VWC	ANG	VWC	*Virgin Enterprise*
390027	69127+69427+69527+69627+68827+69727+69827+69927+69227	MA	VWC	ANG	VWC	*Virgin Buccaneer*
390028	69128+69428+69528+69628+68828+69728+69828+69928+69228	MA	VWC	ANG	VWC	*City of Preston*
390029	69129+69429+69529+69629+68829+69729+69829+69929+69229	MA	VWC	ANG	VWC	*City of Stoke-on-Trent*
390030	69130+69430+69530+69630+68830+69730+69830+69930+69230	MA	VWC	ANG	VWC	*City of Edinburgh*
390031	69131+69431+69531+69631+68831+69731+69831+69931+69231	MA	VWC	ANG	VWC	*City of Liverpool*
390032	69132+69432+69532+69632+68832+69732+69832+69932+69232	MA	VWC	ANG	VWC	*City of Birmingham*
390033	69133+69433+69533+69633+68833+69733+69833+69933+69233	LM	VWC	VIR	-	*(City of Glasgow)*
390034	69134+69434+69534+69634+68834+69734+69834+69934+69234	MA	VWC	ANG	VWC	*City of Carlisle*
390035	69135+69435+69535+69635+68835+69735+69835+69935+69235	MA	VWC	ANG	VWC	*City of Lancaster*
390036	69136+69436+69536+69636+68836+69736+69836+69936+69236	MA	VWC	ANG	VWC	*City of Coventry*
390037	69137+69437+69537+69637+68837+69737+69837+69937+69237	MA	VWC	ANG	VWC	*Virgin Difference*
390038	69138+69438+69538+69638+68838+69738+69838+69938+69238	MA	VWC	ANG	VWC	*City of London*
390039	69139+69439+69539+69639+68839+69739+69839+69939+69239	MA	VWC	ANG	VWC	*Virgin Quest*

Virgin Trains

390040	69140+69440+69540+69640+68840+69740+69840+69940+69240	MA	VWC	ANG	VWC	*Virgin Pathfinder*
390041	69141+69441+69541+69641+68841+69741+69841+69941+69241	MA	VWC	ANG	VWC	*City of Chester*
390042	69142+69442+69542+69642+68842+69742+69842+69942+69242	MA	VWC	ANG	VWC	*City of Bangor / Dinas Bangor*
390043	69143+69443+69543+69643+68843+69743+69843+69943+69243	MA	VWC	ANG	VWC	*Virgin Explorer*
390044	69144+69444+69544+69644+68844+69744+69844+69944+69244	MA	VWC	ANG	VWC	*Virgin Lionheart*
390045	69145+69445+69545+69645+68845+69745+69845+69945+69245	MA	VWC	ANG	VWC	*101 Squadron*
390046	69146+69446+69546+69646+68846+69746+69846+69946+69246	MA	VWC	ANG	VWC	*Virgin Soldiers*
390047	69147+69447+69547+69647+68847+69747+69847+69947+69247	MA	VWC	ANG	VWC	*Clic Sargent*
390048	69148+69448+69548+69648+68848+69748+69848+69948+69248	MA	VWC	ANG	VWC	*Virgin Harrier*
390049	69149+69449+69549+69649+68849+69749+69849+69949+69249	MA	VWC	ANG	VWC	*Virgin Express*
390050	69150+69450+69550+69650+68850+69750+69850+69950+69250	MA	VWC	ANG	VWC	*Virgin Invader*
390051	69151+69451+69551+69651+68851+69751+69851+69951+69251	MA	VWC	ANG	VWC	*Virgin Ambassador*
390052	69152+69452+69552+69652+68852+69752+69852+69952+69252	MA	VWC	ANG	VWC	*Virgin Knight*
390053	69153+69453+69553+69653+68853+69753+69853+69953+69253	MA	VWC	ANG	VWC	*Mission Accomplished*

Above: *The 52 Manchester-based Class 390 'Pendolino' sets operate all Virgin Trains electrified services on the West Coast route. Set No. 3900020 is shown passing Grendon near Stafford on 20 March 2009 forming a London bound service. Additional Alstom-built Pendolino sets are currently on order, as are a number of extra vehicles to strengthen 35 sets to 11 car formations.* **Stacey Thew**

Mk3 Hauled Stock

Vehicle Length: 75ft 0in (22.86m) *Width: 8ft 11in (2.71m)*
Height: 12ft 9in (3.88m) *Bogie Type: BT10*

AJ1G - RFB *Seating 18F*

Number	*Depot*	*Livery*	*Owner*
10212	**WB**	**VWC**	**PTR**

AD1G - FO *Seating 48F*

Number	*Depot*	*Livery*	*Owner*
11007	**WB**	**VWC**	**PTR**
11018	**WB**	**VWC**	**PTR**
11048	**WB**	**VWC**	**PTR**

AC2G - TS0 (*TSOD) *Seating 76/70*S*

Number	*Depot*	*Livery*	*Owner*
12011	**WB**	**VWC**	**PTR**
12078	**WB**	**VWC**	**PTR**
12122*	**WB**	**VWC**	**PTR**
12133	**WB**	**VWC**	**PTR**
12138	**WB**	**VWC**	**PTR**

NL - DVT

Number	*Depot*	*Livery*	*Owner*
82126	**WB**	**VWC**	**PTR**

■ The Virgin West Coast loco-hauled set is operated on the Friday only 18.46 Euston to Preston, as well as providing cover on the Euston - Birmingham corridor. The set is also available for charter hire. Motive power is provided by DBS in the form of a Class 90/0 or a VWC Class 57/3.

Above Right: *Rebuilt from Virgin West Coast stock at Wabtec Doncaster the new Virgin West Coast loco-hauled Mk3 set entered service in summer 2009 allocated to Wembley. TSO No. 12011 is seen coupled to a DBS/ScotRail Class 90.* **John Wills**

Middle Right: *The Virgin West Coast Mk3 set operates with Virgin-branded Mk3 DVT No. 82126. The entire set had been repainted in a similar livery to the 'Pendolino' and 'Voyager' fleets. The vehicle is seen in the yard of Wabtec Doncaster.* **Derek Porter**

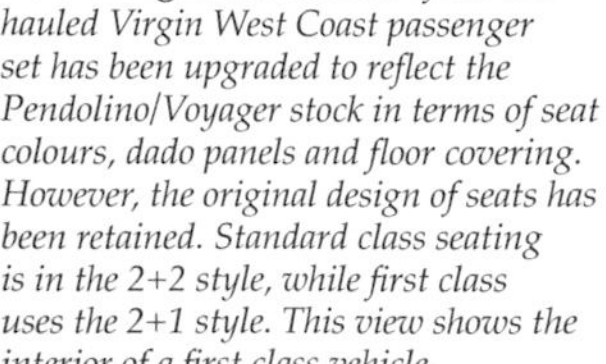

Below Right: *The interior of the loco-hauled Virgin West Coast passenger set has been upgraded to reflect the Pendolino/Voyager stock in terms of seat colours, dado panels and floor covering. However, the original design of seats has been retained. Standard class seating is in the 2+2 style, while first class uses the 2+1 style. This view shows the interior of a first class vehicle.*
Derek Porter

The following vehicles are assigned to form a second West Coast loco hauled train if required in the future:
DBR owned TSOs 12017/054/059/ 094/124.
Cargo-D owned FOs 11064/084/086
Porterbrook-owned DVT 82101

Wrexham & Shropshire Railway

Address: ✉ The Pump House, Cotton Hill, Shrewsbury, SY1 2DP
info@wrexhamandshropshire.co.uk
✆ 0845 260 5233
ⓘ www.wrexhamandshropshire.co.uk

Managing Director: Andy Hamilton
Franchise Dates: Open access operator
Principal Routes: London Marylebone to Wrexham
Parent Company: Wrexham, Shropshire & Marylebone Railway Co - originally a joint venture between Renaissance Trains, Laing Rail and DB Regio.
From January 2010 the Renaissance Trains and Laing Rail share was transferred to DB Regio and the WSR business was operated by Chiltern Railways.

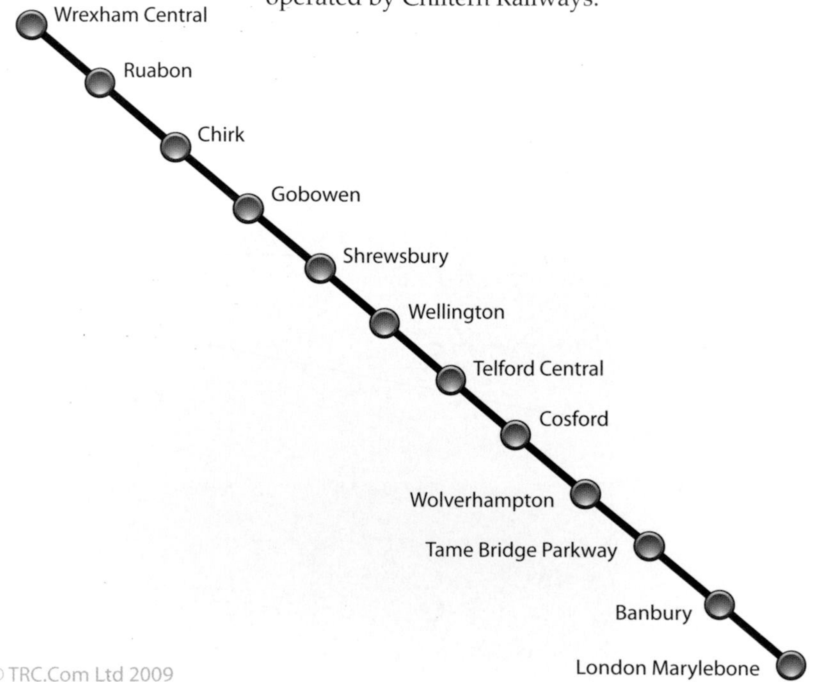

Class 67

Vehicle Length: 64ft 7in (19.68m)
Height: 12ft 9in (3.88m)
Width: 8ft 9in (2.66m)
Engine: EMD 12N-710G3B-EC
Horsepower: 2,980hp (2,223kW)
Electrical Equipment: EMD

Number	Depot	Pool	Livery	Owner	Operator	Name
67010	TO	WAWN	WSR	ANG	DBS/WSR	
67012	TO	WAWN	WSR	ANG	DBS/WSR	A Shropshire Lad
67013	TO	WAWN	WSR	ANG	DBS/WSR	Dyfrbont Pontcysyllte
67014	TO	WAWN	WSR	ANG	DBS/WSR	Thomas Telford
67015	TO	WAWN	WSR	ANG	DBS/WSR	David J. Lloyd

Right: *Although still owned by DBS, five Class 67s are dedicated to the Wrexham & Shropshire service linking London Marylebone with Wrexham. The locos have a slightly modified push-pull system to permit operation with Mk3 DVTs, but otherwise are conventional locos. All are painted in the distinctive two-tone grey of the Wrexham & Shropshire Railway. Maintenance is still carried out by DBS and the locos remain allocated to Toton depot. No. 67012 is seen heading for London Marylebone passing through Washwood Heath.* **John Binch**

Mk3 Hauled Stock (Passenger)

Vehicle Length: 75ft 0in (22.86m)
Height: 12ft 9in (3.88m)
Width: 8ft 11in (2.71m)
Bogie Type: BT10

AJ1G - RFM *Seating 30F*

Number	*Depot*	*Livery*	*Owner*
10208*	CE	WSR	DBR
10215	CE	BLG	DBR
10235	CE	BLG	DBR
10242	CE	BLG	CAD
10246	CE	BLG	CAD
10257	CE	BLG	DBR

** previously 40517*

AD1H - TFO *Seating 48F*

Number	*Depot*	*Livery*	*Owner*
11027	CE	VIR	DBR
11029	CE	BLG	DBR
11031	CE	BLG	DBR
11071	CE	BLG	CAD
11083	CE	BLG	CAD
11097	CE	BLG	DBR

AC2G - TSO *Seating 72S*

Number	*Depot*	*Livery*	*Owner*
12014	CE	BLG	CAD
12038	CE	BLG	CAD
12043	CE	BLG	CAD
12053	CE	BLG	DBR
12119	CE	BLG	CAD
12127	CE	WSR	DBR
12145	CE	WSR	DBR

■ *The following coaches are under modification for WSR at the time of going to press*

10230, 10236, 10255, 12048, 12069, 12072, 12117, 12131, 12169

Mk3 Hauled Stock (NPCCS)

Vehicle Length: 75ft 0in (22.86m)
Height: 12ft 9in (3.88m)
Width: 8ft 11in (2.71m)
Bogie Type: BT7

NZAG - DVT

Number	*Depot*	*Livery*	*Owner*
82301 (82117)	CE	WSR	DBR
82302 (82151)	CE	CRW	DBR
82303 (82135)	CE	WSR	DBR
82304 (82130)	CE	WSR	DBR
82305 (82134)	CE	WSR	DBR

Right: ***Five Mk3 DVTs are set aside for Wrexham & Shropshire use; the vehicles are owned by DB Regio, a part of DBS. All vehicles were refurbished by Axiom Rail, a part of DBS at their plant in Stoke-on-Trent. No. 82305 is seen in this view near Wellington painted in WSR livery. No. 82302 is painted in white and blue Chiltern livery.*** **John Binch**

Advenza Freight / Cotswold Rail

Address (UK): ✉ Advenza Freight Ltd, 105 Great Western Road, Gloucester, GL1 3AN
info@advenza.com ✆ 01452 414422 ⓘ www.advenza.com

■ *This open access operator went into liquidation in October 2009. The assets owned by the company were in the process of disposal when we went to press. The Class 66/8s were immediately returned to the lease owner for new hire.*

Class 08

Vehicle Length: 29ft 3in (8.91m)
Height: 12ft $8^{5}/_{8}$in (3.87m)
Width: 8ft 6in (2.59m)
Engine: English Electric 6K
Horsepower: 400hp (298kW)
Electrical Equipment: English Electric

Number	Depot	Pool	Livery	Owner	Operator
08699	-	MBDL	BLU	CWR	IND
08847(S)	NC	MBDL	CWR	CWR	-

Class 47

Vehicle Length: 63ft 6in (19.35m)
Height: 12ft $10^{3}/_{8}$in (3.91m)
Width: 9ft 2in (2.79m)
Engine: Sulzer 12LDA28C
Horsepower: 2,580hp (1,922kW)
Electrical Equipment: Brush

Number	Depot	Pool	Livery	Owner	Operator	Name/Notes
47237	GL	ADFL	ADV	CWR	-	Stored Gloucester
47375	BH	MBDL	CWR	CWR	-	
47828 (47266/629)	GL	ADFL	CWR	CWR	-	*Joe Strummer*

Left: *Carrying Advenza livery and bodyside branding, Class 47 No. 47237 and Class 57 No. 57006 are seen in the spring of 2008 powering a Gloucester to Plymouth test train at Dawlish Warren, when Advenza Freight were hopeful of winning a new scrap metal contract from the Plymouth area to Cardiff. Both these locomotives are currently stored awaiting sale.* **CJM**

Class 57

Vehicle Length: 63ft 6in (19.38m)
Height: 12ft $10^{1}/_{8}$in (3.91m)
Width: 9ft 2in (2.79m)
Engine: EMD 645-12E3
Horsepower: 2,500hp (1,864kW)
Electrical Equipment: Brush

Number	Depot	Pool	Livery	Owner	Operator	Name/Notes
57005 (47350)	GL	ADFL	ADV	CWR	-	*The Foss Way* - Stored at Cardiff
57006 (47187)	GL	ADFL	ADV	CWR	-	Stored at Heaton

Coaching Stock

Mk2
Vehicle Length: 66ft 0in (20.11m)
Height: 12ft $9^{1}/_{2}$in (3.89m)
Width: 9ft 3in (2.81m)
Seats (total/car): 60S

Mk 3
Vehicle Length: 75ft 0in (22.86m)
Height: 12ft 9in (3.88m)
Width: 8ft 11in (2.71m)
Bogie Type: BT10

Number	Type	Depot	Livery	Operator	Use
5700 (S)	AC2D/TSO	GL	FSW	-	Support vehicle – Stored
5710 (S)	AC2D/TSO	GL	FSW	-	Support vehicle – Stored
6722 (S) (6611)	AN1D/RMBF	OY	FSW	-	Support vehicle – Stored
6724 (S) (6615)	AN1D/RMBF	GL	FSW	-	Support vehicle – Stored
9488	AE2D/BSO	GL	FSW	-	Support vehicle – Stored
10667 (S)	AS4G/SLE	KT	DRS	-	Support vehicle – Stored
10698 (S)	AS4G/SLE	MM	SCT	-	Stored
10733 (S)	AS4G/SLP	MM	ROY	-	Stored
17144 (S) (14144)	AB1D/BFK	LM	ICS	-	Stored
17170 (S) (14170)	AB1D/BFK	LM	ICS	-	Stored

Colas Rail

Address: ✉ Dacre House, 19 Dacre Street, London, SW1H 0DJ
enquiries@colasrail.co.uk
✆ 0207 593 5353
ⓘ www.colasrail.co.uk

Chairman: Charles-Albert Giral

Depot: Tavistock Junction (TJ), Rugby (RU), Eastleigh Works (ZG)

Class 47/7

Vehicle Length: 63ft 6in (19.35m)
Height: 12ft 10⅜in (3.91m)
Width: 9ft 2in (2.79m)
Electric Train Heat fitted

Engine: Sulzer 12LDA28C
Horsepower: 2,580hp (1,922kW)
Electrical Equipment: Brush

Number	*Depot*	*Pool*	*Livery*	*Owner*	*Operator*	*Name*
47727 (47569)	TJ	COLO	COL	COL	COL	*Rebecca*
47739 (47594)	TJ	COLO	COL	COL	COL	*Robin of Templecombe*
47749 (47625)	TJ	COLO	COL	COL	COL	*Demelza*

Right: *After starting life as an infrastructure operator with a fleet of just two Class 47s, Colas Rail are now an established freight haulier, operating a fleet of three Class 47/7 locos in the distinctive orange and lime green livery. No. 47727* Rebecca *is illustrated from its Nos. 2 end 2008.* **CJM**

Below: *In 2009 two of the Colas Class 47s were frequently deployed on the Burton-on-Trent to Dollands Moor export steel train. On 19 March 2009 Nos. 47739 and 47727 pull out of Elford Loop with the Europe bound train.* **Matt Clarke**

Class 66

Vehicle Length: 70ft 0½in (21.34m)
Height: 12ft 10in (3.91m)
Width: 8ft 8¼in (2.65m)
Engine: EMD 12N-710G3B-EC
Horsepower: 3,300hp (2,462kW)
Electrical Equipment: EMD

Number	*Depot*	*Pool*	*Livery*	*Owner*	*Operator*
66841 (66406)	**ZG**	**COLO**	**COL**	**PTR**	**COL**
66842 (66407)	**ZG**	**COLO**	**COL**	**PTR**	**COL**

Below: *Following the demise of freight operater Cotswold/Advenza in October 2009, two of the four Class 66/8s Nos. 66841 and 66842 were transferred to Colas Rail. The pair were quickly repainted into Colas orange, lime green and black by Eastleigh Works. No. 66841 is illustrated.* **Mark V. Pike**

Class 960

Length: 64ft 6in (19.66m)
Height: 12ft 8½in (3.87m)
Width: 9ft 3in (2.81m)
Engine: 2 x Leyland 150hp
Horsepower: 300hp (224kW)

Number	*Depot*	*Livery*	*Owner*	*Operator*	*Note*
977968(S)	**RU**	**YEL**	**COL**	**COL**	*Ex Class 121 55029, Route Training unit*

Left: *Former Class 121 'bubble' car used on Thames Valley services No. 55029 is on the roster of Colas as a route training saloon. In 2009 the vehicle was out of service stored.* **CJM**

DB Schenker

Address (UK): ✉ Lakeside Business Park, Caroline Way, Doncaster, DN4 5PN
info@ews-railway.co.uk
✆ 0870 140 5000
ⓘ www.ews-railway.co.uk

Chief Executive: Keith Heller

Class 08

Vehicle Length: 29ft 3in (8.91m)
Height: 12ft 8⅝in (3.87m)
Width: 8ft 6in (2.59m)
Engine: English Electric 6K
Horsepower: 400hp (298kW)
Electrical Equipment: English Electric

Number	Depot	Pool	Livery	Owner	Operator
08389	TO	WNTS	EWS	DBS	DBS
08393	BS	WNTS	EWS	DBS	DBS
08397(S)	TO	WZTS	EWS	DBS	-
08401(S)	WQ	WSXX	BRD	DBS	-
08405	TO	WSSN	EWS	DBS	DBS
08418(S)	WQ	WZTS	EWS	DBS	-
08428	TO	WSSN	EWS	DBS	DBS
08442(S)	WQ	WSXX	BRT	DBS	-
08466(S)	TO	WNTS	EWS	DBS	-
08480*	WQ	WSXX	EWS	DBS	-
08482	TO	WRLN	EWS	DBS	DBS
08485(S)	WQ	WZTS	BLU	DBS	-
08495¤	TO	WSSN	EWS	DBS	DBS
08499(S)	WQ	WSXX	BLU	DBS	PUL
08500(S)	WQ	WNTS	EWS	DBS	-
08512(S)	WQ	WNTS	EWS	DBS	-
08514(S)	WQ	WNTS	EWS	DBS	-
08516(S)	WQ	WSXX	EWS	DBS	-
08528(S)	WQ	WNTS	BRD	DBS	-
08538(S)	WQ	WNTS	BRD	DBS	-
08540(S)	WQ	WNTS	EWS	DBS	-
08543(S)	WQ	WNYX	BRD	DBS	-
08561(S)	TO	WNXX	BLU	DBS	-
08567	TO	WSSN	EWS	DBS	DBS
08569(S)	WQ	WNYX	EWS	DBS	-
08577(S)	WQ	WNTS	EWS	DBS	-
08578	TO	WSSN	EWS	DBS	DBS
08580(S)	WQ	WNYX	EWS	DBS	-
08593(S)	WQ	WNTS	EWS	DBS	-
08597(S)	WQ	WNTS	EWS	DBS	-
08605¤	TO	WNTR	EWS	DBS	-
08623	TO	WSSI	EWS	DBS	DBS
08630(S)	WQ	WNTS	EWS	DBS	-
08632(S)	TO	WNTR	EWS	DBS	-
08633(S)	WA	WNTR	EWS	DBS	-
08646(S)	MG	WNTS	BRT	DBS	-
08651(S)	WQ	WNYX	BRD	DBS	-
08653	DR	WSSN	EWS	DBS	DBS
08662(S)	WQ	WNTS	EWS	DBS	-
08664(S)	DR	WNTR	EWS	DBS	-
08676	TO	WSSN	EWS	DBS	DBS
08685	TO	WSSI	EWS	DBS	DBS
08689(S)	WQ	WNTS	EWS	DBS	-
08698(S)	WQ	WNTR	EWS	DBS	-
08701¤	TO	WNTR	PCL	DBS	-
08703	DR	WSSK	EWS	DBS	DBS
08706¤(S)	TO	WNTR	EWS	DBS	-
08709	WQ	WNTS	EWS	DBS	-
08711(S)	DR	WNTR	PCL	DBS	DBS
08714	TO	WSSA	EWS	DBS	DBS
08735¤	EH	WSSN	EWS	DBS	DBS
08737(S)	TO	WNTR	EWS	DBS	-
08742(S)	TO	WNTR	PCL	DBS	-
08752	TO	WSSI	EWS	DBS	DBS
08757¤	TO	WSSN	RES	DBS	DBS
08765(S)	WQ	WNTS	EWS	DBS	-
08770	MG	WNTS	BRD	DBS	DBS
08776(S)	WQ	WNTS	BRD	DBS	-
08782	MG	WSSI	BLK	DBS	DBS
08783(S)	WQ	WNTS	EWS	DBS	-
08784¤	WQ	WNTS	EWS	DBS	DBS
08786(S)	DR	WNTS	BRD	DBS	-
08798	TO	WSSN	EWS	DBS	DBS
08799	BZ	WSSN	EWS	DBS	DBS
08802(S)	WQ	WSSN	EWS	DBS	-
08804¤	TO	WNTR	EWS	DBS	-
08824(S)	WQ	WSXX	BLK	DBS	-
08828(S)	WQ	WNYX	EWS	DBS	-
08842(S)	WQ	WNTS	EWS	DBS	-
08844	BS	WNTS	EWS	DBS	DBS
08854(S)	WQ	WNTS	EWS	DBS	-
08856(S)	WQ	WNXX	BLU	DBS	-
08865	TO	WSSK	EWS	DBS	DBS
08866(S)	WQ	WNTS	EWS	DBS	-
08872(S)	WQ	WZTS	EWS	DBS	-
08877(S)	WQ	WSXX	BRD	DBS	-
08879¤	TO	WNTR	EWS	DBS	DBS
08884(S)	WQ	WZTS	BLU	DBS	-
08886(S)	BS	WSSN	EWS	DBS	-
08888¤	TO	WNTR	EWS	DBS	-
08897	DR	WSSN	EWS	DBS	DBS
08904	TO	WSSN	EWS	DBS	DBS
08905	WQ	WNTS	EWS	DBS	-
08907	TO	WSSN	EWS	DBS	DBS
08909	TO	WSSN	EWS	DBS	DBS
08918(S)	TO	WNTS	BRD	DBS	-
08920(S)	WQ	WNXX	BRT	DBS	-
08921(S)	SP	WNTR	EWS	DBS	-
08922(S)	CE	WNTR	BRD	DBS	-
08924(S)	TY	WNTS	EWS	DBS	-
08925(S)	WQ	WNXX	BLU	DBS	-
08941(S)	WQ	WNTS	EWS	DBS	-
08951(S)	TO	WNTS	EWS	DBS	DBS
08953	TO	WSSN	BRD	DBS	DBS
08954(S)	TO	WNXX	TGG	DBS	-
08993+(S)	TO	WNTR	EWS	DBS	-
08994+	DR	WSSN	EWS	DBS	DBS
08995+	TO	WSSN	EWS	DBS	DBS

¤ Remote Control fitted

DB Schenker

Names applied

08442	*Richard J Wenham Eastleigh Depot December 1989 - July 1999*
08482	*Don Gates 1952 - 2000*
08495	*Noel Kirton OBE*
08630	*Bob Brown*
08701	*Type 100*
08738	*Silver Fox*
08799	*Andy Bower*
08844	*Chris Wren 1955-2002*
08872	*Tony Long Stratford Depot 1955-2002*
08905	*Danny Daniels*
08907	*Molly's Day*
08951	*Fred*

* *Numbered - Toton No. 1*
+ *08993 previously No. 08592*
+ *08994 previously No. 08562*
+ *08995 previously No. 08687*

Left: *Carrying standard EWS livery, No. 08482* Don Gates 1952 - 2000 *is seen from its cab end at Eastleigh yard on 27 December 2008.* **Stacey Thew**

Class 09/0

Vehicle Length: 29ft 3in (8.91m)
Height: 12ft 8⅝in (3.87m)
Width: 8ft 6in (2.59m)
Engine: English Electric 6K
Horsepower: 400hp (298kW)
Electrical Equipment: English Electric

Number	*Depot*	*Pool*	*Livery*	*Owner*	*Operator*
09001	DR	WNTS	EWS	DBS	DBS
09003(S)	WQ	WNTS	EWS	DBS	-
09005	TO	WNTS	EWS	DBS	DBS
09006(S)	WQ	WNTS	EWS	DBS	-
09007	TO	WNTR	MLF	DBS	DBS
09008(S)	WQ	WNTS	EWS	DBS	-
09009(S)	WQ	WNXX	EWS	DBS	-
09010(S)	WQ	WNTS	BRD	DBS	-
09011(S)	WQ	WNTS	BRD	DBS	-
09012(S)	WQ	WNXX	BRD	DBS	-
09013(S)	WQ	WNTS	BRD	DBS	-
09014	DR	WNTS	BRD	DBS	DBS
09015(S)	WQ	WNTS	EWS	DBS	-
09016(S)	WQ	WNXX	EWS	DBS	-
09017(S)+	TO	WSSI	EWS	DBS	-
09018(S)	WQ	WNXX	EWS	DBS	-
09019	TO	WSSI	MLF	DBS	DBS
09020(S)	WQ	WNTS	EWS	DBS	-
09022	TO	WSSN	EWS	DBS	DBS
09023	IM	WNTR	EWS	DBS	DBS
09024(S)	WQ	WNTS	MLF	DBS	-

+ 09017 previously numbered 97806

Class 09/1

Vehicle Length: 29ft 3in (8.91m)
Height: 12ft 8⅝in (3.87m)
Width: 8ft 6in (2.59m)
Engine: English Electric 6K
Horsepower: 400hp (298kW)
Electrical Equipment: English Electric

Number		*Depot*	*Pool*	*Livery*	*Owner*	*Operator*
09101(S)	(08833)	DR	WNTR	BRD	DBS	-
09102(S)	(08832)	WQ	WNTS	BRD	DBS	-
09103(S)	(08766)	WQ	WNTS	BRD	DBS	-
09104(S)	(08749)	WQ	WNXX	BRD	DBS	-
09105(S)	(08835)	DR	WNTR	BRD	DBS	-
09106	(08759)	TO	WSSN	BRD	DBS	DBS
09107(S)	(08845)	TO	WNTR	EWS	DBS	-

Class 09/2

Vehicle Length: 29ft 3in (8.91m)
Height: 12ft 8⅝in (3.87m)
Width: 8ft 6in (2.59m)
Engine: English Electric 6K
Horsepower: 400hp (298kW)
Electrical Equipment: English Electric

Number		*Depot*	*Pool*	*Livery*	*Owner*	*Operator*
09201	(08421)	TO	WSSM	BRD	DBS	DBS
09202(S)	(08732)	WQ	WNYX	BRD	DRS	-
09203(S)	(08781)	WQ	WNYX	BRD	DBS	-
09204(S)	(08717)	WQ	WNXX	BRD	DBS	-
09205(S)	(08620)	WQ	WNTS	BRD	DBS	-

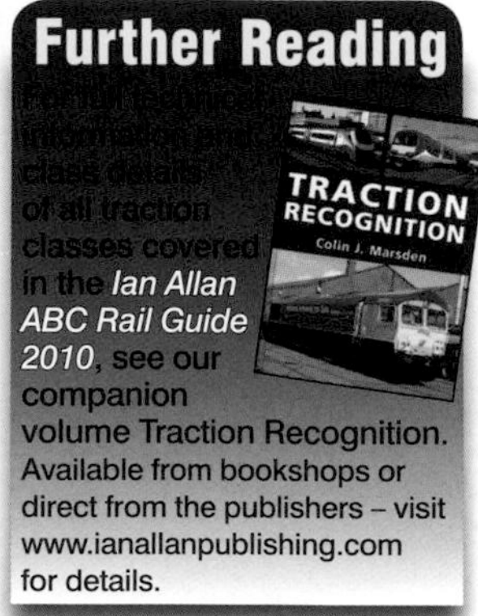

Right: *Looking rather the worse for wear and in need of a repaint, EWS-liveried DBS-operated Class 09/0 No. 09017 passes light engine through Newport station on 12 June 2008.*
Nathan Williamson

Class 37/4

Vehicle Length: 61ft 6in (18.74m)
Height: 13ft 0¼in (3.96m)
Width: 8ft 11⅝in (2.73m)
Electric Train Heat fitted
Engine: English Electric 12CSVT
Horsepower: 1,750hp (1,304kW)
Electrical Equipment: English Electric

Number		*Depot*	*Pool*	*Livery*	*Owner*	*Operator*	*Name*
37401	(37268)	TO	WKBN	EWS	DBS	DBS	
37402(S)	(37274)	TO	WNXX	TLF	DBS	-	*Bont-Y-Bermo*
37405(S)	(37282)	TO	WNTS	EWS	DBS	-	*Strathclyde Region*
37406(S)	(37295)	CD	WNXX	EWS	DBS	-	*The Saltire Society*
37410(S)	(37273)	ZW	WNTS	EWS	DBS	-	
37411(S)	(37290)*	EH	WNTS	GRN	DBS	-	*Caerphilly Castle/Castell Caerffili*
37415(S)	(37277)	EH	WNXX	EWS	DBS	-	
37416(S)	(37302)	EH	WNXX	GSW	DBS	-	
37417(S)	(37269)	EH	WNXX	EWS	DBS	-	*Richard Trevithick*
37419(S)	(37291)	TO	WNTS	DBS	DBS	-	
37422(S)	(37266)	TO	WKBN	EWS	DBS	-	*Cardiff Canton*
37425	(37292)	EH	WKBN	BLL	DBS	DBS	*Pride of the Valleys/Balchder y Cmyoedd*
37426(S)	(37299)	CD	WNXX	EWS	DBS	-	
37427(S)	(37288)	TY	WNXX	EWS	DBS	-	

Class 37/5

Vehicle Length: 61ft 6in (18.74m)
Height: 13ft 0¼in (3.96m)
Width: 8ft 11⅝in (2.73m)
Engine: English Electric 12CSVT
Horsepower: 1,750hp (1,304kW)
Electrical Equipment: English Electric

Number		*Depot*	*Pool*	*Livery*	*Owner*	*Operator*	*Name*
37503(S)	(37017)	DR	WNXX	EWS	DBS	-	
37521(S)	(37117)	DR	WNXX	EWS	DBS	-	
37669(S)	(37129)	TO	WNTS	EWS	DBS	-	
37670(S)	(37182)	CD	WFMU	DBS	DBS	-	*St Blazey T&RS Depot*
37671(S)	(37247)	TO	WNXX	TGG	DBS	-	
37675(S)	(37164)	MG	WNXX	TGG	DBS	-	
37689(S)	(37195)	DR	WNXX	TLF	DBS	-	
37693(S)	(37210)	TO	WNXX	TGG	DBS	-	

Right: *Several of the remaining DBS Class 37s still carry cast nameplates, mainly originating from years past under the EWS or even BR banner. The depot of Canton, located in the city of Cardiff, Wales, Has since the 1960s been associated with the Class and in 2002 this cast plate was unveiled on No. 37422. The name had previously been applied to Class 56 No. 56044.*
Tony Christie

DB Schenker

Class 37/7

Vehicle Length: 61ft 6in (18.74m)
Height: 13ft 0¼in (3.96m)
Width: 8ft 11⅝in (2.73m)
Engine: English Electric 12CSVT
Horsepower: 1,750hp (1,304kW)
Electrical Equipment: English Electric

Number		*Hire No.*	*Depot*	*Pool*	*Livery*	*Owner*	*Operator*
37702	**(37020)**	**L30**	**CON/SS**	**WZKS**	**CON**	**DBS**	**CON**
37703	**(37067)**	**L25**	**CON/SS**	**WZKS**	**CON**	**DBS**	**CON**
37709(S)	**(37014)**		**MH**	**WNXX**	**MLF**	**DBS**	**-**
37714	**(37024)**	**L26**	**CON/SS**	**WZKS**	**CON**	**DBS**	**CON**
37716	**(37094)**	**L23**	**CON/SS**	**WZKS**	**CON**	**DBS**	**CON**
37718	**(37084)**	**L22**	**CON/SS**	**WZKS**	**CON**	**DBS**	**CON**
37800	**(37143)**	**L33**	**CON/SS**	**WZKS**	**CON**	**DBS**	**CON**
37883	**(37176)**	**L28**	**CON/SS**	**WZKS**	**CON**	**DBS**	**CON**
37884	**(37183)**	**L34**	**CON/SS**	**WZKS**	**CON**	**DBS**	**CON**
37886(S)	**(37180)**		**MH**	**WNXX**	**EWS**	**DBS**	**-**
37888	**(37135)**	**L31**	**CON/SS**	**WZKS**	**CON**	**DBS**	**CON**
37891(S)	**(36166)**		**TO**	**WNXX**	**TLF**	**DBS**	**-**
37893(S)	**(37237)**		**BS**	**WNXX**	**EWS**	**DBS**	**-**
37895(S)	**(37283)**		**BS**	**WNXX**	**EWS**	**DBS**	**-**

Above: *In the summer of 2009, DBS authorised the repaint of two of its remaining Class 37s Nos. 37419 and 37670 into the latest corporate red livery, off-set by white DB Schenker bodyside branding and a large German Railways DB sign on the nose end. No. 37670 St Blazey T & RS Depot is seen in multiple with No. 37401 still painted in EWS livery at Llandudno Junction. This loco has now been stored unserviceable.* **Tony Christie**

Class 47/4

Vehicle Length: 63ft 6in (19.35m)
Height: 12ft 10⅜in (3.91m)
Width: 9ft 2in (2.79m)
Electric Train Heat fitted

Engine: Sulzer 12LDA28C
Horsepower: 2,580hp (1,922kW)
Electrical Equipment: Brush

Number	*Depot*	*Pool*	*Livery*	*Owner*	*Operator*	
47799 (47835)	EH	WNXX	ROY	DBS	DBS	*Used for coach pre-heating at Eastleigh*

Class 56

Vehicle Length: 63ft 6in (19.35m)
Height: 13ft 0in (3.96m)
Width: 9ft 2in (2.79m)

Engine: Ruston Paxman 16RK3CT
Horsepower: 3,250hp (2,420kW)
Electrical Equipment: Brush

Number	*Depot*	*Pool*	*Livery*	*Owner*	*Operator*
56006(S)	BH	WNXX	BLU	DBS	-
56007(S)	CE	WZGF	FER	DBS	-
56018(S)	WA	WZGF	FER	DBS	-
56031(S)	CD	WZGF	FER	DBS	-
56032(S)	CD	WZGF	FER	DBS	-
56037(S)	CD	WZTS	EWS	DBS	-
56038(S)	CD	WZGF	FER	DBS	-
56041(S)	HM	WNXX	EWS	DBS	-
56046(S)	TO	WNXX	CIV	DBS	-
56049(S)	CD	WZGF	FER	DBS	-
56051(S)	CD	WZGF	FER	DBS	-
56053(S)	HM	WNXX	TGG	DBS	-
56054(S)	CD	WNXX	TGG	DBS	-
56055(S)	HM	WNXX	LHL	DBS	-
56058(S)	CD	WZGF	FER	DBS	-
56059(S)	EH	WZGF	FER	DBS	-
56060(S)	CD	WZGF	FER	DBS	-
56062(S)	MG	WNXX	EWS	DBS	-
56065(S)	CD	WZGF	FER	DBS	-
56067(S)	CD	WNXX	EWS	DBS	-
56069(S)	CD	WZGF	FER	DBS	-
56070(S)	CE	WNXX	TGG	DBF	-
56071(S)	CD	WZGF	FER	DBS	-
56072(S)	HM	WNXX	TGG	DBS	-
56073(S)	TO	WNXX	TGG	DBS	-
56074(S)	CD	WZGF	FER	DBS	-
56077(S)	CD	WNXX	LHL	DBS	-
56078(S)	CD	WZGF	FER	DBS	-
56081(S)	CD	WZGF	FER	DBS	-
56083(S)	CD	WNXX	LHL	DBS	-
56085(S)	TE	WNXX	LHL	DBS	-
56087(S)	CD	WZGF	FER	DBS	-
56088(S)	TE	WNXX	EWS	DBS	-
56090(S)	CD	WZGF	FER	DBS	-
56091(S)	EH	WZGF	FER	DBS	-
56093(S)	HM	WNXX	TGG	DBS	-
56094(S)	CD	WZGF	FER	DBS	-
56095(S)	EH	WZGF	FER	DBS	-
56096(S)	CD	WZGF	FER	TBS	-
56099(S)	HM	WNXX	TGG	DBS	-
56100(S)	MG	WNXX	LHL	DBS	-
56102(S)	TE	WNXX	LHL	DBS	-
56103(S)	CD	WZGF	FER	DBS	-
56104(S)	CD	WZGF	FER	DBS	-
56105(S)	CD	WZGF	FER	DBS	-
56106(S)	CD	WZGF	FER	DBS	-
56107(S)	CD	WNXX	LHL	DBS	-
56108(S)	TE	WNXX	FER	DBS	-
56109(S)	CD	WNXX	LHL	DBS	-
56110(S)	HM	WNXX	LHL	DBS	-
56111(S)	TE	WNXX	LHL	DBS	-
56112(S)	CE	WNXX	LHL	DBS	-
56113(S)	CD	WZGF	FER	DBS	-
56115(S)	EH	WZGF	FER	DBS	-
56117(S)	EH	WZGF	FER	DBS	-
56120(S)	CD	WNXX	EWS	DBS	-
56127(S)	TE	WNXX	TGG	DBS	-
56129(S)	TE	WNXX	TGG	DBS	-
56133(S)	CE	WZTS	TGG	DBS	-

Below: *DBS-owned Class 56 No. 56094 shows the Fertis hire livery, applied prior to a period of use in France on high speed line construction. The loco is presently stored at Crewe and may well see further hire use.* **Tony Christie**

DB Schenker

Class 58

Vehicle Length: 62ft 9½in (19.13m)	*Engine: Ruston Paxman 12RK3ACT*
Height: 12ft 10in (3.91m)	*Horsepower: 3,300hp (2,460kW)*
Width: 9ft 1in (2.72m)	*Electrical Equipment: Brush*

Number	Hire No.	Depot	Pool	Livery	Owner	Location	Operator	Name
58001		-	WZFF	ETF	DBS	France	ETF	
58002(S)		EH	WZTS	MLF	DBS	UK	-	
58003(S)		TO	WNXX	MLG	DBS	UK	-	
58004		-	WZFF	TSO	DBS	France	TSO	
58005		-	WZFF	ETF	DBS	France	ETF	
58006		-	WZFF	ETF	DBS	France	ETF	
58007		-	WZFF	TSO	DBS	France	TSO	
58008(S)		TO	WNXX	MLF	DBS	UK	-	
58009		-	WZFF	TSO	DBS	France	TSO	
58010		-	WZFF	FER	DBS	France	TSO	
58011		-	WZFF	TSO	DBS	France	TSO	
58012(S)		TO	WNXX	MLG	DBS	UK	-	
58013		-	WZFF	ETF	DBS	France	ETF	
58014(S)		TO	WNXX	MLF	DBS	UK	-	
58015	L54	CON/SS	WZFS	CON	DBS	Spain	CON	
58016(S)		CE	WZFF	FER	DBS	UK	-	
58017(S)		EH	WZTS	MLG	DBS	UK	-	
58018		EH	WZFF	TSO	DBS	France	TSO	
58019(S)		TO	WNXX	MLG	DBS	UK	-	
58020	L43	CON/SS	WZFS	CON	DBS	Spain	CON	
58021		-	WZFF	TSO	DBS	France	TSO	
58022(S)		CD	WNXX	MLG	DBS	UK	-	
58023(S)		TO	WNXX	MLF	DBS	UK	-	
58024	L42	CON/SS	WZFS	CON	DBS	Spain	CON	
58025	L41	CON/SS	WZFS	CON	DBS	Spain	CON	
58026		-	WZTS	TSO	DBS	France	TSO	
58027	L52	CON/SS	WZFS	CON	DBS	Spain	CON	
58028(S)		TO	WNXX	MLG	DBS	UK	-	
58029	L44	CON/SS	WZFS	CON	DBS	Spain	CON	
58030	L46	CON/SS	WZFS	CON	DBS	Spain	CON	
58031	L45	CON/SS	WZFS	CON	DBS	Spain	CON	*Cabellero Ferroviaro*
58032		-	WZFF	ETF	DBS	France	ETF	
58033		-	WZFF	TSO	DBS	France	TSO	
58034		-	WZFF	TSO	DBS	France	TSO	
58035		-	WZFF	TSO	DBS	France	TSO	
58036		-	WZFF	ETF	DBS	France	ETF	
58037(S)		EH	WNXX	EWS	DBS	UK	-	
58038	58-038	-	WZFF	ETF	DBS	France	ETF	
58039	58-039	-	WZFF	ETF	DBS	France	ETF	
58040		-	WZFF	TSO	DBS	France	TSO	
58041	L36	CON/SS	WZFS	CON	DBS	Spain	CON	
58042		-	WZFF	TSO	DBS	France	TSO	
58043	L37	CON/SS	WZFS	CON	DBS	Spain	CON	
58044	58-044	-	WZFF	ETF	DBS	France	ETF	
58045		CE	WNXX	MLG	DBS	UK	-	
58046		-	WZFF	TSO	DBS	France	TSO	
58047	L51	CON/SS	WZFS	CON	DBS	Spain	CON	
58048(S)		CE	WNXX	EWS	DBS	UK	-	
58049		-	WZFF	TSO	DBS	France	ETF	
58050	L53	CON/SS	WZFS	CON	DBS	Spain	CON	

Left: *The BREL/BR Class 58 fleet withdrawn from service when still comparatively new, have seen considerable use in Mainland Europe, beir overhauled and hired to operators in The Neth France and Spain by Axiom Rail, a subsidiar DBS. No. 58027 operating for Continental F Spain is illustrated.* **Enrique Dopico**

Class 59/2

Vehicle Length: 70ft 0½in (21.34m)
Height: 12ft 10in (3.91m)
Width: 8ft 8¼in (2.65m)
Engine: EMD 16-645 E3C
Horsepower: 3,000hp (2,462kW)
Electrical Equipment: EMD

Number	Depot	Pool	Livery	Owner	Operator	Name
59201	TO	WDAK	EWS	DBS	DBS	Vale of York
59202	TO	WDAK	EWS	DBS	DBS	Vale of White Horse
59203	TO	WDAK	EWS	DBS	DBS	Vale of Pickering
59204	TO	WCAM	EWS	DBS	DBS	Vale of Glamorgan
59205	TO	WDAK	EWS	DBS	DBS	L Keith McNair
59206	TO	WDAK	DBS	DBS	DBS	John F. Yeoman Rail Pioneer

Right: *The six strong fleet of General Motors-built Class 59/2s is officially based at Toton, but usually class members can be found operating in the Westbury area on Mendip aggregate workings or powering engineering trains. No. 59202* Vale of White Horse *is seen in this illustration working a weekend engineering train at Dawlish, Devon during track re-laying operations.* **CJM**

Class 60

Vehicle Length: 70ft 0½in (21.34m)
Height: 12ft 10⅝in (3.92m)
Width: 8ft 8in (2.64m)
Engine: Mirrlees MB275T
Horsepower: 3,100hp (2,240kW)
Electrical Equipment: Brush

Number	Depot	Pool	Livery	Owner	Operator	Name
60001(S)	TO	WNTS	EWS	DBS	-	The Railway Observer
60002(S)	TO	WNTR	EWS	DBS	-	High Peak
60003(S)	TO	WNTS	EWS	DBS	-	Freight Transport Association
60004(S)	TO	WNTR	EWS	DBS	-	
60005(S)	TO	WNTS	EWS	DBS	-	
60006(S)	TO	WNTS	COR	DBS	-	
60007(S)	CD	WNTS	LHL	DBS	-	
60008(S)	TO	WNTS	EWS	DBS	-	Sir William McAlpine
60009	TO	WCBI	EWS	DBS	DBS	
60010(S)	TO	WNTR	EWS	DBS	-	
60011(S)	TO	WCAI	MLF	DBS	-	
60012(S)	TO	WNTS	EWS	DBS	-	
60013(S)	TO	WNTR	RFE	DBS	-	Robert Boyle
60014(S)	TO	WNTS	RFE	DBS	-	
60015(S)	TO	WNTS	RFE	DBS	-	Bow Fell
60017(S)	TO	WNTS	EWS	DBS	-	Shotton Works Centenary Year 1996
60018(S)	TO	WNTS	EWS	DBS	-	
60019(S)	TO	WNTR	EWS	DBS	-	Pathfinder Tours 30 Years of Railtouring 1973-2003
60020(S)	TO	WNTS	EWS	DBS	-	
60021(S)	TO	WNTS	EWS	DBS	-	Star of the East
60022(S)	TO	WNTR	EWS	DBS	-	
60023(S)	TO	WNTS	EWS	DBS	-	
60024(S)	TO	WNTR	EWS	DBS	-	
60025(S)	TO	WNTS	EWS	DBS	-	
60026(S)	TO	WNTR	EWS	DBS	-	
60027(S)	TO	WNTR	EWS	DBS	-	
60028(S)	TO	WNTR	RFE	DBS	-	John Flamsteed
60029(S)	TO	WNTS	EWS	DBS	-	Clitheroe Castle
60030(S)	TO	WNTS	EWS	DBS	-	
60031(S)	TO	WNTS	EWS	DBS	-	ABP Connect

DB Schenker

60032(S)	TO	WNTS	EWS	DBS	-	*William Booth*
60033(S)	TO	WNTS	COR	DBS	-	*Tees Steel Express*
60034(S)	TO	WNTS	RFE	DBS	-	*Carnedd Llewelwn*
60035(S)	TO	WNTR	EWS	DBS	-	
60036(S)	TO	WNTS	EWS	DBS	-	*GEFCO*
60037(S)	TO	WNTS	EWS	DBS	-	*Aberddawan / Aberthaw*
60038(S)	TO	WNTR	EWS	DBS	-	*AvestaPolarit*
60039(S)	TO	WNTR	EWS	DBS	-	
60040(S)	TO	WNTR	DBM	DBS	-	*The Territorial Army Centenary*
60041(S)	TO	WNTR	EWS	DBS	-	
60042(S)	TO	WNTS	EWS	DBS	-	*The Hundred of Hoo*
60043(S)	TO	WNTR	EWS	DBS	-	
60044(S)	TO	WNTS	MLF	DBS	-	
60045(S)	TO	WNTR	EWS	DBS	-	*The Permanent Way Institution*
60046(S)	TO	WNTR	RFE	DBS	-	*William Wilberforce*
60047(S)	TO	WNTR	EWS	DBS	-	
60048(S)	TO	WNTR	EWS	DBS	-	*Eastern*
60049	TO	WCAK	EWS	DBS	DBS	
60050(S)	TO	WNTS	EWS	DBS	-	
60051(S)	TO	WNTR	EWS	DBS	-	
60052(S)	TO	WNTS	EWS	DBS	-	*Glofa Twr - The last deep mine in Wales - Tower Colliery*
60053(S)	TO	WNTS	EWS	DBS	-	
60054(S)	TO	WNTR	RFP	DBS	-	*Charles Babbage*
60055(S)	TO	WNTS	RFE	DBS	-	*Thomas Bernardo*
60056(S)	TO	WNTR	RFE	DBS	-	*William Beveridge*
60057(S)	TO	WNTS	RFE	DBS	-	*Adam Smith*
60058(S)	TO	WNTS	EWS	DBS	-	
60059	TO	WCBI	LHL	DBS	DBS	*Swinden Dalesman*
60060(S)	TO	WNTS	RFE	DBS	-	*James Watt*
60061(S)	TO	WNTS	RFE	DBS	-	*Alexander Graham Bell*
60062(S)	TO	WNTS	EWS	DBS	-	
60063(S)	TO	WNTR	RFE	DBS	-	*James Murray*
60064(S)	TO	WNTS	RFE	DBS	-	*Back Tor*
60065(S)	TO	WNTS	EWS	DBS	-	*Spirit of Jaguar*
60066(S)	TO	WNTS	RFE	DBS	-	*John Logie Baird*
60067(S)	TO	WNTS	RFE	DBS	-	*James Clerk-Maxwell*
60068(S)	TO	WNTS	RFE	DBS	-	
60069(S)	TO	WNTS	EWS	DBS	-	*Slioch*
60070(S)	TO	WNTS	TLL	DBS	-	*John Loudon McAdam*
60071	TO	WCBI	EWS	DBS	DBS	*Ribblehead Viaduct*
60072(S)	TO	WNTS	RFE	DBS	-	*Cairn Toul*
60073(S)	TO	WNTR	RFE	DBS	-	*Cairn Gorm*
60074(S)	TO	WNTR	DBB	DBS	-	*Teenage Spirit*
60075(S)	TO	WNTS	EWS	DBS	-	
60076(S)	TO	WNTR	RFE	DBS	-	
60077(S)	TO	WNTR	RFE	DBS	-	
60078(S)	TO	WNTS	MLF	DBS	-	
60079(S)	TO	WNTS	RFE	DBS	-	*Foinaven*
60080(S)	TO	WNTS	EWS	DBS	-	*Bispham Drive Junior School, Toton EWS Rail Safety Competition Winners 2004*
60081(S)	TO	WNTS	GRN	DBS	-	
60082(S)	TO	WNTS	RFE	DBS	-	*Mam Tor*
60083(S)	TO	WNTS	EWS	DBS	-	
60084(S)	TO	WNTR	RFE	DBS	-	*Cross Fell*
60085(S)	TO	WNTR	EWS	DBS	-	*Mini - Pride of Oxford*
60086(S)	TO	WNTS	RFE	DBS	-	*Schiehallion*
60087(S)	TO	WNTS	EWS	DBS	-	*Barry Needham*
60088(S)	TO	WNTS	MLG	DBS	-	*Buachaille Etive Mor*
60089(S)	TO	WNTS	EWS	DBS	-	
60090(S)	TO	WNTS	RFE	DBS	-	*Quinag*
60091(S)	TO	WNTR	RFE	DBS	-	*An Teallach*
60092(S)	CD	WNTR	RFE	DBS	-	*Reginald Munns*
60093(S)	TO	WNTS	EWS	DBS	-	
60094(S)	CD	WNTR	EWS	DBS	-	*Rugby Flyer*

Number	Depot	Pool	Livery	Owner	Operator	Name
60095(S)	TO	WNTR	RFE	DBS	-	
60096	TO	WCAM	EWS	DBS	DBS	
60097(S)	TO	WNTS	EWS	DBS	-	
60098(S)	TO	WNTS	EWS	DBS	-	
60099(S)	TO	WNTS	RFE	DBS	-	*Ben More Assynt*
60100(S)	TO	WNTS	EWS	DBS	-	*Pride of Acton*
60500(S)*	TO	WNTS	EWS	DBS	-	

* Previously numbered 60016

Only a handful of Class 60s still remain in service, mainly due to the downturn in the UK freight industry. No. 60085 is viewed from its No. 1 end. **CJM**

Class 66

Vehicle Length: 70ft 0½in (21.34m)
Height: 12ft 10in (3.91m)
Width: 8ft 8¼in (2.65m)
Engine: EMD 12N-710G3B-EC
Horsepower: 3,300hp (2,462kW)
Electrical Equipment: EMD

Number	*Depot*	*Pool*	*Livery*	*Owner*	*Operator*
66001	TO	WBAN	EWS	ANG	DBS
66002	TO	WBAN	EWS	ANG	DBS
66003	TO	WBAN	EWS	ANG	DBS
66004	TO	WBAK	EWS	ANG	DBS
66005	TO	WBAN	EWS	ANG	DBS
66006	TO	WBAK	EWS	ANG	DBS
66007	TO	WBAI	EWS	ANG	DBS
66008	TO	WBAK	EWS	ANG	DBS
66009	TO	WBAM	EWS	ANG	DBS
66010 E	TO	WBEN	EWS	ANG	DBS
66011	TO	WBAM	EWS	ANG	DBS
66012	TO	WFMU	EWS	ANG	DBS
66013 E	TO	WBAN	EWS	ANG	DBS
66014	TO	WBAM	EWS	ANG	DBS
66015	TO	WBAN	EWS	ANG	DBS
66016	TO	WBAM	EWS	ANG	DBS
66017	TO	WBAI	EWS	ANG	DBS
66018	TO	WFMU	EWS	ANG	DBS
66019	TO	WBAN	EWS	ANG	DBS
66020	TO	WBAI	EWS	ANG	DBS
66021	TO	WBAN	EWS	ANG	DBS
66022 E	TO	WBEN	EWS	ANG	DBS
66023	TO	WBAI	EWS	ANG	DBS
66024	TO	WBAN	EWS	ANG	DBS
66025	TO	WBAN	EWS	ANG	DBS
66026 E	TO	WBEN	EWS	ANG	DBS
66027	TO	WFMU	EWS	ANG	DBS
66028 E	TO	WBEN	EWS	ANG	DBS
66029 E	TO	WBEN	EWS	ANG	DBS
66030	TO	WBAI	EWS	ANG	DBS
66031 E	TO	WFMU	EWS	ANG	DBS
66032 E	TO	WBEN	EWS	ANG	DBS
66033 E	TO	WBEN	EWS	ANG	DBS
66034	TO	WBAN	EWS	ANG	DBS
66035	TO	WBAN	EWS	ANG	DBS
66036 E	TO	WBEN	EWS	ANG	DBS
66037	TO	WBAK	EWS	ANG	DBS
66038 E	TO	WBEN	EWS	ANG	DBS
66039	TO	WBAK	EWS	ANG	DBS
66040	TO	WBAI	EWS	ANG	DBS
66041	TO	WBAI	EWS	ANG	DBS
66042 E	TO	WBEN	EWS	ANG	DBS
66043	TO	WBAN	EWS	ANG	DBS
66044	TO	WBAK	EWS	ANG	DBS
66045 E	TO	WBEN	EWS	ANG	DBS
66046	TO	WBAM	EWS	ANG	DBS
66047	TO	WBAN	EWS	ANG	DBS
66048	TO	WBAN	STO	ANG	DBS
66049 E	TO	WBEN	EWS	ANG	DBS
66050	TO	WBAI	EWS	ANG	DBS
66051	TO	WBAN	EWS	ANG	DBS
66052 E	TO	WBEN	EWS	ANG	DBS
66053	TO	WBAI	EWS	ANG	DBS
66054	TO	WBAI	EWS	ANG	DBS
66055	TO	WBAN	EWS	ANG	DBS
66056	TO	WFMU	EWS	ANG	DBS
66057	TO	WBLI	EWS	ANG	DBS
66058	TO	WBAM	EWS	ANG	DBS
66059	TO	WBAK	EWS	ANG	DBS
66060	TO	WBAN	EWS	ANG	DBS
66061	TO	WBAN	EWS	ANG	DBS
66062 E	TO	WBEN	EWS	ANG	DBS
66063	TO	WFMU	EWS	ANG	DBS
66064 E	TO	WBEN	EWS	ANG	DBS
66065	TO	WBAK	EWS	ANG	DBS

DB Schenker

66066	TO	WBAM	EWS	ANG	DBS
66067	TO	WBAN	EWS	ANG	DBS
66068	TO	WFMU	EWS	ANG	DBS
66069	TO	WBAN	EWS	ANG	DBS
66070	TO	WBAN	EWS	ANG	DBS
66071 E	TO	WBEN	EWS	ANG	DBS
66072 E	TO	WBEN	EWS	ANG	DBS
66073 E	TO	WBEN	EWS	ANG	DBS
66074	TO	WBAK	EWS	ANG	DBS
66075	TO	WBAM	EWS	ANG	DBS
66076	TO	WBAM	EWS	ANG	DBS
66077	TO	WFMU	EWS	ANG	DBS
66078	TO	WBAM	EWS	ANG	DBS
66079	TO	WBAI	EWS	ANG	DBS
66080	TO	WBAM	EWS	ANG	DBS
66081	TO	WBAM	EWS	ANG	DBS
66082	TO	WBAM	EWS	ANG	DBS
66083	TO	WBAN	EWS	ANG	DBS
66084	TO	WBAN	EWS	ANG	DBS
66085	TO	WBAN	EWS	ANG	DBS
66086	TO	WBAN	EWS	ANG	DBS
66087	TO	WBAM	EWS	ANG	DBS
66088	TO	WBAM	EWS	ANG	DBS
66089	TO	WBAI	EWS	ANG	DBS
66090	TO	WBAN	EWS	ANG	DBS
66091	TO	WBAI	EWS	ANG	DBS
66092	TO	WBAN	EWS	ANG	DBS
66093	TO	WBAN	EWS	ANG	DBS
66094	TO	WBAK	EWS	ANG	DBS
66095	TO	WFMU	EWS	ANG	DBS
66096	TO	WBAN	EWS	ANG	DBS
66097	TO	WBAI	EWS	ANG	DBS
66098	TO	WBAM	EWS	ANG	DBS
66099	TO	WBAN	EWS	ANG	DBS
66100	TO	WBBN	EWS	ANG	DBS
66101	TO	WBBN	EWS	ANG	DBS
66102	TO	WBBN	EWS	ANG	DBS
66103	TO	WBAM	EWS	ANG	DBS
66104	TO	WBBN	EWS	ANG	DBS
66105	TO	WBAM	EWS	ANG	DBS
66106	TO	WBBI	EWS	ANG	DBS
66107	TO	WBAN	EWS	ANG	DBS
66108	TO	WFMU	EWS	ANG	DBS
66109	TO	WBAI	EWS	ANG	DBS
66110 E	TO	WBAI	EWS	ANG	DBS
66111	TO	WBBK	EWS	ANG	DBS
66112	TO	WBBN	EWS	ANG	DBS
66113	TO	WFMU	EWS	ANG	DBS
66114	TO	WBBN	EWS	ANG	DBS
66115	TO	WBAN	EWS	ANG	DBS
66116	TO	WBAN	EWS	ANG	DBS
66117	TO	WFMU	EWS	ANG	DBS
66118	TO	WFMU	EWS	ANG	DBS
66119	TO	WBAK	EWS	ANG	DBS
66120	TO	WBAI	EWS	ANG	DBS
66121	TO	WBAN	EWS	ANG	DBS
66122	TO	WBAN	EWS	ANG	DBS
66123 E	TO	WBEN	EWS	ANG	DBS
66124	TO	WBAM	EWS	ANG	DBS
66125	TO	WBAN	EWS	ANG	DBS
66126	TO	WBAN	EWS	ANG	DBS
66127	TO	WBAN	EWS	ANG	DBS
66128	TO	WBAK	EWS	ANG	DBS
66129	TO	WBAM	EWS	ANG	DBS
66130	TO	WBAM	EWS	ANG	DBS
66131	TO	WBAN	EWS	ANG	DBS
66132	TO	WBAM	EWS	ANG	DBS
66133	TO	WBAI	EWS	ANG	DBS
66134	TO	WBAM	EWS	ANG	DBS
66135	TO	WBAI	EWS	ANG	DBS
66136	TO	WBAN	EWS	ANG	DBS
66137	TO	WBAI	EWS	ANG	DBS
66138	TO	WBAN	EWS	ANG	DBS
66139	TO	WBAN	EWS	ANG	DBS
66140	TO	WBAK	EWS	ANG	DBS
66141	TO	WBAN	EWS	ANG	DBS
66142	TO	WBAI	EWS	ANG	DBS
66143	TO	WBAM	EWS	ANG	DBS
66144	TO	WBAM	EWS	ANG	DBS
66145	TO	WFMU	EWS	ANG	DBS
66146	TO	WBAK	EWS	ANG	DBS
66147	TO	WBAN	EWS	ANG	DBS
66148	TO	WBAN	EWS	ANG	DBS
66149	TO	WBAK	EWS	ANG	DBS
66150	TO	WBAM	EWS	ANG	DBS
66151	TO	WBAM	EWS	ANG	DBS
66152	TO	WBAN	DBS	ANG	DBS
66153	TO	WBAN	EWS	ANG	DBS
66154	TO	WBAI	EWS	ANG	DBS
66155	TO	WBAM	EWS	ANG	DBS
66156	TO	WBAN	EWS	ANG	DBS
66157	TO	WBAI	EWS	ANG	DBS
66158	TO	WBAK	EWS	ANG	DBS
66159	TO	WBAN	EWS	ANG	DBS
66160	TO	WBAN	EWS	ANG	DBS
66161	TO	WBAN	EWS	ANG	DBS
66162	TO	WBAN	EWS	ANG	DBS
66163	TO	WBAI	EWS	ANG	DBS
66164	TO	WBAM	EWS	ANG	DBS
66165	TO	WBAN	EWS	ANG	DBS
66166	TO	WBAM	EWS	ANG	DBS
66167	TO	WBAI	EWS	ANG	DBS
66168	TO	WBAN	EWS	ANG	DBS
66169	TO	WBAK	EWS	ANG	DBS
66170	TO	WBAN	EWS	ANG	DBS
66171	TO	WBAI	EWS	ANG	DBS
66172	TO	WFMU	EWS	ANG	DBS
66173	TO	WBAN	EWS	ANG	DBS
66174	TO	WBAN	EWS	ANG	DBS
66175	TO	WBAM	EWS	ANG	DBS
66176	TO	WBAM	EWS	ANG	DBS
66177	TO	WBAK	EWS	ANG	DBS
66178	TO	WBAM	EWS	ANG	DBS
66179 E	TO	WBEN	EWS	ANG	DBS
66180	TO	WBAN	EWS	ANG	DBS
66181	TO	WBAN	EWS	ANG	DBS
66182	TO	WBAM	EWS	ANG	DBS
66183	TO	WBAN	EWS	ANG	DBS
66184	TO	WBAI	EWS	ANG	DBS
66185	TO	WBAM	EWS	ANG	DBS
66186	TO	WBAI	EWS	ANG	DBS
66187	TO	WBAN	EWS	ANG	DBS
66188	TO	WBAN	EWS	ANG	DBS
66189	TO	WBAN	EWS	ANG	DBS
66190 E	TO	WBEN	EWS	ANG	DBS
66191 E	TO	WBEN	EWS	ANG	DBS
66192	TO	WBAK	EWS	ANG	DBS
66193	TO	WBAI	EWS	ANG	DBS

66194	TO	WBAM	EWS	ANG	DBS
66195 E	TO	WBEN	EWS	ANG	DBS
66196	TO	WBAI	EWS	ANG	DBS
66197	TO	WFMU	EWS	ANG	DBS
66198	TO	WBAK	EWS	ANG	DBS
66199	TO	WBAM	EWS	ANG	DBS
66200	TO	WBAK	EWS	ANG	DBS
66201	TO	WBAN	EWS	ANG	DBS
66202 E	TO	WBEN	EWS	ANG	DBS
66203 E	TO	WBEN	EWS	ANG	DBS
66204	TO	WBAN	EWS	ANG	DBS
66205 E	TO	WBEN	EWS	ANG	DBS
66206	TO	WBAN	EWS	ANG	DBS
66207	TO	WBAK	EWS	ANG	DBS
66208 E	TO	WBEN	EWS	ANG	DBS
66209 E	TO	WBEN	EWS	ANG	DBS
66210 E	TO	WBEN	EWS	ANG	DBS
66211 E	TO	WBEN	EWS	ANG	DBS
66212 E	TO	WBEN	EWS	ANG	DBS
66213	TO	WFMU	EWS	ANG	DBS
66214 E	TO	WBEN	EWS	ANG	DBS
66215 E	TO	WBEN	EWS	ANG	DBS
66216 E	TO	WBEN	EWS	ANG	DBS
66217 E	TO	WBEN	EWS	ANG	DBS
66218 E	TO	WBEN	EWS	ANG	DBS
66219 E	TO	WBEN	EWS	ANG	DBS
66220 E	TO	WBEN	EWS	ANG	DBS
66221	TO	WBAM	EWS	ANG	DBS
66222 E	TO	WBEN	EWS	ANG	DBS
66223 E	TO	WBEN	EWS	ANG	DBS
66224 E	TO	WBEN	EWS	ANG	DBS
66225 E	TO	WBEN	EWS	ANG	DBS
66226 E	TO	WBEN	EWS	ANG	DBS
66227	TO	WBAM	EWS	ANG	DBS
66228 E	TO	WBEN	EWS	ANG	DBS
66229 E	TO	WBEN	EWS	ANG	DBS
66230	TO	WBAI	EWS	ANG	DBS
66231 E	TO	WBEN	EWS	ANG	DBS
66232	TO	WBAN	EWS	ANG	DBS
66233 E	TO	WBEN	EWS	ANG	DBS
66234 E	TO	WBEN	EWS	ANG	DBS
66235 E	TO	WBEN	EWS	ANG	DBS
66236 E	TO	WBEN	EWS	ANG	DBS
66237	TO	WBAK	EWS	ANG	DBS
66238	TO	WBAN	EWS	ANG	DBS
66239 E	TO	WBEN	EWS	ANG	DBS
66240 E	TO	WBEN	EWS	ANG	DBS
66241 E	TO	WBEN	EWS	ANG	DBS
66242 E	TO	WBEN	EWS	ANG	DBS
66243 E	TO	WBEN	EWS	ANG	DBS
66244 E	TO	WBEN	EWS	ANG	DBS
66245 E	TO	WBEN	EWS	ANG	DBS
66246 E	TO	WBEN	EWS	ANG	DBS
66247 E	TO	WBEN	EWS	ANG	DBS
66248	TO	WBAN	EWS	ANG	DBS
66249 E	TO	WBEN	EWS	ANG	DBS
66250	TO	WBAK	EWS	ANG	DBS

Names applied

66002	*Lafarge Quorn*
66048	*James the Engine*
66050	*EWS Energy*
66077	*Benjamin Gimbert GC*
66079	*James Nightall GC*
66172	*Paul Melleney*
66200	*Railway Heritage Committee*
66250	*Robert K. Romak* (not standard nameplate)

■ DBS Class 66/0s operated by ECR and marked 'E' on the above listing are usually maintained at Sotteville, France.

Right: *The mainstay of DBS freight power in the UK is the ElectroMotive-built Class 66, of which 250 were ordered soon after EWS took over the UK freight operations. No. 66037 is viewed from its cooler group end at Teignmouth while involved in engineering work.* **CJM**

Class 67

Vehicle Length: 64ft 7in (19.68m)
Height: 12ft 9in (3.88m)
Width: 8ft 9in (2.66m)
Engine: EMD 12N-710G3B-EC
Horsepower: 2,980hp (2,223kW)
Electrical Equipment: EMD

Number	*Depot*	*Pool*	*Livery*	*Owner*	*Operator*	*Name*
67001	TO	WAAN	EWS	ANG	DBS	
67002	TO	WAAN	EWS	ANG	DBS	*Special Delivery*
67003	TO	WAAN	EWS	ANG	DBS	
67004	TO	WABN	EWS	ANG	DBS	*Post Haste*
67005	TO	WAAN	ROY	ANG	DBS	*Queen's Messenger*
67006	TO	WAAN	ROY	ANG	DBS	*Royal Sovereign*
67007	TO	WABN	EWS	ANG	DBS	

DB Schenker

67008	TO	WAAN	EWS	ANG	DBS	
67009	TO	WFMU	EWS	ANG	DBS	
67010	*TO*	*WAWN*	*WSR*	*ANG*	*DBS/WSR*	
67011	TO	WABN	EWS	ANG	DBS	
67012	*TO*	*WAWN*	*WSR*	*ANG*	*DBS/WSR*	*A Shropshire Lad*
67013	*TO*	*WAWN*	*WSR*	*ANG*	*DBS/WSR*	*Dyfrbont Pontcysyllte*
67014	*TO*	*WAWN*	*WSR*	*ANG*	*DBS/WSR*	*Thomas Telford*
67015	*TO*	*WAWN*	*WSR*	*ANG*	*DBS/WSR*	*David J. Lloyd*
67016	TO	WAFN	EWS	ANG	DBS	
67017	TO	WAFN	EWS	ANG	DBS	*Arrow*
67018	TO	WAFN	EWS	ANG	DBS	*Rapid*
67019	TO	WAAN	EWS	ANG	DBS	
67020	TO	WAAN	EWS	ANG	DBS	
67021	TO	WAAN	EWS	ANG	DBS	
67022	TO	WFMU	EWS	ANG	DBS	
67023	TO	WAAN	EWS	ANG	DBS	
67024	TO	WAAN	EWS	ANG	DBS	
67025	TO	WAAN	EWS	ANG	DBS	*Western Star*
67026	TO	WAAN	EWS	ANG	DBS	
67027	TO	WAAN	EWS	ANG	DBS	*Rising Star*
67028	TO	WAAN	EWS	ANG	DBS	
67029	TO	WAAN	EWE	ANG	DBS	*Royal Diamond*
67030	TO	WABN	EWS	ANG	DBS	

Left: *Two of the 30 strong Class 67 fleet are painted in Royal Train livery and used to power the Wolverton-based Royal stock when needed, otherwise the pair Nos. 67005/006 are used within the normal fleet, often being deployed on passenger or charter services. No. 67005 is seen powering an additional service into Dawlish for the 2009 annual air show event.* **CJM**

Class 90

Vehicle Length: 61ft 6in (18.74m)
Height: 13ft 0¼in (3.96m)
Width: 9ft 0in (2.74m)
Power Collection: 25kV ac overhead
Horsepower: 7,860hp (5,860kW)
Electrical Equipment: GEC

Number		*Depot*	*Pool*	*Livery*	*Owner*	*Operator*	*Name*
90017(S)		CE	WNTS	EWS	DBS	-	
90018		CE	WEFE	EWS	DBS	DBS	
90019		CE	WFMU	FGS	DBS	DBS	
90020		CE	WEFE	EWS	DBS	DBS	*Collingwood*
90021	(90221)	CE	WEFE	FGS	DBS	DBS	
90022(S)	(90222)	CE	WNTS	RFE	DBS	-	*Freightconnection*
90023(S)	(90223)	CE	WNTS	EWS	DBS	-	
90024	(90224)	CE	WEFE	FGS	DBS	DBS	
90025(S)	(90225)	CE	WNTS	FGS	DBS	-	
90026(S)		CE	WNTR	EWS	DBS	-	
90027(S)	(90227)	CE	WNTS	RFD	DBS	-	*Allerton T&RS Depot Quality Approved*
90028(S)		CE	WNTS	EWS	DBS	DBS	
90029(S)		CE	WNTS	EWS	DBS	-	*The Institution of Civil Engineers*
90030(S)	(90130)	CE	WNTR	EWS	DBS	-	*Crewe Locomotive Works*
90031(S)	(90131)	CE	WNTS	EWS	DBS	-	*The Railway Children Partnership - Working for Street Children Worldwide*
90032(S)	(90132)	CE	WNTS	EWS	DBS	-	
90033(S)	(90233)	CE	WNTS	RFI	DBS	-	
90034(S)	(90134)	CE	WNTS	EWS	DBS	-	
90035	(90135)	CE	WEFE	EWS	DBS	DBS	
90036	(90136)	CE	WFMU	RFE	DBS	DBS	
90037(S)	(90137)	CE	WNTS	EWS	DBS	-	*Spirit of Dagenham*

90038(S)	(90238)	CE	WNTS	RFI	DBS	-	
90039	(90239)	CE	WEFE	EWS	DBS	DBS	
90040(S)	(90140)	CE	WNTS	EWS	DBS	-	The Railway Mission
90050(S)	(90050)	CE	WNTS	FLG	DBS	-	

Right: *DBS have an ongoing contract with First Scotrail to provide motive power for its Anglo-Scottish sleeper services. Class 90s are used between London and Edinburgh/Glasgow and a small number, such as No. 90021 carry the First Scotrail colours. No. 90021 is seen at Edinburgh.* **Nathan Williamson**

Class 92

Vehicle Length: 70ft 1in (21.34m)
Height: 13ft 0in (3.95m)
Width: 8ft 8in (2.66m)
Power Collection: 25kV ac overhead / 750V dc third rail
Horsepower: ac - 6,700hp (5,000kW) / dc 5,360hp (4,000kW)
Electrical Equipment: Brush

Number	*Depot*	*Pool*	*Livery*	*Owner*	*Operator*	*Name*
92001	CE	WTAE	EWS	HAL	DBS	*Victor Hugo*
92002 (S)	CE	WNTS	RFE	HAL	-	*H G Wells*
92003	CE	WTAE	RFE	HAL	DBS	*Beethoven*
92004 (S)	CE	WNTS	RFE	HAL	-	*Jane Austen*
92005	CE	WTAE	RFE	HAL	DBS	*Mozart*
92007	CE	WTAE	RFE	HAL	DBS	*Schubert*
92008 (S)	CE	WNTR	EPS	HAL	-	*Jules Verne*
92009	CE	WTAE	RFE	HAL	DBS	*Elgar*
92011 (S)	CE	WNTS	RFE	HAL	-	*Handel*
92012	CE	WTAE	RFE	HAL	DBS	*Thomas Hardy*
92013	CE	WFMU	RFE	HAL	DBS	*Puccini*
92015	CE	WFMU	RFE	HAL	DBS	*D H Lawrence*
92016 (S)	CE	WNTS	RFE	HAL	DBS	*Brahms*
92017	CE	WTAE	STO	HAL	DBS	*Bart the Engine*
92019	CE	WTAE	RFE	HAL	DBS	*Wagner*
92023	CE	WTAE	RFE	HAL	DBS	*Charles Dickens*
92024 (S)	CE	WNTS	RFE	HAL	-	*J S Bach*
92025 (S)	CE	WNTS	RFE	HAL	-	*Oscar Wilde*
92026	CE	WTAE	RFE	HAL	DBS	*Britten*
92027 (S)	CE	WNTS	RFE	HAL	-	*George Eliot*
92029 (S)	CE	WNTS	RFE	HAL	-	*Dante*
92030 (S)	CE	WNTR	RFE	HAL	-	*Ashford*
92031 (S)	CE	WNTS	EWS	HAL	-	*The Institute of Logistics and Transport*
92034	CE	WTAE	RFE	HAL	DBS	*Kipling*
92035 (S)	CE	WNTS	RFE	HAL	-	*Mendelssohn*
92036	CE	WFMU	RFE	HAL	DBS	*Bertolt Brecht*
92037	CE	WTAE	RFE	HAL	DBS	*Sullivan*
92039 (S)	CE	WNTS	RFE	HAL	-	*Johann Strauss*
92041	CE	WNTE	RFE	HAL	DBS	*Vaughan Williams*
92042	CE	WFMU	RFE	HAL	DBS	*Honegger*

Right: *The majority of the under used DBS-owned Class 92s still carry the original triple grey livery off-set by Channel Tunnel roundels on the side, together with an EWS sticker on the sides. No. 92041* Vaughan Williams *is seen at Carlisle with a southbound freight from Mossend to Wembley on 15 June 2009.* **Nathan Williamson**

DB Schenker

Hauled Stock (Passenger)

AJ41 - RBR

Number	Depot	Livery	Owner
1658(S)	EH	MAR	DBR
1679	EH	LNE	DBR
1680	CE	LNE	DBR

AD1D - FO

Number	Depot	Livery	Owner
3186	DY	INT	DBR

AD1E - FOT

Number	Depot	Livery	Owner
3255 (3525)	EH	MAR	DBR

AD1F - FO

Number	Depot	Livery	Owner
3269	EH	MAR	DBR
3292	EH	MAR	DBR
3318	EH	MAR	DBR
3331	EH	MAR	DBR
3338(S)	CP	MAR	DBR
3358	EH	MAR	DBR
3368(S)	EH	MAR	DBR
3375(S)	EH	MAR	DBR
3388	EH	MAR	DBR
3399(S)	EH	MAR	DBR
3400	EH	MAR	DBR
3414	EH	MAR	DBR
3424	EH	MAR	DBR

Above: *DBS-operated maroon-liveried Mk2f FO No. 3400.* **Nathan Williamson**

AC21 - TSO

Number	Depot	Livery	Owner
4925(S)	EH	GRN	DBR *(for sale)*
4956(S)	EH	BLG	DBR *(for sale)*
5005(S)	EH	BLG	DBR *(for sale)*
5037(S)	EH	GRN	DBR *(for sale)*

AC2A - TSO

Number	Depot	Livery	Owner
5331	EH	MAR	DBR
5386(S)	EH	MAR	DBR

AC2B - TSO

Number	Depot	Livery	Owner
5482	TO	MAR	DBR

AC2D - TSO

Number	Depot	Livery	Owner
5631	EH	MAR	DBR
5632	EH	MAR	DBR
5657	EH	MAR	DBR

Mk1
Vehicle Length: 64ft 6in (19.65m) *Height: 12ft 9½in (3.89m)*
Width: 9ft 3in (2.81m)

Mk2
Vehicle Length: 66ft 0in (20.11m) *Height: 12ft 9½in (3.89m)*
Width: 9ft 3in (2.81m)

Mk 3
Vehicle Length: 75ft 0in (22.86m) *Height: 12ft 9in (3.88m)*
Width: 8ft 11in (2.71m)

AC2F - TSO

Number	Depot	Livery	Owner
5922	EH	MAR	DBR
5924	EH	MAR	DBR
5954(S)	EH	MAR	DBR
5959	EH	MAR	DBR
6110	EH	MAR	DBR
6139	EH	MAR	DBR
6152	EH	MAR	DBR

Above: *DBS-operated maroon-liveried Mk2f TSO No. 6152.* **Nathan Williamson**

AX51 - GEN

Number	Depot	Livery	Owner
6311 (92911)	TO	BLU	DBR *(for sale)*

AN1D - RMBF

Number	Depot	Livery	Owner
6720 (6602)	CE	MAR	DBR

Above: *RMBF No. 6720 painted in maroon-livery, view from the buffet counter end.* **Nathan Williamson**

AE2D - BSO

Number	Depot	Livery	Owner
9494	EH	MAR	DBR

AE2F - BSO

Number	Depot	Livery	Owner
9529	EH	MAR	DBR

AJ1G - RFM

Number	Depot	Livery	Owner
10205(S) (40503)	LM	SPL	DBR
10211 (40510)	TO	EWE	DBS
10215 (11032)	CE	BLG	DBR/WS
10226(S) (11015)	LM	VIR	DBR
10233(S) (10013)	LM	VIR	DBR
10235 (10015)	CE	BLG	DBR/WS
10236(S) (10018)	ZW	VIR	DBR/WS
10250(S) (10020)	ZW	VIR	DBR
10255(S) (10010)	ZW	VIR	DBR/WS
10257 (10007)	CE	BLG	DBR/WS

AU4G - SLEP

Number	Depot	Livery	Owner
10546	TO	EWE	DBS

AS4G - SLE

Number	Depot	Livery	Owner
10647(S)	LM	INT	DBR
10710(S)	LM	CWR	DBR
10710(S)	LM	COT	DBR
10731(S)	LM	INT	DBR

AD1G - FO

Number	Depot	Livery	Owner
11005(S)	LM	VIR	DBR
11027(S)	CE	VIR	DBR/WS
11029	CE	BLG	DBR/WS
11031	CE	BLG	DBR/WS
11039	TO	EWE	DBS
11040(S)	ZG	VIR	DBR
11041(S)	LM	VIR	DBR
11052(S)	LM	VIR	DBR
11058(S)	LM	VIR	DBR
11097	CE	BLG	DBR/WS

AC2G - TSO

Number	Depot	Livery	Owner
12017	CE	VIR	DBR/VWC
12048(S)	ZW	VIR	DBR/WS
12053	CE	BLG	DBR/WS
12054	CE	VIR	DBR/VWC
12059	CE	VIR	DBR/VWC
12069(S)	ZW	VIR	DBR/WS
12072(S)	ZW	VIR	DBR
12094(S)	CE	VIR	DBR/VWC
12117(S)	ZW	VIR	DBR/WS
12124	CE	VIR	DBR/VWC
12131(S)	ZW	VIR	DBR/WS
12169(S)	ZW	VIR	DBR/WS

AB1D - BFK

Number	Depot	Livery	Owner
17161(S) (14161)	OM	EWS	DBR

AB21 - BSK

Number	Depot	Livery	Owner
35290(S)	CP	CAR	DBR

Saloon

Number	Depot	Livery	Owner
45020	ML	MAR	DBR
45029(S)	ML	EWS	DBR

Below: *The DBS charter rakes, mainly allocated to Eastleigh following the closure in 2009 of Old Oak Common, are frequently used on steam hauled passenger services, such as the annual 'Torbay Express' operating on summer Sundays between Bristol and Kingswear. A maroon EWS passenger set of Mk1s is seen between Churston and Goodrington in the summer of 2009 powered by A1 No. 60163* Tornado. **Tony Christie**

DB Schenker

Hauled Stock (NPCCS)

NZAG - DVT

Number	Depot	Livery	Owner
82108(S)	LM	VIR	DBR
82113(S)	LM	VIR	DBR
82116(S)	LM	VIR	DBR
82120(S)	LM	VIR	DBR
82122(S)	LM	VIR	DBR
82131(S)	LM	VIR	DBR
82137(S)	LM	VIR	DBR
82138(S)	LM	VIR	DBR

Mk 3 (DVT) Height: 12ft 9in (3.88m)
Vehicle Length: 61ft 9in (18.83m) Width: 8ft 11in (2.71m)

82144(S)	LM	VIR	DBR
82146	TO	DBE	DBS
82148(S)	LM	VIR	DBR
82150(S)	LM	VIR	DBR
82301 (82117)	*CE*	*WSR*	*DBR*
*82302 (82151)**	*CE*	*WSR*	*DBR*
82303 (82135)	*CE*	*WSR*	*DBR*
82304 (82130)	*CE*	*WSR*	*DBR*
82305 (82134)	*CE*	*WSR*	*DBR*

NKA1 - H-GUV

Mk1 Height: 12ft 9in (3.88m)
Vehicle Length: 57ft 0in (17.73m) Width: 9ft 3in (2.81m)

Number	Depot	Livery	Owner
92203 (S)	CP	RES	DBS
94103 (W) (95103)	CX	RES	DBS
94104 (S) (95104)	TO	RES	DBS
94106 (S) (95106)	ML	RES	DBS
94113 (S) (95113)	OM	RES	DBS
94116 (S) (95116)	TY	RES	DBS
94121 (S) (95121)	TO	RES	DBS
94137 (S) (95137)	ML	RES	DBS
94147 (S) (95147)	ML	RES	DBS
94150 (S) (95150)	SP	RES	DBS
94153 (S) (95153)	WE	RES	DBS
94155 (S) (95155)	SP	RES	DBS
94160 (S) (95160)	ML	RES	DBS
94166 (S) (95166)	BS	RES	DBS
94168 (S) (95168)	SP	RES	DBS
94170 (S) (95170)	BS	RES	DBS
94176 (S) (95176)	ML	RES	DBS
94177 (S) (95177)	TO	RES	DBS
94190 (S) (95350)	SP	RES	DBS
94191 (S) (95351)	SP	RES	DBS
94192 (S) (95352)	MY	RES	DBS
94195 (S) (95355)	BS	RES	DBS
94196 (S) (95356)	ML	RES	DBS
94197 (S) (95357)	BS	RES	DBS
94199 (S) (95359)	ML	RES	DBS
94203 (S) (95363)	SP	RES	DBS
94207 (S) (95367)	TO	RES	DBS
94208 (S) (95368)	TO	RES	DBS
94209 (W) (95369)	CX	RES	DBS
94213 (S) (95373)	MY	RES	DBS
94214 (S) (95374)	ML	RES	DBS
94217 (S) (93131)	ML	RES	DBS
94221 (S) (93905)	ML	RES	DBS
94222 (S) (93474)	ML	RES	DBS
94225 (S) (93849)	ML	RES	DBS
94227 (S) (93585)	TE	RES	DBS
94229 (S) (93720)	ML	RES	DBS

NAA1 - PCV

Number	Depot	Livery	Owner
94302 (S) (75124)	TY	RES	DBS
94303 (S) (75131)	TY	RES	DBS
94304 (S) (75107)	ML	RES	DBS
94306 (S) (75112)	TY	RES	DBS
94307 (S) (75127)	CX	RES	DBS
94308 (S) (75125)	ML	RES	DBS
94310 (S) (75119)	WE	RES	DBS
94311 (S) (75105)	WE	RES	DBS
94313 (S) (75129)	WE	RES	DBS
94316 (S) (75108)	TO	RES	DBS
94317 (S) (75117)	TO	RES	DBS
94318 (S) (75115)	CX	RES	DBS
94322 (S) (75111)	ML	RES	DBS
94323 (S) (75110)	TY	RES	DBS
94326 (S) (75123)	TY	RES	DBS
94331 (S) (75022)	CX	RES	DBS
94332 (S) (75011)	TY	RES	DBS
94333 (S) (75016)	TY	RES	DBS
94334 (S) (75017)	CD	RES	DBS
94335 (S) (75032)	TY	RES	DBS
94336 (S) (75031)	TY	RES	DBS
94338 (S) (75008)	WE	RES	DBS
94340 (S) (75012)	CD	RES	DBS
94343 (S) (75027)	ML	RES	DBS
94344 (S) (75014)	TO	RES	DBS

NBA1, NOA1, NQA, NRA1 - BVHS

Number	Depot	Livery	Owner
94400 (92524)	CX	RES	DBS
94401 (92224)	ML	RES	DBS
94406 (92956)	ML	RES	DBS
94408 (92981)	TY	RES	DBS
94410 (92941)	WE	RES	DBS
94411 (92945)	CX	RES	DBS
94412 (92945)	ML	RES	DBS
94413 (92236)	ML	RES	DBS
94416 (92746)	MY	RES	DBS
94420 (92263)	ML	RES	DBS
94422 (92651)	TO	RES	DBS
94423 (92914)	BS	RES	DBS
94427 (92754)	WE	RES	DBS
94428 (92166)	MY	RES	DBS
94429 (92232)	TE	RES	DBS
94431 (92604)	ML	RES	DBS
94432 (92999)	MY	RES	DBS
94433 (92643)	ML	RES	DBS
94434 (92584)	TY	RES	DBS
94435 (92134)	TO	RES	DBS
94438 (92251)	TO	RES	DBS
94440 (92645)	MY	RES	DBS

94445 (92615)	WE	RES	DBS
94451 (92257)	WE	RES	DBS
94458 (92974)	CX	RES	DBS
94462 (92270)	CD	RES	DBS
94463 (92995)	TY	RES	DBS
94470 (92113)	TO	RES	DBS
94479 (92132)	TO	RES	DBS
94481 (92641)	CX	RES	DBS
94482 (92639)	MY	RES	DBS
94488 (92105)	CD	RES	DBS
94490 (92230)	ML	RES	DBS
94492 (92721)	WE	RES	DBS
94495 (92755)	TY	RES	DBS
94497 (92717)	ML	RES	DBS
94498 (92555)	ML	RES	DBS
94499 (92577)	CD	BLG	DBS
94501 (92725)	TO	RES	DBS
94504 (92748)	TY	RES	DBS
94512 (92582)	TY	RES	DBS
94514 (92122)	MY	RES	DBS
94515 (92513)	ML	RES	DBS
94518 (92258)	MY	RES	DBS
94519 (92916)	ML	RES	DBS
94520 (92917)	TY	RES	DBS
94521 (92917)	CD	RES	DBS
94522 (92907)	TY	RES	DBS
94525 (92229)	TY	RES	DBS
94526 (92518)	TY	RES	DBS
94527 (92728)	TY	RES	DBS
94528 (92252)	ML	RES	DBS
94529 (92267)	CD	RES	DBS
94530 (94409)	MY	RES	DBS
94531 (94456)	TY	RES	DBS
94532 (94489)	LM	RES	DBS
94534 (94430)	MY	RES	DBS
94536 (94491)	MY	RES	DBS
94538 (94426)	ML	RES	DBS
94539 (92302)	ML	RES	DBS
94540 (92860)	TJ	RES	DBS
94541 (92316)	ML	RES	DBS
94542 (92330)	TY	RES	DBS
94543 (92389)	MY	RES	DBS
94544 (92345)	ML	RES	DBS
94545 (92329)	TE	RES	DBS
94546 (92804)	TY	RES	DBS
94547 (92392)	ML	RES	DBS
94548 (92344)	TY	RES	DBS

NAA1 - PCV

Number	*Depot*	*Livery*	*Owner*
95300 (94300)	ML	RES	DBS
95301 (94301)	ML	RES	DBS

NRA1 - BAA

Number	*Depot*	*Livery*	*Owner*
95400 (95203)	ML	EWS	DBS
95410 (95213)	ML	EWS	DBS

NOA1 - H-GUV

Number	*Depot*	*Livery*	*Owner*
95727 (95127)	WE	RES	DBS
95754 (95154)	TY	RES	DBS
95758 (95158)	SP	RES	DBS
95761 (95161)	WE	RES	DBS
95763 (95163)	BS	RES	DBS

NX5G - NGV

Number	*Depot*	*Livery*	*Owner*
96371(S) (10545)	WB	EPS	DBS
96372(S) (10564)	WB	EPS	DBS
96373(S) (10568)	WB	EPS	DBS
96374(S) (10585)	WB	EPS	DBS
96375(S) (10587)	WB	EPS	DBS

Below: *Mk3 generator van No. 96372, rebuilt from Mk3 Sleeper No. 10564.* **CJM**

Right: *NBA 94423, one of a large number of roller shutter door Royal Mail vans introduced in the 1990s by Rail Express Systems.* **CJM**

Above: *Propelling Control Vehicle No. 94300 was modified as NAA 95300 and is seen at Aberdeen forming an Express Parcels service.* **CJM**

Above: *One of a pair of BAA vans modified for side palette loading using a fork lift. No. 95400 in full EWS livery is seen at Aberdeen.* **CJM**

Euro Cargo Rail A part of DB Schenker

Address: ✉ Immeuble la Palacio, 25-29 Place de la Madeleine, Paris, 75008
info@eurocargorail.com
✆ +33 977 400000
ⓘ www.eurocargorail.com

Class 08

Vehicle Length: 29ft 3in (8.91m)
Height: 12ft 8⅝in (3.87m)
Width: 8ft 6in (2.59m)
Engine: English Electric 6K
Horsepower: 400hp (298kW)
Electrical Equipment: English Electric

Number	Depot	Pool	Livery	Owner	Operator	Name
08738	FN	WSEN	ECR	DBS	ECR *(at Vallourec Steel, Amiens)*	*Silver Fox*
08939	TO	WSEN	ECR	DBS	ECR *(at Vallourec Steel, Amiens)*	

Class 21

Vehicle Length: (21/5) 48ft 2in (14.70m), (21/6) 46ft 3in (14.13m)
Height: (21/5) 13ft 8in (4.16m), (21/6) 13ft 9in (4.19m)
Width: 8ft 8¼in (2.65m)
Engine: (21/5) Caterpiller 3512B DI-TA of 2,011hp
Engine: (21/6) MTU 8V 4000 R41L of 1,475hp
Hydraulic Equipment: Voith

Number	Depot	Pool	Livery	Owner	Operator
21544	DM	WLAN	MAR	ANG	ECR
21545	DM	WLAN	MAR	ANG	ECR
21546	DM	WLAN	MAR	ANG	ECR
21547	DM	WLAN	MAR	ANG	ECR
21610	DM	WLAN	MAR	ANG	ECR
21611	DM	WLAN	MAR	ANG	ECR

Class 77 (JT42CWRM)

Vehicle Length: 70ft 0½in (21.34m)
Height: 12ft 10in (3.91m)
Width: 8ft 8¼in (2.65m)
Engine: EMD 12N-710G3B-EC
Horsepower: 3,300hp (2,462kW)
Electrical Equipment: EMD

Number	Depot	Livery	Owner	Oper'r
77001	ND	ELR	DBS	ECR
77002	ND	ELR	DBS	ECR
77003	ND	ELR	DBS	ECR
77004	ND	ELR	DBS	ECR
77005	ND	ELR	DBS	ECR
77006	ND	ELR	DBS	ECR
77007	ND	ELR	DBS	ECR
77008	ND	ELR	DBS	ECR
77009	ND	ELR	DBS	ECR
77010	ND	ELR	DBS	ECR
77011	ND	ELR	DBS	ECR
77012	ND	ELR	DBS	ECR
77013	ND	ELR	DBS	ECR
77014	ND	ELR	DBS	ECR
77015	ND	ELR	DBS	ECR
77016	ND	ELR	DBS	ECR
77017	ND	ELR	DBS	ECR
77018	ND	ELR	DBS	ECR
77019	ND	ELR	DBS	ECR
77020	ND	ELR	DBS	ECR
77021	ND	ELR	DBS	ECR
77022	ND	ELR	DBS	ECR
77023	ND	ELR	DBS	ECR
77024	ND	ELR	DBS	ECR
77025	ND	ELR	DBS	ECR
77026	ND	ELR	DBS	ECR
77027	ND	ELR	DBS	ECR
77028	ND	ELR	DBS	ECR
77029	ND	ELR	DBS	ECR
77030	ND	ELR	DBS	ECR
77031	ND	ELR	DBS	ECR
77032	ND	ELR	DBS	ECR
77033	ND	ELR	DBS	ECR
77034	ND	ELR	DBS	ECR
77035	ND	ELR	DBS	ECR
77036	ND	ELR	DBS	ECR
77037	ND	ELR	DBS	ECR
77038	ND	ELR	DBS	ECR
77039	ND	ELR	DBS	ECR
77040	ND	ELR	DBS	ECR
77041	ND	ELR	DBS	ECR
77042	ND	ELR	DBS	ECR
77043	ND	ELR	DBS	ECR
77044	ND	ELR	DBS	ECR
77045	ND	ELR	DBS	ECR
77046	ND	ELR	DBS	ECR
77047	ND	ELR	DBS	ECR
77048	ND	ELR	DBS	ECR
77049	ND	ELR	DBS	ECR
77050	ND	ELR	DBS	ECR
77051	ND	ELR	DBS	ECR
77052	ND	ELR	DBS	ECR
77053	ND	ELR	DBS	ECR
77054	ND	ELR	DBS	ECR
77055	ND	ELR	DBS	ECR
77056	ND	ELR	DBS	ECR
77057	ND	ELR	DBS	ECR
77058	ND	ELR	DBS	ECR
77059	ND	ELR	DBS	ECR
77060	ND	ELR	DBS	ECR

■ 20 members of this fleet are scheduled to be transferred to DBS in Germany and re-classified as Class 247.

Left: *The 60 purpose-built Euro Class 66s for Euro Cargo Rail were constructed by Electro Motive Diesels in London, Ontario, Canada in 2008-10 and shipped to the Ned-Trans works in Tilburg, Holland for commissioning. The locos are fitted for full Continental European operation. No. 77044 is seen at the EMD Plant in Canada on 22 February 2009.* **CJM**

Direct Rail Services

Address (UK): ✉ Kingmoor Depot, Etterby Road, Carlisle, Cumbria, CA3 9NZ
info@directrailservices.com
✆ 01228 406600
ⓘ www.directrailservices.com

Managing Director: Neil McNicholas
Depots: Carlisle Kingmoor, Crewe Gresty Bridge

Class 20/3

Vehicle Length: 46ft 9¼in (14.26m)
Height: 12ft 7⅝in (3.84m)
Width: 8ft 9in (2.66m)
Engine: English Electric 8SVT Mk2
Horsepower: 1,000hp (745kW)
Electrical Equipment: English Electric

Number		*Depot*	*Pool*	*Livery*	*Owner*	*Operator*	*Name*
20301	**(20047)**	**KM**	**XHNC**	**DRC**	**DRS**	**DRS**	***Max Joule 1958 - 1999***
20302(S)	**(20084)**	**KM**	**XHSS**	**DRS**	**DRS**	**-**	
20303	**(20127)**	**KM**	**XHNC**	**DRS**	**DRS**	**DRS**	
20304	**(20120)**	**KM**	**XHNC**	**DRS**	**DRS**	**DRS**	
20305(S)	**(20095)**	**KM**	**XHSS**	**DRS**	**DRS**	**-**	***Gresty Bridge***
20306(S)	**(20131)**	**KM**	**XHNC**	**DRS**	**DRS**	**-**	
20307(S)	**(20128)**	**KM**	**XHSS**	**DRS**	**DRS**	**-**	
20308(S)	**(20187)**	**KM**	**XHSS**	**DRC**	**DRS**	**-**	
20309(S)	**(20075)**	**KM**	**XHSS**	**DRC**	**DRS**	**-**	
20310(S)	**(20190)**	**KM**	**XHSS**	**DRS**	**DRS**	**-**	
20311(S)	**(20102)**	**KM**	**XHSS**	**DRS**	**DRS**	**-**	***Class 20 'Fifty'***
20312(S)	**(20042)**	**KM**	**XHSS**	**DRC**	**DRS**	**-**	
20313(S)	**(20194)**	**KM**	**XHSS**	**DRS**	**DRS**	**-**	
20314(S)	**(20117)**	**KM**	**XHSS**	**DRC**	**DRS**	**-**	
20315(S)	**(20104)**	**KM**	**XHSS**	**DRS**	**DRS**	**-**	

Right: *The Direct Rail Services Class 20 fleet are virtually all allocated to the winter RHTT train operation, being out-based from Carlisle to perform rail head cleaning duties with the Network Rail RHTT fleet. Nos. 20314 and 20305 show the nose and cab end layouts at Eastleigh in May 2009.* **Nathan Williamson**

Class 37/0

Vehicle Length: 61ft 6in (18.74m)
Height: 13ft 0¼in (3.96m)
Width: 8ft 11⅝in (2.73m)
Engine: English Electric 12CSVT
Horsepower: 1,750hp (1,304kW)
Electrical Equipment: English Electric

Number	*Depot*	*Pool*	*Livery*	*Owner*	*Operator*	*Name*
37038	**KM**	**XHSS**	**DRS**	**DRS**	**DRS**	
37059	**KM**	**XHNC**	**DRC**	**DRS**	**DRS**	
37069	**KM**	**XHNC**	**DRC**	**DRS**	**DRS**	
37087	**KM**	**XHNC**	**DRS**	**DRS**	**DRS**	***Keighley & Worth Valley Railway***
37194	**KM**	**XHNC**	**DRC**	**DRS**	**DRS**	
37197	**KM**	**XHNC**	**DRS**	**DRS**	**DRS**	
37218	**KM**	**XHNC**	**DRC**	**DRS**	**DRS**	
37229	**KM**	**XHNC**	**DRC**	**DRS**	**DRS**	***Jonty Jarvis***
37259	**KM**	**XHNC**	**DRC**	**DRS**	**DRS**	
37261(S)	**KM**	**XHSS**	**DRS**	**DRS**	**-**	

Direct Rail Services

Class 37/4

Vehicle Length: 61ft 6in (18.74m)
Height: 13ft 0¼in (3.96m)
Width: 8ft 11⅝in (2.73m)
Electric Train Heat fitted

Engine: English Electric 12CSVT
Horsepower: 1,750hp (1,304kW)
Electrical Equipment: English Electric

Number		Depot	Pool	Livery	Owner	Operator	Name
37409	(37270)	KM	XHNC	DRC	DRS	DRS	
37412(S)	(37301)	KM	XHSS	RFT	DRS	-	
37423	(37296)	KM	XHNC	DRC	DRS	DRS	*Spirit of the Lakes*

Class 37/5

Vehicle Length: 61ft 6in (18.74m)
Height: 13ft 0¼in (3.96m)
Width: 8ft 11⅝in (2.73m)

Engine: English Electric 12CSVT
Horsepower: 1,750hp (1,304kW)
Electrical Equipment: English Electric

Number		Depot	Pool	Livery	Owner	Operator	Name
37510		KM	XHNC	DRC	DRS	DRS	
37515(S)		BH	XHSS	DRS	DRS	-	
37667	(37151)	KM	XHNC	DRC	DRS	DRS	
37682(S)	(37236)	KM	XHHP	DRC	DRS	-	
37683(S)	(37187)	KM	XHSS	DRS	DRS	-	
37688	(37205)	KM	XHNC	DRC	DRS	DRS	*Kingmoor TMD*

Class 37/6

Vehicle Length: 61ft 6in (18.74m)
Height: 13ft 0¼in (3.96m)
Width: 8ft 11⅝in (2.73m)

Engine: English Electric 12CSVT
Horsepower: 1,750hp (1,304kW)
Electrical Equipment: English Electric

Number		Depot	Pool	Livery	Owner	Operator	Name
37601	(37501)	KM	XHNC	DRC	DRS	DRS	
37602	(37502)	KM	XHSS	DRS	DRS	-	
37603	(37504)	KM	XHNC	DRC	DRS	DRS	
37604	(37506)	KM	XHNC	DRC	DRS	DRS	
37605	(37507)	KM	XHNC	DRS	DRS	DRS	
37606(S)	(37508)	KM	XHSS	DRS	DRS	-	
37607	(37511)	KM	XHNC	DRS	DRS	DRS	
37608	(37512)	KM	XHNC	DRC	DRS	DRS	
37609	(37514)	KM	XHNC	DRS	DRS	DRS	
37610(S)	(37687)	KM	XHSS	DRC	DRS	-	*T. S. (Ted) Cassady 14.5.61-6.4.08*
37611	(37690)	KM	XHNC	DRC	DRS	DRS	
37612	(37691)	KM	XHNC	DRS	DRS	DRS	

Left: *One of the DRS contracts is to provide motive power for the Network Rail inspection saloons based at Derby. Usually Class 37/4 No. 37423 is used for this work. On 17 March 2009, No. 37423 is seen heading west on the Dawlish Sea Wall hauling inspection saloon No. 975025, rebuilt from a former Hastings DEMU buffet car.* **CJM**

Class 47/4

Vehicle Length: 63ft 6in (19.35m)
Height: 12ft 10⅜in (3.91m)
Width: 9ft 2in (2.79m)
Electric Train Heat fitted
Engine: Sulzer 12LDA28C
Horsepower: 2,580hp (1,922kW)
Electrical Equipment: Brush

Number		Depot	Pool	Livery	Owner	Operator	Name
47501		KM	XHAC	DRC	DRS	DRS	*Craftsman*
47802	(47552)	KM	XHAC	DRC	DRS	DRS	*Pride of Cumbria*
47810	(47247/655)	KM	HNRC	DRC	HNR	DRS	
47832	(47560)	KM	XHAC	DRC	DRS	DRS	*Solway Princess*
47841	(47622)	KM	XHNC	DRC	DRS	DRS	

Class 47/7

Number		Depot	Pool	Livery	Owner	Operator	Name
47703(S)	(47514)	KM	XHSS	FRB	DRS	-	
47709(S)	(47499)	KM	XHHP	DRC	DRS	-	
47712	(47505)	KM	XHAC	DRC	DRS	DRS	*Pride of Carlisle*
47790	(47673)	KM	XHAC	DRC	DRS	DRS	
47791(S)	(47675)	KM	XHSS	RES	DRS	-	

Above: *A handful of Class 47s are operated by DRS for general freight duties, which frequently involves the haulage of Network Rail ballast machines around the network. On 20 April 2009, No. 47832* Solway Princess *passes Dawlish Warren with an Ashford (Kent) to Tavistock Junction track machine transit move.* **CJM**

Class 57/0

Vehicle Length: 63ft 6in (19.38m)
Height: 12ft 10⅛in (3.91m)
Width: 9ft 2in (2.79m)
Engine: EMD 645-12E3
Horsepower: 2,500hp (1,864kW)
Electrical Equipment: Brush

Number	Depot	Pool	Livery	Owner	Operator	Name
57002 (47322)	KM	XHCK	DRC	PTR	DRS	
57003 (47317)	KM	XHCK	DRC	PTR	DRS	

Direct Rail Services

57004 (47347)	KM	XHCK	DRC	PTR	DRS	
57007 (47332)	KM	XHCK	DRC	PTR	DRS	
57008 (47060)	KM	XHCK	DRC	PTR	DRS	*Telford International Railfreight Park June - 2009*
57009 (47079)	KM	XHCK	DRC	PTR	DRS	
57010 (47231)	KM	XHNC	DRC	PTR	DRS	
57011 (47329)	KM	XHNC	DRC	PTR	DRS	
57012 (47204)	KM	XHCK	DRC	PTR	DRS	

Left: *Carrying full DRS Compass livery, Class 57/0 No. 57012 is seen at Newton Abbot in July 2009 while involved in driver's route training in the West Country. The loco's No. 1 end is nearest the camera.* **Nathan Williamson**

Class 66/4

Vehicle Length: 70ft 0½in (21.34m)
Height: 12ft 10in (3.91m)
Width: 8ft 8¼in (2.65m)
Engine: EMD 12N-710G3B-EC
Horsepower: 3,300hp (2,462kW)
Electrical Equipment: EMD

Number	Depot	Pool	Livery	Owner	Operator	Name
66411	KM	XHIM	STO	HAL	DRS	*Eddie the Engine*
66412	KM	XHIM	MAL	HAL	DRS	
66413	KM	XHIM	DRC	HAL	DRS	
66414	KM	XHIM	TES	HAL	DRS	*James the Engine*
66415	KM	XHIM	DRC	HAL	DRS	
66416	KM	XHIM	DRC	HAL	DRS	
66417	KM	XHIM	DRC	HAL	DRS	
66418	KM	XHIM	DRC	HAL	DRS	
66419	KM	XHIM	DRC	HAL	DRS	
66420	KM	XHIM	DRC	HAL	DRS	
66421	KM	XHIM	DRC	HAL	DRS	
66422	KM	XHIM	DRC	HAL	DRS	
66423	KM	XHIM	DRC	HAL	DRS	
66424	KM	XHIM	DRC	HAL	DRS	
66425	KM	XHIM	DRC	HAL	DRS	
66426	KM	XHIM	DRC	HAL	DRS	
66427	KM	XHIM	DRC	HAL	DRS	
66428	KM	XHIM	DRC	HAL	DRS	
66429	KM	XHIM	DRC	HAL	DRS	
66430	KM	XHIM	DRC	HAL	DRS	
66431	KM	XHIM	DRC	HAL	DRS	
66432	KM	XHIM	DRC	HAL	DRS	
66433	KM	XHIM	DRC	HAL	DRS	
66434	KM	XHIM	DRC	HAL	DRS	

Left: *DRS operate a fleet of 24 Class 66/4 locos; these power flask and general freight services throughout the UK including the annual leaf-fall 'Sandite' and 'Water Cannon' services. A pair of locos Nos. 66417 and 66415 pass Dawlish Warren, Devon in May 2008 with a westbound escort coach move to Devonport Dockyard.* **CJM**

Coaching Stock

AJ4I - RBR / RK*

Number	*Depot*	*Livery*	*Owner*
1657	**ZG**	**DRO**	**DRS**
80042 (1646)*	**ZG**	**DRO**	**DRS**

AD1F - FO

Number	*Depot*	*Livery*	*Owner*
3278 (S)	**KM**	**BPM**	**DRS**
3385 (S)	**BH**	**BPM**	**DRS**

AC2F - TSO

Number	*Depot*	*Livery*	*Owner*
5989	**BH**	**DRS**	**DRS**

AC2 - BSO

Number	*Depot*	*Livery*	*Owner*
9419	**KM**	**DRS**	**DRS**
9428	**KM**	**DRS**	**DRS**
9479	**BA**	**DRS**	**DRS**
9513	**BA**	**BPM**	**DRS**

AJ1G - RFM

Number	*Depot*	*Livery*	*Owner*
10237	**BA**	**DRO**	**DRS**

AD1G - FO

Number	*Depot*	*Livery*	*Owner*
11013	**CP**	**DRS**	**DRS**
11019	**CP**	**DRS**	**DRS**
11028	**BA**	**VIR**	**DRS**
11030	**BA**	**DRO**	**DRS**
11033	**CP**	**DRS**	**DRS**
11044	**BA**	**DRO**	**DRS**
11046	**CP**	**DRS**	**DRS**
11054	**BA**	**DRO**	**DRS**

AB1D - BFK

Number	*Depot*	*Livery*	*Owner*
17159	**ZG**	**DRO**	**DRS**

Mk1 *Vehicle Length: 64ft 6in (19.65m)*	*Height: 12ft 9½in (3.89m)* *Width: 9ft 3in (2.81m)*
Mk2 *Vehicle Length: 66ft 0in (20.11m)*	*Height: 12ft 9½in (3.89m)* *Width: 9ft 3in (2.81m)*
Mk 3 *Vehicle Length: 75ft 0in (22.86m)*	*Height: 12ft 9in (3.88m)* *Width: 8ft 11in (2.71m)*

Top: *Painted in all over Blue Pullman livery RBR No. 1657 is shown from its counter end.* **CJM**

Above: *Painted in DRS blue livery BSO No. 9419 one of the operators flask support vehicles is shown from its brake end.* **CJM**

Below: *Mk3 No. 11030 displays the latest DRS Ocean Liner Express livery.* **Nathan Williamson**

■ *At the end of 2009 the DRS 'Ocean Liner Express' set was placed on hold.*

Fastline Freight (Jarvis)

Address (UK): ✉ Meridian House, The Crescent, York, YO24 1AW
info@fastline-group.com
✆ 01904-712712
ⓘ www.fastline-group.com

Chief Executive: Richard Entwistle

Depots: Roberts Road (RR), York (YK)

Class 08

Vehicle Length: 29ft 3in (8.91m)
Height: 12ft $8^5/_8$in (3.87m)
Width: 8ft 6in (2.59m)
Engine: English Electric 6K
Horsepower: 400hp (298kW)
Electrical Equipment: English Electric

Number	*Depot*	*Pool*	*Livery*	*Owner*	*Operator*
08527	**RR**	**HNRL**	**FLF**	**HNR**	**FLF**

Class 56/3

Vehicle Length: 63ft 6in (19.35m)
Height: 13ft 0in (3.96m)
Width: 9ft 2in (2.79m)
Engine: Ruston Paxman 16RK3CT
Horsepower: 3,250hp (2,420kW)
Electrical Equipment: Brush

Number		*Depot*	*Pool*	*Livery*	*Owner*	*Operator*	*Name*
56301(S)	**(56045)**	**RR**	**RCJA**	**FLF**	**JAR**	**-**	
56302(S)	**(56124)**	**RR**	**RCJA**	**FLF**	**JAR**	**-**	***Wilson Walshe***

Left: *The two members of this sub-class are owned by Fastline/Jarvis and are presently stored following the loss of a container contract for which they were converted. No. 56302 is seen at Rugby.* **Tony Christie**

Class 66/3

Vehicle Length: 70ft $0^1/_2$in (21.34m)
Height: 12ft 10in (3.91m)
Width: 8ft $8^1/_4$in (2.65m)
Engine: EMD 12N-710G3B-EC
Horsepower: 3,300hp (2,462kW)
Electrical Equipment: EMD

Number	*Depot*	*Pool*	*Livery*	*Owner*	*Operator*
66301	**RR**	**RCJM**	**FLF**	**BEA**	**FLF**
66302	**RR**	**RCJM**	**FLF**	**BEA**	**FLF**
66303	**RR**	**RCJM**	**FLF**	**BEA**	**FLF**
66304	**RR**	**RCJM**	**FLF**	**BEA**	**FLF**
66305	**RR**	**RCJM**	**FLF**	**BEA**	**FLF**

Left: *The five Fastline Freight Class 66s owned by Bank of Tokyo/Mitsubishi Capital are allocated to Roberts Road, Doncaster and are usually used on the operator's coal flows from the Bristol area to the East Midlands. No. 56303 is seen passing Cossington on 15 September 2008 with a northbound high-capacity coal train.* **John Binch**

Coaching Stock

Mk 3
Vehicle Length: 75ft 0in (22.86m)
Height: 12ft 9in (3.88m)
Width: 8ft 11in (2.71m)

Number		*Type*	*Depot*	*Livery*	*Operator*	*Use*
977989	**(10536)**	**Mk3/SLEP**	**ZA**	**JAR**	**FLF**	**Canteen and Mess coach for Jarvis TRT**

First GBRf

Address: ✉ 15-25 Artillery Lane, London, E1 7HA
info@gbrailfreight.com
✆ 0207 904 3393
ⓘ www.gbrailfreight.com

Managing Director: John Smith
Depots: Peterborough (PT), Wembley (SV)

Class 66/7

Vehicle Length: 70ft 0½in (21.34m)
Height: 12ft 10in (3.91m)
Width: 8ft 8¼in (2.65m)
Engine: EMD 12N-710G3B-EC
Horsepower: 3,300hp (2,462kW)
Electrical Equipment: EMD

Number	Depot	Pool	Livery	Owner	Operator	Name
66701	PT	GBRT	GBR	HSB	GBR	*Whitemoor*
66702	PT	GBRT	GBR	HSB	GBR	*Blue Lightning*
66703	PT	GBCM	GBR	HSB	GBR	*Doncaster PSB 1981 - 2002*
66704	PT	GBRT	GBR	HSB	GBR	*Colchester Power Signalbox*
66705	PT	GBCM	GBR	HSB	GBR	*Golden Jubilee*
66706	PT	GBCM	GBR	HSB	GBR	*Nene Valley*
66707	PT	GBCM	GBR	HSB	GBR	*Sir Sam Fay / Great Central Railway*
66708	PT	GBRT	GBR	HSB	GBR	
66709	PT	GBRT	MED	HSB	GBR	*Joseph Arnold Davies*
66710	PT	GBCM	GBR	HSB	GBR	
66711	PT	GBCM	GBR	HSB	GBR	
66712	PT	GBCM	GBR	HSB	GBR	*Peterborough Power Signalbox*
66713	PT	GBCM	GBR	HSB	GBR	*Forest City*
66714	PT	GBCM	GBR	HSB	GBR	*Cromer Lifeboat*
66715	PT	GBCM	GBR	HSB	GBR	*Valour*
66716	PT	GBCM	GBR	HSB	GBR	*Willesden Traincare Centre*
66717	PT	GBCM	GBR	HSB	GBR	*Good Old Boy*
66718	PT	GBCM	GBM	HSB	GBR	*Gwyneth Dunwoody*
66719	PT	GBCM	GBM	HSB	GBR	*Metro-Land*
66720	PT	GBCM	GBM	HSB	GBR	*Metronet Pathfinder*
66721	PT	GBCM	GBM	HSB	GBR	*Harry Beck*
66722	PT	GBCM	GBM	HSB	GBR	*Sir Edward Watkin*
66723	PT	GBCM	GBF	HSB	GBR	*Chinook*
66724	PT	GBCM	GBF	HSB	GBR	*Drax Power Station*
66725	PT	GBCM	GBF	HSB	GBR	*Sunderland*
66726	PT	GBCM	GBF	HSB	GBR	*Sheffield Wednesday*
66727	PT	GBCM	GBF	HSB	GBR	*Andrew Scott CBE*
66728	PT	GBCM	GBF	PTR	GBR	*Institution of Railway Operators*
66729	PT	GBCM	GBF	PTR	GBR	
66730	PT	GBCM	GBF	PTR	GBR	
66731	PT	GBCM	GBF	PTR	GBR	
66732	PT	GBCM	GBF	PTR	GBR	*GBRf The First Decade 1999-2009 John Smith - MD*

■ *From mid-2009 GBRf hired off-lease Nos. 66401/402/843/844 to cover for modification work on the core GBRf fleet. Allocated to pool GBRT.*

Right: *Several different liveries are carried by the 32 strong First-GBRf fleet of Class 66s. The First 'Barbie' style applied to Nos. 66723-732 is perhaps the most pleasing, as shown on No. 66727.* **CJM**

First/GBRf

Class 73

Vehicle Length: 53ft 8in (16.35m)
Height: 12ft $5^{5}/_{16}$in (3.79m)
Width: 8ft 8in (2.64m)
Power: 750V dc third rail or English Electric 6K
Horsepower: electric - 1,600hp (1,193kW)
Horsepower: diesel - 600hp (447kW)
Electrical Equipment: English Electric

Number		Depot	Pool	Livery	Owner	Operator	Name
73141		SE	GBED	FGF	GBR	GBR	*Charlotte*
73203(S)	(73127)	SE	GBZZ	GAT	GBR	-	
73204	(73125)	SE	GBED	GBR	GBR	GBR	*Janice*
73205	(73124)	SE	GBED	GBR	GBR	GBR	*Jeanette*
73206	(731230	SE	GBED	GBR	GBR	GBR	*Lisa*
73207	(73122)	MR	GBWM	BLL	GBR	GBR	
73208	(73121)	SE	GBED	BLU	PTR	GBR	*Kirsten*
73209(S)	(73120)	SE	GBZZ	GBR	GBR	GBR	*Alison* (Unlikely to be returned to traffic)
73212	(73102)	SE	GBED	NRL	GBR	GBR	
73213	(73112)	SE	GBED	FGF	GBR	GBR	

Left: *Taken over from Network Rail in mid-2009, No. 73141 was the first of the electro-diesel fleet to carry First GBRf 'Barbie' livery, unveiled at Minehead on 11 July 2009 when it was named* Charlotte. *The loco is seen in company with GBRf No. 66732 at Minehead.* **Stacey Thew**

Class 325

Vehicle Length: (Driving) 65ft $0^{3}/_{4}$in (19.82m)
(Inter) 65ft $4^{1}/_{4}$in (19.92m)
Height: 12ft $4^{1}/_{4}$in (3.76m)
Width: 9ft 2in (2.82m)
Horsepower: 1,278hp (990kW)
Seats (total/car): None - luggage space

Number	Formation DTPMV+MPMV+TPMV+DTPMV	Depot	Livery	Owner	Operator	Name
325001	68300+68340+68360+68301	WB	RML	RML	GBR	
325002	68302+68341+68361+68303	WB	RML	RML	GBR	*Royal Mail North Wales & North West*
325003	68304+68342+68362+68305	WB	RML	RML	GBR	
325004	68306+68343+68363+68307	WB	RML	RML	GBR	
325005	68308+68344+68364+68309	WB	RML	RML	GBR	*John Grierson*
325006	68310+68345+68365+68311	WB	RML	RML	GBR	
325007	68312+68346+68366+68313	WB	RML	RML	GBR	*Peter Howarth C.B.E*
325008	68314+68347+68367+68315	WB	RML	RML	GBR	
325009	68316+68348+68368+68317	WB	RML	RML	GBR	
325010	68318+68349+68369+68319	WB	RML	RML	GBR	
325011	68320+68350+68370+68321	WB	RML	RML	GBR	
325012	68322+68351+68371+68323	WB	RML	RML	GBR	
325013	68324+68352+68372+68325	WB	RML	RML	GBR	
325014	68326+68353+68373+68327	WB	RML	RML	GBR	
325015	68328+68354+68374+68329	WB	RML	RML	GBR	
325016	68330+68355+68375+68331	WB	RML	RML	GBR	

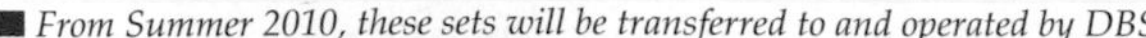
■ *From Summer 2010, these sets will be transferred to and operated by DBS*

Left: *Until spring 2010, First GBRf operate the remains of the UK Royal Mail contract working two south and two northbound mail trains formed of Class 325 stock over the West Coast main line each weekday. On 16 June 2009 set No. 325003 passes south through Lancaster.*
Nathan Williamson

Freightliner

Address: ✉ 3rd Floor, The Podium, 1 Eversholt Street, London NW1 2FL

pressoffice@freightliner.co.uk

✆ 0207 200 3900

ⓘ www.freightliner.com

Chief Executive: Peter Maybury

Managing Director Intermodal: Adam Cunliffe

Managing Director Heavy Haul: Paul Smart

Depots: Freightliner Diesels (FD), Freightliner Electrics (FE), Freightliner Shunters (FS), Ipswich* (IP), Leeds Midland Road (LD), Southampton Maritime (SZ)

* Stabling point

Parent Company: Arcapita

Class 08/0

Vehicle Length: 29ft 3in (8.91m)
Height: 12ft 8⅝in (3.87m)
Width: 8ft 6in (2.59m)

Engine: English Electric 6K
Horsepower: 400hp (298kW)
Electrical Equipment: English Electric

Number	*Depot*	*Pool*	*Livery*	*Owner*	*Operator*
08530(S)	FS	DFLS	FLR	PTR	FLR
08531(S)	FS	DFLS	FLR	PTR	FLR
08575	SZ	DFLS	FLR	PTR	FLR
08585	SZ	DFLS	FLR	PTR	FLR
08624	SZ	DFLS	BLU	PTR	FLR
08691	SZ	DFLS	FLR	FLR	FLR
08785	FD	DFLS	FLR	PTR	FLR
08891	FD	DFLS	FLR	PTR	FLR

Names applied

08585	*Vicky*
08691	*Terri*

Right: *With its cast* Terri *name on the engine room side door, Freightliner green and yellow-liveried No. 08691 stands outside the servicing shed at Southampton Maritime Freightliner Terminal in December 2008.* **Tony Christie**

Class 47/4

Vehicle Length: 63ft 6in (19.35m)
Height: 12ft 10⅜in (3.91m)
Width: 9ft 2in (2.79m)
Electric Train Heat fitted

Engine: Sulzer 12LDA28C
Horsepower: 2,580hp (1,922kW)
Electrical Equipment: Brush

Number	*Depot*	*Pool*	*Livery*	*Owner*	*Operator*	*Note*
47811 (47656)	FD	DFLH	GRN	FLR	FLR	Used as Dagenham pilot

Class 66/5

Vehicle Length: 70ft 0½in (21.34m)
Height: 12ft 10in (3.91m)
Width: 8ft 8¼in (2.65m)

Engine: EMD 12N-710G3B-EC
Horsepower: 3,300hp (2,462kW)
Electrical Equipment: EMD

Number	*Depot*	*Pool*	*Livery*	*Owner*	*Operator*	*Name*
66501	FD	DFGM	FLR	PTR	FLR	*Japan 2001*
66502	FD	DFGM	FLR	PTR	FLR	*Basford Hall Centenary 2001*
66503	FD	DFGM	FLR	PTR	FLR	*The Railway Magazine*
66504	FD	DFGM	FLR	PTR	FLR	
66505	FD	DFRT	FLR	PTR	FLR	
66506	FD	DFHH	FLR	HSB	FLR	*Crewe Regeneration*
66507	FD	DFRT	FLR	HSB	FLR	
66508	FD	DFRT	FLR	HSB	FLR	
66509	FD	DFHH	FLR	HSB	FLR	
66510	FD	DFRT	FLR	HSB	FLR	
66511	FD	DFRT	FLR	HSB	FLR	
66512	FD	DFHH	FLR	HSB	FLR	

Freightliner

66513	FD	DFHH	FLR	HSB	FLR	
66514	FD	DFRT	FLR	HSB	FLR	
66515	FD	DFGM	FLR	HSB	FLR	
66516	FD	DFGM	FLR	HSB	FLR	
66517	FD	DFGM	FLR	HSB	FLR	
66518	FD	DFRT	FLR	HSB	FLR	
66519	FD	DFHH	FLR	HSB	FLR	
66520	FD	DFRT	FLR	HSB	FLR	
66522	LD	DFRT	FLR	HSB	FLR	*east london express*
66523	FD	DFRT	FLR	HSB	FLR	
66524	FD	DFHH	FLR	HSB	FLR	
66525	FD	DFHH	FLR	HSB	FLR	
66526	LD	DFHH	FLR	PTR	FLR	*Driver Steve Dunn (George)*
66527	LD	DFHH	FLR	HSB	FLR	*Don Raider*
66528	FD	DFHH	FLR	PTR	FLR	
66529	FD	DFHH	FLR	PTR	FLR	
66530	FD	DFGM	FLR	PTR	FLR	
66531	FD	DFHH	FLR	PTR	FLR	
66532	FD	DFGM	FLR	PTR	FLR	*P&O Nedlloyd Atlas*
66533	FD	DFGM	FLR	PTR	FLR	*Hanjin Express / Senator Express*
66534	FD	DFGM	FLR	PTR	FLR	*OOCL Express*
66535	FD	DFGM	FLR	PTR	FLR	
66536	FD	DFGM	FLR	PTR	FLR	
66537	FD	DFGM	FLR	PTR	FLR	
66538	FD	DFIM	FLR	HSB	FLR	
66539	FD	DFIM	FLR	HSB	FLR	
66540	FD	DFIM	FLR	HSB	FLR	*Ruby*
66541	FD	DFIM	FLR	HSB	FLR	
66542	FD	DFIM	FLR	HSB	FLR	
66543	FD	DFIM	FLR	HSB	FLR	
66544	LD	DFHG	FLR	PTR	FLR	
66545	LD	DFHG	FLR	PTR	FLR	
66546	LD	DFHG	FLR	PTR	FLR	
66547	LD	DFHG	FLR	PTR	FLR	
66548	LD	DFHG	FLR	PTR	FLR	
66549	LD	DFHG	FLR	PTR	FLR	
66550	LD	DFHG	FLR	PTR	FLR	
66551	LD	DFHG	FLR	PTR	FLR	
66552	LD	DFHG	FLR	PTR	FLR	*Maltby Raider*
66553	LD	DFHG	FLR	PTR	FLR	
66554	LD	DFHG	FLR	HSB	FLR	
66555	LD	DFHG	FLR	HSB	FLR	
66556	LD	DFHG	FLR	HSB	FLR	
66557	LD	DFHG	FLR	HSB	FLR	
66558	LD	DFIM	FLR	HSB	FLR	
66559	FD	DFIM	FLR	HSB	FLR	
66560	FD	DFHG	FLR	HSB	FLR	
66561	FD	DFHG	FLR	HSB	FLR	
66562	FD	DFIM	FLR	HSB	FLR	
66563	FD	DFIM	FLR	HSB	FLR	
66564	FD	DFIM	FLR	HSB	FLR	
66565	FD	DFIM	FLR	HSB	FLR	
66566	FD	DFIM	FLR	HSB	FLR	
66567	FD	DFIM	FLR	HSB	FLR	
66568	FD	DFIM	FLR	HSB	FLR	
66569	FD	DFIM	FLR	HSB	FLR	
66570	FD	DFIM	FLR	HSB	FLR	
66571	FD	DFIM	FLR	HSB	FLR	
66572	FD	DFIM	FLR	HSB	FLR	
66573(S)	FD	DFTZ	FLR	HSB	-	
66574(S)	FD	DFTZ	FLR	HSB	-	
66575	FD	DFIM	FLR	HSB	FLR	
66576	FD	DFIM	FLR	HSB	FLR	*Hamburg Sud Advantage*
66577	FD	DFIM	FLR	HSB	FLR	

66578(S)	FD	DFTZ	FLR	HSB	-	*Scheduled for export to Poland*
66579(S)	FD	DFTZ	FLR	HSB	-	*Scheduled for export to Poland*
66580(S)	FD	DFTZ	FLR	HSB	-	*Scheduled for export to Poland*
66581(S)	FD	DFTZ	FLR	HSB	-	*Scheduled for export to Poland*
66582	*Exported, working in Poland for Freightliner Poland as 66009FPL*					
66583	*Exported, working in Poland for Freightliner Poland as 66010FPL*					
66584	*Exported, working in Poland for Freightliner Poland as 66011FPL*					
66585	FD	DFHG	FLR	HAL	FLR	*The Drax Flyer*
66586	*Exported, working in Poland for Freightliner Poland as 66008FPL*					
66587	FD	DFFT	FLR	HAL	FLR	
66588	FD	DFIN	FLR	HAL	FLR	
66589	FD	DFIN	FLR	HAL	FLR	
66590	FD	DFIN	FLR	HAL	FLR	
66591	FD	DFIN	FLR	LTS	FLR	
66592	FD	DFIN	FLR	LTS	FLR	*Johnson Stevens Agencies*
66593	FD	DFIN	FLR	LTS	FLR	*3MG Mersey Multimodal Gateway*
66594	FD	DFIN	FLR	LTS	FLR	*NYK Spirit of Kyoto*
66595	FD	DFHG	FLR	BEA	FLR	
66596	FD	DFHG	FLR	BEA	FLR	
66597	FD	DFHG	FLR	BEA	FLR	
66598	FD	DFHG	FLR	BEA	FLR	
66599	FD	DFHG	FLR	BEA	FLR	

Class 66/6

Number	*Depot*	*Pool*	*Livery*	*Owner*	*Operator*	*Name*
66601	FD	DFHH	FLR	PTR	FLR	*The Hope Valley*
66602	FD	DFRT	FLR	PTR	FLR	
66603	FD	DFRT	FLR	PTR	FLR	
66604	FD	DFRT	FLR	PTR	FLR	
66605	FD	DFRT	FLR	PTR	FLR	
66606	FD	DFRT	FLR	PTR	FLR	
66607	FD	DFHG	FLR	PTR	FLR	
66608	FD	DFHG	FLR	PTR	FLR	
66609	FD	DFHG	FLR	PTR	FLR	
66610	FD	DFHG	FLR	PTR	FLR	
66611	FD	DFHG	FLR	PTR	FLR	
66612	FD	DFHG	FLG	PTR	FLR	*Forth Raider*
66613	FD	DFHG	FLR	PTR	FLR	
66614	FD	DFHG	FLR	PTR	FLR	
66615	FD	DFHG	FLR	PTR	FLR	
66616	FD	DFHG	FLR	PTR	FLR	
66617	FD	DFHG	FLR	PTR	FLR	
66618	FD	DFHG	FLR	PTR	FLR	*Railways Illustrated Annual Photographic Awards - Alan Barnes*
66619	FD	DFHG	FLR	PTR	FLR	*Derek W. Johnson MBE*
66620	FD	DFHG	FLR	PTR	FLR	
66621	FD	DFHG	FLR	PTR	FLR	
66622	FD	DFHG	FLR	PTR	FLR	
66623	FD	DFHG	AIN	HSB	FLR	*Bill Bolsover*
66624	FD	DFHG	FLR	HSB	FLR	
66625	*Exported, working in Poland for Freightliner Poland as 66601FPL*					

Class 66/9

Number	*Depot*	*Pool*	*Livery*	*Owner*	*Operator*	*Name*
66951	FD	DFHG	FLR	HSB	FLR	
66952	FD	DFHG	FLR	HSB	FLR	
66953	FD	DFHG	FLR	BEA	FLR	
66954	FD	DFIN	FLR	BEA	FLR	
66955	FD	DFIN	FLR	BEA	FLR	
66956	FD	DFIN	FLR	BEA	FLR	
66957	FD	DFIN	FLR	BEA	FLR	*Stephenson Locomotive Society 1909-2009*

Freightliner

Left: *One of the original Freightliner Heavy Haul Class 66/5s No. 66512, showing the early front end lamp cluster design, passes Dawlish Warren on 6 May 2008 with a Westbury to Moorswater cement service.* **CJM**

■ *A number of Freightliner Class 66s are due to come off-lease in 2010.*

Class 70 - PH37ACmi

Vehicle Length: 71ft $2^1/_2$in (21.71m)
Height: 12ft 10in (3.91m)
Width: 8ft 8in (2.64m)
Engine: GE V16-cyliner PowerHaul 616
Horsepower: 3,700hp (2,750kW)
Electrical Equipment: General Electric

Number	*Depot*	*Pool*	*Livery*	*Owner*	*Operator*	*Name/Notes*
70001	FD	DFGI	FLR	LTS	FLR	**PowerHaul** *(Plate not carried)*
70002	FD	DFGH	FLR	LTS	FLR	
70003	FD	DFGH	FLR	LTS	FLR	
70004	FD	DFGH	FLR	LTS	FLR	
70005	FD	DFGH	FLR	LTS	FLR	
70006	FD	DFGH	FLR	LTS	FLR	
70007	FD	DHLT	FLR	LTS	FLR	*Scheduled for delivery September 2010*
70008	FD	DHLT	FLR	LTS	FLR	*Scheduled for delivery September 2010*
70009	FD	DHLT	FLR	LTS	FLR	*Scheduled for delivery September 2010*
70010	FD	DHLT	FLR	LTS	FLR	*Scheduled for delivery September 2010*
70011	FD	DHLT	FLR	LTS	FLR	*Scheduled for delivery September 2010*
70012	FD	DHLT	FLR	LTS	FLR	*Scheduled for delivery September 2010*

■ *Originally 30 locomotives were ordered in 2007 for delivery in 2009-10. In late 2009 it was announced that just 12 locos would be built at this point in time with the remainder of the order being assembled as business demands. Locos 70007-012 are scheduled for delivery to the UK in September 2010.*

Above: *The first two Class 70 Freightliner 'PowerHaul' locomotives arrived in the UK at Newport Docks on 8 November 2009. The locos will be operated by both the Intermodal and Heavy Haul businesses. By early 2010 six locos were delivered to the UK with a further six scheduled for delivery in September 2010. Nos. 70001 and 70002 are seen on the dockside at Newport.* **Chris Perkins**

Class 86/5

Vehicle Length: 58ft 6in (17.83m)
Height: 13ft 0⅝in (3.97m)
Width: 8ft 8¼in (2.64m)
Power Collection: 25kV ac overhead
Horsepower: 5,900hp (4,400kW)
Electrical Equipment: GEC

Number		Depot	Pool	Livery	Owner	Operator
86501	(86608/86408)	FE	DFGC	FLR	FLR	FLR

Class 86/6

Vehicle Length: 58ft 6in (17.83m)
Height: 13ft 0⅝in (3.97m)
Width: 8ft 8¼in (2.64m)
Power Collection: 25kV ac overhead
Horsepower: 5,900hp (4,400kW)
Electrical Equipment: GEC

Number		Depot	Pool	Livery	Owner	Operator
86604	(86404)	FE	DFNC	FLR	FLR	FLR
86605	(86405)	FE	DFNC	FLR	FLR	FLR
86607	(86407)	FE	DFNC	FLR	FLR	FLR
86609	(86409)	FE	DFNC	FLR	PTR	FLR
86610	(86410)	FE	DFNC	FLR	PTR	FLR
86612	(86412)	FE	DFNC	FLR	PTR	FLR
86613	(86413)	FE	DFNC	FLR	PTR	FLR
86614(S)	(86414)	CP	DHLT	FLR	PTR	FLR
86621	(86421)	FE	DFNC	FLR	PTR	FLR
86622	(86422)	FE	DFNC	FLY	PTR	FLR
86627	(86427)	FE	DFNC	FLR	PTR	FLR
86628	(86428)	FE	DFNC	FLR	PTR	FLR
86632	(86432)	FE	DFNC	FLR	PTR	FLR
86637	(86437)	FE	DFNC	FLY	PTR	FLR
86638	(86438)	FE	DFNC	FLR	PTR	FLR
86639	(86439)	FE	DFNC	FLR	PTR	FLR

Right: *The Class 86 fleet operated by Freightliner, work on the North West to Felixstowe via London intermodal services to and from Ipswich. No. 86612 is illustrated stabled at Ipswich Freightliner yard.* **CJM**

Class 90

Vehicle Length: 61ft 6in (18.74m)
Height: 13ft 0¼in (3.96m)
Width: 9ft 0in (2.74m)
Power Collection: 25kV ac overhead
Horsepower: 7,860hp (5,860kW)
Electrical Equipment: GEC

Number	Depot	Pool	Livery	Owner	Operator
90041	CP	DFLC	FLR	PTR	FLR
90042	CP	DFLC	FLY	PTR	FLR
90043	CP	DFLC	FLY	PTR	FLR
90044	CP	DFLC	FLY	PTR	FLR
90045	CP	DFLC	FLY	PTR	FLR
90046	CP	DFLC	FLR	PTR	FLR
90047	CP	DFLC	FLY	PTR	FLR
90048	CP	DFLC	FLY	PTR	FLR
90049	CP	DFLC	FLY	PTR	FLR

Names applied

90043 *Freightliner Coatbridge*

Right: *Nine Class 90s are in the Freightliner pool, owned by Porterbrook. All but two sport the 1995-launched Freightliner double grey livery with red branding. No. 90043* Freightliner Coatbridge *is seen passing Stratford with a liner train bound for Ipswich.* **CJM**

Mendip Rail

Address: ✉ Torr Works, East Cranmore, Shepton Mallet, Somerset, BA4 5SQ
info@mendip-rail.co.uk
✆ 01749 880672
ⓘ www.mendip-rail.co.uk

Managing Director: Alan Taylor
Depots: Merehead (MD), Whatley (WH)
Parent Company: Aggregate Industries and Hanson

Class 08

Vehicle Length: 29ft 3in (8.91m)
Height: 12ft 8⅝in (3.87m)
Width: 8ft 6in (2.59m)
Engine: English Electric 6K
Horsepower: 400hp (298kW)
Electrical Equipment: English Electric

Number	*Depot*	*Pool*	*Livery*	*Owner*	*Operator*
08643	MD	MBDL	GRN	FOS	MRL
08650	MD	MBDL	FOS	FOS	MRL
08652	WH	MBDL	HAN	HAN	MRL
08731	MD	MBDL	BLU	FOS	MRL
08947	WH	MBDL	BLU	FOS	MRL

For an illustration of a Class 08 - see page 183

Class 59/0

Vehicle Length: 70ft 0½in (21.34m)
Height: 12ft 10in (3.91m)
Width: 8ft 8¼in (2.65m)
Engine: EMD 16-645 E3C
Horsepower: 3,000hp (2,462kW)
Electrical Equipment: EMD

Number	*Depot*	*Pool*	*Livery*	*Owner*	*Operator*	*Name*
59001	MD	XYPO	AGI	FOS	MRL	*Yeoman Endeavour*
59002	MD	XYPO	FOS	FOS	MRL	*Alan J Day*
59004	MD	XYPO	FOS	FOS	MRL	*Paul A Hammond*
59005	MD	XYPO	AGI	FOS	MRL	*Kenneth J Painter*

■ *Loco No. 59003* Yeoman Highlander, *originally used by Foster Yeoman in the UK is now owned and operated by Heavy Haul Power International and based in Germany.*

Class 59/1

Number	*Depot*	*Pool*	*Livery*	*Owner*	*Operator*	*Name*
59101	MD	XYPA	HAN	HAN	MRL	*Village of Whatley*
59102	MD	XYPA	HAN	HAN	MRL	*Village of Chantry*
59103	MD	XYPA	HAN	HAN	MRL	*Village of Mells*
59103	MD	XYPA	HAN	HAN	MRL	*Village of Great Elm*

Below: *The first of the build, No. 59001 is shown in full Aggregates Industries livery while on engineering duty.* **CJM**

SW1001 'Switcher'

Vehicle Length: 40ft 6in (12.34m)
Height: 14ft 3in (4.34m)
Width: 10ft 0in (3.04m)
Engine: GM 8-645E
Horsepower: 1,000hp (746kW)
Electrical Equipment: EMD

Number	Depot	Pool	Livery	Owner	Operator	Name
44	MD	-	FOS	FOS	MRL	Yeoman Endeavour II
120	WH	-	HAN	HAN	MRL	

Right: *Built by General Motors Electro Motive Division to a custom sryle based of their 'off-the-shelf' SW1001 switcher design, this loco No. 44* Yeoman Endeavour II *is built to the US loading gauge and cannot leave the confines of Merehead Quarry.* **CJM**

SNCF - French Railways

Address: ✉ Fret-SNCF, 10 Palace de Budapest, Paris, 75009
info@fret-sncf.com
ⓘ fret.sncf.com

Class 92

Vehicle Length: 70ft 1in (21.34m)
Height: 13ft 0in (3.95m)
Width: 8ft 8in (2.66m)
Power Collection: 25kV ac overhead / 750V dc third rail
Horsepower: ac - 6,700hp (5,000kW) / dc 5,360hp (4,000kW)
Electrical Equipment: Brush

Number	Depot	Pool	Livery	Owner	Operator	Name
92006	FN	-	SNF	SNF	SNF	Louis Armand
92014	FN	-	SNF	SNF	SNF	Emile Zola
92018	FN	-	SNF	SNF	SNF	Stendhal
92023	FN	-	SNF	SNF	SNF	Ravel
92033	FN	-	SNF	SNF	SNF	Berlioz

Right: *Under the original concept of the Channel Tunnel, three operators would own specific Class 92s: BR Railfreight, Fret-SNCF (French Railways) and European Passenger Services (EPS). After the demise of the plans for overnight through passenger workings the EPS fleet were stored, while the SNCF fleet operated with the UK fleet for a period. Fret-SNCF No. 92006 stands at the now closed North Pole depot.* **CJM**

Eurotunnel

Address (UK): ✉ The Channel Tunnel Group Ltd, UK Terminal, Ashford Road, Folkestone, CT18 8XX
info@eurotunnel.com
✆ 01303 282222
ⓘ www.eurotunnel.com

Chairman & CEO: Jacques Gounon
Depots: Coquelles, France (CO)

Freight – Europort2

Class 92

Vehicle Length: 70ft 1in (21.34m)
Height: 13ft 0in (3.95m)
Width: 8ft 8in (2.66m)
Power Collection: 25kV ac overhead / 750V dc third rail
Horsepower: ac - 6,700hp (5,000kW) / dc 5,360hp (4,000kW)
Electrical Equipment: Brush

Number	*Depot*	*Pool*	*Livery*	*Owner*	*Operator*	*Name*
92010	CO	PTXX	EU2	EU2	EU2	***Moliere***
92020	CO	PTXX	EU2	EU2	EU2	***Milton***
92021	CO	PTXX	EU2	EU2	EU2	***Purcell***
92028	CO	PTXX	EU2	EU2	EU2	***Saint Saens***
92032	CO	PTXX	EU2	EU2	EU2	***Cesar Franck***
92038	CO	PTXX	EU2	EU2	EU2	***Voltaire***
92040	CO	PTXX	EU2	EU2	EU2	***Goethe***
92043	CO	PTXX	EU2	EU2	EU2	***Debussy***
92044	CO	PTXX	EU2	EU2	EU2	***Couperin***
92045	CO	PTXX	EU2	EU2	EU2	***Chaucer***
92046	CO	PTXX	EU2	EU2	EU2	***Sweelinck***

Left: *Operating under the Europort2 name, the Channel Tunnel operator Eurotunnel has formed a freight operating arm to power through international freight trains via the Channel Tunnel. A total of 11 Class 92s have been sold to Eurotunnel and refurbished to their specification by Brush Traction. A freight operation is due to commence in 2010. No. 92032 'top and tailed' with 92038 form a Europort2 route training through Charing on 3 December 2009.* **Brian Stephenson**

Shuttle

All locomotives allocated to Eurotunnel Maintenance Facility in Coquelles, France, but can be stabled and receive light repair at Cheriton terminal in the UK.

Class 9/0

Vehicle Length: 72ft 2in (22m)
Height: 13ft 9in (4.20m)
Width: 9ft 9in (3.01m)
Power Collection: 25kV ac overhead
Horsepower: 7,720hp (5,760kW)
Electrical Equipment: Brush

Original loco order, many now rebuilt and upgraded to Class 9/8.

Number	Name
9005	***Jessye Norman***
9006	***Regine Crespin***
9007	***Dame Joan Sutherland***
9011	***José Van Dam***
9013	***Maria Callas***
9015	***Lötschberg 1913***
9018	***Wilhelmena Fernandez***
9022	***Dame Janet Baker***
9023	***Dame Elisabeth Legge-Schwarzkopf***
9024	***Gotthard 1882***
9026	***Furkatunnel 1982***
9027	***Barbara Hendricks***
9029	***Thomas Allan***
9031	
9033	***Montserrat Caballe***
9036	***Alan Fondary***
9037	***Gabriel Bacquier***
9040	

Eurotunnel

Class 9/1

Vehicle Length: 72ft 2in (22m)
Height: 13ft 9in (4.20m)
Width: 9ft 9in (3.01m)
Power Collection: 25kV ac overhead
Horsepower: 7,720hp (5,760kW)
Electrical Equipment: Brush

9101 9102 9103 9104 9105 9106 9107 9108 9109 9110 9111 9112 9113

Class 9/7

Vehicle Length: 72ft 2in (22m)
Height: 13ft 9in (4.20m)
Width: 9ft 9in (3.01m)
Power Collection: 25kV ac overhead
Horsepower: 9,387hp (7,000kW)
Electrical Equipment: Brush

9701 9702 9703 9704 9705 9706 9707

Class 9/8

Rebuilt from Class 9/0 locos, 800 added to original running number on conversion.

Vehicle Length: 72ft 2in (22m)
Height: 13ft 9in (4.20m)
Width: 9ft 9in (3.01m)
Power Collection: 25kV ac overhead
Horsepower: 9,387hp (7,000kW)
Electrical Equipment: Brush

9801	*Lesley Garrett*
9802	*Stuart Burrows*
9803	*Benjamin Luxon*
9804	*Victoria de Los Angeles*
9808	*Elisabeth Soderstrom*
9809	*Francois Pollet*
9810	*Jean-Philippe Courtis*
9812	*Luciano Pavarotti*
9814	*Lucia Pop*
9816	*Willard White*
9817	*José Carreras*
9819	*Maria Ewing*
9820	*Nicolai Ghiaurov*
9821	*Teresa Berganza*
9825	
9828	*Dame Kiri Te Kanawa*
9832	*Renata Tebaldi*
9834	*Mirella Freni*
9835	*Nicolai Gedda*
9838	*Hildegard Behrens*

Right: *The entire Eurotunnel fleet of passenger and freight 'Shuttle' locos are based at Coquelles depot in Calais, France. The facility carries out all but workshop overhauls, which are contracted to Brush Traction in the UK. A shuttle passenger loco and a double deck shuttle train is seen in sidings at the Coquelles maintenance facility.* **CJM**

MaK DE1004

Vehicle Length: 54ft 2in (16.50m)
Diesel Engine: MTU 12V396tc
Horsepower: 1,580hp (1,180kW)
Electrical Equipment: BBC

0001 0002 0003 0004 0005

Right: *Emergency rescue of both passenger and freight trains from within the Channel Tunnel, whether operated by EPS, Eurotunnel or the freight operators, falls to Eurotunnel who have a fleet of five Mak DE1004 locos based either side of the Channel Tunnel. These 1,580hp diesel-electric locos have both conventional and Scharfenberg auto couplers. Loco No. 0004 is seen at Coquelles depot.* **CJM**

Hunslet/Schöma

Diesel Engine: Deutz
Horsepower: 200hp (270kW)
Mechanical Equipment: Hunslet

0031	*Frances*
0032	*Elisabeth*
0033	*Silke*
0034	*Amanda*
0035	*Mary*
0036	*Lawrence*
0037	*Lydie*
0038	*Jenny*
0039	*Pacita*
0040	*Jill*
0041	*Kim*
0042	*Nicole*

Network Rail

Address: ✉ Kings Place, 90 York Way, London, N1 9AG
enquiries@networkrail.co.uk
✆ Helpline: 08457 114141, Switchboard: 0203 356 9595
ⓘ www.networkrail.co.uk

Chief Executive: Iain Coucher **Director Operatins:** Robin Gisby
Depot: Edinburgh Craigentinny (EC), Barrow Hill (BH), Derby (DF), Rugby (RU)

Class 31/1 & 31/4

Vehicle Length: 56ft 9in (17.29m)
Height: 12ft 7in (3.91m)
Width: 8ft 9in (2.65m)
31/4 Fitted with electric train heat
Engine: English Electric 12SVT
Horsepower: 1,470hp (1,097kW)
Electrical Equipment: Brush

Number	*Depot*	*Pool*	*Livery*	*Owner*	*Operator*
31105	**DF**	**QADD**	**NRL**	**NRL**	**NRL**
31233	**DF**	**QADD**	**NRL**	**NRL**	**NRL**
31285	**DF**	**QADD**	**NRL**	**NRL**	**NRL**

Number	*Depot*	*Pool*	*Livery*	*Owner*	*Operator*
31465 (31565, 31213)	**DF**	**QADD**	**NRL**	**NRL**	**NRL**

Left: *The Network Rail Class 31 fleet is allocated to the Railway Technical Centre, Derby and power test trains throughout England, Scotland and Wales. The locos have received some modifications for their departmental careers. All are painted in Network Rail yellow livery. No. 31233 is illustrated at Stratford.* **CJM**

Class 43

Vehicle Length: 58ft 5in (18.80m)
Height: 12ft 10in (3.90m)
Width: 8ft 11in (2.73m)
Engine: MTU 16V4000 R31R
Horsepower: 2,250hp (1,680kW)
Electrical Equipment: Brush

Number	*Depot*	*Pool*	*Livery*	*Owner*	*Operator*	*Name*
43013	**EC**	**QCAR**	**NER**	**PTR**	**NRL**	
43014	**EC**	**QCAR**	**NER**	**PTR**	**NRL**	
43062	**EC**	**QCAR**	**NER**	**PTR**	**NRL**	***John Armitt***

Left: *Network Rail's New Measurement Train or NMT operates over the principal main lines carrying out track assessment. Three Edinburgh Craigentinny-based Class 43s share work with the Mk3 test train. All power cars have been re-engined with the latest MTU 4000 engines. No. 43014 is illustrated. Note the nose end camera module.* **CJM**

Class 86

Vehicle Length: 58ft 6in (17.83m)
Height: 13ft 0⅝in (3.97m)
Width: 8ft 8¼in (2.64m)
Power Collection: 25kV ac overhead
Horsepower: 2,950hp (2,200kW)
Electrical Equipment: GEC

Number	*Depot*	*Pool*	*Livery*	*Owner*	*Operator*	*Name*
86424(S) (86024)	**CP**	**QSTR**	**NRL**	**NRL**	**-**	
86901 (86253)	**RU**	**QACL**	**NRL**	**NRL**	**NRL**	***Chief Engineer***
86902 (86210)	**RU**	**QACL**	**NRL**	**NRL**	**NRL**	***Rail Vehicle Engineering***

Right: *The two Network Rail Class 86/9 locos are usually used for overhead power line testing, as load banks to draw current from the overhead wires. Each loco retains one operational power bogie to enable it to be self propelled. The two are seen stabled in the south facing bay at York, during a period of deployment as overhead power contact rail ice scrapers.* **Nathan Williamson**

Class 37 & 97/3

Vehicle Length: 61ft 6in (18.74m)
Height: 13ft 0¼in (3.96m)
Width: 8ft 11⅝in (2.73m)
Engine: English Electric 12CSVT
Horsepower: 1,750hp (1,304kW)
Electrical Equipment: English Electric

Number	*Depot*	*Pool*	*Livery*	*Owner*	*Operator*	*Name*
37198	**BH**	**MBDL**	**NRL**	**NRL**	**NRL**	
97301 (37100)	**BH**	**QETS**	**NRL**	**NRL**	**NRL**	
97302 (37170)	**BH**	**QETS**	**NRL**	**NRL**	**NRL**	
97303 (37178)	**BH**	**QETS**	**NRL**	**NRL**	**NRL**	
97304 (37217)	**BH**	**QETS**	**NRL**	**NRL**	**NRL**	***John Tiley***

Right: *Four former Class 37/0s form the Class 97/3 sub-class. These locos, rebuilt by Barrow Hill are used by Network Rail for the development and testing of the European Railway Traffic Management System (ERTMS) equipment on the Cambrian Lines. The locos are basically a Class 37/0 fitted with cab signalling equipment. No. 97301 is seen passing Borth powering the 08.28 Shrewsbury Howard Street to Aberystwyth on 2 June 2009.* **Richard Jones**

Class 950

Vehicle Length: 64ft 9¾in (19.74m)
Height: 12ft 4½in (3.77m)
Width: 9ft 3⅛in (2.82m)
Engine: 1 x NT855R5 of 285hp per vehicle
Horsepower: 570hp (425kW)
Seats (total/car): 124S, 59S/65S

Number	*Formation*	*Depot*	*Livery*	*Owner*	*Operator*	*Note*
950001	**999600+999601**	**ZA**	**NRL**	**NRL**	**NRL**	*Track assessment train (Class 150 outline)*

Right: *The Class 150/1 outline Network Rail track inspection DMU operates throughout the UK network. One vehicle is basically a passenger carrying vehicle, while the other is an instrumentation and generator coach. The set, No. 950001, is recorded at Newton Abbot, viewed from the instrumentation end.* **Nathan Williamson**

Network Rail

Eurorailscout

Formation	Depot	Livery	Owner	Operator	Notes
999700 + 999701	ZA	NRL	NRL	NRL	Purpose-built Plasser & Theurer UFM160 track inspection machine

■ *This set was transferred to Mainland Europe for track testing work in December 2009.*

Left: *The Network Rail-operated EuroRailScout DMU-based track inspection train, built by Plasser & Theurer of type UFM160, has operated throughout the UK rail network. On 2 November 2006 it was captured passing Charing, Kent while operating over South Eastern tracks.* **Brian Stephenson**

Class 960

Length: 64ft 6in (19.66m)
Height: 12ft 8½in (3.87m)
Width: 9ft 3in (2.81m)
Engine: 2 x Leyland 150hp
Horsepower: 300hp (224kW)
Seats (total/car): None

Number	Formation	Depot	Livery	Owner	Operator	Notes
960201(S)	977975	CF	NRL	NRL	(ATW)	Ex Class 121 55027, Severn Tunnel Train
960202(S)	977976	CF	NRL	NRL	(ATW)	Ex Class 121 55031, Severn Tunnel Train

Left: *Currently stored at Cardiff Canton are the two former Class 121 'bubble' cars converted in the 1990s as a Severn Tunnel emergency train. Considerable structural modification work was done for the emergency train use which has rendered the stock unsuitable for any other deployment.* **Chris Perkins**

De-Icing Cars

Vehicle Length: 66ft 4in (20.22m)
Height: 12ft 4in (3.75m)
Width: 9ft 2in (2.82m)
Horsepower: 500hp (370kW)
Seats (total/car): None

Number	Vehicle	Depot	Livery	Owner	Operator	Notes
489102	68501 (977975)	TN	NRL	NRL	NRL	De-icing vehicle modified from Class 489 DMBS
489105	68504	TN	NRL	GBR	GBR	De-icing vehicle modified from Class 489 DMBS
489106	68505	TN	NRL	GBR	GBR	De-icing vehicle modified from Class 489 DMBS
489109	68508 (977976)	TN	NRL	NRL	NRL	De-icing vehicle modified from Class 489 DMBS

Left: *Former Gatwick Express GLV converted to a de-icing unit No. 68508 leads GBRf Class 73/2 No. 73204 and two further de-icing GLVs, Nos. 68504 and 68505, with a Tonbridge to Dover training run returning back to Tonbridge at Folkestone Warren on 12 January 2008.* **Brian Stephenson**

Hauled Stock

Royal Train

Mk2	
Vehicle Length: 66ft 0in (20.11m)	Height: 12ft 9½in (3.89m)
	Width: 9ft 3in (2.81m)

Mk 3	
Vehicle Length: 75ft 0in (22.86m)	Height: 12ft 9in (3.88m)
	Width: 8ft 11in (2.71m)

Number	Type	Depot	Livery	Operator	Use
2903 (11001)	AT5G	ZN	ROY	NRL/DBS	HM The Queen's Saloon
2904 (12001)	AT5G	ZN	ROY	NRL/DBS	HRH The Duke of Edinburgh's Saloon
2915 (10735)	AT5G	ZN	ROY	NRL/DBS	Royal Household Sleeping Coach
2916 (40512)	AT5G	ZN	ROY	NRL/DBS	HRH The Prince of Wales's Dining Coach
2917 (40514)	AT5G	ZN	ROY	NRL/DBS	Kitchen Car and Royal Household Dining Coach
2918 (40515)	AT5G	ZN	ROY	NRL/DBS	Royal Household Coach
2919 (40518)	AT5G	ZN	ROY	NRL/DBS	Royal Household Coach
2920 (17109)	AT5B	ZN	ROY	NRL/DBS	Generator Coach and Household Sleeping Coach
2921 (17107)	AT5B	ZN	ROY	NRL/DBS	Brake, Coffin Carrier and Household Accommodation
2922	AT5G	ZN	ROY	NRL/DBS	HRH The Prince of Wales's Sleeping Coach
2923	AT5G	ZN	ROY	NRL/DBS	Royal Passenger Saloon

Above: *HM The Queen's saloon No. 2903, rebuilt from prototype HST body shell No. 11001 is viewed from the state entrance end with double inward opening doors at Totnes.* **Nathan Williamson**

Hauled Stock

Number	Type	Depot	Livery	Operator	Use
1205 (6348)	AJIF/RFO	ZA	VIR	NRL	Out of use
1256 (3296)	AJIF/RFO	ZA	NRL	NRL	Special vehicle
5981	AC2F/TSO	ZA	NRL	NRL	Special vehicle
6260 (92116)	AX51/GEN	ZA(S)	RTK	NRL	Generator
6261 (92988)	AX51/GEN	ZA	NRL	NRL	Generator
6262 (92928)	AX51/GEN	ZA(S)	NRL	NRL	Generator
9481	AE2D/BSO	ZA	NRL	NRL	Radio survey coach
9701 (9528)	AF2F/DBSO	ZA	NRL	NRL	Remote driving car (Mentor train)
9702 (9510)	AF2F/DBSO	ZA	NRL	NRL	Remote driving car
9703 (9517)	AF2F/DBSO	ZA	NRL	NRL	Remote driving car
9708 (9530)	AF2F/DBSO	ZA	NRL	NRL	Remote driving car (Structure Gauging)
9714 (9536)	AF2F/DBSO	ZA	NRL	NRL	Remote driving car
72612 (6156)	Mk2f/TSO	ZA	RTB	NRL	Brake force runner
72616 (6007)	Mk2f/TSO	ZA	NRL	NRL	Brake force runner
72630 (6094)	Mk2f/TSO	ZA	NRL	NRL	Brake force runner
72631 (6096)	Mk2f/TSO	ZA	NRL	NRL	Brake force runner
72639 (6070)	Mk2f/TSO	ZA	NRL	NRL	Brake force runner
80211(S)	Mk1/COU	ZA	NRL	NRL	Special vehicle
92114 (81443)	Mk1/BG	ZA	NRL	NRL	Special vehicle
92939 (92039)	Mk1/BG	ZA	INT	NRL	Special vehicle
96210 (96159)	Mk1/BG	ZA	INT	NRL	Special vehicle

Network Rail

99666 (3250)	Mk2e/FO	ZA	NRL	NRL	Ultrasonic Test Train
975025 (60755)	6B Buffet	ZA	GRN	NRL	Control Inspection Saloon *Caroline*
975081 (35313)	Mk1/BSK	ZA	NRL	NRL	Structure Gauging Train
975091 (34615)	Mk1/BSK	ZA	NRL	NRL	Overhead line test coach
975280 (21263)	Mk1/BCK	ZA	NRL	NRL	Staff coach
975464 (35171)	Mk1/BSK	IS	NRL	NRL	Snowblower coach *Ptarmigan*
975486 (34100)	Mk1/BSK	IS	NRL	NRL	Snowblower coach *Polar Bear*
975494 (35082)	Mk1/BSK	MG	NRL	NRL	Re-Railing Train (Margam)
975573 (34729)	Mk1/BSK	MG	NRL	NRL	Re-Railing Train (Margam)
975574 (34599)	Mk1/BSK	TO	NRL	NRL	Re-Railing Train (Toton)
975611 (80915)	Mk1/BG	TO	NRL	NRL	Re-Railing Train (Toton)
975612 (80922)	Mk1/BG	MG	NRL	NRL	Re-Railing Train (Margam)
975613 (80918)	Mk1/BG	TO	NRL	NRL	Re-Railing Train (Toton)
975814 (41000)	HST/TF	EC	NRL	NRL	NMT Conference coach
975984 (40000)	HST/TRUB	EC	NRL	NRL	NMT Lecture coach
977337 (9395)	Mk2/BSO	ZA	NRL	NRL	Track recording - Staff coach
977868 (5846)	Mk2e/TSO	ZA	NRL	NRL	Radio Survey coach
977869 (5858)	Mk2e/TSO	ZA	NRL	NRL	Radio Survey coach
977969 (14112)	Mk2/BFK	ZA	NRL	NRL	Staff coach (Former Royal Saloon 2906)
977974 (5854)	Mk2e/TSO	ZA	NRL	NRL	Laboratory coach (Owned by Delta Rail)
977983 (3407)	Mk2f/FO	ZA	NRL	NRL	Hot Box Detection coach
977984 (40501)	HST/TRFK	EC	NRL	NRL	NMT Staff coach
977985 (6019)	Mk2f/TSO	ZA	NRL	NRL	Structure Gauging Train
977986 (3189)	Mk2d/FO	ZA	NRL	NRL	Track Recording coach
977990 (92937)	Mk1/BG	SP	NRL	NRL	Tool Van
977991 (92991)	Mk1/BG	SP	NRL	NRL	Tool Van
977993 (44053)	HST/TGS	EC	NRL	NRL	NMT Overhead Line Test coach
977994 (44087)	HST/TGS	EC	NRL	NRL	NMT Recording coach
977995 (40719)	HST/TRFM	EC	NRL	NRL	NMT Generator coach
977996 (44062)	HST/TGS	EC	NRL	NRL	NMT Battery coach
977997 (72613)	Mk2f/TSO	ZA	NRL	NRL	Radio Survey Test Vehicle (originally TSO 6126)
999508	Saloon	ZA	NRL	NRL	Track Recording coach
999550	Mk2	ZA	NRL	NRL	Track Recording coach (Purpose built)
999602 (62483)	Mk1/REP	ZA	NRL	SEC	Ultrasonic Test coach, also known as UTC2
999605 (62482)	Mk1/REP	ZA	NRL	NRL	Ultrasonic Test coach
999606 (62356)	Mk1/REP	ZA	NRL	NRL	Ultrasonic Test coach

Left: *Former British Rail BG luggage van No. 92899 has been taken over by Network Rail and is now a generator support coach for a track inspection train. The bodywork still retains four double leaf luggage van doors each side and a central guard's door, but additional ventilation grilles have been made in the bodywork at both ends. Additional power jumper cables have been installed on coach ends. No. 6261 is seen at Bristol Temple Meads in January 2009.* **CJM**

Right: *This former BR Officer's Inspection Coach No. 999508 is now a track recording vehicle and has received suitable body side modifications. Seen at Stratford, instrumentation equipment can be seen on the leading bogie. The coach no longer has certification to be propelled as a leading vehicle, as it would have in the days of an officer's inspection saloon.* **CJM**

Snowploughs

Independent Drift Ploughs

Number	Allocation
ADB965203	Thornaby
ADB965206	Doncaster
ADB965208	Inverness
ADB965209	Bristol Barton H
ADB965210	Tonbridge
ADB965211	Wigan
ADB965217	Mossend
ADB965219	Mossend
ADB965223	Margam
ADB965224	Carlisle
ADB965230	Carlisle
ADB965231	Bristol Barton H
ADB965232	Peterborough
ADB965233	Peterborough
ADB965234	Mossend
ADB965235	Margam
ADB965236	Tonbridge
ADB965237	Wigan
ADB965240	Inverness
ADB965241	Doncaster
ADB965242	Thornaby
ADB965243	Mossend

Right: *Although in the UK we rarely have enough snow these days to require the use of snowploughs, some 22 are still maintained operational by Network Rail. These are allocated in pairs to the principal depots and top either end of a locomotive. Under TOPS classification these ploughs are type ZZA. Nos. ADB965209 and ADB965231 are seen at Bristol Barton Hill depot.* **Tony Christie**

Beilhack Patrol Ploughs (ex-Class 40 bogies)

Right: *In the 1980s 10 Beilhack Patrol ploughs were converted from former Class 40 bogies with added weight blocks; these have seen little use. No. 965579 from Carlisle is illustrated.* **CJM**

Number	Allocation
ADB965576	Mossend
ADB965577	Mossend
ADB965578	Carlisle
ADB965579	Carlisle
ADB965580	Wigan
ADB965581	Wigan
ADB966096	Doncaster
ADB866097	Doncaster
ADB966098	Peterborough
ADB966099	Peterborough

Snow Blowers

Right: *Network Rail operate two high-output snowblowers for dealing with deep drifts. These self propelled units are usually allocated to Motherwell but could operate at any location in the UK. No. 968500 is illustrated with its support train at Ilford.* **CJM**

Number	Allocation
ADB968500	Motherwell
ADB968501	Motherwell

Recovery Cranes

Number	Allocation
ADRC96709 (S)	Thornaby
ADRC96710 (S)	Eastleigh
ADRC96713	Wigan
ADRC96714	Margam
ADRC96715	Toton

Right: *Cowans Sheldon 75 ton recovery crane No. 96713 allocated to Wigan still carries its former depot logo of a Crewe cat when photographed at Taunton in early 2009.* **Kevin Wills**

Multiple Purpose Vehicles MPV

DR97011	High Speed 1 (HS1)
DR97012	High Speed 1 (HS1)
DR97013	High Speed 1 (HS1)
DR97014	High Speed 1 (HS1)
DR98001	West Coast Electrification
DR98002	West Coast Electrification
DR98003	West Coast Electrification
DR98004	West Coast Electrification
DR98005	West Coast Electrification
DR98006	West Coast Electrification
DR98007	West Coast Electrification
DR98008	West Coast Electrification
DR98009	West Coast Electrification
DR98010	West Coast Electrification
DR98011	West Coast Electrification
DR98012	West Coast Electrification
DR98013	West Coast Electrification
DR98014	West Coast Electrification
DR98901+DR98951	Prototype set
DR98902+DR98952	Prototype set
DR98903+DR98953	Prototype set
DR98904+DR98954	Prototype set
DR98905+DR98955	Production set
DR98906+DR98956	Production set
DR98907+DR98957	Production set
DR98908+DR98958	Production set
DR98909+DR98959	Production set
DR98910+DR98960	Production set
DR98911+DR98961	Production set
DR98912+DR98962	Production set
DR98913+DR98963	Production set
DR98914+DR98964	Production set
DR98915+DR98965	Production set
DR98916+DR98966	Production set
DR98917+DR98967	Production set
DR98918+DR98968	Production set
DR98919+DR98969	Production set
DR98920+DR98970	Production set
DR98921+DR98971	Production set
DR98922+DR98972	Production set
DR98923+DR98973	Production set
DR98924+DR98974	Production set
DR98925+DR98975	Production set
DR98926+DR98976	Production set
DR98927+DR98977	Production set
DR98928+DR98978	Production set
DR98929+DR98979	Production set
DR98930+DR98980	Production set
DR98931+DR98981	Production set
DR98932+DR98982	Production set

Below: *Introduced by Railtrack/Network Rail to replace older departmental stock, the Multiple Purpose Vehicles (MPVs) were built by Windhoff in Germany in the 1990s, introduced as two-vehicle sets. A subsequent order for 14 overhead wiring and electrification vehicles were built for West Coast use and four numbered in the DR970xx series for engineering work on HighSpeed 1 between London and the Channel Tunnel. Set No. 98971 + 98921 are seen at Eastleigh loaded with rail cleaning modules.* **CJM**

Serco Railtest

Address: ✉ Derwent House, RTC Business Park, London Road, Derby, DE24 8UP
enquiries@serco.com
✆ 01332 262626
ⓘ www.serco.com

Managing Director: William Roxby Robson, **Depot:** Derby RTC (ZA)

Class 08

Vehicle Length: 29ft 3in (8.91m)
Height: 12ft 8⅝in (3.87m)
Width: 8ft 6in (2.59m)
Engine: English Electric 6K
Horsepower: 400hp (298kW)
Electrical Equipment: English Electric

Number	*Depot*	*Pool*	*Livery*	*Owner*	*Operator*
08417	**ZA**	**CDJD**	**SEC**	**SEC**	**SEC**
08956	**ZA**	**CDJD**	**BLU**	**SEC**	**SEC**

Hauled Stock

Mk2
Vehicle Length: 66ft 0in (20.11m)
Height: 12ft 9½in (3.89m)
Width: 9ft 3in (2.81m)

Mk1 (NPCCS)
Vehicle Length: 57ft 0in (17.73m)
Height: 12ft 9in (3.88m)
Width: 9ft 3in (2.81m)

Number	*Type*	*Depot*	*Livery*	*Owner*	*Operator*
5854	**AC2E/TSO**	**ZA**	**VIR**	**AEA**	**SEC**
6263 (92961)	**AX51/GEN**	**ZA**	**YEL**	**NRL**	**SEC**
6264 (92923)	**AX51/GEN**	**ZA**	**YEL**	**NRL**	**SEC**

Carillion Rail

Address: ✉ 24 Birch Street, Wolverhampton, WV1 4HY
railenquiries@carillionplc.com
✆ 01902 422431
ⓘ www.carillionrail.com

Managing Director: Adam Green, **Depot:** Preston (PR)

Hauled Stock

Mk1
Vehicle Length: 64ft 6in (19.65m)
Height: 12ft 9½in (3.89m)
Width: 9ft 3in (2.81m)

Number	*Type*	*Depot*	*Livery*	*Operator*	*Use*
975699 (35105)	**Mk1/BSK**	**PR**	**BLW**	**CAR**	**Overhead Line Maintainence Train**
975700 (34138)	**Mk1/BSK**	**PR**	**BLW**	**CAR**	**Overhead Line Maintainence Train**
975714 (25466)	**Mk1/SK**	**PR**	**BLW**	**CAR**	**Overhead Line Maintainence Train**
975724 (16079)	**Mk1/CK**	**PR**	**BLW**	**CAR**	**Overhead Line Maintainence Train**
975734 (25695)	**Mk1/SK**	**PR**	**BLW**	**CAR**	**Overhead Line Maintainence Train**
975744 (25440)	**Mk1/SK**	**PR**	**BLW**	**CAR**	**Overhead Line Maintainence Train**

Balfour Beatty Rail Services

Address: ✉ 130 Wilton Road, London, SW1V 4LQ
info@bbrail.com
✆ 0207 216 6800
ⓘ www.bbrail.com

Managing Director: Peter Anderson, **Depot:** Ashford (AD)

Hauled Stock

Mk1
Vehicle Length: 64ft 6in (19.65m)
Height: 12ft 9½in (3.89m)
Width: 9ft 3in (2.81m)

Number	*Type*	*Depot*	*Livery*	*Operator*	*Use*
977163 (35487)	**Mk1/BSK**	**AD**	**BBR**	**BBR**	**Staff & Generator coach**
977165 (35408)	**Mk1/BSK**	**AD**	**BBR**	**BBR**	**Staff & Generator coach**
977166 (35419)	**Mk1/BSK**	**AD**	**BBR**	**BBR**	**Staff & Generator coach**
977167 (35400)	**Mk1/BSK**	**AD**	**BBR**	**BBR**	**Staff & Generator coach**
977168 (35289)	**Mk1/BSK**	**AD**	**BBR**	**BBR**	**Staff & Generator coach**

Alstom Transport

Address: ✉ PO Box 70, Newbold Road, Rugby, Warwickshire, CV21 2WR
info@transport.alstom.com, ✆ 01788 577111, ⓘ www.transport.alstom.com
Managing Director: Paul Robinson
Depot: Chester (CH), Liverpool - Edge Hill (LL), Manchester - Longsight (MA), Wolverhampton - Oxley (OY), Wembley (WB)

Class 08

Vehicle Length: 29ft 3in (8.91m)
Height: 12ft 8⅝in (3.87m)
Width: 8ft 6in (2.59m)
Engine: English Electric 6K
Horsepower: 400hp (298kW)
Electrical Equipment: English Electric

Number	Depot	Pool	Livery	Owner	Operator
08451(S)	AT	ATZZ	GBF	ALS	-
08454	WB	ATLO	BLK	ALS	ALS
08611	AT	ATLO	VT1	ALS	ALS
08617	WB	ATLO	BLK	ALS	ALS
08696	AT	ATLO	GRN	ALS	ALS
08721	AT	ATLO	BLU	ALS	ALS
08790	AT	ATLO	BLU	ALS	ALS
08887(S)	AT	ATZZ	BLK	ALS	-
08934	WB	ATLO	BLK	ALS	ALS

Names applied 08696 *Longsight TMD*, 08721 *M A Smith*, 08790 *Starlet*

Bombardier Transportation

Address: ✉ Litchurch Lane, Derby, DE24 8AD
info@bombardier.com, ✆ 01332 344666, ⓘ www.bombardier.com
Chief Country Representative: Colin Walton
Works: Derby (ZD), Crewe (ZC)

Class 08

Technical data as above

Number	Depot	Pool	Livery	Owner	Operator	Name
08682	ZD	INDL	GRN	BOM	BOM	*Lionheart*
08846	ZD	INDL	BOM	BOM	BOM	

Class 423 (4VEP)

Vehicle Length: 64ft 6in (19.65m)
Height: 12ft 11in (3.93m)
Width: 9ft 0in (2.74m)
Horsepower: 1000hp (745.7kW)
Seats (total/car): Nil
Tractor unit for internal use

Number	Formation DTC+TSO+MBS+DTC	Depot	Livery	Owner	Operator
(42)3905	76397+70904+62266+76398	AF	COX	BOM	BOM (Chart Leaon depot pilot)
(42)3918	76527+70950+62321+76528	AF	COX	BOM	BOM (Chart Leaon depot pilot)

Class 424
Classic

Vehicle Length: 64ft 6in (19.65m)
Height: 12ft 11in (3.93m)
Width: 9ft 0in (2.74m)
Horsepower: Un-powered
Seats (total/car): 64S
Demonstrator vehicle

Number	Formation	Depot	Livery	Owner	Operator	Use
424001(S)	76112	ZB	SIL	BOM	-	Networker Classic demonstrator

Left: *Rebuilt from the frame of a Class 421 (4-CIG) driving car, the Bombardier 'Classic' was one of the many offerings to the rail industry as a low-cost replacement for slam-door stock principally used by the three South-Thames operators. The coach was fully completed at Derby and shown off to potential customers at various locations. One of the most interesting points of this vehicle is that it retained its original Southern Region style semi-rotary power controller and five position ep/Westinghouse brake valve.* **CJM**

Brush-Barclay Ltd

Address: ✉ Caledonia Works, West Langlands Street, Kilmarnock, Ayrshire, Scotland, KA1 2QD

sales@brushtraction.com ✆ 01563 523573, ⓘ www.brushtraction.com

Managing Director: John Bidewell

Right: *The present Brush-Barclay Works in Kilmarnock was previously the Hunslet-Barclay factory, responsible for many major rebuild and refurbishment contracts in recent years, including the Class 155-153 rebuild, the conversion of the PCVs and refurbishment of Scottish EMUs. Class 320 No. 320302 in seen inside the main shop during rebuild.* **CJM**

For Brush Traction - See Train Builders section

Knights Rail Services

Address: ✉ Shoeburyness: Building D23, MoD Shoeburyness, Blackgate Road, Shoeburyness, Essex. SS3 9SR

Eastleigh: Eastleigh Rail Works, Campbell Road, Eastleigh, Hampshire, SO50 5AD

gosborne@knightsrail.co.uk ✆ 01702 299631, ⓘ www.rail-services.net

Managing Director: Bruce Knights

Depots: Eastleigh (ZG), Shoeburyness (SN)

Class 07

Vehicle Length: 26ft 9½in (8.16m)
Height: 12ft 10in (3.91m)
Width: 8ft 6in (2.59m)
Engine: Paxman 6RPHL MkIII
Horsepower: 275hp (205kW)
Electrical Equipment: AEI

Number	*Depot*	*Pool*	*Livery*	*Owner*	*Operator*
07007 (D2991)	**ZG**	**MBDL**	**BLU**	**KRS**	**KRS**

Right: *Originally built in the 1960s by Ruston as diesel-electric shunters for Southampton Docks, this class of shunting locomotive has been associated with Eastleigh ever since, with this example D2991 - TOPS No. 07007 having never left the area from delivery. The loco is seen at Eastleigh Works during the 2009 open weekend.* **Nathan Williamson**

Knights Rail Services

Class 73/1

Vehicle Length: 53ft 8in (16.35m)	*Power: 750V dc third rail or English Electric 6K*
Height: 12ft $5^{5}/_{16}$in (3.79m)	*Horsepower: electric - 1,600hp (1,193kW)*
Width: 8ft 8in (2.64m)	*Horsepower: diesel - 600hp (447kW)*
	Electrical Equipment: English Electric

Number	*Depot*	*Pool*	*Livery*	*Owner*	*Operator*	*Name*
73119	**ZG**	**MBDL**	**BLU**	**KRS**	**KRS**	***Borough of Eastleigh***

Left: *Knights Rail Services Class 73/1 No. 73119* Borough of Eastleigh *has been restored to 1970s BR rail blue, but has a Group Standard headlight and roof mounted aerial. The loco is usually kept at Eastleigh Works.* **Mark Sheen**

Class 421 (4-CIG)

Vehicle Length: 64ft $9^{1}/_{2}$in (19.75m)	*Horsepower: 1,000hp (740kW)*
Height: 12ft $9^{1}/_{4}$in (3.89m)	*Seats (total/car): 42F-192S, 18F-36S/56S/72S/24F-28S*
Width: 9ft 3in (2.81m)	

Number	*Formation* DTC+TSO+MBS+DTC	*Depot*	*Livery*	*Owner*	*Operator*
(42)1881(S)	**76833+71080+62400+76762**	**ZG**	**SWT**	**KRS**	-
(42)1884(S)	**76838+76767**	**ZG**	**SWT**	**KRS**	-

Railcare Ltd

Address: ✉ Wolverton Works, Stratford Road, Wolverton, Milton Keynes, MK12 5NT
info@railcare.com ✆ 08000 741122, ⓘ www.railcare.com

Managing Director: Colin Love

Depot: Glasgow (ZH), Wolverton (ZN)

Class 08

Vehicle Length: 29ft 3in (8.91m)	*Engine: English Electric 6K*
Height: 12ft $8^{5}/_{8}$in (3.87m)	*Horsepower: 400hp (298kW)*
Width: 8ft 6in (2.59m)	*Electrical Equipment: English Electric*

Number	*Depot*	*Pool*	*Livery*	*Owner*	*Operator*	*Name*
08568	**ZH**	**RCZH**	**ALS**	**RCL**	**RCL**	***St Rollox***
08629	**ZN**	**RCZN**	**ROY**	**RCL**	**RCL**	
08649	**ZN**	**RCZN**	**WEX**	**RCL**	**RCL**	***G H Stratton***
08730	**ZH**	**RCZH**	**ALS**	**RCL**	**RCL**	***The Caley***

Left: *Railcare Ltd operate two ex-BR Class 08s at their St Rollox facility in Glasgow; both are painted in two-tone grey and carry local railway names* St Rollox *and* The Caley*. No. 08730 is seen in the works yard in early 2009.* **Bill Wilson**

Rail Vehicle Engineering Ltd

Address: ✉ Vehicles Workshop, RTC Business Park, London Road, Derby, DE24 8UP
enquiries@rvel.co.uk ✆ 01332 331210, ⓘ www.rvel.co.uk

Managing Director: Andy Lynch
Depot: Derby (DF)

Class 31/1

Vehicle Length: 56ft 9in (17.29m)
Height: 12ft 7in (3.91m)
Width: 8ft 9in (2.65m)
Engine: English Electric 12SVT
Horsepower: 1,470hp (1,097kW)
Electrical Equipment: Brush

Number	*Depot*	*Pool*	*Livery*	*Owner*	*Operator*
31106	**DF**	**RVLO**	**BLU**	**HJA**	**RVE**

Class 31/4

Vehicle Length: 56ft 9in (17.29m)
Height: 12ft 7in (3.91m)
Width: 8ft 9in (2.65m)
Fitted with electric train heat
Engine: English Electric 12SVT
Horsepower: 1,470hp (1,097kW)
Electrical Equipment: Brush

Number		*Depot*	*Pool*	*Livery*	*Owner*	*Operator*	*Name*
31454	**(31554, 31228)**	**DF**	**RVLO**	**ICS**	**RMS**	**RVE**	
31459	**(31256)**	**DF**	**RVLO**	**BLK**	**RVE**	**RVE**	***Cerberus***
31468(S)	**(31568, 31321)**	**DF**	**RVLS**	**BLK**	**RMS**	**RVE**	***Hydra***

Class 31/6

Vehicle Length: 56ft 9in (17.29m)
Height: 12ft 7in (3.91m)
Width: 8ft 9in (2.65m)
Fitted with through wiring
Engine: English Electric 12SVT
Horsepower: 1,470hp (1,097kW)
Electrical Equipment: Brush

Number	*Depot*	*Pool*	*Livery*	*Owner*	*Operator*	*Name*
31601 (31186)	**DF**	**RVLO**	**WES**	**RMS**	**RVE**	***Gauge 'O' Guild 1956-2006***
31602 (31191)	**DF**	**RVLO**	**NRL**	**HAN**	**RVE**	***Driver Dave Green 19B***

Above: *Derby-based Rail Vehicle Engineering, an off-shoot of the former FM Rail, operates a number of locos for specialist hire duties such as to Network Rail to power track inspection and test trains. No. 31602 with its unique steam style rounded nameplate* Driver Dave Green 19B *is seen passing Stratford with a single test coach and another Class 31.* **CJM**

Class 56/3

Vehicle Length: 63ft 6in (19.35m)
Height: 13ft 0in (3.96m)
Width: 9ft 2in (2.79m)
Engine: Ruston Paxman 16RK3CT
Horsepower: 3,250hp (2,420kW)
Electrical Equipment: Brush

Number	*Depot*	*Pool*	*Livery*	*Owner*	*Operator*
56303 (56125)	**DF**	**RVLO**	**GRN**	**RVE**	**COL**

Siemens Transportation

Address: ✉ Kings Heath Traincare Facility, Heathfield Way, Kings Heath, Northampton, NN5 7QP
enquiries@siemenstransportation.co.uk ✆ 01604 594500
ⓘ www.siemenstransportation.co.uk

Managing Director UK: Steve Scrimshaw

Depot: Adwick, Manchester (AK), Kings Heath, Northampton (NN), Northam, Southampton (NT)

Class 01 & Unclassified

Number	*Depot*	*Pool*	*Livery*	*Owner*	*Operator*	*Notes*
01551 (H016)	**AK**	**MBDL**	**WAB**	**WAB**	**SIE**	**Operated at Adwick**
Loopy Lou	**NT**	**MBDL**	**SIE**	**SIE**	**SIE**	**Operated at Northam**

Below: *A view inside the Siemens/ South West Trains depot at Northam near Southampton, with Class 450 'Desiro' sets Nos. 450019 and 450013, plus depot pilot* Loopy Lou. **CJM**

Barrier Wagons

Number	*Depot*	*Pool*	*Livery*	*Owner*	*Operator*	*Notes*
6321 (96385, 86515)	**NN**	**SIEM**	**BLU**	**SIE**	**FLR**	**Desiro stock barrier wagon**
6322 (93686, 86859)	**NN**	**SIEM**	**BLU**	**SIE**	**FLR**	**Desiro stock barrier wagon**
6323 (96387, 86973)	**NN**	**SIEM**	**BLU**	**SIE**	**FLR**	**Desiro stock barrier wagon**
6324 (96388, 86562)	**NN**	**SIEM**	**BLU**	**SIE**	**FLR**	**Desiro stock barrier wagon**
6325 (96389, 86135)	**NN**	**SIEM**	**BLU**	**SIE**	**FLR**	**Desiro stock barrier wagon**

Left: *Converted from withdrawn BG stock, the present Desiro barrier wagons were rebuilt to act as barrier trucks to Eurostar stock, fitted with conventional drawgear at one end and a drop head Scharfenberg coupler at the other. After Eurostar use ceased, the vehicles were sold to Siemens to act as barrier vehicles for the electric and diesel 'Desiro' builds. Barrier No. 6322 is seen at Bournemouth.* **CJM**

Wabtec

Address: ✉ PO Box 400, Doncaster Works, Hexthorpe Road, Doncaster, DN1 1SL
wabtecrail@wabtec.com ✆ 01302 340700, ⓘ www.wabtecrail.co.uk

Managing Director: John Meehan
Depot: Doncaster (ZB)

Class 08

Vehicle Length: 29ft 3in (8.91m)
Height: 12ft 8⅝in (3.87m)
Width: 8ft 6in (2.59m)
Engine: English Electric 6K
Horsepower: 400hp (298kW)
Electrical Equipment: English Electric

Number	*Depot*	*Pool*	*Livery*	*Owner*	*Operator*	*Name*
08472	**ZB**	**RFSH**	**GNE**	**WAB**	**NXE**	
08571	**ZB**	**RFSH**	**WAB**	**WAB**	**NXE**	
08596(S)	**ZB**	**RFSH**	**WAB**	**WAB**	**NXE**	
08615	**ZB**	**RFSH**	**WAB**	**WAB**	**NXE**	
08669	**ZB**	**RFSH**	**WAB**	**WAB**	**WAB**	***Bob Machin***
08724	**ZB**	**RFSH**	**WAB**	**WAB**	**WAB**	
08764	**ZB**	**MBDL**	**BLU**	**WAB**	**TRN**	***Old Tom***
08853	**ZB**	**RFSH**	**BLU**	**WAB**	**WAB**	
08871(S)	**ZB**	**RFSH**	**COT**	**WAB**	**WAB**	
08927(S)	**ZB**	**TTLS**	**EWS**	**WAB**	**DBS**	

Pullman Group

Address: ✉ Train Maintenance Depot, Leckwith Road, Cardiff, CF11 8HP
sales@pullmans.net ✆ 029 2036 8850, ⓘ www.pullmans.net

Managing Director: Colin Robinson
Depots: Cardiff Canton

Class 08

Vehicle Length: 29ft 3in (8.91m)
Height: 12ft 8⅝in (3.87m)
Width: 8ft 6in (2.59m)
Engine: English Electric 6K
Horsepower: 400hp (298kW)
Electrical Equipment: English Electric

Number	*Depot*	*Pool*	*Livery*	*Owner*	*Operator*
08499	**CF**	**WSXX**	**BLU**	**DBS**	**PUL**

Owned by DBS, Class 08 No. 08499 is outbased at Pullman Rail, Cardiff where it is used to shunt the company's repair facility. CJM

Europhoenix Ltd

Address: ✉ 58A High Street, Stony Stratford, Milton Keynes, MK11 1AX
info@europhoenix.eu ✆ 01467 624366, ⓘ www.europhoenix.eu

Facilities: Europhoenix purchased the redundant Class 86 locos released from traffic by introduction of new multiple unit rolling stock. The locos are offered to Continental European operators fully refurbished and modified to suit customer needs.

Class 86

Vehicle Length: 58ft 6in (17.83m)
Height: 13ft 0⅝in (3.97m)
Width: 8ft 8¼in (2.64m)
Power Collection: 25kV ac overhead
Horsepower: 5,900hp (4,400kW)
Electrical Equipment: GEC

Number	*Location*	*Hire to*
86212	LM	-
86215	LM	-
86217	LM	-
86218	LM	-
86223	LM	-
86226	LM	-
86228	LM	-
86229	LM	-
86230	LM	-
86231	LM	-
86232	LM	-
86233	LM	-
86234	LM	-
86235	LM	-
86242	LM	-
86245	LM	-
86246	LM	-
86247	LM	-
86248	XX	Floyd (Hungary)
86250	XX	Floyd (Hungary)
86251	LM	-
86701 (86205)	CP*	ETL
86702 (86260)	CP*	ETL

* Spot hire loco, operated by Electric Traction Services

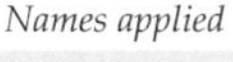

Names applied

86701 ***Orion***
86702 ***Cassiopeia***

Left: *Painted in the spectacular Europhoenix livery, No. 86247 is a demonstrator loco to the Class 86 re-engineering project and is seen at Long Marston. Note the roof level marker light, removal of electric train heat (supply) equipment and new headlight marker/tail light groups.* **CJM**

Porterbrook

Address: ✉ Burdett House, Becket Street, Derby, DE1 1JP
enquiries@porterbrook.co.uk ✆ 01332 262405, ⓘ www.porterbrook.co.uk

Managing Director: Paul Francis

Facilities: Porterbrook Leasing have made available the off-lease Class 87s to mainland European operators, with a significant number being exported to operate in Bulgaria.

Stored in the UK

Number	*Owner*	*Location*
87009	PTR	LM
87011	PTR	LM
87017	PTR	LM
87018	PTR	LM
87020	PTR	LM
87021	PTR	LM
87023	PTR	LM
87025	PTR	LM
87027	PTR	LM
87029	PTR	LM
87030	PTR	LM
87032	PTR	LM
87033	PTR	LM

Exported

Number	*Present operator*
87003	BZK Bulgaria
87004	BZK Bulgaria
87006	BZK Bulgaria
87007	BZK Bulgaria
87008	BZK Bulgaria
87010	BZK Bulgaria
87012	BZK Bulgaria
87013	BZK Bulgaria
87014	BZK Bulgaria
87019	BZK Bulgaria
87020	BZK Bulgaria
87022	BZK Bulgaria
87026	BZK Bulgaria
87028	BZK Bulgaria
87029	BZK Bulgaria
87033	BZK Bulgaria
87034	BZK Bulgaria

Alstom

Address: ✉ PO Box 70, Newbold Road, Rugby, Warwickshire, CV21 2WR
info@transport.alstom.com ✆ 01788 577111, ⓘ www.transport.alstom.com

Managing Director: Paul Robinson

Facilities: Following the assembly of the Virgin Trains Class 390 Pendolino stock, Alstom closed down its UK production facility at Washwood Heath, Birmingham. However, the company still operates from many specialist sites in mainland Europe and if Alstom win further new build contracts in the UK, these will be assembled in Europe.

Bombardier

Address: ✉ Litchurch Lane, Derby, DE24 8AD
info@bombardier.com ✆ 01332 344666, ⓘ www.bombardier.com

Chief Country Representative: Colin Walton

Facilities: Bombardier Transportation is one of the largest transport builders in the world, with offices and building facilities in many countries. Its product range extends well beyond rail vehicles and includes aircraft, boats and leisure equipment.

In terms of the UK two main sites are located in Derby (Litchurch Lane) and Crewe. New build work is undertaken at the Derby site, which mainly concentrates on electric and diesel multiple unit designs.

Brush Traction

Address: ✉ PO Box 17, Loughborough, Leicestershire, LE11 1HS
sales@brushtraction.com ✆ 01509 617000, ⓘ www.brushtraction.com

Managing Director: John Bidewell

Facilities: Brush Traction is now part of the FKI Group and in recent years has been responsible for the majority of UK loco building. The company has been synonymous with loco building for the UK and overseas markets for many years. Although recent main line loco builds have been awarded overseas, the facilities at the Loughborough plant where the Class 31, 47, 60, Eurotunnel Shuttle locos and the Class 57s emerged is still available for new build work. Recently the site has concentrated on re-build operations including the highly successful re-engining of the HST fleet with MTU power units.

Right: *Brush Traction, based in Loughborough, who have been responsible for some of the most significant build contracts in modern traction history have recently completed a major operation to refurbish the majority of Class 43 HST power cars, fitting MTU power units in place of the life expired Paxman engines. First Great Western Nos. 43003 and 43002 are seen inside the main erecting shop in company with two Direct Rail Services Class 37s. Facilities still exist at Brush to undertake new build work if this was required.* **CJM**

Electro-Motive

Address: ✉ Electro-Motive Diesels Inc, 9301 West 55th Street, LaGrange, Illinois, USA 60525
Electro-Motive Diesels Inc, Oxford Street, London, Ontario, Canada
info@emdiesels.com ✆ +1 (800) 255 5355, ⓘ www.emdiesels.com

Facilities: Formerly part of General Motors, Electro-Motive is one of the two largest loco builders in the world. Its main production facility is in London, Ontario, Canada. Production from this sites sees locos transported throughout the world, including the UK and mainland Europe. In terms of the UK the JT42CWRM or Class 66 has been built in copious numbers for many different users. The design has also been built for mainland European operators including DBS subsidiary Euro Cargo Rail. Most recently the JT42CWRM design has been built for use in Egypt.

A new design of JT series loco for UK and mainland Europe use is expected to emerge in 2010.

Above: *The production facility in Oxford Street, London, Canada is visible from the highway and photography of new locos is possible with a big lens from surrounding streets. When new locos are delivered these have to be hauled or driven over the main street into the delivery yard. In this view, two of the Euro Cargo Rail JT42s Nos. 77054 and 77053 are seen in the yard at the rear of the plant awaiting completion.* **CJM**

General Electric

Address: ✉ GE Transportation Rail, 2901 East Lake Road, Erie, Pennsylvania, USA, 16531
UK office: Inspira House, Martinfield, Welwyn Garden City, Herts, AL7 1GW
info@getransportation.com ✆ 01707 383700 ⓘ www.getransportation.com

Chief Executive Officer: Lorenzo Simonelli

Facilities: General Electric have only recently entered the UK loco arena, and are currently fulfilling an order for 'PowerHaul' locomotives for Freightliner. The company operates a huge construction facility in Erie, Pennsylvania, USA from where the UK locos are being built.

Hitachi Europe Ltd

Address: ✉ 16 Upper Woburn Place, London, WC1H 0AF
hirofumi.ojima@hitachi-eu.com ✆ 0207 970 2700, ⓘ www.hitachi-rail.com

Facilities: Hitachi Rail is a relatively new name to the UK rail scene. It won the contract to design, build, test and manage the fleet of Class 395 EMUs for use on the new high speed service from Kent to London St Pancras International using HS1. In 2009 the company formed the construction arm of the consortium awarded the IEP project to design, build and introduce the next generation of high speed passenger trains in the UK.

Hitachi at present do not have construction facilities in the UK and the Class 395s together with the first 60 vehicles of the IEP have been and will be constructed in Japan and shipped to the UK. Hitachi intend to open a construction site in the UK.

Siemens Transportation Ltd

Address: ✉ Ashby Park, Ashby de la Zouch, Leicestershire, LE65 1JD
✉ uk.mobility@siemens.com ✆ 01530 258000
ⓘ www.siemens.co.uk/mobility

Managing Director UK: Steve Scrimshaw

Facilities: Siemens are now an established provider of UK EMU and DMU rolling stock with various derivatives of their 'Desiro' product line. Siemens while having maintenance facilities in the UK, perform all new build work in mainland Europe at their Krefeld/Uerdingen factory in Germany. Testing of vehicles is performed in Germany before delivery at the world famous test track at Wildenrath.

Above: *To enable testing of all types of electric Desiro stock on the Wildenrath test track in Germany, the previously overhead electrified test circuit was energised with the 750V dc third rail system, the 'live' rail being visible behind plastic covers in this view of a Class 360/1 being put through its paces on the test track.* **CJM**

Right: *On the basis of the success of the Desiro trains all round the world, Siemens has developed the Desiro City, a new platform concept for rail rapid transit, regional transport and inter-regional rail services in the UK. The lightweight design combined with an intelligent vehicle control system reduces overall energy consumption by up to 50 per cent and is a likely contender for future electrification projects, including the Thameslink order.* **Siemens**

British American Railway Services

Previously RMS Locotec, RT Rail, Dartmoor Railway, Weardale Railway and ECT Mainline Rail

Address: ✉ London Riverside, London SE1 2AQ
President: Ed Ellis
Depots: RMS Wakefield (ZS)
UK operation is part of Iowa Pacific Holdings

Class 08

Vehicle Length: 29ft 3in (8.91m)
Height: 12ft 8⅝in (3.87m)
Width: 8ft 6in (2.59m)
Engine: English Electric 6K
Horsepower: 400hp (298kW)
Electrical Equipment: English Electric

Number	*Depot*	*Pool*	*Livery*	*Owner*	*Operator*
08308	**IS**	**MRSO**	**FSR**	**ECT**	**FSR**
08423	**ZS**	**INDL**	**RMS**	**RMS**	**IND**
08573	**ZB**	**MRSO**	**WHT**	**ECT**	**LUL**
08588	**ZB**	**MRSO**	**BLK**	**ECT**	**IND**
08598	**ZS**	**MBDL**	**YEL**	**RMS**	**IND**
08613	**BH**	**MOLO**	**BLU**	**RMS**	**IND**
08622	**ZS**	**INDL**	**BLU**	**RMS**	**IND**
08750	**ZB**	**MRSO**	**BLK**	**ECT**	**FCC**
08754	**ZB**	**MRSO**	**BLU**	**ECT**	**IND**
08756	**MR**	**MRSO**	**GRY**	**ECT**	**GBR**
08762	**ZB**	**MRSO**	**BLK**	**ECT**	**WAB**
08870	**ZS**	**MBDL**	**BLG**	**RMS**	**IND**
08873	**ZB**	**MRSO**	**RFG**	**ECT**	**IND**
08885	**ZS**	**INDL**	**GBR**	**RMS**	**GBR**
08936	**ZS**	**MBDL**	**BLU**	**RMS**	**IND**

Class 20

Vehicle Length: 46ft 9¼in (14.26m)
Height: 12ft 7⅝in (3.84m)
Width: 8ft 9in (2.66m)
Engine: English Electric 8SVT Mk2
Horsepower: 1,000hp (745kW)
Electrical Equipment: English Electric

Number	*Depot*	*Pool*	*Livery*	*Owner*	*Operator*
20189	**WR**	**MOLO**	**GRN**	**C20**	**LUL**
20227	**WR**	**MOLO**	**RFG**	**C20**	**LUL**

Class 31/4 & 31/6

Vehicle Length: 56ft 9in (17.29m)
Height: 12ft 7in (3.91m)
Width: 8ft 9in (2.65m)
31/4 Fitted with electric train heat
Engine: English Electric 12SVT
Horsepower: 1,470hp (1,097kW)
Electrical Equipment: Brush

Number	*Depot*	*Pool*	*Livery*	*Owner*	*Operator*
31452 (31552/279)	**DF**	**RVLO**	**DCG**	**ECT**	**ECT**

31454, 31468, 31601 - See Rail Vehicle Engineering section

Class 73

Vehicle Length: 53ft 8in (16.35m)
Height: 12ft 5$\frac{5}{16}$in (3.79m)
Width: 8ft 8in (2.64m)
Power: 750V dc third rail or English Electric 6K
Horsepower: electric - 1,600hp (1,193kW)
Horsepower: diesel - 600hp (447kW)
Electrical Equipment: English Electric

Number	*Depot*	*Pool*	*Livery*	*Owner*	*Operator*	*Name*
73107	**SE**	**MBED**	**GRY**	**RTR**	**ECT**	***Spitfire***
73201 (73142)	**SE**	**MBED**	**BLU**	**PTR**	**ECT**	***Broadlands***

Left: *Former Southern Region Royal Train locomotive, Class 73 No. 73142, (now 73201) carries 1970s BR rail blue and has been re-united with its* Broadlands *nameplates. The loco is seen at Eastleigh in May 2009.* **Nathan Williamson**

HSBC Rail

Address: ✉ PO Box 29499, 1 Eversholt Street, London, NW1 2ZF
wendyfiler@hsbc.com ✆ 0207 380 5040, ⓘ www.hsbc.co.uk
Chief Operating Officer: Mary Kenny

Angel Trains

Address: ✉ Portland House, Bressenden Place, London, SW1E 5BH
reception@angeltrains.co.uk ✆ 0207 592 0500, ⓘ www.angeltrains.co.uk
Chief Executive: Malcolm Brown
Owned by: Babcock Brown, AMP Capital & Deutsche Bank

Porterbrook

Address: ✉ Burdett House, Becket Street, Derby, DE1 1JP
enquiries@porterbrook.co.uk ✆ 01332 262405, ⓘ www.porterbrook.co.uk
Managing Director: Paul Francis
Owned by: Antin Infrastructure Partners, Deutsche Bank & Lloyds TSB

Above: *Funded and owned by HSBC Rail, Class 66/7 No. 66722 is operated by First GBRf and branded in the light blue and range Metronet London Underground livery. As and when First GBRf finish their use with this loco it will be returned to its ase owner and made available for other operators to hire.* **CJM**

etails of vehicles owned by the main UK rail lease companies are found in the Passenger d Freight Operator sections. Off lease stock details can be found in the Vehicles Off Lease section

Harry Needle Railroad Company

Address: ✉ Harry Needle Railway Shed, Barrow Hill Roundhouse, Campbell Drive, Chesterfield, Derbyshire, S43 2PR

Managing Director: Harry Needle

Depots: Barrow Hill (BH)

Harry Needle Railroad Company also operates as a scrap dealer in dismantling locomotives and rolling stock.

Class 01

Number	*Depot*	*Pool*	*Livery*	*Owner*	*Operator*
01552 (TH167V)	BH	HNRL	IND	HNR	IND
01553 (12082)	BH	HNRL	HNR	HNR	IND
01564 (12088)	BH	HNRL	BLK	HNR	IND

Class 07

Vehicle Length: 26ft 9½in (8.16m)
Height: 12ft 10in (3.91m)
Width: 8ft 6in (2.59m)
Engine: Paxman 6RPHL MkIII
Horsepower: 275hp (205kW)
Electrical Equipment: AEI

Number	*Depot*	*Pool*	*Livery*	*Owner*	*Operator*
07001	BH	HNRS	HNR	HNR	IND

Class 08

Vehicle Length: 29ft 3in (8.91m)
Height: 12ft 8⅝in (3.87m)
Width: 8ft 6in (2.59m)
Engine: English Electric 6K
Horsepower: 400hp (298kW)
Electrical Equipment: English Electric

Number	*Depot*	*Pool*	*Livery*	*Owner*	*Operator*
08492	BH	HNRL	BLU	HNR	HNR
08502	BH	HNRL	NOR	HNR	NOR
08502(S)	BH	HNRS	IND	HNR	-
08507	CZ	HNRL	HNR	HNR	BOM
08517(S)	LM	HNRS	BLU	HNR	-
08527	RR	HNRL	JAR	HNR	FLF
08668(S)	BH	HNRS	BLU	HNR	-
08695	BH	HNRL	EWS	HNR	HNR
08813(S)	LM	HNRS	GRY	HNR	-
08818	BH	HNRL	HNR	HNR	IND
08827(S)	LM	HNRS	BLU	HNR	-
08834	BH	HNRL	DRS	HNR	OLD
08868	CP	HNRL	BLU	HNR	LNW
08869(S)	LM	HNRS	GRN	HNR	-
08892	BH	HNRL	DRS	HNR	HNR
08929(S)	LM	HNRS	BLK	HNR	-
08943	ZC	HNRL	GRN	HNR	BOM

Names applied

08502	*Lybert Dickinson*
08818	*Molly*

Left: *Former BR Class 11 diesel-electric 0-6-0 shunter No. 12082 is operated by Harry Needle Railroad Co as a hire loco. It is painted in HNRC house colours and officially classified as a Class 01 and numbered 01553 under the current TOPS classificat system. The loco, fitted with air br equipment, is seen at Long Marst* **Kevin Wills**

Class 20/0

Vehicle Length: 46ft $9^{1}/_{4}$in (14.26m)	Engine: English Electric 8SVT Mk2
Height: 12ft $7^{5}/_{8}$in (3.84m)	Horsepower: 1,000hp (745kW)
Width: 8ft 9in (2.66m)	Electrical Equipment: English Electric

Number	Depot	Pool	Livery	Owner	Operator
20016(S)	LM	HNRS	BLU	HNR	-
20032(S)	LM	HNRS	BLU	HNR	-
20056	BH	HNRL	COR	HNR	COR
20057(S)	LM	HNRS	BLU	HNR	-
20066	BH	HNRL	COR	HNR	COR
20072(S)	LM	HNRS	BLU	HNR	-
20081(S)	LM	HNRS	BLU	HNR	-
20088(S)	LM	HNRS	RFG	HNR	-
20092(S)	BH	HNRS	LAF	HNR	-
20096	BH	HNRL	BLU	HNR	HNR
20105(S)	BH	HNRS	RFG	HNR	-
20107(S)	BH	HNRS	BLU	HNR	-
20121(S)	BH	HNRS	BLU	HNR	-
20132(S)	BH	HNRS	GRN	HNR	-
20138(S)	LM	HNRS	RFT	HNR	-
20168	EA	HNRL	LAF	HNR	LAF
20197(S)	LM	HNRS	BLU	HNR	-

Names applied

20168	*Sir George Earle*

Class 20/9

Number		Depot	Pool	Livery	Owner	Operator
20901	(20101)	BH	HNRL	TLG	HNR	ADV
20902(S)	(20060)	LM	HNRS	DRS	HNR	-
20903(S)	(20083)	LM	HNRS	DRS	HNR	-
20904(S)	(20041)	LM	HNRS	DRS	HNR	-
20905	(20225)	BH	HNRL	TLG	HNR	ADV
20906	(20219)	LM	HNRL	DRS	HNR	HNR

Right: *All six of the original Hunslet-Barclay Class 20/9s still remain; having worked for DRS in the interim period, all six are now owned by HNRC. Two, Nos. 20901/05 are operational in two-tone grey, while the remainder are in ex DRS colours. No. 20901 is seen at Bristol (above) and No. 20902 at Long Marston (below).*
Stacey Thew/CJM

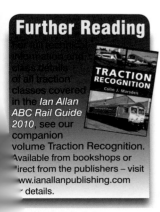

HNRC

Class 37/0

Vehicle Length: 61ft 6in (18.74m)
Height: 13ft 0¼in (3.96m)
Width: 8ft 11⅝in (2.73m)
Engine: English Electric 12CSVT
Horsepower: 1,750hp (1,304kW)
Electrical Equipment: English Electric

Number	*Depot*	*Pool*	*Livery*	*Owner*	*Operator*
37029(S)	**LM**	**HNRS**	**DRS**	**HNR**	**-**
37057(S)	**BH**	**HNRS**	**EWS**	**HNR**	**-**
37165(S) (37374)	**CS**	**HNRS**	**CIV**	**HNR**	**-**

Class 37/4

Vehicle Length: 61ft 6in (18.74m)
Height: 13ft 0¼in (3.96m)
Width: 8ft 11⅝in (2.73m)
Electric Train Heat fitted
Engine: English Electric 12CSVT
Horsepower: 1,750hp (1,304kW)
Electrical Equipment: English Electric

Number	*Depot*	*Pool*	*Livery*	*Owner*	*Operator*
37412(S) (37301)	**LM**	**HNRS**	**TLF**	**HNR**	**-**

Class 37/5

Vehicle Length: 61ft 6in (18.74m)
Height: 13ft 0¼in (3.96m)
Width: 8ft 11⅝in (2.73m)
Engine: English Electric 12CSVT
Horsepower: 1,750hp (1,304kW)
Electrical Equipment: English Electric

Number	*Depot*	*Pool*	*Livery*	*Owner*	*Operator*
37672(S) (37189)	**LM**	**HNRS**	**TLF**	**HNR**	**-**
37680(S) (37224)	**BH**	**HNRS**	**TLF**	**HNR**	**-**
37696(S) (37228)	**BH**	**HNRS**	**TGG**	**HNR**	**-**

Class 47

Vehicle Length: 63ft 6in (19.35m)
Height: 12ft 10⅜in (3.91m)
Width: 9ft 2in (2.79m)
Electric Train Heat fitted to Class 47/4 and 47/7
Engine: Sulzer 12LDA28C
Horsepower: 2,580hp (1,922kW)
Electrical Equipment: Brush

Number	*Depot*	*Pool*	*Livery*	*Owner*	*Operator*
47150(S)	**BA**	**HNRS**	**FLG**	**HNR**	**-**
47289(S)	**BA**	**HNRS**	**FL1**	**HNR**	**-**
47295(S)	**LM**	**HNRS**	**FL1**	**HNR**	**-**

Number	*Depot*	*Pool*	*Livery*	*Owner*	*Opertor*
47810 (47247/655)	**BH**	**HNRL**	**DRU**	**HNR**	**DRS**
47813 (47129/658)	**BH**	**HNRL**	**CWR**	**HNR**	**HNR**
47818 (47240/663)	**BH**	**HNRL**	**DRU**	**HNR**	**HNR**
47829(S) (47264/619)	**LM**	**HNRS**	**POL**	**HNR**	**-**
47714 (47511)	**OD**	**HNRL**	**ANG**	**HNR**	**SEC***

* Working at Old Dalby

Below: *In mid-2009 the ownership of three Cotswold Class 47s was transferred to HNRC. Painted in Cotswold silver livery, Class 47 No. 47810* Captain Sensible *(now de-named), is seen at Gloucester.* **CJM**

Electric Traction Limited

Address: ✉ Woodlands, Manse Road, Inverurie, Scotland AB51 3UJ

Depots: Long Marston (LM)

Electric Traction Ltd provide spot hire of Class 86 and 87 traction, as well as providing engineering and graphic design services to the rail industry.

Class 86

Vehicle Length: 58ft 6in (17.83m)
Height: 13ft 0⅝in (3.97m)
Width: 8ft 8¼in (2.64m)
Power Collection: 25kV ac overhead
Horsepower: 5,900hp (4,400kW)
Electrical Equipment: GEC

Number	*Depot*	*Pool*	*Livery*	*Owner*	*Operator*	*Name*
86101	WA	ACAC	BLU	ETL	ETL	
86701 (86205)	CP	ETLO	ETL	ETL	ETL	*Orion*
86702 (86260)	CP	ETLO	ETL	ETL	ETL	*Cassiopeia*

Right: *Class 86 No. 86702, the former No. 86260 is seen painted in ETL silver and red livery at Long Marston depot, alongside a Class 87 owned by Porterbrook.* **CJM**

Hauled stock

Mk1 Car Carrier (side load)
Vehicle Length: 57ft 0in (17.73m)
Height: 12ft 9in (3.88m)
Width: 9ft 3in (2.81m)

Number	*Depot*	*Livery*	*Owner*	*Operator*
96101 (93741/86741)	LM	BLG	ETL	ETL

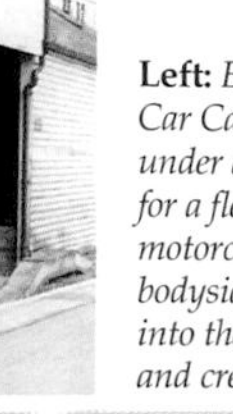

Left: *Electric Traction Ltd (ETL) own the unique prototype Car Carrier wagon; converted from a mail van at Marcroft under a finance deal with HSBC, the vehicle was a prototype for a fleet of side-loading car carriers which could load/unload motorcars from a standard railway platform. Six hinged bodyside sections drop down and lift up allowing a flat access into the vehicle. The prototype vehicle painted in HSBC blue and cream is seen at Exeter.* **CJM**

Class 87

Vehicle Length: 58ft 6in (17.83m)
Height: 13ft 1¼in (3.99m)
Width: 8ft 8¼in (2.64m)
Power Collection: 25kV ac overhead
Horsepower: 7,860hp (5,680kW)
Electrical Equipment: GEC

Number	*Depot*	*Pool*	*Livery*	*Owner*	*Operator*	*Name*
87002	CP	ETLO	BLU	ETL	ETL	*Royal Sovereign*

Right: *In immaculate rail blue-livery, Class 87 No. 87002* Royal Sovereign *shows the high quality external finish given to the ETL operated loco fleet. No. 87002 is certified for full Network Rail ac operation.* **CJM**

Cargo-D

Address: ✉ 32 Sydney Road, Haywards Heath, West Sussex, RH16 1QA
info@cargo-d.co.uk ✆ 07970 344046, ⓘ www.cargo-d.co.uk

Commercial Director: Mark Honey

Cargo-D also owns the rail passenger charter business Rail Blue Charters

Hauled stock

Mk2 *Height: 12ft 9½in (3.89m)*
Vehicle Length: 66ft 0in (20.11m) *Width: 9ft 3in (2.81m)*

Number	*Type*	*Depot*	*Livery*	*Operator*
1252 (3280)	AJ1F/RFO	LM	VIR	CAD
1254 (3391)	AJ1F/RFO	BH	BLG	WCR
3366	AD1F/FO	BH	BLG	CAD
3374	AD1F/FO	BH	BLG	WCR
5810	AC2E/TSO	BH	BLG	CAD
5901	AC2F/TSO	BH	BLG	CAD
5919	AC2F/TSO	BH	BLG	CAD
5941	AC2F/TSO	BH	BLG	CAD
5971	AC2F/TSO	BH	BLG	WCR
5995	AC25/TSO	BH	BLG	CAD
6001	AC2F/TSO	BH	BLG	CAD
6008	AC2F/TSO	BK	BLG	FGW
6045	AC2F/TSO	BH	VIR	CAD
6046	AC2F/TSO	BH	BLG	CAD
6064	AC2F/TSO	BK	BLG	FGW
6117	AC2F/TSO	BK	BLG	FGW
6122	AC2F/TSO	BH	BLG	WCR
6134	AC2F/TSO	KT	ICS	CAD
6151	AC2F/TSO	BH	BLG	CAD
6173	AC2F/TSO	BH	BLG	WCR
9506	AE2E/BSO	BH	BLG	CAD*
9508	AE2E/BSO	BK	BLG	FGW

Mk 3 *Height: 12ft 9in (3.88m)*
Vehicle Length: 75ft 0in (22.86m) *Width: 8ft 11in (2.71m)*

Number	*Type*	*Depot*	*Livery*	*Operator*
10202 (40504)	AJ1G/RFM	CF	ATW	CAD
10213(S) (11050)	AJ1G/RFM	HT	VIR	CAD
10242 (10002)	AJ1G/RFM	CE	BLG	WSR
10246 (10014)	AJ1G/RFM	CE	BLG	WSR
10249 (10012)	AJ1G/RFM	CF	ATW	ATW
10588	AU4G/SLEP	CE	BLG	CAD
11064	AD1H/FO	CE	BLG	CAD
11065	AD1H/FO	CE	BLG	CAD
11071	AD1H/FO	CE	BLG	WSR
11079	AD1H/FO	CE	VIR	CAD
11083	AD1H/FOD	CE	BLG	WSR
11084	AD1H/FO	WB	BLG	CAD/VWC
11086	AD1H/FO	WB	BLG	CAD/VWC
11089	AD1H/FO	CE	BLG	CAD
12014	AC2G/TSO	CE	BLG	WSR
12017	AC2G/TSO	WB	VIR	WSR/VWC
12038	AC2G/TSO	CE	BLG	WSR
12043	AC2G/TSO	CE	BLG	WSR
12059	AC2G/TSO	WB	VIR	WSR/VWC
12094	AC2G/TSO	WB	VIR	WSR/VWC
12119	AC2G/TSO	CE	BLG	WSR

** Leased from HSBC*

Below: *The standard livery for Cargo-D owned rolling stock is traditional 1970s-80s BR blue and grey, complete with Inter-City branding, taking one back to the early days of the Mk3 stock. Looking very smart at London Marylebone, TSO No. 12143 was photographed on 1 November 2008.* **Nathan Williamson**

Hanson Traction

Address: ✉ 38 St James Road, Ilkley, West Yorkshire, LS29 9PY
info@ hansontraction.co.uk ✆ 07710 132741, ⓘ www.hansontraction.co.uk
Commercial Director: Garcia Hanson

Class 31/1 & 31/6

Vehicle Length: 56ft 9in (17.29m)
Height: 12ft 7in (3.91m)
Width: 8ft 9in (2.65m)
Fitted with through wiring
Engine: English Electric 12SVT
Horsepower: 1,470hp (1,097kW)
Electrical Equipment: Brush

Number	Depot	Pool	Livery	Owner	Operator	Name
31190	WZ	HTLX	GRN	HAN	- (Spot hire)	
31602 (31191)	DF	RVLO	NRL	HAN	RVE	Driver Dave Green 19B

Class 47/0

Vehicle Length: 63ft 6in (19.35m)
Height: 12ft 10⅜in (3.91m)
Width: 9ft 2in (2.79m)
Engine: Sulzer 12LDA28C
Horsepower: 2,580hp (1,922kW)
Electrical Equipment: Brush

Number	Depot	Pool	Livery	Owner	Name
47270	WZ	BREL	BLU	HAN	*Swift*

Class 56

Vehicle Length: 63ft 6in (19.35m)
Height: 13ft 0in (3.96m)
Width: 9ft 2in (2.79m)
Engine: Ruston Paxman 16RK3CT
Horsepower: 3,250hp (2,420kW)
Electrical Equipment: Brush

Number		Depot	Pool	Livery	Owner	Operator	Name
56311	(56057)	WZ	HTLX	GRY	HAN	COL	
56312	(56003)	WZ	HTLX	PUR	HAN	COL	*Artemis*
(56313) (S)	56128	WZ	HTLX	FRB	HAN	-	
(56314) (S)	56114	WF	HTLX	HAN	HAN	-	

bove: *Hanson Tractions Nos. 56311 and 56312 pass Lower Moor on the Cotswold Line between Norton Junction and esham powering train 6Z56 from Long Marston to Washwood Heath on 14 November 2008.* **Jack Boskett**

anson Traction also own Class 31s Nos. 31190/459 which are operated by Rail Vehicle Engineering Ltd, and Class 50 No. 8 at the East Lancs Railway.

Listings provide details of locomotives and stock, authorised for operation on the UK National Rail network and could be seen operating special and charter services.
Preserved locomotives authorised for main line operation are found in the preserved section.

Bo'ness and Kinneil Railway

Number	Type	Depot	Livery	Operator	Use
464	AO3/BCK	BT	CAL	BOK	Charter train use
1375 (99803)	AO2/TK	BT	CAL	BOK	Charter train use
3096 (99827)	AD11/FO	BT	MAR	BOK	Charter train use
3115	AD11/FO	BT	MAR	BOK	Charter train use
3150	AD11/FO	BT	MAR	BOK	Charter train use
4831 (99824)	AC21/TSO	BT	MAR	BOK	Charter train use
4832 (99823)	AC21/TSO	BT	CHC	BOK	Charter train use
4836 (99831)	AC21/TSO	BT	MAR	BOK	Charter train use
4856 (99829)	AC21/TSO	BT	MAR	BOK	Charter train use
5028 (99830)	AC21/TSO	BT	CAR	BOK	Charter train use
5412	AC2A/TSO	BT	MAR	BOK	Charter train use
13229 (99826)	AA11/FK	BT	MAR	BOK	Charter train use
13230 (99828)	AA11/FK	BT	MAR	BOK	Charter train use

Flying Scotsman Railway Ltd

Number	Type	Depot	Livery	Operator	Notes/Name
316 (S) (975608)	AO11/PFK	CS	PUL	FSL	Pullman *Magpie*
321 (S)	AO11/PFK	CS	PUL	FSL	Pullman *Swift*
337 (S)	AO11/PSK	CS	PUL	FSL	Pullman Car No. 337

Great Scottish & Western Railway Co

Number	Type	Depot	Livery	Operator	Notes/Name
313 (S) (99964)	AO11/PFK	CS	MAR	GSW	Royal Scotsman - *Finch*
317 (99967)	AO11/PFK	CS	MAR	GSW	Royal Scotsman - *Raven*
319 (99965)	AO11/PFK	CS	MAR	GSW	Royal Scotsman - *Snipe*
324 (99961)	AO11/PFP	CS	MAR	GSW	Royal Scotsman - *Amber*
329 (99962)	AO11/PFP	CS	MAR	GSW	Royal Scotsman - *Pearl*
331 (99963)	AO11/PFP	CS	MAR	GSW	Royal Scotsman - *Topaz*
1999 (99131)	AO10/SAL	CS	MAR	GSW	Royal Scotsman - *Lochaber*

Jeremy Hoskins

Number	Type	Depot	Livery	Operator	Notes/Name
3125 (S)	AD11/FO	TM	CHC	JHS	*Loch Shiel*
3148 (S) (3610)	AD11/FO	CS	MAR	JHS	

Mid-Hants Railway

Number	Type	Depot	Livery	Operator
1105 (99531/302)	AJ41/RG	RL	GRN	MHR
21252	AB31/BCK	RL	GRN	MHR

North Yorkshire Moors Railway

Class 25

Vehicle Length: 50ft 6in (15.39m)
Height: 12ft 8in (3.86m)
Width: 9ft 1in (2.76m)
Engine: Sulzer 6LDA28B
Horsepower: 1,250hp (932kW)
Electrical Equipment: Brush

Number	Depot	Pool	Livery	Owner	Operator	Name	Notes
25278	NY	MBDL	GRN	NYM	NYM	*Sybilia*	Restricted main line use

Coaching Stock

Number	Type	Depot	Livery	Operator	
1823	AN21/RMB	NY	MAR	NYM	
3860	AC21/TSO	NY	MAR	NYM	
3872	AC21/TSO	NY	CAR	NYM	
3948	AC2I/TSO	NY	CAR	NYM	Spare vehicle
4198	AC21/TSO	NY	CAR	NYM	
4252	AC21/TSO	NY	CAR	NYM	
4290	AC21/TSO	NY	MAR	NYM	
4455	AC21/TSO	NY	CAR	NYM	
4786	AC21/TSO	NY	MAR	NYM	
4817	AC21/TSO	NY	CHC	NYM	
5000	AC21/TSO	NY	MAR	NYM	
5029	AC21/TSO	NY	CHC	NYM	
9267	AE21/BSO	NY	CHC	NYM	
9274	AE21/BSO	NY	CHC	NYM	
16156 (7156)	AA31/CK	NY	MAR	NYM	
35089	AB2I/BSK	NY	MAR	NYM	

Railfilms Limited

Number	Type	Depot	Livery	Operator	Notes/Name
310 (99107)	AO11/PFL	EH	PUL	RAF	*Pegasus*
1659	AJ41/RBR	EH	PUL	RAF	*Camelot*
3188	AD1D/FO	EH	PUL	RAF	*Sovereign*
3231	AD1E/FO	EH	PUL	RAF	*Apollo*
5067 (99993)	AC21/TSO	CP	MAR	RAF	
13508 (S)	AA1B/FK	CS	MAR	RAF	
21224 (S)	AB31/BCK	TM	RIV	RAF	Director's Saloon

Right: *Railfilms-owned Pullman No. 310* Pegasus *is 'The Trianon Bar' and provides luxurious accommodation on VIP charter trains. The vehicle is seen from the bar end at Carnforth soon after restoration. This coach is also allocated the number 99107.* **CJM**

Ridings Railtours

Number	Type	Depot	Livery	Operator
5520 (S)	AC2C/TSO	SV	PUL	RRS
13581 (S)	AA1D/FK	SV	ICS	RRS
13583 (S)	AA1D/FK	SV	ICS	RRS

Riviera Trains

Class 47

Vehicle Length: 63ft 6in (19.35m)
Height: 12ft 10⅜in (3.91m)
Width: 9ft 2in (2.79m)
Electric Train Heat fitted
Engine: Sulzer 12LDA28C
Horsepower: 2,580hp (1,922kW)
Electrical Equipment: Brush

Number	Depot	Pool	Livery	Owner	Operator	Name
47575 (S)	CQ	RTLS	RES	RIV	-	
47747 (47615)	CP	RTLO	EWS	RIV	RIV	
47769 (47491)	CP	RTLO	VIR	RIV	RIV	

Riviera

47805 (47650)	CP	RTLO	RIV	RIV	RIV	*Talisman*
47812 D1916 (47657)	CP	RTLO	GRN	RIV	RIV	
47815 (47660)	CP	RTLO	GRN	RIV	RIV	*Great Western*
47839 (47621)	CP	RTLO	RIV	RIV	RIV	*Pegasus*
47843 (47623)	CP	RTLO	RIV	RIV	RIV	*Vulcan*
47847 (47577)	CP	RTLO	RIV	RIV	RIV	
47848 (47632)	CP	RTLO	RIV	RIV	RIV	*Titan Star*
47853 (47614)	CP	RTLO	XP6	RIV	RIV	*Rail Express*

Left: *The Class 47s operated by Riviera Trains can be found throughout the country, powering charter and special services. No. 47853 painted in its original XP64 livery which it carried in 1964 as No. D1733, is seen passing along the Dawlish Sea Wall powering a pair of FGW high speed train barrier coaches.* **CJM**

Coaching Stock

Number	*Type*	*Depot*	*Livery*	*Operator*	*Notes/Name*
1200 (6459)	AJ1F/RFO	EH	RIV	RIV	Set 04 - The Great Briton - *Amber*
1212 (6453)	AJ1F/RFO	EH	VIR	RIV	Set 05 - The Norfolkman
1250 (3372)	AJ1F/RFO	EH	VIR	RIV	Set 07 - The West Coast Set
1260 (S) (3378)	AJ1F/RFO	EH	RIV	RIV	
1651	AJ41/RBR	EH	MAR	RIV	Set 02 - The Royal Scot Set
1671	AJ41/RBR	EH	MAR	RIV	Set 02 - The Royal Scot Set
1683	AJ41/RBR	CP	BLU	RIV	Set 04 - The Great Briton - *Carol*
1691	AJ41/RBR	CP	CCM	RIV	Set 02 - The Royal Scot Set
1692	AJ41/RBR	CP	CHC	RIV	Set 01 - The British Classic Set
1698 (S)	AJ41/RBR	EH	LNR	RIV	
1699	AJ41/RBR	CP	BLU	RIV	Set 04 - The Great Briton
1813	AN21/RMB	CP	MAR	RIV	Set 03
1832	AN21/RMB	EH	CCM	RIV	
1842	AN21/RMB	EH	CCM	RIV	Set 02 - The Royal Scot Set
1863	AN21/RMB	EH	CHC	RIV	Set 01 - British Classic Set
2834 (S) (21267)	AU51/SLSC	EH	LNR	RIV	
3066 (99566)	AD11/FO	EH	CCM	RIV	Set 02 - The Royal Scot Set
3068 (99568)	AD11/FO	EH	CCM	RIV	Set 02 - The Royal Scot Set
3069 (99540)	AD11/FO	EH	CCM	RIV	Set 02 - The Royal Scot Set
3097	AD11/FO	EH	CCM	RIV	Set 02 - The Royal Scot Set
3098	AD11/FO	EH	CHC	RIV	Set 01 - The British Classic Set
3107	AD11/FO	EH	CHC	RIV	Set 01 - The British Classic Set
3110 (99124)	AD11/FO	EH	CHC	RIV	Set 01 - The British Classic Set
3112 (99357)	AD11/FO	EH	CHC	RIV	Set 01 - The British Classic Set
3114 (S)	AD11/FO	EH	GRN	RIV	
3119	AD11/FO	EH	CCM	RIV	Set 02 - The Royal Scot Set
3120	AD11/FO	EH	CCM	RIV	Set 03
3121	AD11/FO	EH	LNE	RIV	Set 02 - The Royal Scot Set
3122	AD11/FO	EH	CHC	RIV	Set 01 - British Classic Set
3123	AD11/FO	EH	LNE	RIV	Set 03
3124 (S)	AD11/FO	EH	GRN	RIV	
3127 (S)	AD11/FO	EH	GRN	RIV	
3131 (S) (99190)	AD11/FO	EH	MAR	RIV	
3132 (S) (99191)	AD11/FO	EH	MAR	RIV	
3133 (S) (99192)	AD11/FO	EH	MAR	RIV	

3140	AD11/FO	EH	CHC	RIV	Set 01 - British Classic Set
3141 (3608)	AD11/FO	EH	MRN	RIV	Set 03
3144 (3602)	AD11/FO	EH	MRN	RIV	Set 03
3146	AD11/FO	EH	MRN	RIV	Set 03
3147 (3604)	AD11/FO	EH	LNE	RIV	Set 03
3149	AD11/FO	EH	CCM	RIV	Set 02 - The Royal Scot Set
3181 (S)	AD1D/FO	EH	RIV	RIV	*Topaz*
3223 (S)	AD1E/FO	EH	RIV	RIV	*Diamond*
3228	AD1E/FO	EH	RIV	RIV	Set 05 - The Norfolkman - *Amethyst*
3240 (S)	AD1E/FO	EH	RIV	RIV	*Sapphire*
3244	AD1E/FO	EH	RIV	RIV	Set 05 - The Norfolkman - *Emerald*
3277	AD1F/FO	EH	ANG	RIV	Set 05 - The Norfolkman
3279	AD1F/FO	EH	MAR	RIV	Set 05 - The Norfolkman
3295	AD1F/FO	EH	ANG	RIV	Set 05 - The Norfolkman
3304	AD1F/FO	EH	VIR	RIV	Set 07 - West Coast Set
3314	AD1F/FO	EH	VIR	RIV	Set 07 - West Coast Set
3325	AD1F/FO	EH	VIR	RIV	Set 07 - West Coast Set
3330	AD1F/FO	EH	RIV	RIV	Set 04 - The Great Briton - *Brunel*
3333	AD1F/FO	EH	VIR	RIV	Set 07 - The West Coast Set
3334	AD1F/FO	EH	ANG	RIV	Set 05 - The Norfolkman
3336	AD1F/FO	EH	ANG	RIV	Set 05 - The Norfolkman
3340	AD1F/FO	EH	VIR	RIV	Set 07 - The West Coast Set
3344	AD1F/FO	EH	RIV	RIV	Set 07 - The West Coast Set
3345	ADIF/FO	EH	VIR	RIV	Set 07 - The West Coast Set
3348	AD1F/FO	EH	RIV	RIV	Set 04 - The Great Briton - *Gainsborough*
3356	AD1F/FO	EH	RIV	RIV	Set 04 - The Great Briton - *Tennyson*
3364	AD1F/FO	EH	RIV	RIV	Set 04 - The Great Briton - *Shakespeare*
3379	AD1F/FO	EH	ANG	RIV	
3384	AD1F/FO	EH	RIV	RIV	Set 04 - The Great Briton - *Dickens*
3386	AD1F/FO	EH	VIR	RIV	Set 07 - The West Coast Set
3390	AD1F/FO	EH	RIV	RIV	Set 04 - The Great Briton - *Constable*
3397	AD1F/FO	EH	RIV	RIV	Set 04 - The Great Briton - *Wordsworth*
3417	AD1F/FO	EH	ANG	RIV	
3426	AD1F/FO	EH	RIV	RIV	Set 04 - The Great Briton - *Elgar*
4902	AC21/TSO	EH	CHC	RIV	Set 01 - British Classic Set
4927	AC21/TSO	EH	CHC	RIV	Set 01 - British Classic Set
4946 (S) (99000)	AC21/TSO	EH	MAR	RIV	
4949	AC21/TSO	EH	MAR	RIV	Set 03
4959 (S)	AC21/TSO	EH	BLG	RIV	
4986	AC21/TSO	EH	GRN	RIV	Set 03
4991 (S)	AC21/TSO	EH	BLG	RIV	
4996 (S) (99001)	AC21/TSO	EH	MAR	RIV	
4998	AC21/TSO	EH	MAR	RIV	Set 03
4999 (S)	AC21/TSO	EH	BLG	RIV	
5007 (S)	AC21/TSO	EH	GRN	RIV	
5008 (99002)	AC21/TSO	EH	MAN	RIV	Set 03
5009	AC21/TSO	EH	CHC	RIV	Set 01 - British Classic Set
5023	AC21/TSO	EH	MRN	RIV	Set 03
5027 (S)	AC21/TSO	EH	GRN	RIV	
5040	AC21/TSO	EH	CHC	RIV	Set 01 - British Classic Set
5276	AC2A/TSO	EH	RIV	RIV	Set 02 - The Royal Scot Set
5292	AC2A/TSO	EH	RIV	RIV	Set 02 - The Royal Scot Set
5309 (S)	AC2A/TSO	EH	CHC	RIV	
5322	AC2A/TSO	EH	RIV	RIV	Set 02 - The Royal Scot Set
5341	AC2A/TSO	EH	CCM	RIV	Set 02 - The Royal Scot Set
5350	AC2A/TSO	EH	CHC	RIV	Set 01 - British Classic Set - *Dawn*
5365 (S)	AC2A/TSO	EH	RIV	RIV	*Deborah*
5366	AC2A/TSO	EH	RIV	RIV	Set 02 - The Royal Scot Set
5376 (S)	AC2A/TSO	EH	RIV	RIV	*Michaela*
5494 (S)	AC2B/TSO	SV	NSE	RIV	
5647 (S)	AC2D/TSO	EH	RIV	RIV	
5739 (S)	AC2D/TSO	SV	NWM	RIV	
5748	AC2E/TSO	EH	ICS	RIV	
5769	AC2E/TSO	EH	ICS	RIV	Set 07 - The West Coast Set
5792	AC2E/TSO	EH	VIR	RIV	Set 07 - The West Coast Set

Riviera

5910	AC2F/TSO	EH	VIR	RIV	Set 07 - The West Coast Set
5911 (S)	AC2F/TSO	EH	VIR	RIV	
5921	AC2F/TSO	EH	ANG	RIV	Set 05 - The Norfolkman
5929	AC2F/TSO	EH	ANG	RIV	Set 05 - The Norfolkman
5934	AC2F/TSO	EH	VIR	RIV	Set 07 - The West Coast Set
5937 (S)	AC2F/TSO	EH	VIR	RIV	
5945	AC2F/TSO	EH	VIR	RIV	Set 07 - The West Coast Set
5946	AC2F/TSO	EH	VIR	RIV	Set 07 - The West Coast Set
5952 (S)	AC2F/TSO	EH	VIR	RIV	
5955 (S)	AC2F/TSO	EH	VIR	RIV	
5961	AC2F/TSO	EH	VIR	RIV	Set 07 - The West Coast Set
5964	AC2F/TSO	EH	ANG	RIV	Set 05 - The Norfolkman
5984	AC2F/TSO	EH	VIR	RIV	Set 07 - The West Coast Set
5985	AC2F/TSO	EH	ANG	RIV	Set 05 - The Norfolkman
5987	AC2F/TSO	EH	VIR	RIV	Set 07 - The West Coast Set
5997	AC2F/TSO	EH	VIR	RIV	Set 07 - The West Coast Set
5998	AC2F/TSO	EH	ANG	RIV	Set 05 - The Norfolkman
6006	AC2F/TSO	EH	ANG	RIV	Set 05 - The Norfolkman
6024 (S)	AC2F/TSO	EH	VIR	RIV	
6027	AC2F/TSO	EH	VIR	RIV	Set 07 - The West Coast Set
6038 (S)	AC2F/TSO	EH	VIR	RIV	
6042	AC2F/TSO	EH	ANG	RIV	Set 05 - The Norfolkman
6051	AC2F/TSO	EH	VIR	RIV	Set 07 - The West Coast Set
6054	AC2F/TSO	EH	VIR	RIV	Set 07 - The West Coast Set
6056 (S)	AC2F/TSO	EH	VIR	RIV	
6067 (S)	AC2F/TSO	EH	VIR	RIV	
6104	AC2F/TSO	EH	VIR	RIV	Set 07 - The West Coast Set
6107	AC2F/TSO	EH	VIR	RIV	
6138	AC2F/TSO	EH	RIV	RIV	Set 07 - The West Coast Set
6141	AC2F/TSO	EH	RIV	RIV	Set 07 - The West Coast Set
6153 (S)	AC2F/TSO	ZG	VIR	RIV	
6158	AC2F/TSO	EH	VIR	RIV	Set 07 - The West Coast Set
6176 (S)	AC2F/TSO	EH	VIR	RIV	
6177	AC2F/TSO	EH	RIV	RIV	
6310 (81448)	AX51/GEN	EH	CHC	RIV	
6320 (5033)	AZ5Z/SAL	SK	MRN	RIV	
6720 (6602)	AN1D/RMBF	EH	MRN	RIV	
9504	AC2E/BSO	EH	VIR	RIV	Set 07 - The West Coast Set
9507	AC2E/BSO	EH	RIV	RIV	
9520	AE2F/BSO	EH	RIV	RIV	Set 07 - The West Coast Set
9526	AC2F/BSO	EH	RIV	RIV	
9527	AC2F/BSO	EH	VIR	RIV	Set 07 - The West Coast Set
9537	AE2F/BSO	EH	RIV	RIV	Set 07 - The West Coast Set
17015 (14015)	AB11/BFK	EH	CHC	RIV	Set 02 - The Royal Scot Set
17056 (S) (14056)	AB1A/BFK	EH	MAR	RIV	
17077 (14077)	AB1A/BFK	EH	RIV	RIV	Set 04 - The Great Briton - *Catherine*
17105 (2905)	AX5B/BFK	EH	RIV	RIV	Set 02 - Staff Couchette
21245 (99356)	AB31/BCK	EH	MAR	RIV	Set 03
21269 (S)	AB31/BCK	EH	LNE	RIV	
21272 (99129)	AB31/BCK	EH	CHC	RIV	Set 01 - British Classic Set
35469 (99763)	AB21/BSK	EH	CCM	RIV	Set 03
80041 (1690)	AK51/RK	EH	MAR	RIV	Set 03 - Pride of the Nation

Left: *Catering vehicle RFO No. 1200 was a rebuild from coach No. 6459; the vehicle is painted in lined Riviera blue and cream. The coach operates from Eastleigh and is part of 'The Great Briton' charter set.* **Tony Christie**

Scottish Railway Preservation Society

Number	Type	Depot	Livery	Operator
1730	AJ41/RBR	BT	MAR	SRP
1859 (99822)	AN21/RMB	BT	MAR	SRP
21241	AB31/BCK	BT	CHC	SRP
35185	AB21/BSK	BT	MAR	SRP

Stratford Class 47 Group

Vehicle Length: 63ft 6in (19.35m)
Height: 12ft 10⅜in (3.91m)
Width: 9ft 2in (2.79m)
Electric Train Heat fitted
Engine: Sulzer 12LDA28C
Horsepower: 2,580hp (1,922kW)
Electrical Equipment: Brush

Number	Depot	Pool	Livery	Owner	Operator	Name
47580 (47732)	TM	MBDL	LLB	S4G	S4G	*County of Essex*

Right: *A Class 47 which is superbly restored to main line certified condition is Stratford Class 47 Group owned No. 47580* County of Essex*, restored to Stratford depot 1980s condition in large logo blue livery complete with Stratford cockney sparrow logo. The loco is viewed from its No. 2 end at Long Marston where it was one of the prime exhibits for the 2009 open weekend.* **CJM**

Venice Simplon Orient Express (VSOE)

Number	Name	Type	Depot	Livery	Operator	Notes
213 (99535)	*Minerva*	AO40/PFP	SL	PUL	VSO	
239 (S)	*Agatha*	AO40/PFP	SL	PUL	VSO	
243 (99541)	*Lucille*	AO40/PFP	SL	PUL	VSO	
245 (99534)	*Ibis*	AO40/PFK	SL	PUL	VSO	
254 (99536)	*Zena*	AO40/PFP	SL	PUL	VSO	
255 (99539)	*Ione*	AO40/PFK	SL	PUL	VSO	
261 (S)	Car No. 83	AO40/PTP	SL	PUL	VSO	
264 (S)	*Ruth*	AO40/PCK	SL	PUL	VSO	
280 (99537)	*Audrey*	AO40/PFK	SL	PUL	VSO	
281 (99546)	*Gwen*	AO40/PFK	SL	PUL	VSO	
283 (S)	*Mona*	AO40/PFK	SL	PUL	VSO	
284 (99543)	*Vera*	AO40/PFK	SL	PUL	VSO	
285 (S)	Car No. 85	AO40/PTP	SL	PUL	VSO	
286 (S)	Car No. 86	AO40/PTP	SL	PUL	VSO	
288 (S)	Car No. 88	AO40/PTB	SL	PUL	VSO	
292 (S)	Car No. 92	AO40/PTB	SL	PUL	VSO	
293 (S)	Car No. 93	AO40/PTB	SL	PUL	VSO	
301 (99530)	*Perseus*	AO41/PFP	SL	PUL	VSO	
302 (99531)	*Phoenix*	AO41/PFP	SL	PUL	VSO	
307 (S)	*Carina*	AO41/PFK	SL	PUL	VSO	
308 (99532)	*Cygnus*	AO41/PFP	SL	PUL	VSO	
325 (2907)		AJ11/RFO	CP	PUL	VSO	
1566		AK51/RKB	CP	VSN	VSO	
1953		AJ41/RBR	CP	VSN	VSO	

VSOE

3174	*Glamis*	AD1D/FO	CP	VSN	VSO	
3182	*Warwick*	AD1D/FO	CP	VSN	VSO	
3232		AD1E/FO	BH	BLG	VSO	
3247	*Chatsworth*	AD1E/FO	CP	VSN	VSO	
3267	*Belvoir*	AD1E/FO	CP	VSN	VSO	
3273	*Alnwick*	AD1E/FO	CP	VSN	VSO	
3275	*Harlech*	AD1E/FO	CP	VSN	VSO	
6313 (92167)		AX51/GEN	SL	PUL	VSO	
9502		AE2E/BSO	SL	PUL	VSO	
10541 (99968)		AO4G/SSV	CS	MRN	VSO	Royal Scotsman - State Car 5
10556 (99969)		AO4G/SSV	CS	MRN	VSO	Royal Scotsman - Service Car
10569 (S)	*Leviathan*	AU4G/SLEP	CP	PUL	VSO	
10729	*Crewe*	AS4G/SLE	CP	VSN	VSO	
10734 (2914)	*Balmoral*	AS4G/SLE	CP	VSN	VSO	
17080 (35516)		AB1A/BFK	CP	VSN	VSO	
17167 (14167)	*Aspinal*	AB1D/BFK	CP	VSN	VSO	
35466 (99545)		AB21/BSK	SL	PUL	VSO	
92904		NBA	CP	PUL	VSO	

Above: *VSOE first class Pullman car No. 99536 or 254 Zena is illustrated formed in the VSOE British Pullman train while working a London Victoria to Truro charter.* **CJM**

Left: *In addition to the luxury British Pullman train formed of historic Pullman vehicles, the company operates a sizeable fleet of ex-BR Mk1 and Mk2 stock converted to Pullman standards which operate under the Northern Bell name. Former Mk2 FO 3275 painted in mock Pullman colours and named* Harlech *is viewed at Exeter on a charter from Bristol.* **CJM**

Vintage Trains

Class 47

Vehicle Length: 63ft 6in (19.35m)
Height: 12ft $10\frac{3}{8}$in (3.91m)
Width: 9ft 2in (2.79m)
Electric Train Heat fitted
Engine: Sulzer 12LDA28C
Horsepower: 2,580hp (1,922kW)
Electrical Equipment: Brush

Number	*Depot*	*Pool*	*Livery*	*Owner*	*Operator*
47773 (47541)	**TM**	**MBDL**	**GRN**	**VTN**	**VTN**

Right: *Preserved by Vintage Trains and based at Tyseley, ex-Res Class 47 No. 47773 is now painted in two-tone green livery and certified for main line operation. It is used for main line charter and hire work. It is seen here leading a WCRC train at Kingswear.* **Tony Christie**

Coaching Stock

Number	*Type*	*Depot*	*Livery*	*Owner*	*Operator*
335 (99361)	**AO11/PSK**	**TM**	**PUL**	**VTN**	**VTN**
349 (99349)	**AO11/PSP**	**TM**	**PUL**	**VTN**	**VTN**
353 (99353)	**AO11/PSP**	**TM**	**PUL**	**VTN**	**VTN**
17018 (99108)	**AB11/BFK**	**TM**	**CHC**	**VTN**	**VTN**

West Coast Railway Company

Class 03

Vehicle Length: 26ft 3in (7.92m)
Height: 12ft $7\frac{7}{16}$in (3.72m)
Width: 8ft 6in (2.59m)
Engine: Gardner 8L3
Horsepower: 204hp (149kW)
Mechanical Equipment: Wilson-Drewry

Number	*Depot*	*Pool*	*Livery*	*Owner*	*Operator*	*Name*
03196	**CS**	**MBDL**	**GRN**	**WCR**	**WCR**	***Joyce***
D2381	**CS**	**MBDL**	**BLK**	**WCR**	**WCR**	

Class 08

Vehicle Length: 29ft 3in (8.91m)
Height: 12ft $8\frac{5}{8}$in (3.87m)
Width: 8ft 6in (2.59m)
Engine: English Electric 6K
Horsepower: 400hp (298kW)
Electrical Equipment: English Electric

Number	*Depot*	*Pool*	*Livery*	*Owner*	*Operator*	*Name*
08678	**CS**	**MBDL**	**GLX**	**WCR**	**WCR**	***Artila***

Class 33

Vehicle Length: 50ft 9in (15.47m)
Height: 12ft 8in (3.86m)
Width: 33/0, 33/1 9ft 3in (2.81m), 33/2 8ft 8in (2.64m)
Engine: English Electric 12CSVT
Horsepower: 1,750hp (1,304kW)
Electrical Equipment: English Electric

Number	*Depot*	*Pool*	*Livery*	*Owner*	*Operator*	*Name*
33025	**CS**	**MBDL**	**WCR**	**WCR**	**WCR**	***Glen Falloch***
33029	**CS**	**MBDL**	**WCR**	**WCR**	**WCR**	***Glen Roy***
33030 (S)	**CS**	**MBDL**	**DRS**	**WCR**	**-**	
33207	**CS**	**MBDL**	**WCR**	**WCR**	**WCR**	***Jim Martin***

ight: ***The West Coast Railway Co WCRC) has a very pleasing deep aroon livery applied to its motive wer, with a neat West Coast lways bodyside branding. The ry is displayed on Class 33/0*** **33025 Glen Falloch,** ***stabled at r St Davids.*** **Tony Christie**

WCRC

Class 37

Vehicle Length: 61ft 6in (18.74m)	*Engine: English Electric 12CSVT*
Height: 13ft 0¼in (3.96m)	*Horsepower: 1,750hp (1,304kW)*
Width: 8ft 11⅝in (2.73m)	*Electrical Equipment: English Electric*

Number	*Depot*	*Pool*	*Livery*	*Owner*	*Operator*	*Name*
37108 (37325)	**CS**	**MBDL**	**GSR**	**WCR**	**WCR**	
37214	**CS**	**MBDL**	**WCR**	**WCR**	**WCR**	***Loch Laidon***
37248 (S)	**CS**	**MBDL**	**WCR**	**TTT**	**WCR**	
37516 (S) (37086)	**CS**	**MBDL**	**WCR**	**WCR**	**-**	
37517 (S) (37018)	**CS**	**MBDL**	**LHL**	**WCR**	**-**	
37668 (S) (37257)	**CS**	**MBDL**	**EWS**	**WCR**	**-**	***Loch Rannoch***
37676 (37126)	**CS**	**MBDL**	**WCR**	**WCR**	**WCR**	
37685 (S) (37234)	**CS**	**MBDL**	**ICS**	**WCR**	**-**	
37706 (37016)	**CS**	**MBDL**	**WCR**	**WCR**	**WCR**	
37710 (S) (37044)	**CS**	**MBDL**	**LHL**	**WCR**	**-**	
37712 (37102)	**CS**	**MBDL**	**WCR**	**WCR**	**WCR**	

Class 47

Vehicle Length: 63ft 6in (19.35m)	*Engine: Sulzer 12LDA28C*
Height: 12ft 10⅜in (3.91m)	*Horsepower: 2,580hp (1,922kW)*
Width: 9ft 2in (2.79m)	*Electrical Equipment: Brush*
Electric Train Heat fitted to Class 47/4, 47/7 and 47/8	

Number	*Depot*	*Pool*	*Livery*	*Owner*	*Operator*	*Name*
47194 (S)	**CS**	**MBDL**	**TLF**	**WCR**	**-**	
47245	**CS**	**MBDL**	**WCR**	**WCR**	**WCR**	
47489 (S)	**CS**	**MBDL**	**PCL**	**WCR**	**-**	
47492	**CS**	**MBDL**	**RES**	**WCR**	**WCR**	
47525 (S)	**CS**	**MBDL**	**RFD**	**WCR**	**-**	
47526 (S)	**CS**	**MBDL**	**BLU**	**WCR**	**-**	
47760 (47562)	**CS**	**MBDL**	**WCR**	**WCR**	**WCR**	
47770 (S) (47500)	**CS**	**MBDL**	**RES**	**WCR**	**-**	
47772 (S) (47537)	**CS**	**MBDL**	**RES**	**WCR**	**-**	
47776 (S) (47578)	**CS**	**MBDL**	**RES**	**WCR**	**-**	
47786 (47821)	**CS**	**MBDL**	**WCR**	**WCR**	**WCR**	***Roy Castle OBE***
47787 (47823)	**CS**	**MBDL**	**WCR**	**WCR**	**WCR**	***Windsor Castle***
47804 (47792)	**CS**	**MBDL**	**WCR**	**WCR**	**WCR**	
47826 (47637)	**CS**	**MBDL**	**WCR**	**WCR**	**WCR**	
47851/D1648 (47639)	**CS**	**MBDL**	**GRN**	**WCR**	**WCR**	***Traction Magazine***
47854 (47674)	**CS**	**MBDL**	**WCR**	**WCR**	**WCR**	

Class 57

Vehicle Length: 63ft 6in (19.38m)	*Engine: EMD 645-12E3*
Height: 12ft 10⅛in (3.91m)	*Horsepower: 2,500hp (1,860kW)*
Width: 9ft 2in (2.79m)	*Electrical Equipment: Brush*

Number	*Depot*	*Pool*	*Livery*	*Owner*	*Operator*
57601 (47825)	**CS**	**MBDL**	**WCR**	**WCR**	**WCR**

Not all locomotives owned by West Coast Railways are in front line condition and use. A number are stored at the operator's Carnforth base, some are used for spares while others might return to use if business opportunities arise. Here several locos are seen awaiting attention in the yard at Carnforth on 27 July 2008. **Jack Boskett**

Coaching Stock

Number	Name	Type	Depot	Livery	Operator	Notes
159 (99980)		AO10/SAL	CS	-	WCR	Former LNWR saloon
326 (S) (99402)	*Emerald*	AO11/PFP	CS	PUL	WCR	
348 (99348)	Car No. 348	AO11/PSP	CS	WCR	WCR	
350 (99350)	Car No. 350	AO11/PSP	CS	GRN	WCR	
352 (99352)	Car No. 352	AO11/PSP	CS	PUL	WCR	
354 (99354)	*The Hadrian Bar*	AO11/PSP	CS	PUL	WCR	
504 (99678)	*Ullswater*	AP1Z/PFK	CS	PUL	WCR	
506 (99679)	*Windermere*	AP1Z/PFK	CS	PUL	WCR	
546 (S) (99670)	*City of Manchester*	AQ1Z/PFP	CS	PUL	WCR	
548 (99671)	*Grasmere*	AQ1Z/PFP	CS	PUL	WCR	
549 (99672)	*Bassenthwaite*	AQ1Z/PFP	CS	PUL	WCR	
550 (99673)	*Rydal Water*	AQ1Z/PFP	CS	PUL	WCR	
551 (99674)	*Buttermere*	AQ1Z/PFP	CS	PUL	WCR	
552 (99675)	*Ennerdale Water*	AQ1Z/PFP	CS	PUL	WCR	
553 (99676)	*Crummock Water*	AQ1Z/PFP	CS	PUL	WCR	
586 (99677)	*Derwent Water*	AR1Z/PFB	CS	PUL	WCR	
807 (99881)		AO10/SAL	CS	-	WCR	Former GNR Saloon
1644 (S)		AJ41/RBR	CS	ICS	WCR	
1650 (S)		AJ41/RBR	CS	ICS	WCR	
1652 (S)		AJ41/RBR	CS	ICS	WCR	
1655 (S)		AJ41/RBR	CS	ICS	WCR	
1663 (S)		AJ41/RBR	CS	ICS	WCR	
1670 (S)		AJ41/RBR	CS	ICS	WCR	
1800 (5970)	*Tintagel*	AN2F/RSS	CS	CHC	WCR	
1840		AN21/RMB	CS	GRN	WCR	Set - The Green Train
1860		AN21/RMB	CS	WCR	WCR	
1861 (99132)		AN21/RMB	CS	WCR	WCR	
1882 (99311)		AN21/RMB	CS	WCR	WCR	
1961		AJ41/RBR	CS	GRN	WCR	Set - The Green Train
2127 (S)		AO11/SLF	CS	MAR	WCR	
2833 (21270)		AU51/SLSC	CS	BLU	WCR	
3105 (99121)	*Julia*	AD11/FO	CS	WCR	WCR	
3106	*Alexandra*	AD11/FO	CS	WCR	WCR	
3113 (99125)	*Jessica*	AD11/FO	CS	WCR	WCR	
3117 (99127)		AD11/FO	CS	WCR	WCR	
3128 (99371)	*Victoria*	AD11/FO	CS	WCR	WCR	
3130 (99128)		AD11/FO	CS	WCR	WCR	
3136 (3605)	*Diana*	AD11/FO	CS	WCR	WCR	
3143 (3609)	*Patricia*	AD11/FO	CS	WCR	WCR	
3309		AD1F/FO	CS	ICS	WCR	
3313 (S)		AD1F/FO	CS	BPM	WCR	Blue Pullman vehicle
3326 (S)		AD1F/FO	CS	BPM	WCR	Blue Pullman vehicle
3350 (S)		AD1F/FO	CS	BPM	WCR	Blue Pullman vehicle
3352 (S)		AD1F/FO	CS	BPM	WCR	Blue Pullman vehicle
3359		AD1F/FO	CS	WCR	WCR	
3360		AD1F/FO	CS	ICS	WCR	
3362		AD1F/FO	CS	ICS	WCR	
3392 (S)		AD1F/FO	CS	BPM	WCR	Blue Pullman vehicle
3395 (S)		AD1F/FO	CS	BPM	WCR	Blue Pullman vehicle
3408		AD1F/FO	CS	WCR	WCR	
3416		AD1F/FO	CS	ICS	WCR	
3431 (S)		AD1F/FO	CS	BPM	WCR	Blue Pullman vehicle
3766 (99317)		AC21/SO	CS	WCR	WCR	
4860 (S) (99193)		AC21/TSO	CS	MAR	WCR	
4905		AC21/TSO	CS	WCR	WCR	
4912 (99318)		AC21/TSO	CS	WCR	WCR	
4931 (99329)		AC21/TSO	CS	WCR	WCR	
4932 (S)		AC21/TSO	CS	BLG	WCR	
4940		AC21/TSO	CS	WCR	WCR	
4951		AC21/TSO	CS	WCR	WCR	
4954 (99326)		AC21/TSO	CS	WCR	WCR	
4958		AC21/TSO	CS	WCR	WCR	
4960		AC21/TSO	CS	WCR	WCR	
4973		AC21/TSO	CS	WCR	WCR	

WCRC

4984		AC21/TSO	CS	WCR	WCR	
4994		AC21/TSO	CS	WCR	WCR	
4997 (S)		AC21/TSO	CS	BLG	WCR	
5032 (99194)		AC21/TSO	CS	WCR	WCR	
5033 (99328)		AC21/TSO	CS	WCR	WCR	
5035 (99195)		AC21/TSO	CS	WCR	WCR	
5044 (99327)		AC21/TSO	CS	WCR	WCR	
5125 (S)		AC2Z/TSO	BH	GRN	WCR	
5171		AC2Z/TSO	CS	GRN	WCR	
5200		AC2Z/TSO	CS	GRN	WCR	
5216		AC2Z/TSO	CS	GRN	WCR	
5222		AC2Z/TSO	CS	MAR	WCR	
5229	*The Green Knight*	AC2Z/SO	CS	CHC	WTN	
5236		AC2Z/SO	CS	GRN	WCR	
5237		AD2Z/SO	CS	GRN	WCR	
5239	*The Red Knight*	AD2Z/SO	CS	CHC	WTN	
5249		AD2Z/SO	CS	GRN	WCR	
5278	*Melisande*	AC2A/TSO	CS	CHC	WTN	
5299 (S) (99321)		AC2A/TSO	CS	WCR	WCR	
5419	*Sir Launcelot*	AC2A/TSO	CS	CHC	WTN	
5453		AC2B/TSO	CS	WCR	WCR	
5463 (S)		AC2B/TSO	CS	WCR	WCR	
5478		AC2B/TSO	CS	WCR	WCR	
5487		AC2B/TSO	CS	WCR	WCR	
5491		AC2B/TSO	CS	WCR	WCR	
5569		AC2C/TSO	CS	WCR	WCR	
5600 (S) (99322)		AC2C/TSO	CS	WCR	WCR	
5669 (S)		AC2D/TSO	EM	BPM	CWR	Blue Pullman vehicle
5727 (S) (99325)		AC2D/TSO	CS	WCR	WCR	
5756 (S)		AC2E/TSO	CS	WCR	WCR	
5874		AC2E/TSO	CS	WCR	WCR	
5917 (S)		AC2F/TSO	CS	VIR	WCR	At Hellifield
5928		AC2F/TSO	EH	CHC	WCR	
6000		AC2F/TSO	CS	WCR	WCR	
6014 (S)		AC2F/TSO	CS	ICS	WCR	At Hellifield
6022		AC2F/TSO	CS	WCR	WCR	
6041		AC2F/TSO	CS	WCR	WCR	
6103		AC2F/TSO	CS	WCR	WCR	
6115 (S)		AC2F/TSO	CS	WCR	WCR	
6135 (S)		AC2F/TSO	CS	ICS	WCR	At Hellifield
6148 (S)		AC2F/TSO	CS	ICS	WCR	At Hellifield
6312 (92925)		AX51/GEN	CS	PUL	WCR	
9391	*Pendragon*	AE2Z/BSO	CS	PUL	WTN	
9493 (S)		AE2D/BSO	EM	BPM	CWR	Blue Pullman vehicle
6523 (S) (5568)		AG2C/TSOT	CS	WCR	WCR	
6528 (5592)		AG2C/TSOT	CS	WCR	WCR	
9104 (S) (9401)		AH2Z/BSOT	CS	WCR	WCR	
9392		AE2Z/BSO	CS	WCR	WCR	Set - The Green Train
9440		AE2C/BSO	CS	WCR	WCR	
9448 (S)		AE2C/BSO	CS	WCR	WCR	
13306 (S)		AA11/FK	CS	WCR	WCR	
13320 (S)		AA11/FK	CS	WCR	WCR	
13321 (S) (99316)		AA11/FK	CS	MAR	WCR	
13440 (S)		AA1A/FK	CS	GRN	WCR	Set - The Green Train
17102 (99680)		AB1A/BFK	CS	MAB	WCR	
17168 (S) (99319)		AB1D/BFK	CS	WCR	WCR	
18756 (99721)		AA21/SK	CS	WCR	WCR	
18767 (99710)		AA21/SK	CS	WCR	WCR	
18806 (99722)		AA21/SK	CS	WCR	WCR	
18808 (99706)		AA21/SK	CS	WCR	WCR	
18837 (S) (99717)		AA21/SK	CS	WCR	WCR	
18862 (99718)		AA21/SK	CS	WCR	WCR	
18893 (S) (99712)		AA21/SK	CS	CHC	WCR	
19013 (S) (99713)		AA21/SK	CS	MAR	WCR	
19208 (99884)	Car No. 84	AA21/SK	CS	WCR	WCR	
21256 (99304)		AB31/BCK	CS	WCR	WCR	
21266		AB31/BCK	CS	WCR	WCR	
35407 (99886)		AB21/BSK	CJ	-	WCR	Finished in LNWR livery

34525 (S) (99966)	AR51/GEN	CS	WCR	WCR	
35459 (99723)	AB21/BSK	CS	WCR	WCR	
45018 (99052)	AO10/SAL	CJ	QOS	WCR	
45026 (S)	SAL	CS	MAR	WCR	LMS Inspection Saloon

Above: *West Coast Railway liveried and owned Brake Composite Corridor No. 21266.* **Nathan Williamson**

Below: *A number of former BR operated Metro-Cammell Pullman cars are now owned and operated by West Coast Railways, offering a high-quality travelling environment in two-one seating with an at-seat silver service dining facility. Car No. 99352, the original BR Pullman No. 352 is illustrated, painted in standard West Coast Railway livery.* **Nathan Williamson**

Loco Support Coaches

Most preserved locomotives authorised for main line operation, either steam or diesel, operate with a support coach conveying owners' representatives, engineering staff and light maintenance equipment. Support coaches can be allocated to a specific locomotive or operate with a pool of locos.

Number	*Type*	*Depot*	*Livery*	*Support Coach for*
14007 (99782) *Mercator*	AB11/BSK	BH	MAR	61264
17013 (14013) *Botaurus*	AB11/BFK	SH	PUL	60019
17019 (99792)	AB11/BFK	CS	MAR	30777 or 70013
17025 (14025)	AB11/BFK	CS	MAR	45690
17041 (99141)	AB1Z/BFK	BQ	MAR	71000
17096	AB1B/BFK	SL	CHC	35028
21096 (99080)	AB31/BCK	NY	MAR	60007
21232 (99040)	AB31/BCK	SK	MAR	46233
21236 (99120)	AB31/BCK	ZG	GRN	30828
21268	AB31/BCK	SH	MAR	46100
35317	AD21/BSK	BQ	GRN	30850
35322 (99035)	AB21/BSK	CJ	LNW	70000
35329	AB21/BSK	RL	GRN	Mid Hants fleet
35333 (99180)	AB21/BSK	DI	CHC	6024
35449 (99241)	AB21/BSK	BQ	MAR	45231
35453	AB21/BSK	DI	CHC	5051
35457 (99995)	AB21/BSK	NY	MAR	60532
35461 (99720)	AB21/BSK	TM	CHC	5029
35463 (99312)	AB21/BSK	CS	WCR	WCR fleet
35464	AB21/BSK	PR	MAR	Swanage Railway
35465 (99991)	AB21/BSK	BQ	CCM	46201
35468 (99953)	AB21/BSK	NY	MAR	NYMR fleet
35470	AB21/BSK	TM	CHC	Vintage Trains fleet
35476 (99041)	AB21/BSK	SK	MAR	46233
35479	AB21/BSK	KR	CHC	SVR fleet
35486 (99405)	AB21/BSK	--	MAR	60009 or 61994
35508	AB1C/BSK	BQ	MAR	East Lancs fleet
35517 (17088)	ABIK/BSKk	BQ	MAR	East Lancs fleet
35518 (17097)	AB11/BFK	SH	GRN	34067
80204 (35297)	NNX	CS	MAR	WCRC fleet
80217 (35299)	NNX	CS	MAR	WCRC fleet
80220 (35276)	NNX	NY	MAR	62005

Left: *Viewed at Carnforth is support coach 80204, modified with roller shutter door from BSK No. 35297. This vehicle is a support coach which can be used with GW 'Castle' No. 5972, or LMS locos 46115 or 48151.* **Nathan Williamson**

Left: *In keeping with the colours of the Great Western Railway, the support coach 35333 for preserved ex-GWR 'King' No. 6024* King Edward I *is chocolate and cream. The coach is viewed at St Blazey depot while the loco was operating charter traffic in Cornwall.* **Tony Christie**

Locomotives

Number	Class	Owner	Location
57001	57/0	PTR	LB
66403	66/4	PTR	WB
66404	66/4	PTR	WB
66405	66/4	PTR	WB
66410	66/4	PTR	WB
87009	87/0	PTR	LM
87011	87/0	PTR	LM
87017	87/0	PTR	LM
87018	87/0	PTR	LM
87020	87/0	PTR	LM
87021	87/0	PTR	LM
87023	87/0	PTR	LM
87025	87/0	PTR	LM
87027	87/0	PTR	LM
87029	87/0	PTR	LM
87030	87/0	PTR	LM
87031	87/0	PTR	LM
87032	87/0	PTR	LM
87033	87/0	PTR	LM

Right: *Porterbrook Leasing-owned Class 87/0 No. 87023 stands in the yard of Motorail Logistics at Long Marston. This loco is scheduled for restoration and sale to Bulgaria.* **CJM**

Diesel Multiple Units

At the time of writing no DMU stock was off-lease

Electric Multiple Units

Number	Class	Owner	Location
316997	316	SEC	EH#
310049	310	HSB	KT
310050	310	HSB	PY
310051	310	HSB	PY
310059	310	HSB	PY
310069	310	HSB	PY
310070	310	HSB	PY
310102	310	HSB	PY
310108	310	HSB	PY
310110	310	HSB	PY
310111	310	HSB	PY
321407	321/4	HSB	ZG¤
321408	321/4	HSB	ZG
321409	321/4	HSB	ZG
321410	321/4	HSB	ZG¤
321418	321/4	HSB	ZG
321419	321/4	HSB	ZG
321420	321/4	HSB	ZG
321426	321/4	HSB	ZB§
321428	321/4	HSB	ZG§
321429	321/4	HSB	ZG§
321430	321/4	HSB	ZG§
321431	321/4	HSB	ZG§
321432	321/4	HSB	SO§
321433	321/4	HSB	ZG§
365526	365	HSB	ZC*
390033	390	ANG	LM*
- Cars 69633 & 69733 at Fire Service Training School, Moreton-in-Marsh			
508201	508	ANG	AF
508202	508	ANG	AF
508203	508	ANG	SL
508204	508	ANG	AF
508205	508	ANG	SL
508206	508	ANG	AF
508207	508	ANG	SL
508208	508	ANG	GI
508209	508	ANG	AF
508210	508	ANG	SL
508211	508	ANG	SL
508212	508	ANG	GI
508301	508	ANG	ZG
508302	508	ANG	ZG
508303	508	ANG	ZG

* Collision damage
\# Holec test set
¤ For FCC
§ For NEEA

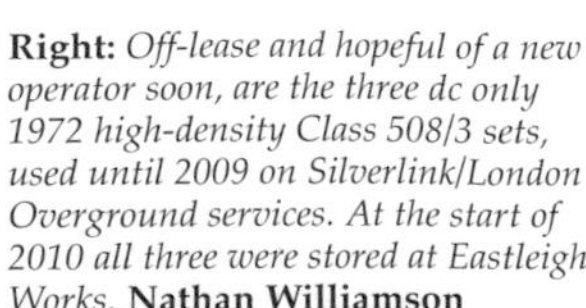

Right: *Off-lease and hopeful of a new operator soon, are the three dc only 1972 high-density Class 508/3 sets, used until 2009 on Silverlink/London Overground services. At the start of 2010 all three were stored at Eastleigh Works.* **Nathan Williamson**

Off Lease Rolling Stock

Coaching Stock - Passenger

Number	Type	Owner	Location
1203 (3291)	RFO	HSB	CD
1204 (3401)	RFO	HSB	PY
1207 (6422)	RFO	HSB	ZG
1209 (6457)	RFO	HSB	ZH
1211 (3305)	RFO	HSB	LM
1214 (6433)	RFO	HSB	KT
1219 (3418)	RFO	HSB	KT
1221 (3371)	RFO	HSB	ZG
1253 (3432)	RFO	HSB	LM
1256 (3296)	RFO	HSB	ZA
1258 (3322)	RFO	HSB	KT
3229	FO	HSB	KT
3303	FO	HSB	OC
3351	FO	HSB	TM
3434	FO	HSB	OY
3438	FO	HSB	LM
5148	TSO	HSB	TM
5179	TSO	HSB	TM
5183	TSO	HSB	TM
5186	TSO	HSB	TM
5193	TSO	HSB	TM
5194	TSO	HSB	TM
5212	TSO	HSB	TM
5221	TSO	HSB	TM
5636	TSO	HSB	PM
5679	TSO	HSB	KT
5737	TSO	HSB	KT
5740	TSO	HSB	KT
5745	TSO	HSB	KT
5750	TSO	HSB	KT
5754	TSO	HSB	KT
5788	TSO	HSB	KT
5789	TSO	HSB	LM
5793	TSO	HSB	KT
5797	TSO	HSB	LM
5821	TSO	HSB	KT
5866	TSO	HSB	GL
5881	TSO	HSB	KT
5886	TSO	HSB	KT
5888	TSO	HSB	KT
5899	TSO	HSB	KT
5900	TSO	HSB	KT
5903	TSO	HSB	KT
5905	TSO	HSB	KT
5906	TSO	HSB	BH
5908	TSO	HSB	ZG
5912	TSO	HSB	KT
5925	TSO	HSB	LM
5930	TSO	HSB	KT
5933	TSO	HSB	ZG
5936	TSO	HSB	LM
5940	TSO	HSB	ZG
5943	TSO	HSB	ZG¤
5947	TSO	HSB	ZG¤
5948	TSO	HSB	ZG¤
5949	TSO	HSB	ZG¤
5957	TSO	HSB	ZG¤
5958	TSO	HSB	GL
5960	TSO	HSB	KT
5962	TSO	HSB	KT
5969	TSO	HSB	ZG
5977	TSO	HSB	ZG¤
5978	TSO	HSB	ZG
5980	TSO	HSB	ZG¤
5981	TSO	HSB	ZA
5983	TSO	HSB	KT
5991	TSO	HSB	KT
5997	TSO	HSB	ZH
6009	TSO	HSB	ZG¤
6012	TSO	HSB	ZG¤
6016	TSO	HSB	ZG
6021	TSO	HSB	ZG
6028	TSO	HSB	ZG
6029	TSO	HSB	ZG¤
6031	TSO	HSB	ZG¤
6037	TSO	HSB	ZG¤
6049	TSO	HSB	KT
6050	TSO	HSB	ZG
6052	TSO	HSB	KT
6053	TSO	HSB	KT
6059	TSO	HSB	KT
6061	TSO	HSB	ZG¤
6073	TSO	HSB	KT
6101	TSO	HSB	ZG
6120	TSO	HSB	KT
6121	TSO	HSB	KT
6136	TSO	HSB	ZG
6150	TSO	HSB	ZG
6151	TSO	HSB	ZG
6160	TSO	HSB	LM
6164	TSO	HSB	KT
6168	TSO	HSB	GL
6175	TSO	HSB	ZG¤
6179	TSO	HSB	ZG¤

¤ For export to New Zealand

Number	Type	Owner	Location
9480	BSO	HSB	KT
9481	BSO	HSB	ZA
9490	BSO	HSB	KT
9496	BSO	HSB	TM
9497	BSO	HSB	KT
9498	BSO	HSB	KT
9500	BSO	HSB	LM
9505	BSO	HSB	LM
9516	BSO	HSB	KT
9522	BSO	HSB	KT
9523	BSO	HSB	KT
9525	BSO	HSB	BH
9538	BSO	HSB	KT
9704	DBSO	HSB	ZG
9705	DBSO	HSB	ZG
9707	DBSO	HSB	ZG
9709	DBSO	HSB	ZG
9710	DBSO	HSB	ZG
10204 (40502)	RFM	PTR	3M
10231 (10016)	RFM	PTR	LM
10240 (10003)	RFM	PTR	LM
10245 (10019)	RFM	PTR	ZB
10253 (10026)	RFM	PTR	LM
10256 (10028)	RFM	PTR	GW¶
10259 (10025)	RFM	PTR	LM
10260 (10001)	RFM	PTR	GW¶

¶ Instruction vehicle - Shields

Number	Type	Owner	Location
10540	SLE	PTR	OM
10547	SLE	PTR	IS
10596	SLE	PTR	LM
10661	Concept vehicle at Wolverton		
10682	SLE	PTR	TO
11006	FO	PTR	LM
11011	FO	PTR	LM
11026	FO	PTR	LM
12008	TSO	PTR	ZB
12022	TSO	PTR	ZB
12029	TSO	PTR	LM
12036	TSO	PTR	LM
12045	TSO	PTR	LM
12047	TSO	PTR	LM
12078	TSO	PTR	ZB
12083	TSO	PTR	LM
12087	TSO	PTR	LM
12095	TSO	PTR	LM
12101	TSO	PTR	LM
12134	TSO	PTR	LM
12142	TSO	PTR	LM
12144	TSO	PTR	LM
12156	TSO	PTR	LM
12158	TSO	PTR	BN
12160	TSO	PTR	LM
12163	TSO	PTR	BN

Coaching Stock - HST

Number	Type	Owner	Location
40208 (40008)	TRSB	ANG	ZG
40209 (40009)	TRSB	ANG	ZG
40228 (40028)	TRSB	ANG	ZG
40402 (40002)	TRSB	PTR	LM
40403 (40003)	TRSB	PTR	LM
40416 (40016)	TRSB	PTR	LM
40417 (40017)	TRSB	PTR	ZK
40419 (40019)	TRSB	PTR	LM
40425 (40025)	TRSB	PTR	ZK
40434 (40034)	TRSB	PTR	LM
40717 (40317)	TRSB	ANG	ZG
40731 (40331)	TRSB	ANG	ZG
40747 (40347)	TRSB	ANG	ZG

Coaching Stock - NPCCS

Number	Type	Owner	Location
82106	DVT	PTR	ZB
82109	DVT	PTR	ZB
82110	DVT	PTR	LM
82111	DVT	PTR	LM
82115	DVT	PTR	ZN
82124	DVT	PTR	LM
82125	DVT	PTR	LM
82126	DVT	PTR	ZB

82128	DVT	PTR	LM
82129	DVT	PTR	LM
82140	DVT	PTR	LM
82141	DVT	PTR	LM
82145	DVT	PTR	LM
82149	DVT	PTR	FC
92159 (81534)	BG	HSB	KT
92901 (92001)	BG	HSB	WB
92931 (92031)	BG	HSB	PY
96100 (93734)	GUV	HSB	TM
96139 (93751)	GUV	HSB	WB
96175 (93628)	GUV	HSB	CS
96181 (93875)	GUV	HSB	LM
96602 (96150)	NV	HSB	LM
96603 (96155)	NV	HSB	LM
96604 (96156)	NV	HSB	LM
96605 (96157)	NV	HSB	LM
96606 (96213)	NV	HSB	LM
96607 (96215)	NV	HSB	LM
96608 (96216)	NV	HSB	LM
96609 (96217)	NV	HSB	LM

Above: *The eight HSBC-owned side-loading Motorail vehicles used for a short time to carry motor cars between London Paddington and Penzance as part of the Night Riviera services, are all stored at Long Marston with little hope of finding further work. No. 96604 is illustrated.* **CJM**

Below: *Much speculation has always surrounded the possibility of rebuilding the large number of off-lease Mk3 sleeping cars into day saloons. However, even after a prototype was modified, no follow-on contracts were placed. Here we see Porterbrook-owned concept vehicle No. 10661 at Wolverton Works; note the rounded windows at the far end.* **CJM**

Preserved Motive Power

Preserved motive power is listed in this section. Those in a red type face are authorised for main line operation. For information on preserved steam traction and railway centres, please refer to our sister publication *Railways Restored*, published by Ian Allan publishing.

Locomotives

Main line certified shown in red

Prototype Locomotives

Number	*Operator/Base*	*Status*
LMS7050	NRM	STC
LMS7051	MID	OPR
LMS7069	GWR	RES
D0226	KWV	OPR
18000	BHR	STC
DELTIC	NRM	STC

Non Classified

Number	*Operator/Base*	*Status*
D2511	KWV	OPR
D2767	BKR	OPR
D2774	STR	RES
DS75	NRS	STC

Class 01

Number	*Operator/Base*	*Status*
D2953	PRL	OPR
D2956	ELR	OPR

Class 02

Number	*Operator/Base*	*Status*
D2854	PRL	OPR
D2858	MRC	RES
D2860	NRM	OPR
D2866	PRL	RES
D2867	BAT	OPR
D2868	PRL	OPR

Class 03

Number	*Operator/Base*	*Status*
03018	MFM	RES
03020	LDL	STO
03022	SWI	OPR
D2023	KES	OPR
D2024	KES	STO
03027	PRL	RES
03037	PRL	OPR
D2041	COL	OPR
D2046	PVR	RES
D2051	NNR	STO
03059	IOW	OPR
03062	ELR	OPR
03063	NNR	OPR
03066	BHR	OPR
03069	GWR	OPR
03072	LHR	OPR
03073	RAC	OPR
03078	TYN	OPR
03079	DER	OPR
03081	MFM	RES
03084	ECC	OPR
03089	MFM	OPR
03090	NRS	OPR
03094	CRT	OPR
03099	PRL	OPR
03113	PRL	RES
D2117	LHR	OPR
D2118	PRL	RES
03119	WSR	OPR
03120	FHL	OPR
03128	APF	STO
D2133	WSR	OPR
03134	DEE	OPR
D2138	MRC	OPR
D2139	PRL	RES
03141	PRB	RES
03144	WEN	OPR
03145	MOL	OPR
D2148	RIB	OPR
03152	SWI	OPR
03158	LWR	OPR
03162	LAN	OPR
03170	BAT	OPR
D2178	GWI	OPR
D2182	GWR	OPR
D2184	COL	OPR
03189	RIB	RES
D2192	PDR	OPR
D2199	PRL	OPR
03371	ROW	OPR
03399	MFM	OPR

Class 04

Number	*Operator/Base*	*Status*
D2203	EMB	OPR
D2205	WSR	STO
D2207	NYM	OPR
D2229	PRL	RES
D2245	BAT	STO
D2246	SDR	OPR
D2271	WSR	STO
D2272	PRL	RES
D2279	EAR	OPR
D2280	NNR	RES
D2284	PRL	OPR
D2298	BRC	OPR
D2302	BHR	OPR
D2310	BAT	OPR
D2324	BHR	STO
D2325	MFM	OPR
D2334	CVR	OPR
D2337	PRL	RES

Class 05

Number	*Operator/Base*	*Status*
05001	IOW	OPR
D2578	MOL	OPR
D2587	PRL	RES
D2595	RIB	OPR

Class 06

Number	*Operator/Base*	*Status*
06003	PRL	OPR

Class 07

Number	*Operator/Base*	*Status*
07005	GCR	RES
07010	AVR	OPR
07011	SEL	OPR
07012	APF	RES
07013	PRL	RES

Class 08

Number	*Operator/Base*	*Status*
D3000	APF	RES
D3002	PVR	OPR
D3014	PDR	OPR
08011	CPR	OPR
08012	CRT	OPR
08015	SVR	OPR
08016	PRL	OPR
08021	BRM	OPR
08022	CWR	OPR
08032	MHR	OPR
08046	CRB	OPR
08054	EMB	OPR
08060	CWR	OPR
08064	NRS	OPR
D3101	GCR	OPR
08102	LWR	OPR
08108	KES	OPR
08114	GCR	OPR
08123	CWR	OPR
08133	SVR	OPR
D3255	CVR	STO
08164	ELR	OPR
08168	BAT	OPR
D3261	SWI	RES
08195	LAN	OPR
08220	NHC	STO
08238	DFR	OPR
08266	KWV	OPR
08288	MHR	OPR
08359	TSR	OPR
08377	WSR	OPR
08388	NHD	STO
08436	SWN	OPR
08443	BKR	RES
08444	BWR	OPR
08471	SVR	OPR
08473	DFR	STO
08476	SWN	OPR
08479	ELR	OPR
08481	VOG	RES
08490	STR	OPR
08556	NYM	OPR
08590	MRC	OPR
08604	DID	OPR
08631	MNR	OPR
08635	SVR	RES
08683	GWR	RES
08694	GCR	RES
08700	ELR	OPR
08734	DFR	STO
08767	NNR	OPR
08769	SVR	OPR
08772	NNR	OPR
08773	EMB	OPR
08780	SOU	OPR
08830	RAC	OPR
08850	NYM	OPR§
08891	SVR	RES
08911	NRM	OPR
08937	DAR	OPR
08944	ELR	OPR

§ Battersby-Whitby only

Class 09

09002	SDR	RES
09004	SPV	OPR
09025	SWI	OPR

Class 10

D3452	BWR	OPR
D3489	SPV	OPR
D4067	GCR	OPR
D4092	BHR	RES

Class 11

12049	MHR	OPR
12052	CRB	STO
12061	PRL	RES
12077	MRC	OPR
12093	CRB	OPR
12099	SVR	OPR
12131	NNR	OPR

Class 12

15224	SPV	OPR

Class 14

D9500	PRL	RES
D9502	PRL	STO
D9504	NVR	OPR
D9513	EMB	OPR
D9516	NVR	OPR
D9520	NVR	OPR
D9521	DFR	OPR
D9523	NVR	OPR
D9524	EHC	RES
D9525	PRL	OPR
D9526	WSR	OPR
D9531	ELR	RES
D9537	RIP	RES
D9539	RIB	OPR
D9551	DEE	OPR
D9553	GWR	STO
D9555	DFR	OPR

Class 15

D8233	ELR	RES

Class 17

D8568	CPR	RES

Class 20

D8000	NRM	OPR
20001	ECC	OPR
20007	GCR	OPR
20020	BKR	RES
20031	KWV	OPR
20048	MRC	RES
20059	BRM	RES
20069	MNR	OPR
20087	ELR	OPR
20098	GCR	RES
20110	SDR	OPR
20118	SDR	OPR
20137	GWR	OPR
20142	BHR	OPR
20154	GCR	OPR
20166	WEN	OPR
20169	SRC	RES
20177	BRM	STO
20188	SVR	OPR
20189	MRC	OPR
20205	MRC	RES
20214	LHR	OPR
20227	MRC	OPR

Class 24

24032	NYM	RES
24054	ELR	OPR
24061	NYM	RES
24082	GWR	OPR

Class 25

25035	GCR	OPR
25057	NNR	OPR
25059	KWV	OPR
25067	BAT	OPR
25072	CRB	RES
25083	CRB	RES
25173	WSR	OPR
25185	PDR	OPR
25191	NYM	STO
25235	BKR	RES
25244	EKR	STO
25262	SDR	OPR
25265	GCR	RES
25278	NYM	OPR
25279	GCR	OPR
25283	DFR	RES
25309	WCR	RES
25313	WEN	RES
25321	MRC	OPR
25322	CVR	RES

Class 26

26001	CRB	OPR
26002	STR	RES
26004	BKR	STO
26007	BHR	OPR
26010	LAN	OPR
26011	BHR	RES
26014	CRB	OPR
26024	BKR	OPR
26025	STR	RES
26035	CRB	RES
26038	CAN	RES
26040	MET	RES
26043	GWR	RES

Class 27

27001	BKR	OPR
27005	BKR	STO
27007	MHR	RES
27024	LHR	OPR
27050	STR	RES
27056	GCR	OPR
27059	SVR	RES
27066	DFR	OPR

Class 28

D5705	ELR	RES

Class 31

D5500	NRM	OPR
31101	BAT	RES
31108	MRC	OPR
31119	EMB	OPR
31130	BAT	OPR
31144	NHD	RES
31162	EHC	OPR
31163	CPR	OPR
31203	PBR	OPR
31206	RST	OPR
31207	NNR	OPR
31210	DFR	RES
31235	MNR	OPR
31255	COL	OPR
31270	PRL	OPR
31271	NVR	OPR
31289	NLR	OPR
31327	STR	OPR
31410	SRC	RES
31414	ECC	OPR
31415	BHR	RES
31418	MRC	RES
31422	RVE	RES
31435	EMB	OPR
31438	MNR	OPR
31461	BAT	STO
31463	GCR	OPR
31466	DFR	OPR
31530	MNR	RES

Class 33

33002	SDR	OPR
33008	BAT	RES
33012	SWN	OPR
33018	MRC	STO
33019	BAT	OPR
33021	BRM	RES
33035	BHR	RES
33046	MRC	STO
33048	WSR	OPR
33052	KES	OPR
33053	MHR	OPR
33057	WSR	RES
33063	SPV	OPR
33065	SPV	RES
33102	CVR	RES
33103	BHR	RES
33108	BHR	RES
33109	ELR	OPR
33110	BWR	RES
33111	SWN	OPR
33116	GCR	OPR
33117	ELR	RES
33201	MRC	OPR
33202	MFM	OPR
33208	MHR	OPR

Class 35

D7017	WSR	OPR
D7018	WSR	RES
D7029	SVR	RES
D7076	ELR	OPR

Class 37

D6700	NRM/NYM	OPR
37003	MNR	OPR
37009	GCR	RES
37023	ALY	RES

37025	BKR	RES
37032	NNR	RES
37037	SDR	OPR
37075	CVR	OPR
37097	CRB	OPR
37109	ELR	OPR
37116	CPR	OPR
37142	BWR	OPR
37146	SRC	RES
37152	PRL	RES
37175	BKR	RES
37188	PRL	RES
37207	PVR	RES
37215	GWR	OPR
37216	PBR	OPR
37219	CPR	OPR
37227	BAT	OPR
37240	LAN	OPR
37250	EDR	RES
37254	SPV	OPR
37255	GCR	OPR
37263	DFR	RES
37264	BRM	RES
37275	BHR	OPR
37294	EMB	RES
37308	EHD	RES
37314	MRC	OPR
37324	GWR	OPR
37372	BHR	RES
37403	BKR	RES
37407	CVR	STO
37413	BKR	RES
37418	ELR	RES
37421	PBR	RES
37424	CVR	STO
37518	NVR	OPR
37674	SRC	RES
37679	NLR	RES
37901	ELR	OPR
37905	BAT	OPR
37906	SVR	OPR

Class 40

D200	NRM	RES
40012	MRC	OPR
40013	BHR	OPR
40106	NVR	OPR
40118	BRM	RES
40135	ELR	OPR
40145	ELR	OPR

Class 41

41001	NRM	STC

Class 42

D821	SVR	OPR
D832	WSR	OPR

Class 44

D4	MRC	RES
44008	PRL	OPR

Class 45

45014	BAT	STO
45041	MRC	OPR
45060	BHR	RES
45105	BHR	RES
45108	MRC	RES
45118	NLR	RES
45125	GCR	OPR
45132	MHR	RES
45133	MRC	RES
45135	ELR	RES
45149	GWR	RES

Class 46

46010	GCN	OPR
46035	RAC	STO
46045	MRC	OPR

Class 47

47004	EMB	OPR
47105	GWR	OPR
47117	GCR	OPR
47192	DAR	OPR
47205	NLR	OPR
47292	GCR	OPR
47306	BWR	OPR
47367	NNR	OPR
47376	GWR	RES
47401	MRC	OPR
47402	ELR	OPR
47417	MRC	RES
47449	LAN	OPR
47484	GDM	STO
47524	CVR	RES
47540	WEN	STO
47580	BRM	OPR
47596	MNR	RES
47635	PRL	OPR
47640	BAT	OPR
47643	BKR	OPR
47701	DAR	OPR
47703	WEN	OPR
47714	GCR	OPR
47715	WEN	OPR
47716	BHR	RES
47746	MLM	STO
47765	GCR	RES
47768	BIR¤	OPR
47771	COL	RES
47785	ECC	RES
47793	MFM	OPR
47798	NRM	OPR
47840	WST	OPR

¤ *For sale*

Class 50

50002	SDR	RES
50007	MRC	OPR
50008	ELR	OPR
50015	ELR	OPR
50017	PVR	RES
50019	MNR	OPR
50021	BRM	RES
50026	EHD	RES
50027	NYM	OPR
50029	PRL	STO
50030	PRL	RES
50031	SVR	RES
50033	BRM	STO
50135	EHD	OPR
50042	BWR	OPR
50044	SVR	OPR
50049	SVR	OPR
50050	YEO	RES

Class 52

D1010	WSR	OPR
D1013	SVR	OPR
D1015	EHD	OPR
D1023	NRM	OPR
D1041	ELR	STO
D1048	MRC	RES
D1062	SVR	OPR

Class 55

55002	NRM	RES
55009	BHR	OPR
55015	BHR	RES
55016	ELR	OPR
55019	BHR	OPR
55022	ELR	OPR

Class 56

56040	MNR	OPR
56086	BAT	RES
56097	GCR	OPR
56098	BAT	RES
56101	BHR	RES

Class 97

97650	LWR	OPR
97651	STR	OPR
97654	PRL	OPR

Class 71

71001	NRM	STO

Class 73

73001	DFR	OPR
73003	SWI	OPR
73005	SVR	RES
73006	SVR	OPR
73101	AVR	OPR
73103	ALY	STO
73104	WED	STO
73110	GCR	OPR
73114	BAT	OPR
73117	BHR	OPR
73118	VOG	OPR
73128	PBR	OPR
73129	GWR	OPR
73130	SLN	OPR
73134	BHR	OPR
73136	BLU	OPR
73138	MLM	OPR
73139	WED	OPR
73140	SPV	OPR
73210	MNR	OPR
73211	SLN	RES

Class 76

E26020	NRM	STC

Class 77

E27000	MRC	STC
E27001	MSM	STC

Class 81

81002	BHR	STC

Class 82

82008	BHR	STC

Class 83

83012	BHR	STC

Class 84

84001	BHR	STC

Class 85

85101	BHR	STC

Class 86

86101	BHR	OPR
86213¤	WB	OPR/WB
86233	MLM	STC
86259	BRM	OPR
86401¤	MLM	OPR/WB

Class 87

87001	NRM	STC
87002	MLM	OPR
87035	RAC	RES

Class 89

89001	BHR	STC

London Transport

12	LUL	OPR

¤ In use at depot shown for carriage heating

Right: *Love it or hate it, Fifty Fund-owned No. 50035 was repainted in 2009 in Loadhaul black and orange livery and renumbered as 50135, to show how the loco might have looked under the BR shadow privatisation freight banner. No. 50135 is seen at Long Marston.* **CJM**

Diesel Units

Number	*Base*
Unclassied	
APT-E	NRS
LEV1	NNR
RB004	TEL
79018	MRC
79612	MRC
79900	ECC
79960	NNR
79962	KWV
79963	NNR
79964	KWV
79976	GCR
79978	COL
Class 100	
56301	MNR
Class 101	
50222	BIR
50256	EKR
50338	BIR
51505	ECC
51187	CRT
51188	ECC
51189	KWV
51192	ELR
51205	CRT
51210	WEN
51226	MNR
51228	NNR
51247	WEN
51427	GCR
51434	MNR
51499	MNR
51503	MNR
51505	EAR
51511	NYM
51512	CRT
51213	EAR
51803	KWV
53160	CHS
53164	CHS
53170	MRC
53193	GCR
53203	GCR
53204	NYM
53253	MRC
53266	GCR
53321	GCR
53746	WEN
54055	CRT
54062	NNR
54365	EAR
54408	SPV
56343	EKR
56352	ELR
56358	EAR
59117	MNR
59539	NYM
Class 104	
50447	LAN
50454	LAN
50479	TEL
50528	LAN
50531	TEL
50556	TEL
54207	APF
59228	TEL
Class 105	
51485	ELR
56121	ELR
56456	LAN
Class 107	
51990	STR
52005	NVR
52006	AVR
52008	STR
52025	AVR
52030	STR
59791	NVR
Class 108	
50599	EAR
50619	DFR
50632	PBR
50929	KWV
50980	BWR
51562	NRM
51565	KWV
51566	DFR
51567	MRC
51568	KEI
51571	KES
51572	WEN
51907	LAN
51909	AVR
51914	DFR
51919	BVR
51922	NRM
51933	DFR
51941	SVR
51942	PBR
51947	BWR
51950	GWR
51973	MRC
52044	PBR
52048	BVR
52053	KEI
52054	BWR
52062	GWR
52064	SVR
53628	KEI
53645	GCR
53926	GCR
53971	KES
54223	EAR
54270	PBR
54279	LDL
54490	LAN
54504	SWN
56208	SVR
56224	ECC
56271	AVR
56484	MRC
56491	KEI
56492	DFR
56495	KLR
59245	APF
59250	SVR
59387	DFR
59389	GCR
Class 109	
50416	LAN
56171	LAN
Class 110	
51813	WEN
51842	WEN
52071	LHR
52077	LHR
59701	WEN
Class 111	
59575	MRC
Class 114	
50015	MRC
50019	MRC
54057	STR
56006	MRC
56015	MRC

Class 115
51655 (BIR)¤
51663 WSR
51669 SPV
51677 (BIR)¤
51849 SPV
51852 WSR
51859 WSR
51880 WSR
51886 BRC
51887 WSR
51899 BRC
59659 SDR
59664 (BIR)¤
59678 WSR
59719 SDR
59740 SDR
59761 BRC

Class 116
51131 BAT
51138 GCR
51151 GCR
51321 BAT
59003 PDR
59004 PDR
59444 CHS

Class 117
51339 (BIR)¤
51341 MRC
51342 EPO
51346 SWN
51347 GWI
51351 PBR
51353 MRC
51356 SWN
51359 NLR
51360 ECC
51363 MHR
51365 PVR
51367 STR
51372 TIT
51381 MFM
51382 (BIR)¤
51384 EPO
51388 SWN
51392 SWN
51395 MRC
51397 PBR
51398 MRC
51400 WEN
51401 GWI
51402 STR
51405 MHR
51407 PVR
59486 MRC
59488 PDR
59492 SWN
59494 PDR
59500 WEN
59503 PDR
59506 WSR
59507 PDR
59508 GWI
59509 WEN
59510 MHR
59513 PDR
59514 SWI
59516 SWN
59517 PDR
59520 PBR
59521 MRC
59522 CHS
59603 CHS

Class 119
51073 ECC
51074 SWI
51104 SWI

Class 120
59276 GCR

Class 121
55023 CPR
55028 SWN
55033 COL
56287 COL
54289 ECC

Class 122
55000 SDR
55001 ELR
55003 MHR
55005 BAT
55006 ECC
55009 MNR
55012 SHI

Class 126
51017 BKR
51043 BKR
59404 BKR
79443 BKR

Class 127
51592 SDR
51604 SDR
51616 GCR
51618 LAN
51622 GCR
55966 MRC
55976 MRC
59609 MRC

Class 140
140001 - 55500/01 KEI

Class 141
141103 WED
141110 WED
141108 COL
141113 MRC

Class 201 & 202
60116 HAD
60118 HAD
60501 HAD
60529 HAD
201001 HAD

Class 205
60117 PBR
60822 LDL
60828 PBR
60154 X 1101 EKR
60800 X 1101 EKR
70549 ELR
Set 205009 EDR
Set 205025 MHR
Set 205028 DAR
Set 205032 DAR
Set 205033 LDL
Set 205205 EPO

Class 207
60127 SWI
60130 X 207202 ELR
60142 SPV
60145 SEL
60149 SEL
60616 SPV
60901 SWI
60904 X 207202 ELR
60916 SPV

901001 CVR

¤ *For sale*

Below: *Two Class 127 diesel-hydraulic driving cars are preserved on the South Devon Railway, Nos. 51592 and 51604. Both are restored to green livery. The pair see little work as DHMU stock, but are sometimes hauled by diesel locos during gala events. The pair are seen at Buckfastleigh.* **CJM**

Electric Units

Unclassified
28249 NRM
29666 MRC
29670 MRC

79998 DEE
79999 DEE

BEL
85 SOU
87 KEI
91 RAM

BIL
10656 (2090)NRS
12123 (2090) NRS

COR
10096 EKR
11161 EKR
11179 NRM
11201 BLU
11825 EKR

DD
13004 NIR

Class 302
75033 MFM
75250 MFM

Class 303
303032 SHP

Class 306
306017 KIN

Class 309
309616 COV
309624 COV

Class 405 (SUB)
S8143S NRM
4732 COV

Class 411/412 (CEP)
61742 DAR
61743 DAR
61798 EVR
61799 EVR
61804 EVR
61805 EVR
70229 EVR
70257 GCR
70273 DFR
70284 NIR
70292 SMP
70296 NIR
70354 EVR
70527 WRN
70531 SMP
70539 EVR
70576 SNI
70607 EVR
Set 1198 PBR
Set 7105 EKR

Class 414 (HAP)
61275 NRM
61287 (4311) COV
75395 NRM
75407 (4311) COV

Class 415 (EPB)
14351 (5176) NIR
14352 (5176) NIR
15345 COV
15396 (5176) NIR

Class 416 (EPB)
65302 FIN
65304 FIN
65373 (5759) EKR
77558 (5759) EKR
14573 (6307) COV
16117 (6307) COV
65321 (5791) COV
77112 (5793) COV

Class 419 (MLV)
68001 EKR
68002 EKR
68003 EVR
68004 MNR
68005 EVR
68008 EKR
68009 EKR

Class 421 (CIG)
62364 DFR
62384 GCR
62378 DFR
62887 LWR
69339 GCR
76726 DFR
76740 DFR
76746 GCR
76797 DFR
76811 DFR
76812 DAR
76817 GCR
Set 1399 PBR

Class 422 (BEP)
69304 NIR
69310 DAR
69318 COL
69332 DAR
69333 LDL
69337 HAD

Class 423 (VEP)
(42)3417 KRS
62351 CVR
71032 CVR
76529 CVR
76712 CVR
76875 NRM

Class 457
67300 COV

Class 488
72501 ECC
72617 ECC

Class 489
68500 ECC
68506 ECC

Class 501
61183 COV
75186 COV

Class 502
28361 TEB
29896 TEB

Class 503
28690 COV
29298 COV
29720 COV

Class 504
65451 ELR
77172 ELR

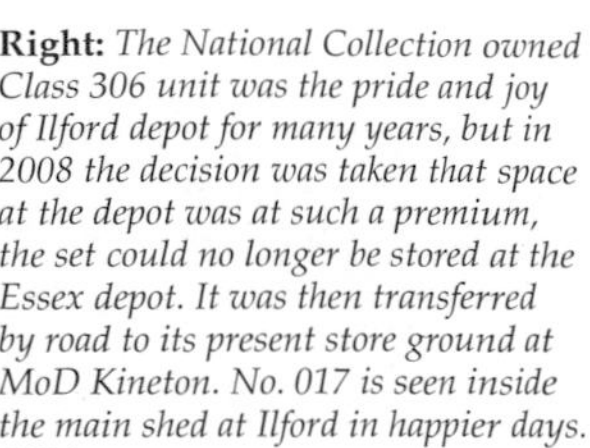

Right: *The National Collection owned Class 306 unit was the pride and joy of Ilford depot for many years, but in 2008 the decision was taken that space at the depot was at such a premium, the set could no longer be stored at the Essex depot. It was then transferred by road to its present store ground at MoD Kineton. No. 017 is seen inside the main shed at Ilford in happier days.* **CJM**

These lists give details of former UK diesel and electric locos exported for further use overseas and are understood to still be operational.

Class 03

D2013 Italy
D2032 Italy
D2033 Italy
D2036 Italy

Class 04

D2216 Italy
D2232 Italy
D2289 Italy
D2295 Italy

Class 08

D3047 Lamco Liberia
D3092 Lamco Liberia
D3094 Lamco Liberia
D3098 Lamco Liberia
D3100 Lamco Liberia

Class 10

D3639 Conakry (Guinae)
D3649 Conakry (Guinae)

Class 14

D9534 Bruges

Class 37

37702 Continental Rail, Spain
37703 Continental Rail, Spain
37714 Continental Rail, Spain
37716 Continental Rail, Spain
37718 Continental Rail, Spain
37800 Continental Rail, Spain
37883 Continental Rail, Spain
37884 Continental Rail, Spain
37888 Continental Rail, Spain

Class 58

58001 ETF France
58004 TSO France
58005 ETF France
58006 ETF France
58007 TSO France
58009 TSO France
58010 TSO France
58011 TSO France
58013 ETF France
58015 Continental Rail, Spain
58018 TSO France
58020 Continental Rail, Spain
58021 TSO France
58024 Continental Rail, Spain
58025 Continental Rail, Spain
58026 TSO France
58027 Continental Rail, Spain
58029 Continental Rail, Spain
58030 Continental Rail, Spain
58031 Continental Rail, Spain
58032 ETF France
58033 TSO France
58034 TSO France
58035 TSO France
58036 ETF France
58038 ETF France
58039 ETF France
58040 TSO France
58041 Continental Rail, Spain
58042 TSO France
58043 Continental Rail, Spain
58044 ETF France
58046 TSO France
58047 Continental Rail, Spain
58049 ETF France
58050 Continental Rail, Spain

Class 59

59003 HHPI, Germany

Class 66

66010 ECR, France
66013 ECR, France
66022 ECR, France
66026 ECR, France
66028 ECR, France
66029 ECR, France
66031 ECR, France
66032 ECR, France
66033 ECR, France
66036 ECR, France
66038 ECR, France
66042 ECR, France
66045 ECR, France
66049 ECR, France
66052 ECR, France
66062 ECR, France
66064 ECR, France
66071 ECR, France
66072 ECR, France
66073 ECR, France

Below: *Class 37/7 No. 37883, also carrying its Continental Rail identity of L28 stands under the rail loading cranes at Vilafranca del Penedes, Spain. After departure from the UK, wing mirrors and a cab nose headlight were fitted. The locos still retain their BR style couplings and drawgear as well as blue star multiple control.* **Gavin Lake**

66110	ECR, France
66123	ECR, France
66179	ECR, France
66190	ECR, France
66191	ECR, France
66195	ECR, France
66202	ECR, France
66203	ECR, France
66205	ECR, France
66208	ECR, France
66209	ECR, France
66210	ECR, France
66211	ECR, France
66212	ECR, France
66214	ECR, France
66215	ECR, France
66216	ECR, France
66217	ECR, France
66218	ECR, France
66219	ECR, France
66220	ECR, France
66222	ECR, France
66223	ECR, France
66224	ECR, France
66225	ECR, France
66226	ECR, France
66228	ECR, France
66229	ECR, France
66231	ECR, France
66233	ECR, France
66234	ECR, France
66235	ECR, France
66236	ECR, France
66239	ECR, France
66240	ECR, France
66241	ECR, France
66242	ECR, France
66243	ECR, France
66244	ECR, France
66245	ECR, France
66246	ECR, France
66247	ECR, France
66249	ECR, France
66582	Freightliner, Poland
66583	Freightliner, Poland
66584	Freightliner, Poland
66586	Freightliner, Poland
66625	Freightliner, Poland

Class 86

86248	Floyd, Hungary As 0450-001-7
86250	Floyd, Hungary As 0450-002-5

Class 87

87003	BZK Bulgaria
87004	BZK Bulgaria
87006	BZK Bulgaria
87007	BZK Bulgaria
87008	BZK Bulgaria
87010	BZK Bulgaria
87012	BZK Bulgaria
87013	BZK Bulgaria
87014	BZK Bulgaria
87019	BZK Bulgaria
87020	BZK Bulgaria
87022	BZK Bulgaria
87026	BZK Bulgaria
87028	BZK Bulgaria
87029	BZK Bulgaria
87033	BZK Bulgaria
87034	BZK Bulgaria

Right: *Looking rather work worn and covered in dust, Continental Rail-operated Class 58s Nos. 58042 and 58031 pose in the yard at Bobadilla, Spain.* **Gavin Lake**

Below: *Class 87s Nos. 87003 and 87006 are seen at the BZK depot at Sofia in Bulgaria on 24 May 2009 undergoing modifications prior to entering traffic. Note new position of horn and headlights and the very appealing 'cow catcher'!* **Philip Wormald**

As of autumn 2009, although much has been discussed about new train orders for the UK very few new build contracts are in place.

We have recently seen the completion of the Class 395 order for Southeastern to provide high speed services between Kent and London St Pancras International. These units will also be the stock used for the 'shuttle' services between London St Pancras and Stratford International for the 2012 Olympic Games, with the service marketed under the 'Javelin' title.

In 2009 the Class 350 sets were fully delivered for London Midland, allowing the cascade of Class 321 stock to other routes, while the Class 377s originally ordered for Southern were delivered for First Capital Connect.

New stock currently on order is:

Class 172/0 - 'Bombardier Turbostar' sets 172001-172008 - 16 vehicles for London Overground to replace ageing Class 150 stock.

Class 172/1 - 'Bombardier Turbostar' sets 172101-172104 - eight vehicles for Chiltern to assist with route growth.

Class 172/22 - 'Bombardier Turbostar' sets 172211-172222 - 24 vehicles formed as two-car sets for London Midland to replace Class 150 stock in the Midlands.

Class 172/23 - 'Bombardier Turbostar' sets 172331-172345 - 45 vehicles formed as three-car sets for London Midland to replace Class 150 stock in the Midlands.

Class 378/0 - 'Bombardier Capitalstar' sets 378001-378024 - 72 vehicles formed into three car sets for London Overground for dual ac/dc operation. These sets will subsequently be upgraded to four-car sets by the addition of a MSO at which time sets will be renumbered into the 378/2 range by adding 200 to the existing running number.

Class 378/1 - 'Bombardier Capitalstar' sets 378136-378154 - 80 vehicles formed as four-car units for dc operation.

Class 378/2 - 'Bombardier Capitalstar' sets 378225-378238 - 56 vehicles formed as four-car units with ac/dc operation.

Class 379/0 - 'Bombardier Electrostar' sets 379001-379030 - 120 vehicles formed as four-car units for East Anglia Liverpool Street - Stansted Airport route.

Class 380/0 'Desiro' sets 380001-380022 - 66 vehicles formed as three-car sets for Scotland Ayrshire routes.

Class 378/1 - 'Desiro' sets 380101-380116 - 64 vehicles formed as four-car sets for Scotland Ayrshire routes.

Class 390 - 'Pendolino' 106 vehicles in total, formed as two additional carriages for existing sets, plus four extra complete train sets.

Locomotives

Class 70 - Up to 30 new heavy Co-Co diesel-electric locos for Freightliner, built by General Electric.

Thameslink / CrossRail - Massive new EMU orders will be placed for these projects. A number of companies will be bidding including Siemens offering their 'Desiro City' train, Alstom and Bombardier.

Intercity Express Programme (IEP) - This is the UK Government's derived name for the replacement of the UK High Speed Train (HST) fleet. Even though the majority of sets have now been refurbished, the performance and passenger environment falls way short of present day and projected aspirations of passengers.

Hitachi Super Express (HSE) Train - In February 2009 Agility Trains a partnership between Barclays Private Equity, Hitachi and John Lang was announced as the preferred bidder for the IEP project. Agility Trains have said that the new fleet of trains will be known as the Hitachi Super Express (HSE) Train. The first area to see HSE trains will be the East Coast from 2013, with between then and 2018 some 1,400 vehicles entering service. The trains will be built in full electric, bi-mode and hybrid configurations in 5 and 10 car formations.

The actual order details have yet to be announced and will be further complicated by the mid-2009 announcement of the electrification of the Great Western route between London and Swansea, Bristol, Oxford and Newbury.

Above: *An artist's impression of how the Hitachi Super Express (HSE) train might look. This image shows a possible style for the hybrid train diesel power car.* **Hitachi**

A number of preserved steam locomotives have been allocated five-digit TOPS numbers to allow their operation over the National Network. The numbers allocated are shown below; not all locos may currently be authorised for use on Network rail metals.

TOPS No.	Railway No.	Type	Name
98166	1466	GWR 14xx	
98150	1450	GWR 14xx	
98186	686	0-6-0T	*Lady Armaghdale*
98212	41312	LMS 2MT	
98219	55189	CR 0-4-4T	
98221	46521	LMS 2MT	
98238	1638	GWR 16xx	
98240	3440	GWR 34xx	*City of Truro*
98241	46441	LMS 2MT	
98243	46443	LMS 2MT	
98253	30053	SR M7	
98254	58926	LNWR 2F	
98273	65243	NBR J36	*Maude*
98315	7715	GWR 57xx	
98321	69621	GER N7	*A. J. Hill*
98372	30072	SR USA	
98400	41000	LMS 4P	
98406	43106	LMS 4MT	
98414	75014	BR 4MT	
98425	7325	GWR 7321	
98426	31625	SR U	
98427	44027	LMS 4F	
98435	80135	BR 4MT	
98455	4555	GWR 45xx	
98457	9600	GWR 8750	
98460	7760	GWR 57xx	
98466	9466	GWR 94xx	
98469	75069	BR 4MT	
98472	5572	GWR 4575	
98476	76079	BR 4MT	
98478	68078	WD 4F	
98479	80079	BR 4MT	
98480	80080	BR 4MT	
98482	3882	0-6-0ST	*Barbara*
98488	4588	GWR 4575	
98494	65894	LNER J27	
98498	80098	BR 4MT	
98500	45000	LMS 5MT	
98502	7802	GWR 78xx	*Bradley Manor*
98505	45305	LMS 5MT	*Alderman A E Draper*
98507	45407	LMS 5MT	*Lancashire Fusilier*
98510	45110	LMS 5MT	
98512	7812	GWR 78xx	*Erlestoke Manor*
98519	7819	GWR 78xx	*Hinton Manor*
98525	45025	LMS 5MT	
98526	30925	SR V	*Cheltenham*
98529	73129	BR 5MT	
98530	4930	GWR 49xx	*Hagley Hall*
98531	45231	LMS 5MT	*Sherwood Forrester*
98532	44932	LMS 5MT	
98536	4936	GWR 49xx	*Kinlet Hall*
98549	4965	GWR 49xx	*Rood Ashton Hall*
98553	4953	GWR 49xx	*Pitchford Hall*
98560	6960	GWR 6959	*Raveningham Hall*
98564	61264	LNER B1	
98565	42765	LMS 6P5F	
98567	44767	LMS 5MT	*George Stephenson*
98568	42968	LMS 5MT	
98571	44871	LMS 5MT	
98572	5972	GWR 49xx	*Olton Hall*
98577	30777	SR N15	*Sir Lamiel*
98596	73096	BR 5MT	
98598	6998	GWR 6959	*Burton Agnes Hall*
98605	62005	LNER K1	
98628	30828	SR S15	
98641	30841	SR S15	
98642	61994	LNER K4	*The Great Marquess*
98690	45690	LMS 6P5F	*Leander*
98693	45593	LMS 6P5F	*Kolhapur*
98696	45596	LMS 6P5F	*Bahamas*
98700	70000	BR 7P	*Britannia*
98701	34101	SR WC	*Hartland*
98709	53809	SDJR 7F	
98713	70013	BR 7P	*Oliver Cromwell*
98715	46115	LMS 7P	*Scots Guardsman*
98716	34016	SR WC	*Bodmin*
98727	34027	SR WC	*Taw Valley*
98728	5029	GWR 4073	*Nunney Castle*
98729	7029	GWR 4073	*Clun Castle*
98750	30850	SR LN	*Lord Nelson*
98751	5051	GWR 4073	*Earl Bathurst*
98767	34067	SR BB	*Tangmere*
98771	60800	LNER V2	*Green Arrow*
98772	34072	SR BB	*257 Squadron*
98780	5080	GWR 4073	*Defiant*
98792	34092	SR WC	*City of Wells*
98800	6000	GWR 60xx	*King George V*
98801	46201	LMS 8P	*Princess Elizabeth*
98802	71000	BR 8P	*Duke of Gloucester*
98803	46203	LMS 8P	*Princess Margaret Rose*
98805	35005	SR MN	*Canadian Pacific*
98809	60009	LNER A4	*Union of South Africa*
98824	6024	GWR 60xx	*King Edward I*
98828	35028	SR MN	*Clan Line*
98829	46229	LMS 8P	*Duchess of Hamilton*
98832	60532	LNER A2	*Blue Peter*
98834	46233	LMS 8P	*Duchess of Sutherland*
98851	48151	LMS 8F	
98857	2857	GWR 28xx	
98863	60163	LNER A1	*Tornado*
98868	60022	LNER A4	*Mallard*
98872	60103	LNER A3	*Flying Scotsman*
98873	48773	LMS 8F	
98898	60007	LNER A4	*Sir Nigel Gresley*
98920	92220	BR 9F	*Evening Star*

Above: *Although carrying its original steam loco number of 70013, this loco is registered on TOPS as No. 98713.*
Stacey Thew

Ex-BR Industrial Locos

Over the years a number of former BR locomotives have after withdrawal from normal duties taken up use for industrial operators. The list below represents those which are understood to still be in existence in late 2009. Some locos operated at preservation sites are deemed to be 'industrial' but these are grouped in the preserved section.

Class 03

03112 (D2112)	Port of Boston
03179 *Clive*	First Capital Connect, Hornsey Depot

Class 08

08202	The Potter Group, Knowsley, Merseyside
08320 (400D) *Susan*	Imerys Clay Company, Burngullow
08331 (H001)	Midland Railway-Butterley
08375	Prologis Park, Coventry
08398 (402D) *Annabel*	Imerys Clay Company, Bugle
08411	Colne Valley Railway
08441	Colne Valley Railway
08445	Castle Cement, Stamford
08447	Deanside Transit, Hillington, Glasgow
08460	Felixstowe Dock & Railway
08484 *Captain Nathaniel Darell*	Felixstowe Dock & Railway
08503	Rye Farm, Wishaw
08511	Felixstowe Dock & Railway
08523	Celtic Energy, Onllwyn Washery
08535	Corus, Shotton
08598 (H016)	The Potter Group, Knowsley
08600	LH Group Services, Barton-under-Needwood
08613	Corus, Shotton Works
08622 (H028) (7)	P & D Ports Teesport
08643	Aggregate Industries, Whatley
08650 *Isle of Grain*	Aggregate Industries, Isle of Grain
08652	Hanson Aggregates, Whatley Quarry
08668	St. Modwen Storage, Long Marston
08670	Colne Valley Railway
08704 (D3871)	Port of Boston, Boston Docks
08728	St. Modwen Storage, Long Marston
08731	Aggregate Industries, Merehead
08743 *Bryan Turner*	SembCorp Utilities Teesside, Wilton
08774 *Arthur Vernon Dawson*	AV Dawson, Middlesbrough
08787	Hanson Aggregates, Machen
08807	AV Dawson, Middlesbrough
08809	Corus, Shotton
08813	St. Modwen Storage, Long Marston
08818 *Molly*	Faber Prest Ports, Flixborough Wharf

Left: *Former BR Class 08 No. 08937 is now operated by Aggregate Industries at Meldon Quarry on the edge of Dartmoor in Devon. Like many industrial locos this example has gained a cast nameplate, in this case* Bluebell Mel. **CJM**

08823 (D3991)	Manchester Ship Canal, Trafford Park
08827	St. Modwen Storage, Long Marston
08869	St. Modwen Storage, Long Marston
08870 (H024)	Castle Cement, Ketton
08873	Manchester Ship Canal, Trafford Park
08881 (D4095)	Lafarge Aggregates, Mountsorrel
08903 *John W. Antill*	SembCorp Utilities Teesside, Wilton
08912	AV Dawson, Middlesbrough
08913	Manchester Ship Canal Co, Trafford Park (at L H Group)
08915	Stephenson Railway Museum
08928	St. Modwen Storage, Long Marston
08933	Aggregate Industried, Merehead
08936	Corus, Shotton Works
08937 *Bluebell Mel*	Aggregate Industries, Meldon Quarry
08947	Aggregate Industries, Merehead

Class 11

12082 (01553)	Deanside Transit, Hillington, Glasgow
12088	Johnson's, Widdrington Disposal Point

Class 14

D9529 (14029)	Aggregate Industries, Bardon Quarry

Class 20

20056 (81)	Corus, Appleby-Frodingham
20066 (82)	Corus, Appleby-Frodingham

Class 56

56009 (56201)	Brush Traction, Loughborough

Class 73

73133	Colas, Tavistock Junction (Scheduled to move to Rugby)

Below: *After withdrawal from the BR freight sector, Class 56 No. 56009, one of the original Romanian-built locos, was sold to Brush Traction of Loughborough for use as a power unit test bed as part of a then Class 56 overhaul project. The loco was painted in turquoise blue and renumbered as 56201. The loco is seen in the Brush yard in 2008.* **CJM**

Industrial

Transport for London
London Underground

Address: ✉ Floor 11, Windsor House, 50 Victoria Street, London SW1H 0TL
pressoffice@tfl.gov.uk
✆ 0845 604 4141
ⓘ www.tfl.gov.uk

Managing Director: Mike Brown

Operations: The London Underground system, now operated by Transport for London (TfL), operates services on 10 lines in and around the capital and uses a mix of surface and tunnel stock.

Bakerloo Line	Tube Line. Operates services between Elephant & Castle and Harrow & Wealdstone. **Rolling Stock:** 1972 Mk2, livery - red, white and blue, allocated to Stonebridge Park. Scheduled for replacement in 2018.
Central Line	Tube Line. Operates services between West Ruislip / Ealing and Epping **Rolling Stock:** 1992, livery - red, white and blue, allocated to Hainault.
Circle Line	Sub-Surface Line. Operates circle network in Central London and the branch from Edgware Road to Hammersmith. **Rolling Stock:** 'C' stock, introduced 1969-78, livery - red, white and blue, allocated to Hammersnith.
District Line	Sub-Surface Line. Operates services between Wimbledon, Richmond, Ealing, Edgware Road, Kensington Olympia to Upminster. **Rolling Stock:** 'C' and 'D' stock, livery - red, white and blue, allocated to Ealing Common and Upminster.
Jubilee Line	Tube Line. Operates services between Stanmore and Stratford. **Rolling Stock:** 1996, livery - red, white and blue, allocated to Wembley Park.
Metropolitan Line	Sub-Surface Line. Operates services between Amersham, Chesham, Watford and Uxbridge to Aldgate. **Rolling Stock:** 'A' stock, livery - red, white and blue, allocated to Wembley Park, due for replacement with 'S' stock in 2010-2011.
Northern Line	Tube Line. Operates services between Morden and Edgware, Mill Hill East and High Barnet. **Rolling Stock:** 1995 Stock, livery - red, white and blue, allocated to Morden.
Piccadilly Line	Tube Line. Operates services between Heathrow Airport / Uxbridge and Cockfosters. **Rolling Stock:** 1973 Stock, livery - red, white and blue, allocated to Northfields and Cockfosters. Stock due for replacement in 2014.
Victoria Line	Tube Line. Operates services between Brixton and Walthamstow Central **Rolling Stock:** 1967 Stock, livery - red, white and blue, allocated to Northumberland Park.
Waterloo & City Line	Tube Line. Operates services between Waterloo and Bank **Rolling Stock:** 1992 Stock, livery - red, white and blue, allocated to Waterloo.

Above: *Two trains of 1972 Mk2 stock operating on the Bakerloo Line pass at Willesden Junction. The Bakerloo Line shares Network Rail tracks operated by London Overground between Queens Park and Harrow, providing a very frequent service via the expanding passenger interchange at Willesden Junction. The tracks on the left of this view are the freight only line linking the North London line with the West Coast route.* **CJM**

Below: *The shortest of the London Underground 'tube' lines is the Waterloo & City line, linking Waterloo with Bank station in the City of London. The self contained line uses a batch of modified 1992 Central Line units, which were originally introduced on line modernisation by the then Network SouthEast. Car No. 65503 is seen in one of the two platforms at Bank station on 11 November 2009.* **John Binch**

For space reasons, we are unable in this publication to provide vehicle numbers for London Underground stock.

Above: *London Underground's Northern Line, running from Morden in the south to High Barnet, Mill Hill East and Edgware in the north, uses 1995 stock built by Alstom of Birmingham. A total of 106 trains operate the line and all are allocated to Morden depot. On 11 November 2009, car No. 51611 leads a train set at Finchley Central.* **John Binch**

Transport for London Docklands Light Railway

Contact details as London Underground.

Operations: The Docklands Light Railway, operates between Bank and Tower Gateway and Woolwich Arsenal, Beckton and Stratford, as well as a Lewisham to Stratford service.

Class B90 (twin)

Train Length: 94ft 5in (28.80m)
Width: 8ft 7in (2.65m)
Power Supply: 750V dc third rail
Seating: 52 + 4 tip-up
Horsepower: 375hp (280kW)
Electrical Equipment: Brush

22	25	28	31	34	37	40	43
23	26	29	32	35	38	41	44
24	27	30	33	36	39	42	

Class B92 (twin)

Train Length: 94ft 5in (28.80m)
Width: 8ft 7in (2.65m)
Power Supply: 750V dc third rail
Seating: 54 + 4 tip-up
Horsepower: 375hp (280kW)
Electrical Equipment: Brush

45	51	57	63	69	75	81	87
46	52	58	64	70	76	82	88
47	53	59	65	71	77	83	89
48	54	60	66	72	78	84	90
49	55	61	67	73	79	85	91
50	56	62	68	74	80	86	

Class B2K (twin)

Train Length: 94ft 5in (28.80m)
Width: 8ft 7in (2.65m)
Power Supply: 750V dc third rail
Seating: 52 + 4 tip-up
Horsepower: 375hp (280kW)
Electrical Equipment: Brush

01	03	05	07	09	11	13	15
02	04	06	08	10	12	14	16

92	93	94	95	96	97	98	99

Class B07 (twin)

Train Length: 94ft 5in (28.80m)
Width: 8ft 7in (2.65m)
Power Supply: 750V dc third rail
Seating: 52 + 4 tip-up
Horsepower: 375hp (280kW)
Electrical Equipment: Bombardier
To be extended to three-car sets in time for 2012 Olympic Games

101	108	115	122	129	136	143	150
102	109	116	123	130	137	144	151
103	110	117	124	131	138	145	152
104	111	118	125	132	139	146	153
105	112	119	126	133	140	147	154
106	113	120	127	134	141	148	155
107	114	121	128	135	142	149	

Left: *Class B90 Docklands set No. 27 is illustrated at Poplar in August 2009. 23 sets of this fleet, built in 1991-92 by BN in Belgium, can be found usually working in pairs throughout the expanding DLR network. The livery shown is DLR red with advertising branding.* **Tony Christie**

Transport for London Croydon Tramlink

Contact details as London Underground
Operations: The Croydon Tramlink operates between Croydon and Wimbledon, New Addington, Beckenham, and Elmers End.

Six-axle stock

Train Length: 98ft 9in (30.1m)
Width: 8ft 7in (2.65m)
Power Supply: 750V dc overhead
Seating: 70
Horsepower: 643hp (480kW)
Electrical Equipment: Bombardier

2530	2533	2536	2539	2542	2545	2548	2551
2531	2534	2537	2540	2543	2546	2549	2552
2532	2535	2538	2541	2544	2547	2550	2553

Name applied

2535	*Stephen Parascandolo 1980-2007*

Left: *When the Croydon Tramlink was under development it was agreed that the fleet would be numbered continuing on from the previous trams, withdrawn from the area in the 1960s. In spring 2009, set No. 2548 painted in grey, green and blue livery is seen at East Croydon station with a service to New Addington.* **John Binch**

Manchester Metrolink

Address: ✉ Greater Manchester PTE, 2 Piccadilly Gardens, Manchester, M1 3BG
Metrolink House, Queens Road, Manchester M6 0RY
customerservices@metrolink.co.uk
✆ 0161 224 1000
ⓘ www.metrolink.co.uk

Metrolink is operated for GMPTE by Stagecoach Group.

Operations: Manchester Metrolink operates a street and dedicated track tram system around Manchester. Services operate from the City Centre to Bury, Altrincham and Eccles.

Six-axle stock

Train Length: 95ft 1in (29m)
Width: 8ft 7in (2.65m)
Power Supply: 750V dc overhead
Seating: 82 + 4 tip-up
Horsepower: 697hp (520kW)
Electrical Equipment: Firema

No.	Name	No.	Name	No.	Name
1001	*System One*	1010		1019	
1002		1011	*System One*	1020	*Lancashire Fusilier*
1003		1012		1021	*Starlight Express*
1004	*The Robert Owen*	1013		1022	*Poppy Appeal*
1005	*The Railway Mission*	1014	*The Great Manchester Runner*	1023	
1006		1015	*Burma Star*	1024	
1007	*East Lancashire Railway*	1016		1025	
1008		1017	*Bury Hospice*	1026	
1009	*Virgin Megastores*	1018			

Six-axle stock

Train Length: 95ft 1in (29m)
Width: 8ft 7in (2.65m)
Power Supply: 750V dc overhead
Seating: 82 + 4 tip-up
Horsepower: 697hp (520kW)
Electrical Equipment: Ansaldo

No.	Name	No.	Name	No.	Name
2001(S)		2003	*Traveller 2000*	2005	*W H Smith West One*
2002		2004		2006	

Left: *On 4 June 2009, Firema trams Nos. 1011* System One *and 1021* Starlight Express *stand at Altrincham, which is an interchange station with Network Rail. On the right, Northern Rail Class 142 No. 142037 pauses with the 15.17 Manchester Piccadilly to Chester service.* **John Binch**

M5000 stock

Train Length: 93ft 1in (28.4m)
Width: 8ft 7in (2.65m)
Power Supply: 750V dc overhead
Seating: 52 + 8 tip-up
Horsepower: 643hp (480kW)
Electrical Equipment: Bombardier

3001	3007	3013	3019	3025	3031	3037
3002	3008	3014	3020	3026	3032	3038
3003	3009	3015	3021	3027	3033	3039
3004	3010	3016	3022	3028	3034	3040
3005	3011	3017	3023	3029	3035	
3006	3012	3018	3024	3030	3036	

Nottingham Express Transit

Address: ✉ Transdev Tram UK Ltd, Garrick House, 74 Chiswick High Road, London, W4 1SY
Nottingham City Transport Ltd, Lower Parliament Street, Nottingham, NG1 1GG
info@thetram.net ✆ 0115 942 7777, ⓘ www.thetram.net

Operations: Nottingham Express Transit (NET) operate trams between Hucknell and Nottingham.

Six-axle stock

Train Length: 108ft 3in (29m)
Width: 7ft 9in (2.4m)
Power Supply: 750V dc overhead
Seating: 54 + 4 tip-up
Horsepower: 697hp (520kW)
Electrical Equipment: Bombardier

No.	Name
201	*Torvill and Dean*
202	*DH Lawrence*
203	*Bendigo Thompson*
204	*Erica Beardsmore*
205	*Lord Byron*
206	*Angela Alcock*
207	*Mavis Worthington*
208	*Dinah Minton*
209	*Sid Standard*
210	*Sir Jesse Boot*
211	*Robin Hood*
212	*William Booth*
213	*Mary Potter*
214	*Dennis McCarthy*
215	*Brian Clough*

Right: *Following the public inquiry held in the autumn of 2007, the Government has awarded a Transport and Works Act Order (TWAO) for the proposed Phase Two extension of the Nottingham Express Transit system to Chilwell and Clifton (via Beeston). Bombardier Incentro tram No. 204* Erica Beardsmore *stands at the Station Street terminus on 15 May 2009, with the 13.42 service to Phoenix Park.* **John Binch**

Midland Metro

Address: ✉ Travel West Midlands, PO Box 3565, Birmingham, B1 3JR
info@travelmetro.co.uk ✆ 0121 254 7272, ⓘ www.travelmetro.co.uk

Operations: Midland Metro operates trams between Birmingham Snow Hill and Wolverhampton.

Six-axle stock

Train Length: 108ft 3in (29m)
Width: 7ft 9in (2.4m)
Power Supply: 750V dc overhead
Seating: 54 + 4 tip-up
Horsepower: 697hp (520kW)
Electrical Equipment: Bombardier

No.	Name
01(S)	*Sir Frank Whittle*
02	
03	*Ray Lewis*
04	
05	*Sister Dora*
06	*Alan Garner*
07	*Billy Wright*
08	*Joseph Chamberlain*
09	*Jeff Astle*
10	*John Stanley Webb*
11	*Theresa Stewart*
12	
13	*Anthony Nolan*
14	*Jim Eames*
15	*Agenoria*
16	*Gerwyn John*

Right: *Painted in revised Network West Midlands tram livery of pink and silver, set No. 09* Jeff Astle *is viewed at Priestfield on 31 August 2008.* **John Binch**

Sheffield Super Tram

Address: ✉ Stagecoach Supertram, Nunnery Depot, Woodburn Road, Sheffield, S9 3LS

enquiries@supertram.com

✆ 0114 272 8282

ⓘ www.supertram.com

Operations: Sheffield Super Tram operates services within Sheffield City Centre and to Herdings Park, Halfway, Meadowhall Interchange, Middlewood and Malin Bridge.

Six-axle stock

Train Length: 113ft 6in (34.75m)
Width: 8ft 7in (2.65m)
Power Supply: 750V dc overhead
Seating: 80 + 6 tip-up
Horsepower: 800hp (596kW)
Electrical Equipment: Siemens

101	105	109	113	117	121	125
102	106	110	114	118	122	
103	107	111	115	119	123	
104	108	112	116	120	124	

Left: *On 13 September 2008, Sheffield Super Tram No. 110, painted in Stagecoach blue swirl 'Desiro' style livery departs from the Sheffield Midland Station / Sheffield Hallam University stop with a Malin Bridge to Halfway service.* **John Binch**

Tyne & Wear Metro

Address: ✉ Tyne & Wear Passenger Transport Executive (NEXUS), Nexus House, 33 St James Boulevard, Newcastle upon Tyne, NE1 4AX

enquiries@nexus.co.uk

✆ 0191 203 3333

ⓘ www.nexus.org.uk

Operations: Tyne & Wear Metro operates tram services within Newcastle City Centre and to Whitley Bay, Newcastle Airport, South Shields, Sunderland and South Hylton.

Six-axle stock

Train Length: 91ft 3in (27.80m)
Width: 8ft 7in (2.65m)
Power Supply: 1500V dc overhead
Seating: 68 tip-up
Horsepower: 500hp (374kW)
Electrical Equipment: Siemens

4001	4011	4021	4031	4041	4051	4061
4002	4012	4022	4032	4042	4052	4062
4003	4013	4023	4033	4043	4053	4063
4004	4014	4024	4034	4044	4054	4064
4005	4015	4025	4035	4045	4055	4065
4006	4016	4026	4036	4046	4056	4066
4007	4017	4027	4037	4047	4057	4067
4008	4018	4028	4038	4048	4058	4068
4009	4019	4029	4039	4049	4059	4069
4010	4020	4030	4040	4050	4060	4070

4071	4074	4077	4080	4083	4086	4089
4072	4075	4078	4081	4084	4087	4090
4073	4076	4079	4082	4085	4088	

Name applied

4026	*George Stephenson*
4041	*Harry Cowans*
4060	*Thomas Bewick*
4064	*Michael Campbell*
4065	*Dame Catherine Cookson*
4073	*Danny Marshall*
4077	*Robert Stephenson*
4078	*Ellen Wilkinson*

Right: *Painted in the distinctive Tyne & Wear Metro (NEXUS) red and yellow livery, set No. 4003 leads another set at Felling on 30 July 2008.* **Dave McAlone**

Glasgow Subway

Address: ✉ SPT, Consort House, 12 West George Street, Glasgow, G2 1HN

enquiry@spt.co.uk

✆ 0141 332 6811

ⓘ www.spt.co.uk

Glasgow Subway is operated for Strathclyde Partnership for Transport (SPT)

Operations: Circular network around Glasgow City Centre.

Single Power Cars

Length: 42ft 2in (12.81m)
Width: 7ft 7in (2.34m)
Power Supply: 600V dc third rail
Seating: 36S
Horsepower: 190hp (142.4kW)
Electrical Equipment: GEC

101	105	109	113	117	121	125	129	133
102	106	110	114	118	122	126	130	
103	107	111	115	119	123	127	131	
104	108	112	116	120	124	128	132	

Trailer Cars

Length: 41ft 6in (12.70m)
Width: 7ft 7in (2.34m)
Seating: 40S

201	202	203	204	205	206	207	208

Right: *The circular Glasgow Underground rail system, operating to the west side of the city, has its depot located at Broomloan, a spur off the passenger circuit near Govan. Two sets, one painted in carmine and cream and the other in 'clockwork orange' livery, are seen 'on shed'.* **Brian Morrison**

Livery Codes

ABL	Arriva Trains Blue
ADV	Advenza Freight, blue with yellow branding
AGI	Aggregate Industries green, silver and green
AIN	Aggregate Industries - blue
ALS	Alstom Transportation
ANG	Anglia - mid blue
ANN	Anglia - turquoise/white with National Express East Anglia branding
ATE	Arriva Trains Executive- turquoise/cream with branding
ATW	Arriva Trains Wales - turquoise/cream
AXC	Arriva Cross Country - brown, silver, pink
BBR	Balfour Beatty Rail blue/white
BLG	Blue and Grey
BLK	Black
BLL	BR rail blue with large logo
BLU	Blue
BLW	Carillion Rail blue/white
BOM	Bombardier Transportation
BPM	Blue Pullman - Nankin blue and white
BRD	BR Departmental mid grey
BRT	BR Trainload two-tone grey
c2c	c2c - blue/pink
CAL	Caledonian Railway
CAR	Carmine & Cream
CEN	Central Trains blue and two-tone green
CHC	Chocolate & Cream
CIV	BR Civil Engineers - grey and yellow
COL	Colas - Orange, lime green and black
CON	Continental Rail - light/mid blue
COR	Corus Steel - light blue or yellow
COX	Connex white and yellow
CRW	Chilton Railways - while/blue
CTL	Central Trains blue, green with yellow doors
CWR	Cotswold Rail - silver with branding
DBB	DB Schenker - light blue
DBM	DB Schenker - maroon
DBS	DB Schenker - red
DCG	Devon & Cornwal Railway - green
DRC	Direct Rail Services - blue compass branding
DRO	Direct Rail Services Ocean Liner - blue
DRS	Direct Rail Services - blue
DRU	Direct Rail Services - unbranded blue
ECR	European Cargo Rail - grey
ECT	East Coast branded National Express livery
EMT	East Midlands Trains, white, blue, swirl cab ends
EPS	European Passenger Services
EPX	Europhoenix red/silver
ETF	ETF Rail - yellow with green band
EU2	Eurotunnel - Europort2
EUS	Eurostar - white,yellow and blue
EWE	English Welsh Scottish Executive
EWS	English Welsh Scottish - red with gold band
FCC	First Capital Connect, First Group Urban Lights - mauve/blue with pink, blue and white lower branding
FER	Fertis - grey with branding
FGB	First Great Western blue
FGF	First Group - GBRf (Barbie)
FGL	First Great Western local lines
FGN	First Great Western branded Northern blue
FGS	First Group Scotrail with EWS branding
FGT	First Great Western, Thames/London area branding
FGW	First Great Western, as FST with FGW branding
FHT	First Hull Trains, as FST with Hull Trains branding
FLF	Fastline Freight - grey with yellow/white chevrons
FLG	Freightliner green unbranded
FLR	Freightliner - green/yellow
FLY	Freightliner grey
FNA	First livery with National Express East Anglia branding
FOS	Foster Yeoman
FRB	Fragonset black
FSN	Northern branded First Group
FSP	First Scotrail Strathclyde carmine and cream (some with turquoise band)
FSR	First Scotrail, as FST with FSR branding
FSS	First Scotrail, blue with white Saltair branding
FTP	First TransPennine, as FST with FTP branding
FST	First Group - dark blue, pink and white swirl
FSW	First Group - green and white with gold branding
GAT	Gatwick Express, white, mid-grey and red with red doors
GBF	First GB Railfreight - swirl
GBM	First GB Railfreight Metronet
GBR	First GB Railfreight - blue
GLX	Glaxochem - grey, blue and black
GNE	Great North Eastern Railway - blue
GRN	Green
GRY	Grey
GSW	Great Scottish & Western Railway - maroon
GTL	Grand Central Railway - black
GWG	First Great Western - green
HAN	Hanson
HEC	Heathrow Connect - grey, orange
HEX	Heathrow Express - silver, grey
HNR	Harry Needle Railroad - yellow/grey
HS1	High Speed 1 - blue with powder blue doors
ICS	InterCity Swallow - two-tone grey off-set with red and white body band
IND	Industrial colours of operator
INT	InterCity two-tone grey off-set with red and white body band
JAR	Jarvis maroon
LAF	Lafarge Aggregates - green/white
LHL	Loadhaul Freight - black and orange
LLB	Large Logo Blue
LMI	London Midland grey, green and black
LNE	LNER tourist green/cream
LOG	London Overground, white and blue with orange doors
LUL	London Underground red
MAB	Statesman Pullman - maroon/beige
MAI	MainTrain - blue with branding
MAL	Malcome Rail
MAR	Maroon

Data Tables

MED	Medite - black
MEA	Merseyrail advertising
MER	Merseyrail, silver and yellow
MLF	Mainline Freight - aircraft blue
MLG	Mainline Freight - branded double grey
MML	Midland Main Line - turquoise/white
NE2	National Express with c2c branding
NGE	National Great Eastern , First Great Eastern grey/blue with cab end swirl, branded National Express
NOM	Northern Rail - blue Metro branded
NOR	Northern - blue, purple grey
NRL	Network Rail - yellow with branding
NSE	Network SouthEast - red, white and blue
NUB	Northern Rail blue - unbranded ScotRail
NWT	North West Trains - dark blue
NXA	National Express East Anglia
NXE	National Express East Coast
NXG	National Express East Coast branding on GNER blue livery
ONE	One Anglia mid-blue
ORN	One Railway with National Express branding
PCL	BR Parcels red/grey
POL	Police livery
PTR	Porterbrook
PUL	Pullman - umber/cream
PUR	Artemis purple
QOS	Queen of Scots Pullman
RES	Rail express systems - red and graphite
RFD	Railfreight Distribution
RFE	Railfreight grey with EWS branding
RFG	Railfreight grey
RFI	Railfreight International
RFP	Railfreight with Petroleum branding
RFT	BR Railfreight - Grey, red and yellow, with large logo and numbers
RIV	Riviera Trains - maroon
RML	Royal Mail Limited - red
ROY	Royal Train - claret
RTB	Railtrack - blue
RTK	Railtrack - grey/brown
SCE	Stagecoach - white with East Midlands branding
SCT	Scotrail Calidonian Sleeper - mauve/ white
SEC	Serco
SET	South Eastern Trains - white with branding
SGK	Southern Gatwick Express - blue, white and red with swirl ends
SIL	Silver
SKL	Silverlink London Overground, SLK with London Overground branding
SLF	Silverlink, with First Great Western branding
SLK	Silverlink, mauve, green and white
SNF	Railfreight grey with SNCF branding
SNT	SNCF domestic on Eurostar, silver, while and yellow
SOU	Southern - white, black and green
SPL	Special livery
STN	Stansted Express
STO	Stobart Rail
SWM	South West Trains main line white and blue
SWO	South West Trains outer suburban blue
SWS	South West Trains suburban red
SWT	South West Trains blue, red, grey
TES	Tesco
TEX	TransPennine Express - As FST with TPE brand
TGG	Transrail Grey with 'T' branding
THM	Thameslink - blue, white, yellow
TLF	Trainload Freight - grey
TLL	Trainload grey with Loadhaul branding
TLP	Thameslink promotional multi-coloured stripes
TPD	Trans Pennine/Central Trains logo
TSO	Travaux du Sud Ouest - yellow
TTG	Two-tone grey
VIR	Virgin - red/grey
VSN	VSOE Northern
VT1	Virgin - red/grey unbranded
VWC	Virgin West Coast, silver, red, white and black
WAB	Wabtec Rail - black
WAG	West Anglia Great Norther - purple
WAL	Wales & Borders 'Alphaline' silver/grey
WCR	West Coast Railway - maroon
WES	Wessex Trains - maroon
WEX	Wessex Rail Engineering
WET	Wessex Trains - silver, maroon/pink doors
WHT	White
WMD	West Midlands Network, light blue and green
WSR	Wrexham & Shropshire two-tone grey
YEL	Yellow
XCM	AXC branding on MML or CTR livery
XP4	BR XP64 colours

Right: *Showing standard Southern livery of mid-green and white, off-set by dark green passenger doors and a Southern logo applied in the middle of the lower body panel, Class 377 No. 377409 is viewed at Clapham Junction.* CJM

Operational Pool Codes

ADFL	Advenza Freight - Freight locos
ATLO	West Coast Traincare - Locomotives
ATTB	West Coast Traincare - Class 57/3 with Dellner
ATZZ	West Coast Traincare - Locos for disposal
BREL	Boden Rail Locomotives
CDJD	Serco Railtest - Shunting locos
COLO	Colas Rail - Operational locomotives
CREL	Cotswold Rail - Locomotives
DFFT	Freightliner - Restricted duties
DFGC	Freightliner Class 86/5 trials locomotive
DFGH	Freightliner - Heavy Haul Class 70
DFGI	Freightliner - Intermodal Class 70
DFGM	Freightliner - Intermodal Class 66/5
DFHG	Freightliner - Heavy Haul Class 66/5 & 66/6
DFHH	Freightliner - Heavy Haul Class 66/5 & 66/6
DFIM	Freightliner - Intermodal Class 66/5
DFIN	Freightliner - Intermodal - low emisson
DFLC	Freightliner - Class 90
DFLS	Freightliner - Class 08
DFNC	Freightliner - Class 86/6
DFRT	Freightliner - Class 66 Infrastructure contracts
DHLT	Freightliner - Awaiting repairs
EFOO	First Great Western - Class 57
EFPC	First Great Western - HST power cars
EFSH	First Great Western - Class 08
EHPC	CrossCountry Trains - HST power cars
EJLO	London Midland - Class 08
EMPC	East Midlands Trains - HST power cars
EMSL	East Midlands Trains - Class 08
EPXX	Europhoenix Class 86
GBCM	First/GBRf - Class 66 commercial contracts
GBED	First/GBRf - Class 73
GBRT	First/GBRf - Class 66 Network Rail contracts
GBWM	First/GBRf - Whitemoor
GBZZ	First/GBRf - Stored locomotives
GCHP	Grand Central - HST power cars
GPSS	Eurostar UK - Class 08
HNRL	Harry Needle Railroad - Class 08, 20 hire locos
HNRS	Harry Needle Railroad - Stored locomotives
HTCX	Hanson Traction - Class 56
HYWD	South West Trains - Class 73
IANA	National Express East Anglia - Class 90
IECA	National Express East Coast - Class 91
IECP	National Express East Coast - HST power cars
INDL	Industrial (unofficial code)
IVGA	Gatwick Express - Class 73/2
IWCA	Virgin West Coast - Class 57/3
MBDL	Private operators - Diesel traction
MBED	Private operators - Class 73
MRSO	Mainline Rail - Class 08
PTXX	Eurotunnel - Europort2 Class 92
QACL	Network Rail - Class 86 load banks
QADD	Network Rail - Class 31
QCAR	Network Rail - HST power cars
QETS	Network Rail - Class 97/3
QSTR	Network Rail - stored locos
RCJA	Fastline Freight - Class 56
RCJM	Fastline Freight - Class 66
RCZH	Railcare Springburn - Class 08
RCZN	Railcare Wolverton - Class 08
RFSH	Wabtec Rail Doncaster - Class 08
RVLO	Rail Vehicle Engineering Derby - Locos
RVLS	Rail Vehicle Engineering Derby - Stored locos
SIEM	Siemens Transportation - Barriers
TTLS	Traditional Traction - Locomotives
WAAN	DB Schenker - Class 67
WABN	DB Schenker - Class 67 RETB fitted
WAFN	DB Schenker - Class 67 hire to FGW
WAWN	Wrexham & Shropshire Railway - Class 67
WBAI	DB Schenker - Class 66 Industrial
WBAK	DB Schenker - Class 66 Construction
WBAM	DB Schenker - Class 66 Energy
WBAN	DB Schenker - Class 66 Network
WBBI	DB Schenker - Class 66 Industrial RETB fitted
WBBM	DB Schenker - Class 66 Energy RETB fitted
WBBN	DB Schenker - Class 66 Network RETB fitted
WBEN	DB Schenker - Class 66 Euro Cargo Rail mods
WBLI	DB Schenker - Class 66 Industrial Auto coupler
WCAI	DB Schenker - Class 60 Industrial 990 gal fuel
WCAK	DB Schenker - Class 60 Construction 990 gal fuel
WCAM	DB Schenker - Class 60 Energy 990 gal fuel
WCBK	DB Schenker - Class 60 Construct'n 1150 gal fuel
WDAK	DB Schenker - Class 59/2 Construction
WEFE	DB Schenker - Class 90
WFMS	DB Schenker - Class 60 Fleet Management
WFMU	DB Schenker - Fleet Management
WKBN	DB Schenker - Class 37 Network RETB fitted
WLAN	DB Schenker - Euro Cargo Rail Class 21
WNTR	DB Schenker - Stored locos - reserve
WNTS	DB Schenker - Stored locos - serviceable
WNXX	DB Schenker - Stored locos - unserviceable
WNYX	DB Schenker - Stored locos - parts recovery
WNZX	DB Schenker - Awaiting Disposal
WRLN	DB Schenker - Class 08, 09 - North London
WSEN	DB Schenker - Euro Cargo Rail - Class 08
WSSA	DB Schenker - Class 08, 09 - Axiom Rail
WSSI	DB Schenker - Class 08, 09 Industrial
WSSK	DB Schenker - Class 08, 09 Construction
WSSM	DB Schenker - Class 08, 09 Energy
WSSN	DB Schenker - Class 08, 09 Network
WSXX	DB Schenker - Class 08, 09 Stored
WTAE	DB Schenker - Class 92 Network
WZFF	DB Schenker - Class 58 France
WZFS	DB Schenker - Class 58 Spain
WZGF	DB Schenker - Class 56, 92 France
WZTS	DB Schenker - Class 08, 56, 58 Stored (hire pool)
XHAC	Direct Rail Services - Class 47
XHCK	Direct Rail Services - Class 57
XHHP	Direct Rail Services - Holding Pool
XHIM	Direct Rail Services - Class 66 - Intermodal
XHNC	Direct Rail Services - Nuclear Traffic
XHSS	Direct Rail Services - Stored
XYPA	Mendip Rail - Hanson Group
XYPO	Mendip Rail - Foster Yeoman (Aggregate Inds)

Pools are only given for locomotive groups which are included in this book. Pool codes for multiple units are not included.

Preserved site codes

ALY	Allelys, Studley
APF	Appleby-Frodingham RPS
AVR	Avon Valley Railway
BAT	Battlefield Line
BHR	Barrow Hill Roundhouse
BIR	Barry Island Railway
BKR	Bo'ness & Kinneil Railway
BLU	Bluebell Railway
BRC	Buckinghamshire Railway Centre
BRM	Birmingham Railway Museum, Tyseley
BVR	Bridgend Valleys Railway
BWR	Bodmin & Wenford Railway
CAN	Canton (Pullman Rail)
CHS	Chasewater Railway
COL	Colne Valley Railway
COV	Coventry Electric Railway Museum
CPR	Chinnor & Princes Risborough Railway
CRB	Caledonian Railway, Brechin
CRT	Cambrian Railway Trust
CVR	Churnet Valley Railway
CWR	Cholsey & Wallingford Railway
DAR	Dartmoor Railway
DEE	Royal Deeside Railway
DER	Derwent Valley Railway
DFR	Dean Forest Railway
DID	Didcot Railway Centre
EAR	East Anglican Rly Museum
ECC	Ecclesbourne Valley Railway
EDR	Edin Valley Railway
EHC	Elsecar Heritage Centre
EHD	Eastleigh DBS Depot
EKR	East Kent Railway
ELR	East Lancashire Railway
EMB	Embsay Steam Railway
EPO	Epping - Ongar Railway
FHL	Fawley Hall (Private)
FIN	Finmere Station, Oxfordshire
GCN	Great Central Railway (North)
GCR	Great Central Railway
GKR	Graham Kirk Rail
GWI	Gwili Railway
GWR	Gloucestershire & Warwickshire Railway
HAD	Hastings Diesels
IOW	Isle of Wight Railway
KEI	Keith & Dufftown Railway
KES	Kent & East Sussex Railway
KIN	MoD Kineton
KWV	Keighley & Worth Valley Railway
LAN	Llangollen Railway
LDL	Lavender Line
LHR	Lakeside & Haverthwaite Railway
LNW	London North Western, Crewe
LWR	Lincolnshire Wolds Railway
MET	Methill (Private)
MFM	Mangapps Farm Railway Museum
MHR	Mid Hants Railway
MID	Middleton Railway
MLM	Motorail - Long Marston
MOR	Morton-on-Lugg
MRC	Middleton Railway Centre
MSM	Museum of Science & Industry, Manchester
NHD	Newton Heath Depot
NIR	Northamptonshire Ironstone Railway
NLR	Northampton & Lamport Railway
NNR	North Norfolk Railway
NRM	National Railway Museum, York
NRS	National Railway Museum, Shildon
NYM	North Yorkshire Moors Railway
PBR	Pontypool & Blaenavon Railway
PDR	Paignton & Dartmouth Railway
PRL	Peak Rail
PVR	Plym Valley Railway
RAC	Railway Age, Crewe
RAM	Rampart, Derby
RIB	Ribble Steam Railway
RIP	Rippingdale Station
ROW	Rowley Mill
RST	Rushden Station Transport Museum
SEL	St Leonards Railway Engineering
SHP	Summerlee Heritage Park
SLN	Stewarts Lane Depot
SNI	Snibston Railway
SPV	Spa Valley Railway
SRC	Stainmore Railway Co
STR	Strathspay Railway
SVR	Severn Valley Railway
SWI	Swindon & Cricklade Railway
SWN	Swanage Railway
TEB	Friends of 502 Group, Tebay
TEL	Telford Horsehay Steam Trust
TIT	Titley Junction
TSR	Telford Steam Railway
TYN	North Tyneside Railway
VOG	Vale of Glamorgan Railway
WCR	West Coast Railway Co
WED	Weardale Railway
WEN	Wensleydale Railway
WSR	West Somerset Railway
XXX	Private unspecified site
YEO	Yeovil Railway Centre

Status

	Status
OPR	Operational
OPR	Operational Main Line certified
RES	Under restoration
STC	Static exhibit
STO	Stored

Depot Codes

Code	Facility	Name	Operator
AB	SD	Aberdeen Guild Street	DBS
AC	CSD	Aberdeen Clayhills	ICE
AD	EMUD	Ashford Hitachi	HIT/SET
AF	T&RSMD	Ashford Chart Leacon	BOM
AH	MoD	Ashchurch	MoD
AK	DMUD	Ardwick	SIE/FTP
AL	DMUD	Aylesbury	CRW
AN	TMD/WRD	Allerton, Liverpool	DBS
AP	TMD	Ashford Rail Plant	BBR
AS	Store	Allelys	ALL
AT	TMD	Various sites	ALS
AW	SD	Washwood Heath	DBS
AY	SD	Ayr	DBS
AZ	TMD	Ashford	BBR
BA	TMD	Crewe Basford Hall	FLR, DBS
BC	MoD	Bicester	MoD
BD	T&RSMD	Birkenhead North	MER
BF	EMUD	Bedford Cauldwell Walk	FCC
BG	SD	Hull Botanic Gardens	NOR
BH	Eng	Barrow Hill Roundhouse	BHE
BI	EMUD	Brighton	SOU
BK	T&RSMD	Barton Hill	DBS
BM	T&RSMD	Bournemouth	SWT
BN	T&RSMD	Bounds Green	ICE
BP	SD	Blackpool CS	NOR
BQ	TMD	Bury	ELR
BR	SD	Bristol Kingsland Road	NRL, FLR
BS	TMD	Bescot	DBS
BT	TMD	Bo'ness	BOK
BW	SD	Barrow-in-Furness	NOR
BZ	T&RSMD	St Blazey	DBS
CA	SD	Cambridge Coldhams Ln	AXI
CB	STORE	Crewe Brook Sidings	DBS
CC	SD	Clacton	SIE, NXA
CD	SD	Crewe Diesel	RIV, DBS
CE	IEMD	Crewe Electric	DBS
CF	DMUD	Cardiff Canton	PUL, ATW
CG	TMD	Crewe Gresty Bridge	DRS
CH	DMUD	Chester	ALS, ATW
CJ	SD	Clapham Junction	SWT
CK	DMUD	Corkerhill	FSR
CL	Store	Carlisle Upperby	DBS
CM	SD	Camden	LMI
CO	IEMD	Coquelles (France)	EUR
CP	CARMD	Crewe Carriage Shed	LNW
CQ	T&RSMD	Crewe Railway Age	CHC
CR	SD	Colchester	NXA
CS	T&RSMD	Carnforth	WCR
CT	SD	Cleethorpes	FTP
CW	MoD	Caerwent	MoD
CX	Store	Cardiff Tidal	DBS
CY	Store	Crewe Coal/South Yards	DRS
CZ	TMD	Central Rivers	BOM
DD	SD	Doncaster Wood Yard	DBS
DF	T&RSMD	Rail Vehicle Engineering	RVE
DI	Pres	Didcot Railway Centre	GWS
DM	TMD	Dollands Moor	DBS
DR	TMD	Doncaster Carr	DBS
DT	SD	Didcot Triangle	DBS
DV	SD	Dover	SET
DW	SD	Doncaster West Yard	NRL, WAB
DY	T&RSMD	Derby Etches Park	EMT
EA	SD	Earles Sidings	DBS
EC	T&RSMD	Craigentinny (Edinburgh)	ICE
ED	DMUD	Eastfield	FSR
EF	MPVD	Effingham Junction	AMS
EH	SD	Eastleigh	DBS
EM	EMUD	East Ham	c2c
EN	CARMD	Euston Downside	NRL
EU	SD	Euston Station Sidings	VWC
EZ	DMUD	Exeter	FGW
FB	Store	Ferrybridge	DBS
FC*		Fire College (Morton-on-Lugg)	
FD	Mobile	Diesel loco	FLR
FE	Mobile	Electric loco	FLR
FF	TRSMD	Forest - Brussels	SNCB, NMBS, EUS
FH	TRACK	Frodingham	GRP
FN	Hire	France	ECR
FP	CSD	Ferme Park	ICE
FR	EMUD	Fratton	SWT
FS	Mobile	Diesel Shunter	FLR
FW	SD	Fort William	DBS
FX	TMD	Felixstowe	FDH
GI	EMUD	Gillingham	SET
GL	TMD	Gloucester	CWR, ADV
GP	SD	Grove Park	SET
GW	EMUD	Glasgow Shields	FSR
HA	TMD	Haymarket	FSR
HD	SD	Holyhead	ATW
HE	EMUD	Hornsey	FCC
HF	SD	Hereford	DBS
HG	Store	Hither Green	DBS
HI	TM	Hitchin	BBR
HJ	SD	Hoo Junction	DBS
HM	SD/WRD	Healey Mills	DBS
HT	T&RSMD	Heaton	NOR, GTL
HY	SD	Oxford Hinksey Yard	NRL
IL	T&RSMD	Ilford	NXA
IM	SD	Immingham	DBS
IP	SD	Ipswich	FLR
IS	TMD	Inverness	FSR
KC	Store	Carlisle Currock WRD	DBS
KD	SD	Kingmoor Yard	DRS
KK	EMUD	Kirkdale	MER
KM	TMD	Carlisle Kingmoor	DRS
KR	T&RSMD	Kidderminster	SVR
KT	MoD	Kineton	MoD
KY	SD/WRD	Knottingley	DBS
LA	T&RSMD	Laira	FGW
LB	Eng	Loughborough	BTL
LD	TMD	Leeds Midland Road	FLR
LE	T&RSMD	Landore	FGW
LG	T&RSMD	Longsight Electric	ALT
LH	Eng	LH Group	LHG
LL	CSD	Liverpool Edge Hill	ALS
LM	Store	Long Marston	MLS
LO	T&RSMD	Longsight Diesel	NOR
LR	SD	Leicester	DBS
LT	MoD	Longtown	MoD

LU	MoD	Ludgershall	MoD
LY	T&RSMD	Le Landy - Paris	SNCF, EUS
MA	CARMD	Manchester International	ALS
MD	TMD	Merehead	MRL
MG	TMD	Margam	DBS
MH	SD	Millerhill	DBS
ML	SD	Motherwell	DBS
MM	Store	Moreton in Marsh	CWR
MN	DMUD	Machynlleth	ATW
MR	SD	March	GBR
MQ	Store	Meldon Quarry	BAR
MW	MoD	Marchwood Military Port	MoD
MY	SD/Store	Mossend Yard	DBS, FLR
NB	SD	New Brighton	MER
NC	T&RSMD	Norwich Crown Point	NXA
ND	Works	NedTrans, Tilburg	NDZ
NH	DMUD	Newton Heath	NOR
NL	T&RSMD	Neville Hill (Leeds)	EMT, ICE
NM	SD	Nottingham Eastcroft	EMT
NN	EMUD	Northampton, Kings Heath	SIE, LMI
NT	EMUD	Northam	SIE, SWT
NY	T&RSMD	Grosmont	NYM
OD	Eng	Old Dalby	ALS
OH	EMUD	Old Oak Common Electric	SIE
ON	SD	Orpington	SET
OO	HSTMD	Old Oak Common HST	FGW
OX	CSD	Oxford Carriage Sidings	FGW
OY	CARMD	Oxley	ALS
PB	SD	Peterborough	DBS
PC	TRSMD	Polmadie	ALS
PE	SD	Peterborough Nene	FCC
PF	SD	Peak Forest	DBS
PG	TRSMD	Peterborough	GBR
PH	SD	Perth	FSR
PM	TRSMD	St Philip's Marsh (Bristol)	FGW
PN	SD	Preston Station	NOR
PQ	SD	Harwich Parkeston Quay	DBS
PT	SD	Peterborough	GBR
PY	MoD	Shoeburyness (Pigs Bay)	MoD, KRS
PZ	TRSMD	Penzance (Long Rock)	FGW
RE	EMUD	Ramsgate	SET
RG	DMUD	Reading	FGW
RH	SD	Redhill	DBS
RL	TRSMD	Ropley	MHR
RO	SD	Rotherham Steel	DBS
RR	TMD	Roberts Road	JAR, FLF
RU	TMD	Rugby Rail Plant	GRP
RY	EMUD	Ryde	SWT
SA	DMUD	Salisbury	SWT
SB	TMD	Shrewsbury	NOR
SE	TRSMD	St Leonards	SLR
SG	EMUD	Slade Green	SET
SH	CARMD	Southall Railway Centre	WCR
SI	EMUD	Soho	LMI
SJ	TRSMD	Stourbridge Junction	LMI
SK	TRSMD	Swanwick	MRC
SL	TRSMD	Stewarts Lane	DBS, VSO, SOU
SM	SD	Sheffield Station	NOR
SN	SD	Shoeburyness	c2c
SO*		Southend	
SP	CRDC	Springs Branch	DBS
SQ	SD	Stockport	NOR
ST	SD	Southport	MER
SU	TRSMD	Selhurst	SOU
SX	SD	Shrewsbury	ATW
SZ	TMD	Southampton Maritime	FLR
TB	SD	Three Bridges	DBS
TE	TMD	Thornaby/Tees Yard	DBS
TF	SD	Orient Way	NXA
TG	SD	Tonbridge	GBR
TI	TRSMD	Temple Mills	EUS
TJ	TMD	Tavistock Junction	COL
TM	SD	Tyseley Loco Works	BRM
TN	SD	Taunton Fairwater	NRL, FLR
TO	TMD	Toton	DBS
TS	DMUD	Tyseley	LMI
TT	Store	Toton Training Compound	DBS
TY	Store	Tyne Yard	DBS
VI	SD	Victoria	SET
VR	SD	Aberystwyth	ATW
VZ	EMUD	Strawberry Hill	SIE, SWT
WA	SD	Warrington Arpley	DBS
WB	TRSMD	Wembley	ALS
WD	EMUD	East Wimbledon	SWT
WE	SD	Willesden Brent	DBS
WF	SD	Wansford	NVR
WH	Eng	Whatley	MRL
WK	SD	West Kirby	MER
WN	EMUD	Willesden	LOG
WP	SD	Worksop	DBS
WS	SD	Worcester	LMI
WW	SD	West Worthing	SOU
WY	SD/CSD	Westbury Yard	DBS
WZ*	TRSMD	Washwood Heath	HAN
XW	TMD	Crofton	BOM
XX	-	Exported	-
YK	DMUD	Siemens York	SIE, FTP
YL	TMD	York Leeman Road	JAR, FLF
YM	Store	National Railway Museum	NRM
YN	SD	York North Yard	DBS
YO	SD	Yoker	FSR
ZA	Eng	RTC Derby	SER, NRL, AEA
ZB	Eng	Doncaster	WAB
ZC	Eng	Crewe	BOM
ZD	Eng	Derby Litchurch Lane	BOM
ZG	Eng	Eastleigh Works	KRS
ZH	Eng	Glasgow	RCL
ZI	Eng	Ilford	BOM
ZK	Eng	Kilmarnock	BTL
ZL	Eng	Cardiff Canton	PUL
ZN	Eng	Wolverton	RCL
ZS	Eng	Locotech Wakefield	BAR
ZW	Eng	Stoke-on-Trent (Marcroft)	AXI
3M*		3M Industries, Bracknell	

* Unofficial code

Operator Codes

ADV	Advenza Freight
ALL	Allelys Heavy Haul
ALS	Alstom
AMS	Amec Spie Rail
ATW	Arriva Trains Wales
AXC	Arriva Cross Country
AXI	Axiom Rail
BAR	British American Railway Services
BBR	Balfour Beatty
BHE	Barrow Hill Roundhouse
BOK	Bo'ness and Kinneil
BOM	Bombardier
BRM	Birmingham Railway Museum
BTL	Brush Traction Limited
C2C	C2C Rail
CAD	Cargo-D
CAR	Carillion
CHS	Crewe Heritage Centre
COL	Colas Rail
CON	Continental Rail (Spain)
COR	Corus Steel
CRW	Chiltern Railways
CWR	Cotswold Rail
DBS	DB Schenker West
DRS	Direct Rail Services
ECR	Euro Cargo Rail (DBS)
ELR	East Lancashire Railway
EMT	East Midlands Trains
ETF	ETF Freight (France)
ETL	Electric Traction Ltd
EU2	Eurotunnel Europort2
EUR	Eurotunnel
EUS	Eurostar
FCC	First Capital Connect
FDH	Felixstowe Dock & Harbour
FGW	First Great Western
FHT	First Hull Trains
FLF	Fastline Freight
FLR	Freightliner
FMR	FM Rail
FSL	Flying Scotsman Railway Ltd
FSR	First ScotRail
FTP	First TransPennine
GBR	GB Railfreight
GRP	Grant Rail Plant
GTL	Grand Central Railway
GWS	Great Western Society
HEC	Heathrow Connect
HEX	Heathrow Express
HIT	Hitachi
HNR	Harry Needle Railroad
ICE	Inter City East Coast
IND	Industrial operator
JAR	Jarvis
JHS	Jeremy Hoskins
KRS	Knights Rail Services
LAF	Lafarge Aggregates
LMI	London Midland
LNW	L&WR Railway Co
LOG	London Overground
LUL	London Underground Ltd
MER	Merseyrail
MHR	Mid Hants Railway
MoD	Ministry of Defence
MRC	Midland Railway Centre
MRL	Mendip Rail Ltd
MRS	Motorail Logistics
NDZ	NedTrains
NOR	Northern Rail
NRL	Network Rail
NRM	National Railway Museum
NVR	Nene Valley Railway
NXA	National Express East Anglia
NYM	North Yorkshire Moors Railway
OLD	Old Dalby Test Track
PUL	Pullman Group
RAF	Railfilms Ltd
RCL	Railcare Ltd
RIV	Riviera Trains
RRS	Ridings Railtours
RVE	Rail Vehicle Engineering
S4G	Stratford 47 Group
SEC	Serco
SET	Southeastern Trains
SIE	Siemens
SIL	Stagecoach Island Line
SLR	St Leonards Rail Engineereing
SNB	Societe National des Chemins de fer de Belges
SNF	Societe National des Chemins de fer Francais
SOU	Southern
SRP	Scottish Railway Preservation Society
SVR	Severn Valley Railway
SWT	South West Trains
TRN	Transfessa
TSO	Travaux du Sud Ouest (France)
VSO	Venice Simplon Orient Express
VTN	Vintage Trains
VWC	Virgin West Coast
WAB	Wabtec
WCR	West Coast Railway Co
WSR	Wrexham & Shropshire Railway
WTN	Wessex Trains

Owner Codes

Code	Owner
AEA	AEA Rail Technology
ALS	Alstom
ANG	Angel Trains
ATW	Arriva Trains Wales
BAA	British Airports Authority
BCC	Bridgend County Council
BEA	Beacon Rail
BOM	Bombardier
BOT	Bank of Tokyo (Mitsubishi)
BTM	BTMU Capital Corporation
C20	Class 20 Locomotive Ltd
CAD	Cargo-D
CCC	Cardiff County Council
COL	Colas Rail
CRW	Chiltern Railways
CWR	Cotswold Rail
DBR	DB Regio
DBS	DB Schenker West
DRS	Direct Rail Services
ECR	Euro Cargo Rail (DBS)
ECT	ECT Main Line Rail
EMT	East Midlands Trains
ETL	Electric Traction Ltd
EU2	Eurotunnel Europort2
EUR	Eurotunnel
EUS	Eurostar
HAN	Hanson
FGP	First Group
FLF	Fastline Freight
FLR	Freightliner
FOS	Foster Yeoman
GBR	GB Railfreight
GTL	Grand Central Railway Ltd
HAL	Halifax Assets Finance Ltd
HAN	Hanson Traction
HBS	Halifax-Bank of Scotland
HJA	Howard Johnson Associates
HNR	Harry Needle Railroad
HSB	HSBC Bank
JAR	Jarvis
KRS	Knights Rail Services
LTS	Lloyds TSB Finance
NRL	Network Rail
NYM	North Yorkshire Moors Railway
PTR	Porterbrook
QWR	QW Rail Leasing
RCL	Railcare Limited
RIV	Riviera Trains
RML	Royal Mail
RMS	RMS Locotech
RTR	RT Rail
RVE	Rail Vehicle Engineering
SEC	Serco
S4G	Stratford Class 47 Group
SIE	Siemens
SOU	Southern (Govia)
SNB	Societe National des Chemins de fer de Belges
SNF	Societe National des Chemins de fer Francais
SWT	South West Trains (Stagecoach)
VTN	Vintage Trains
WAB	Wabtec
WCR	West Coast Railway Co
WYP	West Yorkshire PTE

Below: *Owned by the Dean Forest Diesel Association and usually used on the Severn Valley Railway to power engineering trains, Eastleigh-built electro-diesel No. 73006 is restored to 1980s rail blue livery. In this view the loco is seen at Long Marston, alongside Class 86 No. 86233 painted in mock electric blue with small yellow warning ends.* **CJM**

Station three-letter Codes

Abbey Wood	ABW
Aber	ABE
Abercynon	ACY
Aberdare	ABA
Aberdeen	ABD
Aberdour	AUR
Aberdovey	AVY
Abererch	ABH
Abergavenny	AGV
Abergele & Pensarn	AGL
Aberystwyth	AYW
Accrington	ACR
Achanalt	AAT
Achnasheen	ACN
Achnashellach	ACH
Acklington	ACK
Acle	ACL
Acocks Green	ACG
Acton Bridge	ACB
Acton Central	ACC
Acton Main Line	AML
Adderley Park	ADD
Addiewell	ADW
Addlestone	ASN
Adisham	ADM
Adlington (Cheshire)	ADC
Adlington (Lancs)	ADL
Adwick	AWK
Aigburth	AIG
Ainsdale	ANS
Aintree	AIN
Airbles	AIR
Airdrie	ADR
Albany Park	AYP
Albrighton	ALB
Alderley Edge	ALD
Aldermaston	AMT
Aldershot	AHT
Aldrington	AGT
Alexandra Palace	AAP
Alexandra Parade	AXP
Alexandria	ALX
Alfreton	ALF
Allens West	ALW
Alloa	ALO
Alness	ASS
Alnmouth	ALM
Alresford	ALR
Alsager	ASG
Althorne	ALN
Althorpe	ALP
Altnabreac	ABC
Alton	AON
Altrincham	ALT
Alvechurch	ALV
Ambergate	AMB
Amberley	AMY
Amersham	AMR
Ammanford	AMF
Ancaster	ANC
Anderston	AND
Andover	ADV
Anerley	ANZ
Angel Road	AGR
Angmering	ANG
Annan	ANN
Anniesland	ANL
Ansdell & Fairhaven	AFV
Appleby	APP
Appledore (Kent)	APD
Appleford	APF
Appley Bridge	APB
Apsley	APS
Arbroath	ARB
Ardgay	ARD
Ardlui	AUI
Ardrossan Harbour	ADS
Ardrossan South Beach	ASB
Ardrossan Town	ADN
Ardwick	ADK
Argyle Street	AGS
Arisaig	ARG
Arlesey	ARL
Armathwaite	AWT
Arnside	ARN
Arram	ARR
Arrochar & Tarbet	ART
Arundel	ARU
Ascot	ACT
Ascott-u-Wychwood	AUW
Ash	ASH
Ash Vale	AHV
Ashburys	ABY
Ashchurch	ASC
Ashfield	ASF
Ashford International	AFK
Ashford (Eurostar)	ASI
Ashford (Surrey)	AFS
Ashley	ASY
Ashtead	AHD
Ashton-under-Lyne	AHN
Ashurst	AHS
Ashurst New Forest	ANF
Ashwell & Morden	AWM
Askam	ASK
Aslockton	ALK
Aspatria	ASP
Aspley Guise	APG
Aston	AST
Atherstone	ATH
Atherton	ATN
Attadale	ATT
Attenborough	ATB
Attleborough	ATL
Auchinleck	AUK
Audley End	AUD
Aughton Park	AUG
Aviemore	AVM
Avoncliff	AVF
Avonmouth	AVN
Axminster	AXM
Aylesbury	AYS
Aylesbury Parkway	AVP
Aylesford	AYL
Aylesham	AYH
Ayr	AYR
Bache	BAC
Baglan	BAJ
Bagshot	BAG
Baildon	BLD
Baillieston	BIO
Balcombe	BAB
Baldock	BDK
Balham	BAL
Balloch	BHC
Balmossie	BSI
Bamber Bridge	BMB
Bamford	BAM
Banavie	BNV
Banbury	BAN
Bangor (Gwynedd)	BNG
Bank Hall	BAH
Banstead	BAD
Barassie	BSS
Barbican	ZBB
Bardon Mill	BLL
Bare Lane	BAR
Bargeddie	BGI
Bargoed	BGD
Barking	BKG
Barking Underground	ZBK
Barlaston	BRT
Barming	BMG
Barmouth	BRM
Barnehurst	BNH
Barnes	BNS
Barnes Bridge	BNI
Barnetby	BTB
Barnham	BAA
Barnhill	BNL
Barnsley	BNY
Barnstaple	BNP
Barnt Green	BTG
Barrhead	BRR
Barrhill	BRL
Barrow Haven	BAV
Barrow Upon Soar	BWS
Barrow-in-Furness	BIF
Barry	BRY
Barry Docks	BYD
Barry Island	BYI
Barry Links	BYL
Barton-on-Humber	BAU
Basildon	BSO
Basingstoke	BSK
Bat & Ball	BBL
Bath Spa	BTH
Bathgate	BHG
Batley	BTL
Battersby	BTT
Battersea Park	BAK
Battle	BAT
Battlesbridge	BLB
Bayford	BAY
Beaconsfield	BCF
Bearley	BER
Bearsden	BRN
Bearsted	BSD
Beasdale	BSL
Beaulieu Road	BEU
Beauly	BEL
Bebington	BEB
Beccles	BCC
Beckenham Hill	BEC
Beckenham Junction	BKJ
Bedford	BDM
Bedford St Johns	BSJ
Bedhampton	BDH
Bedminster	BMT
Bedworth	BEH
Bedwyn	BDW
Beeston	BEE
Bekesbourne	BKS
Belle Vue	BLV
Bellgrove	BLG
Bellingham	BGM
Bellshill	BLH
Belmont	BLM
Belper	BLP
Beltring	BEG
Belvedere	BVD
Bempton	BEM
Ben Rhydding	BEY
Benfleet	BEF
Bentham	BEN
Bentley	BTY
Bentley (South Yorks)	BYK
Bere Alston	BAS
Bere Ferrers	BFE
Berkhamsted	BKM
Berkswell	BKW
Berney Arms	BYA
Berry Brow	BBW
Berrylands	BRS
Berwick	BRK
Berwick-upon-Tweed	BWK
Bescar Lane	BES
Bescot Stadium	BSC
Betchworth	BTO
Bethnal Green	BET
Betws-y-Coed	BYC
Beverley	BEV
Bexhill	BEX
Bexley	BXY
Bexleyheath	BXH
Bicester North	BCS
Bicester Town	BIT
Bickley	BKL
Bidston	BID
Biggleswade	BIW
Bilbrook	BBK
Billericay	BIC
Billingham	BIL
Billingshurst	BIG
Bingham	BIN
Bingley	BIY
Birchgrove	BCG
Birchington-on-Sea	BCH
Birchwood	BWD
Birkbeck	BIK
Birkdale	BDL
Birkenhead Central	BKC
Birkenhead North	BKN
Birkenhead Park	BKP
Birmingham Int	BHI
Birmingham Moor St	BMO
Birmingham New St	BHM
Birmingham Snow Hill	BSW
Bishop Auckland	BIA
Bishopbriggs	BBG
Bishops Stortford	BIS
Bishopstone	BIP
Bishopton	BPT
Bitterne	BTE
Blackburn	BBN
Blackheath	BKH
Blackhorse Road	BHO
Blackpool North	BPN
Blackpool P Beach	BPB
Blackpool South	BPS
Blackrod	BLK
Blackwater	BAW
Blaenau Ffestiniog	BFF
Blair Atholl	BLA
Blairhill	BAI
Blake Street	BKT
Blakedown	BKD
Blantyre	BLT
Blaydon	BLO
Bleasby	BSB
Bletchley	BLY
Bloxwich	BLX
Bloxwich North	BWN
Blundellsands & Crosby	BLN
Blythe Bridge	BYB
Bodmin Parkway	BOD
Bodorgan	BOR
Bognor Regis	BOG
Bogston	BGS
Bolton	BON
Bolton-on-Dearne	BTD
Bookham	BKA

Bootle	BOC
Bootle New Strand	BNW
Bootle Oriel Road	BOT
Bordesley	BBS
Borough Green	BRG
Borth	BRH
Bosham	BOH
Boston	BSN
Botley	BOE
Bottesford	BTF
Bourne End	BNE
Bournemouth	BMH
Bournville	BRV
Bow Brickhill	BWB
Bowes Park	BOP
Bowling	BWG
Boxhill & Westhumble	BXW
Bracknell	BCE
Bradford Forster Sq	BDQ
Bradford Interchange	BDI
Bradford-on-Avon	BOA
Brading	BDN
Braintree	BTR
Braintree Freeport	BTP
Bramhall	BML
Bramley	BLE
Bramley (Hants)	BMY
Brampton (Cumbria)	BMP
Brampton (Suffolk)	BRP
Branchton	BCN
Brandon	BND
Branksome	BSM
Braystones	BYS
Bredbury	BDY
Breich	BRC
Brentford	BFD
Brentwood	BRE
Bricket Wood	BWO
Bridge of Allan	BEA
Bridge of Orchy	BRO
Bridgend	BGN
Bridgeton	BDG
Bridgwater	BWT
Bridlington	BDT
Brierfield	BRF
Brigg	BGG
Brighouse	BGH
Brighton	BTN
Brimsdown	BMD
Brinnington	BNT
Bristol Parkway	BPW
Bristol Temple Meads	BRI
Brithdir	BHD
British Steel Redcar	RBS
Briton Ferry	BNF
Brixton	BRX
Broad Green	BGE
Broadbottom	BDB
Broadstairs	BSR
Brockenhurst	BCU
Brockholes	BHS
Brockley	BCY
Bromborough	BOM
Bromborough Rake	BMR
Bromley Cross	BMC
Bromley North	BMN
Bromley South	BMS
Bromsgrove	BMV
Brondesbury	BSY
Brondesbury Park	BSP
Brookmans Park	BPK
Brookwood	BKO
Broome	BME
Broomfleet	BMF
Brora	BRA
Brough	BUH
Broughty Ferry	BYF
Broxbourne	BXB
Bruce Grove	BCV
Brundall	BDA
Brundall Gardens	BGA
Brunstane	BSU
Brunswick	BRW
Bruton	BRU
Bryn	BYN
Buckenham	BUC
Buckley	BCK
Bucknell	BUK
Bugle	BGL
Builth Road	BHR
Bulwell	BLW
Bures	BUE
Burgess Hill	BUG
Burley Park	BUY
Burley-in-Wharfedale	BUW
Burnage	BNA
Burneside	BUD
Burnham	BNM
Burnham-on-Crouch	BUU
Burnley Barracks	BUB
Burnley Central	BNC
Burnley Manchester Rd	BYM
Burnside	BUI
Burntisland	BTS
Burscough Bridge	BCB
Burscough Junction	BCJ
Bursledon	BUO
Burton Joyce	BUJ
Burton-on-Trent	BUT
Bury St Edmunds	BSE
Busby	BUS
Bush Hill Park	BHK
Bushey	BSH
Butlers Lane	BUL
Buxted	BXD
Buxton	BUX
Byfleet & New Haw	BFN
Bynea	BYE
Cadoxton	CAD
Caergwrle	CGW
Caerphilly	CPH
Caersws	CWS
Caldicot	CDT
Caledonian Rd & Bby	CIR
Calstock	CSK
Cam & Dursley	CDU
Camberley	CAM
Camborne	CBN
Cambridge	CBG
Cambridge Heath	CBH
Cambuslang	CBL
Camden Road	CMD
Camelon	CMO
Canley	CNL
Cannock	CAO
Canonbury	CNN
Canterbury East	CBE
Canterbury West	CBW
Cantley	CNY
Capenhurst	CPU
Carbis Bay	CBB
Cardenden	CDD
Cardiff Bay	CDB
Cardiff Central	CDF
Cardiff Queen Street	CDQ
Cardonald	CDO
Cardross	CDR
Carfin	CRF
Cark	CAK
Carlisle	CAR
Carlton	CTO
Carluke	CLU
Carmarthen	CMN
Carmyle	CML
Carnforth	CNF
Carnoustie	CAN
Carntyne	CAY
Carpenders Park	CPK
Carrbridge	CAG
Carshalton	CSH
Carshalton Beeches	CSB
Carstairs	CRS
Cartsdyke	CDY
Castle Bar Park	CBP
Castle Cary	CLC
Castleford	CFD
Castleton	CAS
Castleton Moor	CSM
Caterham	CAT
Catford	CTF
Catford Bridge	CFB
Cathays	CYS
Cathcart	CCT
Cattal	CTL
Causeland	CAU
Cefn-y-Bedd	CYB
Chadwell Heath	CTH
Chafford Hundred	CFH
Chalfont & Latimer	CFO
Chalkwell	CHW
Chandlers Ford	CFR
Chapel-en-le-Frith	CEF
Chapelton	CPN
Chapeltown	CLN
Chappel & Wakes Colne	CWC
Charing	CHG
Charing Cross (FSR)	CHC
Charlbury	CBY
Charlton	CTN
Chartham	CRT
Chassen Road	CSR
Chatelherault	CTE
Chatham	CTM
Chathill	CHT
Cheadle Hulme	CHU
Cheam	CHE
Cheddington	CED
Chelford	CEL
Chelmsford	CHM
Chelsfield	CLD
Cheltenham Spa	CNM
Chepstow	CPW
Cherry Tree	CYT
Chertsey	CHY
Cheshunt	CHN
Chessington North	CSN
Chessington South	CSS
Chester	CTR
Chester Road	CRD
Chesterfield	CHD
Chester-le-Street	CLS
Chestfield & Swalecliffe	CSW
Chetnole	CNO
Chichester	CCH
Chilham	CIL
Chilworth	CHL
Chingford	CHI
Chinley	CLY
Chippenham	CPM
Chipstead	CHP
Chirk	CRK
Chislehurst	CIT
Chiswick	CHK
Cholsey	CHO
Chorley	CRL
Chorleywood	CLW
Christchurch	CHR
Christs Hospital	CHH
Church & Oswaldtwistle	CTW
Church Fenton	CHF
Church Stretton	CTT
Cilmeri	CIM
City Thameslink	CTK
Clacton on Sea	CLT
Clandon	CLA
Clapham High Street	CLP
Clapham Junction	CLJ
Clapham (Yorkshire)	CPY
Clapton	CPT
Clarbeston Road	CLR
Clarkston	CKS
Claverdon	CLV
Claygate	CLG
Cleethorpes	CLE
Cleland	CEA
Clifton	CLI
Clifton Down	CFN
Clitheroe	CLH
Clock House	CLK
Clunderwen	CUW
Clydebank	CYK
Coatbridge Central	CBC
Coatbridge Sunnyside	CBS
Coatdyke	COA
Cobham & Stoke d'An	CSD
Codsall	CSL
Cogan	CGN
Colchester	COL
Colchester Town	CET
Coleshill Parkway	CEH
Collingham	CLM
Collington	CLL
Colne	CNE
Colwall	CWL
Colwyn Bay	CWB
Combe	CME
Commondale	COM
Congleton	CNG
Conisbrough	CNS
Connel Ferry	CON
Cononley	CEY
Conway Park	CNP
Conwy	CNW
Cooden Beach	COB
Cookham	COO
Cooksbridge	CBR
Coombe Halt	COE
Copplestone	COP
Corbridge	CRB
Corby	COR
Corkerhill	CKH
Corkickle	CKL
Corpach	CPA
Corrour	CRR
Coryton	COY
Coseley	CSY
Cosford	COS
Cosham	CSA
Cottingham	CGM
Cottingley	COT
Coulsdon South	CDS
Coventry	COV
Cowden	CWN
Cowdenbeath	COW
Cradley Heath	CRA
Craigendoran	CGD
Cramlington	CRM
Craven Arms	CRV
Crawley	CRW
Crayford	CRY

Crediton	CDI
Cressing	CES
Cressington	CSG
Creswell	CWD
Crewe	CRE
Crewkerne	CKN
Crews Hill	CWH
Crianlarich	CNR
Criccieth	CCC
Cricklewood	CRI
Croftfoot	CFF
Crofton Park	CFT
Cromer	CMR
Cromford	CMF
Crookston	CKT
Cross Gates	CRG
Crossflatts	CFL
Crosshill	COI
Crosskeys	CKY
Crossmyloof	CMY
Croston	CSO
Crouch Hill	CRH
Crowborough	COH
Crowhurst	CWU
Crowle	CWE
Crowthorne	CRN
Croy	CRO
Crystal Palace	CYP
Cuddington	CUD
Cuffley	CUF
Culham	CUM
Culrain	CUA
Cumbernauld	CUB
Cupar	CUP
Curriehill	CUH
Cuxton	CUX
Cwmbach	CMH
Cwmbran	CWM
Cynghordy	CYN
Dagenham Dock	DDK
Daisy Hill	DSY
Dalgety Bay	DAG
Dalmally	DAL
Dalmarnock	DAK
Dalmeny	DAM
Dalmuir	DMR
Dalreoch	DLR
Dalry	DLY
Dalston	DLS
Dalston Kingsland	DLK
Dalton	DLT
Dalwhinnie	DLW
Danby	DNY
Danescourt	DCT
Danzey	DZY
Darlington	DAR
Darnall	DAN
Darsham	DSM
Dartford	DFD
Darton	DRT
Darwen	DWN
Datchet	DAT
Davenport	DVN
Dawlish	DWL
Dawlish Warren	DWW
Deal	DEA
Dean	DEN
Dean Lane	DNN
Deansgate	DGT
Deganwy	DGY
Deighton	DHN
Delamere	DLM
Denby Dale	DBD
Denham	DNM
Denham Golf Club	DGC
Denmark Hill	DMK
Dent	DNT
Denton	DTN
Deptford	DEP
Derby	DBY
Derby Road	DBR
Derker	DKR
Devonport	DPT
Dewsbury	DEW
Didcot Parkway	DID
Digby & Sowton	DIG
Dilton Marsh	DMH
Dinas Powys	DNS
Dinas Rhondda	DMG
Dingle Road	DGL
Dingwall	DIN
Dinsdale	DND
Dinting	DTG
Disley	DSL
Diss	DIS
Dockyard	DOC
Dodworth	DOD
Dolau	DOL
Doleham	DLH
Dolgarrog	DLG
Dolwyddelan	DWD
Doncaster	DON
Dorchester South	DCH
Dorchester West	DCW
Dore	DOR
Dorking	DKG
Dorking Deepdene	DPD
Dorking West	DKT
Dormans	DMS
Dorridge	DDG
Dove Holes	DVH
Dover Priory	DVP
Dovercourt	DVC
Dovey Junction	DVY
Downham Market	DOW
Drayton Green	DRG
Drayton Park	DYP
Drem	DRM
Driffield	DRF
Drigg	DRI
Droitwich Spa	DTW
Dronfield	DRO
Drumchapel	DMC
Drumfrochar	DFR
Drumgelloch	DRU
Drumry	DMY
Dublin Ferryport	DFP
Dublin Port - Stena	DPS
Duddeston	DUD
Dudley Port	DDP
Duffield	DFI
Duirinish	DRN
Duke Street	DST
Dullingham	DUL
Dumbarton Central	DBC
Dumbarton East	DBE
Dumbreck	DUM
Dumfries	DMF
Dumpton Park	DMP
Dunbar	DUN
Dunblane	DBL
Duncraig	DCG
Dundee	DEE
Dunfermline Q'n Margaret	DFL
Dunfermline Town	DFE
Dunkeld & Birnam	DKD
Dunlop	DNL
Dunrobin Castle	DNO
Dunston	DOT
Dunton Green	DNG
Durham	DHM
Durrington-on-Sea	DUR
Dyce	DYC
Dyffryn Ardudwy	DYF
Eaglescliffe	EAG
Ealing Broadway	EAL
Earlestown	ERL
Earley	EAR
Earlsfield	EAD
Earlswood (Surrey)	ELD
Earlswood (Midlands)	EWD
East Croydon	ECR
East Didsbury	EDY
East Dulwich	EDW
East Farleigh	EFL
East Garforth	EGF
East Grinstead	EGR
East Kilbride	EKL
East Malling	EML
East Midlands Parkway	EMD
East Tilbury	ETL
East Worthing	EWR
Eastbourne	EBN
Eastbrook	EBK
Easterhouse	EST
Eastham Rake	ERA
Eastleigh	ESL
Eastrington	EGN
Ebbw Vale Parkway	EBV
Eccles	ECC
Eccles Road	ECS
Eccleston Park	ECL
Edale	EDL
Eden Park	EDN
Edenbridge	EBR
Edenbridge Town	EBT
Edge Hill	EDG
Edinburgh Park	EDP
Edinburgh Waverley	EDB
Edmonton Green	EDR
Effingham Junction	EFF
Eggesford	EGG
Egham	EGH
Egton	EGT
Elephant & Castle	EPH
Elgin	ELG
Ellesmere Port	ELP
Elmers End	ELE
Elmstead Woods	ESD
Elmswell	ESW
Elsecar	ELR
Elsenham	ESM
Elstree & Borehamwood	ELS
Eltham	ELW
Elton & Orston	ELO
Ely	ELY
Emerson Park	EMP
Emsworth	EMS
Enfield Chase	ENC
Enfield Lock	ENL
Enfield Town	ENF
Entwistle	ENT
Epsom	EPS
Epsom Downs	EPD
Erdington	ERD
Eridge	ERI
Erith	ERH
Esher	ESH
Essex Road	EXR
Etchingham	ETC
Euxton Balshaw Lane	EBA
Evesham	EVE
Ewell East	EWE
Ewell West	EWW
Exeter Central	EXC
Exeter St David's	EXD
Exeter St Thomas	EXT
Exhibition Centre	EXG
Exmouth	EXM
Exton	EXN
Eynsford	EYN
Failsworth	FLS
Fairbourne	FRB
Fairfield	FRF
Fairlie	FRL
Fairwater	FRW
Falconwood	FCN
Falkirk Grahamston	FKG
Falkirk High	FKK
Falls of Cruachan	FOC
Falmer	FMR
Falmouth Docks	FAL
Falmouth Town	FMT
Fareham	FRM
Farnborough (Main)	FNB
Farnborough North	FNN
Farncombe	FNC
Farnham	FNH
Farningham Road	FNR
Farnworth	FNW
Farringdon	ZFD
Fauldhouse	FLD
Faversham	FAV
Faygate	FGT
Fazakerley	FAZ
Fearn	FRN
Featherstone	FEA
Felixstowe	FLX
Feltham	FEL
Feniton	FNT
Fenny Stratford	FEN
Fernhill	FER
Ferriby	FRY
Ferryside	FYS
Ffairfach	FFA
Filey	FIL
Filton Abbey Wood	FIT
Finchley Rd & Frognal	FNY
Finsbury Park	FPK
Finstock	FIN
Fishbourne (Sussex)	FSB
Fishersgate	FSG
Fishguard Harbour	FGH
Fiskerton	FSK
Fitzwilliam	FZW
Five Ways	FWY
Fleet	FLE
Flimby	FLM
Flint	FLN
Flitwick	FLT
Flixton	FLI
Flowery Field	FLF
Folkestone Central	FKC
Folkestone West	FKW
Ford	FOD
Forest Gate	FOG
Forest Hill	FOH
Formby	FBY
Forres	FOR
Forsinard	FRS
Fort Matilda	FTM
Fort William	FTW
Four Oaks	FOK
Foxfield	FOX
Foxton	FXN
Frant	FRT
Fratton	FTN
Freshfield	FRE
Freshford	FFD
Frimley	FML
Frinton on Sea	FRI
Frizinghall	FZH
Frodsham	FRD
Frome	FRO

Fulwell	FLW
Furness Vale	FNV
Furze Platt	FZP
Gainsborough Central	GNB
Gainsborough Lea Rd	GBL
Garelochhead	GCH
Garforth	GRF
Gargrave	GGV
Garrowhill	GAR
Garscadden	GRS
Garsdale	GSD
Garston (Hertfordshire)	GSN
Garswood	GSW
Gartcosh	GRH
Garth (Bridgend)	GMG
Garth (Powys)	GTH
Garve	GVE
Gathurst	GST
Gatley	GTY
Gatwick Airport	GTW
Georgemas Junction	GGJ
Gerrards Cross	GER
Gidea Park	GDP
Giffnock	GFN
Giggleswick	GIG
Gilberdyke	GBD
Gilfach Fargoed	GFF
Gillingham (Dorset)	GIL
Gillingham (Kent)	GLM
Gilshochill	GSC
Gipsy Hill	GIP
Girvan	GIR
Glaisdale	GLS
Glan Conwy	GCW
Glasgow Central	GLC
Glasgow Queen Street	GLQ
Glasshoughton	GLH
Glazebrook	GLZ
Gleneagles	GLE
Glenfinnan	GLF
Glengarnock	GLG
Glenrothes with Thornton	GLT
Glossop	GLO
Gloucester	GCR
Glynde	GLY
Gobowen	GOB
Godalming	GOD
Godley	GDL
Godstone	GDN
Goldthorpe	GOE
Golf Street	GOF
Golspie	GOL
Gomshall	GOM
Goodmayes	GMY
Goole	GOO
Goostrey	GTR
Gordon Hill	GDH
Goring & Streatley	GOR
Goring-by-Sea	GBS
Gorton	GTO
Gospel Oak	GPO
Gourock	GRK
Gowerton	GWN
Goxhill	GOX
Grange Park	GPK
Grange-Over-Sands	GOS
Grangetown	GTN
Grantham	GRA
Grateley	GRT
Gravelly Hill	GVH
Gravesend	GRV
Grays	GRY
Great Ayton	GTA
Great Bentley	GRB
Great Chesterford	GRC
Great Coates	GCT
Great Malvern	GMV
Great Missenden	GMN
Great Yarmouth	GYM
Green Lane	GNL
Green Road	GNR
Greenbank	GBK
Greenfaulds	GRL
Greenfield	GNF
Greenford	GFD
Greenhithe for Bluewater	GNH
Greenock Central	GKC
Greenock West	GKW
Greenwich	GNW
Gretna Green	GEA
Grimsby Docks	GMD
Grimsby Town	GMB
Grindleford	GRN
Grosmont	GMT
Grove Park	GRP
Guide Bridge	GUI
Guildford	GLD
Guiseley	GSY
Gunnersbury	GUN
Gunnislake	GSL
Gunton	GNT
Gwersyllt	GWE
Gypsy Lane	GYP
Habrough	HAB
Hackbridge	HCB
Hackney Central	HKC
Hackney Downs	HAC
Hackney Wick	HKW
Haddenham & T Parkway	HDM
Haddiscoe	HAD
Hadfield	HDF
Hadley Wood	HDW
Hag Fold	HGF
Hagley	HAG
Hairmyres	HMY
Hale	HAL
Halesworth	HAS
Halewood	HED
Halifax	HFX
Hall Green	HLG
Hall I Th Wood	HID
Hall Road	HLR
Halling	HAI
Haltwhistle	HWH
Ham Street	HMT
Hamble	HME
Hamilton Central	HNC
Hamilton Square	BKQ
Hamilton West	HNW
Hammerton	HMM
Hampden Park	HMD
Hampstead Heath	HDH
Hampton	HMP
Hampton Court	HMC
Hampton Wick	HMW
Hampton-in-Arden	HIA
Hamstead	HSD
Hamworthy	HAM
Hanborough	HND
Handforth	HTH
Hanwell	HAN
Hapton	HPN
Harlech	HRL
Harlesden	HDN
Harling Road	HRD
Harlington	HLN
Harlow Mill	HWM
Harlow Town	HWN
Harold Wood	HRO
Harpenden	HPD
Harrietsham	HRM
Harringay	HGY
Harringay Green Lanes	HRY
Harrington	HRR
Harrogate	HGT
Harrow & Wealdstone	HRW
Harrow-on-the-Hill	HOH
Hartford	HTF
Hartlebury	HBY
Hartlepool	HPL
Hartwood	HTW
Harwich International	HPQ
Harwich Town	HWC
Haslemere	HSL
Hassocks	HSK
Hastings	HGS
Hatch End	HTE
Hatfield	HAT
Hatfield & Stainforth	HFS
Hatfield Peverel	HAP
Hathersage	HSG
Hattersley	HTY
Hatton	HTN
Havant	HAV
Havenhouse	HVN
Haverfordwest	HVF
Hawarden	HWD
Hawarden Bridge	HWB
Hawkhead	HKH
Haydon Bridge	HDB
Haydons Road	HYR
Hayes & Harlington	HAY
Hayes (Kent)	HYS
Hayle	HYL
Haymarket	HYM
Haywards Heath	HHE
Hazel Grove	HAZ
Headcorn	HCN
Headingley	HDY
Headstone Lane	HDL
Heald Green	HDG
Healing	HLI
Heath High Level	HHL
Heath Low Level	HLL
Heathrow Airport T123	HXX
Heathrow Airport T4	HAF
Heathrow Terminal 5	HWV
Heaton Chapel	HTC
Hebden Bridge	HBD
Heckington	HEC
Hedge End	HDE
Hednesford	HNF
Heighington	HEI
Helensburgh Central	HLC
Helensburgh Upper	HLU
Hellifield	HLD
Helmsdale	HMS
Helsby	HSB
Hemel Hempstead	HML
Hendon	HEN
Hengoed	HNG
Henley-in-Arden	HNL
Henley-on-Thames	HOT
Hensall	HEL
Hereford	HFD
Herne Bay	HNB
Herne Hill	HNH
Hersham	HER
Hertford East	HFE
Hertford North	HFN
Hessle	HES
Heswall	HSW
Hever	HEV
Heworth	HEW
Hexham	HEX
Heyford	HYD
Heysham Port	HHB
High Brooms	HIB
High St (Glasgow)	HST
High Street Kensington	ZHS
High Wycombe	HWY
Higham	HGM
Highams Park	HIP
Highbridge & Burnham	HIG
Highbury & Islington	HHY
Hightown	HTO
Hildenborough	HLB
Hillfoot	HLF
Hillington East	HLE
Hillington West	HLW
Hillside	HIL
Hilsea	HLS
Hinchley Wood	HYW
Hinckley	HNK
Hindley	HIN
Hinton Admiral	HNA
Hitchin	HIT
Hither Green	HGR
Hockley	HOC
Hollingbourne	HBN
Hollinwood	HOD
Holmes Chapel	HCH
Holmwood	HLM
Holton Heath	HOL
Holyhead	HHD
Holytown	HLY
Homerton	HMN
Honeybourne	HYB
Honiton	HON
Honley	HOY
Honor Oak Park	HPA
Hook	HOK
Hooton	HOO
Hope (Derbyshire)	HOP
Hope (Flintshire)	HPE
Hopton Heath	HPT
Horley	HOR
Hornbeam Park	HBP
Hornsey	HRN
Horsforth	HRS
Horsham	HRH
Horsley	HSY
Horton-in-Ribblesdale	HIR
Horwich Parkway	HWI
Hoscar	HSC
Hough Green	HGN
Hounslow	HOU
Hove	HOV
Hoveton & Wroxham	HXM
How Wood	HWW
Howden	HOW
Howwood (Renfrew)	HOZ
Hoylake	HYK
Hubberts Bridge	HBB
Hucknall	HKN
Huddersfield	HUD
Hull Paragon	HUL
Humphrey Park	HUP
Huncoat	HCT
Hungerford	HGD
Hunmanby	HUB
Huntingdon	HUN
Huntly	HNT
Hunts Cross	HNX
Hurst Green	HUR
Hutton Cranswick	HUT
Huyton	HUY
Hyde Central	HYC
Hyde North	HYT
Hykeham	HKM
Hyndland	HYN
Hythe	HYH
IBM	IBM
Ifield	IFI

Ilford	IFD
Ilkley	ILK
Imperial Wharf	IMW
Ince	INC
Ince & Elton	INE
Ingatestone	INT
Insch	INS
Invergordon	IGD
Invergowrie	ING
Inverkeithing	INK
Inverkip	INP
Inverness	INV
Invershin	INH
Inverurie	INR
Ipswich	IPS
Irlam	IRL
Irvine	IRV
Isleworth	ISL
Islip	ISP
Iver	IVR
Ivybridge	IVY
Jewellery Quarter	JEQ
Johnston	JOH
Johnstone	JHN
Jordanhill	JOR
Kearsley	KSL
Kearsney	KSN
Keighley	KEI
Keith	KEH
Kelvedon	KEL
Kelvindale	KVD
Kemble	KEM
Kempston Hardwick	KMH
Kempton Park	KMP
Kemsing	KMS
Kemsley	KML
Kendal	KEN
Kenley	KLY
Kennett	KNE
Kennishead	KNS
Kensal Green	KNL
Kensal Rise	KNR
Kensington Olympia	KPA
Kent House	KTH
Kentish Town	KTN
Kentish Town West	KTW
Kenton	KNT
Kents Bank	KBK
Kettering	KET
Kew Bridge	KWB
Kew Gardens	KWG
Keyham	KEY
Keynsham	KYN
Kidbrooke	KDB
Kidderminster	KID
Kidsgrove	KDG
Kidwelly	KWL
Kilburn High Road	KBN
Kildale	KLD
Kildonan	KIL
Kilgetty	KGT
Kilmarnock	KMK
Kilmaurs	KLM
Kilpatrick	KPT
Kilwinning	KWN
Kinbrace	KBC
Kingham	KGM
Kinghorn	KGH
Kings Langley	KGL
King's Lynn	KLN
Kings Norton	KNN
Kings Nympton	KGN
Kings Park	KGP
Kings Sutton	KGS
Kingsknowe	KGE
Kingston	KNG
Kingswood	KND
Kingussie	KIN
Kintbury	KIT
Kirby Cross	KBX
Kirk Sandall	KKS
Kirkby	KIR
Kirkby in Ashfield	KKB
Kirkby Stephen	KSW
Kirkby-in-Furness	KBF
Kirkcaldy	KDY
Kirkconnel	KRK
Kirkdale	KKD
Kirkham & Wesham	KKM
Kirkhill	KKH
Kirknewton	KKN
Kirkwood	KWD
Kirton Lindsey	KTL
Kiveton Bridge	KIV
Kiveton Park	KVP
Knaresborough	KNA
Knebworth	KBW
Knighton	KNI
Knockholt	KCK
Knottingley	KNO
Knucklas	KNU
Knutsford	KNF
Kyle of Lochalsh	KYL
Ladybank	LDY
Ladywell	LAD
Laindon	LAI
Lairg	LRG
Lake	LKE
Lakenheath	LAK
Lamphey	LAM
Lanark	LNK
Lancaster	LAN
Lancing	LAC
Landywood	LAW
Langbank	LGB
Langho	LHO
Langley	LNY
Langley Green	LGG
Langley Mill	LGM
Langside	LGS
Langwathby	LGW
Langwith-Whaley Thorns	LAG
Lapford	LAP
Lapworth	LPW
Larbert	LBT
Largs	LAR
Larkhall	LRH
Lawrence Hill	LWH
Layton	LAY
Lazonby & Kirkoswald	LZB
Lea Green	LEG
Lea Hall	LEH
Leagrave	LEA
Lealholm	LHM
Leamington Spa	LMS
Leasowe	LSW
Leatherhead	LHD
Ledbury	LED
Lee	LEE
Leeds	LDS
Leicester	LEI
Leigh (Kent)	LIH
Leigh-on-Sea	LES
Leighton Buzzard	LBZ
Lelant	LEL
Lelant Saltings	LTS
Lenham	LEN
Lenzie	LNZ
Leominster	LEO
Letchworth Garden City	LET
Leuchars (St Andrews)	LEU
Levenshulme	LVM
Lewes	LWS
Lewisham	LEW
Leyland	LEY
Leyton Midland Road	LEM
Leytonstone High Road	LER
Lichfield City	LIC
Lichfield Trent Valley	LTV
Lidlington	LID
Limehouse	LHS
Lincoln Central	LCN
Lingfield	LFD
Lingwood	LGD
Linlithgow	LIN
Liphook	LIP
Liskeard	LSK
Liss	LIS
Lisvane & Thornhill	LVT
Little Kimble	LTK
Little Sutton	LTT
Littleborough	LTL
Littlehampton	LIT
Littlehaven	LVN
Littleport	LTP
Liverpool Central	LVC
Liverpool James Street	LVJ
Liverpool Lime Street	LIV
Liverpool South Parkway	LPY
Livingston North	LSN
Livingston South	LVG
Llanaber	LLA
Llanbedr	LBR
Llanbister Road	LLT
Llanbradach	LNB
Llandaf	LLN
Llandanwg	LDN
Llandecwyn	LLC
Llandeilo	LLL
Llandovery	LLV
Llandrindod	LLO
Llandudno	LLD
Llandudno Junction	LLJ
Llandybie	LLI
Llanelli	LLE
Llanfairfechan	LLF
Llanfairpwll	LPG
Llangadog	LLG
Llangammarch	LLM
Llangennech	LLH
Llangynllo	LGO
Llanharan	LLR
Llanhilleth	LTH
Llanishen	LLS
Llanrwst	LWR
Llansamlet	LAS
Llantwit Major	LWM
Llanwrda	LNR
Llanwrtyd	LNW
Llwyngwril	LLW
Llwynypia	LLY
Loch Awe	LHA
Loch Eil Outward Bound	LHE
Lochailort	LCL
Locheilside	LCS
Lochgelly	LCG
Lochluichart	LCC
Lochwinnoch	LHW
Lockerbie	LOC
Lockwood	LCK
London Blackfriars	BFR
London Bridge	LBG
London Cannon Street	CST
London Charing Cross	CHX
London Euston	EUS
London Fenchurch St	FST
London Fields	LOF
London King's Cross	KGX
London Liverpool St	LST
London Marylebone	MYB
London Paddington	PAD
London Road (Brighton)	LRB
London Road (Guildford)	LRD
London St Pancras	STP
London Victoria	VIC
London Waterloo	WAT
London Waterloo East	WAE
Long Buckby	LBK
Long Eaton	LGE
Long Preston	LPR
Longbeck	LGK
Longbridge	LOB
Longcross	LNG
Longfield	LGF
Longniddry	LND
Longport	LPT
Longton	LGN
Looe	LOO
Lostock	LOT
Lostock Gralam	LTG
Lostock Hall	LOH
Lostwithiel	LOS
Loughborough	LBO
Loughborough Junction	LGJ
Lowdham	LOW
Lower Sydenham	LSY
Lowestoft	LWT
Ludlow	LUD
Luton	LUT
Luton Airport Parkway	LTN
Luxulyan	LUX
Lydney	LYD
Lye	LYE
Lymington Pier	LYP
Lymington Town	LYT
Lympstone Commando	LYC
Lympstone Village	LYM
Lytham	LTM
Macclesfield	MAC
Machynlleth	MCN
Maesteg	MST
Maesteg (Ewenny Rd)	MEW
Maghull	MAG
Maiden Newton	MDN
Maidenhead	MAI
Maidstone Barracks	MDB
Maidstone East	MDE
Maidstone West	MDW
Malden Manor	MAL
Mallaig	MLG
Malton	MLT
Malvern Link	MVL
Manchester Airport	MIA
Manchester Oxford Rd	MCO
Manchester Piccadilly	MAN
Manchester United FC	MUF
Manchester Victoria	MCV
Manea	MNE
Manningtree	MNG
Manor Park	MNP
Manor Road	MNR
Manorbier	MRB
Manors	MAS
Mansfield	MFT
Mansfield Woodhouse	MSW
March	MCH
Marden	MRN
Margate	MAR
Market Harborough	MHR
Market Rasen	MKR

Markinch	MNC
Marks Tey	MKT
Marlow	MLW
Marple	MPL
Marsden	MSN
Marske	MSK
Marston Green	MGN
Martin Mill	MTM
Martins Heron	MAO
Marton	MTO
Maryhill	MYH
Maryland	MYL
Maryport	MRY
Matlock	MAT
Matlock Bath	MTB
Mauldeth Road	MAU
Maxwell Park	MAX
Maybole	MAY
Maze Hill	MZH
Meadowhall	MHS
Meldreth	MEL
Melksham	MKM
Melton	MES
Melton Mowbray	MMO
Menheniot	MEN
Menston	MNN
Meols	MEO
Meols Cop	MEC
Meopham	MEP
Merrytown	MEY
Merstham	MHM
Merthyr Tydfil	MER
Merthyr Vale	MEV
Metheringham	MGM
MetroCentre	MCE
Mexborough	MEX
Micheldever	MIC
Micklefield	MIK
Middlesbrough	MBR
Middlewood	MDL
Midgham	MDG
Milford Haven	MFH
Milford (Surrey)	MLF
Mill Hill Broadway	MIL
Mill Hill (Lancashire)	MLH
Millbrook (Bedfordshire)	MLB
Millbrook (Hants)	MBK
Milliken Park	MIN
Millom	MLM
Mills Hill	MIH
Milngavie	MLN
Milnrow	MLR
Milton Keynes Central	MKC
Minffordd	MFF
Minster	MSR
Mirfield	MIR
Mistley	MIS
Mitcham Eastfields	MTC
Mitcham Junction	MIJ
Mobberley	MOB
Monifieth	MON
Monks Risborough	MRS
Montpelier	MTP
Montrose	MTS
Moorfields	MRF
Moorgate	ZMG
Moorside	MSD
Moorthorpe	MRP
Morar	MRR
Morchard Road	MRD
Morden South	MDS
Morecambe	MCM
Moreton (Dorset)	MTN
Moreton (Merseyside)	MRT
Moreton-in-Marsh	MIM
Morfa Mawddach	MFA
Morley	MLY
Morpeth	MPT
Mortimer	MOR
Mortlake	MTL
Moses Gate	MSS
Moss Side	MOS
Mossley	MSL
Mossley Hill	MSH
Mosspark	MPK
Moston	MSO
Motherwell	MTH
Motspur Park	MOT
Mottingham	MTG
Mottisfont & Dunbridge	DBG
Mouldsworth	MLD
Moulsecoomb	MCB
Mount Florida	MFL
Mount Vernon	MTV
Mountain Ash	MTA
Muir of Ord	MOO
Muirend	MUI
Musselburgh	MUB
Mytholmroyd	MYT
Nafferton	NFN
Nailsea & Backwell	NLS
Nairn	NRN
Nantwich	NAN
Narberth	NAR
Narborough	NBR
Navigation Road	NVR
Neath	NTH
Needham Market	NMT
Neilston	NEI
Nelson	NEL
Neston	NES
Netherfield	NET
Nethertown	NRT
Netley	NTL
New Barnet	NBA
New Beckenham	NBC
New Brighton	NBN
New Clee	NCE
New Cross	NWX
New Cross Gate	NXG
New Cumnock	NCK
New Eltham	NEH
New Hey	NHY
New Holland	NHL
New Hythe	NHE
New Lane	NLN
New Malden	NEM
New Mills Central	NMC
New Mills Newtown	NMN
New Milton	NWM
New Pudsey	NPD
New Southgate	NSG
Newark Castle	NCT
Newark North Gate	NNG
Newbridge	NBE
Newbury	NBY
Newbury Racecourse	NRC
Newcastle	NCL
Newcraighall	NEW
Newhaven Harbour	NVH
Newhaven Town	NVN
Newington	NGT
Newmarket	NMK
Newport (Essex)	NWE
Newport (S. Wales)	NWP
Newquay	NQY
Newstead	NSD
Newton Abbot	NTA
Newton Aycliffe	NAY
Newton for Hyde	NWN
Newton (Lanarks)	NTN
Newton St Cyres	NTC
Newton-le-Willows	NLW
Newtonmore	NWR
Newton-on-Ayr	NOA
Newtown (Powys)	NWT
Ninian Park	NNP
Nitshill	NIT
Norbiton	NBT
Norbury	NRB
Normans Bay	NSB
Normanton	NOR
North Berwick	NBW
North Camp	NCM
North Dulwich	NDL
North Fambridge	NFA
North Llanrwst	NLR
North Queensferry	NQU
North Road	NRD
North Sheen	NSH
North Walsham	NWA
North Wembley	NWB
Northallerton	NTR
Northampton	NMP
Northfield	NFD
Northfleet	NFL
Northolt Park	NLT
Northumberland Park	NUM
Northwich	NWI
Norton Bridge	NTB
Norwich	NRW
Norwood Junction	NWD
Nottingham	NOT
Nuneaton	NUN
Nunhead	NHD
Nunthorpe	NNT
Nutbourne	NUT
Nutfield	NUF
Oakengates	OKN
Oakham	OKM
Oakleigh Park	OKL
Oban	OBN
Ockendon	OCK
Ockley	OLY
Old Hill	OHL
Old Roan	ORN
Old Street	OLD
Oldfield Park	OLF
Oldham Mumps	OLM
Oldham Werneth	OLW
Olton	OLT
Ore	ORE
Ormskirk	OMS
Orpington	ORP
Orrell	ORR
Orrell Park	OPK
Otford	OTF
Oulton Broad North	OUN
Oulton Broad South	OUS
Outwood	OUT
Overpool	OVE
Overton	OVR
Oxenholme Lake District	OXN
Oxford	OXF
Oxshott	OXS
Oxted	OXT
Paddock Wood	PDW
Padgate	PDG
Paignton	PGN
Paisley Canal	PCN
Paisley Gilmour Street	PYG
Paisley St James	PYJ
Palmers Green	PAL
Pangbourne	PAN
Pannal	PNL
Pantyffynnon	PTF
Par	PAR
Parbold	PBL
Park Street	PKT
Parkstone (Dorset)	PKS
Parson Street	PSN
Partick	PTK
Parton	PRN
Patchway	PWY
Patricroft	PAT
Patterton	PTT
Peartree	PEA
Peckham Rye	PMR
Pegswood	PEG
Pemberton	PEM
Pembrey & Burry Port	PBY
Pembroke	PMB
Pembroke Dock	PMD
Penally	PNA
Penarth	PEN
Pencoed	PCD
Pengam	PGM
Penge East	PNE
Penge West	PNW
Penhelig	PHG
Penistone	PNS
Penkridge	PKG
Penmaenmawr	PMW
Penmere	PNM
Penrhiwceiber	PER
Penrhyndeudraeth	PRH
Penrith	PNR
Penryn	PYN
Pensarn (Gwynedd)	PES
Penshurst	PHR
Pentre-Bach	PTB
Pen-y-Bont	PNY
Penychain	BPC
Penyffordd	PNF
Penzance	PNZ
Perranwell	PRW
Perry Barr	PRY
Pershore	PSH
Perth	PTH
Peterborough	PBO
Petersfield	PTR
Petts Wood	PET
Pevensey & Westham	PEV
Pevensey Bay	PEB
Pewsey	PEW
Pilning	PIL
Pinhoe	PIN
Pitlochry	PIT
Pitsea	PSE
Pleasington	PLS
Plockton	PLK
Pluckley	PLC
Plumley	PLM
Plumpton	PMP
Plumstead	PLU
Plymouth	PLY
Pokesdown	POK
Polegate	PLG
Polesworth	PSW
Pollokshaws East	PWE
Pollokshaws West	PWW
Pollokshields East	PLE
Pollokshields West	PLW
Polmont	PMT
Polsloe Bridge	POL
Ponders End	PON
Pontarddulais	PTD
Pontefract Baghill	PFR
Pontefract Monkhill	PFM
Pontefract Tanshelf	POT

Pontlottyn	PLT
Pontyclun	PYC
Pont-y-Pant	PYP
Pontypool & New Inn	PPL
Pontypridd	PPD
Poole	POO
Poppleton	POP
Port Glasgow	PTG
Port Sunlight	PSL
Port Talbot Parkway	PTA
Portchester	PTC
Porth	POR
Porthmadog	PTM
Portlethen	PLN
Portslade	PLD
Portsmouth & Southsea	PMS
Portsmouth Arms	PMA
Portsmouth Harbour	PMH
Possilpark & Parkhouse	PPK
Potters Bar	PBR
Poulton-le-Fylde	PFY
Poynton	PYT
Prees	PRS
Prescot	PSC
Prestatyn	PRT
Prestbury	PRB
Preston	PRE
Preston Park	PRP
Prestonpans	PST
Prestwick Int Airport	PRA
Prestwick Town	PTW
Priesthill & Darnley	PTL
Princes Risborough	PRR
Prittlewell	PRL
Prudhoe	PRU
Pulborough	PUL
Purfleet	PFL
Purley	PUR
Purley Oaks	PUO
Putney	PUT
Pwllheli	PWL
Pyle	PYL
Quakers Yard	QYD
Queenborough	QBR
Queens Park (Glasgow)	QPK
Queens Park (London)	QPW
Queens Road, Peckham	QRP
Queenstown Road	QRB
Quintrel Downs	QUI
Radcliffe (Notts)	RDF
Radlett	RDT
Radley	RAD
Radyr	RDR
Rainford	RNF
Rainham (Essex)	RNM
Rainham (Kent)	RAI
Rainhill	RNH
Ramsgate	RAM
Ramsgreave & Wilpshire	RGW
Rannoch	RAN
Rauceby	RAU
Ravenglass for Eskdale	RAV
Ravensbourne	RVB
Ravensthorpe	RVN
Rawcliffe	RWC
Rayleigh	RLG
Raynes Park	RAY
Reading	RDG
Reading West	RDW
Rectory Road	REC
Redbridge	RDB
Redcar Central	RCC
Redcar East	RCE
Reddish North	RDN
Reddish South	RDS
Redditch	RDC
Redhill	RDH
Redland	RDA
Redruth	RED
Reedham (Norfolk)	REE
Reedham (Surrey)	RHM
Reigate	REI
Renton	RTN
Retford	RET
Rhiwbina	RHI
Rhoose Cardiff Int Airport	RIA
Rhosneigr	RHO
Rhyl	RHL
Rhymney	RHY
Ribblehead	RHD
Rice Lane	RIL
Richmond	RMD
Rickmansworth	RIC
Riddlesdown	RDD
Ridgmont	RID
Riding Mill	RDM
Risca & Pontymister	RCA
Rishton	RIS
Robertsbridge	RBR
Roby	ROB
Rochdale	RCD
Roche	ROC
Rochester	RTR
Rochford	RFD
Rock Ferry	RFY
Rogart	ROG
Rogerstone	ROR
Rolleston	ROL
Roman Bridge	RMB
Romford	RMF
Romiley	RML
Romsey	ROM
Roose	ROO
Rose Grove	RSG
Rose Hill Marple	RSH
Rosyth	ROS
Rotherham Central	RMC
Roughton Road	RNR
Rowlands Castle	RLN
Rowley Regis	ROW
Roy Bridge	RYB
Roydon	RYN
Royston	RYS
Ruabon	RUA
Rufford	RUF
Rugby	RUG
Rugeley Town	RGT
Rugeley Trent Valley	RGL
Runcorn	RUN
Runcorn East	RUE
Ruskington	RKT
Ruswarp	RUS
Rutherglen	RUT
Ryde St Johns Road	RYR
Ryde Esplanade	RYD
Ryde Pier Head	RYP
Ryder Brow	RRB
Rye	RYE
Rye House	RYH
Salford Central	SFD
Salford Crescent	SLD
Salfords	SAF
Salhouse	SAH
Salisbury	SAL
Saltaire	SAE
Saltash	STS
Saltburn	SLB
Saltcoats	SLT
Saltmarshe	SAM
Salwick	SLW
Sandal & Agbrigg	SNA
Sandbach	SDB
Sanderstead	SNR
Sandhills	SDL
Sandhurst	SND
Sandling	SDG
Sandown	SAN
Sandplace	SDP
Sandwell & Dudley	SAD
Sandwich	SDW
Sandy	SDY
Sankey for Penketh	SNK
Sanquhar	SQH
Sarn	SRR
Saundersfoot	SDF
Saunderton	SDR
Sawbridgeworth	SAW
Saxilby	SXY
Saxmundham	SAX
Scarborough	SCA
Scotscalder	SCT
Scotstounhill	SCH
Scunthorpe	SCU
Sea Mills	SML
Seaford	SEF
Seaforth & Litherland	SFL
Seaham	SEA
Seamer	SEM
Seascale	SSC
Seaton Carew	SEC
Seer Green & Jordans	SRG
Selby	SBY
Selhurst	SRS
Sellafield	SEL
Selling	SEG
Selly Oak	SLY
Settle	SET
Seven Kings	SVK
Seven Sisters	SVS
Sevenoaks	SEV
Severn Beach	SVB
Severn Tunnel Junction	STJ
Shalford	SFR
Shanklin	SHN
Shaw & Crompton	SHA
Shawford	SHW
Shawlands	SHL
Sheerness-on-Sea	SSS
Sheffield	SHF
Shelford	SED
Shenfield	SNF
Shenstone	SEN
Shepherd's Bush	SPB
Shepherds Well	SPH
Shepley	SPY
Shepperton	SHP
Shepreth	STH
Sherborne	SHE
Sherburn-in-Elmet	SIE
Sheringham	SHM
Shettleston	SLS
Shieldmuir	SDM
Shifnal	SFN
Shildon	SHD
Shiplake	SHI
Shipley	SHY
Shippea Hill	SPP
Shipton	SIP
Shirebrook	SHB
Shirehampton	SHH
Shireoaks	SRO
Shirley	SRL
Shoeburyness	SRY
Sholing	SHO
Shoreham (Kent)	SEH
Shoreham-by-Sea	SSE
Shortlands	SRT
Shotton	SHT
Shotts	SHS
Shrewsbury	SHR
Sidcup	SID
Sileby	SIL
Silecroft	SIC
Silkstone Common	SLK
Silver Street	SLV
Silverdale	SVR
Singer	SIN
Sittingbourne	SIT
Skegness	SKG
Skewen	SKE
Skipton	SKI
Slade Green	SGR
Slaithwaite	SWT
Slateford	SLA
Sleaford	SLR
Sleights	SLH
Slough	SLO
Small Heath	SMA
Smallbrook Junction	SAB
Smethwick Galton Bridge	SGB
Smethwick Rolfe Street	SMR
Smitham	SMI
Smithy Bridge	SMB
Snaith	SNI
Snodland	SDA
Snowdown	SWO
Sole Street	SOR
Solihull	SOL
Somerleyton	SYT
South Acton	SAT
South Bank	SBK
South Bermondsey	SBM
South Croydon	SCY
South Elmsall	SES
South Greenford	SGN
South Gyle	SGL
South Hampstead	SOH
South Kenton	SOK
South Merton	SMO
South Milford	SOM
South Ruislip	SRU
South Tottenham	STO
South Wigston	SWS
South Woodham Ferrers	SOF
Southall	STL
Southampton Airport	SOA
Southampton Central	SOU
Southbourne	SOB
Southbury	SBU
Southease	SEE
Southend Central	SOC
Southend East	SOE
Southend Victoria	SOV
Southminster	SMN
Southport	SOP
Southwick	SWK
Sowerby Bridge	SOW
Spalding	SPA
Spean Bridge	SBR
Spital	SPI
Spondon	SPO
Spooner Row	SPN
Spring Road	SRI
Springburn	SPR
Springfield	SPF
Squires Gate	SQU
St Albans	SAC
St Albans Abbey	SAA
St Andrews Road	SAR
St Annes-on-the-Sea	SAS
St Austell	SAU
St Bees	SBS
St Budeaux Ferry Road	SBF
St Budeaux Victoria Rd	SBV

St Columb Road	SCR
St Denys	SDN
St Erth	SER
St Germans	SGM
St Helens Central	SNH
St Helens Junction	SHJ
St Helier	SIH
St Ives (Cornwall)	SIV
St James Park	SJP
St James Street	SJS
St Johns	SAJ
St Keyne	SKN
St Leonards Warrior Sq	SLQ
St Margarets (London)	SMG
St Margarets (Herts)	SMT
St Mary Cray	SMY
St Michaels	STM
St Neots	SNO
St Pancras International	SPX
Stafford	STA
Staines	SNS
Stallingborough	SLL
Stalybridge	SYB
Stamford	SMD
Stamford Hill	SMH
Stanford-le-Hope	SFO
Stanlow & Thornton	SNT
Stansted Airport	SSD
Stansted Mountfitchet	SST
Staplehurst	SPU
Stapleton Road	SRD
Starbeck	SBE
Starcross	SCS
Staveley (Cumbria)	SVL
Stechford	SCF
Steeton & Silsden	SON
Stepps	SPS
Stevenage	SVG
Stevenston	STV
Stewartby	SWR
Stewarton	STT
Stirling	STG
Stockport	SPT
Stocksfield	SKS
Stocksmoor	SSM
Stockton	STK
Stoke Mandeville	SKM
Stoke Newington	SKW
Stoke-on-Trent	SOT
Stone	SNE
Stone Crossing	SCG
Stonebridge Park	SBP
Stonegate	SOG
Stonehaven	STN
Stonehouse	SHU
Stoneleigh	SNL
Stourbridge Junction	SBJ
Stourbridge Town	SBT
Stowmarket	SMK
Stranraer	STR
Stratford (London)	SRA
Stratford-upon-Avon	SAV
Strathcarron	STC
Strawberry Hill	STW
Streatham	STE
Streatham Common	SRC
Streatham Hill	SRH
Streethouse	SHC
Strines	SRN
Stromeferry	STF
Strood	SOO
Stroud	STD
Sturry	STU
Styal	SYA
Sudbury	SUY
Sudbury & Harrow Road	SUD

Sudbury Hill Harrow	SDH
Sugar Loaf	SUG
Summerston	SUM
Sunbury	SUU
Sunderland	SUN
Sundridge Park	SUP
Sunningdale	SNG
Sunnymeads	SNY
Surbiton	SUR
Sutton Coldfield	SUT
Sutton Common	SUC
Sutton Parkway	SPK
Sutton (Surrey)	SUO
Swale	SWL
Swanley	SAY
Swanscombe	SWM
Swansea	SWA
Swanwick	SNW
Sway	SWY
Swaythling	SWG
Swinderby	SWD
Swindon	SWI
Swineshead	SWE
Swinton (Gr Manchester)	SNN
Swinton (Yorks)	SWN
Sydenham	SYD
Sydenham Hill	SYH
Syon Lane	SYL
Syston	SYS
Tackley	TAC
Tadworth	TAD
Taffs Well	TAF
Tain	TAI
Talsarnau	TAL
Talybont	TLB
Tal-y-Cafn	TLC
Tame Bridge Parkway	TAB
Tamworth	TAM
Taplow	TAP
Tattenham Corner	TAT
Taunton	TAU
Taynuilt	TAY
Teddington	TED
Tees-side Airport	TEA
Teignmouth	TGM
Telford Central	TFC
Templecombe	TMC
Tenby	TEN
Teynham	TEY
Thames Ditton	THD
Thatcham	THA
Thatto Heath	THH
The Hawthorns	THW
The Lakes	TLK
Theale	THE
Theobalds Grove	TEO
Thetford	TTF
Thirsk	THI
Thornaby	TBY
Thorne North	TNN
Thorne South	TNS
Thornford	THO
Thornliebank	THB
Thornton Abbey	TNA
Thornton Heath	TTH
Thorntonhall	THT
Thorpe Bay	TPB
Thorpe Culvert	TPC
Thorpe-le-Soken	TLS
Three Bridges	TBD
Three Oaks	TOK
Thurgarton	THU
Thurnscoe	THC
Thurso	THS
Thurston	TRS
Tilbury Town	TIL

Tile Hill	THL
Tilehurst	TLH
Tipton	TIP
Tir-Phil	TIR
Tisbury	TIS
Tiverton Parkway	TVP
Todmorden	TOD
Tolworth	TOL
Ton Pentre	TPN
Tonbridge	TON
Tondu	TDU
Tonfanau	TNF
Tonypandy	TNP
Tooting	TOO
Topsham	TOP
Torquay	TQY
Torre	TRR
Totnes	TOT
Tottenham Hale	TOM
Totton	TTN
Town Green	TWN
Trafford Park	TRA
Trefforest	TRF
Trefforest Estate	TRE
Trehafod	TRH
Treherbert	TRB
Treorchy	TRY
Trimley	TRM
Tring	TRI
Troed-y-rhiw	TRD
Troon	TRN
Trowbridge	TRO
Truro	TRU
Tulloch	TUL
Tulse Hill	TUH
Tunbridge Wells	TBW
Turkey Street	TUR
Tutbury & Hatton	TUT
Twickenham	TWI
Twyford	TWY
Ty Croes	TYC
Ty Glas	TGS
Tygwyn	TYG
Tyndrum Lower	TYL
Tyseley	TYS
Tywyn	TYW
Uckfield	UCK
Uddingston	UDD
Ulceby	ULC
Ulleskelf	ULL
Ulverston	ULV
Umberleigh	UMB
University	UNI
Uphall	UHA
Upholland	UPL
Upminster	UPM
Upper Halliford	UPH
Upper Holloway	UHL
Upper Tyndrum	UTY
Upper Warlingham	UWL
Upton	UPT
Upwey	UPW
Urmston	URM
Uttoxeter	UTT
Valley	VAL
Vauxhall	VXH
Virginia Water	VIR
Waddon	WDO
Wadhurst	WAD
Wainfleet	WFL
Wakefield Kirkgate	WKK
Wakefield Westgate	WKF
Walkden	WKD
Wallasey Grove Road	WLG
Wallasey Village	WLV
Wallington	WLT

Wallyford	WAF
Walmer	WAM
Walsall	WSL
Walsden	WDN
Waltham Cross	WLC
Walthamstow Central	WHC
Walthamstow Queen's Rd	WMW
Walton (Merseyside)	WAO
Walton on the Naze	WON
Walton-on-Thames	WAL
Wanborough	WAN
Wandsworth Common	WSW
Wandsworth Road	WWR
Wandsworth Town	WNT
Wanstead Park	WNP
Warblington	WBL
Ware	WAR
Wareham	WRM
Wargrave	WGV
Warminster	WMN
Warnham	WNH
Warrington Bank Quay	WBQ
Warrington Central	WAC
Warwick	WRW
Warwick Parkway	WRP
Water Orton	WTO
Waterbeach	WBC
Wateringbury	WTR
Waterloo (Merseyside)	WLO
Watford High Street	WFH
Watford Junction	WFJ
Watford North	WFN
Watlington	WTG
Watton-at-Stone	WAS
Waun-Gron Park	WNG
Wavertree Tech Park	WAV
Wedgwood	WED
Weeley	WEE
Weeton	WET
Welham Green	WMG
Welling	WLI
Wellingborough	WEL
Wellington (Shropshire)	WLN
Welshpool	WLP
Welwyn Garden City	WGC
Welwyn North	WLW
Wem	WEM
Wembley Central	WMB
Wembley Stadium	WCX
Wemyss Bay	WMS
Wendover	WND
Wennington	WNN
West Allerton	WSA
West Brompton	WBP
West Byfleet	WBY
West Calder	WCL
West Croydon	WCY
West Drayton	WDT
West Dulwich	WDU
West Ealing	WEA
West Ham	WEH
West Hampstead	WHD
West Hampstead T'link	WHP
West Horndon	WHR
West Kilbride	WKB
West Kirby	WKI
West Malling	WMA
West Norwood	WNW
West Ruislip	WRU
West Runton	WRN
West St Leonards	WLD
West Sutton	WSU
West Wickham	WWI
West Worthing	WWO
Westbury (Wilts)	WSB
Westcliff	WCF

Westcombe Park	WCB
Westenhanger	WHA
Wester Hailes	WTA
Westerfield	WFI
Westerton	WES
Westgate-on-Sea	WGA
Westhoughton	WHG
Weston Milton	WNM
Weston-super-Mare	WSM
Wetheral	WRL
Weybridge	WYB
Weymouth	WEY
Whaley Bridge	WBR
Whalley	WHE
Whatstandwell	WTS
Whifflet	WFF
Whimple	WHM
Whinhill	WNL
Whiston	WHN
Whitby	WTB
Whitchurch (Cardiff)	WHT
Whitchurch (Hants)	WCH
Whitchurch (Shropshire)	WTC
White Hart Lane	WHL
White Notley	WNY
Whitecraigs	WCR
Whitehaven	WTH
Whitland	WTL
Whitley Bridge	WBD
Whitlocks End	WTE
Whitstable	WHI
Whittlesea	WLE
Whittlesford Parkway	WLF
Whitton	WTN
Whitwell	WWL
Whyteleafe	WHY
Whyteleafe South	WHS
Wick	WCK
Wickford	WIC
Wickham Market	WCM
Widdrington	WDD
Widnes	WID
Widney Manor	WMR
Wigan North Western	WGN
Wigan Wallgate	WGW
Wigton	WGT
Wildmill	WMI
Willesden Junction	WIJ
Williamwood	WLM
Willington	WIL
Wilmcote	WMC
Wilmslow	WML
Wilnecote	WNE
Wimbledon	WIM
Wimbledon Chase	WBO
Winchelsea	WSE
Winchester	WIN
Winchfield	WNF
Winchmore Hill	WIH
Windermere	WDM
Windsor & Eton Central	WNC
Windsor & Eton Riverside	WNR
Winnersh	WNS
Winnersh Triangle	WTI
Winsford	WSF
Wishaw	WSH
Witham	WTM
Witley	WTY
Witton	WTT
Wivelsfield	WVF
Wivenhoe	WIV
Woburn Sands	WOB
Woking	WOK
Wokingham	WKM
Woldingham	WOH
Wolverhampton	WVH
Wolverton	WOL
Wombwell	WOM
Wood End	WDE
Wood Street	WST
Woodbridge	WDB
Woodgrange Park	WGR
Woodhall	WDL
Woodhouse	WDH
Woodlesford	WDS
Woodley	WLY
Woodmansterne	WME
Woodsmoor	WSR
Wool	WOO
Woolston	WLS
Woolwich Arsenal	WWA
Woolwich Dockyard	WWD
Wootton Wawen	WWW
Worcester Foregate St	WOF
Worcester Park	WCP
Worcester Shrub Hill	WOS
Workington	WKG
Worksop	WRK
Worle	WOR
Worplesdon	WPL
Worstead	WRT
Worthing	WRH
Wrabness	WRB
Wraysbury	WRY
Wrenbury	WRE
Wressle	WRS
Wrexham Central	WXC
Wrexham General	WRX
Wye	WYE
Wylam	WYM
Wylde Green	WYL
Wymondham	WMD
Wythall	WYT
Yalding	YAL
Yardley Wood	YRD
Yarm	YRM
Yate	YAE
Yatton	YAT
Yeoford	YEO
Yeovil Junction	YVJ
Yeovil Pen Mill	YVP
Yetminster	YET
Ynyswen	YNW
Yoker	YOK
York	YRK
Yorton	YRT
Ystrad Mynach	YSM
Ystrad Rhondda	YSR

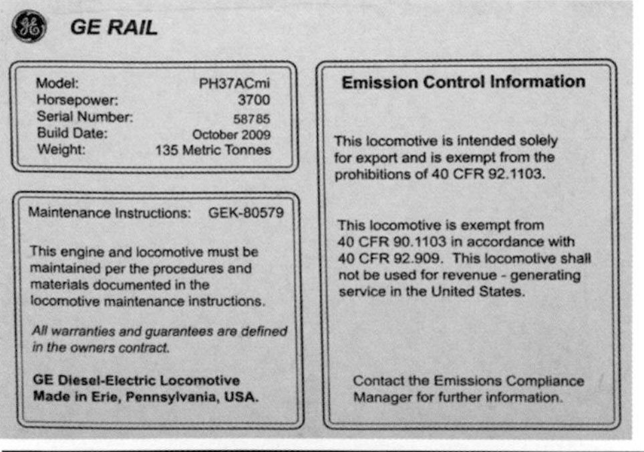

Left: *Builders technical plate from Class 70 'PowerHaul' loco, showing the US classification PH37ACmi, the horsepower of 3,700, its construction serial number (works number) 58785, its build date of October 2009 and weight of 135 metric tonnes. Other information relates to maintenance instructions, and emissions certification, specially noting that the loco cannot operate in revenue service in the USA.*
Kevin Wills

DMU and EMU Vehicle Codes

BDMSO	Battery Driving Motor Standard Open
DM	Driving Motor
DMBS	Driving Motor Brake Standard
DMCL	Driving Motor Composite Lavatory
DMCO	Driving Motor Composite Open
DMF	Driving Motor First
DMFO	Driving Motor Brake Open
DMFLO	Driving Motor First Luggage Open
DMRFO	Driving Motor Restaurant First Open
DMS	Driving Motor Standard
DMSL	Driving Motor Standard Lavatory
DMSO	Driving Motor Standard Open
DTCO	Driving Trailer Composite Open
DTPMV	Driving Trailer Parcels Mail Van
DTSO	Driving Trailer Standard Open
MBC	Motor Brake Composite
MBSO	Motor Brake Standard Open
MC	Motor Composite
MFL	Motor First Lavatory
MPMV	Motor Parcels Mail Van
MS	Motor Standard
MSL	Motor Standard Lavatory
MSLRB	Motor Standard Lavatory Restaurant Buffet
MSO	Motor Standard Open
MSRMB	Motor Standard Restaurant Micro Buffet
PTSO	Pantograph Trailer Standard Open
RB	Restaurant Buffet
TBFO	Trailer Brake First Open
TCO	Trailer Composite Open
TFO	Trailer First Open
TPMV	Trailer Parcels Mail Van
TSO	Trailer Standard Open
TSRMB	Trailer Standard Restaurant Micro Buffet

(A) - A Car
(B) - B Car

Railtour Operators

Darjeeling Tours: Lime Tree Lodge, Thorpe Road, Mattersey, Doncaster, DN10 5ED 01777 817798 www.darjeelingtours.co.uk Enthusiast holidays for steam and modern traction, mainly to India but also includes USA and New Zealand.

East European Railtours: 'Birchwood' Shatterford, Nr Bewdley, Worcestershire, DY12 1TP www.easteuroperailtours.com Tours for steam enthusiasts to Europe and China plus rail tourist holidays to Europe, China and New Zealand.

Far Rail Tours: PO Box 5700, Doncaster, DN1 2YF. 07930 958941 www.farrail.com Tours worldwide visiting active steam railways.

Ffestiniog Travel: First Floor Unit 6, Snowdonia Business Park, Penrhyndeudraeth, Gwynedd, LL48 6LD 01766 772957 www.festtravel.co.uk Worldwide railway holidays from a few days and up to a month.

Green Express Railtours: 66 Stonegate, Hunmanby, Filey, YO14 0PP 01723 891400 www.greenexpressrailtours.co.uk Steam and diesel tours.

Kingfisher Railtours: Felmersham Mills Road, Osmington Mills, Weymouth, Dorset, DT3 6HE www.kingfisherrailtours.co.uk Steam hauled excursions throughout Britain as well as steam and diesel hauled land cruise trains.

Pathfinder Tours: Stag House, Gydynap Lane, Inchbrook, Woodchester, Gloucestershire, GL5 5EZ. 01453 835414/834477. www.pathfindertours.co.uk Enthusiast tours and general excursions with dining options using steam and diesel traction.

Ptg Tours: Gable House, Letcombe Hill, East Challow, Oxfordshire, OX12 9RW 01235 768855 www.ptg.co.uk Enthusiast tours and holidays mainly in Europe but with yearly trips to the USA and Cuba.

Rail-Blue Charters: 0161 8500559. www.rail-bluecharters.co.uk Enthusiast tours with diesel & electric traction with some dining options.

Railtours: The Travel Bureau, The Cottage, High Street, Wombourne, West Midlands, WV5 9DN 01902 324343 www.railtoursholidays.co.uk Holidays worldwide for steam and modern traction enthusiasts.

Railway Touring Company: 14a Tuesday Market Place, Kings Lynn, Norfolk, PE30 1JN 01553 661500 www.railwaytouring.co.uk Tours behind steam, either day trips, tours or long haul holidays in the UK and worldwide.

Retro Railtours: 2 Brookfield Grove, Ashton-under-Lyne, Lancashire, OL6 6TL 0161 3309055. www.retrorailtours.co.uk Enthusiast tours with dining options.

Saltburn Railtours: 01287 625956 www.saltburnrailtours.co.uk Steam and diesel tours using WCRC Pullman coaches with dining options.

Scottish Railway Preservation Society Railtours: 3 South Cathkin Farm Cottages, Glasgow, G73 5RG. 01698 263814/457777 www.srps.org.uk Steam and diesel hauled tours originating in Scotland; some tours have meal options.

Spitfire Railtours: PO Box 824, Taunton, TA1 9ET. 0870 8793675. www.spitfirerailtours.co.uk Heritage diesel & electric traction mainline enthusiast tours with dining options on some tours.

Statesman Rail Ltd: PO Box 83, St. Erth, Hayle, Cornwall, TR27 9AD. 0845 3102458 www.statesmanrail.com Luxury land cruise trains with dining options plus regular steam excursions over the Settle & Carlisle Railway.

Uk Railtours: PO Box 350, Welwyn, AL6 0WG. 01438 715050 www.ukrailtours.com Steam and diesel excursions plus excursions using the Ocean Liner Express stock.

West Coast Railways: Jesson Way, Crag Bank, Carnforth, Lancashire, LA5 9UR 0845 4153131. www.westcoastrailway.co.uk Steam and diesel enthusiast tours, excursions and weekend tours plus regular steam trains such as the Jacobite.

UK Railway Magazines

MODERN RAILWAYS

Published monthly by Ian Allan Publishing Ltd., Riverdene Business Park, Molesey Road, Hersham, Surrey, KT12 4RG.
01932 266622, modern.railways@googlemail.com
Edited by James Abbot, priced £3.80. Contains news and feature articles on the current railway scene at home and abroad with a bias towards industry coverage.

RAILWAYS ILLUSTRATED

Published monthly by Ian Allan Publishing Ltd, Riverdene Business Park, Molesey Road, Hersham, Surrey, KT12 4RG. 01932 266622, pip.dunn@eastfieldmedia.com Edited by Pip Dunn, priced £3.70. Feature articles and news on the current scene at home and abroad with a bias towards the heritage railways and preservation.

MODERN LOCOMOTIVES ILLUSTRATED

Published bi-monthly by the Railway Centre.Com Ltd, PO Box 45, Dawlish, Devon, EX7 9XY, 01626 862320.
editor@modern-locoillustrated.com Edited by Colin Marsden, priced £4.20. Each issue deals with one class or related classes of modern traction with full fleet listings, scale drawings and detail photographs.

RAIL EXPRESS

Published monthly by Foursight Publications Ltd., 20 Park Street, Kings Cliffe, Peterborough, PE8 6XN. 01780 470086, editor@railexpress.co.uk Edited by Philip Sutton, priced £3.95. Contains a mixture of news of the current scene both mainline and heritage railways, feature articles, traction & rolling stock updates plus a modelling supplement.

TODAY'S RAILWAYS (UK)

Published monthly by Platform 5, 3 Wyvern House, Sark Road, Sheffield, S2 4HG. 0114 2552625. editorial@platform5.com Edited by Peter Fox, priced £3.95. Contains news and feature articles on the current scene with some articles on the Irish and heritage scenes. Includes listings for updating the Platform 5 pocket books each month.

TODAY'S RAILWAYS (EUROPE)

Published monthly by Platform 5, 3 Wyvern House, Sark Road, Sheffield, S2 4HG. 0114 2552625. davidhaydock@orange.fr Edited by David Haydock, priced £4.15. Feature articles and news from around Europe plus some heritage coverage.

RAILWAY MAGAZINE

Published monthly by IPC Media, Blue Fin Buildings, 110 Southwark Street, London SE1 0SU. 020 31484683. railways@ipcmedia.com Edited by Nick Pigott, priced £3.75. With feature articles on the current and historic steam and diesel scene around the world. Plus current news for the mainline network, heritage railways and the narrow gauge scenes.

RAIL

Published fortnightly by Bauer Media, Bushfield House, Orton Centre, Peterborough, Cambridgeshire, PE2 5UW. Edited by Nigel Harris, priced £3.20. Feature articles on the current scene with a bias towards industry coverage.

TRACTION

Published monthly by Warners Group Publications PLC, The Maltings, West Street, Bourne, Lincolnshire, PE10 9PH. davidb@warnersgroup.co.uk Edited by Richard Wilson, priced £3.75.
Articles on first and second generation diesels at work, plus coverage of heritage diesels still at work and current preservation scene.

STEAM RAILWAY

Published monthly by Bauer Media, Bushfield House, Orton Centre, Peterborough, Cambridgeshire, PE2 5UW. steam.railway@bauermedia.co.uk Edited by Danny Hopkins, priced £3.70. Articles on the current steam scene on the mainline and preserved railways with coverage of narrow gauge and steam around the world.

HERITAGE RAILWAY

Published monthly by Mortons Media Ltd, PO Box 99, Horncastle, Lincolnshire, LN9 6JR. rjones@mortons.co.uk Edited by Robin Jones, priced at £3.60. Articles on the preserved railway scene, mainly steam but with some diesel coverage.

RAILNEWS

Published monthly by Railnews Ltd, King's Cross Business Centre, 180-186 King's Cross Road, London, WC1X 9DE. newsdesk@railnews.co.uk Edited by Sim Harris. Monthly rail staff magazine/paper available on subscription. website www.railnews.co.uk

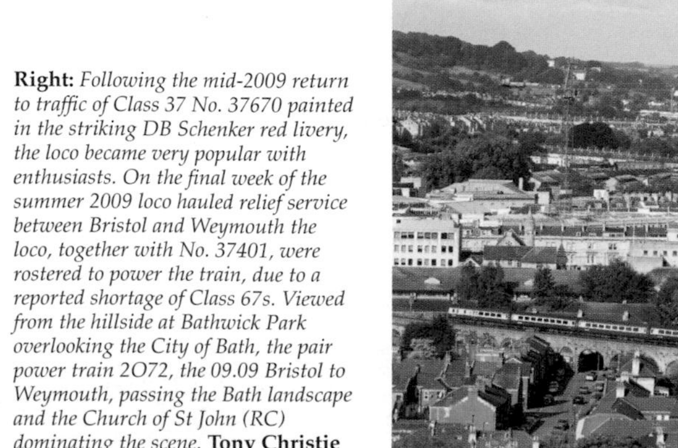

Right: *Following the mid-2009 return to traffic of Class 37 No. 37670 painted in the striking DB Schenker red livery, the loco became very popular with enthusiasts. On the final week of the summer 2009 loco hauled relief service between Bristol and Weymouth the loco, together with No. 37401, were rostered to power the train, due to a reported shortage of Class 67s. Viewed from the hillside at Bathwick Park overlooking the City of Bath, the pair power train 2O72, the 09.09 Bristol to Weymouth, passing the Bath landscape and the Church of St John (RC) dominating the scene.* **Tony Christie**

Number Cross-Link

This cross number check list indicates in which section of the ABC Rail Guide 2010 full details of rolling stock can be found.

Locomotives - Diesel & Electric

Number	Section
D0226	PRE
D4	PRE
D200	PRE
D821	PRE
D832	PRE
D1010	PRE
D1013	PRE
D1015	PRE
D1023	PRE
D1041	PRE
D1048	PRE
D1062	PRE
D2023	PRE
D2024	PRE
D2041	PRE
D2046	PRE
D2051	PRE
D2117	PRE
D2118	PRE
D2133	PRE
D2138	PRE
D2139	PRE
D2148	PRE
D2178	PRE
D2182	PRE
D2184	PRE
D2192	PRE
D2199	PRE
D2203	PRE
D2205	PRE
D2207	PRE
D2229	PRE
D2245	PRE
D2246	PRE
D2271	PRE
D2272	PRE
D2279	PRE
D2280	PRE
D2284	PRE
D2298	PRE
D2302	PRE
D2310	PRE
D2324	PRE
D2325	PRE
D2334	PRE
D2337	PRE
D2511	PRE
D2578	PRE
D2587	PRE
D2595	PRE
D2767	PRE
D2774	PRE
D2854	PRE
D2858	PRE
D2860	PRE
D2866	PRE
D2867	PRE
D2868	PRE
D2953	PRE
D2956	PRE
D3000	PRE
D3002	PRE
D3014	PRE
D3101	PRE
D3255	PRE
D3261	PRE
D3452	PRE
D3489	PRE
D4067	PRE
D4092	PRE
D5500	PRE
D5705	PRE
D6700	PRE
D7017	PRE
D7018	PRE
D7029	PRE
D7076	PRE
D8000	PRE
D8233	PRE
D8568	PRE
D9500	PRE
D9502	PRE
D9504	PRE
D9513	PRE
D9516	PRE
D9520	PRE
D9521	PRE
D9523	PRE
D9524	PRE
D9525	PRE
D9526	PRE
D9529	IND
D9531	PRE
D9537	PRE
D9539	PRE
D9551	PRE
D9553	PRE
D9555	PRE
DELTIC	PRE
DS75	PRE
LMS7050	PRE
LMS7051	PRE
LMS7069	PRE
E26020	PRE
E27000	PRE
E27001	PRE
9005	EUR
9006	EUR
9007	EUR
9011	EUR
9013	EUR
9015	EUR
9018	EUR
9022	EUR
9023	EUR
9024	EUR
9026	EUR
9027	EUR
9029	EUR
9031	EUR
9033	EUR
9036	EUR
9037	EUR
9040	EUR
9101	EUR
9102	EUR
9103	EUR
9104	EUR
9105	EUR
9106	EUR
9107	EUR
9108	EUR
9109	EUR
9110	EUR
9111	EUR
9112	EUR
9113	EUR
9701	EUR
9702	EUR
9703	EUR
9704	EUR
9705	EUR
9706	EUR
9707	EUR
9801	EUR
9802	EUR
9803	EUR
9804	EUR
9808	EUR
9809	EUR
9810	EUR
9812	EUR
9814	EUR
9816	EUR
9817	EUR
9819	EUR
9820	EUR
9821	EUR
9825	EUR
9828	EUR
9832	EUR
9834	EUR
9835	EUR
9838	EUR
01551	SIE
01552	HNR
01553	HNR
01564	HNR
01568	JAR
03018	PRE
03020	PRE
03022	PRE
03027	PRE
03037	PRE
03059	PRE
03062	PRE
03066	PRE
03069	PRE
03072	PRE
03073	PRE
03078	PRE
03079	PRE
03081	PRE
03084	PRE
03089	PRE
03090	PRE
03094	PRE
03099	PRE
03112	IND
03113	PRE
03119	PRE
03120	PRE
03128	PRE
03134	PRE
03141	PRE
03144	PRE
03145	PRE
03152	PRE
03158	PRE
03162	PRE
03170	PRE
03179	IND
03189	PRE
03371	PRE
03399	PRE
05001	PRE
06003	PRE
07001	HNR
07005	PRE
07007	KRS
07010	PRE
07011	PRE
07012	PRE
07013	PRE
08011	PRE
08012	PRE
08015	PRE
08016	PRE
08021	PRE
08022	PRE
08032	PRE
08046	PRE
08054	PRE
08060	PRE
08064	PRE
08102	PRE
08108	PRE
08114	PRE
08123	PRE
08133	PRE
08164	PRE
08168	PRE
08195	PRE
08202	IND
08220	PRE
08238	PRE
08266	PRE
08266	PRE
08308	BAR
08320	IND
08331	IND
08359	PRE
08375	IND
08377	PRE
08388	PRE
08389	DBS
08393	DBS
08397	DBS
08398	IND
08401	DBS
08405	DBS
08410	FGW
08411	IND
08417	SEC
08418	DBS
08423	BAR
08428	DBS
08436	PRE
08441	IND
08442	DBS
08443	PRE
08444	PRE
08445	IND
08447	IND
08451	ALS
08454	ALS
08460	IND
08466	DBS
08471	PRE
08472	WAB
08473	PRE

08476	PRE
08479	PRE
08480	DBS
08481	PRE
08482	DBS
08483	FGW
08484	IND
08485	DBS
08490	PRE
08492	HNR
08499	PUL
08500	DBS
08502	HNR
08503	IND
08507	HNR
08511	IND
08512	DBS
08514	DBS
08516	DBS
08517	HNR
08523	IND
08525	EMT
08527	FLR
08530	FLR
08531	FLR
08535	IND
08528	DBS
08538	DBS
08540	DBS
08543	DBS
08556	PRE
08561	DBS
08567	DBS
08568	RCL
08569	DBS
08571	WAB
08573	BAR
08575	FLR
08577	DBS
08578	DBS
08580	DBS
08585	FLR
08588	BAR
08590	PRE
08593	DBS
08596	WAB
08597	DBS
08598	BAR
08600	IND
08604	PRE
08605	DBS
08611	ALS
08613	BAR
08615	WAB
08616	LMI
08617	ALS
08622	BAR
08623	DBS
08624	FLR
08629	RCL
08630	DBS
08631	PRE
08632	DBS
08633	DBS
08635	PRE
08641	FGW
08643	MRL
08644	FGW
08645	FGW
08649	RCL
08650	MRL
08651	DBS
08652	MRL
08653	DBS
08662	DBS
08663	FGW
08664	DBS
08668	HNR
08669	WAB
08670	IND
08676	DBS
08678	WCR
08682	BOM
08683	PRE
08685	DBS
08689	DBS
08690	EMT
08691	FLR
08694	PRE
08695	HNR
08696	ALS
08697	EMT
08698	DBS
08699	CWR
08700	PRE
08701	DBS
08703	DBS
08704	IND
08706	DBS
08711	DBS
08714	DBS
08721	ALS
08724	WAB
08728	IND
08730	RCL
08731	MRL
08734	PRE
08735	DBS
08737	DBS
08738	DBS
08742	DBS
08743	IND
08750	BAR
08752	DBS
08754	BAR
08756	BAR
08757	DBS
08762	BAR
08764	WAB
08765	DBS
08767	PRE
08769	PRE
08770	DBS
08772	PRE
08773	PRE
08774	IND
08776	DBS
08780	PRE
08782	DBS
08783	DBS
08784	DBS
08785	FLR
08786	DBS
08787	IND
08790	ALS
08795	FGW
08798	DBS
08799	DBS
08802	DBS
08804	DBS
08805	LMI
08807	IND
08809	CWR
08813	HNR
08818	HNR
08822	FGW
08823	IND
08824	DBS
08827	HNR
08828	DBS
08830	PRE
08834	HNR
08836	FGW
08842	DBS
08844	DBS
08846	BOM
08847	CWR
08850	PRE
08853	WAB
08854	DBS
08856	DBS
08865	DBS
08866	DBS
08868	HNR
08869	HNR
08870	BAR
08871	WAB
08872	DBS
08873	BAR
08877	DBS
08879	DBS
08881	IND
08884	DBS
08885	BAR
08887	ALS
08886	DBS
08888	DBS
08891	FLR
08892	HNR
08896	PRE
08897	DBS
08899	EMT
08903	IND
08904	DBS
08905	DBS
08907	DBS
08908	EMT
08909	DBS
08911	PRE
08912	IND
08913	IND
08915	IND
08918	DBS
08920	DBS
08921	DBS
08922	DBS
08924	DBS
08925	DBS
08927	WAB
08928	IND
08929	HNR
08933	IND
08934	ALS
08936	BAR
08937	PRE
08939	DBS
08941	DBS
08943	BOM
08944	PRE
08947	MRL
08948	EUS
08950	EMT
08951	DBS
08953	DBS
08954	DBS
08956	SEC
08993	DBS
08994	DBS
08995	DBS
09001	DBS
09002	PRE
09003	DBS
09004	PRE
09005	DBS
09006	DBS
09007	DBS
09008	DBS
09009	DBS
09010	DBS
09011	DBS
09012	DBS
09013	DBS
09014	DBS
09015	DBS
09016	DBS
09017	DBS
09018	DBS
09019	DBS
09020	DBS
09022	DBS
09023	DBS
09024	DBS
09025	PRE
09101	DBS
09102	DBS
09103	DBS
09104	DBS
09105	DBS
09106	DBS
09107	DBS
09201	DBS
09202	DBS
09203	DBS
09204	DBS
09205	DBS
12049	PRE
12052	PRE
12061	PRE
12077	PRE
12082	IND
12088	IND
12093	PRE
12099	PRE
12131	PRE
15224	PRE
18000	PRE
20001	PRE
20007	PRE
20016	HNR
20020	PRE
20031	PRE
20032	HNR
20048	PRE
20056	HNR
20057	HNR
20059	PRE
20066	HNR
20069	PRE
20072	HNR
20081	HNR
20087	PRE
20088	HNR
20092	HNR
20096	HNR
20098	PRE
20105	HNR
20107	HNR
20110	PRE
20118	PRE
20121	HNR
20132	HNR
20137	PRE
20138	HNR
20142	PRE
20154	PRE
20166	PRE
20168	HNR
20169	PRE
20177	PRE
20188	PRE
20189	BAR
20197	HNR
20205	PRE
20214	PRE
20215	HNR
20227	BAR
20301	DRS
20302	DRS
20303	DRS
20304	DRS

20305	DRS	26043	PRE	33052	PRE	37294	PRE	37689	DBS
20306	DRS			33053	PRE	37308	PRE	37693	DBS
20307	DRS	27001	PRE	33057	PRE	37314	PRE	37696	HNR
20308	DRS	27005	PRE	33063	PRE	37324	PRE	38698	DBS
20309	DRS	27007	PRE	33065	PRE	37372	PRE	37702	DBS
20310	DRS	27024	PRE	33102	PRE	37401	DBS	37703	DBS
20311	DRS	27050	PRE	33103	PRE	37403	PRE	37706	WCR
20312	DRS	27056	PRE	33108	PRE	37402	DBS	37709	DBS
20313	DRS	27059	PRE	33109	PRE	37405	DBS	37710	WCR
20314	DRS	27066	PRE	33110	PRE	37406	DBS	37712	WCR
20315	DRS			33111	PRE	37407	PRE	37714	DBS
20901	HNR	31101	PRE	33116	PRE	37409	DRS	37716	DBS
20902	HNR	31105	NRL	33117	PRE	37410	DBS	37718	DBS
20903	HNR	31108	PRE	33201	PRE	37411	DBS	37800	DBS
20904	HNR	31106	RVE	33202	PRE	37412	HNR	37883	DBS
20905	HNR	31119	PRE	33207	WCR	37413	PRE	37884	DBS
20906	HNR	31130	PRE	33208	PRE	37415	DBS	37886	DBS
		31144	PRE			37416	DBS	37888	DBS
21544	ECR	31162	PRE	37003	PRE	37417	DBS	37890	DBS
21545	ECR	31163	PRE	37009	PRE	37418	PRE	37891	DBS
21546	ECR	31190	HAN	37023	PRE	37419	DBS	37893	DBS
21547	ECR	31203	PRE	37025	PRE	37421	PRE	37893	DBS
21610	ECR	31206	PRE	37029	HNR	37423	DRS	37901	PRE
21611	ECR	31207	PRE	37032	PRE	37424	PRE	37905	PRE
		31210	PRE	37037	PRE	37425	DBS	37906	PRE
24032	PRE	31233	NRL	37038	DRS	37426	DBS		
24054	PRE	31235	PRE	37042	DBS	37427	DBS	40012	PRE
24061	PRE	31270	PRE	37057	HNR	37428	DBS	40013	PRE
24082	PRE	31271	PRE	37059	DRS	37503	DBS	40106	PRE
		31285	NRL	37069	DRS	37510	DRS	40118	PRE
25035	PRE	31289	PRE	37075	PRE	37515	DRS	40135	PRE
25057	PRE	31327	PRE	37087	DRS	37516	WCR	40145	PRE
25059	PRE	31410	PRE	37097	PRE	37517	WCR		
25067	PRE	31414	PRE	37108	WCR	37518	PRE	41001	PRE
25072	PRE	31415	PRE	37109	PRE	37521	DBS		
25083	PRE	31418	PRE	37116	PRE	37601	DRS	43002	FGW
25173	PRE	31422	PRE	37142	PRE	37602	DRS	43003	FGW
25185	PRE	31435	PRE	37146	PRE	37603	DRS	43004	FGW
25191	PRE	31438	PRE	37152	PRE	37604	DRS	43005	FGW
25235	PRE	31452	RVE	37165	HNR	37605	DRS	43009	FGW
25244	PRE	31454	RVE	37175	PRE	37606	DRS	43010	FGW
25262	PRE	31459	RVE	37188	PRE	37607	DRS	43012	FGW
26265	PRE	31461	PRE	37194	DRS	37608	DRS	43013	NRL
25278	NYM	31463	PRE	37197	DRS	37609	DRS	43014	NRL
25279	PRE	31465	NRL	37198	NRL	37610	DRS	43015	FGW
25283	PRE	31466	PRE	37207	PRE	37611	DRS	43016	FGW
25309	PRE	31468	RVE	37214	WCR	37612	DRS	43017	FGW
25311	PRE	31530	PRE	37215	PRE	37667	DRS	43018	FGW
25321	PRE	31601	RVE	37216	PRE	37668	WCR	43020	FGW
25322	PRE	31602	RVE	37218	DRS	37669	DBS	43021	FGW
				37219	PRE	37670	DBS	43022	FGW
26001	PRE	33002	PRE	37227	PRE	37671	DBS	43023	FGW
26002	PRE	33008	PRE	37229	DRS	37672	HNR	43024	FGW
26004	PRE	33012	PRE	37240	PRE	37674	PRE	43025	FGW
26007	PRE	33018	PRE	37248	WCR	37675	DBS	43026	FGW
26010	PRE	33019	PRE	37250	PRE	37676	WCR	43027	FGW
26011	PRE	33021	PRE	37254	PRE	37679	PRE	43028	FGW
26014	PRE	33025	WCR	37255	PRE	37680	HNR	43029	FGW
26024	PRE	33029	WCR	37259	DRS	37682	DRS	43030	FGW
26025	PRE	33030	WCR	37261	DRS	37683	DRS	43031	FGW
26035	PRE	33035	PRE	37263	PRE	37684	DBS	43032	FGW
26038	PRE	33046	PRE	37264	PRE	37685	WCR	43033	FGW
26040	PRE	33048	PRE	37275	PRE	37688	DRS	43034	FGW

Number	Operator
43035	FGW
43036	FGW
43037	FGW
43040	FGW
43041	FGW
43042	FGW
43043	EMT
43044	EMT
43045	EMT
43046	EMT
43047	EMT
43048	EMT
43049	EMT
43050	EMT
43052	EMT
43053	FGW
43054	EMT
43055	EMT
43056	FGW
43058	EMT
43059	EMT
43060	EMT
43061	EMT
43062	NRL
43063	FGW
43064	EMT
43065	GTL
43066	EMT
43067	GTL
43068	GTL
43069	FGW
43070	FGW
43071	FGW
43072	EMT
43073	EMT
43074	EMT
43075	EMT
43076	EMT
43078	FGW
43079	FGW
43080	GTL
43081	EMT
43082	EMT
43083	EMT
43084	GTL
43086	FGW
43087	FGW
43088	FGW
43089	EMT
43091	FGW
43092	FGW
43093	FGW
43094	FGW
43097	FGW
43098	FGW
43122	FGW
43123	GTL
43124	FGW
43125	FGW
43126	FGW
43127	FGW
43128	FGW
43129	FGW
43130	FGW
43131	FGW
43132	FGW
43133	FGW
43134	FGW
43135	FGW
43136	FGW
43137	FGW
43138	FGW
43139	FGW
43140	FGW
43141	FGW
43142	FGW
43143	FGW
43144	FGW
43145	FGW
43146	FGW
43147	FGW
43148	FGW
43149	FGW
43150	FGW
43151	FGW
43152	FGW
43153	FGW
43154	FGW
43155	FGW
43156	FGW
43158	FGW
43159	FGW
43160	FGW
43161	FGW
43162	FGW
43163	FGW
43164	FGW
43165	FGW
43168	FGW
43169	FGW
43170	FGW
43171	FGW
43172	FGW
43174	FGW
43175	FGW
43176	FGW
43177	FGW
43179	FGW
43180	FGW
43181	FGW
43182	FGW
43183	FGW
43185	FGW
43186	FGW
43187	FGW
43188	FGW
43189	FGW
43190	FGW
43191	FGW
43192	FGW
43193	FGW
43194	FGW
43195	FGW
43196	FGW
43197	FGW
43198	FGW
43206	ICE
43207	AXC
43208	ICE
43238	ICE
43239	ICE
43251	ICE
43257	ICE
43277	ICE
43285	AXC
43290	ICE
43295	ICE
43296	ICE
43299	ICE
43300	ICE
43301	AXC
43302	ICE
43303	AXC
43304	AXC
43305	ICE
43306	ICE
43307	ICE
43308	ICE
43309	ICE
43310	ICE
43311	ICE
43312	ICE
43313	ICE
43314	ICE
43315	ICE
43316	ICE
43317	ICE
43318	ICE
43319	ICE
43320	ICE
43321	AXC
43357	AXC
43366	AXC
43367	ICE
43378	AXC
43384	AXC
44008	PRE
45014	PRE
45041	PRE
45060	PRE
45105	PRE
45108	PRE
45118	PRE
45125	PRE
45132	PRE
45133	PRE
45135	PRE
45149	PRE
46010	PRE
46035	PRE
46045	PRE
47004	PRE
47105	PRE
47117	PRE
47150	HNR
47192	PRE
47194	WCR
47205	PRE
47237	CWR
47245	WCR
47270	HAN
47289	HNR
47292	PRE
47295	HNR
47306	PRE
47367	PRE
47376	PRE
47401	PRE
47402	PRE
47417	PRE
47449	PRE
47484	PRE
47489	WCR
47492	WCR
47501	DRS
47525	WCR
47524	PRE
47526	WCR
47575	RIV
47580	PRE
47596	PRE
47635	PRE
47640	PRE
47643	PRE
47701	PRE
47703	PRE
47709	DRS
47712	DRS
47714	PRE
47715	PRE
47716	PRE
47727	COL
47739	COL
47746	PRE
47747	RIV
47749	COL
47760	WCR
47763	PRE
47768	PRE
47769	RIV
47770	WCR
47771	PRE
47772	WCR
47773	VTN
47776	WCR
47785	PRE
47786	WCR
47787	WCR
47790	DRS
47791	DRS
47792	WCR
47793	PRE
47798	PRE
47799	DBS
47802	DRS
47804	WCR
47805	RIV
47810	HNR
47812	RIV
47813	HNR
47815	RIV
47818	HNR
47826	WCR
47828	CWR
47829	HNR
47832	DRS
47839	RIV
47840	PRE
47841	DRS
47843	RIV
47847	RIV
47848	RIV
47851	WCR
47853	RIV
47854	WCR
50002	PRE
50007	PRE
50008	PRE
50015	PRE
50017	PRE
50019	PRE
50021	PRE
50026	PRE
50027	PRE
50029	PRE
50030	PRE
50031	PRE
50033	PRE
50135	PRE
50042	PRE
50044	PRE
50049	PRE
50050	PRE
55002	PRE
55009	PRE
55015	PRE
55016	PRE
55019	PRE
55022	PRE
56006	DBS
56007	DBS
56009	IND
56018	DBS
56027	HAN
56031	DBS
56032	DBS
56033	DBS
56037	DBS
56038	DBS
56040	PRE
56041	DBS
56046	DBS
56048	DBS
56049	DBS
56051	DBS
56053	DBS
56054	DBS
56055	DBS

56056	DBS
56058	DBS
56059	DBS
56060	DBS
56062	DBS
56065	DBS
56067	DBS
56068	DBS
56069	DBS
56070	DBS
56071	DBS
56072	DBS
56073	DBS
56074	DBS
56077	DBS
56078	DBS
56079	DBS
56081	DBS
56083	DBS
56085	DBS
56086	PRE
56087	DBS
56088	DBS
56090	DBS
56091	DBS
56093	DBS
56094	DBS
56095	DBS
56096	DBS
56097	PRE
56098	PRE
56099	DBS
56100	DBS
56101	PRE
56102	DBS
56103	DBS
56104	DBS
56105	DBS
56106	DBS
56107	DBS
56108	DBS
56109	DBS
56110	DBS
56111	DBS
56112	DBS
56113	DBS
56114	HAN
56115	DBS
56116	DBS
56117	DBS
56118	DBS
56120	DBS
56127	DBS
56129	DBS
56133	DBS
56134	DBS
56301	FLF
56302	FLF
56303	RVE
56311	HAN
56312	HAN
56313	HAN
56314	HAN
57001	OLS
57002	DRS
57003	DRS
57004	DRS
57005	CWR
57006	CWR
57007	DRS
57008	DRS
57009	DRS
57010	DRS
57011	DRS
57012	DRS
57301	VWC
57302	VWC
57303	VWC
57304	VWC
57305	VWC
57306	VWC
57307	VWC
57308	VWC
57309	VWC
57310	VWC
57311	VWC
57312	VWC
57313	ATW
57314	ATW
57315	ATW
57316	ATW
57601	WCR
57602	FGW
57603	FGW
57604	FGW
57605	FGW
58001	DBS
58002	DBS
58003	DBS
58004	DBS
58005	DBS
58006	DBS
58007	DBS
58008	DBS
58009	DBS
58010	DBS
58011	DBS
58012	DBS
58013	DBS
58014	DBS
58015	DBS
58016	DBS
58017	DBS
58018	DBS
58019	DBS
58020	DBS
58021	DBS
58022	DBS
58023	DBS
58024	DBS
58025	DBS
58026	DBS
58027	DBS
58028	DBS
58029	DBS
58030	DBS
58031	DBS
58032	DBS
58033	DBS
58034	DBS
58035	DBS
58036	DBS
58037	DBS
58038	DBS
58039	DBS
58040	DBS
58041	DBS
58042	DBS
58043	DBS
58044	DBS
58045	DBS
58046	DBS
58047	DBS
58048	DBS
58049	DBS
58050	DBS
59001	MRL
59002	MRL
59003	EXP
59004	MRL
59005	MRL
59101	MRL
59102	MRL
59103	MRL
59104	MRL
59201	DBS
59202	DBS
59203	DBS
59204	DBS
59205	DBS
59206	DBS
60001	DBS
60002	DBS
60003	DBS
60004	DBS
60005	DBS
60006	DBS
60007	DBS
60008	DBS
60009	DBS
60010	DBS
60011	DBS
60012	DBS
60013	DBS
60014	DBS
60015	DBS
60017	DBS
60018	DBS
60019	DBS
60020	DBS
60021	DBS
60022	DBS
60023	DBS
60024	DBS
60025	DBS
60026	DBS
60027	DBS
60028	DBS
60029	DBS
60030	DBS
60031	DBS
60032	DBS
60033	DBS
60034	DBS
60035	DBS
60036	DBS
60037	DBS
60038	DBS
60039	DBS
60040	DBS
60041	DBS
60042	DBS
60043	DBS
60044	DBS
60045	DBS
60046	DBS
60047	DBS
60048	DBS
60049	DBS
60050	DBS
60051	DBS
60052	DBS
60053	DBS
60054	DBS
60055	DBS
60056	DBS
60057	DBS
60058	DBS
60059	DBS
60060	DBS
60061	DBS
60062	DBS
60063	DBS
60064	DBS
60065	DBS
60066	DBS
60067	DBS
60068	DBS
60069	DBS
60070	DBS
60071	DBS
60072	DBS
60073	DBS
60074	DBS
60075	DBS
60076	DBS
60077	DBS
60078	DBS
60079	DBS
60080	DBS
60081	DBS
60082	DBS
60083	DBS
60084	DBS
60085	DBS
60086	DBS
60087	DBS
60088	DBS
60089	DBS
60090	DBS
60091	DBS
60092	DBS
60093	DBS
60094	DBS
60095	DBS
60096	DBS
60097	DBS
60098	DBS
60099	DBS
60100	DBS
60500	DBS
66001	DBS
66002	DBS
66003	DBS
66004	DBS
66005	DBS
66006	DBS
66007	DBS
66008	DBS
66009	DBS
66010	DBS
66011	DBS
66012	DBS
66013	DBS
66014	DBS
66015	DBS
66016	DBS
66017	DBS
66018	DBS
66019	DBS
66020	DBS
66021	DBS
66022	DBS
66023	DBS
66024	DBS
66025	DBS
66026	DBS
66027	DBS
66028	DBS
66029	DBS
66030	DBS
66031	DBS
66032	DBS
66033	DBS
66034	DBS
66035	DBS
66036	DBS
66037	DBS
66038	DBS
66039	DBS
66040	DBS
66041	DBS
66042	DBS
66043	DBS
66044	DBS
66045	DBS
66046	DBS
66047	DBS
66048	DBS
66049	DBS
66050	DBS

66051	DBS
66052	DBS
66053	DBS
66054	DBS
66055	DBS
66056	DBS
66057	DBS
66058	DBS
66059	DBS
66060	DBS
66061	DBS
66062	DBS
66063	DBS
66064	DBS
66065	DBS
66066	DBS
66067	DBS
66068	DBS
66069	DBS
66070	DBS
66071	DBS
66072	DBS
66073	DBS
66074	DBS
66075	DBS
66076	DBS
66077	DBS
66078	DBS
66079	DBS
66080	DBS
66081	DBS
66082	DBS
66083	DBS
66084	DBS
66085	DBS
66086	DBS
66087	DBS
66088	DBS
66089	DBS
66090	DBS
66091	DBS
66092	DBS
66093	DBS
66094	DBS
66095	DBS
66096	DBS
66097	DBS
66098	DBS
66099	DBS
66100	DBS
66101	DBS
66102	DBS
66103	DBS
66104	DBS
66105	DBS
66106	DBS
66107	DBS
66108	DBS
66109	DBS
66110	DBS
66111	DBS
66112	DBS
66113	DBS
66114	DBS
66115	DBS
66116	DBS
66117	DBS
66118	DBS
66119	DBS
66120	DBS
66121	DBS
66122	DBS
66123	DBS
66124	DBS
66125	DBS
66126	DBS
66127	DBS
66128	DBS
66129	DBS
66130	DBS
66131	DBS
66132	DBS
66133	DBS
66134	DBS
66135	DBS
66136	DBS
66137	DBS
66138	DBS
66139	DBS
66140	DBS
66141	DBS
66142	DBS
66143	DBS
66144	DBS
66145	DBS
66146	DBS
66147	DBS
66148	DBS
66149	DBS
66150	DBS
66151	DBS
66152	DBS
66153	DBS
66154	DBS
66155	DBS
66156	DBS
66157	DBS
66158	DBS
66159	DBS
66160	DBS
66161	DBS
66162	DBS
66163	DBS
66164	DBS
66165	DBS
66166	DBS
66167	DBS
66168	DBS
66169	DBS
66170	DBS
66171	DBS
66172	DBS
66173	DBS
66174	DBS
66175	DBS
66176	DBS
66177	DBS
66178	DBS
66179	DBS
66180	DBS
66181	DBS
66182	DBS
66183	DBS
66184	DBS
66185	DBS
66186	DBS
66187	DBS
66188	DBS
66189	DBS
66190	DBS
66191	DBS
66192	DBS
66193	DBS
66194	DBS
66195	DBS
66196	DBS
66197	DBS
66198	DBS
66199	DBS
66200	DBS
66201	DBS
66202	DBS
66203	DBS
66204	DBS
66205	DBS
66206	DBS
66207	DBS
66208	DBS
66209	DBS
66210	DBS
66211	DBS
66212	DBS
66213	DBS
66214	DBS
66215	DBS
66216	DBS
66217	DBS
66218	DBS
66219	DBS
66220	DBS
66221	DBS
66222	DBS
66223	DBS
66224	DBS
66225	DBS
66226	DBS
66227	DBS
66228	DBS
66229	DBS
66230	DBS
66231	DBS
66232	DBS
66233	DBS
66234	DBS
66235	DBS
66236	DBS
66237	DBS
66238	DBS
66239	DBS
66240	DBS
66241	DBS
66242	DBS
66243	DBS
66244	DBS
66245	DBS
66246	DBS
66247	DBS
66248	DBS
66249	DBS
66250	DBS
66301	FLF
66302	FLF
66303	FLF
66304	FLF
66305	FLF
66401	GBR
66402	GBR
66403	OLS
66404	OLS
66405	OLS
66410	OLS
66411	DRS
66412	DRS
66413	DRS
66414	DRS
66415	DRS
66416	DRS
66417	DRS
66418	DRS
66419	DRS
66420	DRS
66421	DRS
66422	DRS
66423	DRS
66424	DRS
66425	DRS
66426	DRS
66427	DRS
66428	DRS
66429	DRS
66430	DRS
66431	DRS
66432	DRS
66433	DRS
66434	DRS
66501	FLR
66502	FLR
66503	FLR
66504	FLR
66505	FLR
66506	FLR
66507	FLR
66508	FLR
66509	FLR
66510	FLR
66511	FLR
66512	FLR
66513	FLR
66514	FLR
66515	FLR
66516	FLR
66517	FLR
66518	FLR
66519	FLR
66520	FLR
66521	FLR
66522	FLR
66523	FLR
66524	FLR
66525	FLR
66526	FLR
66527	FLR
66528	FLR
66529	FLR
66530	FLR
66531	FLR
66532	FLR
66533	FLR
66534	FLR
66535	FLR
66536	FLR
66537	FLR
66538	FLR
66539	FLR
66540	FLR
66541	FLR
66542	FLR
66543	FLR
66544	FLR
66545	FLR
66546	FLR
66547	FLR
66548	FLR
66549	FLR
66550	FLR
66551	FLR
66552	FLR
66553	FLR
66554	FLR
66555	FLR
66556	FLR
66557	FLR
66558	FLR
66559	FLR
66560	FLR
66561	FLR
66562	FLR
66563	FLR
66564	FLR
66565	FLR
66566	FLR
66567	FLR
66568	FLR
66569	FLR
66570	FLR
66571	FLR
66572	FLR
66573	FLR
66574	FLR
66575	FLR
66576	FLR
66577	FLR
66578	FLR
66579	FLR
66580	FLR

66581	FLR
66582	FLR
66583	FLR
66584	FLR
66585	FLR
66586	FLR
66587	FLR
66588	FLR
66589	FLR
66590	FLR
66591	FLR
66592	FLR
66593	FLR
66594	FLR
66595	FLR
66596	FLR
66597	FLR
66598	FLR
66599	FLR
66601	FLR
66602	FLR
66603	FLR
66604	FLR
66605	FLR
66606	FLR
66607	FLR
66608	FLR
66609	FLR
66610	FLR
66611	FLR
66612	FLR
66613	FLR
66614	FLR
66615	FLR
66616	FLR
66617	FLR
66618	FLR
66619	FLR
66620	FLR
66621	FLR
66622	FLR
66623	FLR
66624	FLR
66625	FLR
66701	GBR
66702	GBR
66703	GBR
66704	GBR
66705	GBR
66706	GBR
66707	GBR
66708	GBR
66709	GBR
66710	GBR
66711	GBR
66712	GBR
66713	GBR
66714	GBR
66715	GBR
66716	GBR
66717	GBR
66718	GBR
66719	GBR
66720	GBR
66721	GBR
66722	GBR
66723	GBR
66724	GBR
66725	GBR
66726	GBR
66727	GBR
66728	GBR
66729	GBR
66730	GBR
66731	GBR
66841	CWR
66842	CWR
66843	CWR
66844	CWR
66951	FLR
66952	FLR
66953	FLR
66954	FLR
66955	FLR
66956	FLR
66957	FLR
67001	DBS
67002	DBS
67003	DBS
67004	DBS
67005	DBS
67006	DBS
67007	DBS
67008	DBS
67009	DBS
67010	WSR
67011	DBS
67016	DBS
67012	WSR
67013	WSR
67014	WSR
67015	WSR
67017	DBS
67018	DBS
67019	DBS
67020	DBS
67021	DBS
67022	DBS
67023	DBS
67024	DBS
67025	DBS
67026	DBS
67027	DBS
67028	DBS
67029	DBS
67030	DBS
70001	FLR
70002	FLR
70003	FLR
70004	FLR
70005	FLR
70006	FLR
70007	FLR
70008	FLR
70009	FLR
70010	FLR
70011	FLR
70012	FLR
71001	PRE
73001	PRE
73003	PRE
73005	PRE
73006	PRE
73101	PRE
73103	PRE
73104	PRE
73107	BAR
73109	SWT
73110	PRE
73114	PRE
73117	PRE
73118	PRE
73119	KRS
73128	PRE
73129	PRE
73130	PRE
73133	IND
73134	PRE
73136	PRE
73138	PRE
73139	PRE
73140	PRE
73141	GBR
73201	BAR
73202	SOU
73203	GBR
73204	GBR
73205	GBR
73206	GBR
73207	GBR
73208	GBR
73209	GBR
73210	PRE
73211	PRE
73212	GBR
73213	GBR
77001	ECR
77002	ECR
77003	ECR
77004	ECR
77005	ECR
77006	ECR
77007	ECR
77008	ECR
77009	ECR
77010	ECR
77011	ECR
77012	ECR
77013	ECR
77014	ECR
77015	ECR
77016	ECR
77017	ECR
77018	ECR
77019	ECR
77020	ECR
77021	ECR
77022	ECR
77023	ECR
77024	ECR
77025	ECR
77026	ECR
77027	ECR
77028	ECR
77029	ECR
77030	ECR
77031	ECR
77032	ECR
77033	ECR
77034	ECR
77035	ECR
77036	ECR
77037	ECR
77038	ECR
77039	ECR
77040	ECR
77041	ECR
77042	ECR
77043	ECR
77044	ECR
77045	ECR
77046	ECR
77047	ECR
77048	ECR
77049	ECR
77050	ECR
77051	ECR
77052	ECR
77053	ECR
77054	ECR
77055	ECR
77056	ECR
77057	ECR
77058	ECR
77059	ECR
77060	ECR
81002	PRE
82008	PRE
83012	PRE
84001	PRE
85101	PRE
86101	ETL
86205	EPX
86212	EPX
86213	PRE
86215	EPX
86217	EPX
86218	EPX
86223	EPX
86226	EPX
86228	EPX
86229	EPX
86230	EPX
86231	EPX
86232	EPX
86233	PRE
86234	EPX
86235	EPX
86242	EPX
86245	EPX
86246	EPX
86247	EPX
86248	EPX
86250	EXP
86251	EPX
86258	EPX
86259	PRE
86260	ETL
86401	PRE
86424	NRL
86501	FLR
86602	FLR
86604	FLR
86605	FLR
86607	FLR
86609	FLR
86610	FLR
86612	FLR
86613	FLR
86614	FLR
86621	FLR
86622	FLR
86623	FLR
86627	FLR
86628	FLR
86632	FLR
86633	FLR
86635	FLR
86637	FLR
86638	FLR
86639	FLR
86701	ETL
86702	ETL
86901	NRL
86902	NRL
87001	PRE
87002	PRE
87003	EXP
87002	ETL
87004	EXP
87006	EXP
87007	EXP
87008	EXP
87009	OLS
87010	EXP
87011	OLS
87012	EXP

87013 OLS
87014 EXP
87017 OLS
87018 OLS
87019 EXP
87020 EXP
87021 OLS
87022 EXP
87023 OLS
87025 OLS
87026 EXP
87027 OLS
87028 EXP
87029 EXP
87030 OLS
87031 ETS
87032 OLS
87033 EXP
87034 EXP
87035 PRE

89001 PRE

90001 NXA
90002 NXA
90003 NXA
90004 NXA
90005 NXA
90006 NXA
90007 NXA
90008 NXA
90009 NXA
90010 NXA
90011 NXA
90012 NXA
90013 NXA
90014 NXA
90015 NXA
90017 DBS
90018 DBS
90019 DBS
90020 DBS
90021 DBS
90022 DBS
90023 DBS
90024 DBS
90025 DBS
90026 DBS
90027 DBS
90028 DBS
90029 DBS
90030 DBS
90031 DBS
90032 DBS
90033 DBS
90034 DBS
90035 DBS
90036 DBS
90037 DBS
90038 DBS
90039 DBS
90040 DBS
90042 FLR
90043 FLR
90044 FLR
90045 FLR
90046 FLR
90047 FLR
90048 FLR
90049 FLR
90050 FLR

91101 ICE
91102 ICE
91103 ICE
91104 ICE
91105 ICE
91106 ICE
91107 ICE
91108 ICE
91109 ICE
91110 ICE
91111 ICE
91112 ICE
91113 ICE
91114 ICE
91115 ICE
91116 ICE
91117 ICE
91118 ICE
91119 ICE
91120 ICE
91121 ICE
91122 ICE
91124 ICE
91125 ICE
91126 ICE
91127 ICE
91128 ICE
91129 ICE
91130 ICE
91131 ICE
91132 ICE

92001 DBS
92002 DBS
92003 DBS
92004 DBS
92005 DBS
92006 SNF
92007 DBS
92008 DBS
92009 DBS
92010 EUR
92011 DBS
92012 DBS
92013 DBS
92014 SNF
92015 DBS
92016 DBS
92017 DBS
92018 SNF
92019 DBS
92020 EUR
92021 EUR
92022 DBS
92023 SNF
92024 DBS
92025 DBS
92026 DBS
92027 DBS
92028 EUR
92029 DBS
92030 DBS
92031 DBS
92032 EUR
92033 SNF
92034 DBS
92035 DBS
92036 DBS
92038 EUR
92039 DBS
92040 EUR
92041 EUR
92042 DBS
92043 EUR
92044 EUR
92045 EUR
92046 EUR

97301 NRL
97302 NRL
97303 NRL
97304 NRL

97650 PRE
97651 PRE
97654 PRE

Diesel Multiple Units

APT-E PRE
LEV1 PRE
RB004 PRE

50015 PRE
50019 PRE
50222 PRE
50256 PRE
50338 PRE
50416 PRE
50447 PRE
50454 PRE
50479 PRE
50528 PRE
50531 PRE
50556 PRE
50599 PRE
50619 PRE
50632 PRE
50929 PRE
50980 PRE

51017 PRE
51043 PRE
51073 PRE
51074 PRE
51104 PRE
51131 PRE
51138 PRE
51151 PRE
51187 PRE
51188 PRE
51189 PRE
51192 PRE
51205 PRE
51210 PRE
51226 PRE
51228 PRE
51247 PRE
51321 PRE
51339 PRE
51341 PRE
51342 PRE
51346 PRE
51347 PRE
51351 PRE
51353 PRE
51356 PRE
51359 PRE
51360 PRE
51363 PRE
51365 PRE
51367 PRE
51372 PRE
51381 PRE
51382 PRE
51384 PRE
51388 PRE
51392 PRE
51395 PRE
51397 PRE
51398 PRE
51400 PRE
51401 PRE
51402 PRE
51405 PRE
51407 PRE
51434 PRE
51485 PRE
51499 PRE
51503 PRE
51505 PRE
51511 PRE
51512 PRE
51513 PRE
51562 PRE
51565 PRE
51566 PRE
51567 PRE
51568 PRE
51571 PRE
51572 PRE
51592 PRE
51604 PRE
51616 PRE
51618 PRE
51622 PRE
51655 PRE
51663 PRE
51669 PRE
51677 PRE
51803 PRE
51813 PRE
51842 PRE
51849 PRE
51852 PRE
51859 PRE
51880 PRE
51886 PRE
51887 PRE
51899 PRE
51907 PRE
51909 PRE
51914 PRE
51919 PRE
51922 PRE
51933 PRE
51941 PRE
51942 PRE
51947 PRE
51950 PRE
51973 PRE
51990 PRE

52005 PRE
52006 PRE
52008 PRE
52025 PRE
52030 PRE
52044 PRE
52048 PRE
52053 PRE
52054 PRE
52062 PRE
52064 PRE
52071 PRE
52077 PRE

53160 PRE
53164 PRE
53170 PRE
53193 PRE
53203 PRE
53204 PRE
53253 PRE
53266 PRE
53321 PRE
53628 PRE
53645 PRE
53746 PRE
53926 PRE
53971 PRE
54055 PRE
54057 PRE
54062 PRE
54207 PRE
54223 PRE
54270 PRE
54279 PRE
54289 PRE
54365 PRE
54408 PRE
54490 PRE
54504 PRE

Number	Operator
55000	PRE
55001	PRE
55003	PRE
55005	PRE
55006	PRE
55009	PRE
55012	PRE
55023	PRE
55028	PRE
55032	ATW
55033	PRE
55966	PRE
55976	PRE
56006	PRE
56015	PRE
56121	PRE
56171	PRE
56208	PRE
56224	PRE
56271	PRE
56287	PRE
56301	PRE
56343	PRE
56352	PRE
56358	PRE
56456	PRE
56484	PRE
56491	PRE
56492	PRE
56495	PRE
59003	PRE
59004	PRE
59117	PRE
59228	PRE
59245	PRE
59250	PRE
59276	PRE
59387	PRE
59389	PRE
59404	PRE
59444	PRE
59486	PRE
59488	PRE
59492	PRE
59494	PRE
59500	PRE
59503	PRE
59506	PRE
59507	PRE
59508	PRE
59509	PRE
59510	PRE
59513	PRE
59514	PRE
59516	PRE
59517	PRE
59520	PRE
59521	PRE
59522	PRE
59539	PRE
59575	PRE
59603	PRE
59609	PRE
59659	PRE
59664	PRE
59678	PRE
59701	PRE
59719	PRE
59740	PRE
59761	PRE
59791	PRE
60117	PRE
60127	PRE
60142	PRE
60145	PRE
60149	PRE
60616	PRE
60822	PRE
60828	PRE
60901	PRE
60904	PRE
60916	PRE
70549	PRE
79018	PRE
79612	PRE
79900	PRE
79960	PRE
79962	PRE
79963	PRE
79964	PRE
79976	PRE
79978	PRE
121032	ATW
139001	LMI
139002	LMI
140001	PRE
142001	FGW
142002	ATW
142003	NOR
142004	NOR
142005	NOR
142006	ATW
142007	NOR
142009	FGW
142010	ATW
142011	NOR
142012	NOR
142013	NOR
142014	NOR
142015	NOR
142016	NOR
142017	NOR
142018	NOR
142019	NOR
142020	NOR
142021	NOR
142022	NOR
142023	NOR
142024	NOR
142025	NOR
142026	NOR
142027	NOR
142028	NOR
142029	FGW
142030	FGW
142031	NOR
142032	NOR
142033	NOR
142034	NOR
142035	NOR
142036	NOR
142037	NOR
142038	NOR
142039	NOR
142040	NOR
142041	NOR
142042	NOR
142043	NOR
142044	NOR
142045	NOR
142046	NOR
142047	NOR
142048	NOR
142049	NOR
142050	NOR
142051	NOR
142052	NOR
142053	NOR
142054	NOR
142055	NOR
142056	NOR
142057	NOR
142058	NOR
142060	NOR
142061	NOR
142062	NOR
142063	FGW
142064	FGW
142065	NOR
142066	NOR
142067	NOR
142068	FGW
142069	ATW
142070	NOR
142071	NOR
142072	ATW
142073	ATW
142074	ATW
142075	ATW
142076	ATW
142077	ATW
142078	NOR
142079	NOR
142080	ATW
142081	ATW
142082	ATW
142083	ATW
142084	NOR
142085	ATW
142086	NOR
142087	NOR
142088	NOR
142089	NOR
142090	NOR
142091	NOR
142092	NOR
142093	NOR
142094	NOR
142095	NOR
142096	NOR
143601	ATW
143602	ATW
143603	FGW
143604	ATW
143605	ATW
143606	ATW
143607	ATW
143608	ATW
143609	ATW
143610	ATW
143611	FGW
143612	FGW
143614	ATW
143615	ATW
143617	FGW
143618	FGW
143619	FGW
143620	FGW
143621	FGW
143622	ATW
143623	ATW
143624	ATW
143625	ATW
144001	NOR
144002	NOR
144003	NOR
144004	NOR
144005	NOR
144006	NOR
144007	NOR
144008	NOR
144009	NOR
144010	NOR
144011	NOR
144012	NOR
144013	NOR
144014	NOR
144015	NOR
144016	NOR
144017	NOR
144018	NOR
144019	NOR
144020	NOR
144021	NOR
144022	NOR
144023	NOR
150001	LMI
150002	LMI
150003	LMI
150005	LMI
150007	LMI
150009	LMI
150010	LMI
150011	LMI
150012	LMI
150013	LMI
150014	LMI
150015	LMI
150016	LMI
150017	LMI
150018	LMI
150019	LMI
150101	LMI
150102	LMI
150104	LMI
150106	LMI
150108	LMI
150120	LOG
150121	FGW
150123	LOG
150122	LMI
150124	LMI
150125	LMI
150126	LMI
150127	FGW
150128	LOG
150129	LOG
150130	LOG
150131	LOG
150132	LMI
150133	NOR
150134	NOR
150135	NOR
150136	NOR
150137	NOR
150138	NOR
150139	NOR
150140	NOR
150141	NOR
150142	NOR
150143	NOR
150144	NOR
150145	NOR
150146	NOR
150147	NOR
150148	NOR
150149	NOR
150150	NOR
150201	NOR
150203	NOR
150205	NOR
150207	NOR
150208	ATW
150211	NOR
150214	LMI
150215	NOR
150216	LMI
150218	NOR
150219	FGW
150221	FGW
150222	NOR
150223	NOR
150224	NOR

Number	Operator
150225	NOR
150228	NOR
150232	FGW
150233	FGW
150234	FGW
150236	ATW
150238	FGW
150239	FGW
150240	ATW
150241	ATW
150242	ATW
150243	FGW
150244	FGW
150245	ATW
150246	FGW
150247	FGW
150248	FGW
150249	FGW
150250	ATW
150251	ATW
150252	ATW
150253	ATW
150254	ATW
150256	ATW
150258	ATW
150259	ATW
150260	ATW
150261	FGW
150262	ATW
150263	FGW
150264	ATW
150265	FGW
150266	FGW
150267	ATW
150268	NOR
150269	NOR
150270	NOR
150271	NOR
150272	NOR
150273	NOR
150274	NOR
150275	NOR
150276	NOR
150277	NOR
150278	ATW
150279	ATW
150280	ATW
150281	ATW
150282	ATW
150283	ATW
150284	ATW
150285	ATW
153301	NOR
153302	EMT
153303	ATW
153304	NOR
153305	FGW
153306	NXA
153307	NOR
153308	EMT
153309	NXA
153310	EMT
153311	EMT
153312	ATW
153313	EMT
153314	NXA
153315	NOR
153316	NOR
153317	NOR
153318	FGW
153319	EMT
153320	ATW
153321	EMT
153322	NXA
153323	ATW
153324	NOR
153325	LMI
153326	EMT
153327	ATW
153328	NOR
153329	FGW
153330	NOR
153331	NOR
153332	NOR
153333	LMI
153334	LMI
153335	NXA
153351	NOR
153352	NOR
153353	ATW
153354	LMI
153355	EMT
153356	LMI
153357	EMT
153358	NOR
153359	NOR
153360	NOR
153361	FGW
153362	ATW
153363	NOR
153364	LMI
153365	LMI
153366	LMI
153367	ATW
153368	FGW
153369	FGW
153370	FGW
153371	LMI
153372	FGW
153373	FGW
153374	EMT
153375	LMI
153376	EMT
153377	FGW
153378	NOR
153379	EMT
153380	FGW
153381	EMT
153382	FGW
153383	EMT
153384	EMT
153385	EMT
155341	NOR
155342	NOR
155343	NOR
155344	NOR
155345	NOR
155346	NOR
155347	NOR
156401	EMT
156402	NXA
156403	EMT
156404	EMT
156405	EMT
156406	EMT
156407	NXA
156408	EMT
156409	NXA
156410	EMT
156411	EMT
156412	NXA
156413	EMT
156414	EMT
156415	EMT
156416	NXA
156417	NXA
156418	NXA
156419	NXA
156420	NOR
156421	NOR
156422	NXA
156423	NOR
156424	NOR
156425	NOR
156426	NOR
156427	NOR
156428	NOR
156429	NOR
156431	FSR
156432	FSR
156433	FSR
156434	FSR
156435	FSR
156436	FSR
156437	FSR
156438	NOR
156439	FSR
156440	NOR
156441	NOR
156442	FSR
156443	NOR
156444	NOR
156445	FSR
156446	FSR
156447	FSR
156448	NOR
156449	FSR
156450	FSR
156451	NOR
156452	NOR
156453	FSR
156454	NOR
156455	NOR
156456	FSR
156457	FSR
156458	FSR
156459	NOR
156460	NOR
156461	NOR
156462	FSR
156463	NOR
156464	NOR
156465	FSR
156466	NOR
156467	FSR
156468	NOR
156469	NOR
156470	NOR
156471	NOR
156472	NOR
156473	NOR
156474	FSR
156475	NOR
156476	FSR
156477	FSR
156478	FSR
156479	NOR
156480	NOR
156481	NOR
156482	NOR
156483	NOR
156484	NOR
156485	FSR
156486	NOR
156487	NOR
156488	NOR
156489	NOR
156490	NOR
156491	NOR
156492	FSR
156493	FSR
156494	FSR
156495	FSR
156496	FSR
156497	NOR
156498	NOR
156499	FSR
156500	FSR
156501	FSR
156502	FSR
156503	FSR
156504	FSR
156505	FSR
156506	FSR
156507	FSR
156508	FSR
156509	FSR
156510	FSR
156511	FSR
156512	FSR
156513	FSR
156514	FSR
158701	FSR
158702	FSR
158703	FSR
158704	FSR
158705	FSR
158706	FSR
158707	FSR
158708	FSR
158709	FSR
158710	FSR
158711	FSR
158712	FSR
158713	FSR
158714	FSR
158715	FSR
158716	FSR
158717	FSR
158718	FSR
158719	FSR
158720	FSR
158721	FSR
158722	FSR
158723	FSR
158724	FSR
158725	FSR
158726	FSR
158727	FSR
158728	FSR
158729	FSR
158730	FSR
158731	FSR
158732	FSR
158733	FSR
158734	FSR
158735	FSR
158736	FSR
158737	FSR
158738	FSR
158739	FSR
158740	FSR
158741	FSR
158745	FGW
158752	NOR
158753	NOR
158754	NOR
158755	NOR
158756	NOR
158757	NOR
158758	NOR
158759	NOR
158763	FGW
158766	FGW
158767	FGW
158769	FGW
158770	EMT
158773	EMT
158774	EMT
158777	EMT
158780	EMT
158783	EMT
158782	FSR
158784	NOR
158785	EMT
158786	FSR
158787	NOR
158788	EMT
158789	FSR
158790	NOR
158791	NOR

Number	Operator
158792	NOR
158793	NOR
158794	NOR
158795	NOR
158796	NOR
158797	NOR
158798	FGW
158799	EMT
158806	EMT
158810	EMT
158812	EMT
158813	EMT
158815	NOR
158816	NOR
158817	NOR
158818	ATW
158819	ATW
158820	ATW
158821	ATW
158822	ATW
158823	ATW
158824	ATW
158825	ATW
158826	ATW
158827	ATW
158828	ATW
158829	ATW
158830	ATW
158831	ATW
158832	ATW
158833	ATW
158834	ATW
158835	ATW
158836	ATW
158837	ATW
158838	ATW
158839	ATW
158840	ATW
158841	ATW
158843	NOR
158844	NOR
158845	NOR
158846	EMT
158847	EMT
158848	NOR
158849	NOR
158850	NOR
158851	NOR
158852	EMT
158853	NOR
158854	EMT
158855	NOR
158856	EMT
158857	EMT
158858	EMT
158859	NOR
158860	NOR
158861	NOR
158862	EMT
158863	EMT
158864	EMT
158865	EMT
158866	EMT
158867	FSR
158868	FSR
158869	FSR
158870	FSR
158872	NOR
158880	SWT
158881	SWT
158882	SWT
158883	SWT
158884	SWT
158885	SWT
158886	SWT
158887	SWT
158888	SWT
158889	SWT
158890	SWT
158901	NOR
158902	NOR
158903	NOR
158904	NOR
158905	NOR
158906	NOR
158907	NOR
158908	NOR
158909	NOR
158910	NOR
158950	FGW
158951	FGW
158952	FGW
158953	FGW
158954	FGW
158955	FGW
158956	FGW
158957	FGW
158958	FGW
158959	FGW
159001	SWT
159002	SWT
159003	SWT
159004	SWT
159005	SWT
159006	SWT
159007	SWT
159008	SWT
159009	SWT
159010	SWT
159011	SWT
159012	SWT
159013	SWT
159014	SWT
159015	SWT
159016	SWT
159017	SWT
159018	SWT
159019	SWT
159020	SWT
159021	SWT
159022	SWT
159101	SWT
159102	SWT
159103	SWT
159104	SWT
159105	SWT
159106	SWT
159107	SWT
159108	SWT
165001	CRW
165002	CRW
165003	CRW
165004	CRW
165005	CRW
165006	CRW
165007	CRW
165008	CRW
165009	CRW
165010	CRW
165011	CRW
165012	CRW
165013	CRW
165014	CRW
165015	CRW
165016	CRW
165017	CRW
165018	CRW
165019	CRW
165020	CRW
165021	CRW
165022	CRW
165023	CRW
165024	CRW
165025	CRW
165026	CRW
165027	CRW
165028	CRW
165029	CRW
165030	CRW
165031	CRW
165032	CRW
165033	CRW
165034	CRW
165035	CRW
165036	CRW
165037	CRW
165038	CRW
165039	CRW
165101	FGW
165102	FGW
165103	FGW
165104	FGW
165105	FGW
165106	FGW
165107	FGW
165108	FGW
165109	FGW
165110	FGW
165111	FGW
165112	FGW
165113	FGW
165114	FGW
165115	FGW
165116	FGW
165117	FGW
165118	FGW
165119	FGW
165120	FGW
165121	FGW
165122	FGW
165123	FGW
165124	FGW
165125	FGW
165126	FGW
166201	FGW
166202	FGW
166203	FGW
166204	FGW
166205	FGW
166206	FGW
166207	FGW
166208	FGW
166209	FGW
166210	FGW
166211	FGW
166212	FGW
166213	FGW
166214	FGW
166215	FGW
166216	FGW
166217	FGW
166218	FGW
166219	FGW
166220	FGW
166221	FGW
168001	CRW
168002	CRW
168003	CRW
168004	CRW
168005	CRW
168106	CRW
168107	CRW
168108	CRW
168109	CRW
168110	CRW
168112	CRW
168113	CRW
168214	CRW
168215	CRW
168216	CRW
168217	CRW
168218	CRW
168219	CRW
170101	AXC
170102	AXC
170103	AXC
170104	AXC
170105	AXC
170106	AXC
170107	AXC
170108	AXC
170109	AXC
170110	AXC
170111	AXC
170112	AXC
170113	AXC
170114	AXC
170115	AXC
170116	AXC
170117	AXC
170201	NXA
170202	NXA
170203	NXA
170204	NXA
170205	NXA
170206	NXA
170207	NXA
170208	NXA
170270	NXA
170271	NXA
170272	NXA
170273	NXA
170301	FTP
170302	FTP
170303	FTP
170304	FTP
170305	FTP
170306	FTP
170307	FTP
170308	FTP
170309	FTP
170393	FSR
170394	FSR
170395	FSR
170397	AXC
170398	AXC
170401	FSR
170402	FSR
170403	FSR
170404	FSR
170405	FSR
170406	FSR
170407	FSR
170408	FSR
170409	FSR
170410	FSR
170411	FSR
170412	FSR
170413	FSR
170414	FSR
170415	FSR
170416	FSR
170417	FSR
170418	FSR
170419	FSR
170420	FSR
170421	FSR
170422	FSR
170423	FSR
170424	FSR
170425	FSR
170426	FSR
170427	FSR
170428	FSR
170429	FSR
170430	FSR
170431	FSR
170432	FSR
170433	FSR
170434	FSR
170450	FSR

Number	Operator
170451	FSR
170452	FSR
170453	FSR
170454	FSR
170455	FSR
170456	FSR
170457	FSR
170458	FSR
170459	FSR
170460	FSR
170461	FSR
170470	FSR
170471	FSR
170472	FSR
170473	FSR
170474	FSR
170475	FSR
170476	FSR
170477	FSR
170478	FSR
170501	LMI
170502	LMI
170503	LMI
170504	LMI
170505	LMI
170506	LMI
170507	LMI
170508	LMI
170509	LMI
170510	LMI
170511	LMI
170512	LMI
170513	LMI
170514	LMI
170515	LMI
170516	LMI
170517	LMI
170518	AXC
170519	AXC
170520	AXC
170521	AXC
170522	AXC
170523	AXC
170630	LMI
170631	LMI
170632	LMI
170633	LMI
170634	LMI
170635	LMI
170636	AXC
170637	AXC
170638	AXC
170639	AXC
171721	SOU
171722	SOU
171723	SOU
171724	SOU
171725	SOU
171726	SOU
171727	SOU
171728	SOU
171729	SOU
171730	SOU
171801	SOU
171802	SOU
171803	SOU
171804	SOU
171805	SOU
171806	SOU
172001	LOG
172002	LOG
172003	LOG
172004	LOG
172005	LOG
172006	LOG
172007	LOG
172008	LOG
172101	CRW
172102	CRW
172103	CRW
172104	CRW
172211	LMI
172212	LMI
172213	LMI
172214	LMI
172215	LMI
172216	LMI
172217	LMI
172218	LMI
172219	LMI
172220	LMI
172221	LMI
172222	LMI
172331	LMI
172332	LMI
172333	LMI
172334	LMI
172335	LMI
172336	LMI
172337	LMI
172338	LMI
172339	LMI
172340	LMI
172341	LMI
172342	LMI
172343	LMI
172344	LMI
172345	LMI
175001	ATW
175002	ATW
175003	ATW
175004	ATW
175005	ATW
175006	ATW
175007	ATW
175008	ATW
175009	ATW
175010	ATW
175011	ATW
175101	ATW
175102	ATW
175103	ATW
175104	ATW
175105	ATW
175106	ATW
175107	ATW
175108	ATW
175109	ATW
175110	ATW
175111	ATW
175112	ATW
175113	ATW
175114	ATW
175115	ATW
175116	ATW
180101	GTL
180102	ICE
180103	ICE
180104	ICE
180105	GTL
180106	ICE
180107	GTL
180108	ICE
180109	FHT
180110	FHT
180111	FHT
180112	GTL
180113	FHT
180114	GTL
185101	FTP
185102	FTP
185103	FTP
185104	FTP
185105	FTP
185106	FTP
185107	FTP
185108	FTP
185109	FTP
185110	FTP
185111	FTP
185112	FTP
185113	FTP
185114	FTP
185115	FTP
185116	FTP
185117	FTP
185118	FTP
185119	FTP
185120	FTP
185121	FTP
185122	FTP
185123	FTP
185124	FTP
185125	FTP
185126	FTP
185127	FTP
185128	FTP
185129	FTP
185130	FTP
185131	FTP
185132	FTP
185133	FTP
185134	FTP
185135	FTP
185136	FTP
185137	FTP
185138	FTP
185139	FTP
185140	FTP
185141	FTP
185142	FTP
185143	FTP
185144	FTP
185145	FTP
185146	FTP
185147	FTP
185148	FTP
185149	FTP
185150	FTP
185151	FTP
201001	PRE
205009	PRE
205025	PRE
205028	PRE
205032	PRE
205033	PRE
205101	PRE
205205	PRE
202202	PRE
220001	AXC
220002	AXC
220003	AXC
220004	AXC
220005	AXC
220006	AXC
220007	AXC
220008	AXC
220009	AXC
220010	AXC
220011	AXC
220012	AXC
220013	AXC
220014	AXC
220015	AXC
220016	AXC
220017	AXC
220018	AXC
220019	AXC
220020	AXC
220021	AXC
220022	AXC
220023	AXC
220024	AXC
220025	AXC
220026	AXC
220027	AXC
220028	AXC
220029	AXC
220030	AXC
220031	AXC
220032	AXC
220033	AXC
220034	AXC
221101	VWC
221102	VWC
221103	VWC
221104	VWC
221105	VWC
221106	VWC
221107	VWC
221108	VWC
221109	VWC
221110	VWC
221111	VWC
221112	VWC
221113	VWC
221114	VWC
221115	VWC
221116	VWC
221117	VWC
221118	VWC
221119	AXC
221120	AXC
221121	AXC
221122	AXC
221123	AXC
221124	AXC
221125	AXC
221126	AXC
221127	AXC
221128	AXC
221129	AXC
221130	AXC
221131	AXC
221132	AXC
221133	AXC
221134	AXC
221135	AXC
221136	AXC
221137	AXC
221138	AXC
221139	AXC
221140	AXC
221141	AXC
221142	VWC
221143	VWC
221144	VWC
222001	EMT
222002	EMT
222003	EMT
222004	EMT
222005	EMT
222006	EMT
222007	EMT
222008	EMT
222009	EMT
222010	EMT
222011	EMT
222012	EMT
222013	EMT
222014	EMT
222015	EMT
222016	EMT
222017	EMT
222018	EMT

222019	EMT
222020	EMT
222021	EMT
222022	EMT
222023	EMT
222101	EMT
222102	EMT
222103	EMT
222104	EMT

Electric Multiple Units

85	PRE
87	PRE
91	PRE
2090	PRE
4732	PRE
5176	PRE
5759	PRE
5791	PRE
5793	PRE
6307	PRE
7105	PRE
8143	PRE
10096	PRE
11161	PRE
11179	PRE
11201	PRE
11825	PRE
13004	PRE
15345	PRE
28249	PRE
28361	PRE
28690	PRE
29298	PRE
29666	PRE
29670	PRE
29720	PRE
29896	PRE
61183	PRE
61275	PRE
61287	PRE
61742	PRE
61743	PRE
61798	PRE
61799	PRE
61804	PRE
61805	PRE
62351	PRE
62364	PRE
62384	PRE
62378	PRE
62887	PRE
65451	PRE
65302	PRE
65304	PRE
67300	PRE
68001	PRE
68002	PRE
68003	PRE
68004	PRE
68005	PRE
68008	PRE
68009	PRE
68500	PRE
68506	PRE
69304	PRE
69310	PRE
69318	PRE
69332	PRE
69333	PRE
69337	PRE
69339	PRE
70229	PRE
70257	PRE
70273	PRE
70284	PRE
70292	PRE
70296	PRE
70354	PRE
70527	PRE
70531	PRE
70539	PRE
70576	PRE
70607	PRE
71032	PRE
72501	PRE
72617	PRE
75033	PRE
75186	PRE
75250	PRE
75395	PRE
75407	PRE
76529	PRE
76712	PRE
76726	PRE
76740	PRE
76746	PRE
76797	PRE
76811	PRE
76812	PRE
76817	PRE
76875	PRE
77172	PRE
79998	PRE
79999	PRE
303032	PRE
306017	PRE
309616	PRE
309624	PRE
310049	OLS
310050	OLS
310051	OLS
310059	OLS
310069	OLS
310070	OLS
310102	OLS
310110	OLS
310111	OLS
313018	FCC
313024	FCC
313025	FCC
313026	FCC
313027	FCC
313028	FCC
313029	FCC
313030	FCC
313031	FCC
313032	FCC
313033	FCC
313035	FCC
313036	FCC
313037	FCC
313038	FCC
313039	FCC
313040	FCC
313041	FCC
313042	FCC
313043	FCC
313044	FCC
313045	FCC
313046	FCC
313047	FCC
313048	FCC
313049	FCC
313050	FCC
313051	FCC
313052	FCC
313053	FCC
313054	FCC
313055	FCC
313056	FCC
313057	FCC
313058	FCC
313059	FCC
313060	FCC
313061	FCC
313062	FCC
313063	FCC
313064	FCC
313101	LOG
313102	LOG
313103	LOG
313104	LOG
313105	LOG
313106	LOG
313107	LOG
313108	LOG
313109	LOG
313110	LOG
313111	LOG
313112	LOG
313113	LOG
313114	LOG
313115	LOG
313116	LOG
313117	LOG
313119	LOG
313120	LOG
313121	LOG
313122	LOG
313123	LOG
313134	LOG
314201	FSR
314202	FSR
314203	FSR
314204	FSR
314205	FSR
314206	FSR
314207	FSR
314208	FSR
314209	FSR
314210	FSR
314211	FSR
314212	FSR
314213	FSR
314214	FSR
314215	FSR
314216	FSR
315801	NXA
315802	NXA
315803	NXA
315804	NXA
315805	NXA
315806	NXA
315807	NXA
315808	NXA
315809	NXA
315810	NXA
315811	NXA
315812	NXA
315813	NXA
315814	NXA
315815	NXA
315816	NXA
315817	NXA
315818	NXA
315819	NXA
315820	NXA
315821	NXA
315822	NXA
315823	NXA
315824	NXA
315825	NXA
315826	NXA
315827	NXA
315828	NXA
315829	NXA
315830	NXA
315831	NXA
315832	NXA
315833	NXA
315834	NXA
315835	NXA
315836	NXA
315837	NXA
315838	NXA
315839	NXA
315840	NXA
315841	NXA
315842	NXA
315843	NXA
315844	NXA
315845	NXA
315846	NXA
315847	NXA
315848	NXA
315849	NXA
315850	NXA
315851	NXA
315852	NXA
315853	NXA
315854	NXA
315855	NXA
315856	NXA
315857	NXA
315858	NXA
315859	NXA
315860	NXA
315861	NXA
316997	OLS
317337	FCC
317338	FCC
317339	FCC
317340	FCC
317341	FCC
317342	FCC
317343	FCC
317344	FCC
317345	FCC
317346	FCC
317347	FCC
317348	FCC
317501	NXA
317502	NXA
317503	NXA
317504	NXA
317505	NXA
317506	NXA
317507	NXA
317508	NXA
317509	NXA
317510	NXA
317511	NXA
317512	NXA
317513	NXA
317514	NXA
317515	NXA

Number	Operator
317649	NXA
317650	NXA
317651	NXA
317652	NXA
317653	NXA
317654	NXA
317655	NXA
317656	NXA
317657	NXA
317658	NXA
317659	NXA
317660	NXA
317661	NXA
317662	NXA
317663	NXA
317664	NXA
317665	NXA
317666	NXA
317667	NXA
317668	NXA
317669	NXA
317670	NXA
317671	NXA
317672	NXA
317708	NXA
317709	NXA
317710	NXA
317714	NXA
317719	NXA
317722	NXA
317723	NXA
317729	NXA
317732	NXA
317881	NXA
317882	NXA
317883	NXA
317884	NXA
317885	NXA
317886	NXA
317887	NXA
317888	NXA
317889	NXA
317890	NXA
317891	NXA
317892	NXA
318250	FSR
318251	FSR
318252	FSR
318253	FSR
318254	FSR
318255	FSR
318256	FSR
318257	FSR
318258	FSR
318259	FSR
318260	FSR
318261	FSR
318262	FSR
318263	FSR
318264	FSR
318265	FSR
318266	FSR
318267	FSR
318268	FSR
318269	FSR
318270	FSR
319001	FCC
319002	FCC
319003	FCC
319004	FCC
319005	FCC
319006	FCC
319007	FCC
319008	FCC
319009	FCC
319010	FCC
319011	FCC
319012	FCC
319013	FCC
319214	FCC
319215	FCC
319216	FCC
319217	FCC
319218	FCC
319219	FCC
319220	FCC
319361	FCC
319362	FCC
319363	FCC
319364	FCC
319365	FCC
319366	FCC
319367	FCC
319368	FCC
319369	FCC
319370	FCC
319371	FCC
319372	FCC
319373	FCC
319374	FCC
319375	FCC
319376	FCC
319377	FCC
319378	FCC
319379	FCC
319380	FCC
319381	FCC
319382	FCC
319383	FCC
319384	FCC
319385	FCC
319386	FCC
319421	FCC
319422	FCC
319423	FCC
319424	FCC
319425	FCC
319426	FCC
319427	FCC
319428	FCC
319429	FCC
319430	FCC
319431	FCC
319432	FCC
319433	FCC
319434	FCC
319435	FCC
319436	FCC
319437	FCC
319438	FCC
319439	FCC
319440	FCC
319441	FCC
319442	FCC
319443	FCC
319444	FCC
319445	FCC
319446	FCC
319447	FCC
319448	FCC
319449	FCC
319450	FCC
319451	FCC
319452	FCC
319453	FCC
319454	FCC
319455	FCC
319456	FCC
319457	FCC
319458	FCC
319459	FCC
319460	FCC
320301	FSR
320302	FSR
320303	FSR
320304	FSR
320305	FSR
320306	FSR
320307	FSR
320308	FSR
320309	FSR
320310	FSR
320311	FSR
320312	FSR
320313	FSR
320314	FSR
320315	FSR
320316	FSR
320317	FSR
320318	FSR
320319	FSR
320320	FSR
320321	FSR
320322	FSR
321301	NXA
321302	NXA
321303	NXA
321304	NXA
321305	NXA
321306	NXA
321307	NXA
321308	NXA
321309	NXA
321310	NXA
321311	NXA
321312	NXA
321313	NXA
321314	NXA
321315	NXA
321316	NXA
321317	NXA
321318	NXA
321319	NXA
321320	NXA
321321	NXA
321322	NXA
321323	NXA
321324	NXA
321325	NXA
321326	NXA
321327	NXA
321328	NXA
321329	NXA
321330	NXA
321331	NXA
321332	NXA
321333	NXA
321334	NXA
321335	NXA
321336	NXA
321337	NXA
321338	NXA
321339	NXA
321340	NXA
321341	NXA
321342	NXA
321343	NXA
321344	NXA
321345	NXA
321346	NXA
321347	NXA
321348	NXA
321349	NXA
321350	NXA
321351	NXA
321352	NXA
321353	NXA
321354	NXA
321355	NXA
321356	NXA
321357	NXA
321358	NXA
321359	NXA
321360	NXA
321361	NXA
321362	NXA
321363	NXA
321364	NXA
321365	NXA
321366	NXA
321401	FCC
321402	FCC
321403	FCC
321404	FCC
321405	FCC
321406	FCC
321407	OLS
321408	OLS
321409	OLS
321410	OLS
321411	LMI
321412	LMI
321413	LMI
321414	LMI
321415	LMI
321416	LMI
321417	LMI
321418	OLS
321419	OLS
321420	OLS
321421	NXA
321422	NXA
321423	NXA
321424	NXA
321425	NXA
321426	NXA
321427	NXA
321428	NXA
321429	NXA
321430	NXA
321431	NXA
321432	NXA
321433	NXA
321434	NXA
321435	NXA
321436	NXA
321437	NXA
321438	NXA
321439	NXA
321440	NXA
321441	NXA
321442	NXA
321443	NXA
321444	NXA
321445	NXA
321446	NXA
321447	NXA
321448	NXA
322481	FSR
322482	FSR
322483	FSR
322484	FSR
322485	FSR
323201	LMI
323202	LMI
323203	LMI
323204	LMI
323205	LMI
323206	LMI
323207	LMI
323208	LMI
323209	LMI
323210	LMI
323211	LMI
323212	LMI
323213	LMI
323214	LMI
323215	LMI
323216	LMI
323217	LMI

323218	LMI
323219	LMI
323220	LMI
323221	LMI
323222	LMI
323223	NOR
323224	NOR
323225	NOR
323226	NOR
323227	NOR
323228	NOR
323229	NOR
323230	NOR
323231	NOR
323232	NOR
323233	NOR
323234	NOR
323235	NOR
323236	NOR
323237	NOR
323238	NOR
323239	NOR
323240	LMI
323241	LMI
323242	LMI
323243	LMI
325001	GBR
325002	GBR
325003	GBR
325004	GBR
325005	GBR
325006	GBR
325007	GBR
325008	GBR
325009	GBR
325010	GBR
325011	GBR
325012	GBR
325013	GBR
325014	GBR
325015	GBR
325016	GBR
332001	HEX
332002	HEX
332003	HEX
332004	HEX
332005	HEX
332006	HEX
332007	HEX
332008	HEX
332009	HEX
332010	HEX
332011	HEX
332012	HEX
332013	HEX
332014	HEX
333001	NOR
333002	NOR
333003	NOR
333004	NOR
333005	NOR
333006	NOR
333007	NOR
333008	NOR
333009	NOR
333010	NOR
333011	NOR
333012	NOR
333013	NOR
333014	NOR
333015	NOR
333016	NOR
334001	FSR
334002	FSR
334003	FSR
334004	FSR
334005	FSR
334006	FSR
334007	FSR
334008	FSR
334009	FSR
334010	FSR
334011	FSR
334012	FSR
334013	FSR
334014	FSR
334015	FSR
334016	FSR
334017	FSR
334018	FSR
334019	FSR
334020	FSR
334021	FSR
334022	FSR
334023	FSR
334024	FSR
334025	FSR
334026	FSR
334027	FSR
334028	FSR
334029	FSR
334030	FSR
334031	FSR
334032	FSR
334033	FSR
334034	FSR
334035	FSR
334036	FSR
334037	FSR
334038	FSR
334039	FSR
334040	FSR
350101	LMI
350102	LMI
350103	LMI
350104	LMI
350105	LMI
350106	LMI
350107	LMI
350108	LMI
350109	LMI
350110	LMI
350111	LMI
350112	LMI
350113	LMI
350114	LMI
350115	LMI
350116	LMI
350117	LMI
350118	LMI
350119	LMI
350120	LMI
350121	LMI
350122	LMI
350123	LMI
350124	LMI
350125	LMI
350126	LMI
350127	LMI
350128	LMI
350129	LMI
350130	LMI
350231	LMI
350232	LMI
350233	LMI
350234	LMI
350235	LMI
350236	LMI
350237	LMI
350238	LMI
350239	LMI
350240	LMI
350241	LMI
350242	LMI
350243	LMI
350244	LMI
350245	LMI
350246	LMI
350247	LMI
350248	LMI
350249	LMI
350250	LMI
350251	LMI
350252	LMI
350253	LMI
350254	LMI
350255	LMI
350256	LMI
350257	LMI
350258	LMI
350259	LMI
350260	LMI
350261	LMI
350262	LMI
350263	LMI
350264	LMI
350265	LMI
350266	LMI
350267	LMI
357001	C2C
357002	C2C
357003	C2C
357004	C2C
357005	C2C
357006	C2C
357007	C2C
357008	C2C
357009	C2C
357010	C2C
357011	C2C
357012	C2C
357013	C2C
357014	C2C
357015	C2C
357016	C2C
357017	C2C
357018	C2C
357019	C2C
357020	C2C
357021	C2C
357022	C2C
357023	C2C
357024	C2C
357025	C2C
357026	C2C
357027	C2C
357028	C2C
357029	C2C
357030	C2C
357031	C2C
357032	C2C
357033	C2C
357034	C2C
357035	C2C
357036	C2C
357037	C2C
357038	C2C
357039	C2C
357040	C2C
357041	C2C
357042	C2C
357043	C2C
357044	C2C
357045	C2C
357046	C2C
357201	C2C
357202	C2C
357203	C2C
357204	C2C
357205	C2C
357206	C2C
357207	C2C
357208	C2C
357209	C2C
357210	C2C
357211	C2C
357212	C2C
357213	C2C
357214	C2C
357215	C2C
357216	C2C
357217	C2C
357218	C2C
357219	C2C
357220	C2C
357221	C2C
357222	C2C
357223	C2C
357224	C2C
357225	C2C
357226	C2C
357227	C2C
357228	C2C
360101	NXA
360102	NXA
360103	NXA
360104	NXA
360105	NXA
360106	NXA
360107	NXA
360108	NXA
360109	NXA
360110	NXA
360111	NXA
360112	NXA
360113	NXA
360114	NXA
360115	NXA
360116	NXA
360117	NXA
360118	NXA
360119	NXA
360120	NXA
360121	NXA
360201	HEC
360202	HEC
360203	HEC
360204	HEC
360205	HEC
365501	FCC
365502	FCC
365503	FCC
365504	FCC
365505	FCC
365506	FCC
365507	FCC
365508	FCC
365509	FCC
365510	FCC
365511	FCC
365512	FCC
365513	FCC
365514	FCC
365515	FCC
365516	FCC
365517	FCC
365518	FCC
365519	FCC
365520	FCC
365521	FCC
365522	FCC
365523	FCC
365524	FCC
365525	FCC
365526	OLS
365527	FCC
365528	FCC

365529 FCC
365530 FCC
365531 FCC
365532 FCC
365533 FCC
365534 FCC
365535 FCC
365536 FCC
365537 FCC
365538 FCC
365539 FCC
365540 FCC
365541 FCC

373001 EUS
373002 EUS
373003 EUS
373004 EUS
373005 EUS
373006 EUS
373007 EUS
373008 EUS
373009 EUS
373010 EUS
373011 EUS
373012 EUS
373013 EUS
373014 EUS
373015 EUS
373016 EUS
373017 EUS
373018 EUS
373019 EUS
373020 EUS
373021 EUS
373022 EUS
373101 EUS
373102 EUS
373103 EUS
373104 EUS
373105 EUS
373106 EUS
373107 EUS
373108 EUS
373201 EUS
373202 EUS
373203 EUS
373204 EUS
373205 EUS
373206 EUS
373207 EUS
373208 EUS
373209 EUS
373210 EUS
373211 EUS
373212 EUS
373213 EUS
373214 EUS
373215 EUS
373216 EUS
373217 EUS
373218 EUS
373219 EUS
373220 EUS
373221 EUS
373222 EUS
373223 EUS
373224 EUS
373225 EUS
373226 EUS
373227 EUS
373228 EUS
373229 EUS
373230 EUS
373231 EUS
373232 EUS
373301 EUS
373302 EUS
373303 EUS
373304 EUS
373305 EUS
373306 EUS
373307 EUS
373308 EUS
373309 EUS
373310 EUS
373311 EUS
373312 EUS
373313 EUS
373314 EUS

375301 SET
375302 SET
375303 SET
375304 SET
375305 SET
375306 SET
375307 SET
375308 SET
375309 SET
375310 SET
375601 SET
375602 SET
375603 SET
375604 SET
375605 SET
375606 SET
375607 SET
375608 SET
375609 SET
375610 SET
375611 SET
375612 SET
375613 SET
375614 SET
375615 SET
375616 SET
375617 SET
375618 SET
375619 SET
375620 SET
375621 SET
375622 SET
375623 SET
375624 SET
375625 SET
375626 SET
375627 SET
375628 SET
375629 SET
375630 SET
375701 SET
375702 SET
375703 SET
375704 SET
375705 SET
375706 SET
375707 SET
375708 SET
375709 SET
375710 SET
375711 SET
375712 SET
375713 SET
375714 SET
375715 SET
375801 SET
375802 SET
375803 SET
375804 SET
375805 SET
375806 SET
375807 SET
375808 SET
375809 SET
375810 SET
375811 SET
375812 SET
375813 SET
375814 SET
375815 SET
375816 SET
375817 SET
375818 SET
375819 SET
375820 SET
375821 SET
375822 SET
375823 SET
375824 SET
375825 SET
375826 SET
375827 SET
375828 SET
375829 SET
375830 SET
375901 SET
375902 SET
375903 SET
375904 SET
375905 SET
375906 SET
375907 SET
375908 SET
375909 SET
375910 SET
375911 SET
375912 SET
375913 SET
375914 SET
375915 SET
375916 SET
375917 SET
375918 SET
375919 SET
375920 SET
375921 SET
375922 SET
375923 SET
375924 SET
375925 SET
375926 SET
375927 SET

376001 SET
376002 SET
376003 SET
376004 SET
376005 SET
376006 SET
376007 SET
376008 SET
376009 SET
376010 SET
376011 SET
376012 SET
376013 SET
376014 SET
376015 SET
376016 SET
376017 SET
376018 SET
376019 SET
376020 SET
376021 SET
376022 SET
376023 SET
376024 SET
376025 SET
376026 SET
376027 SET
376028 SET
376029 SET
376030 SET
376031 SET
376032 SET
376033 SET
376034 SET
376035 SET
376036 SET

377101 SOU
377102 SOU
377103 SOU
377104 SOU
377105 SOU
377106 SOU
377107 SOU
377108 SOU
377109 SOU
377110 SOU
377111 SOU
377112 SOU
377113 SOU
377114 SOU
377115 SOU
377116 SOU
377117 SOU
377118 SOU
377119 SOU
377120 SOU
377121 SOU
377122 SOU
377123 SOU
377124 SOU
377125 SOU
377126 SOU
377127 SOU
377128 SOU
377129 SOU
377130 SOU
377131 SOU
377132 SOU
377133 SOU
377134 SOU
377135 SOU
377136 SOU
377137 SOU
377138 SOU
377139 SOU
377140 SOU
377141 SOU
377142 SOU
377143 SOU
377144 SOU
377145 SOU
377146 SOU
377147 SOU
377148 SOU
377149 SOU
377150 SOU
377151 SOU
377152 SOU
377153 SOU
377154 SOU
377155 SOU
377156 SOU
377157 SOU
377158 SOU
377159 SOU
377160 SOU
377161 SOU
377162 SOU
377163 SOU
377164 SOU
377201 SOU
377202 SOU
377203 SOU
377204 SOU
377205 SOU
377206 SOU
377207 SOU
377208 SOU
377209 SOU
377210 SOU

Number	Operator
377211	SOU
377212	SOU
377213	SOU
377214	SOU
377215	SOU
377301	SOU
377302	SOU
377303	SOU
377304	SOU
377305	SOU
377306	SOU
377307	SOU
377308	SOU
377309	SOU
377310	SOU
377311	SOU
377312	SOU
377313	SOU
377314	SOU
377315	SOU
377316	SOU
377317	SOU
377318	SOU
377319	SOU
377320	SOU
377321	SOU
377322	SOU
377323	SOU
377324	SOU
377325	SOU
377326	SOU
377327	SOU
377328	SOU
377401	SOU
377402	SOU
377403	SOU
377404	SOU
377405	SOU
377406	SOU
377407	SOU
377408	SOU
377409	SOU
377410	SOU
377411	SOU
377412	SOU
377413	SOU
377414	SOU
377415	SOU
377416	SOU
377417	SOU
377418	SOU
377419	SOU
377420	SOU
377421	SOU
377422	SOU
377423	SOU
377424	SOU
377425	SOU
377426	SOU
377427	SOU
377428	SOU
377429	SOU
377430	SOU
377431	SOU
377432	SOU
377433	SOU
377434	SOU
377435	SOU
377436	SOU
377437	SOU
377438	SOU
377439	SOU
377440	SOU
377441	SOU
377442	SOU
377443	SOU
377444	SOU
377445	SOU
377446	SOU
377447	SOU
377448	SOU
377449	SOU
377450	SOU
377451	SOU
377452	SOU
377453	SOU
377454	SOU
377455	SOU
377456	SOU
377457	SOU
377458	SOU
377459	SOU
377460	SOU
377461	SOU
377462	SOU
377463	SOU
377464	SOU
377465	SOU
377466	SOU
377467	SOU
377468	SOU
377469	SOU
377470	SOU
377471	SOU
377472	SOU
377473	SOU
377474	SOU
377475	SOU
377501	FCC
377502	FCC
377503	FCC
377504	FCC
377505	FCC
377506	FCC
377507	FCC
377508	FCC
377509	FCC
377510	FCC
377511	FCC
377512	FCC
377513	FCC
377514	FCC
377515	FCC
377516	FCC
377517	FCC
377518	FCC
377519	FCC
377520	FCC
377521	FCC
377522	FCC
377523	FCC
378001	LOG
378002	LOG
378003	LOG
378004	LOG
378005	LOG
378006	LOG
378007	LOG
378008	LOG
378009	LOG
378010	LOG
378011	LOG
378012	LOG
378013	LOG
378014	LOG
378015	LOG
378016	LOG
378017	LOG
378018	LOG
378019	LOG
378020	LOG
378021	LOG
378022	LOG
378023	LOG
378024	LOG
378135	LOG
378135	LOG
378136	LOG
378137	LOG
378138	LOG
378139	LOG
378140	LOG
378141	LOG
378142	LOG
378143	LOG
378144	LOG
378145	LOG
378146	LOG
378147	LOG
378148	LOG
378149	LOG
378150	LOG
378151	LOG
378152	LOG
378153	LOG
378154	LOG
378225	LOG
378226	LOG
378227	LOG
378228	LOG
378229	LOG
378230	LOG
378231	LOG
378232	LOG
378233	LOG
378234	LOG
378235	LOG
378236	LOG
390001	VWC
390002	VWC
390003	VWC
390004	VWC
390005	VWC
390006	VWC
390007	VWC
390008	VWC
390009	VWC
390010	VWC
390011	VWC
390012	VWC
390013	VWC
390014	VWC
390015	VWC
390016	VWC
390017	VWC
390018	VWC
390019	VWC
390020	VWC
390021	VWC
390022	VWC
390023	VWC
390024	VWC
390025	VWC
390026	VWC
390027	VWC
390028	VWC
390029	VWC
390030	VWC
390031	VWC
390032	VWC
390033	OLS
390034	VWC
390035	VWC
390036	VWC
390037	VWC
390038	VWC
390039	VWC
390040	VWC
390041	VWC
390042	VWC
390043	VWC
390044	VWC
390045	VWC
390046	VWC
390047	VWC
390048	VWC
390049	VWC
390050	VWC
390051	VWC
390052	VWC
390053	VWC
395001	SET
395002	SET
395003	SET
395004	SET
395005	SET
395006	SET
395007	SET
395008	SET
395009	SET
395010	SET
395011	SET
395012	SET
395013	SET
395014	SET
395015	SET
395016	SET
395017	SET
395018	SET
395019	SET
395020	SET
395021	SET
395022	SET
395023	SET
395024	SET
395025	SET
395026	SET
395027	SET
395028	SET
395029	SET
411198	PRE
421304	KRS
421399	PRE
421497	SWT
421498	SWT
421884	KRS
423576	KRS
424001	BOM
442401	SOU
442402	SOU
442403	SOU
442404	SOU
442405	SOU
442406	SOU
442407	SOU
442408	SOU
442409	SOU
442410	SOU
442411	SOU
442412	SOU
442413	SOU
442414	SOU
442415	SOU
442416	SOU
442417	SOU
442418	SOU
442419	SOU
442420	SOU
442421	SOU
442422	SOU
442423	SOU
442424	SOU
444001	SWT
444002	SWT
444003	SWT
444004	SWT
444005	SWT

444006	SWT
444007	SWT
444008	SWT
444009	SWT
444010	SWT
444011	SWT
444012	SWT
444013	SWT
444014	SWT
444015	SWT
444016	SWT
444017	SWT
444018	SWT
444019	SWT
444020	SWT
444021	SWT
444022	SWT
444023	SWT
444024	SWT
444025	SWT
444026	SWT
444027	SWT
444028	SWT
444029	SWT
444030	SWT
444031	SWT
444032	SWT
444033	SWT
444034	SWT
444035	SWT
444036	SWT
444037	SWT
444038	SWT
444039	SWT
444040	SWT
444041	SWT
444042	SWT
444043	SWT
444044	SWT
444045	SWT
450001	SWT
450002	SWT
450003	SWT
450004	SWT
450005	SWT
450006	SWT
450007	SWT
450008	SWT
450009	SWT
450010	SWT
450011	SWT
450012	SWT
450013	SWT
450014	SWT
450015	SWT
450016	SWT
450017	SWT
450018	SWT
450019	SWT
450020	SWT
450021	SWT
450022	SWT
450023	SWT
450024	SWT
450025	SWT
450026	SWT
450027	SWT
450028	SWT
450029	SWT
450030	SWT
450031	SWT
450032	SWT
450033	SWT
450034	SWT
450035	SWT
450036	SWT
450037	SWT
450038	SWT
450039	SWT
450040	SWT
450041	SWT
450042	SWT
450071	SWT
450072	SWT
450073	SWT
450074	SWT
450075	SWT
450076	SWT
450077	SWT
450078	SWT
450079	SWT
450080	SWT
450081	SWT
450082	SWT
450083	SWT
450084	SWT
450085	SWT
450086	SWT
450087	SWT
450088	SWT
450089	SWT
450090	SWT
450091	SWT
450092	SWT
450093	SWT
450094	SWT
450095	SWT
450096	SWT
450097	SWT
450098	SWT
450099	SWT
450100	SWT
450101	SWT
450102	SWT
450103	SWT
450104	SWT
450105	SWT
450106	SWT
450107	SWT
450108	SWT
450109	SWT
450110	SWT
450111	SWT
450112	SWT
450113	SWT
450114	SWT
450115	SWT
450116	SWT
450117	SWT
450118	SWT
450119	SWT
450120	SWT
450121	SWT
450122	SWT
450123	SWT
450124	SWT
450125	SWT
450126	SWT
450127	SWT
450543	SWT
450544	SWT
450545	SWT
450546	SWT
450547	SWT
450548	SWT
450549	SWT
450550	SWT
450551	SWT
450552	SWT
450553	SWT
450554	SWT
450555	SWT
450556	SWT
450557	SWT
450558	SWT
450559	SWT
450560	SWT
450561	SWT
450562	SWT
450563	SWT
450564	SWT
450565	SWT
450566	SWT
450567	SWT
450568	SWT
450569	SWT
450570	SWT
455701	SWT
455702	SWT
455703	SWT
455704	SWT
455705	SWT
455706	SWT
455707	SWT
455708	SWT
455709	SWT
455710	SWT
455711	SWT
455712	SWT
455713	SWT
455714	SWT
455715	SWT
455716	SWT
455717	SWT
455718	SWT
455719	SWT
455720	SWT
455721	SWT
455722	SWT
455723	SWT
455724	SWT
455725	SWT
455726	SWT
455727	SWT
455728	SWT
455729	SWT
455730	SWT
455731	SWT
455732	SWT
455733	SWT
455734	SWT
455735	SWT
455736	SWT
455737	SWT
455738	SWT
455739	SWT
455740	SWT
455741	SWT
455742	SWT
455750	SWT
455801	SOU
455802	SOU
455803	SOU
455804	SOU
455805	SOU
455806	SOU
455807	SOU
455808	SOU
455809	SOU
455810	SOU
455811	SOU
455812	SOU
455813	SOU
455814	SOU
455815	SOU
455816	SOU
455817	SOU
455818	SOU
455819	SOU
455820	SOU
455821	SOU
455822	SOU
455823	SOU
455824	SOU
455825	SOU
455826	SOU
455827	SOU
455828	SOU
455829	SOU
455830	SOU
455831	SOU
455832	SOU
455833	SOU
455834	SOU
455835	SOU
455836	SOU
455837	SOU
455838	SOU
455839	SOU
455840	SOU
455841	SOU
455842	SOU
455843	SOU
455844	SOU
455845	SOU
455846	SOU
455847	SWT
455848	SWT
455849	SWT
455850	SWT
455851	SWT
455852	SWT
455853	SWT
455854	SWT
455855	SWT
455856	SWT
455857	SWT
455858	SWT
455859	SWT
455860	SWT
455861	SWT
455862	SWT
455863	SWT
455864	SWT
455865	SWT
455866	SWT
455867	SWT
455868	SWT
455869	SWT
455870	SWT
455871	SWT
455872	SWT
455873	SWT
455874	SWT
455901	SWT
455902	SWT
455903	SWT
455904	SWT
455905	SWT
455906	SWT
455907	SWT
455908	SWT
455909	SWT
455910	SWT
455911	SWT
455912	SWT
455913	SWT
455914	SWT
455915	SWT
455916	SWT
455917	SWT
455918	SWT
455919	SWT
455920	SWT
456001	SOU
456002	SOU
456003	SOU
456004	SOU
456005	SOU
456006	SOU
456007	SOU
456008	SOU

Number	Operator
456009	SOU
456010	SOU
456011	SOU
456012	SOU
456013	SOU
456014	SOU
456015	SOU
456016	SOU
456017	SOU
456018	SOU
456019	SOU
456020	SOU
456021	SOU
456022	SOU
456023	SOU
456024	SOU
458001	SWT
458002	SWT
458003	SWT
458004	SWT
458005	SWT
458006	SWT
458007	SWT
458008	SWT
458009	SWT
458010	SWT
458011	SWT
458012	SWT
458013	SWT
458014	SWT
458015	SWT
458016	SWT
458017	SWT
458018	SWT
458019	SWT
458020	SWT
458021	SWT
458022	SWT
458023	SWT
458024	SWT
458025	SWT
458026	SWT
458027	SWT
458028	SWT
458029	SWT
458030	SWT
460001	SOU
460002	SOU
460003	SOU
460004	SOU
460005	SOU
460006	SOU
460007	SOU
460008	SOU
465001	SET
465002	SET
465003	SET
465004	SET
465005	SET
465006	SET
465007	SET
465008	SET
465009	SET
465010	SET
465011	SET
465012	SET
465013	SET
465014	SET
465015	SET
465016	SET
465017	SET
465018	SET
465019	SET
465020	SET
465021	SET
465022	SET
465023	SET
465024	SET
465025	SET
465026	SET
465027	SET
465028	SET
465029	SET
465030	SET
465031	SET
465032	SET
465033	SET
465034	SET
465035	SET
465036	SET
465037	SET
465038	SET
465039	SET
465040	SET
465041	SET
465042	SET
465043	SET
465044	SET
465045	SET
465046	SET
465047	SET
465048	SET
465049	SET
465050	SET
465151	SET
465152	SET
465153	SET
465154	SET
465155	SET
465156	SET
465157	SET
465158	SET
465159	SET
465160	SET
465161	SET
465162	SET
465163	SET
465164	SET
465165	SET
465166	SET
465167	SET
465168	SET
465169	SET
465170	SET
465171	SET
465172	SET
465173	SET
465174	SET
465175	SET
465176	SET
465177	SET
465178	SET
465179	SET
465180	SET
465181	SET
465182	SET
465183	SET
465184	SET
465185	SET
465186	SET
465187	SET
465188	SET
465189	SET
465190	SET
465191	SET
465192	SET
465193	SET
465194	SET
465195	SET
465196	SET
465197	SET
465235	SET
465236	SET
465237	SET
465238	SET
465239	SET
465240	SET
465241	SET
465242	SET
465243	SET
465244	SET
465245	SET
465246	SET
465247	SET
465248	SET
465249	SET
465250	SET
465901	SET
465902	SET
465903	SET
465904	SET
465905	SET
465906	SET
465907	SET
465908	SET
465909	SET
465910	SET
465911	SET
465912	SET
465913	SET
465914	SET
465915	SET
465916	SET
465917	SET
465918	SET
465919	SET
465920	SET
465921	SET
465922	SET
465923	SET
465924	SET
465925	SET
465926	SET
465927	SET
465928	SET
465929	SET
465930	SET
465931	SET
465932	SET
465933	SET
465934	SET
466001	SET
466002	SET
466003	SET
466004	SET
466005	SET
466006	SET
466007	SET
466008	SET
466009	SET
466010	SET
466011	SET
466012	SET
466013	SET
466014	SET
466015	SET
466016	SET
466017	SET
466018	SET
466019	SET
466020	SET
466021	SET
466022	SET
466023	SET
466024	SET
466025	SET
466026	SET
466027	SET
466028	SET
466029	SET
466030	SET
466031	SET
466032	SET
466033	SET
466034	SET
466035	SET
466036	SET
466037	SET
466038	SET
466039	SET
466040	SET
466041	SET
466042	SET
466043	SET
483002	SIL
483004	SIL
483006	SIL
483007	SIL
483008	SIL
483009	SIL
489102	NRL
489105	NRL
489106	NRL
489109	NRL
507001	MER
507002	MER
507003	MER
507004	MER
507005	MER
507006	MER
507007	MER
507008	MER
507009	MER
507010	MER
507011	MER
507012	MER
507013	MER
507014	MER
507015	MER
507016	MER
507017	MER
507018	MER
507019	MER
507020	MER
507021	MER
507023	MER
507024	MER
507025	MER
507026	MER
507027	MER
507028	MER
507029	MER
507030	MER
507031	MER
507032	MER
507033	MER
508103	MER
508104	MER
508108	MER
508110	MER
508111	MER
508112	MER
508114	MER
508115	MER
508117	MER
508120	MER
508122	MER
508123	MER
508124	MER
508125	MER
508126	MER
508127	MER
508128	MER
508130	MER
508131	MER
508134	MER
508136	MER

508137 MER
508138 MER
508139 MER
508140 MER
508141 MER
508143 MER
508201 OLS
508202 OLS
508203 OLS
508204 OLS
508205 OLS
508206 OLS
508207 OLS
508208 OLS
508209 OLS
508210 OLS
508211 OLS
508212 OLS
508301 OLS
508302 OLS
503303 OLS

901001 PRE

Coaching Stock
41 WCR
159 WCR
213 VSO
239 VSO
243 VSO
245 VSO
254 VSO
255 VSO
261 VSO
264 VSO
280 VSO
281 VSO
283 VSO
284 VSO
285 VSO
286 VSO
288 VSO
292 VSO
293 VSO
301 VSO
302 VSO
307 VSO
308 VSO
310 RAF
313 GSW
316 FSL
317 GSW
319 GSW
321 FSL
324 GSW
325 VSO
326 WCR
329 GSW
331 GSW
335 VTN
337 FSL
348 WCR
349 VTN
350 WCR
352 WCR
353 VTN
354 WCR
464 BOK
504 WCR
506 WCR
546 WCR
548 WCR
549 WCR
550 WCR
551 WCR
552 WCR
553 WCR
586 WCR
807 WCR

1105 MHR
1200 RIV
1203 OLS
1204 OLS
1205 NRL
1207 OLS
1209 OLS
1211 OLS
1212 RIV
1214 OLS
1219 OLS
1221 OLS
1250 RIV
1252 CAD
1253 OLS
1254 CAD
1256 NRL
1258 OLS
1260 RIV
1375 BOK
1566 VSO
1644 WCR
1650 WCR
1651 RIV
1652 WCR
1655 WCR
1657 DRS
1658 DBS
1659 RAF
1663 WCR
1670 WCR
1671 RIV
1679 DBS
1680 DBS
1683 RIV
1691 RIV
1692 RIV
1698 RIV
1699 RIV
1730 SRP
1800 WCR
1813 RIV
1823 NYM
1832 RIV
1840 WCR
1842 RIV
1859 SRP
1860 WCR
1861 WCR
1863 RIV
1882 WCR
1953 VSO
1961 WCR
1999 GSW

2127 WCR
2833 WCR
2834 RIV
2902 NRL
2904 NRL
2915 NRL
2916 NRL
2917 NRL
2918 NRL
2919 NRL
2920 NRL
2921 NRL
2922 NRL
2923 NRL

3066 RIV
3068 RIV
3069 RIV
3096 BOK
3097 RIV
3098 RIV
3105 WCR
3106 WCR
3107 RIV
3110 RIV
3112 RIV
3113 WCR
3114 RIV
3115 BOK
3117 WCR
3119 RIV
3120 RIV
3121 RIV
3122 RIV
3123 RIV
3124 RIV
3125 JHS
3127 RIV
3128 WCR
3130 WCR
3131 RIV
3132 RIV
3133 RIV
3136 WCR
3140 RIV
3141 RIV
3143 WCR
3144 RIV
3146 RIV
3147 RIV
3148 JHS
3149 RIV
3150 BOK
3174 VSO
3181 RIV
3182 VSO
3186 DBS
3188 RAF
3223 RIV
3228 RIV
3229 OLS
3231 RAF
3232 VSO
3240 RIV
3244 RIV
3247 VSO
3255 DBS
3267 VSO
3269 DBS
3273 VSO
3275 VSO
3277 RIV
3278 DRS
3279 RIV
3292 DBS
3295 RIV
3303 OLS
3304 RIV
3309 WCR
3313 WCR
3314 RIV
3318 DBS
3325 RIV
3326 WCR
3330 RIV
3331 DBS
3333 RIV
3334 RIV
3336 RIV
3338 DBS
3340 RIV
3344 RIV
3345 RIV
3348 RIV
3350 WCR
3351 OLS
3352 WCR
3356 RIV
3358 DBS
3359 WCR
3360 WCR
3362 WCR
3364 RIV
3366 CAD
3368 DBS
3374 CAD
3375 DBS
3379 RIV
3384 RIV
3385 DRS
3386 RIV
3388 DBS
3390 RIV
3392 WCR
3395 WCR
3397 RIV
3399 DBS
3400 DBS
3408 WCR
3414 DBS
3416 WCR
3417 RIV
3424 DBS
3426 RIV
3431 WCR
3434 OLS
3438 OLS
3766 WCR
3860 NYM
3872 NYM
3948 NYM

4198 NYM
4252 NYM
4290 NYM
4326 RIV
4455 NYM
4786 NYM
4817 NYM
4831 BOK
4832 BOK
4836 BOK
4856 BOK
4860 WCR
4902 RIV
4905 WCR
4912 WCR
4925 DBS
4927 RIV
4931 WCR
4932 WCR
4940 WCR
4946 RIV
4949 RIV
4951 WCR
4954 WCR
4956 DBS
4958 WCR
4959 RIV
4960 WCR
4973 WCR
4984 WCR
4986 RIV
4991 RIV
4994 WCR
4996 RIV
4997 WCR
4998 RIV
4999 RIV

5000 NYM
5005 DBS
5007 RIV
5008 RIV
5009 RIV
5023 RIV
5027 RIV
5028 BOK
5029 NYM
5032 WCR

Number	Operator
5033	WCR
5035	WCR
5037	DBS
5040	RIV
5044	WCR
5067	RAF
5125	WCR
5148	OLS
5171	WCR
5179	OLS
5183	OLS
5186	OLS
5193	OLS
5194	OLS
5200	WCR
5212	OLS
5216	WCR
5221	OLS
5222	WCR
5229	WCR
5236	WCR
5237	WCR
5239	WCR
5249	WCR
5276	RIV
5278	WCR
5292	RIV
5299	WCR
5309	RIV
5322	RIV
5331	DBS
5341	RIV
5350	RIV
5365	RIV
5366	RIV
5376	RIV
5386	DBS
5412	BOK
5419	WCR
5453	WCR
5463	WCR
5467	RIV
5478	WCR
5482	DBS
5487	WCR
5491	WCR
5494	RIV
5520	RRS
5569	WCR
5600	WCR
5631	DBS
5632	DBS
5636	OLS
5647	RIV
5657	DBS
5669	WCR
5679	OLS
5700	CWR
5727	WCR
5737	OLS
5739	RIV
5740	OLS
5745	OLS
5748	RIV
5750	OLS
5754	OLS
5756	WCR
5769	RIV
5788	OLS
5789	OLS
5791	CAD
5792	RIV
5793	OLS
5797	OLS
5810	CAD
5821	OLS
5853	ATW
5854	SEC
5866	OLS
5869	ATW
5874	WCR
5881	OLS
5886	OLS
5888	OLS
5899	OLS
5900	OLS
5901	CAD
5903	OLS
5905	OLS
5906	OLS
5908	OLS
5910	RIV
5911	RIV
5912	OLS
5913	ATW
5917	WCR
5919	CAD
5921	RIV
5922	DBS
5924	DBS
5925	OLS
5928	WCR
5929	RIV
5930	OLS
5933	OLS
5934	RIV
5936	OLS
5937	RIV
5940	OLS
5943	OLS
5945	RIV
5946	RIV
5947	OLS
5948	OLS
5949	OLS
5952	RIV
5954	DBS
5955	RIV
5957	OLS
5958	OLS
5959	DBS
5960	OLS
5961	RIV
5962	OLS
5964	RIV
5965	ATW
5969	OLS
5976	ATW
5977	OLS
5978	OLS
5980	OLS
5981	NRL
5984	RIV
5985	RIV
5983	OLS
5987	RIV
5989	DRS
5991	OLS
5995	CAD
5997	RIV
5998	RIV
6000	WCR
6001	CAD
6006	RIV
6008	CAD
6009	OLS
6012	OLS
6013	ATW
6014	WCR
6016	OLS
6021	OLS
6022	WCR
6024	RIV
6027	RIV
6028	OLS
6029	OLS
6031	OLS
6035	ATW
6036	DBS
6037	OLS
6038	RIV
6041	WCR
6042	RIV
6045	CAD
6046	CAD
6049	OLS
6050	OLS
6051	RIV
6052	OLS
6053	OLS
6054	RIV
6055	RIV
6056	RIV
6059	OLS
6061	OLS
6064	CAD
6067	RIV
6073	OLS
6101	OLS
6103	WCR
6104	RIV
6107	RIV
6110	DBS
6115	WCR
6117	CAD
6119	ATW
6120	OLS
6121	OLS
6122	CAD
6134	CAD
6135	WCR
6136	OLS
6137	ATW
6138	RIV
6139	DBS
6141	RIV
6148	WCR
6150	OLS
6151	OLS
6152	DBS
6153	RIV
6158	RIV
6160	OLS
6162	ATW
6164	OLS
6168	OLS
6170	ATW
6173	CAD
6175	OLS
6176	RIV
6177	RIV
6179	OLS
6183	ATW
6310	RIV
6311	DBS
6312	WCR
6313	VSO
6320	RIV
6321	SIE
6322	SIE
6323	SIE
6324	SIE
6325	SIE
6330	FGW
6336	FGW
6338	FGW
6340	ICE
6344	ICE
6346	ICE
6348	FGW
6352	ICE
6353	ICE
6354	ICE
6355	ICE
6358	ICE
6359	ICE
6392	EMT
6395	EMT
6397	EMT
6398	EMT
6399	EMT
6523	WCR
6528	WCR
6700	FSR
6701	FSR
6702	FSR
6703	FSR
6704	FSR
6705	FSR
6706	FSR
6707	FSR
6708	FSR
6720	RIV
6722	CWR
6723	CWR
6724	CWR
9104	WCR
9267	NYM
9274	NYM
9391	WCR
9392	WCR
9393	ICE
9394	ICE
9419	DRS
9428	DRS
9440	WCR
9448	WCR
9479	DRS
9480	OLS
9481	NRL
9488	CWR
9490	OLS
9493	WCR
9494	DBS
9496	OLS
9497	OLS
9498	OLS
9500	OLS
9502	VSO
9503	ATW
9504	RIV
9505	OLS
9506	CAD
9507	RIV
9508	CAD
9509	ATW
9513	DRS
9516	OLS
9520	RIV
9521	ATW
9522	OLS
9523	OLS
9524	ATW
9525	OLS
9526	RIV
9527	RIV
9529	DBS
9537	RIV
9538	OLS
9539	ATW
9701	NRL
9702	NRL
9703	NRL
9704	OLS
9705	OLS
9707	OLS
9708	NRL
9709	OLS
9710	OLS
9714	NRL
10200	NXA
10202	CAD

Number	Operator
10203	NXA
10204	3MP
10205	DBS
10206	NXA
10208	WSR
10211	DBS
10212	VWC
10213	CAD
10214	NXA
10215	WSR
10216	NXA
10217	VWC
10219	FGW
10223	NXA
10225	FGW
10226	DBS
10228	NXA
10229	NXA
10230	WSR
10231	OLS
10232	FGW
10233	DBS
10235	WSR
10236	WSR
10237	DRS
10240	OLS
10241	NXA
10242	WSR
10245	OLS
10246	WSR
10247	NXA
10249	CAD
10250	DBS
10253	OLS
10255	WSR
10256	OLS
10257	WSR
10259	OLS
10260	OLS
10300	ICE
10301	ICE
10302	ICE
10303	ICE
10304	ICE
10305	ICE
10306	ICE
10307	ICE
10308	ICE
10309	ICE
10310	ICE
10311	ICE
10312	ICE
10313	ICE
10314	ICE
10317	ICE
10318	ICE
10319	ICE
10320	ICE
10321	ICE
10323	ICE
10324	ICE
10325	ICE
10326	ICE
10328	ICE
10329	ICE
10330	ICE
10331	ICE
10332	ICE
10333	ICE
10401	NXA
10402	NXA
10403	NXA
10404	NXA
10405	NXA
10406	NXA
10501	FSR
10502	FSR
10504	FSR
10506	FSR
10507	FSR
10508	FSR
10513	FSR
10516	FSR
10519	FSR
10520	FSR
10522	FSR
10523	FSR
10526	FSR
10527	FSR
10529	FSR
10531	FSR
10532	FGW
10534	FGW
10540	OLS
10541	VSO
10542	FSR
10543	FSR
10544	FSR
10546	DBS
10547	OLS
10548	FSR
10551	FSR
10556	VSO
10562	FSR
10563	FGW
10565	FSR
10569	VSO
10580	FSR
10584	FGW
10588	CAD
10589	FGW
10590	FGW
10594	FGW
10596	OLS
10597	FSR
10598	FSR
10600	FSR
10601	FGW
10605	FSR
10607	FSR
10610	FSR
10612	FGW
10613	FSR
10614	FSR
10616	FGW
10617	FSR
10647	DBS
10648	FSR
10650	FSR
10666	FSR
10667	CWR
10675	FSR
10680	FSR
10682	OLS
10683	FSR
10688	FSR
10689	FSR
10690	FSR
10693	FSR
10698	CWR
10699	FSR
10701	DBS
10703	FSR
10706	FSR
10710	DBS
10713	OLS
10714	FSR
10718	FSR
10719	FSR
10722	FSR
10723	FSR
10729	VSO
10731	DBS
10733	CWR
11005	DBS
11006	OLS
11007	VWC
11011	OLS
11013	DRS
11018	VWC
11019	DRS
11021	NXA
11026	OLS
11027	WSR
11029	WSR
11030	DRS
11031	WSR
11033	DRS
11039	DBS
11040	DBS
11042	DBS
11044	DRS
11046	DRS
11048	VWC
11052	DBS
11054	DRS
11058	DBS
11064	VWC
11065	CAD
11066	NXA
11067	NXA
11068	NXA
11069	NXA
11070	NXA
11071	WSR
11072	NXA
11073	NXA
11074	NXA
11075	NXA
11076	NXA
11077	NXA
11078	NXA
11079	CAD
11080	NXA
11081	NXA
11082	NXA
11083	WSR
11084	VWC
11085	NXA
11086	VWC
11087	NXA
11088	NXA
11089	CAD
11090	NXA
11091	NXA
11092	NXA
11093	NXA
11094	NXA
11095	NXA
11096	NXA
11097	WSR
11098	NXA
11099	NXA
11100	NXA
11101	NXA
11201	ICE
11219	ICE
11229	ICE
11237	ICE
11241	ICE
11244	ICE
11273	ICE
11277	ICE
11278	ICE
11279	ICE
11280	ICE
11281	ICE
11282	ICE
11283	ICE
11284	ICE
11285	ICE
11286	ICE
11287	ICE
11288	ICE
11289	ICE
11290	ICE
11291	ICE
11292	ICE
11293	ICE
11294	ICE
11295	ICE
11298	ICE
11299	ICE
11301	ICE
11302	ICE
11303	ICE
11304	ICE
11305	ICE
11306	ICE
11307	ICE
11308	ICE
11309	ICE
11310	ICE
11311	ICE
11312	ICE
11313	ICE
11314	ICE
11315	ICE
11316	ICE
11317	ICE
11318	ICE
11319	ICE
11320	ICE
11321	ICE
11322	ICE
11323	ICE
11324	ICE
11325	ICE
11326	ICE
11327	ICE
11328	ICE
11329	ICE
11330	ICE
11401	ICE
11402	ICE
11403	ICE
11404	ICE
11405	ICE
11406	ICE
11407	ICE
11408	ICE
11409	ICE
11410	ICE
11411	ICE
11412	ICE
11413	ICE
11414	ICE
11415	ICE
11416	ICE
11417	ICE
11418	ICE
11419	ICE
11420	ICE
11421	ICE
11422	ICE
11423	ICE
11424	ICE
11425	ICE
11426	ICE
11427	ICE
11428	ICE
11429	ICE
11430	ICE
11998	ICE
11999	ICE
12005	NXA
12009	NXA
12011	VWC
12012	NXA
12013	NXA
12014	WSR
12015	NXA
12016	NXA

12017	VWC	12107	NXA	12315	ICE	12453	ICE	17056	RIV
12019	NXA	12108	NXA	12316	ICE	12454	ICE	17077	RIV
12021	NXA	12109	NXA	12317	ICE	12456	ICE	17080	VSO
12022	OLS	12110	NXA	12318	ICE	12457	ICE	17096	SUP
12024	NXA	12111	NXA	12319	ICE	12458	ICE	17102	WCR
12026	NXA	12114	NXA	12320	ICE	12459	ICE	17105	RIV
12027	NXA	12115	NXA	12321	ICE	12460	ICE	17144	CWR
12029	OLS	12116	NXA	12322	ICE	12461	ICE	17159	DRS
12030	NXA	12117	WSR	12323	ICE	12462	ICE	17168	WCR
12031	NXA	12118	NXA	12324	ICE	12463	ICE	17170	CWR
12032	NXA	12119	WSR	12325	ICE	12464	ICE	17161	DBS
12034	NXA	12120	NXA	12326	ICE	12465	ICE	17167	VSO
12035	NXA	12122	VWC	12327	ICE	12466	ICE	17173	FGW
12036	OLS	12124	VWC	12328	ICE	12467	ICE	17174	FGW
12037	NXA	12125	NXA	12329	ICE	12468	ICE	17175	FGW
12038	WSR	12126	NXA	12330	ICE	12469	ICE		
12040	NXA	12127	WSR	12331	ICE	12470	ICE	18756	WCR
12041	NXA	12129	NXA	12400	ICE	12471	ICE	18767	WCR
12042	NXA	12130	NXA	12401	ICE	12472	ICE	18806	WCR
12043	WSR	12131	WSR	12402	ICE	12473	ICE	18808	WCR
12045	OLS	12132	NXA	12403	ICE	12474	ICE	18837	WCR
12046	NXA	12133	VWC	12404	ICE	12476	ICE	18862	WCR
12047	OLS	12134	OLS	12405	ICE	12477	ICE	18893	WCR
12048	WSR	12137	NXA	12406	ICE	12478	ICE		
12049	NXA	12138	VWC	12407	ICE	12480	ICE	19013	WCR
12051	NXA	12139	OLS	12409	ICE	12481	ICE	19208	WCR
12053	WSR	12141	NXA	12410	ICE	12483	ICE		
12054	VWC	12142	OLS	12411	ICE	12484	ICE	21096	SUP
12056	NXA	12143	NXA	12414	ICE	12485	ICE	21224	RAF
12057	NXA	12144	OLS	12415	ICE	12486	ICE	21232	SUP
12059	VWC	12145	WSR	12417	ICE	12488	ICE	21236	SUP
12060	NXA	12146	NXA	12419	ICE	12489	ICE	21241	SRP
12061	NXA	12147	NXA	12420	ICE	12513	ICE	21245	RIV
12062	NXA	12148	NXA	12421	ICE	12514	ICE	21252	MHR
12063	OLS	12150	NXA	12422	ICE	12515	ICE	21256	WCR
12064	NXA	12151	NXA	12423	ICE	12518	ICE	21266	WCR
12065	OLS	12153	NXA	12424	ICE	12519	ICE	21268	SUP
12066	NXA	12154	NXA	12425	ICE	12520	ICE	21269	RIV
12067	NXA	12156	OLS	12426	ICE	12522	ICE	21272	RIV
12069	WSR	12158	OLS	12427	ICE	12526	ICE		
12072	WSR	12159	NXA	12428	ICE	12533	ICE	34525	WCR
12073	NXA	12160	OLS	12429	ICE	12534	ICE	35089	NYM
12078	OLS	12161	FGW	12430	ICE	12538	ICE	35185	SRP
12079	NXA	12163	OLS	12431	ICE			35290	DBS
12081	NXA	12164	NXA	12432	ICE	13306	WCR	35317	SUP
12082	NXA	12166	NXA	12433	ICE	13320	WCR	35322	SUP
12083	OLS	12167	NXA	12434	ICE	13321	WCR	35329	SUP
12084	NXA	12169	WSR	12436	ICE	13229	BOK	35333	SUP
12087	OLS	12170	NXA	12437	ICE	13230	BOK	35407	WCR
12089	NXA	12171	NXA	12438	ICE	13440	WCR	35449	SUP
12090	NXA	12300	ICE	12439	ICE	13508	RAF	35453	SUP
12091	NXA	12301	ICE	12440	ICE	13581	RRS	35457	SUP
12092	OLS	12302	ICE	12441	ICE	13583	RRS	35459	WCR
12093	NXA	12303	ICE	12442	ICE			35461	SUP
12094	VWC	12304	ICE	12443	ICE	14007	SUP	35463	SUP
12095	OLS	12305	ICE	12444	ICE	16156	NYM	35464	SUP
12097	NXA	12307	ICE	12445	ICE			35465	SUP
12098	NXA	12308	ICE	12446	ICE	17013	SUP	35466	VSO
12099	NXA	12309	ICE	12447	ICE	17015	RIV	35468	SUP
12100	FGW	12310	ICE	12448	ICE	17018	VTN	35469	RIV
12101	OLS	12311	ICE	12449	ICE	17019	SUP	35470	SUP
12103	NXA	12312	ICE	12450	ICE	17025	SUP	35476	SUP
12105	NXA	12313	ICE	12452	ICE	17041	SUP	35479	SUP

Number	Operator
35486	SUP
35508	SUP
35517	SUP
35518	SUP
40101	FGW
40102	FGW
40103	FGW
40104	FGW
40105	FGW
40106	FGW
40107	FGW
40108	FGW
40109	FGW
40110	FGW
40111	FGW
40112	FGW
40113	FGW
40114	FGW
40115	FGW
40116	FGW
40117	FGW
40118	FGW
40204	FGW
40205	FGW
40207	FGW
40208	FGW
40209	FGW
40210	FGW
40221	FGW
40228	FGW
40231	FGW
40402	OLS
40403	OLS
40416	OLS
40417	OLS
40419	OLS
40424	GTL
40425	OLS
40426	GTL
40433	GTL
40434	OLS
40700	EMT
40701	ICE
40702	ICE
40703	FGW
40704	ICE
40705	ICE
40706	ICE
40707	FGW
40708	ICE
40709	FGW
40710	FGW
40711	ICE
40712	FGW
40713	FGW
40714	FGW
40715	FGW
40716	FGW
40717	FGW
40718	FGW
40720	ICE
40721	FGW
40722	FGW
40724	FGW
40725	FGW
40726	FGW
40727	FGW
40728	EMT
40729	EMT
40730	EMT
40731	FGW
40733	FGW
40734	FGW
40735	ICE
40736	FGW
40737	ICE
40738	FGW
40739	FGW
40740	ICE
40741	EMT
40742	ICE
40743	FGW
40744	FGW
40745	FGW
40746	EMT
40747	FGW
40748	ICE
40749	EMT
40750	ICE
40751	EMT
40752	FGW
40753	EMT
40754	EMT
40755	FGW
40756	EMT
40757	FGW
40801	FGW
40802	FGW
40803	FGW
40806	FGW
40807	FGW
40808	FGW
40809	FGW
40810	FGW
40900	FGW
40901	FGW
40902	FGW
40903	FGW
40904	FGW
41003	FGW
41004	FGW
41005	FGW
41006	FGW
41007	FGW
41008	FGW
41009	FGW
41010	FGW
41011	FGW
41012	FGW
41015	FGW
41016	FGW
41017	FGW
41018	FGW
41019	FGW
41020	FGW
41021	FGW
41022	FGW
41023	FGW
41024	FGW
41026	AXC
41027	FGW
41028	FGW
41029	FGW
41030	FGW
41031	FGW
41032	FGW
41033	FGW
41034	FGW
41035	AXC
41037	FGW
41038	FGW
41039	ICE
41040	ICE
41041	EMT
41044	ICE
41045	FGW
41046	EMT
41051	FGW
41052	FGW
41055	FGW
41056	FGW
41057	EMT
41058	ICE
41059	FGW
41061	EMT
41062	EMT
41063	EMT
41064	EMT
41065	FGW
41066	ICE
41067	EMT
41068	EMT
41069	EMT
41070	EMT
41071	EMT
41072	EMT
41075	EMT
41076	EMT
41077	EMT
41078	EMT
41079	EMT
41081	FGW
41083	ICE
41084	EMT
41085	FGW
41086	FGW
41087	ICE
41088	ICE
41089	FGW
41090	ICE
41091	ICE
41092	ICE
41093	FGW
41094	FGW
41095	ICE
41096	FGW
41097	ICE
41098	ICE
41099	ICE
41100	ICE
41101	FGW
41102	FGW
41103	FGW
41104	FGW
41105	FGW
41106	FGW
41108	FGW
41109	FGW
41110	FGW
41111	EMT
41112	EMT
41113	EMT
41114	FGW
41115	ICE
41116	FGW
41117	EMT
41118	ICE
41119	FGW
41120	ICE
41121	FGW
41122	FGW
41123	FGW
41124	FGW
41125	FGW
41126	FGW
41127	FGW
41128	FGW
41129	FGW
41130	FGW
41131	FGW
41132	FGW
41133	FGW
41134	FGW
41135	FGW
41136	FGW
41137	FGW
41138	FGW
41139	FGW
41140	FGW
41141	FGW
41142	FGW
41143	FGW
41144	FGW
41145	FGW
41146	FGW
41147	FGW
41148	FGW
41149	FGW
41150	ICE
41151	ICE
41152	ICE
41153	FGW
41154	EMT
41155	FGW
41156	EMT
41157	FGW
41158	FGW
41159	ICE
41160	FGW
41161	FGW
41162	FGW
41163	FGW
41164	ICE
41165	ICE
41166	FGW
41167	FGW
41168	FGW
41169	FGW
41170	ICE
41176	FGW
41179	FGW
41180	FGW
41181	FGW
41182	FGW
41183	FGW
41184	FGW
41185	ICE
41186	FGW
41187	FGW
41189	FGW
41190	ICE
41191	FGW
41192	FGW
41193	AXC
41194	AXC
41195	AXC
41201	GTL
41202	GTL
41203	GTL
41204	GTL
41205	GTL
41206	GTL
42003	FGW
42004	FGW
42005	FGW
42006	FGW
42007	FGW
42008	FGW
42009	FGW
42010	FGW
42012	FGW
42013	FGW
42014	FGW
42015	FGW
42016	FGW
42019	FGW
42021	FGW
42023	FGW
42024	FGW
42025	FGW
42026	FGW
42027	FGW
42028	FGW
42029	FGW
42030	FGW
42031	FGW
42032	FGW
42033	FGW
42034	FGW
42035	FGW
42036	AXC
42037	AXC

42038	AXC	42105	FGW	42171	ICE	42237	ICE	42307	ICE
42039	FGW	42106	ICE	42172	ICE	42238	ICE	42308	FGW
42040	FGW	42107	FGW	42173	FGW	42239	ICE	42309	FGW
42041	FGW	42108	FGW	42174	FGW	42240	ICE	42310	FGW
42042	FGW	42109	ICE	42175	FGW	42241	ICE	42314	FGW
42043	FGW	42110	ICE	42176	FGW	42242	ICE	42315	FGW
42044	FGW	42111	EMT	42177	FGW	42243	ICE	42316	FGW
42045	FGW	42112	EMT	42178	FGW	42244	ICE	42317	FGW
42046	FGW	42113	EMT	42179	ICE	42245	FGW	42319	FGW
42047	FGW	42115	FGW	42180	ICE	42247	FGW	42320	FGW
42048	FGW	42116	ICE	42181	ICE	42248	FGW	42321	FGW
42049	FGW	42117	ICE	42182	ICE	42249	FGW	42322	ICE
42050	FGW	42118	FGW	42183	FGW	42250	FGW	42323	ICE
42051	AXC	42119	EMT	42184	FGW	42251	FGW	42324	EMT
42052	AXC	42120	EMT	42185	FGW	42252	FGW	42325	FGW
42053	AXC	42121	EMT	42186	ICE	42253	FGW	42326	ICE
42054	FGW	42123	EMT	42187	FGW	42254	FGW	42327	EMT
42055	FGW	42124	EMT	42188	ICE	42255	FGW	42328	EMT
42056	FGW	42125	EMT	42189	ICE	42256	FGW	42329	EMT
42057	ICE	42126	FGW	42190	ICE	42257	FGW	42330	ICE
42058	ICE	42127	ICE	42194	EMT	42258	FGW	42331	EMT
42059	ICE	42128	ICE	42195	FGW	42259	FGW	42332	FGW
42060	FGW	42129	FGW	42196	FGW	42260	FGW	42333	FGW
42061	FGW	42130	ICE	42197	FGW	42261	FGW	42334	FGW
42062	FGW	42131	EMT	42198	ICE	42262	FGW	42335	EMT
42063	ICE	42132	EMT	42199	ICE	42263	FGW	42336	FGW
42064	ICE	42133	EMT	42200	FGW	42264	FGW	42337	EMT
42065	ICE	42134	ICE	42201	FGW	42265	FGW	42338	FGW
42066	FGW	42135	EMT	42202	FGW	42266	FGW	42339	EMT
42067	FGW	42136	EMT	42203	FGW	42267	FGW	42340	ICE
42068	FGW	42137	EMT	42204	FGW	42268	FGW	42341	EMT
42069	FGW	42138	FGW	42205	EMT	42269	FGW	42342	AXC
42070	FGW	42139	EMT	42206	FGW	42271	FGW	42343	FGW
42071	FGW	42140	EMT	42207	FGW	42272	FGW	42344	FGW
42072	FGW	42141	EMT	42208	FGW	42273	FGW	42345	FGW
42073	FGW	42143	FGW	42209	FGW	42275	FGW	42346	FGW
42074	FGW	42144	FGW	42210	EMT	42276	FGW	42347	FGW
42075	FGW	42145	FGW	42211	FGW	42277	FGW	42348	FGW
42076	FGW	42146	ICE	42212	FGW	42279	FGW	42349	FGW
42077	FGW	42147	ICE	42213	FGW	42280	FGW	42350	FGW
42078	FGW	42148	EMT	42214	FGW	42281	FGW	42351	FGW
42079	FGW	42149	EMT	42215	ICE	42283	FGW	42352	ICE
42080	FGW	42150	ICE	42216	FGW	42284	FGW	42353	FGW
42081	FGW	42151	EMT	42217	FGW	42285	FGW	42354	ICE
42083	FGW	42152	EMT	42218	FGW	42286	ICE	42355	ICE
42084	FGW	42153	EMT	42219	ICE	42287	FGW	42356	FGW
42085	FGW	42154	ICE	42220	EMT	42288	FGW	42357	ICE
42087	FGW	42155	EMT	42221	FGW	42289	FGW	42360	FGW
42089	FGW	42156	EMT	42222	FGW	42290	AXC	42361	FGW
42090	FGW	42157	EMT	42223	FGW	42291	FGW	42362	FGW
42091	ICE	42158	ICE	42224	FGW	42292	FGW	42363	ICE
42092	FGW	42159	ICE	42225	EMT	42293	FGW	42364	FGW
42093	FGW	42160	ICE	42226	ICE	42294	FGW	42365	FGW
42094	FGW	42161	ICE	42227	EMT	42295	FGW	42366	AXC
42095	FGW	42162	FGW	42228	ICE	42296	FGW	42367	AXC
42096	FGW	42163	ICE	42229	EMT	42297	FGW	42368	AXC
42097	AXC	42164	EMT	42230	EMT	42300	FGW	42369	AXC
42098	FGW	42165	EMT	42231	FGW	42301	FGW	42370	AXC
42099	FGW	42166	FGW	42232	FGW	42302	FGW	42371	AXC
42100	EMT	42167	FGW	42233	FGW	42303	FGW	42372	AXC
42101	FGW	42168	FGW	42234	AXC	42304	FGW	42373	AXC
42102	FGW	42169	FGW	42235	ICE	42305	FGW	42374	AXC
42103	FGW	42170	FGW	42236	FGW	42306	ICE	42375	AXC

42376 AXC
42377 AXC
42378 AXC
42379 AXC
42380 AXC
42381 FGW
42401 GTL
42402 GTL
42403 GTL
42404 GTL
42405 GTL
42406 GTL
42407 GTL
42408 GTL
42409 GTL

44000 FGW
44001 FGW
44002 FGW
44003 FGW
44004 FGW
44005 FGW
44007 FGW
44008 FGW
44009 FGW
44010 FGW
44011 FGW
44012 AXC
44013 FGW
44014 FGW
44015 FGW
44016 FGW
44017 AXC
44018 FGW
44019 ICE
44020 FGW
44021 AXC
44022 FGW
44023 FGW
44024 FGW
44025 FGW
44026 FGW
44027 EMT
44028 FGW
44029 FGW
44030 FGW
44031 ICE
44032 FGW
44033 FGW
44034 FGW
44035 FGW
44036 FGW
44037 FGW
44038 FGW
44039 FGW
44040 FGW
44041 EMT
44042 FGW
44043 FGW
44044 EMT
44045 ICE
44046 EMT
44047 EMT
44048 EMT
44049 FGW
44050 ICE
44051 EMT
44052 AXC
44054 EMT
44055 FGW
44056 ICE
44057 ICE
44058 ICE
44059 FGW
44060 FGW
44061 ICE
44063 ICE
44064 FGW
44065 GTL
44066 FGW
44067 FGW
44068 FGW
44069 FGW
44070 EMT
44071 EMT
44072 AXC
44073 EMT
44074 FGW
44075 ICE
44076 FGW
44077 ICE
44078 FGW
44079 FGW
44080 ICE
44081 FGW
44083 ICE
44085 EMT
44086 FGW
44088 GTL
44089 GTL
44090 FGW
44091 FGW
44093 FGW
44094 ICE
44097 FGW
44098 ICE
44100 FGW
44101 FGW

45001 AXC
45002 AXC
45003 AXC
45004 AXC
45005 AXC

45018 WCR
45020 DBS
45026 WCR
45029 DBS

80041 RIV
80042 DRS

99035 SUP
99040 SUP
99041 SUP
99080 SUP
99108 VTN
99120 SUP
99121 WCR
99125 WCR
99127 WCR
99128 WCR
99132 WCR
99193 WCR
99194 WCR
99195 WCR
99241 SUP
99304 WCR
99311 WCR
99312 SUP
99316 WCR
99317 WCR
99318 WCR
99319 WCR
99321 WCR
99322 WCR
99325 WCR
99326 WCR
99327 WCR
99328 WCR
99329 WCR
99348 WCR
99349 VTN
99350 WCR
99353 VTN
99354 WCR
99361 VTN
99371 WCR
99402 WCR
99405 SUP
99530 VSO
99531 VSO
99532 VSO
99534 VSO
99535 VSO
99536 VSO
99537 VSO
99539 VSO
99541 VSO
99543 VSO
99545 VSO
99546 VSO
99678 WCR
99679 WCR
99670 WCR
99671 WCR
99672 WCR
99673 WCR
99674 WCR
99675 WCR
99676 WCR
99677 WCR
99680 WCR
99706 WCR
99710 WCR
99712 WCR
99713 WCR
99717 WCR
99718 WCR
99721 WCR
99722 WCR
99723 WCR
99782 SUP
99792 SUP
99884 WCR
99953 SUP
99966 WCR
99968 VSO
99969 VSO
99991 SUP
99995 SUP

NPCCS Stock

6260 NRL
6261 NRL
6262 NRL
6263 SEC
6264 SEC
6356 FMR
6357 FMR

9701 NRL
9702 NRL
9703 NRL
9708 NRL
9714 NRL

72612 NRL
72613 NRL
72616 NRL
72630 NRL
72631 NRL
72639 NRL

80204 SUP
80211 NRL
80217 SUP
80220 SUP

82101 VWC
82102 NXA
82103 NXA
82104 NXA
82105 NXA
82106 OLS
82107 NXA
82108 DBS
82109 OLS
82110 OLS
82111 OLS
82112 NXA
82113 DBS
82114 NXA
82115 OLS
82116 DBS
82118 NXA
82120 DBS
82121 NXA
82122 DBS
82124 OLS
82125 OLS
82126 VWC
82127 NXA
82128 OLS
82129 OLS
82131 DBS
82132 NXA
82133 NXA
82136 NXA
82137 DBS
82138 DBS
82139 NXA
82140 OLS
82141 OLS
82143 NXA
82144 DBS
82145 OLS
82146 DBS
82148 DBS
82149 OLS
82150 DBS
82151 DBS
82152 NXA
82301 WSR
82302 WSR
82303 WSR
82304 WSR
82305 WSR
82200 ICE
82201 ICE
82202 ICE
82203 ICE
82204 ICE
82205 ICE
82206 ICE
82207 ICE
82208 ICE
82209 ICE
82210 ICE
82211 ICE
82212 ICE
82213 ICE
82214 ICE
82215 ICE
82216 ICE
82217 ICE
82218 ICE
82219 ICE
82220 ICE
82222 ICE
82223 ICE
82224 ICE
82225 ICE
82226 ICE
82227 ICE
82228 ICE
82229 ICE
82230 ICE
82231 ICE
92114 NRL
92159 OLS
92203 DBS
92901 OLS
92904 VSO

Number	Operator
92931	OLS
92939	NRL
94103	DBS
94104	DBS
94106	DBS
94113	DBS
94116	DBS
94121	DBS
94137	DBS
94147	DBS
94150	DBS
94153	DBS
94155	DBS
94160	DBS
94166	DBS
94168	DBS
94170	DBS
94176	DBS
94177	DBS
94190	DBS
94191	DBS
94192	DBS
94195	DBS
94196	DBS
94197	DBS
94199	DBS
94203	DBS
94207	DBS
94208	DBS
94209	DBS
94213	DBS
94214	DBS
94217	DBS
94221	DBS
94222	DBS
94225	DBS
94227	DBS
94229	DBS
94302	DBS
94303	DBS
94304	DBS
94306	DBS
94307	DBS
94308	DBS
94310	DBS
94311	DBS
94313	DBS
94316	DBS
94317	DBS
94318	DBS
94322	DBS
94323	DBS
94326	DBS
94331	DBS
94332	DBS
94333	DBS
94334	DBS
94335	DBS
94336	DBS
94338	DBS
94340	DBS
94343	DBS
94344	DBS
94400	DBS
94401	DBS
94406	DBS
94408	DBS
94410	DBS
94411	DBS
94412	DBS
94413	DBS
94416	DBS
94420	DBS
94422	DBS
94423	DBS
94427	DBS
94428	DBS
94429	DBS
94431	DBS
94432	DBS
94433	DBS
94434	DBS
94435	DBS
94438	DBS
94440	DBS
94445	DBS
94451	DBS
94458	DBS
94462	DBS
94463	DBS
94470	DBS
94479	DBS
94481	DBS
94482	DBS
94488	DBS
94490	DBS
94492	DBS
94495	DBS
94497	DBS
94498	DBS
94499	DBS
94501	DBS
94504	DBS
94512	DBS
94514	DBS
94515	DBS
94518	DBS
94519	DBS
94520	DBS
94521	DBS
94522	DBS
94525	DBS
94526	DBS
94527	DBS
94528	DBS
94529	DBS
94530	DBS
94531	DBS
94532	DBS
94534	DBS
94536	DBS
94538	DBS
94539	DBS
94540	DBS
94541	DBS
94542	DBS
94543	DBS
94544	DBS
94545	DBS
94546	DBS
94547	DBS
94548	DBS
95300	DBS
95301	DBS
95400	DBS
95410	DBS
95727	DBS
95754	DBS
95758	DBS
95761	DBS
95763	DBS
96100	OLS
96139	OLS
96175	OLS
96181	OLS
96602	OLS
96603	OLS
96604	OLS
96605	OLS
96606	OLS
96607	OLS
96608	OLS
96609	OLS
99666	NRL

Service Stock

Number	Operator
950001	NRL
960010	CRW
960013	CRW
960014	CRW
960015	CRW
960021	CRW
960201	NRL
960202	NRL
960301	CRW
975025	NRL
975081	NRL
975091	NRL
975280	NRL
975464	NRL
975486	NRL
975494	NRL
975573	NRL
975574	NRL
975611	NRL
975612	NRL
975613	NRL
975699	CAR
975700	CAR
975714	CAR
975724	CAR
975734	CAR
975744	CAR
975814	NRL
975984	NRL
977163	BBR
977165	BBR
977166	BBR
977167	BBR
977168	BBR
977337	NRL
977868	NRL
977869	NRL
977968	COL
977969	NRL
977974	NRL
977983	NRL
977984	NRL
977985	NRL
977986	NRL
977989	FLF
977990	NRL
977991	NRL
977993	NRL
977994	NRL
977995	NRL
977996	NRL
977997	NRL
999508	NRL
999550	NRL
999602	NRL
999605	NRL
999606	NRL

Number Cross-Link Codes

3MP	3M Productions
ALS	Alstom
ATW	Arriva Trains Wales
AXC	Arriva Cross Country
BAR	British American Railway
BOK	Bo'ness & Kinneil Railway
BOM	Bombardier Transportation
C2C	c2c Railway
CAD	Cargo D
COL	Colas
CRW	Chiltern Railways
CWR	Cotswold Rail
DBS	DB Schenker
DRS	Direct Rail Services
ECR	Euro Cargo Rail
EMT	East Midlands Trains
EPX	Euro Phoenix Ltd
ETL	Electric Traction Ltd
EUR	Eurotunnel
EUR	Euro Port 2
EUS	Eurostar UK
EXP	Exported
FCC	First Capital Connect
FGW	First Great Western
FHT	First Hull Trains
FLF	Fastline Freight
FLR	Freightliner
FMR	FM Rail
FSL	Flying Scotsman Railway Ltd
FSR	First ScotRail
FTP	First TransPennine
GBR	GB Railfreight
GSW	Great Scottish & Western Rly
GTL	Grand Central Railway
HAN	Hanson Traction
HEC	Heathrow Connect
HEX	Heathrow Express
HNR	Harry Needle Railroad Co
IND	Industrial
JAR	Jarvis
JHS	Jeremy Hoskins
KRS	Knights Rail Services
LMI	London Midland
LOG	London Overground
MER	Mersey Rail
MHR	Mid Hants Railway
MRL	Mendip Rail Ltd
NOR	Northern
NRL	Network Rail Limited
NXA	National Express East Anglia
NXE	National Express East Coast
NYM	North Yorkshire Moors Railway
OLS	Off Lease
PRE	Preserved
PUL	Pullman Rail
RAF	Railfilms
RCL	Railcare
RIV	Riviera
RRS	Ridings Railtours
RVE	Rail Vehicle Engineering
SEC	Serco Railtest
SET	South Eastern Trains
SIE	Siemens
SIL	Stagecoach Island Line
SNF	SNCF (French Railways)
SOU	Southern
SRP	Scottish Railway Preservation Soc
SUP	Support Coaches
SWT	South West Trains
VSO	Venice Simplon Orient Express
VTN	Vintage Trains
VWC	Virgin West Coast
WAB	Wabtec
WCR	West Coast Railway
WSR	Wrexham & Shropshire Railway
WTN	Wessex Trains

Above: *Modern traction preservation is now big business in the UK, with a large number of superbly restored shunting and main line locomotives operating on preserved lines. Normally based on the South Devon Railway, green-liveried No. D6737 is seen on the West Somerset Railway on 14 June 2008 piloting Class 33 No. D6566 out of Watchet bound for Minehead.* **CJM**

Left: *A popular location to observe and photograph passenger and freight trains is Gloucester station; passenger services operated by First Great Western and CrossCountry, together with freights operated by DBS and DRS are frequently seen. On 2 July 2009 DBS Class 66 No. 66012 passes through the station with the 08.54 Margam to Lackenby while Class 153 No. 153369 and Advenza-liveried Class 66 No. 66842 stand in the yard.* **CJM**

BR Green Diesels

32-911A Class 108 3-Car DMU BR Green with Yellow Warning Panels 8 DCC

With the formation of British Railways in 1948 engineers quickly started to design and build diesel locomotives with the long-term aim of replacing steam motive power. A variety of types soon started to appear in the early 1950's. These prototypes were tested over all parts of the railway network, the results being evaluated and incorporated into the designs being proposed for mass production. Orders were placed and construction began in the many railway workshops which manufactured long-service designs such as the Class 20 Freig Locomotive and the universal Type 4/Class 47 Diesel Locomotiv

Passenger Diesel Multiple Units (known as DMU's) also bega to appear fairly early in the 1950's and a great variety of thes versatile units were produced to replace 100's of steam engin classes on Branchline and commuter trains through the UK.

32-401DS Class 25 BR Two Tone Green D7638 DCC SOUND

31-342 Class 04 BR Green Late Crest D2264

32-034 Class 20 BR Green 8164

32-678DS Class 45 BR Green D55

32-529 Class 55 BR Two Tone Green D9017

32-801 Class 47 BR Two Tone Green 1764 21 DCC

All products are designated an Era symbol using the Bachmann Product Period Key, as seen on our website.
Era 5 signifies locomotives suitable for period 1957 - 1966 British Railways Late Crest.
Era 6 signifies locomotives suitable for period 1967 - 1971 British Railways Blue Pre-TOPS.

OO Scale **Bachmann Europe Plc.** Moat Way, Barwell, Leicestershire. LE9 8EY
www.bachmann.co.uk